LITERARY CRITICISM
Idea and Act

The English Institute, 1939-1972
Selected Essays

LITERARY CRITICISM
Idea and Act

The English Institute, 1939-1972
Selected Essays

Edited with an Introduction by

W. K. WIMSATT

UNIVERSITY OF CALIFORNIA PRESS
Berkeley / Los Angeles / London

University of California Press
Berkeley and Los Angeles, California

University of California Press, Ltd.
London, England

Copyright © 1974 by
The Regents of the University of California

ISBN: 0-520-02585-7
Library of Congress Catalog Card Number: 73-85797

Designed by Jim Mennick
Printed in the United States of America

For Cleanth and Tinkham Brooks

Contents

Introduction

I

SIXTY-THREE "eager scholars" registered for the inaugural English Institute at Columbia University in August and September 1939.[1] Tucker Brooke . . . Carleton Brown . . . Arthur Case . . . Walter Graham . . . Miles Hanley . . . T. O. Mabbott . . . Hereward Price . . . George Sherburn . . . Rosemond Tuve . . . George Whicher. The roster of such stalwarts appears, as an afterthought, in the fourth volume of Institute Essays, published in 1943. Professor Rudolf Kirk, who, in virtue of his having edited the first four volumes of the *Annual* and having written the prefaces of the second, third, and fourth, may be looked on as the earliest historian of the Institute, tells us that the plan was conceived by "two plotters" in a Greenwich Village restaurant on January 27, 1938. The Institute was projected "amid rumours of war." Its early meetings benefited from the restraint on summer travel to foreign libraries resulting from the actual outbreak. What is more important, the meetings erupted, in their casual way, out of a certain now celebrated unrest—an uneasy question about "history" and "criticism" —which had invaded the profession of English literary scholarship in America during the 1930s. A serious call to a review of purposes had been sounded in the semicentennial Presidential Address of Professor John Livingston Lowes before the Modern Language Association of America in 1933, and no less in a companion address by Professor Carleton Brown, veteran Secretary of the Association. Brown became President of the Association in 1936, and he was the Chairman of the Supervising Committee of the Institute for its first two years.

It seems extravagant in retrospect, but that first gathering of the Institute, in South Hall, the new library building at Columbia, continued for nearly two full weeks. The registrants had an opportunity

[1] I adapt some parts of the opening paragraphs of a foreword which I wrote for a small retrospective anthology of Institute essays in 1963.

of hearing and discussing twenty-four morning papers (in four series: on English and American dialects, on editing Middle English texts, on editing correspondences, and on the social backgrounds of drama). They could hear no fewer than nine evening lectures, by as many learned speakers, on such business-like topics as the finding of literary documents, the screening of graduate students, the selection of a topic of research.

In a second year, William Y. Tindall, David Daiches, Cleanth Brooks, Allen Tate, and W. H. Auden were speakers on a program entitled simply "Literary Criticism." A third year introduced the novel theme of explication ("Literary Criticism: The Interpretation of Poetry"). Horace Gregory, Lionel Trilling, Cleanth Brooks, and Frederick A. Pottle performed a memorable feat in demonstrating four ways of talking about a single lyric poem—Wordsworth's "Ode: Intimations of Immortality."

Pearl Harbor came soon after. After a short meeting on the Labor Day weekend of 1942, the Institute disappeared for the space of three years. It was revived in 1946. It flourished.

I do not attempt an anecdotal history. South Hall (1939–1940), Room 307 in Philosophy Hall (1941–1953), the Men's Faculty Club (1954–1957), Earl Hall, the Religious Studies center (1958–1961), and for a long later stretch (1962–1971) Wollman Auditorium in the new Ferris Booth Hall in the southwest corner of the campus—these will evoke different memories for frequenters of the Institute during different periods of its history. But time (Mutabilitie), which has worked such shifts even in so stably dedicated an enterprise, has recently brought even a greater one, the beginning of a new era, as the academic year at Columbia has made a recession to the first weeks of September, and the Institute has moved to Cambridge, the Harvard Yard.

The history of the Institute, so far as it has been deliberately recorded, appears at the end of each volume of essays: a short and simple annal (1) naming the current Secretary of the Institute and the nine members (including the Chairman) of the Supervising Committee for the preceding year; (2) giving the program for that year; (3) listing the registrants—in later years usually to a number between two and three hundred.

II

The essays for the first eleven years, 1939–1942, 1946–1952 (published in 1940–1943, 1947–1952, and 1954), had from the start tended to reflect the harmoniously heterogeneous makeup of the Institute, dividing their tables of contents as fairly as possible among diverse programs. The volumes were in short miscellanies. After the meeting of 1953, the Institute Supervising Committee and the editors of the Columbia University Press joined in the view that a more coherent annual volume was desirable. A small volume of partly borrowed essays on Ezra Pound, edited by Lewis Leary and published in 1954, assisted the start of a delayed-publication and stockpiling plan. The present editor had the satisfaction of drawing on two programs relating to comedy, presented in successive years, 1953 and 1954, to shape a collection entitled *English Stage Comedy,* published in 1955.

Volumes of Institute Essays which appeared in subsequent years have all had special themes and corresponding titles. Eighteen years of focal interests at the Institute meetings are synopsized in the titles of these volumes and the names of the editors.

Mark Schorer, *Society and Self in the Novel,* 1956 (from 1955)

Northrop Frye, *Sound and Poetry,* 1957 (from 1955 and 1956)

M. H. Abrams, *Literature and Belief,* 1958 (from 1956 and 1957)

Harold C. Martin, *Style in Prose Fiction,* 1959 (from 1957 and 1958)

Richard Ellmann, *Edwardians and Late Victorians,* 1960 (from 1958 and 1959)

Dorothy Bethurum, *Critical Approaches to Medieval Literature,* 1960, extra volume (from 1958 and 1959)

William Nelson, *Form and Convention in the Poetry of Edmund Spenser,* 1961 (from 1959 and 1960)

R. W. B. Lewis, *The Presence of Walt Whitman,* 1962 (from 1960 and 1961)

Northrop Frye, *Romanticism Reconsidered,* 1963 (four papers from a single program directed by Frye in 1962)

John Gassner, *Ideas in the Drama,* 1964 (from 1962 and 1963)

Joseph H. Summers, *The Lyric and Dramatic Milton,* 1965 (from 1963 and 1964)

Murray Krieger, *Northrop Frye in Modern Criticism,* 1966 (three essays from a program of 1965, with responses by Krieger and Frye)

Philip Damon, *Literary Criticism and Historical Understanding*, 1967
(from 1966)

Roy Harvey Pearce, *Experience in the Novel*, 1968 (from 1967)

Norman Rabkin, *Reinterpretations of Elizabethan Drama*, 1969 (from
1968, with invited additions)

Reuben A. Brower, *Forms of Lyric*, 1970 (from 1968 and 1969)

J. Hillis Miller, *Aspects of Narrative*, 1971 (from 1969 and 1970)

Geoffrey Hartman, *New Perspectives on Coleridge and Wordsworth*,
1972 (from 1970 and 1971)

Seymour Chatman, *Recent Linguistics and Literary Study*, 1973 (from
1971 and 1972)

III

The programs of the English Institute for the years 1939–1972 record
the reading in all of 522 papers—daytime and nighttime. The *Essays*
(or *Papers*) published in the corresponding volumes, 1940–1973, total
221. The annual volumes have struggled to keep up with and do justice
to an ever-various performance. In a complementary sense, they have,
from the start, worked as a gradually clarifying selector of critical
themes. Various kinds of interest have found various other outlets. Professor Fredson Bowers, editor of *Studies in Bibliography*, published at
the University of Virginia, and Professor David Erdman, editor of *The
Bulletin of the New York Public Library*, ought to be named as special
friends of the several publishing ambitions of the English Institute.[2]

For reasons ranging from the failure of tape-recording procedures
to an occasional tendency of well-planned programs to fall apart in
actual miscellaneity, a number of individually excellent Institute critical
papers have escaped the editors of subsequent volumes. Published in
periodicals or as parts of longer works by their authors, these papers have
often undergone alterations, especially expansions, which raise a difficult
question about the identity of what was read at the Institute. The voice
once heard merges with the world of print.[3]

[2] See, for example: *Studies in Bibliography*, vols. 3–5 (The University of Virginia, 1950–1952); *The Bulletin of the New York Public Library*, June 1962–October 1963; *Literature as a Mode of Travel*, ed. Warner G. Rice, The New York Public
Library, 1963; and *Blake's Visionary Forms Dramatic*, ed. David Erdman and John
E. Grant, The Princeton University Press, 1970.

[3] The Institute program of 1960, for example, looks forward to three books:
Harold Bloom's *Visionary Company* (1961), Bernard N. Schilling's *Dryden and the*

In the selection of essays for this volume (see the table of Contents), one consideration has been contrast. Anyone who will read (I.1) James M. Osborn's "Search for English Literary Documents" (1939) and immediately afterwards (I.5) Wallace Stevens' "Imagination as Value" (1948) must be impressed by the range of interests represented in early Institute Confrontations—from the detective work and diplomacy promoting the physical transmission of the poet's texts all the way to the penetralia of the temple of creative imagination. A climax of this decade in American criticism was to be reached in the encyclopedic *Theory of Literature* published by René Wellek and Austin Warren in 1949. Wellek's Institute paper (I.3) "The Parallelism between Literature and the Arts" (1941) and also his "Periods and Movements in Literary History" (1940) contributed substantially, in ways that the titles will suggest, to the scope of that book. Plenary expressions of certain "new" critical ideas might come only some years later. Cleanth Brooks in "Implications of an Organic Theory of Poetry," read in a program "Literature and Belief" (1957), of which he was the director, subsumed much that had occurred in American criticism since his Institute paper of 1940, "The Poem as Organism: Modern Critical Procedure." (Brooks's *Well Wrought Urn* had appeared in 1947.) In the same program of 1957, Meyer Abrams's (I.9) "Belief and the Suspension of Disbelief," proceeding from the direction of Kantian disinterest and Coleridgean organicism, joins the new critic in an ample united front. (The simple, photographically supposed landscape had never been a feature of interest to the American metaphysical school, so that Abrams's masterpiece of a few years earlier, *The Mirror and the Lamp, Romantic Theory and the Critical Tradition*, 1953, had entered a highly congenial climate.) Father Walter J. Ong's paper "Voice a Summons to Belief" (1957) (continuing the "personalist" strain of another of his essays, "The Jinnee in the Well-Wrought Urn," *Essays in Criticism*, 1954) was a counter-aesthetic, with affinities for the Genevan (and then incipient Baltimorean) centers of Gallic "consciousness." Father Ong's earlier Institute paper (I.8), "Ramus, Rhetoric, and the Pre-Newtonian Mind" (1952) and (I.7) Philip Wheelwright's Aristotelian "Mimesis and Katharsis: An Archetypal Consideration" (1951) are excellent

---

Conservative Myth (1961), and Richard S. Sylvester's edition of More's *History of King Richard III* (1963); that of 1961, to Jean H. Hagstrum's *William Blake: Poet and Painter* (1964); and that of 1962, to Monroe K. Spears's *The Poetry of W. H. Auden* (1963) and John G. Blair's *The Poetic Art of W. H. Auden* (1965).

illustrations of an interest in classical poetics and rhetoric that moved
readily in rapport with American analytic criticism in those years.
(Father Ong's *Ramus: Method and the Decay of Dialogue* appeared in
1958. Wheelwright's *Burning Fountain, A Study in the Language of
Symbolism,* 1954, was an anthropologically and psychologically glowing, at moments a luridly illuminated, contribution to the semantic or
symbolic dimension of the new school. The word "archetypal," appearing somewhat intrusively in his Aristotelian title of 1951, will suggest
the wide gathering of interests which joined in the writings of this imaginatively learned scholar.)

Two Institute essays, separated by nine years, exemplify, once
more, though in a different way, the principle of extreme contrast.
D. W. Robertson's "Historical Criticism" (1950) and E. Talbot
Donaldson's (I.10) "Patristic Exegesis in the Criticism of Medieval
Literature: The Opposition" (1958) were challenge and response in
a debate about a special code of historically arguable rules for reading
the medieval poem. This heated concern of the 1950s afforded an instructive model of a clash between two conceptions of history as
hermeneutic authority that is no doubt destined for many a return. It
rehearsed in one very specific field of historical expertise the wider
historical issue which during the late 1930s had done much to initiate
the conferences of the Institute.

The drive of the well-equipped theoretical intelligence toward the
definition of some schematic goal (some kernel in the poetic husk) is
no doubt never defeasible for very long. It searches, relentlessly, its opportunities for reassertion against the aesthetic intuition. The more
specifically identifiable this drive, however, the less likely it may be to
succeed. The categories of the fourfold patristic exegesis were indeed
to play a new role in academic criticism, but they were not the complete, the exquisitely abstracted, machine of an immediate great future.
A succession of Institute papers during the 1940s—(I.2) W. H. Auden's
"Mimesis and Allegory" (1940), (I.4) Donald A. Stauffer's "The
Modern Myth of the Modern Myth" (1947), Richard Chase's "Myth
as Literature" (1947), (I.5) Wallace Stevens' "Imagination as Value"
(1948), and (I.6) Leslie Fiedler's "Defence of the Illusion and the
Creation of Myth . . ." (1948)—testify to what we may conceive as a
deep yearning on the part of literary criticism to discover and assert
some system of fundamental poetic meanings to replace others of which
the contemporary mind might seem to stand largely bereft. The hope
for the deliberate reinvention of a sustaining "myth" is most promi-

nently and logically examined in Stauffer's masterly paper—very relevantly enriched by a series of examples from the career of Yeats. The stage had already been set, the empty yearning space had been implicitly defined, into which in the same year (1947) stepped the young Canadian professor Northrop Frye with *Fearful Symmetry, A Study of William Blake.* This was an elaboration of the Blakean "Prophecies" which was immediately recognized to have "extraordinary possibilities for expansion and development" in our own day. The last chapter was indeed an open forecast of a vast general application. In an Institute paper of 1948, "The Argument of Comedy," Frye moved immediately ahead, giving in effect a preview of the quasi-Aristotelian comic mythos which would be the center of the central third Essay of his *Anatomy of Criticism,* 1957. He returned to the Institute in 1950 with "Blake's Treatment of the Archetypes," a reordered synopsis of the mythic content of *Fearful Symmetry,* ending with another patent prediction of the yet unnamed system of 1957. Geoffrey H. Hartman's "Ghostlier Demarcations" (I.12), part of an Institute special panel upon Frye (1965), correctly located the archetypes as the supreme fiction of a modern trend toward the democratization, or "demystification," of criticism (or of the literary norms) or—conversely, as it may be put if we look from the other end—toward the romantic sacralization of literature itself— the imagination as value. (Meyer Abrams's second great work on romanticism, *Natural Supernaturalism,* 1971, has been one kind of realization of that trend.) A certain high principle, an ascetic severity, which strains and blanches the modern mythoi, is exquisitely narrated by Lionel Trilling in (I.11) "The Fate of Pleasure: Wordsworth to Dostoevsky" (1962). In an essay of 1966, "Structuralism: The Anglo-American Adventure" (*Yale French Studies,* 36–37), Geoffrey Hartman would go on to intimate affinities between the American secularizing effort and the Parisian "structuralist" ambience of the 1960s, the latter a subject that a few years later (1971) was sampled for the Institute by Hugh Davidson in (I.13) "Sign, Sense, and Roland Barthes." The radically linguistic aspect of Parisian structuralism linked Davidson's paper in the same program (1971) with George Steiner's clarion (I.14) concerning some currently home-grown schematisms, "Whorf, Chomsky, and the Student of Literature."

The distinction between I, *Idea* in literary criticism, and II, *Act,* admits of no rigor in application. Still the colorations can be on the whole very different. Series II (see the table of Contents) is critical history of literature, or historico-critical moments and synopses arranged in the historical order: specifically, that of English literature from 1600, the date of Shakespeare's *Twelfth Night*, to 1950, the approximate *terminus ad quem* of Arthur Mizener's retrospect of twentieth-century poetic drama (II.17).

Two excursuses, one near the beginning, into romance parody, the other (double) near the end, into the Parisian Theater, have been invited by the quality of the papers and their brevity and by what seemed to me a not remote relevance to the adjacent English topics. Certain other possible sources of amplification have not been tapped.[4] In the laborious selection of the thirty-four essays which compose this volume, the criteria of quality, of auctorial distribution, and of cohesive variety have competed fiercely. Many other individual papers, a number of other basic patterns, might have emerged. I have chosen, or in a sense have created, one pattern that lies near the heart of Institute concerns, and I think that I have, within necessary limits of length, come close to maximizing it.

It is possible that in adopting the order of literary history (1600–1950) I have obscured developments in the methods of American criticism that have occurred during the course of the Institute's thirty odd years (1939–1972). I do not really think so. The excellence of these essays, considered individually, lies in their lovingly and thoughtfully close scrutiny of the literary objects, in their originality of insight, in their clarity of exposition. Taken together, they have I believe the merit of a nearly continuous montage of vignettes of English literary history.

The editorial task has been happily promoted by the varieties of focus which I have advertized in the heading: Works, Authors, Periods, Types.

The 1940s were the heyday of the essay devoted entirely to the analysis of a single short poem. A masterpiece of the mode appears in (II.9) Cleanth Brooks on "Marvell's Horatian Ode." Ray L. Heffner's study of unifying symbols in Jonson's *Silent Woman* and *Bartholomew Fair* (II.5) has obvious connections with the school of lyric analysis. I have taken two relatively late Shakespearean examples, John Hollander's (II.1) "*Musica Mundana* and *Twelfth Night*," in part for its extra dimension of musicology (a trial piece for his *Untuning of the Sky*, 1961), and Stephen Booth's (II.2) "On the Value of *Hamlet*," in part

---

[4] E.g., the poetry of Chaucer and his contemporaries, American literature, rhetorical and metrical analysis.

for its novel exploitation of clashing elements in that puzzling play. C. L. Barber's (II.7) "A Mask Presented . . ." studies a drama of different magnitude and style in Milton's *Comus*. (This paper of 1964 at the Institute followed by ten years the same author's exposition of ritual and mythic features in Shakespeare's *Henry IV*, published in the *Institute Essays* in 1955 and incorporated in his book of 1959, *Shakespeare's Festal Comedy*.)

The essay framing and describing a single author's book of short poems and arguing their unity or their significance in the author's career may be viewed as a specialty of Louis L. Martz, demonstrated at the Institute in his paper of 1960 on Spenser's *Amoretti* and in a second (II.8, 1964), on Milton's volume of 1645. Helen Vendler's essay (II.6) "The Re-invented Poem . . ." also deals with a single collection of poems, Herbert's *Temple*, marking, for the first time, I believe, a structural feature of extraordinary interest, which I notice more explicitly below. Martha England's essay on "The Satiric Blake" (II.12) is mainly about one work, *An Island in the Moon*, developing an external or antecedent feature in a surprising way which too I will note again briefly below. Hugh Kenner's "Urban Apocalypse" (II.20) is a visit to Eliot's *Waste Land* occasioned not only by the anniversary (1972) but by the manuscript revelations of 1971.

Two essays—(II.13), Harold Bloom on Coleridge, and (II.15), Northrop Frye on Dickens—embrace the works of a single author as subject entity, but in widely different ways. Five essays—(II.10), Marvin Mudrick on comedy of manners, (II.11), W. K. Wimsatt on eighteenth-century lyrics, (II.14), Martin Price on irrelevant details in novels, (II.16), Richard Ellmann on the Edwardians, and (II.17), Arthur Mizener on poetic drama—are synoptic efforts which in one degree or another merge ideas of period with ideas of type.

A certain braggadocio of scholarly idiom and of publishers' assertions might lead us to believe that we live in a universe of continual "breakthrough," where each new book of a theoretical slant is bound to have the profoundest consequences for the adventuring practical critic of tomorrow. My own notion is that so far as any critic deliberately tries to make this come true, the fact is deplorable. We need not admire or participate in that kind of guildhall practicality in order to hold theory of literature in the highest esteem. Theory ought to be interesting in itself. At the same time, it can be, and ought to be, tonic and nourishing. Theory produces an indirect general improvement in

practical discourse. Some degree of *general* or virtual correspondence
between the theories of an era and the practical criticism are no doubt
almost always to be observed.

The analytic procedures recommended by the "new" criticism and
the ironies to which it gave so much attention appear pervasively, more
or less, in essays of nearly all the other tendencies during the decades of
the Institute. Historical research, having in the phase of the 1940s
staged some excited counter-demonstrations, steadily began to co-opt,
or be co-opted by, analytic sensitivity. Critics of the 1950s and 1960s,
Martz, Barber, Vendler, Booth, illustrate (as Brooks, Trilling, and
others had done before) the essential nullity of a supposed contest. The
semantic or rhetorico-verbal accent of the era comes out strongly in
Mudrick's insistent translation of socio-ethical values in Jonson and
Congreve into achievements of verbal ordonnance (II.10). Classical
and medieval grammatico-rhetorical ideas (like those in Father Ong's
I.8 on Ramus) were applied by Hugh Kenner (1952) in a portrayal not
only of a background Dublin verbal world but of the elaborately
figured art, against that ground, practiced by Joyce.

With so much desacralization abroad on the winds of mythopoeic
theory, it would have been strange if the conception had not managed
to blend with many practical analyses. Delicately shaded instances are
to be read in Barber's study of pagan-Christian equivalences in *Comus*
(II.7), in Trilling's classic metaphorization of Wordsworth's intimations of immortality (1941), in the several essays of 1960 on Whitman's
"Out of the Cradle," in Ellmann's discovery of sacramental symbols
released for secular duty everywhere in Edwardian literature (II.16).
Northrop Frye's essay on "Dickens and the Comedy of Humors"
(II.15) is not only an attractive exposition of Dickens but one of the
few best examples the editor has seen of Frye's archetypes in action.
Frye is the only critic who has ever really been able to put his system
into action. Frye's Institute essay on Blake's archetypes (1950)—the
"ghostlier demarcations"—urgently invites contrast with (II.12, 1968)
Martha England's lavishly historical painting of the satiric Blake, probable apprentice of Samuel Foote's mimic tea parties in the Haymarket.

The motif of secularization shows a fairly close affinity for another,
more recently and tentatively emergent, that of poetic alteration or
emendation—or, in a slightly wider perspective, openness or "virtuality"
of meaning.[5] *Metamorphoses* is another name for *Fables of Identity*.

---

[5] I borrow the latter term from chess problems, where the thematically relevant
and strongly invited, yet actually precluded, solution—"virtual play"—has been a

Modification of models, or at the very slenderest a slightly askew, or faintly burlesque, self-consciousness in the act of "imitation," is inevitably a part of each phase in a neo-classic succession. It is intrinsic to the juncture of "tradition and the individual talent." W. K. Wimsatt's (II.11), on derivative poems of the eighteenth century, touches modestly, to a large extent inadvertently, on the theme of correction. Harold Bloom's (II.13), tracing the anguish of the not-quite-"strong" poet Coleridge in a struggle with the father-poet Milton, boldly applies the term "misprision" to the process of poetic alteration and divides it into six grades with as many esoteric names. Bloom may be said to be the proprietor of the new concept in its most advanced version. His recent book *The Anxiety of Influence* (1972) is a rhapsodically eloquent exposition. Daniel Seltzer's evocative (II.3) "Shakespeare's Text and Modern Productions" expounds another kind of willful misprision, a rewarding violence, committed against the revered text by the modern theatrical inheritor. The *Lear* inspired by Samuel Beckett and Jan Kott and produced a few years ago by Peter Brook will serve as paradigm of the "reimaged" Shakespeare. Paul de Man's *Blindness & Insight* (1971), incorporating his Institute essay of 1969, "Lyric and Modernity," carries a thesis about misprision boldly into the realm of modern literary criticism itself—where the best performers appear to begin with misinterpretation and by that path proceed to their own best insights.

But a poet may engage in correcting or transcending not only his father but himself in his earlier work. (This was notably illustrated by Louis Martz in a paper in the Institute volume of 1958 on the progressive dissatisfactions of Wallace Stevens.) And correction may both *occur* (psychologically) during an author's act of composition and in a resulting sense *be built in* (structurally and dramatically) as a part of the achieved work. (In the latter sense it can in fact appear in the work *without* any change of mind on the part of the author in the process of writing, and it is perhaps just as well if the critic does not often ask any questions about that.) Martin Price's (II.14), delicately pondering the ways in which the novelist's "solidity of specification" may exceed, or appear to exceed, the demands of relevance—and yet after all may emerge as an extra kind of relevance—is an essay that seems to me to verge on problems of auto-correction. Helen Vendler's (II.6) "The Re-

---

growing discovery for the past twenty years. The resemblance of the conception to certain open-ended, hopscotch, aleatory, and labyrinthine arrangements in modern fiction may be recognized. The theme has been notably exploited in some of the novels of Vladimir Nabokov. See a forthcoming article by Janet Gezari in *Poétique*.

invented Poem: George Herbert's Alternatives" shows dramatized or incorporated correction perhaps at its maximum éclat, in the short metaphysical and religious poem, where context and tradition are urgently present to remind us of what may be expected, but where the poet's last stanza often executes an evasion or substitution—which too we find eminently in place and acceptable. The latter twist is the poetic secret—and the secret of Mrs. Vendler's fine essay. Hugh Kenner's "Urban Apocalypse" (II.20, 1972), through the happy event of so large an assemblage of early drafts for Eliot's *Waste Land* at length coming to light, is able to expound something like a maximum instance of a poet's voice in selective engagement with those of his sources and instructors—modern and ancient—and his laborious recovery of a masterpiece from "the wreckage of a far different" initial "conception." It is easy to contend with fathers, to revolt against them, easy to reshape, to recolor, to contaminate received materials, easy to make our own mistakes and to reverse them, to change our minds and even to incorporate changes in our works. But not easy to execute any of these commonplaces with the kind of special reason and authority that turns them into wit, and imagination.

The English Institute Supervising Committees and their Chairmen from 1969 to 1973 have been the sponsors of this anthology. My thanks are due especially to Irvin Ehrenpreis and J. Hillis Miller.

Four student helpers, Walter Schindler, Robert Young, Steven Brooks, and John Crigler, have been companions in the enterprise.

My colleagues Geoffrey Hartman, Paul de Man, James M. Osborn, and Maynard Mack, and the Secretary of the Institute, Charles Owen, have all generously contributed both advice and comfort.

Helene Fineman read the proof. Cynthia Brodhead made the index.

W. K. WIMSATT

Silliman College
Yale University
The Vernal Equinox, 1974

Part I. IDEA:

The Nature of Literature and of Literary Study, 1939–1971

I. 1

The Search for English Literary Documents[1]

JAMES M. OSBORN

Yale University

AMONG THE various activities which pass under the name "literary scholarship" it is generally agreed that the finding of documents is not the most important. And yet I imagine it will also be agreed that the study of documents (using the word in the widest sense) is the primary task of the literary researcher. Documents are the basic evidence to be gathered and sorted before attempts are made to explain what an author wrote or why he wrote it. Finding literary documents is thus the foundation of literary research, upon which interpretative criticism must rest. It is scarcely necessary to emphasize the importance of knowing your subject or author thoroughly before you set out to find new manuscripts. By having a greater mastery of detail than your predecessors, you will find significance in documents they passed over.[2] But in the absence of such knowledge, information will be overlooked and the next man to cover the ground may make a monkey out of you.

In the following remarks I shall take the term "literary documents" to include every piece of evidence which throws light on the text of a literary work or on the life of the author. These documents fall into three categories, which may be briefly distinguished as official, personal,

[1] This paper, delivered at the first session of the English Institute in August 1939 before the outbreak of World War II, contained several references to persons, periodicals, and even institutions now deceased or defunct. These passages have been revised, and a few illustrative examples have been inserted in the notes. The paper was published in the *Institute Annual*, 1940.

[2] For example, the manuscript horoscope of Sir Philip Sidney. See the author's *Young Philip Sidney*, 1972, Appendix 1.

and textual documents. Official documents are those which have passed through the hands of an office holder in the performance of his duties. Personal documents are the letters, diaries, notebooks, and other personal papers of the author. And textual documents include manuscript copies of literary work, whether or not in the author's holograph, as well as proof sheets or other versions of the text before it reached final revised form.

Of these three groups, official documents are frequently given the position of stepchildren and barely allowed a place on the fringe of literary research. We have much to learn on this subject from our cousins the historians. Except for Chaucerians and Shakespeareans, whose research techniques have led literary scholarship for two hundred years, our profession has made little use of official archives. It is true that each year more and more students of literature are seen in the Public Record Office, but even so, the caverns of that institution will not be exhausted for many generations to come. Moreover, literary researchers are too often satisfied with public records at second hand, going no further than the printed calendars and indexes instead of scrutinizing the documents themselves. Yet the calendars are often most untrustworthy: [3] Percy Simpson has reported some instances in which the meaning in the calendar is quite the opposite of that in the actual document. Another trouble is that pilgrimages to Chancery Lane are frequently made without remembering that the Public Record Office may contain only a small portion of the documents that are involved in an investigation. Municipal, manorial, and ecclesiastical records are as much neglected today as those of the Public Record Office were yesterday.

This situation is understandable. To the neophyte the ocean of documents appears as wide and as trackless as the Pacific did to Keats's "stout Cortez." American life is organized differently from that of Great Britain, and our scholars are often baffled when confronted by the ancient legal, ecclesiastical, and governmental structures of England. To be specific, how many persons can distinguish a "Coram Rege Roll" from a "Pipe Roll," or the Pells office from the Petty Bag office? And how many graduate students of pre-Georgian literary history are encouraged to make a study of diplomatic? Indeed, the majority of our graduate students are turned out as finished products without receiving any specific training in research among manuscripts.

---

[3] *Ibid.*, p. 166; the *Calendar of State Papers Venetian* mistranslates and misdates Sidney's Patent to Bear Arms.

In the matter of official documents even their seniors are handi-capped, for no proper guidebook has been written especially to help literary scholars find their way among the bulging archives of Great Britain.[4] Perhaps the best practical procedure is to observe the methods of those who have gone over the field with care. For the Elizabethan period Sir Edmund Chambers's treatment of the records in his *William Shakespeare* is a model. Much can be also learned from the Marlowe researches of Hotson, Brooke, Bakeless, and Eccles. Specialists in the later centuries may well examine R. C. Bald's documentary researches on John Donne. Another fine example may be seen in Dixon Wecter's brilliant monograph on *Edmund Burke and His Kinsmen*. The digger after biographical facts who will honestly compare Bald's or Wecter's documentary researches with his own will profit much. He will either be immensely stimulated or be content to relapse into the tranquillity of administrative work. Chambers, Wecter, Hotson, and others show by example the type of documentary evidence that other scholrs may hope to discover in their own researches.

The other two categories, personal documents and textual docu-ments, present enough common problems to be discussed jointly, with occasional digressions. In pursuing these problems one must use a variety of methods, devices, and techniques, the choice depending on the nature of the documents sought. One should first make a funda-mental distinction between documents that have been exposed to public view and those that are in the hands of the original owners or their descendants. In effect, the distinction is between documents that have passed through the auction rooms or the hands of dealers and those that have not.

Seeking the latter class of documents, those that have never been on the market, is like prospecting for oil. The rewards are those of oil-prospecting, too, for one good strike may compensate for many disap-pointments. There are four places where such hidden documents are likely to be found. The most natural is in the possession of the heirs of

---

[4] Much helpful information may be obtained from V. H. Galbraith's *Introduc-tion to the Use of the Public Records* (rev. ed., 1952) and the *Guide to the Con-tents of the Public Record Office* (3 vols., 1968). Read carefully for the types of records, the rules of access and the regulations concerning photocopies and publication rights. M. F. Bond's *Guide to the Records of Parliament* (1971) is indispensable for investigation within that area. Similarly, for records of the Corporation of London and those in the Guildhall Library, see the *Guide* (1951) by P. E. Jones and R. Smith. Local archives present particular problems. Consult H. Hull, *A Repertory of British Archives*, for information and addresses of local record associations.

the author in question, and in their garrets you may discover a cache to
rival the Malahide papers. The finding of heirs involves a little genealogical work, usually not difficult. If the ordinary genealogical tools are
inadequate, good use can sometimes be made of obituary articles in
newspapers, especially of the nineteenth century and after. In other
cases, effective use can be made of wills, for the law requires that the
wills of all British subjects be recorded at the Probate Registry, located
in Somerset House. After paying a modest fee you may there inspect
registered copies of wills, but much time will be saved if you will send the
fee by mail and ask that a photocopy be sent. Those who have wasted
an afternoon in the dark chambers of Somerset House will be pleased
to know that wills before 1900 are being moved to the Public Record
Office where no fee is required. Requests concerning wills known to
exist may be addressed to Jeffrey R. Ede, Director of the PRO, with a
money order for several dollars to cover costs and postage. For more
complicated requests, a list of qualified professional searchers can be obtained upon application. Some wills are not lodged there, but for most
modern wills, the authorities will tell the inquirer where they can be
found.

The second likely place to look for hidden documents is in the
possession of the heirs of an author's friends, correspondents, and patrons. Perhaps the outstanding discovery of this sort was the Boswell
bonanza at Fettercairn House, in the possession of the descendants of
Sir William Forbes, Boswell's literary executor. The first scholar to
make a systematic census of heirs was Edmond Malone, who did so
while searching for Dryden papers. He drew up a list of "Persons in
whose cabinets letters written by Dryden may probably be found," [5]
which is still consulted by Dryden scholars. Malone's example may be
profitably followed by those who wish to be systematic in their research.

Naturally, one needs tact in approaching the present representatives
of English worthies. Most Englishmen of high position resent being
molested, especially by Americans. To the great families it is generally
necessary to present an introduction, and one is not always easily obtained. Highly practical discussion of this difficult problem will be
found in Gordon N. Ray's valuable paper, *The Private Collector and
the Literary Scholar* (Clark Memorial Library Seminar, 1969, pp. 32–
42). The British assume the right to privacy, and expect social etiquette
to be observed. Idle curiosity repels the owner of a private library. The

[5] *The Prose Works of John Dryden*, 1800, I, 567–69.

demands of your scholarly project impose no obligation on him as they may on an institutional library. Facilities for making photocopies are difficult to arrange, even if the owner wishes to provide them.

The neophyte scholar embarking on a research visit to England can attempt to enlist the help of the Cultural Attaché at the American Embassy in London. (Remember, however, that his help represents a personal courtesy, not your right as a taxpayer.) He can provide you with a "To Whom It May Concern" introduction if you provide him in advance with proper documentation in Xerox form. This should include evidence of your university appointment, with reference to travel or research grants, if any, and a detailed description of your research project. Make an effort to address the Cultural Attaché by name; it can be found in the *Foreign Service List* at your university library. He may be even more helpful if you can talk with him and arouse his interest in your work: personal phone calls from the Embassy have opened doors where letters proved unavailing.

When writing to titled personages, be sure to study the correct form of address. This can be found in *Whitaker's Almanack*, under the heading "Address." The easiest explanation of such delicate matters occurs in Donald Greene's "Note on Titles" in his *Age of Exuberance*, 1970, pp. 53–55. A glance at *Who's Who* may provide some idea of the individual's interests and tastes; other information may be found by checking in a recent volume of the peerage (Burke's or Debrett's), or for commoners in the *Landed Gentry*. If possible, try in a subtle manner to appeal to family pride. Send them one of your books or articles in which their illustrious forebear plays a role, for though the article may not be read by them, it will have a psychological effect. Moreover, it will show that you have more than curiosity to recommend your petition. Sometimes I have sent a typewritten account of information, preferably new, about their ancestor with the request that it be added to the family archives, a gesture that has usually been well received.

A device that a member of this institute found useful in gaining admission to the papers in one of the great ducal houses may be mentioned. By digging around a bit he learned the shelf mark of one manuscript in the library, and although it was of no interest to him, he wrote and asked to be allowed to come and consult it. Permission was granted. After sitting with the decoy manuscript open before him for a while, our friend returned it to the librarian, and asked to see the set of papers in which he was really interested. The librarian was obliging, and the sought-for documents were produced for examination. Obviously this device should not be tried by every neophyte.

The attitudes of humbler families may be far different. Often they are pleased by attention and willing to assist in every way possible the glorification of their literary ancestor. An exceptional incident occurred when one of our countrymen applied to their heirs of an eighteenth-century poet for the use of papers in their possession and was told that he could use them only upon payment of twenty pounds. After having recovered from the blow, he agreed to pay provided they would sign an agreement prepared by a lawyer granting him exclusive publishing rights to the collection. Thus he ended by getting more than his money's worth.

The third possible source of literary materials is the author's publishing house. Among its papers, highly interesting documents may be discovered, such as proof sheets, financial agreements, and letters in which the author discusses his own writings. Once again the Dryden researches of Edmond Malone provide an example of a new technique. From the heirs of Jacob Tonson he obtained a treasure trove. Reputedly the house of Murray still owns manuscripts written by Byron and his contemporaries. For modern authors, the publisher's files are invaluable. An illustration is found in the widely dispersed papers of John Lane, the publisher of the *Yellow Book* and friend to two generations of literary men. If the Lane papers could have been preserved intact, they would have constituted an unrivaled reservoir of information on the poets and the literature of his time.

American publishers have shown more responsibility to posterity, and many of them make a practice of sending most of their papers to the Library of Congress or to other suitable institutions. Columbia University houses the archives of Random House and many from Simon and Schuster. The Scribners' correspondence is at Princeton and the Knopf papers at the University of Texas. Harper's have divided their archives between Yale and the Morgan Library. Research on the papers of American authors should begin with the index of P. H. Hamer's *Guide to Archives and Manuscripts in the United States*. Next, consult indexes to the continuing *National Union Catalogue of Manuscript Collections* which describe collections of papers "housed permanently in American repositories that are regularly open to scholars." Bulk measurements, such as number of boxes or feet of shelving, indicate the size of each collection. Researchers in British subjects should not neglect these important volumes, though the vast archives of American papers overshadow those originating overseas.

A fourth source is the literary remains of earlier scholars, which are often worth attention, since in addition to valuable hints they may contain copies of important documents. For example, when Francis Child was preparing his great edition of *English and Scottish Popular Ballads,* he derived substantial help from the collections of David Herd. Herd was an Edinburgh accountant who had published only a small selection of ballads, but had made extensive collections. Another interesting example is Walter Graham's experience in tracking down Addison letters. He learned that a long series known to be among the State Papers in Dublin had been burned in the Irish Rebellion of 1916. But by a happy stroke Graham found that his predecessor in Addison research, A. C. Guthkelch, had made transcripts of them. The letters have been printed from these copies.

A special category must be made for the documents described in the reports of the Historical Manuscripts Commission. Like those discussed previously, most of them are in the possession of the original owners, but with the significant difference that in trailing these manuscripts there is some specific information to go by. The first step is to discover if manuscripts relevant to your research are recorded. Here the *Index to Persons* will prove indispensable: two volumes (1938) cover HMC Reports published from 1870 to 1911; three additional volumes (1966) index Reports published 1911–1957. The next step will be to determine whether the manuscripts are still in the possession of the same family or if they have been sold in the years since the report was printed.

Here the National Register of Archives (Quality Court, Chancery Lane, London W.C.2) may be invaluable for your purposes. A full description of its resources and index system is in Philip Hepworth's *Selected Biographical Sources* (1971, the Library Association, 7 Ridgmount Street, London W.C.1), a volume worth careful study by any research student in British history or literature. If a visit to the National Register of Archives can supply no further information, then application may be made directly to the present representative of the former owner. Because only a hundred years have elapsed since the earliest reports were issued, the present generation of owners is easily traceable. In making overtures to them, one should take the same types of precaution that I mentioned earlier—introductions whenever possible, and tact always. And do not neglect the new HMC reports that appear from time to time.[6]

A great change in technique is required when we pass from the pursuit of documents that are still in the original place of deposit and begin to search for those that have been placed on the market and have been scattered to the seven seas. The earlier method was to get permission to fish in private waters and then to rely on skill with the rod and hook. But to catch fish that have found their way into the sea, one must use a net. And the net must be spread wide so that good luck may supplement piscatory prowess.

When a scholar sets out to use a net, it is advisable to let the rest of the world know what kind of quarry he seeks, since help may come from unsuspected quarters. Letters to the *Times Literary Supplement* and its American counterparts will cost no more than a few stamps and an hour at the typewriter, and although such announcements often fail to bring a response, many searchers have had lucky results. The officials of many American libraries, notably the Folger, take their responsibility seriously, and usually reply with a list of their holdings on the subject.

Sometimes it is wise to insert paid advertisements in the British newspapers. If you try this, remember that the *Times* is not the only important paper in England. Choose the *Telegraph* or other papers that the propertied class who own manuscripts might read, and do not forget the local newspapers. The scholar writing on Sir Thomas Browne, for example, should try the Norwich papers, and for Henry MacKenzie, the newspapers in Edinburgh. When searching for local materials it is well to correspond with a local antiquary. In case you cannot discover one easily, write to the vicar of the local church, for in many cases he will be the very man you seek. His name can usually be found in *Crockford's Clerical Directory*. Remember that vicars are traditionally as poor as church mice, so send a money order for a few dollars to cover postage and the effort required to answer. The warmth of cooperation may surprise you. Before asking for search of a parish register, check available books to learn whether those you seek are

---

[6] While one is using these valuable reports, their limitations should not be forgotten. The failure of a report to list certain manuscripts is no reason to suppose that they are not in fact to be found in the collection. And many important collections of papers are in existence which, for one reason or another, have never been reported on.

extant. A. M. Burke's *Key to the Ancient Parish Registers of England and Wales* lists these registers alphabetically for each parish.

Another way of making your research known involves direct communication with workers in the same or neighboring fields. Your work on Eustace Budgell will benefit if you correspond with students working on Addison, or Pope, or the Augustan theatre, or Grub Street. Before approaching them, make sure that you have read articles or books pertinent to your inquiries. If you have information to offer, suggest an exchange. Since generosity begets generosity, enclose several items with your initial letter. Even if you receive only a third as much in return, that amount will be all gain. Once cordial relations have been established with fellow laborers, the fruits of time will be yours. And don't be backward in talking to other scholars about your subject, for many significant clues can be picked up in conversation.

As for documents that have appeared on the market, the chances are nine to one that they are still preserved somewhere. The tenth instance allows for accidents, especially fires and other calamities. The reason they have been preserved is that once a man has paid cash for anything, he and his heirs will thenceforth consider it a potential source of ready money. There are three places where you can look for such documents: in the hands of dealers, on the shelves of collectors, or in the vaults of institutions. Most of such items pass through the hands of dealers more than once, and some of them a dozen times, as collectors die, become financially embarrassed or bored with their collections. But sooner or later, through gift or purchase, nearly all documents of any value reach a permanent home in some institution. This trend, and the fact that saleable documents are usually preserved somewhere, should be considered corollaries of documentary research.

The relations between you, as a manuscript seeker, and the dealer, as manuscript merchant, must receive your attention. Most dealers are well versed in literary lore, a type of information which may be invaluable on certain occasions. In transactions with them, however, do not lose sight of the facts that the dealer is a merchant and that he is not in business because he loves to read *Paracelsus* or *Gondibert*. Most dealers are kindly disposed toward scholars, and at your request, many of them will allow you to make copies of low- or medium-priced documents. But they rightly feel that the existence of a duplicate lowers the marketability of their merchandise, and so they may demur if you ask for copies of expensive manuscripts.

It is highly desirable to establish personal relations with at least one dealer, preferably the one who is most active and learned in your field. For medievalists and Elizabethans, Goldschmidt, H. P. Kraus and Quaritch might be most satisfactory; for the Restoration and the eighteenth century, Theodore Hofmann is knowledgeable, as are Winifred Myers and Maggs Brothers. Among American dealers who specialize in manuscripts, Mary Benjamin, Kenneth Rendell, Paul Richards and John Fleming may be named.

The best way to build up personal relations with a dealer is, naturally, to give him an occasional order. If it happens that you are not in a position to buy even a few dollars' worth of merchandise per year from your chosen dealer, you may be able to arrange with your college library to route a few of their orders or inquiries through his firm. If the dealer knows you have his interests at heart, he will not forget your interests, and when he sees a letter or diary that is essential for, let us say, your definitive biography of Eustace Budgell, he may pass along a hint of its whereabouts. Even more important, the dealer may offer you or your library a chance to acquire important documents that he has purchased privately. For example, the late Gabriel Wells obtained from the heirs of John G. Lockhart the heavily annotated proof sheets of Lockhart's *Life of Scott*. He promptly offered them to a scholar who, he knew, would be interested in them. Without the existence of this personal relationship, the documents might have been sold privately and have remained inaccessible, if not unknown, for decades to come. The scholar who is alert will find frequent opportunities to purchase, at fair market prices, documents that are of definite literary importance. Except for the "high spots," literary manuscripts are often good investments for the working scholar.

But regardless of your success in establishing personal relations with someone in the trade, it is necessary to keep an eagle eye on the catalogues of the principal dealers in order that knowledge of available manuscripts may not escape you. Most dealers will send you their catalogues if encouraged to do so. Furthermore, you must see that your university library does not lack them. Catalogue reading can become a time-consuming habit if one does not keep in mind the law of diminishing returns, yet I have heard no less a scholar than David Nichol Smith declare that booksellers' catalogues had made a definite contribution to his education.

For work that is intended to be definitive in scope, it is necessary to make a systematic perusal of the back numbers of catalogues issued by the principal manuscript dealers since the beginning of the nineteenth century. Those of Thomas Thorpe abound with information about letters and other documents, now unlocated, which presumably exist somewhere. During earlier decades of this century, the catalogues of Robinson, Dobell, Colbeck, Radford and Bernard Halliday (all now discontinued), offered much remarkable manuscript material, as did those of firms still vigorous, especially Maggs and Quaritch. The task of skimming through these early catalogues may take several weeks but it will yield information about documents whose existence might not otherwise be known to you.

Analogous to the catalogues of dealers are those of the leading auction houses, Sotheby's and Christies' in England, as well as Hodgson's, now out of business, but whose old catalogues contain much of interest. In New York, Charles Hamilton and Parke-Bernet are active in manuscript sales. The catalogues of Parke-Bernet's predecessor, Anderson-American Art Gallery, may be checked for sales of the booming 1920s. Every university library should subscribe to current catalogues of rare book and manuscripts, and in my opinion serious literary historians should themselves subscribe to the Sotheby catalogues. Each year many highly important manuscripts are placed on the market for the first time. Even the shelf-worn stock sold by the trade, usually catalogued as "Other Properties," may be important for your purpose. It is more important to examine the auction catalogues of former years than the catalogues of dealers, although actually the two complement each other. These catalogues often reproduce passages from interesting documents, which may be useful to you even if the original cannot be found. Some day there may be an index to the most important contents of these sale catalogues, but at present each man must traverse the ground for himself. In such a search there is another tool, of limited utility—the sizeable list of "Autographs and Manuscripts" sold at auction, printed at the end of *Book Prices Current*; volumes covering the years 1941–1965 contain cumulative indexes.

To keep well informed about newly available manuscripts, several other steps may be taken. Most of the important libraries include in their annual reports a summary of their principal acquisitions. These publications can be inspected in your library or, better yet, can be subscribed for directly. The *Annual Report* of the Curators of the Bodleian and the British Museum Quarterly can be obtained for a small sum. Interim reports are found in the publications of many American libraries, among them the John Carter Brown, the Newberry, the Huntington, the Folger, Princeton, Texas, and Yale, to mention only a few examples.

The *Bulletin* of the Institute of Historical Research devotes several pages to news about historical manuscripts that have recently changed ownership. One section lists those acquired by British libraries and permanent repositories; the other part is called "Migrations" and lists manuscripts sold at auction, offered by dealers, or otherwise changing hands among private parties. Fortunately the editor's definition of "historical manuscripts" is broad enough to include many documents of interest to literary researchers. Perhaps some day one of our periodicals will publish a similar list called "The Migrations of Literary Manuscripts." It is urgently needed.

When you begin to seek manuscripts that have already passed from dealers to collectors, a different set of problems must be faced. Probably the most difficult situation is that in which the manuscript and its location are known, but the collector wishes to keep his prize to himself. Generally, there is little that can be done in such a case. The best approach is through some intermediary who has the collector's confidence, for example, someone with whom he sits on a board of directors, or one of his cronies at the Grolier Club. But even the best ambassador will fail if the collector is a real hoarder, or if, as has occurred in several notorious cases, his collections are in pawn. But such collectors are the exception; most of them are generous almost to the point of cordiality in allowing *bone fide* students to use their treasures. Many collectors consider themselves patrons of learning and the arts. A psychological factor is also involved—one of the motives behind collecting is the hope of obtaining erudition vicariously. So, too, attention from a scholar implies that the manuscript in question was worth the price the collector paid for it. Once access to the inner sanctum has been granted, most collectors will display their rarities as long as you show a polite interest, for you may be the first intelligent audience in months. It is needless to warn you against the greatest insult you can make to any collector: never imply that he has paid too much for anything. And don't expect him to know much about literary or bibliographical matters outside his own collection.

To locate manuscripts in collections unknown to you, about all that can be done is to trust to luck and keep on trying.[7] Here is where

---

[7] A number of collectors have published accounts of the manuscripts that they have brought together. It is worth while to look over the following, in particular:

personal relations with a dealer bear fruit. Sometimes his knowledge will be confidential, but at other times the information can be passed along openly. Whatever the topic of your research may be, it is advisable to assume that someone somewhere has made a collection on the subject. Inquiries should be made before the work has advanced very far, but even then you may discover a collection of your special material after plans for publication have been made. Arthur Case had this experience with his valuable bibliography of *Poetical Miscellanies*. The book was already in proof when he learned that, unknown to specialists, the world's best collection of miscellanies was in Chicago, not ten miles from his own door.

In attempting to find such collections, only a few blind steps can be taken. First, consult the directory (1973) of members of The Manuscript Society, and subsequent issues of their journal, *Manuscripts*. Though mostly concerned with American autographs, when used intelligently, *Manuscripts* will yield valuable clues. Secondly, the dealer with whom you have contact may know of a collection on the subject you seek, or he might be persuaded to keep his ear to the ground. Any collector with whom you are acquainted should also be questioned. And if a choice manuscript appears at an auction, tracing it may lead to a whole collection of material useful to you. Similar clues can be derived from tracing the ownership of manuscripts loaned for exhibitions. De Ricci's *Census* is also useful within the limits of time and geography that governed its compilation.[8]

The greatest private collections in the world are, however, mere molehills compared to those amassed by the great national and institutional libraries. As I suggested a moment ago, nearly all documents sooner or later come to rest in permanent repositories. This process is nowhere better revealed than at the Bodleian, which was the national repository for one hundred and fifty years before the British Museum came into existence. And the great component collections still kept under the names of their donors—Laud, Selden, Junius, Tanner, Rawlinson, Malone, Douce, and others—show that Bodley's manuscript trea-

---

Catalogue of the Collection of Autograph Letters Formed by Alfred Morrison, 1885; *Meditations of an Autograph Collector*, by A. H. Joline, New York, 1902; *An Autograph Collection*, by Lady Charnwood, London, 1930; *The R. B. Adam Johnsonian Collection*, 1929 (now part of the Hyde Collection, Somerville, New Jersey); the facsimile reprint of the catalogues 1831–71 of the Phillipps Collection, 1968.

[8] Seymour De Ricci, *A Census of Medieval and Renaissance Manuscripts in the United States and Canada*, 3 vols., New York, 1935–37, and the important *Supplement*, 1962.

sures essentially consist of great collections arranged next to one another. The British Museum, of course, was founded on the great Cottonian and Harleian collections, to which many other notable ones have been added. The same is true to a limited degree of even the modern libraries like the John Rylands and the Huntington.

For most seekers of English literary documents, the British Museum is the first port of call. But that is no reason to rush there blindly before investigating how many of its treasures would be available without the expense of a trans-Atlantic ticket. Most Americans wait until they have entered the portals at Great Russell Street before making a systematic search of the catalogues of the Museum's manuscripts; indeed, the average graduate student does not know that these catalogues are available in his university library. By going through them carefully, one can determine how much preliminary material is available, and microfilms or photostats can be ordered without waiting for a traveling fellowship or a sabbatical year. It is my observation that most traveling fellows who journey to England spend at least half their working time there hovering over materials that could have been photostated and sent to them in America. A shelf load of microfilms or photocopies can be bought for the price of a ticket. Of course, other values are derived from a literary pilgrimage to England, but often the amount of completed research fails to justify the financial sacrifices involved.

These comments apply to the first steps in manuscript research: learning what materials exist on a chosen subject, and preliminary work on them. After these preliminary steps, scholarly use of the manuscripts requires that you see the documents themselves. Important evidence is often missed by the student dependent on photocopies. Differences in ink, over-scorings and later additions may not show distinctly. Differences in paper, especially in watermarks, require actual handling of the documents. Photographic employees often decide what to copy, and sometimes omit leaves bearing only a postmark or a docket inscription. Bindings and end-papers often reveal provenance from book-plates, signatures, and dealers' pencilings. Moreover, most private owners and many institutions are reluctant to allow photocopies out of their control. Beginning students have so frequently indulged in lazy microfilm-ordering sprees that curators of manuscript collections have become wary. Indeed, one of the dividends resulting from work-on-the-spot arises from developing a relationship with the curator or custodian in charge of the manuscripts. Once a personal relationship exists, a few minutes of polite conversation might elicit more information than could be gained in a dozen exchanges of letters.

Thus expensive journeys for research should be made only after adequate preparation; the printed catalogues to the great British libraries should be exhausted before searching for a seat in the overcrowded reading rooms. The catalogues of manuscripts in the Bodleian and the British Museum, not to mention others, are the most neglected tools for research in English literature. For browsing purposes, their pages are a scholar's delight.[9] In addition to the printed catalogues, there is in the Student's Manuscript Room at the Museum a series of class (e.g., poetry, letters, etc.) catalogues, of which only one copy exists. They are described in T. C. Skeats's *Catalogues of the Manuscript Collections in the British Museum* (rev. edn. 1962). If your subject is a fairly specific one—a biography of Eustace Budgell, to use our former example—a letter can be sent directly to the superintendent of the Manuscript Room asking him to send a list of entries which may appear in the class catalogues under the name Budgell. This will be done without charge, but further work, such as transcribing and photographing, involves a small fee.

If your research concerns a poet or a type of poetry, full use should be made of Margaret Crum's *First-Line Index to English Poetry in the Manuscripts of the Bodleian Library, 1500–1800* (1969). These two thick volumes lead you to manuscript texts of 23,000 poems, most of which have never reached print. An interleaved copy at Yale contains entries for manuscript poems in the Osborn Collection; 3,500 other poems in this collection and "not in Crum" are listed in a card file. The Huntington Library has a first-line index of its manuscript poems, as has the Folger Library, as far as the year 1700. The British Museum first-line index occupies fourteen folio volumes listing over 17,000 poems but omits those containing bawdy words, among them, many by the Earl of Rochester; a microfilm copy (six reels) is available at Yale.[10] When properly used, these first-line indexes may add poems to the canon of your chosen author, Budgell.

The same type of written inquiry may be sent to the Bodleian as to the British Museum, but their slip index to the manuscripts is based

[9] Interesting documents are sometimes found in "grangerized" volumes, of which the British Museum copy of Moore's *Life of Byron* is perhaps the best known.

[10] See the author's discussion, "Fingerprinting Poems" in *Books and Libraries*, University of Kansas, April, 1972.

on the printed catalogues, and so it will add little to what you have already found in them. The University Library at Cambridge does not contain manuscripts comparable to the Bodleian or the British Museum, but its catalogues should not be neglected. Some of the colleges, especially Trinity and St. Johns, have very valuable collections, particularly of medieval and Elizabethan literature. Their catalogues, like those of the Oxford colleges, the Rylands Library, the Bretherton Library, the Hunterian Library, and the National Library of Scotland, should be systematically examined before written inquiries are made. You may be surprised at the richness of their contents. Indeed, our pride in the Pierpont Morgan and other great manuscript collections in the United States is rudely deflated when the contents of some of the smaller English libraries, for example, Corpus Christi College, Cambridge, are compared with them. Students whose researches center on Anglo-Saxon documents or Chaucer manuscripts do not need to have this truth emphasized. Only one complete Anglo-Saxon document is on this side of the Atlantic, the "Blickling Homilies" in the Scheide Collection at Princeton. While stressing the riches of these smaller British libraries, I do not wish to imply that the holdings of American libraries are inconsiderable. But the value and extent of their manuscript treasures are so well known that a delineation of the subject would be superfluous. And the intelligent assistance rendered by the authorities at the Folger, the Huntington, the Pierpont Morgan, the Boston Public, the Historical Society of Pennsylvania, and a score of other libraries should be a source of national pride.

The most systematic method of determining whether these institutions in Europe and in America have any manuscripts of use to you is to conduct a so-called census by mail. If your query is brief and specific, then a reply postcard may be used. For longer inquiries, a form letter is preferable, prepared so that information may be supplied in blank spaces on the letter before it is returned to you.

Once you have made full use of the printed catalogues and have supplemented them with postal inquiries, the time will have come to go to the places where you suspect manuscripts will be found. Many important discoveries have resulted from this simple procedure of going to the places concerned. Perhaps the most spectacular example is that of James Clifford who set out on a bicycle to visit all the haunts of Mrs. Thrale-Piozzi. At a remote farmhouse in a Welsh valley, he was finally rewarded by discovering several bushels of manuscripts, including some of Dr. Johnson and Fanny Burney. Back in London, he visited the brewery that had once belonged to Thrale, and there he uncovered a hundred more letters. Just being on the spot and active in the pursuit may result in unexpected good fortune. The luck of Anna Kitchel is also an example to be remembered. While riding on a London bus, she was discussing her pursuit of materials about George Henry Lewes. The woman sitting in front of her turned suddenly and asked, "Would you be interested in Lewes's diaries?"

Less dramatic discoveries are also to be made in the libraries among uncatalogued and miscatalogued documents. Arthur Case's discovery of the anecdotes about Pope which Spence had sent Warburton is a clear instance of an important document being miscatalogued. If you will "go to the places" and make a thorough examination of the evidence, you cannot fail to discover new documents or find new significance in some of the old ones. In the phrase of Wilmarth Lewis, "expose yourself to luck."

Thus the finding of literary documents, like the finding of anything else, depends less on the devices, tricks, and techniques than on the amount of diligence, common sense, and imagination put into the task. It is after you have found the documents that the real work will begin.

I. 2

Mimesis and Allegory*

W. H. AUDEN

New School for Social Research

SOCIETIES COME to grief if and when they are confronted by problems for which their technique or their metaphysics or both are inadequate, and every technical advance requires a parallel advance in metaphysics. What we call civilization, that is, a rational order of activities and societies, each aware of its special function and of its relation to others, would have been impossible without the monotheistic concept of fate, a common horizon against which even the gods must play their parts, the assumption that throughout the universe there is one set of laws which the universe obeys and which cannot be altered by anybody's art.

One, at least, of the causes for the breakdown of classical civilization was a failure to relate this abstract concept to the concrete phenomenal world; it remained a high-brow satisfaction only. History can always be counted upon to show that a false proposition is not true and that a relative presupposition is not absolute; but it cannot of itself produce absolute presuppositions. The man in the Athenian street lost his faith in the gods, but the philosophers were unable to replace that faith by anything he could understand from his own experience, so that he easily stepped into the nihilistic conclusion expressed by Euripides in Hecuba: "The Gods are strong and convention which rules them. For by convention we believe in the Gods and define justice and injustice." By rejecting as heresies both Arianism and Manicheeism, the Christian Church was able to relate the universal to the

* Read at the Institute in September 1940. Published in the *Institute Annual*, 1941.

particular, the spiritual to the material, and made the technical advance of civilization possible.

Again, the invention of the microscope needed to be balanced by the idealism of Berkeley. Unless it had been realized that the existence of a world of nature—"of things to which events happen, things which move"[1]—was not a proposition to be proved true or false by experiment, but an absolute presupposition, an act of faith, science might well have wasted its time trying to prove that matter existed.

What is unique about our present crisis is that there seem so few technical reasons for it; the conquest of material nature is already a fact. If we are going to break down, it seems, then, that our failure will be largely a metaphysical failure. And what is true for life as a whole is true for art in particular. An unsound aesthetic or no aesthetic at all can be as damaging to art as an unsound ethic can be to conduct.

I have entitled this paper "Mimesis and Allegory" in order to have terms for two apparently contradictory characteristics of art. In the first place we expect art, in some way or other, to be like Life, though we may severally mean very different things by "like" and by "life." To one, art may mean a representation of the facts of the phenomenal world in the same order and with the same emphasis as they are presented to consciousness by the senses; to another, a representation of mental images in the same order and with the same emphasis as they are presented to consciousness from the unconscious; to a third, a revelation of the laws which govern life.

At the same time the very name "art" implies that it is in some way or other unlike life. Even the most ardent realist must use a medium which is not identical with his subject. Richard Strauss might exclaim joyfully, "Soon we shall be able to imitate exactly the sound of a fork on a plate," but it would never have occurred to him simply to use a fork as an orchestral instrument. In primitive societies the difference between art and life is only vaguely realized. The incantation of a curse is believed to be as practically effective as a stab with a knife, but aesthetics only begins when it is realized that one man curses another precisely because he knows he is unable to murder him. It is unlike life for other reasons, too: the life it is attempting to represent may be too abstract to be communicable without giving a special case, or too uniquely personal to be communicable without giving the gen-

[1] R. G. Collingwood, *An Essay on Metaphysics*, Oxford, 1940.

eral case, or in some way so forbidden and unpleasant that it must be referred to in terms of something which, though related to it, is pleasant and acceptable.

I have used only two terms to keep the antithesis simple. In fact, of course, there are two kinds of "unlikeness"—allegory and symbolism. Allegory is a conscious rhetorical device; one of its forms is metaphor. A symbol is any object to which value is attached in excess of its apparent value. What is only allegorical for one, may be symbolic for another. A foreigner sees an American cartoon of an elephant and a donkey and recognizes an allegory of two political parties. For a passionate Republican the elephant may attract all the emotions connected with his father, liberty, and God, and the donkey may remind him, not only of the man in the White House, but of his childish nightmares, blood, impotence, and death.

Allegory, being a conscious figure of expression, is one-dimensional and flat; symbolism is ambiguous and round, for which reason, perhaps, artists like Melville who use symbols, appear more "realistic" than allegorists like Langland or Bunyan. Precisely because the significance of the symbol is vaguer and further removed from the sign, its representation must be more exact. Further, since the creation of a work of art is, in the artist's experience, a conscious act, and the significance of a symbol is unconscious, the artist himself will tend to give an allegorical interpretation of figures which are really symbolic. The aesthetic of Dryden and Pope, with its emphasis on wit and fancy rather than on imagination, is one-sided because the artist's experience of what he is doing is one-sided. The artist is inclined to overstress the conscious element in his work, while the uncreative reader overstresses the unconscious element. The romantic aesthetic is a reader's aesthetic.

I am going to center my remarks in the work of one man, Richard Wagner. I choose him because he seems to me the greatest and the most typical modern artist, the forerunner, and in many ways the creator, of both the high-brow and the low-brow tastes of our time.

Before Proust or Joyce, it was Wagner who, under the banner of realism, recreated the world in his own image. With one hand he pointed toward the photographic realism of Zola, with the other toward the symbolic and the heroic. Before Mr. Goldwyn was born, it was Wagner who discovered that crowds will go to see a show just because it has cost a million dollars and there will be real horses on the stage. It was Wagner who saw that if Work A is twice as long as Work

B the public will think Work A is twice as serious. At the same time it was Wagner who set a standard for the expression of subtle emotional nuances which not even Henry James surpassed. But it was Wagner also who, with his unscrupulous stimulation of the nerves by orchestral colors and noise, created a taste for the Wurlitzer. It was Wagner who showed the surrealists that the primitive, the illogical, the chance-determined was the true revolutionary art and who preceded Sibelius and Gertrude Stein in the discovery that if you repeat the same thing four times it has little effect, but that a remarkable effect can be gained by repeating it four hundred times. With the possible exception of Goethe's *Faust*, his operas are the first major works which did not assume the Christian beliefs, and, finally, as the inventor of artistic nationalism his political influence, as we know to our cost, has been profound. We are all his heirs, whether we like it or not, and he was greater than we are.

He had the naïveté of decadence. That was his spontaneity. He believed in it, he did not stop before any logic of decadence. The others hesitate; that distinguishes them; nothing else. The incomplete is set aside by the presence of the complete. Wagner was complete. He was courage, he was will, he was conviction in corruption.[2]

Let us take the *Ring*. What is it *about?* In what ways is it an imitation of the life we know or a part of it, and in what ways is it an allegorical picture? At once we come up against a paradox. The plot and the characters are clearly allegorical, yet within the limits of the operatic form the treatment is as realistic, in Zola's sense, as possible. Wagner broke away from the Italian tradition of formal arias and ensembles on the ground that they were artificial, and he developed the recitative into "infinite melody" conforming to the rhythms of the natural speaking voice. Let us first take the story, the allegory. In general terms it is about the passing away of an old order. Since history is a continuous dynamic process, such a situation continually reoccurs; what order is allegorized by the Gods of Valhalla will depend upon the historical period or geographical location of the audience. From Wagner's point of view, however, the allegory concerned a particular order. The historian will see a picture of a nineteenth-century struggle in Germany between a reactionary nobility (the gods), the money-grabbing bourgeoisie (the dwarfs), and the powerful but stupid proletariat (the

[2] Nietzsche, *The Case of Wagner*, tr. by Thomas Common, p. 50.

giants), from all of whom Germany is delivered by the hero who is afraid of none of them (Siegfried) and the emancipated woman (Brünnehilde). And it is in this sense, despite Brünnehilde's lack of interest in cooking and children, that the Nazis have taken it.

But this interpretation becomes difficult in *Götterdämmerung*. Siegfried and Brünnehilde do not create the new world, they go up in flames with the old, and the "Ring" of civilization goes back to the primitive Rhine. We are given to understand that the new world will be re-created, but it is left vague how and by whom. Again, if we take it as a particular allegory, that is, as a picture of conscious human beings capable of reasoning and free will, the behavior of the characters is odd, not because they make mistakes for which later they will have to suffer, but because they know beforehand that they are mistakes. In *Oedipus Rex* the audience knows what Oedipus is doing, but he himself is ignorant. In the *Ring*, on the other hand, the actors are never tired of explaining exactly what is going to happen and how awful it will be; they deny their own knowledge. For example, Valhalla is set alight by faggots from the World Ash Tree. Why does Wotan leave such dangerous and inflammable material there? If Wotan knows that his power depends upon keeping treaties, why does he build Valhalla by a trick? If he is able to create a saving race who hate the gods, why does he have to give way to Fricka? If he knows that all he fashions are slaves, why does he choose to beget them, or, if he so chooses, why does he mind? He says: "Though the gods are ending, I feel no anguish since it works my will." If so, why does he postpone the ending for so long? Alberich forswears love, but he is shown as a person who already is incapable of it.

The critic is compelled by these difficulties to remember that Wagner began as a political revolutionary and then became interested in Schopenhauer, who taught him that the will was evil and that history was an endless cycle.

Suppose we try another interpretation, the psychoanalytical. Assuming that all actions in the phenomenal world are dramatizations of transphenomenal conflicts, what does the story mean? The Rhine is the unconscious mind, Valhalla the conscious; the gods are the conscious faculties of thinking and feeling, the dwarfs and giants, the unconscious faculties of intuition and sensation. The treasure of the unconscious instincts can only be fashioned into the *Ring* of art and civilization by one who will renounce the incest wish, and can only be forged into the sword of purposive action by the one who is not afraid of them. The intellect (Wotan) is unable to obey its own logic because it is always being swayed by emotions (women) and cannot renounce the infantile incest wish (Wotan begets Brünnehilde upon Erda).

The whole cycle of the *Ring*, indeed, is full of incest; it is precisely this love that is never renounced. As a political allegory the birth of a hero through the incest of Siegmund and Sieglinde may be sound— only those who are not bound by the tabus of their culture can reform it—but as a psychological allegory, incest is a regressive step.

Again, it is in *Götterdämmerung* that the allegory becomes so vague. When, in the third act of *Siegfried*, the young hero awakens Brünnehilde, the libretto makes it very clear that he regards her as a mother and that she regards him as a son, even, in a sense, a rejuvenated father. What one would expect in *Götterdämmerung* is a dramatization of growing up: Brünnehilde would marry Gunther and Siegfried, Gutrune; but such behavior is portrayed as infidelity occasioned by magic and fatal to them both. The final moral would seem to be: civilization can only be built by those who renounce incest, but those who renounce incest are destroyed and destroy civilization at the same time.

Just as an irregularity in the orbit of a planet can lead to the discovery of a hitherto unknown planet, so discrepancy in an allegory points to something of which the artist himself was unaware. Believing that he is allegorizing A, he may unconsciously be imitating B: to find B, the critic must turn his attention from the work of art to its creator.

Every artist attempts to give an objective picture of the world, but since he is himself a part of it, such objectivity can never be complete; and Wagner was less objective than most. With his extraordinary acumen Nietzsche put his finger on this.

The Wagnerian heroines each and all, when one has only stripped them of their heroic trappings, are the counterparts of Madame Bovary. Yes, taken as a whole, Wagner appears to have no interest in any other problems than those which at present interest pretty Parisian decadents. Always just five steps from the hospital. Nothing but quite modern problems, nothing but problems of a great city.[3]

What from Wagner's point of view was an allegory of the destruction of a moribund order and the emergence of a heroic, becomes, then, an imitation of bourgeois life in an industrial civilization. Hence

[3] Nietzsche: *The Case of Wagner*, p. 34.

Wagner's popularity. Little people frightened of losing their jobs and bewildered by the perplexity of modern life do feel that they are in the hands of a fate they cannot control; they are often seized with the desire to smash everything; they do, like Tristan, welcome the night of dreams as a relief from the dullness of their working day; they are bewildered by the rebellion of their children.

This becomes even more obvious when we consider Wagner, not as a citizen, but as an artist. In his own life he suffered a great deal, and suffering was what he understood how to express. The illogical behavior of his characters becomes intelligible when we realize that its purpose is to allow Wagner to go on writing the kind of music he was good at writing.

In the expression of physical suffering (Amfortas), the suffering of unrequited love (Hans Sachs), the suffering of self-love (Tristan and Isolde), the suffering of betrayed love (Brünnehilde), the sufferings, in short, of failure, Wagner is one of the greatest geniuses who ever lived. But only in the expression, "the imitation," of suffering; happiness, social life, mystical joy, and success were beyond him. His finest passages are monologues, and the introduction of more than two people onto a stage usually ruins the music. Even the finale of *Die Meistersinger* suggests a military parade, something unspontaneous. The contrast between the lack of will shown by his characters and Wagner's own amazing will power is extraordinary. This is perhaps to be expected. From Luther, saying, "I can no other," to Hitler, looking at the ruins of Warsaw and saying, "Why do they try to resist my destiny?" strong-willed persons have usually been determinists, and in the case of an artist this tendency is encouraged by his relation to his medium. All the more so if, like Wagner or Whitman, he breaks with the traditional forms; everything in the creative act seems unconsciously determined, an authoritative personal utterance.

In what respects, then, can Wagner's work be called good or bad? Suppose the critic says that art should be true to life and that by true to life he means an exposition of events as governed by certain laws; will his verdict depend upon his beliefs? Will the critic find the *Ring* good if he is a disciple of Schopenhauer and bad if he is, let us say, a Roman Catholic? If, on the other hand, by "true to life" is meant an accurate representation of the conduct and beliefs of particular people living in a particular historical period, does the value of the *Ring* depend upon the historical and psychological perspective of the audience? Is it false to the ingenuous who take it at its face value and true to the sophisticated who are able to see what the allegory is really about?

I must confess that I cannot myself solve this dilemma. My personal experience tells me that, while one does not necessarily have to accept the beliefs expressed in a work of art in order to appreciate it, they cannot be ignored and that sometimes they seem so silly as to arouse aesthetic dislike. Again, observation of others leads me to think that of two people who respond favorably to the same work, one may respond in a way which suggests the illegitimate satisfaction of bad art and the other in a way which one recognizes as a response to good art.

Lastly, I suspect that when one likes a work containing beliefs with which one disagrees, one does not, as Coleridge thought, "willingly suspend belief," but tries rather to allegorize them, to see them in historical relation to a historical absolute background of one's own beliefs, and that is why readers of poetry who have not yet learned this mental habit or lack the necessary historical knowledge are inclined, as Dr. I. A. Richards has shown in his *Practical Criticism*, to insist upon identity of belief.

Such questions necessarily involve morals. We have two kinds of experience: the first, objective experience of the world outside consciousness, entering as sensory images or as memories from our unconscious; this kind of experience is governed by causal necessity, that is, it is presented to us independently of our will, and it is either pleasant or unpleasant. The second, subjective, or consciousness of our own conscious faults: this kind of experience is accessible to the will, and is governed by whatever is our conception of logical and moral necessity; it is here that ethical judgments are made, and conduct decided—experience here is either good or evil. Similarly there are two classes of events: those which we cannot alter or prevent by our own actions, and those which we can. Of the first, some, like war, floods, disease, the stars, and so forth, are unalterable because they are larger and stronger than we; others, simply because they have already occurred. If we call unpleasant events which are unalterable tribulations, and evil events which are preventable temptations, then science and art are both concerned primarily with tribulations, but in different ways. The aim of science is to convert tribulations into temptations, an insoluble problem of passive endurance into a soluble problem of conduct, the unpleasant into the evil. Let us take psychotherapy as an example. Imagine a

puritanical young man tormented by phantasies that he is cutting
women's throats. He is restrained from doing so not only by his consciousness but also by fear of the police and public opinion. He tries to
suppress his phantasies; he fails; they get worse. He suffers in tribulation till he goes to a psychologist and with his help unravels his complex and is cured, that is, the phantasies cease, his attitude toward
women becomes normal, and he no longer believes that sexual desire is
in all circumstances wicked. Presently he falls in love with a married
woman. This time no psychologist can help him; the police are indifferent. He is faced with a conscious temptation; he alone can decide
whether to yield or to resist. Science has not made him better or worse;
it has only increased his responsibility.

But there are always tribulations which science has not yet been
able to change into temptations and which it will never be able to
change because they have already happened. It is with these that art is
concerned; the Muses are the daughters of memory. For if past events
cannot be altered, our attitude toward them can. They can be accepted;
their relation to each other and the present can be understood. The
moralist's attack on art comes from his confusion of art with science. A
book, for example, about sharecroppers is scientifically valuable in
proportion to its power to change conditions; it is aesthetically valuable
in proportion to its power to help sharecroppers endure with understanding these conditions until they are changed. Naturally enough,
these two values do not always coincide. When we say that art is beyond good and evil, what we really mean is that "good" and "evil" are
terms which can only be applied to our own conscious choices, but not
to the past, because it cannot be undone, or to the world outside ourselves, because it is not our own property. We do not mean that art has
no moral effect, but only that the latter depends upon our individual
responses.

Many people who demand that art be moral only want to be told
that moral behavior is easy and makes one happy and rich. But if the
respectable citizen falls into error, so does the anarchist bohemian. The
romantic rebels from Baudelaire down to the "art for art's sake" school
of the nineties were, in fact, intensely and all too moral. Their fundamental premise was a simple one: the "good" equals what the bourgeoisie do not do. The bourgeoisie manufacture, therefore manufac-
turers such as Alberich are bad. The bourgeoisie think incest wicked,
therefore heroes like Siegmund will commit incest. Comedy may be

possible on such a negative basis, but not tragedy. To the bourgeois who is incapable of loving another sufficiently ever to want to commit suicide, *Romeo and Juliet* can only be a psychological case history—a sordid police-court case. To the bohemian who regards any restriction on his sex impulses as absurd and, for others at least, if not for himself, approves of suicide, the play can only be a romantic comedy, a beautiful fairy tale. It becomes a tragedy only if we admit that Romeo and Juliet are superior to ourselves in the intensity of their love, but that, even so, suicide is morally wrong. It is not a police-court case, because we are made to realize how great is their temptation to die; it is not a comedy, because they finally succumb.

Both these false moral attitudes result from an attempt to find in art a bolster or substitute for a faith in which people no longer believe and are symptoms of the romantic revolt against Protestantism. Protestantism, like democracy, is based upon the assumption that controversy is a form of coöperation, and ultimately the only way of arriving at truth, and that the average man is sufficiently energetic and interested in truth to take his part in looking for it, sufficiently intelligent to recognize logical necessity, and sufficiently humble to obey it. If he is lazy or bored or stupid or conceited, it must fail, because you must either look for the truth yourself or accept as true what someone else tells you; truth will not come to you of its own accord.

Kierkegaard puts this very well:

Luther set up the highest spiritual principle: pure inwardness. It may become so dangerous that . . . in Protestantism a point may be reached at which worldliness may be honoured and highly valued as—piety. And this—as I maintain—cannot happen in Catholicism. But why can it not happen in Catholicism? Because Catholicism has the universal premise that we men are pretty well rascals. And why can it happen in Protestantism? Because the Protestant principle is related to a particular premise: a man who sits in the anguish of death, in fear and trembling and much tribulation—and of these there are not many in any one generation.[4]

The romantic movement has been, *au fond*, an attempt to find a new nonsupernatural Catholicism, and because art is a shared thing and so in this sense catholic, one of the romantic symptoms has been an enormous exaggeration of the importance of art as a guide to life, and, within art itself, an emphasis on the unconscious, the childish, and the irrational in the hope that in these lie human unity. The change

[4] *Journals of Søren Kierkegaard*, London, 1938, p. 513.

can be seen clearly if we compare a Wagner opera with one by Mozart. If, by the life that art is to imitate, we mean our conscious and social daily life, then Mozart is the more realistic. If, on the other hand, we mean our unconscious dream life, then Wagner is the better imitator.

The modern artist is in a dilemma. If he has beliefs, realizing that he cannot assume them in his audience, he is tempted to underline them in his work and to become a preacher of pious religious or political sermons to the faithful. If he has none, he is drawn either like Wagner to a mythical symbolism, or, like *Time* magazine to realistic reporting, evading the problem of belief by presenting something which is as ambiguous as life itself and so putting the audience vis-à-vis his work in the same situation as he is toward life. I. A. Richards is right, I think, in his account of how art organizes attitudes, but the criterion by which we judge the value of such an organization lies outside art. That this is not always obvious is only because the works which we subject to analysis are usually very short. If we confine our attention to the movements of the sun and of the earth, our observations can be coördinated equally well by a Ptolemaic or a Copernican theory; it is only when we consider them within a larger field that the former hypothesis becomes inadequate. Similarly, it is only when we approach a large work of art, such as the *Ring*, that the problem of belief becomes acute. Perhaps that is why most modern works are small or, if large like those of Wagner, Proust, and Joyce, memorable in detail rather than as wholes.

One solution, and it is highly recommended by many, is some new form of catholic belief; but whether the freedom of choice, the specialization of occupation, and the detachment of community from locality created by science can now permit anything along such lines, except crude slogans imposed by ruthless force, is doubtful. The alternative is the acceptance by every individual of his aloneness and his responsibility for it, the overcoming of his natural distaste or ineptitude for thinking about anything that is not immediately and obviously connected with his job, and a willingness continually to reëxamine his absolute assumptions in the light of his own experience and that of others. Art is not metaphysics any more than it is conduct, and the artist is usually unwise to insist too directly in his art upon his beliefs; but without an adequate and conscious metaphysics in the background, art's imitation of life inevitably becomes, either a photostatic copy of the accidental details of life without pattern or significance, or a personal allegory of the artist's individual dementia, of interest primarily to the psychologist and the historian.

The choice was put to them whether they would like to be kings or kings' couriers. Like children, they all wanted to be couriers. So now there are a great many couriers, they post through the world and, as there are no kings left, shout to each other their meaningless and obsolete messages. They would gladly put an end to their wretched lives but they dare not because of their oath of service.[5]

[5] Franz Kafka, *The Great Wall of China*, London, 1933, p. 265.

I. 3

The Parallelism between Literature and the Arts[*]

RENÉ WELLEK

The State University of Iowa

THE TITLE of my address, "the parallelism between literature and the arts," may sound, I fear, somewhat cryptic and vague. I chose it because I could not think of a simple title which would clearly indicate my problem: what use is there, for the study of literature, in the comparisons and parallels drawn between literature and the arts? Which of these methods are legitimate and have led to illuminating results? Are we justified in assuming a unitary time-spirit which pervades all the arts of a given period and makes parallels between the arts not only possible but also necessary? These are large questions, and I should like to define my problem even more narrowly, as I do not want to forget that I am speaking at the *English* Institute and don't want to indulge in too general aesthetic speculations or theories belonging properly to a philosophy of history.

I am thus not concerned with the question of the manifold relationships between the arts. There is no particular theoretical problem in the fact that the arts are in constant interrelationship, as are all human activities. Literature has sometimes drawn inspiration from paintings or pieces of sculpture or music. Other works of art have become the theme of poetry just as any other piece or section of reality. In surveying the history of English poetry alone we need only to think of the tapestries and pageants which seem to have inspired Spenser, the paintings of Claude Lorrain and Salvatore Rosa which influenced

[*] Read at the Institute in 1941. Published in the *Institute Annual*, 1942.

eighteenth-century landscape poetry, or recall Keats's "Ode on a Grecian Urn." Here is a wide field of study still only partially explored by Miss Manwaring, Professor Tinker, Sidney Colvin, and others.[1] I need not stress the fact that literature can become the theme of painting or that music, especially vocal and program music, has drawn on literary inspiration, just as literature, especially the lyric, has coöperated closely with music. There is an increasing number of studies of medieval carols or Elizabethan lyrics which stress the close association with the musical setting, and in art history a whole group of scholars (Erwin Panofsky, Fritz Saxl, and others) has grown up who study the conceptual and symbolic meanings of works of art and thus frequently also their literary relations and inspirations. As we shall hear other speakers exemplify these fascinating methods, I can turn with less compunction to the more general and theoretical question of the comparison between the arts.

I can only touch briefly on one problem: the question of the confusion of the arts. This is the topic of Lessing's *Laokoön* and Irving Babbitt's *New Laokoön:* whether one art should or should not try to achieve the effects of another art—whether poetry, for example, can make visual descriptions or achieve musical sound effects. As a matter of history the arts have tried to borrow effects from each other, and the critical question whether they are always successful or whether that success is desirable may be left unanswered today.

What I want to discuss is not a new and esoteric question. It dates back to antiquity. Simonides, as reported by Plutarch, was the originator of the phrase "painting is mute poetry and poetry speaking painting." [2] In the eighteenth century innumerable comparisons were made between the composition of Spenser's *Faerie Queene* and the glorious disorder of a Gothic cathedral.[3] Then August Wilhelm Schlegel stressed the sculpturesque qualities of classical literature and the pictorial quali-

[1] Elizabeth W. Manwaring, *Italian Landscape in Eighteenth Century England,* New York, 1925; Chauncey Brewster Tinker, *Painter and Poet; Studies in the Literary Relations of English Painting,* Cambridge, Mass., 1938; Sir Sidney Colvin, *John Keats,* London, 1917; also Warren H. Smith, *Architecture in English Fiction,* New Haven, 1934.

[2] Plutarch, *On the Fame of the Athenians,* chap. iii. *Moralia,* Loeb Library ed., IV, 500.

[3] For example, in John Hughes's Preface to his edition of the *Faerie Queene* (1715), and in Richard Hurd's *Letters on Chivalry and Romance* (1762). Cf. pp. 102–3 of my book *The Rise of English Literary History,* Chapel Hill, 1941.

ties of modern romantic poetry.[4] To Schelling is usually ascribed the
saying that "architecture is frozen music." [5] These parallels became
more and more concrete and widespread in the nineteenth century; for
instance, the German dramatist Otto Ludwig drew an elaborate comparison between a sonata and a Shakespearean drama.[6] These analogies
have found more and more favor also with academic and analytical
scholars. Early in this century the well-known German art historian
August Schmarsow did much to introduce the term "rhythm" into
architecture, and he even drew up an amusing scheme of an alcaic
verse pattern for which he claimed decorative value.[7]

In 1915 the famous Swiss art historian, Heinrich Wölfflin, published his *Principles of Art History*, a book which was destined to influence literary history profoundly. Wölfflin tries to distinguish between Renaissance and baroque art on purely structural grounds. He
constructed a scheme of contraries which are applicable to any kind
of picture or piece of sculpture or architecture in the period. Renaissance art, he showed, is "linear," while baroque art is "pictorial." "Linear" suggests that the outlines of figures or objects are drawn clearly,
while "pictorial" means that light and color blur the outlines of objects
and are the principles of composition. Renaissance painting uses a
"closed" form, a symmetrical, balanced grouping of figures or surfaces

---

[4] August Wilhelm Schlegel, "Vorlesungen über schöne Litteratur und Kunst,
Erster Teil (1801–2), Die Kunstlehre," in *Deutsche Literaturdenkmale des 18. und
19. Jahrhunderts*, ed. by B. Seuffert, Heilbronn, 1884, p. 156, and *Über dramatische
Kunst und Litteratur*, Heidelberg, 1808, I, 13, 15–16. O. Walzel, in *Wechselseitige
Erhellung der Künste*, Berlin, 1917, pp. 32–33, shows that Schlegel was partly an-
ticipated by the Dutch eighteenth-century Platonist, Franz Hemsterhuis.

[5] There is a quarrel about the priority for this saying. Dorothea Schlegel, in a
letter dated August 7, 1816, claims it for Friedrich Schlegel (see Dorothea von
Schlegel, *Briefwechsel*, ed. by J. M. Raich, Mainz, 1881, II, 373). "Im Dom zu
Köln z. B. verstand ich zum erstenmal, was eine Fuge ist und sein soll. Daher kam
ja der so oft von den Platten bekrittelte und bespöttelte Ausdruck Friedrichs von der
versteinerten Musik." Goethe (*Maximen*, No. 1133) ascribes the saying to Schelling
and this seems to be borne out by his *Vorlesungen über Philosophie der Kunst*, given
in 1802–3, but published only in *Sämtliche Werke*. Abteilung I, V, 576, 593. Stutt-
gart, 1859. Schelling there calls architecture "die erstarrte Musik." Still it is not
impossible that Friedrich Schlegel was the originator of the witticism. Ascriptions to
Schopenhauer or to Ruskin (Theodore Meyer Greene, *The Arts and the Art of
Criticism*, Princeton, 1940, p. 72) are false.

[6] Otto Ludwig, "Über Shakespeares Komposition," in his *Werke*, ed. by
A. Stern, V, 89.

[7] August Schmarsow, *Kompositionsgesetze in der Kunst des Mittelalters*, Leipzig, 1915, I, 88 ff. The verse-pattern also in Walzel, *op. cit.*, p. 24.

while baroque prefers an "open" form: an unsymmetrical composition
which puts emphasis on a corner of a picture rather than on its center
or points beyond the frame of the picture. Renaissance pictures are
"flat" or, at least, composed on different recessive planes, while baroque
pictures are "deep" or seem to lead the eye into a distant and indistinct
background. Two further such contraries are developed in detail and it
is argued that these principles of composition can be found in all art
and must be found always in this combination and this temporal sequence. Wölfflin's brilliant formal analyses of pictures soon excited the
envy and competition of literary historians. In 1916 Professor Oskar
Walzel, fresh from the reading of Wölfflin's *Principles of Art History*,
attempted to transfer to literature the categories established by Wölfflin's contrast between Renaissance and baroque art. Walzel took one
of these pairs of contraries, the "closed" and "open" form, and applied
it to Shakespeare.[8] Studying the composition of Shakespeare's plays he
came to the conclusion that Shakespeare belongs to the baroque, as his
plays are not built in the symmetrical manner found by Wölfflin in
Renaissance pictures. The number of minor characters, their unsymmetrical grouping, the varying emphasis on different acts of the play
—all these characteristics are supposed to show that Shakespeare's
technique is the same as that of baroque art, while Corneille or Racine
who composed their tragedies around one central figure and distributed
the emphasis among the acts according to an Aristotelian pattern, belong to the Renaissance type. Thus, on the basis of a single criterion,
transfered from painting to drama, Shakespeare and Racine exchanged
places. Actually we have learned only what we knew long before, that
is, that Shakespeare violated the unities. But it would be unjust to criticize Oskar Walzel too severely; he himself realized the limitations of
the method and in his little book on *Wechselseitige Erhellung der
Künste* (1917) puts its claim very cautiously and modestly.[9]

But these restraints were thrown to the winds by Oswald Spengler,
who was then writing his amazing work of analogizing ingenuity, *The
Decline of the West* (1918). Most scholars today profess to ignore
Spengler, and there is no necessity to warn against his extravagancies.

---

[8] "Shakespeares dramatische Baukunst," in *Jahrbuch der Shakespearegesellschaft*,
LII (1916), 17 ff., reprinted in *Das Wortkunstwerk: Mittel seiner Erforschung*,
Leipzig, 1926, pp. 302–25.
   [9] However, *Gehalt und Gestalt im Kunstwerk des Dichters* (Berlin-Potsdam,
1925) makes extravagant claims for his method. Cf. especially pp. 265 ff. and 282 ff.

But one should not underrate his enormous direct and especially indirect influence on the effort to set up analogies among the arts. He
revived and deeply impressed on recent scholars the concept of organic,
necessary evolution from flowering to decay and erected into a dogma
the idea that a period is a closed organic whole. He claims that it is
possible from the scattered details of ornaments, architecture, writing,
or from scattered data of a political, economic, and religious nature to
reconstruct the history of whole centuries or to divine from details of
the artistic forms the contemporary constitution of a state and from
the mathematics of a time to draw conclusions as to economic conditions.[10] Everything in Spengler thus parallels everything. Where there
is a discrepancy, Spengler knows how to resolve it into some higher
whole. The analogizing between the arts breaks out into a veritable
riot of metaphors. Spengler speaks, for example, of the "visible chamber music of the bent furniture, the mirror rooms, pastorals and por-
celain groups of the eighteenth century," he mentions the "Titian
style of the madrigal," and refers to the *allegro feroce* of Franz Hals
and the *andante con moto* of Van Dyck," and he elaborately compares
Rembrandt to the music of his times. In Rembrandt he finds a *"basso
continuo* of the costume, above which play the *motifs* of the head." [11]
All this may be very ingenious and amusing, but at closer inspection it
amounts to little more than assertions that certain moods induced by
a picture suggest the mood of some musical composition, which, to
support the theory, must be contemporary. In isolation this a harmless
game, but Spengler's method, prepared as it was by suggestions in
Schlegel and others, soon found its scholarly glorification in "Geistesgeschichte," a large-scale movement in German scholarship of the last
twenty years. The term is sometimes used as referring to any type of
"intellectual history," and thus in its broader sense it remains outside
our discussion. But usually, to quote one of its exponents, "Geistesgeschichte" aims to "reconstruct the spirit of a time from the different
objectivations of an age—from its religion down to its costumes. We
look for the totality behind the objects and explain all facts by this
spirit of the time." [12] Thus a universal analogizing between the arts is

[10] *Der Untergang des Abendlandes*, München, 1923, I, 151.

[11] *Ibid.*, pp. 297, 299, 322, 339, and similar examples throughout the two
volumes.

[12] The quotation from M. W. Eppelsheimer, "Das Renaissance-Problem," in
Deutsche Vierteljahrschrift für Literaturwissenschaft und Geistesgeschichte, II
(1933), 497.

at the very center of the method which has stimulated a veritable flood of writings on the "Gothic" man, the spirit of the baroque, and so forth. Most relevant to our purpose are the attempts to transfer terms originally defined in art history to the history of literature. Today periods in the history of literature, instead of being, as they used to be, either political concepts transferred to literature or literary terms and slogans, have come more and more under the spell of the divisions in art history.

The term "baroque" is the most obvious case in point. Fritz Strich, Arthur Hübscher, and Herbert Cysarz have interpreted German seventeenth-century literature in terms of the baroque in the fine arts,[13] and the method has been applied also to the English seventeenth century. There is a whole book by Paul Meissner called *Die geisteswissenschaftlichen Grundlagen des englischen Literaturbarocks* (1934), which seems to me, in spite of its learning, the *reductio ad absurdum* of the method. Meissner defines the baroque as a conflict of antithetic tendencies and pursues this formula for the "time-spirit" relentlessly through all human activities from technology to exploration, from traveling to religion. All the wealth of materials is nicely ordered into categories such as expansion and concentration, macrocosmos and microcosmos, sin and salvation, faith and reason, absolutism and democracy, "atectonics" and "tectonics." A method of universal analogizing arrives at the triumphant conclusion that the baroque age showed conflict, contradiction, and tension throughout its manifestations. There were active men interested in conquering nature and praising war, there were passionate collectors, travelers, adventurers; but there were also contemplative men who sought out solitude or founded secret societies. Some people were fascinated by the new astronomy, while others analyzed personal states of mind like the diarists or drew the individual features of men like the painters of portraits. There were those believing in the divine right of kings and others believing in an equalitarian democracy. Everything exemplifies, thus, the principle either of concentration or of expansion. If you want concentration in literature, you are presented with the plain style of prose stimulated by the Royal

13 F. Strich, "Der lyrische Stil des 17. Jahrhunderts," in *Abhandlungen zur deutschen Literaturgeschichte Festschrift für Franz Muncker*, München, 1916, pp. 21 ff.; A. Hübscher, "Barock als Gestaltung antithetischen Lebensgefühls," *Euphorion*, XXIV (1925), pp. 517–62, 759–805; Herbert Cysarz, *Deutsche Barockdichtung*, Leipzig, 1924. See the excellent review by J. Körner, "Barocke Barockforschung," *Historische Zeitschrift*, CXXXIII (1925), 455–64.

Society after the Restoration. If you want expansion, you are shown the long sentences of Milton or Sir Thomas Browne. Mr. Meissner never stops to ask whether the very same scheme of contraries could not be extracted from any other age. Nor does he, of course, raise the question whether we could not impose a completely different scheme of contraries on the seventeenth century and even on exactly the same quotations culled from his wide reading.[14]

Similarly Ludwig Pfandl, in his very learned and informative *Geschichte der spanischen Nationalliteratur in ihrer Blütezeit* (1929), which is also available in a Spanish translation, gave us a slightly varied formula for the baroque in Spain. It is supposed to show how the innate Spanish dualism of realism and idealism was during the baroque age "expanded and exaggerated" in an antithesis of naturalism and illusionism. Under these categories a varied scheme of subdivisions of symbolism, the cult of genius, the humanization of the supernatural, and so forth, marshals a wealth of information which, however, frequently amounts to no more than telling us that there were nuns and prostitutes, beggars and rich men, in seventeenth-century Spain; that some people danced the indecent *zarabanda,* while others (or the same) went to masses, that some professed the creed of Epicurus, while others were pessimistic and melancholy, had headaches (*jaqueca*), and thought of death.[15]

The phrase "the baroque Shakespeare," tentatively proposed by Walzel, has caught on amazingly. In a book by Helene Richter, *Shakespeare der Mensch* (1923), Shakespeare is made out to be a typical baroque man. Even his career described a curve or zigzag line: he reached his aims always by devious ways, and this is, of course, an "unmistakable analogy to the baroque." Miss Richter also applies one of Wölfflin's principles to the *Merchant of Venice.* The composition of baroque pictures in diagonals leading the eye toward a distant prospect in the rear is there paralleled. "The diagonal of ideas connects the foreground of concrete vital truth with backgrounds of world-wide distance and extension." [16] But even this verbiage was easily surpassed by later German scholars. In *Shakespeares Macbeth als Drama des Barock* (1936) Max Deutschbein presents us with several graphic pictures of

[14] Cf. the acute criticism by R. S. Crane in the *Philological Quarterly,* XIV (1935), 152–54.
[15] Ludwig Pfandl, *Geschichte der spanischen Nationalliteratur in ihrer Blütezeit,* Freiburg-im-Breisgau, 1929, pp. 213, 225, 227, 228, *et passim.*
[16] Helene Richter, *Shakespeare der Mensch,* Halle, 1923, pp. 84, 88.

the composition of *Macbeth*. A very nice ellipse is drawn with the words "Grace" and "Realm of Darkness" written around it, and "Lady Macbeth" and "Weird Sisters" placed at the focal points. We are then told that this represents the "inner form" of Macbeth which determines the baroque character of the drama, because the baroque style "has a pronounced predilection for the oval groundplan, as shown frequently in the groundplans of baroque churches and castles." [17] Here, then, a completely arbitrary geometrical pattern is drawn up by the ingenious professor, and then this drawing is used as a proof for the baroque character of *Macbeth*, as the ellipse is supposed to be a specific form of baroque architecture. To dismiss this whole undertaking, it is not even necessary to doubt whether the ellipse is so frequent in baroque churches as Deutschbein seems to imply.

Bernard Fehr, in a series of articles in English on the "Antagonism of Forms in the Eighteenth Century," [18] made a similar attempt to interpret poetry in terms of architecture. He takes eight lines from Pope's *Moral Essays* and then draws parallel lines for each verse which he interrupts wherever there is a caesura. The result is that these lines, in his own words, "make up a body of equidistant parallels like the string courses and cornices of a Palladian building." Moreover, "they rhyme scheme *aa, bb, cc* . . . breaks up the parallel into a flight of couples to be compared to the colonnades of the pavilions so fashionable in Pope's day." Mr. Fehr never asks the question whether any set of end-stopped lines, rhymed or unrhymed, with any place for the caesura would not lend themselves to exactly the same depiction in parallel lines and thus invite the same comparison with Palladian architecture or whether any couplets should not be, on the same principle, compared to colonnades of pavilions. Mr. Fehr, however, is not content with having demonstrated the parallel between Pope's verse and a Palladan building. He picks a passage from a poem by David Mallet, which happens to be a long pseudo-Miltonic period in blank verse, and represents it, by the same method, as a serpentine line. Thus Mallet and Thomson and many others who wrote blank verse with long sentences overflowing the limits of a single line are shown to be baroque, for convolutions and cork-screw pillars are baroque and look exactly like

[17] Max Deutschbein, *Shakespeares Macbeth als Drama des Barock*, Leipzig (s. d. 1936?), pp. 26–28.

[18] Bernard Fehr, "The Antagonism of Forms in the Eighteenth Century," *English Studies*, XVIII (1936), 115–21, 193–205, and XIX (1937), 1–13, 49–57; especially XVIII, 193, 194, 197, 199, 202, and XIX, 57.

the picture of the verse drawn by Mr. Fehr. But Mallet's lines lend themselves to a further analogizing with architecture. The sentence quoted has clauses and even subclauses, and these suggest to Fehr "in opposition to Pope's double rows of columns, the broken frontage of a baroque building and the recesses and advances of its groundplan, such as may be noted in Blenheim Castle." "This presupposes," he continues ingenuously, "that we look upon a principal sentence as a movement on the front vertical plane, and that anything interrupting an initial or later stage of this movement—from the slightest appositional adjunct or adverbial phrase to the longest subordinate clause—is to be taken as a recess." With the same method any writer who uses subordinate clauses, from Demosthenes and Cicero down to Mr. Fehr himself, could be proved to be baroque. The whole amazing jugglery is only possible because he takes seriously the purely graphic arrangement of a line on a page in print and devises a completely arbitrary translation into architectural terms, which has not even the merit of being specific. No wonder that he comes to such conclusions that all run-on-line blank verse is baroque, that therefore Wordsworth is baroque, while Keats mysteriously "adapted his eyes to a pre-baroque mode of seeing." Thus the baroque has finally stretched to include both Shakespeare and Wordsworth, and almost everybody, with the exception of the strictest classicists, between them.

This foray of art history or rather pseudo-art history into the study of literature is not, of course, confined to the baroque. There is, for example, a book by Friedrich Schürr, *Das altfranzösische Epos* (1926), which in its subtitle tells us that it is a contribution to the history of the style and inner form of Gothic. In the text the parallelism between a Gothic cathedral and a French epic poem is pursued with relentless vigor. For example, the widespread use of parallels and repetitions in action, themes, and motifs in the epic is quoted as argument for an architectonic composition of these epics which can be easily enough demonstrated to agree with the "principle" of all Gothic art: "repetition with variation," which we find in the flying buttresses, pillars, and pointed arches of the Gothic cathedrals.[19] That pattern and variation are devices of practically all art of all times is an objection which is not even considered by Mr. Schürr. There are other books of this type, one by Friedrich Brie on the rococo epic in English literature which centers in the *Rape of the Lock* and many studies trying to trans-

[19] Friedrich Schürr, *Das altfranzösische Epos*, München, 1926, p. 148.

fer the term "Empire," "Biedermeier" or "impressionism" from painting and decorative arts to literature.[20]

Most widely known is possibly Fritz Strich's attempt in his *Deutsche Klassik und Romantik* (1922) to describe the opposition between German classicism and romanticism by an application of Wölfflin's categories evolved for the Renaissance and the baroque. The baroque characteristics hold good for romanticism, the Renaissance for classicism. Strich's special contribution is the interpretation he gives to Wölfflin's contraries of closed and open forms. "Closed" form means to him complete, perfect classical form, which expresses a longing for timeless values; while the "open," unfinished, fragmentary or blurred form of romantic poetry expresses man's longing for the infinite, for eternity. Thus, by a simple equivocation between finished and finite, unfinished and infinite, an elaborate structure of metaphysical implications is erected and much opportunity for clever juxtapositions is gained.[21]

It would not have been worth while to discuss these books if they were merely isolated perversions on the fringes of scholarship. Actually all the books mentioned are thoroughly representative of a much larger literature written by the most prominent scholars of Germany, many in high academic positions, and,—it would be unjust not to recognize it,— by scholars of real learning and comprehension. "Geistesgeschichte" is, besides, not a local phenomenon any more, but is spreading to publications in English, though, on the whole, the greater common sense and ingrained empiricism of most non-German scholars have saved them from some of the worst quibbling, extended metaphors, and easy formulas of the Germans. The few writers who have used the term "baroque" in English literature have been extraordinarily cautious. In his studies of the *Baroque Style in Prose* Morris William Croll has proceeded by strictly empirical methods: he has analyzed and observed with great sensitivity the types of prose rhythm and sentence structure current in the seventeenth century. The term "baroque" is used to label

[20] Friedrich Brie, *Englische Rokokoepik*, München, 1927; "Empire," in Helene Richter, *Lord Byron; Persönlichkeit und Werk*, Halle, 1929. On "Biedermeier" in literature, see R. Majut, "Das Literarische Biedermeier," in *Germanisch-romanische Monatsschrift*, XX (1932), pp. 401–24, and P. Kluckhohn, "Zur Biedermeier-Diskussion," *Deutsche Vierteljahrschrift*, XIV (1936), 495 ff.

[21] Fritz Strich, *Deutsche Klassik und Romantik; oder Vollendung und Unendlichkeit*, München, 1922, *passim;* see also the criticism in Martin Schütze, *Academic Illusions*, Chicago, 1933, pp. 13, 16.

the ornate style of the age. Parallels to painting occur only as illustrations, for example, in analyzing a loose sentence by Sir Thomas Browne, Mr. Croll suggests that it "closely parallels the technique of an El Greco composition, where broken and tortuous lines in the body of the design prepare the eye for curves that leap upward beyond the limits of the canvas." [22] Wölfflin's "open" form is obviously in the mind of the author, but no far-reaching conclusions or speculations are tied to these remarks. Austin Warren, also, in his book on *Richard Crashaw: a Study in Baroque Sensibility* (1939), though he describes Bernini's St. Theresa and uses the term "baroque," carefully keeps to an analysis of the actual poems in terms of their verse, imagery, and symbolism. There is no particular objection to the use of this term as an alternative to metaphysical, concettist, and so forth, as long as we give it a strictly literary meaning.

Somewhat earlier Mr. F. W. Bateson, to whom we are all indebted for the *Cambridge Bibliography of English Literature*, took up the term "baroque" but applied it to eighteenth-century Miltonic poetry, in his stimulating book on *English Poetry and the English Language* (1934). Thomson, Young, Gray, and Collins make on him the same impression as baroque architecture by their orderly disorder and artificial excitement. He characterizes them in terms quoted from Geoffrey Scott's *Architecture of Humanism* (1914), a book which, partly under the influence of the early studies of Wölfflin, described baroque architecture along the lines of distinctions between picturesque versus linear, and unclear versus clear forms. Mr. Bateson also argues that the eighteenth-century term "sublime," as expounded by Burke, in its love of the obscure and confused is a description of the baroque and that the function of the invocations, personifications, and stock phrases in Thomson, Young and the others is "identical with that of baroque ornament." [23] One might ask whether all poetic diction, including that of the Scottish Chaucerians and the Italian sonneteers and even the Silver Latin poets would not, according to the same criteria, have to be considered "baroque ornament." Baroque thus loses any useful connotation and becomes a term for anything decorative, tawdry, and conventionalized.

[22] Especially Morris W. Croll, "The Baroque Style in Prose," in *Studies in English Philology; a Miscellany in Honor of Frederick Klaeber*, ed. by K. Malone and M. B. Rund, Minneapolis, 1929, pp. 427–56. The quotation is from p. 451.

[23] F. W. Bateson, *English Poetry and the English Language*, Oxford, 1934; especially pp. 76–77.

Sprague Allen's two-volume study of *Tides in English Taste* (1937) examines the relationships between the arts in concrete terms, only rarely attempting speculations about far-reaching parallelisms. Mr. Allen suggests such similarities as those between the still fundamentally Gothic architecture of the Tudor period with the early Tudor drama, full of medieval remnants, overlaid by imitations of Seneca. He sees also a parallel between the Palladian adaptations of Tudor houses and the "improving" of Shakespeare during the Restoration. More doubtful seems a parallel he draws between the rococo in the arts and the eighteenth-century attack on the unities in the drama. The similarity is merely in the dissatisfaction with rigid symmetrical form.[24] Even more fanciful is the parallel recently drawn by the eminent Italian scholar, Mario Praz, between Milton and Poussin.[25] He tries to show that Milton preferred design to color and tells us that Poussin modeled his figures first in wax in order to study their attitudes before he painted his pictures. But then Signor Praz goes on to say that

Milton also modelled his verse in wax before working it in English. The wax pattern of Milton was the Latin construction; he handles so to say the classical flesh of the words before dressing it in English attire . . . his sentences marched at the pace of Roman legions; there was an enchanted air about it all, as in Poussin's pictures.

As a matter of fact, Milton did not write first in Latin and then in English; and the similarity between Poussin's wax figures and Milton's search for Latinized constructions seems very remote. Nor is there much light in the comparison of Milton's sentences with the pace of Roman legions or in a purely emotive statement that "there was an enchanted air about it all" in Milton as in Poussin. Mr. Laurence Binyon, in a chatty lecture on *English Poetry in Its Relation to Painting and the Other Arts* (1918), spoke of the "organ-music" of Milton's rhythm, which seems hardly compatible with the pace of Roman legions, and had paralleled Milton with both Michelangelo and Veronese rather than with Poussin.[26] A German scholar compared the tension and bold arch of Milton's sentences with the cupola of St. Paul's Cathedral,

[24] Beverly Sprague Allen, *Tides in English Taste*. Cambridge, Mass., 2 vols., 1937, I, 17–18, 78–79; II, 107–8.

[25] Mario Praz, "Milton and Poussin," in *Seventeenth Century Studies Presented to Sir Herbert Grierson*, Oxford, 1938, pp. 192–210; especially pp. 204–5.

[26] Laurence Binyon, "English Poetry in Its Relation to Painting and the Other Arts," in *Proceedings of the British Academy*, VIII (1918), 381–402; especially 389.

while Mr. Herbert Read is reminded of Dryden by the buildings of Sir Christopher Wren.[27]

Mr. Read, in his express discussion of "Parallels in English Painting and Poetry," published in his volume of essays In Defence of Shelley (1936), compares Turner with Keats, while Mr. Binyon thought rather of Shelley. But these are all only vague impressions, and there is also little more than a comparison of landscape types and moods in Mr. Read's statement that "an early landscape of Gainsborough's matches the unrhymed rhythms of Collins' 'Ode to Evening,' whilst the still freer and more naturalistic treatment of Gainsborough's later landscapes approaches to the poetic objectivity of Wordsworth." Only once, in his survey of the whole history, does Mr. Read attempt a structural parallel between painting and poetry. He compares Anglo-Saxon ornament with Anglo-Saxon meter.

I wish to suggest that the same spirit which expressed itself in linear emphasis in the case of drawing, when it came to verse expressed itself in alliteration. Alliteration is a horizontal movement across the structure of verse; it is linear abstraction within verbal expression. In a corresponding way, the play of lines in a drawing will show a continual repetition of the same motive, a kind of linear alliteration.[28]

Mr. Read does not see that the term "horizontal" applied to alliteration refers purely to the graphic picture on a page and might be applied to any repetition within a verse, for instance, the repeated accents of normal blank verse which would be even more regularly placed than the alliterations. The view that repetitive ornament is a kind of alliteration could be equally upheld as to classical columns, Gothic arches, meanders and arabesques, in short to any repetitive device, and thus the whole parallel falls to the ground. I don't want, however, to press these statements, but merely to take them as examples. They show how parallelism between poetry and painting are spreading and that most of them point only to the slightest and most tenuous thematic or emotional similarities.

I should have created a wrong impression, if this little survey of books and examples were understood to imply a wholesale dismissal of the problem. I am rather pleading for clear distinctions between the dif-

[27] Gustav Hübener, Die stilistische Spannung in Miltons Paradise Lost, Halle, 1913, p. 57. H. Read, In Defence of Shelley and Other Essays, London, 1936, p. 233.

[28] Herbert Read, op. cit., pp. 230, 243, 246.

ferent methods in use and a scheme of relationships and emphases. A clarification of the place and function of each special method and a realization of their difficulties and limitations may help us in formulating a new approach. Let me attempt such a sketch.

Most of our criticism in literature and the arts is still purely emotive: it judges works of art in terms of their emotional effect on the reader or spectator and describes this effect by exclamations, suggested moods or scenes, and so forth. However disguised, much criticism amounts to the labeling of works of art by emotional terms like "joyful," "gay," "melancholy," and so forth, or, in modern psychological terms, as inducing a balance of impulses—a "patterning" and "ordering" of our mind, to use the terms introduced by Mr. I. A. Richards. Many parallels between the fine arts and literature amount to an assertion that this picture and that poem induce the same mood in me: for example, that I feel light-hearted and gay in hearing a minuet of Mozart, seeing a landscape by Watteau, and reading an Anacreontic poem. But this is the kind of parallelism which is of little worth for purposes of scholarly analysis: joy induced by a piece of music is, not joy in general or even joy of a particular shade, but is an emotion closely following and thus tied to the pattern of the music. We experience emotions which have only a general tone in common with those of real life, and even if we define these emotions as closely as we can, we are still quite removed from the specific object which induced them. I cannot see any light in Mr. Richards's main theory, that poetry and art put into order the chaos of our impulses. He is driven to admit that a balanced poise might be achieved by a bad as well as a good poem, by a carpet as well as a sonata, and thus has nothing to do with the actual object of our study: the work of art.[29] Parallels between the arts which remain inside the individual reactions of a reader or spectator and are content with describing some emotional similarity of our reactions to two arts will, therefore, never lend themselves to verification and thus to a coöperative advance in our knowledge.

Another common approach is the intentions and theories of the artists. No doubt, we can show that there are some similarities in the theories and formulas behind the different arts, in the neoclassical or the romantic movements, and we can find also professions of intentions of the individual artists in the different arts which sound identical or

[29] I. A. Richards, *Principles of Literary Criticism*, London, 1925, p. 125. Cf. *ibid.*, p. 248.

similar. But these intentions may not have any definite relation to the finished work of art; they may go far beyond it, they may contradict its results, or they may fall short of the accomplished object. They can at the most serve as a useful commentary or as signposts pointing to problems, but they require much analysis and interpretation to be of any use in the comparison of the arts. A good example is the professed classicism of most baroque artists. Bernini, for example, gave a lecture to the Paris Academy, asserting that he followed the Greek sculptors, and the architect of a most rococo building, the Zwinger in Dresden, Daniel Adam Pöppelmann, wrote a whole little book demonstrating the agreement of his building with the chastest principles of Vitruvius.[30] Similarly, the metaphysical poets in England never thought of their own work as deviating from classical standards, nor did they ever invent a distinct aesthetic for their extremely different practice except that they spoke about "strong lines" and praised wit and obscurity.[31] "Classicism" in music must mean something very different from its use in literature for the simple reason that no real classical music (with the exception of a few fragments) was known and could thus shape the evolution of music as literature was actually shaped by the precepts and practice of antiquity. Likewise painting, before the excavation of the frescoes in Pompeii and Herculaneum, can scarcely be described as influenced by classical painting in spite of the frequent reference to classical theories and Greek painters like Apelles and possibly some remote pictorial traditions which must have descended from antiquity through the Middle Ages. Sculpture and architecture, however, were to an extent far exceeding the other arts, including literature, determined by classical models and their derivatives. Thus theories and conscious intentions mean something very different in the various arts and say little or nothing about the concrete results of an artist's activity: his work and its specific content and form.

How little decisive for an understanding of a concrete work of art may be the approach through the personality of the author can best be seen in the rare cases when artist and poet are identical. For example, a comparison of the poetry and the paintings of Blake or Rossetti will show that the character, not merely the technical quality of their paint-

---

[30] Described in Oscar Walzel's article, "Künstlerische Absicht," in *Germanisch-romanische Monatsschrift*, VIII (1920), 329 ff.

[31] The aesthetic views of the metaphysicals collected in Robert Lathrop Sharp's *From Donne to Dryden*, Chapel Hill, 1940, and in Leah Jones, *The Divine Science*, New York, 1940.

ing and poetry, is very different and even divergent. I think of the grotesque little animal which is supposed to illustrate "Tiger! Tiger! Burning bright." Without daring to dogmatize about Michelangelo, I would venture the opinion that in structure and quality there is little comparison between his *Sonnets* and his sculpture and paintings, though we can find the same Neoplatonic ideas in all and may discover some psychological similarities.[32] This shows that the "medium" of a work of art (an unfortunate question-begging term) is not merely a technical obstacle to be overcome by the artist in order to express his personality, but a factor pre-formed by tradition and thus has a powerful determining character which shapes and modifies the approach and expression of the individual artist. The artist does not conceive in general mental terms, but in terms of concrete material; and the concrete medium has its own history, frequently very different from that of any other medium.

More valuable than the approach through the artist's intentions and theories is a comparison of the arts on the basis of their common social and cultural background. Certainly it is possible to describe the common temporal, local, or social nourishing soil of the arts and literature and thus to point to common influences working on them. But many parallels between the arts are possible only because they ignore the utterly different social background to which the individual work of art appealed or from which it seems to be derived. The social classes either creating or demanding a certain type of art may be quite different at any one time or place. Certainly the Gothic cathedrals have a different social background from the French epic; and sculpture frequently appeals to and is paid for by a very different audience from the novel. Just as fallacious as the assumption of a common social background of the arts at a given time and place is the usual assumption that the intellectual background is necessarily identical and effective in all the arts. Literature, because it shades off almost imperceptibly into the vehicle of science and philosophy, is in closest touch with the technical philosophy of a time. But even there the assumption that poetry mirrors the thought of an age is not always true, as witness the gulf between the poetic thought of the romantic age in England and the prevalent common-sense and utilitarian philosophy of the time. It is even more hazardous to interpret painting in the light of contemporary philosophy: to mention only one example, Károly Tolnai has attempted to interpret

---

[32] See Erwin Panofsky, "The Neoplatonic Movement and Michelangelo," in his *Studies in Iconology*, New York, 1939, pp. 171 ff.

the pictures of the elder Brueghel in evidence of a pantheistic monism paralleling Cusanus or Paracelsus and anticipating Spinoza and Goethe.[33] Even more dangerous is an "explanation" of the arts in terms of a "time-spirit," a sort of mystical integral which is positively vicious when hypostatized and made absolute and is useful only as a pointer toward a problem. But the German "Geistesgeschichte" has usually merely succeeded in transferring criteria from one series to the whole and has then characterized the times and in them every individual work of art in terms of such vague contraries as "rationalism" and "irrationalism." The genuine parallelisms which follow from the identical or similar social or intellectual background scarcely ever have been analyzed in concrete terms. I want only to suggest that we have rarely had studies which would concretely show how, for example, all the arts in a given time or setting expand or narrow their field over the objects of "nature" or how the norms of art are tied to specific social classes and thus subject to uniform changes or how aesthetic values change with social revolutions. Here is a wide field for investigation which has been scarcely touched and promises concrete results for the comparison of the arts. Of course, only similar influences on the evolution of the different arts can be proved by this method, *not* any necessary parallelism.

Obviously, the most central approach to a comparison of the arts is based on an analysis of the actual objects of art, and thus of their structural relationships. There will never be a proper history of an art, not to speak of a comparative history of the arts, unless we concentrate on an analysis of the works themselves and relegate to the background studies in the psychology of the reader and the spectator or the author and the artist as well as studies in the cultural and social background, however illuminating they may be from their own point of view. Unfortunately it seems to me that hitherto we have had scarcely any tools for such a comparison between the arts. Here a very difficult question arises: what are the common and the comparable elements of the arts? I hardly need to say that I see no light in a theory like Croce's, which concentrates all aesthetic problems on the act of intuition, mysteriously identified with expression. Croce asserts the nonexistence of modes of expression and condemns "any attempt at an aesthetic classification of the arts as absurd" and thus *a fortiori* rejects all distinction between

33 Charles de Tolnay, *Pierre Bruegel l'Ancien*, 2 vols., Bruxelles, 1935; see also *Die Zeichnungen Peter Breugels*. München, 1925; cf. Carl Neumann's criticism in *Deutsche Vierteljahrschrift*, IV (1926), 308 ff.

genres or types.[34] Nor is much gained for our problem by John Dewey's insistence in his *Art as Experience* (1934) that there is a common substance among the arts because there are "general conditions without which an experience is not possible." [35] I am not prepared to deny that there is a common denominator in the act of all artistic creation or, for that matter, in all human creation, activity, and experience. But these are solutions which do not help us in comparing the arts. More concretely, Theodore Meyer Greene, in his *Arts and the Art of Criticism* (1940), defines the comparable elements of the arts as complexity, integration, and rhythm, and he argues eloquently, as John Dewey had done before him, for the applicability of the term "rhythm" to the plastic arts.[36] I have no time to enter into this controversy, but it seems to me that it is impossible to overcome the profound distinction between the rhythm of a piece of music and the rhythm of a colonnade, where neither the order nor the tempo is imposed by the structure of the work itself. Complexity and integration are merely other terms for "variety" and "unity" and thus of only very limited use. Few concrete attempts to arrive at such common denominators among the arts on a structural basis have gone any further. Mr. Birckhoff, a Harvard mathematician, in a book on *Aesthetic Measure* (1933), has with apparent success tried to find a common mathematical basis for simple art forms and music and he has included a study of the "musicality" of verse which is also defined in mathematical equations and coefficients. I have my doubts whether the problem of euphony in verse can be solved in isolation from meaning, and Mr. Birckhoff's high grades for poems by Edgar Allan Poe seem to confirm such an assumption, but his ingenious attempt, if accepted, would tend rather to widen the gulf between the essentially "literary" qualities of poetry and the other arts which share much more fully in "aesthetic measure" than literature.

Thus, the application of Wölfflin's *Principles of Art History* to literature is the one concrete attempt to find a common ground among

[34] Benedetto Croce, *Aesthetic*, translated by D. Ainslie, London, 1909, pp. 62, 110, 188, *et passim*.

[35] John Dewey, *Art as Experience*, New York, 1934, p. 212.

[36] Greene, *op. cit.*, pp. 213 ff.; especially 221–26. John Dewey, *op. cit.*, pp. 175 ff., 218 ff. Arguments against the use of rhythm in the plastic arts in Ernst Meumann, *Untersuchungen zur Psychologie und Aesthetik des Rhythmus*, Leipzig, 1894, and in Fritz Medicus, "Das Problem einer vergleichenden Geschichte der Künste," in *Philosophie der Literaturwissenschaft*, ed. by E. Ermatinger, Berlin, 1930, pp. 195 ff.

the arts based on an analysis of structure. Wölfflin's analysis is frequently admirably concrete and sensitive. Used with caution, his terms "open" and "closed" form, "linear" and "pictorial," "flat" and "deep," and so forth seem to point to real distinctions in the history of art, illuminating for the contrast between the High Renaissance and the baroque. The art historians will have to decide whether the terms are particularly useful in analyzing the arts of other times and places, but one cannot suppress the obvious criticism that Wölfflin provides us with only one set of contraries which applied to the whole history of the arts seems a clumsy instrument of distinction. But transferred to literature and thus deprived of the concrete meaning attached to them by Wölfflin, these concepts seem to lose almost all meaning. They help us merely to arrange works of art into two categories which, when examined in detail, amount only to the old distinction between classic and romantic, severe and loose structure, plastic and picturesque art: a dualism which was known to the Schlegels and to Schiller and Coleridge and was arrived at by them through ideological and literary arguments. Wölfflin's one set of contraries manages to group all classical and pseudoclassical art together, on the one hand, and on the other to combine very divergent movements such as the Gothic, the baroque, and romanticism. This theory seems to me to obscure the undoubted and extremely important continuity between the Renaissance and baroque just as its application to German literature by Strich [37] makes an artificial contrast between the pseudoclassical stage in the development of Schiller and Goethe and the romantic movement of the early nineteenth century, while it must leave the "Storm and Stress" unexplained and incomprehensible. Actually, the German literature at the turn of the eighteenth and nineteenth centuries forms a comparative unity which it seems absurd to break up into an irreconcilable antithesis. Thus, Wölfflin's theory may help us in classifying works of art and establishing or rather confirming the old action-reaction, convention-revolt, or see-saw type of dualistic evolutionary scheme, which, however, confronted with the reality of the complex process of literature, falls far short of coping with the complex pattern of the actual development.

The transfer of Wölfflin's pairs of concepts also leaves one important problem completely unsolved. We cannot explain in any way the undoubted fact that the arts did not evolve with the same speed at the same time. Literature seems sometimes to linger behind the arts:

[37] In Fritz Strich, *loc. cit.*

for instance, we can scarcely speak of an English literature when the great English cathedrals were being built. At other times music lags behind literature and the other arts; for instance, we cannot speak of "romantic" music before 1800, while much romantic poetry preceded that date. We have difficulty in accounting for the fact that there was "picturesque" poetry at least sixty years before the picturesque invaded architecture [38] or for the fact, mentioned by Burckhardt,[39] that *Nencia*, the description of peasant life by Lorenzo Magnifico, preceded by some eighty years the first genre pictures of Jacopo Bassano and his school. Even if these few examples were wrongly chosen and could be refuted, they raise a question which, I think, cannot be answered by an oversimple theory according to which, let us say, music is always lagging by a generation after poetry. Obviously a correlation with social factors should be attempted, and these factors will vary in every single instance.

We are finally confronted with the problem that certain times or nations were extremely productive only in one or two arts, while either completely barren or merely imitative and derivative in others. The flowering of Elizabethan literature, which was not accompanied by any comparable flowering of the fine arts, is a case in point, and little, it seems to me, is gained by speculations to the effect that the national soul, in some way, concentrated on one art or that, as M. Legouis phrases it in his *History of English Literature*,[40] "Spenser would have become a Titian or Veronese had he been born in Italy or a Rubens or Rembrandt in the Netherlands." In the case of English literature it is easy to suggest that Puritanism was responsible for the neglect of the fine arts, but that is scarcely enough to account for the differences between the productivity in very secular literature and the comparative barrenness in painting. But all this leads us far afield into concrete historical questions which I have not time to argue in full.

I merely wanted to suggest further problems in order to support my conclusions. The various arts—the plastic arts, literature, and music—have each their individual evolution, with a different tempo and a different internal structure of elements. No doubt they are in constant relationship with each other, but these relationships are not influences

[38] See Christopher Hussey, *The Picturesque; Studies in a Point of View*, London, 1927, p. 5.

[39] Jakob Burckhardt, *Die Kultur der Renaissance in Italien*, Phaidon, Vienna, pp. 202–3.

[40] E. Legouis and L. Cazamian, *Histoire de la littérature anglaise*, Paris, 1924, p. 279.

which start from one point and determine the evolution of the other arts; they have to be conceived rather as a complex scheme of dialectical relationships which work both ways, from one art to another and *vice versa*, and may be completely transformed within the art which they have entered. It is not a simple affair of a "time-spirit" determining and permeating each and every art. We must conceive of the sum-total of man's cultural activities as of a whole system of self-evolving series, each having its own set of norms which is not necessarily identical with those of the neighboring series. The task of art historians in the widest sense, including historians of literature and of music, is to evolve a descriptive set of terms in each art, based on the specific characteristics of each art. Thus poetry today needs a new poetics, a technique of analysis which cannot be arrived at by a simple transfer or adaptation of terms from the fine arts. Only when we have evolved a successful system of terms for the analysis of literary works of art can we delimit literary periods, which, as I showed in my lecture last year, can be best conceived in terms of dominant systems of norms, and not as metaphysical entities dominated by a "time-spirit." [41] Having established such outlines of strictly literary evolution, we then can ask the question whether this evolution is, in some way, similar to the similarly established evolution of the other arts. The answer will be, as we can see, not a flat "yes" or "no." It will take the form of an intricate pattern of coincidences and divergences rather than parallel lines.

Thus, to summarize briefly, I should like to argue that the current methods for the comparison of the arts are of little value. They are based either on vague similarities of emotional effects or on a community of intentions, theories, and slogans which may not be very concretely related to the actual works of arts. Or, more usefully, they are based on a community of antecedents in the social or general cultural background, but even here the community is frequently merely presupposed, and the mysterious unifying "time-spirit" is usually little more than a vague abstraction or empty formula. Finally, most usefully, this community among the arts has been and should be studied in the structural relationships between the arts, but, in practice, the one widely used scheme for the approximation of the arts, Wölfflin's series of contrary concepts, leads only to the establishment of a very general community between the arts and literature by the distinction of two stylistic

[41] See my "Periods and Movements in Literary History," in *English Institute Annual*, 1940, New York, 1941, pp. 73–93.

types and their supposed alteration in the course of history. The vaguely emotive, the fancifully metaphorical, and the drearily speculative analogizing between the arts should be recognized as blind alleys, and the problem should be approached anew.

It might sound distressingly vague and abstract, if I should suggest that the approximation among the arts which would lead to concrete possibilities of comparison might be sought in an attempt to reduce all the arts to branches of semiology, or to so many systems of signs. These systems of signs might be conceived as enforcing certain systems of norms which imply groups of values. In such terms as signs, norms, and values I would look for a description of the common basis of the arts. But I propose such a distant solution only hesitatingly, knowing very well that this would involve the presentation of a system of aesthetics which I am not prepared to develop today.

I. 4

The Modern Myth
of the Modern Myth[*]

DONALD A. STAUFFER

Princeton University

A FABLE, said La Fontaine, is "a lie that tells the truth." I should like to define "myth" in similar terms of rough justice. The myth, as I conceive it, tends toward a lie at least to the extent that it is not verifiable in science or history. And it tells the truth to the extent that people *believe* that it tells the truth. As Julius Caesar said, "Most people believe what they want to believe." The myth helps them in their beliefs. It satisfies a desire or a need. It answers a riddle. It gives us a home, so that the universe is no longer so dizzying, or frightful, or empty. When we are looking toward a quarter of the sky for a constellation that will orient us in our wandering, there, in the center of our field of vision, glimmers the shadow shape of myth, faint stars that seem to form a pattern, and for a moment we know that we are not lost.

Goethe has said that for modern times, the subject for great art is the portrayal of the soul of man. Let us accept this idea for a moment, and also conceive of myth as something that gives man through a fiction a clearer knowledge of himself, or a belief that he possesses such knowledge. Then we might also accept Salvador de Madariaga's statement that the great modern myths are to be found in the persons and actions of such figures as Don Juan, Hamlet, and Don Quixote. Here are aspects of the human spirit given such a complete life of their own, so widely familiar—we may even say so widely believed in—that each

* Read at the Institute in 1947. Published in the *Institute Essays*, 1948.

of us knows himself better in the reckless, or melancholic, or quixotic mood because of acquaintance with these mythical creations.

But in what sense do we believe in Don Juan? Is he any more than a joint heritage of the European community, a convenient clotheshorse on which, borrowed from Mozart's modifications, George Bernard Shaw can hang his own ideas in the dream scene of *Man and Superman?* And tomorrow might we not see a movie called *Don Juan in Hollywood,* with no more belief in its subject, or indignation at the violation of belief, than such a movie would probably imply?

The question which I am obviously raising is the embarrassing question of the relation of art and belief. The commonsense answer, that no one mistakes the imagined world for the historical world, was long ago given by Dr. Johnson when he demolished the credibility of the theater: "It is false [he said] that any representation is mistaken for reality; that any dramatic fable in its *materiality* was ever credible, or for a single moment was ever credited."

Yet if we do not credit the fable, how can it affect us? Critics from ancient down to very recent times have felt that art does and should move us to action, in which term might be included what I. A. Richards calls "attitudes" and what I would prefer to call moral beliefs that lead toward action. How can we be moved by something we don't believe in? When Theodore Roosevelt used to present his argument for the necessity of war by asking: "What would you do if someone struck your wife?" the necessity for physical action depended upon one's belief in the reality of one's wife. But if I asked you: "What would you do if someone struck Hamlet?" I would have framed a question that most of us could agree upon as ridiculous. We are back at Dr. Johnson's dictum that no dramatic fable in its materiality was ever credited.

Let us make another start. Assumptions which we act upon instinctively are based on beliefs. Therefore, if we study our assumptions and actions, we may be able to assess our beliefs, though they vary from tepidity to fanaticism, and though they are in themselves intangible. In the physical world, the law of gravity is intangible. Yet all of us assume that the effects of disregarding it would be tangible enough. So heartily do we believe in it that none of us will start for a stroll by stepping out of a third-story window. What happens when we consider our assumptions, not in the physical but the moral world? I doubt if any one of us assumes that he is in danger of being shot or stabbed to death by his neighbor. It is possible, though it seems to me improbable, that we refrain from murder because of the social penalties. Those of us who refrain from murder because we believe that God gave Moses on the mount the Ten Commandments are living in a vital myth. And those of us who, upon analyzing our more irreligious minds, decide that we refrain from murder perhaps because of the presence of an inner law—a kind of handy check that operates for the sake of preserving the species—are also acting upon a belief, usually unanalyzed and undoubtedly harder to state or even to agree upon precisely because it has no story, no myth, to cling to.

After this expatiation among beliefs and skepticism and climates of opinion, it is time to set some bounds to our subject. Let us define myth for the purposes of speculation and of getting on with the argument. A myth is a story which cannot with any success be reasonably accredited, but which is accepted without reasoning to such an extent that people act upon its assumptions. Under this definition, a person living within a myth is not aware of its mythical nature. As soon as he consciously thinks of it as something made up, or invented, or codified by custom, it has ceased to be a live myth and has become a curiosity, or a superstition, or a deliberate fiction. As long as the myth remains living, we live within it instinctively.

S. Thompson in his *The Folktale* writes: "Of all the words used to distinguish the classes of prose narrative, myth is the most confusing. The difficulty is that it has been discussed too long and that it has been used in too many different senses." In Professor Thompson's eyes, however, myth implies "a world supposed to have preceded the present order. It tells of sacred beings and of semi-divine heroes and of the origins of all things, usually thru the agency of these sacred beings. Myths are intimately connected with religious beliefs and practices of the people." They are "given religious significance." [1]

Does this conception make myth sound so far-away and long-ago that there is no possibility of us enlightened moderns possessing any myths? I believe not. I would accept Mr. Thompson's definition, and would lay stress upon three points: (1) that myths do not deal directly with the present order—since the present order affords too great a chance of incipient myth being proved and thus becoming history, or disproved and thus becoming a hoax; (2) that myths deal with sacred beings or at least with supermortals; and (3) that myths are connected

[1] *The Folktale* (New York, The Dryden Press, 1946), p. 9. Reprinted by permission of the publishers.

with beliefs—religious beliefs, if you will. In my own terms, a myth is living only while we live within it, accepting it without question.

I believe I can illustrate what I mean simply and easily. In talking about the possibility of modern myths with an intelligent woman, I speculated concerning whether we had created in America a myth of Abraham Lincoln. I was careful to say that I realized Lincoln was an historical character, but that I believed we had made him something more than mortal, that to the average American Abraham Lincoln, singlehanded, tragically and humorously smiling, had freed the slaves and preserved the Union, dying sacrificially, a one-man hecatomb, the fulcrum of American history and the symbol of the United States. My explanation did not protect me: my friend was indignant. In her eyes, to call Lincoln a myth was almost blasphemous: it was a vile attack— more vile because indirect—on his humility, on his great sense of brotherhood, on his passion for human equality. I inquired, in some embarrassment, whether any mere human being could fulfill in his mere mortal life all the functions that popular American history has demanded of Lincoln. Her answer was: "Yes! Lincoln did!" I submit that my friend was living in a living myth. Since I am living in the myth, too, I am not going to waste time in the nefarious attempt to show that Lincoln popularly conceived is a "myth" in quotation marks. And the shades of Washington and Jefferson may rest in peace as well. As for Woodrow Wilson and Franklin Roosevelt, they are on their long journey and their backs are toward us; when they turn their faces, transfigured, in some fifty years shall we say, they too may look at us under the aspect of myth.

Yet only out of some such material may we moderns draw our scanty store of genuine myths. The ambient atmosphere of our times allows us to breathe only history. If a man has not lived historically, he cannot be alive. The mustard seed of doubt destroys any structure of myth in the sense in which I am using this word. That is why Davy Crockett has more chance of being an American myth than Davy Jones; that is why Paul Revere and his galloping horse is a better subject than Paul Bunyan and his blue ox. It is possible to accept Shelley's dictum that the great imaginative creators are "the mirrors of the gigantic shadows which futurity casts upon the present" and to build on this dictum a fanciful mythology that shows the American soul expressing its desires—perhaps its future—in bright fantasies. It would be an interesting gallery, from Captain Ahab to Paul Bunyan; it would draw on the movies and the comic strips and would include Charlie Chaplin and Bill Hart and Mickey Mouse and Li'l Abner and Mauldin's G.I.s and the Timid Soul and Terry and the Pirates and Buck Rogers—and above all Superman with his mastery of space and matter and his simple virtue coupled with absolute physical power. But this is not scientific enough to suit us today. It is based too largely on what might have happened or what may happen; it is the soul of America dreaming on things to come—which is a waste of time until they get here. We are a hopeful people, but we are also from Missouri: we believe in the future, but we will believe in it even more when we can see it.

I seem to be cutting down on the possibilities for a modern myth. It cannot exist in the future and elicit widespread belief; it cannot exist too far back in the past because there is not enough certainty then that it really happened, *wie es eigentlich gewesen*. (Many of us would turn Christians more easily if there were evidence to show that the apple Eve ate was a genuine Grimes Golden or Bellflower.) We need for our myths actors doing great deeds in some period which we can accept as historical.

Yet we are further handicapped because we believe in the natural, not the supernatural; and we do not believe that many men have been capable of great deeds. That in itself would be super-natural. We subscribe to the idea of the liberty of the individual, but we prefer that he exercise that liberty in being just like all the rest of us.

The modern myth-maker is confronted by a dilemma: democracy and science have opened up two great *fields* for mythology, in which belief is almost omnipresent; at the same time democracy and science have dwarfed the importance of the human actors without which a myth, in our definition, cannot truly take on flesh. If our definition were not so disconcertingly rigid—that a myth should tell a story with human actors—it would be easier to conceive of modern myths. For in the larger terms of a *conception* commonly accepted and believed in without proof, we have today two great myths: the myth of science and the myth of the state. The myth of science makes us trust the world of matter, because it is subject to the controlled observation of specialists; but it takes away from us trust in ourselves, except when we are operating as scientists. We believe in matter and motion, and we shall believe in our minds when they too have been charted as electrical impulses in the laboratory. We believe that we are composed of elements, but we know not what we do. The myth of the atom is popularly accepted, although scientists are not so certain in their description of this fiction as were the theologians of the Middle Ages in ordering the angels. Yet we shall continue to believe in the invisible atom and doubt the invisible angels; we shall disregard the upward movement of the soul, whose nature is the nature of a wing, and remain content to scrutinize the Brownian movement in a suspended drop of oil in a near-vacuum. A doctor today takes care of the health of the physical body; in earlier times a doctor was a wise man who understood the health of the soul. I am not denying that the myth of science works; it could not work so well today if it had not been popularly accepted and believed in for three hundred years. From the success with which the assumptions of materialism have been applied in science derives also in part our worship of economics. I am arguing that economics also furnish the grounds for a living myth: if I mentioned the miracle of the loaves and fishes, or the precept of casting our bread upon the waters, as possible aids to the millions who are starving in India, the frivolity of my non-economic approach would rouse the indignation of every honest citizen. We believe in economics; we do not believe in miracles or symbolic parables.

The other great ground for modern myth rears up a giant more terrible than any Gargantua or Micromégas or Brobdingnagian—the Giant of the State. When Shakespeare's Menenius, and Plutarch's before him, told the story of the classes of Rome constituting the various organs of the body politic, we had an exercise in fancy. It is no fancy today—it is a living myth. We are no more than corpuscles in the body politic. We can see the frightening unimportance of individuals in the Fascist and Nazi states so recently destroyed, and sense it, perhaps, in the Communist practice. Yet we are aware, too, that in acknowledging and combating such creations of political megalomania—effective because the world accepts them so readily—we have ourselves become controlled corpuscles in the body politic to an extent unprecedented in anything that has ever gone by the name of republic or democracy. The sheer brutal size and omnipresence of the state is crowding individual spirit out of the world, which is smaller than we think.

I take it that the English Institute believes in spirit and the individual, or would like to believe in them. Of what significance they are to society is sufficiently evident in the space such a five-day conference as this does not receive in the newspapers. We talk about the spirit and the individual, the necessary grounds for myth in the sense in which I use it; the world today believes in matter and the state. This is the century of the atomic bomb and of socialism. To science each of us is so many percent of phosphorus or of water; to the state each of us is a taxpayer, a maker of x's to indicate a choice on a ballot, a prospective soldier or recipient of government checks. Is this the human material out of which myths may be made?

This, then, is the narrow circle from which I do not think we shall soon escape: a living myth is a story of extraordinary human action which is widely accepted without question; we accept without question only the ideas of science and the state; the ideas of science and the state, since they minimize extraordinary human action, make a living myth almost impossible to conceive. Yet still, in the midst of our despair, we hope. "Surely some revelation is at hand." To bring it about we consider the possibility, which in my mind is a contradiction in terms, of constructing or inventing myths without belief. That is why I have called this paper "The Modern Myth of the Modern Myth." We are asking for too easy a solution. We are prescribing a quack salve for a deep-rooted disease. Knowing too much and too little psychology, too much and too little sociology, and practically nothing about the manner in which belief operates in art, we are proposing from the heights of our skeptical sophistication a cure for the great modern spiritual vacuum by suggesting that the world be offered some handy, newly concocted, modern myths. Who will believe them? On what grounds? And if they are not accepted so deeply that they guide our actions, how do they differ from the daily monotony of realistic novels on the one hand, whose invention is so pallid that they must be protected by guarantees that none of the historical characters in the novel is historical; or on the other from the escapes into fantasy that are either coy and gamesome or hysterical?

A society that possesses myths is a healthy human society. If we did not know this from our own study of history, we could find it out from Arnold Toynbee (whose knowledge is so wide that he like Einstein is a candidate around whom the myths of the twenty-first century might easily grow). Yet myths will not come into being because some convention votes that they are a good thing to have, or because some poet in sudden whim decides to invent them. They will come into being, as they probably have in the past, only out of deep and long-continued passion, crystallized and given shape, perhaps, by some deeply passionate seer-artist, and slowly absorbed into a common culture because they reflect or create profound convictions, and satisfy the impossible desires of that culture.

So far I have advanced the tragically ironical reasons why modern myth-making seems to me difficult if not almost impossible. I shall now want to reverse the field and consider the most serious, the most conscious, and the most nearly successful attempt at such myth-making. But first I should like to give as a coda to this initial section a quick restatement of my essential positions, in words culled here and there from a representative and sensitive contemporary. Only when we realize the difficulty of myth-making today may we properly value our closest approximation to the myth-maker.

Cyril Connolly, a sensitive critic, is living in an unquiet grave with his eyes wide open. He finds today a triple decadence: of language, of society, and of the myth. "Decadence of the myth," he says, "for there is no longer a unifying belief (as in Christianity or in Renaissance Man) to give to a writer a sense of awe, and of awe which he shares with the mass of humanity." Validity of the myth and vigor of belief, as he sees it, are two of the requisites for a work of art. Yet he immediately adds, from his unquiet grave: "The strength of belief in a myth whose validity is diminishing will not produce such great art as the strength of belief in one which is valid, and *none is valid today.*"

He freely acknowledges that the mythoclasts seem always to be right, for our capacity for reverence so easily turns into superstition (or that modern equivalent of superstition, a neurosis). Yet that will not stop man's sense of reverence which, says Mr. Connolly, man continually exudes like a secretion; and reverence tends to turn even the immediate toward myth. In individual history, he says, "The three or four people whom I have loved seem utterly set apart from the others in my life; angelic, ageless creatures, more alive than the living, embalmed perpetually in their all-devouring myth." And in social history, "Lenin, the father figure mummified, replaces the Byzantine Christ."

Myth-making may be not only dangerous, but also a *cowardly* attempt to escape. "Cowardice in living," he writes. "Evasion through comfort, through society, through acquisitiveness, through the book-bed-bath defence system, above all through the past, the flight to the romantic womb of history, into primitive myth-making."

And yet—and yet—in spite of all dangers and difficulties and despairs, the artist, murdering impossibilities, even today has his function. This is Mr. Connolly's text: "Today the function of the artist is to bring imagination to science and science to imagination, where they meet, in the myth." His language here approximates Wordsworth at his most philosophically mythopoeic: "Poetry is the breath and finer spirit of all knowledge; it is the impassioned expression which is in the countenance of all science." Or as Shelley phrases it: "[The poetic faculty] creates new materials of knowledge." And in Shelley's negative statement of the same thing, the obverse of Shelley's coin: "There is no want of knowledge respecting what is wisest and best in morals, government, and political economy, or at least, what is wiser and better than what men now practice and endure. But . . . we want the creative faculty to imagine that which we know."

Shelley's words on the rarity of this creative passionate energy or belief that alone can make great art come close to the memorable phrase of the modern poet, whose career we cannot consider with too great seriousness, and who says: "It is so many years before one can believe enough in what one feels even to know what the feeling is." It is William Butler Yeats speaking. His passion, the unpredictable sallies of his imagination, his piercing philosophical mind, his single dedication to a long and *directed* career as poet, and finally—is it the luck of the Irish?—his genius, make him a safe guide in seeking what may be done in modern times toward the establishment of myth.

He began as a late Pre-Raphaelite idle singer of an empty day. His early imaginative poems are merely desultory wish-fulfillments. Mr. Connolly's flight to the romantic past is almost a gallop in Yeats, when we encounter a poem (1889) called "Anashuya and Vijaya" and find ourselves in "A little Indian temple in the Golden Age." And perhaps the Indian philosopher of another of his early poems believes that God is a moorfowl, or a lotus, or a roebuck, or a peacock, or a combination of all of these. But probably the Indian himself doesn't believe this, and certainly neither Yeats nor the reader. But then, Yeats is young, he is not yet twenty when he writes, this is his first volume of verse, and he knows himself that he is at the "Crossways."

Being a poet, Yeats has an eye for the actual, and an inner eye for the ideal. How combine them in a myth? In the 1890s he tries two roads-of-the-chameleon. One approach is the deliberate creation of all-inclusive symbols. Perhaps under the influence of Shelley's and Spenser's idealism, and of Blake's private cosmos and galvanized symbols, he creates his symbol of the Rose. What is the Rose? "The quality symbolized as The Rose," he writes, "differs from the Intellectual Beauty of Shelley and of Spenser" in that he "imagined it as suffering with man and not as something pursued and seen from afar." Yet he realizes this significance only thirty-two or thirty-three years after the event. In the 1890s the Rose might be the Rose of the World, or of Peace, or of Battle, or the Secret Rose, or the Rose upon the Rood of Time, or the Rose in a Lover's Heart, or a "Red Rose, proud Rose, sad Rose of all my days!" And that is too much to ask of any rose! He might well say with Blake, "Oh Rose, thou art sick!" and abandon—until much later he successfully turns it to a new use—the attempt at myth through arbitrary amorphous symbols.

His second approach to myth is the expected and normal one. He turns to the past of his race. The attempt is as heroic (and even longer continued) and perhaps as fruitless, as his own Cuchulain battling against the waves with his sword. In his dramas and closet-dramas and poems, from the time he was twenty until he was seventy he worked over with love and admiration and care those great shadowy figures of Aengus the Master of Love, and Fergus and Cuchulain, and Cathleen the daughter of Houlihan, and Oisin and Baile and Aillin, and Forgael, and Deirdre and Queen Maeve. If Yeats is right in his belief that no great passion ever dies, but lives on in the great mind and memory of the world, always endowed with the possibility of breaking out of eternity into particular time and space, then perhaps his strong imaginings have done, or still may do, what he hoped from them: they may give the Irish a sense of pride in their own history, give them semimythical noble ancestors that might make the Irish nation noble as Thebes and Troy made Greece and Rome. Yet many of these creations had to meet the hard test of the theater, before the eyes of the people whom they were designed to educate. The myths did not convince them; and seeing them unconvinced, Yeats apparently lost his conviction in turn.

I must do some drastic collapsing in talking about Yeats's most obviously mythical subjects, for the obvious things are not the important things in this extraordinary long and vital career at myth-making. He diminished his emphasis on Irish legend when he found that the epic heroes and the fairy hosts of the Sidhe inhabited a land of shadowy waters, as unreal as Tennyson's Lotus-Eaters or Morris's Earthly Paradise. If his first volume could take as a theme:

My songs of old earth's dreamy youth . . .
Dream, dream, for this is also sooth,

he learns, in twenty-five years, to cast away the embroidery of old my-
thologies:

For there's more enterprise
In walking naked.

One road toward greater reality lies among the people—the songs
and ballads of the peasants, the superstitions and half-presences of the
folk. But Yeats's imagination was never as coy as Barrie's, nor as deliberately cunning as Kipling's, so that he has left us no Peter Pan or
Puck of Pook's Hill.

Another road is the hymning of Ireland in her time of greatness in
the historical past—in the eighteenth century. His four chivalric horse-
men are Swift, Berkeley, Goldsmith, and Burke. Yet again, his sense
of humor—which is but another aspect of a sense of balance and a sense
of reality—protects him from impossible constructions, and only Swift
in his hands attains anything like mythical proportions.

These two roads run parallel in another quest: figures invented, or
possessing a basis in history, fairly close to present times, who, like the
main characters in historical novels, are freely enough imagined to live
easily and significantly in their own passions, but who are given reality
by actual humble Irish backgrounds. Demonstrable geography and
history chain them to the physical world. The argument would run that
since Aherne and Robartes can stop on a bridge and talk about Yeats
working in his tower, and since Yeats and the tower and the bridge are
real, then Aherne and Robartes may also be believed in. Yeats, in divers
of his writings, gave his imagination discipline in constructing reality
in this careful conjuration of such figures as Michael Robartes, Red
Hanrahan, Blind Raftery, and Mary Hynes.

But again, they can hardly be considered myths, for they have no
commonly accepted connotations. How many of us would immediately
and naturally associate Blind Raftery with art, in Yeats's personal and
historical figure of the blind Irish singer and poet? How many would
see Mary Hynes as the symbol of the world's beauty?

Along the last road which he chose, Yeats deliberately substituted
universally familiar figures for his local loyalties. Helen of Troy replaces
Mary Hynes; Homer is more easily understood as a symbol for the
artist than is Blind Raftery. Solomon and Sheba, Leda, the Virgin

Mary, Saint Veronica—such names figure in the titles of his later poems, and what they stand for, even though Yeats may shape it to his own purposes, may be more easily and commonly understood. To sustain his own unique thought, therefore, Yeats in the end turns to the great myths of Greece, Christianity, and world history.

So far we have been discussing merely the means for myth-making. What are the beliefs that in Yeats's mind were seeking embodiment? They may be summed up simply: the belief in free spirit. As a single extended illustration of the belief in spirit, I need do no more than mention Yeats's fantastic and continuous inquiry into the occult, from Madame Blavatsky and theosophy and Eastern mysticism down to table-tipping, telepathy, and Rosicrucianism. These quixotic and erratic quests form a lifelong declaration that for Yeats the world of matter, or the world of science, or the world of reason, is not enough. Reality for Yeats, even more than for most poets, lies somewhere in the spirit.

As for the *free* spirit, in a world of increasing bondages and pressures and conformities and uniformities, Yeats dedicated himself unswervingly to the freedom of the individual. It is typical of him to write in 1905 (he was thinking of Synge's *Playboy of the Western World*): "We will have a hard fight before we get *the right of every man to see the world in his own way* admitted." In the realms of social ideas and intellectual fashions, he felt it his duty to constitute himself a member of his majesty's loyal opposition, no matter who might be the reigning majesty. He seems at times contemptuous of liberty and democracy. But the liberty he scorned was one of easy privileges, half-formed opinions, and evaded responsibilities. He did not so much disdain the common man and little people as commonness in any man and littleness of soul. His so-called Fascism is but a belief that we must recover from the errors of too much liberty—"the building up of authority, the restoration of discipline, the discovery of a life sufficiently heroic to live without the opium dream" (1924).

This, then, is the goal: the discovery of a life sufficiently heroic. It cannot be found in artificial political unity, "which is the decadence of every civilization." It must be found in the individual human being. And probably it must be found there by the artist. "The arts are, I believe," Yeats writes in 1898, "about to take upon their shoulders the burdens that have fallen from the shoulders of the priests." He knew it was no simple task, nor a popular assignment. And it was a lonely one.

Perhaps he felt the truth of what A. C. Benson wrote to him in 1923 when he was awarded the Nobel Prize: "I am sure you differ from all writers of the time in having the best sort of detachment—the detachment from the urgent *present* which ends by bringing an artist, if he is a great artist, into line with the great spirits of the past and future."

At any rate, Yeats can speculate in such terms as these: "The first nation which can possess the three convictions, God, Freedom and Immortality, affirmed by Kant as *free powers*, will control the moral energies of the soul." Yet this is no easy goal, to be reached by conventions, or programs, or acts of the will. Yeats is not satisfied with Eliot's Anglicanism nor with French Neo-Thomism at one end, nor with the Fascist and Bolshevist idea of the state at the other. His belief can be attained neither by any metaphysics nor by any economic theory. "That belief which I call free powers is free because we cannot distinguish between the things believed in and the belief." Here he is speaking in terms of his own distinction between allegory (which is artificial and rational) and symbolism (which is organic and inevitable); and he is speaking almost in the terms of my assumed definition of myth as a story in which we live instinctively and without analysis.

To set up this belief in free powers in which the belief and the powers are indistinguishable, Yeats devotes the great period of his life as a poet—the quarter century preceding 1933—to the construction of a system. As he writes to his father: "Much of your thought resembles mine . . . but mine is part of a religious system more or less logically worked out. A system which will, I hope, interest you as a form of poetry. I find the setting of it in order has helped my verse, has given me a new framework and new patterns. One goes on year after year getting the disorder of one's mind in order, and this is the real impulse to create."

The system, which gives structure to many of his greatest poems, is most fully presented in his book *A Vision*. No philosophy, psychology, and theory of world history has ever been presented in such mathematically perfect, geometric form. The artist's eye has glimpsed this vision of formal beauty; but the reader is mistaking the nature of the artist's mind if he takes the form mechanically and literally. He should be warned by Yeats's own statement that the system should interest his father "as a form of *poetry*." And he should remember John Butler Yeats writing to his son: "You [became a poet] because you had convictions of the kind that *could be best expressed in verse*, i.e. convictions that were *desires*, and such as could never be imprisoned in opinions."

Yeats's diagrams of the Great Wheel and the Historical Cones, therefore, his speculations on the twenty-six Phases of the Moon in which human incarnations are possible, and on the Great Year of the Ancients, are all to be taken with a grain of Attic, or Irish, salt. "If you *believe* in magic," as Yeats says in a flash of his chameleon wit, "it ceases to be magical." The road of a poet is no concrete turnpike. It is the road of the chameleon. The poet sets up tentative fictions, until he finds those in which he can believe—or better, until he finds those where the question of belief does not even come up.

A *Vision* (1924) presents an enthralling study in its delicate balances between fantasy and revelation. Two of its great intuitions are the importance of Desire in human life, and the Duality of Truth. Body seeks soul; soul seeks body; all living qualities desire their opposites, and in fact cannot be understood without them. Solomon yearns toward Sheba, Sheba toward Solomon; and Wisdom without Beauty, Beauty without Wisdom, are meaningless. This is the condition of the world— a world given structure by antitheses and antinomies, a world in which Chance is ever present and Choice is always necessary, a world which, with its returning cycles and revolving diametrically opposed desires, will persist in its great pattern this side eternity, an eternity which will be crowed in when Chance is one with Choice at last.

Yeats has given mysterious power to his symbols—so that the great Blakean figure of the archer, shooting her arrow of desire into another dimension from the flat circle and cycle of history, recurs in the memory. And the old myths and accepted stories—of Dionysus, of the Trojan War, of the birth of Christ—are caught up into a single coherent imaginative pattern of which we today are a part. The vision is not smaller in scope than Dante's. It takes as its province all time and all space. In place of Dante's descending *bolge* in the Inferno and ascending ledges on the Mount of Purgatory, Yeats has created the twenty-eight Phases of the Moon on a scale where he can group Shakespeare, Balzac, and Napoleon in one phase, or in another, Queen Victoria, Galsworthy, and Lady Gregory.

How should the system, the vision, be taken? To consider its artificiality absurd is not so absurd as to fail in understanding how the mind of a poet works, how he inhabits the world of Make-Believe taken in a literal sense, how he functions as the unacknowledged legislator of the world, how he creates visions that have an odd habit of solidifying into reality. He builds a structure with gossamer, and before we know it, he has made a bridge across Chaos. The first section of Yeats's poem "The Second Coming" has become famous because it describes—it has never been better done—the world of the 1930s. The poem was published in 1921. Yet since it was principally concerned with looking forward to the year 2000, and since it shows Yeats's power of fusing old materials into new myths at its most intense and most characteristic, its last section may be quoted in full:

> Surely some revelation is at hand;
> Surely the Second Coming is at hand.
> The Second Coming! Hardly are those words out
> When a vast image out of *Spiritus Mundi*
> Troubles my sight: somewhere in sands of the desert
> A shape with lion body and a head of a man,
> A gaze blank and pitiless as the sun,
> Is moving its slow thighs, while all about it
> Reel shadows of the indignant desert birds.
> The darkness drops again: but now I know
> That twenty centuries of stony sleep
> Were vexed to nightmare by a rocking cradle,
> And what rough beast, its hour come round at last,
> Slouches towards Bethlehem to be born?

The creative poetic power is at work—making from materials available to all those patterns toward which life may move, if only the patterns are seen clearly and believed in. The materials available to all! How much of the nobility with which Yeats has invested his ideals of tradition, of ceremony, of aristocracy, of custom may we assume sprang from Yeats's association with an actual Lady Gregory at an actual Coole Park? How much of the bravery of his mythical heroes came from the veins of the men he knew, the martyrs and the patriots of the Irish rebellion, so that Cuchulain is but a mythical magnification of Pearse and Connolly? The great Rose Tree of Ireland must grow, and must be watered. And yet, said Pearse to Connolly,

> There's nothing but our own red blood
> Can make a right Rose Tree.

Perhaps this is the only source and soil of all myth—our own red blood. And how many of his eagle spirits, his Queen Maeves, his heroes impossibly brave and gay, found their first inceptions in memories of

Maud Gonne?—"Angelic, ageless creatures, more alive than the living, embalmed perpetually in their all-devouring myth."

However it was done, the poetic process, mixing memory and desire, continued for fifty years in this one man. And the results, though they celebrate personality and individuality, take on that accessibility to the experience of all men which is an essential attribute of the greatest poetry and of myth.

His Byzantium poems, perhaps his best known, are part of the great myth of cyclical history which is a part of his greater myth of *A Vision*. They are complex and they are personal. Yeats believed in the Great Mind and the Great Memory; he believed that this great mind and great memory could be evoked by symbols. Perhaps they can. At any rate, before we dismiss these poetic symbols and myths of Byzantium, we had better also dismiss Plato's Golden Year. And we must also sweep away as refuse Oswald Spengler and Arnold Toynbee.

I venture to suggest that perhaps Yeats's greatest mythical creation is himself. Living in a world which is frightening principally because it is so limited, so sordidly tied down to a mechanical multitude of tiny facts, so thoroughly small and dry, he broke the Lilliputian threads and stood up in all the dignity of an imaginative artist, to the full height of a man. His short play *The King's Threshold* (1904) creates as its protagonist a rebel poet who will starve on the steps of power rather than submit to mere authority. The King speaks of this hero:

> No fever or sickness. He has chosen death:
> Refusing to eat or drink, that he may bring
> Disgrace upon me; for there is a custom,
> An old and foolish custom, that if a man
> Be wronged, or think that he is wronged, and starve
> Upon another's threshold till he die,
> The common people, for all time to come,
> Will raise a heavy cry against that threshold,
> Even though it be the king's.

Yeats himself chose to make that gesture. Like that of his Countess Cathleen, such lonely sacrifice of self is made, not forgetful of the people, but for their sake. It is therefore possible for one blind reviewer, on Yeats's death, to reprimand him with being so far removed from his times; and for T. S. Eliot to say of him: "He was one of those few whose history is the history of their own time, who are a part of the consciousness of an age which cannot be understood without them."

Time alone will tell whether or not through his life Yeats has not also achieved "perfection of the work," and has become, by the imaginative art with which he dramatized himself and his relation to his world, a heartening hero, a myth, for "the common people, for all time to come."

We would not really be able to tell whether Yeats had created any myths, or prepared the ground for possible myths, unless we could get a point for perspective some hundred years, say, in the future. And by that time, since the Second Coming is at hand, it might be too late. If there were more men of Yeats's stature, and bold passion, I would not be so sure that the modern myth is no more than a "modern myth" in the most discouragingly cynical sense. At the very least, we cannot but admire his energy. We cannot but be grateful to him for showing us the fascination of what's difficult, and for affirming the mythological basis of all morality in the line he quotes: "In dreams begins responsibility." And to Yeats, more than to any twentieth-century artist, we owe an immense debt for shooting the golden arrow of desire beyond the bounds and atmosphere of the flat world of society and science. He has almost created, or singlehanded he has almost revived, the myth that individual man is a free spirit.

I. 5

Imagination as Value*

WALLACE STEVENS

IT DOES NOT seem possible to say of the imagination that it has a certain single characteristic which of itself gives it a certain single value as, for example, good or evil. To say such a thing would be the same thing as to say that the reason is good or evil or, for that matter, that human nature is good or evil. Since that is my first point, let us discuss it.

Pascal called the imagination the mistress of the world. But as he seems never to have spoken well of it, it is certain that he did not use this phrase to speak well of it. He called it the deceptive element in man, the mistress of error and duplicity, and yet not always that, since there would be an infallible measure of truth if there was an infallible measure of untruth. But being most often false, imagination gives no sign of its quality and indicates in the same way both the true and the false. A little farther on in his *Pensées*, Pascal speaks of magistrates, their red robes, their ermines in which they swathe themselves, like furry cats, the palaces in which they sit in judgment, the fleurs de lis, and the whole necessary, august apparatus. He says, and he enjoys his own malice in saying it, that if medical men did not have their cassocks and the mules they wear, and if doctors did not have their square hats and robes four times too large, they would never have been able to dupe the world, which is incapable of resisting so genuine a display. He refers to soldiers and kings, of whom he speaks with complete caution and respect, saying that they establish themselves by force, the others "par grimace." He justifies monarchs by the strength they possess and says that it is necessary to have a well-defined reason to regard like

---

* Read at the Institute in 1948. Published in the *Institute Essays*, 1949.

anyone else the Grand Seigneur surrounded, in his superb seraglio, by forty thousand janissaries.

However this may be, if respect for magistrates can be established by their robes and ermines, and if justice can be made to prevail by the appearance of the seats of justice, and if vast populations can be brought to live peacefully in their homes and to lie down at night with a sense of security and to get up in the morning confident that the great machine of organized society is ready to carry them on, merely by dressing a few men in uniform and sending them out to patrol the streets, the sort of thing that was the object of Pascal's ridicule and that was, to his way of thinking, an evil, or something of an evil, becomes to our way of thinking a potent good. The truth is, of course, that we do not really control vast populations in this way. Pascal knew perfectly well that the chancellor had force behind him. If he felt in his day that medicine was an imaginary science, he would not feel so today. After all, Pascal's understanding of the imagination was a part of his understanding of everything else. As he lay dying, he experienced a violent convulsion. His sister who attended him described the scene. He had repeatedly asked that he might receive communion. His sister wrote:

"God, who wished to reward a desire so fervent and so just, suspended this convulsion as by a miracle and restored his judgment completely as in the perfection of his health, in a manner that the parish priest, entering into his room with the sacrament, cried to him: 'Here is he whom you have so much desired.' These words completely roused him and as the priest approached to give him communion, he made an effort, he raised himself halfway without help to receive it with more respect; and the priest having interrogated him, following the custom, on the principal mysteries of the faith, he responded distinctly: 'Yes, monsieur, I believe all that with all my heart.' Then he received the sacred wafer and extreme unction with feelings so tender that he poured out tears. He replied to everything, thanked the priest and as the priest blessed him with the holy ciborium, he said, 'Let God never forsake me.' "

Thus, in the very act of dying, he clung to what he himself had called the delusive faculty. When I said a moment ago that he had never spoken well of it, I did not overlook the fact that "this superb power, the enemy of reason," to use his own words, did not, and could not, always seem the same to him. In a moment of indifference, he said that the imagination disposes all things and that it is the imagination that creates beauty, justice, and happiness. In these various ways, the example of Pascal demonstrates how the good of the imagination may be evil and its evil good. The imagination is the power of the mind over the possibilities of things; but if this constitutes a certain single characteristic, it is the source not of a certain single value but of as many values as reside in the possibilities of things.

A second difficulty about value is the difference between the imagination as metaphysics and as a power of the mind over external objects, that is to say, reality. Ernst Cassirer in *An Essay on Man* says,

In romantic thought the theory of poetic imagination had reached its climax. Imagination is no longer that special human activity which builds up the human world of art. It now has universal metaphysical value. Poetic imagination is the only clue to reality. Fichte's idealism is based upon his conception of "productive imagination." Schelling declared in his *System of Transcendental Idealism* that art is the consummation of philosophy. In nature, in morality, in history we are still living in the propylaeum of philosophical wisdom; in art we enter into the sanctuary itself. . . . The true poem is not the work of the individual artist; it is the universe itself, the one work of art which is forever perfecting itself.[1]

Professor Cassirer speaks of this as "exuberant and ecstatic praise of poetic imagination." In addition, it is the language of what he calls "romantic thought," and by romantic thought he means metaphysics. When I speak of the power of the mind over external objects, I have in mind, as external objects, works of art as, for example, the sculptures of Michael Angelo with what Walter Pater calls "their wonderful strength verging, as in the things of the imagination great strength always does, on what is singular or strange" or, in architecture, the formidable public buildings of the British, or the architecture and decoration of churches, as, say, in the case of the Jesuit church at Lucerne, where one might so easily pass from the real to the visionary without consciousness of change. Imagination, as metaphysics, leads us in one direction and, as art, in another.

When we consider the imagination as metaphysics, we realize that it is in the nature of the imagination itself that we should be quick to accept it as the only clue to reality. But alas! we are no sooner so disposed than we encounter the logical positivists. In *Language, Truth and Logic*, Professor Ayer says that

[1] Ernst Cassirer, *An Essay on Man* (New Haven, Yale University Press, 1944), pp. 155–56.

it is fashionable to speak of the metaphysician as a kind of misplaced poet. As his statements have no literal meaning, they are not subject to any criteria of truth or falsehood: but they may still serve to express, or arouse, emotion, and thus be subject to ethical or aesthetic standards. And it is suggested that they may have considerable value, as means of moral inspiration, or even as works of art. In this way, an attempt is made to compensate the metaphysician for his extrusion from philosophy.[2]

It appears from this that the imagination as metaphysics, from the point of view of the logical positivist, has at least seeming values. The *New Statesman* of London has recently published letters growing out of a letter sent to it by a visitor to Oxford, who reported that Professor Ayer's book had "acquired almost the status of a philosophic Bible." This led Professor Joad to look up the book and see for himself. He reported that the book teaches that "If . . . God is a metaphysical term, if, that is to say, He belongs to a reality which transcends the world of sense-experience . . . to say that He exists is neither true nor false. This position . . . is neither atheist nor agnostic; it cuts deeper than either, by asserting that all talk about God, whether pro or anti, is twaddle." What is true of one metaphysical term is true of all.

Then, too, before going on, we must somehow cleanse the imagination of the romantic. We feel, without being particularly intelligent about it, that the imagination as metaphysics will survive logical positivism unscathed. At the same time, we feel, and with the sharpest possible intelligence, that it is not worthy to survive if it is to be identified with the romantic. The imagination is one of the great human powers. The romantic belittles it. The imagination is the liberty of the mind. The romantic is a failure to make use of that liberty. It is to the imagination what sentimentality is to feeling. It is a failure of the imagination precisely as sentimentality is a failure of feeling. The imagination is the only genius. It is intrepid and eager, and the extreme of its achievement lies in abstraction. The achievement of the romantic, on the contrary, lies in minor wish-fulfillments, and it is incapable of abstraction. In any case, and without continuing to contrast the two things, one wants to elicit a sense of the imagination as something vital. In that sense one must deal with it as metaphysics.

If we escape destruction at the hands of the logical positivists, and if we cleanse the imagination of the taint of the romantic, we still face Freud. What would he have said of the imagination as the clue to

[2] Alfred J. Ayer, *Language, Truth and Logic* (New York, Oxford University Press, 1936), pp. 36–37.

reality and of a culture based on the imagination? Before jumping to the conclusion that at last there is no escape, is it not possible that he might have said that in a civilization based on science there could be a science of illusions? He does in fact say that "so long as a man's early years are influenced by the religious thought-inhibition . . . as well as by the sexual one, we cannot really say what he is actually like." If, when the primacy of the intelligence has been achieved, one can really say what a man is actually like, what could be more natural than a science of illusions? Moreover, if the imagination is not quite the clue to reality now, might it not become so then? As for the present, what have we, if we do not have science, except the imagination? And who is to say of its deliberate fictions arising out of the contemporary mind that they are not the forerunners of some such science? There is more than the romantic in the statement that the true work of art, whatever it may be, is not the work of the individual artist. It is time and it is place, as these perfect themselves.

To regard the imagination as metaphysics is to think of it as part of life, and to think of it as part of life is to realize the extent of artifice. We live in the mind. One way of demonstrating what it means to live in the mind is to imagine a discussion of the world between two people born blind, able to describe their images, so far as they have images, without the use of images derived from other people. It would not be our world that would be discussed. Still another illustration may help. A man in Paris does not imagine the same sort of thing that a native of Uganda imagines. If each could transmit his imagination to the other, so that the man in Paris, lying awake at night, could suddenly hear a footfall that meant the presence of some inimical and merciless monstrosity, and if the man in Uganda found himself in, say, the Münster at Basel and experienced what is to be experienced there, what words would the Parisian find to forestall his fate, and what understanding would the Ugandan have of his incredible delirium? If we live in the mind, we live with the imagination. It is a commonplace to realize the extent of artifice in the external world and to say that Florence is more imaginative than Dublin, that blue and white Munich is more imaginative than white and green Havana, and so on; or to say that, in this town, no single public object of the imagination exists, while, in the Vatican City, say, no public object exists that is not an object of the imagination. What is engaging us at the moment has nothing to do with the external world. We are concerned with the extent of artifice within us and, almost parenthetically, with the question of its value.

What, then, is it to live in the mind with the imagination, yet not too near to the fountains of its rhetoric, so that one does not have a consciousness only of grandeurs, of incessant departures from the idiom, and of inherent altitudes? Only the reason stands between it and the reality for which the two are engaged in a struggle. We have no particular interest in this struggle because we know that it will continue to go on and that there will never be an outcome. We lose sight of it until Pascal, or someone else, reminds us of it. We say that it is merely a routine, and the more we think about it the less able we are to see that it has heroic aspects or that the spirit is at stake or that it may involve the loss of the world. Is there in fact any struggle at all, and is the idea of one merely a bit of academic junk? Do not the two carry on together in the mind like two brothers or two sisters or even like young Darby and young Joan? Darby says, "It is often true that what is most rational appears to be most imaginative, as in the case of Picasso." Joan replies, "It is often true, also, that what is most imaginative appears to be most rational, as in the case of Joyce. Life is hard and dear, and it is the hardness that makes it dear." And Darby says, "Speaking of Joyce and the coexistence of opposites, do you remember the story that Joyce tells of Pascal in A Portrait of the Artist as a Young Man?" Stephen said,

—Pascal, if I remember rightly, would not suffer his mother to kiss him as he feared the contact of her sex.—
—Pascal was a pig—said Cranly.
—Aloysius Gonzaga, I think, was of the same mind—Stephen said.
—And he was another pig then—said Cranly.
—The church calls him a saint—Stephen objected.

How is it that we should be speaking of the prize of the spirit and of the loss, or gain, of the world, in connection with the relations between reason and the imagination? It may be historically true that the reason of a few men has always been the reason of the world. Notwithstanding this, we live today in a time dominated by great masses of men; and, while the reason of a few men may underlie what they do, they act as their imaginations impel them to act. The world may, certainly, be lost to the poet, but it is not lost to the imagination. I speak of the poet because we think of him as the orator of the imagination. And I say that the world is lost to him, certainly, because, for one thing, the great poems of heaven and hell have been written and the great poem of the earth remains to be written. I suppose it is that poem that will constitute the true prize of the spirit, and that until it is written many lesser things will be so regarded, including conquests that are not unimaginable. One wants to consider the imagination on its most momentous scale. Today this scale is not the scale of poetry, nor of any form of literature or art. It is the scale of international politics and in particular of communism. Communism is not the measure of humanity. But I limit myself to an allusion to it as a phenomenon of the imagination. Surely the diffusion of communism exhibits imagination on its most momentous scale. This is because whether or not communism is the measure of humanity the words themselves echo back to us that it has for the present taken the measure of an important part of humanity. With the collapse of other beliefs, this grubby faith promises a practicable earthly paradise. The only earthly paradise that even the best of other faiths has been able to promise has been one in man's noblest image, and this has always required an imagination that has not yet been included in the fortunes of mankind.

The difference between an imagination that is engaged by the materialism of communism and one that is engaged by the projects of idealism is a difference in nature. It is not that the imagination is versatile, but that there are different imaginations. The commonest idea of an imaginative object is something large. But apparently with the Japanese it is the other way round, and with them the commonest idea of an imaginative object is something small. With the Hindu it appears to be something vermicular; with the Chinese, something round; and with the Dutch, something square. If these evidences do not establish the point, it can hardly be because the point needs establishing. A comparison between the Bible and poetry is relevant. It cannot be said that the Bible, the most widely distributed book in the world, is the poorest. Nor can it be said that it owes its distribution to the poetry it contains. If poetry should address itself to the same needs and aspirations, the same hopes and fears, to which the Bible addresses itself, it might rival it in distribution. Poetry does not address itself to beliefs. Nor could it ever invent an ancient world full of figures that had been known and become endeared to its readers for centuries. Consequently, when critics of poetry call upon it to do some of the things that the Bible does, they overlook the certainty that the Biblical imagination is one thing and the poetic imagination, inevitably, something else.

We cannot look at the past or the future except by means of the imagination, but again the imagination of backward glances is one thing and the imagination of looks ahead something else. Even the psychologists concede this present particular, for, with them, memory involves a reproductive power and looks ahead involve a creative power: the power of our expectations. When we speak of the life of the imagination, we do not mean man's life as it is affected by his imagination but the life of the faculty itself. Accordingly, when we think of the permeation of man's life by the imagination, we must think of it as a life permeated not by a single thing but by a class of things. We use our imagination with respect to every man of whom we take notice when by a glance we make up our mind about him. The differences so defined entail differences of value. The imagination that is satisfied by politics, whatever the nature of the politics, has not the same value as the imagination that seeks to satisfy, say, the universal mind, which, in the case of a poet, would be the imagination that tries to penetrate to basic images, basic emotions, and so to compose a fundamental poetry even older than the ancient world. Perhaps, one drifts off into rhetoric here, but then there is nothing more congenial than that to the imagination.

Of imaginative life as social form, let me distinguish at once between everyday living and the activity of cultural organization. A theater is a social form, but it is also a cultural organization, and it is not my purpose to discuss the imagination as an institution. Having in mind the extent to which the imagination pervades life, it seems curious that it does not pervade, or even create, social form more widely. It is an activity like seeing things or hearing things, or any other sensory activity. Perhaps, if one collected instances of imaginative life as social form over a period of time, one might amass a prodigious number from among the customs of our lives. Our social attitudes, social distinctions, and the insignia of social distinctions are instances. A ceremonious baptism, a ceremonious wedding, a ceremonious funeral are instances. It takes very little, however, to make a social form arising from the imagination stand out from the normal, and the fact that a form is abnormal is an argument for its suppression. Normal people do not accept something abnormal because it has its origin in an abnormal force like the imagination, nor at all until they have somehow normalized it as by familiarity. Costume is an instance of imaginative life as social form. At the same time it is an instance of the acceptance of something incessantly abnormal by reducing it to the normal. It cannot be said that life as we live it from day to day wears an imaginative aspect. On the other hand, it can be said that the aspect of life as we live it from day to day conceals the imagination as social form. No one doubts that the forms of daily living secrete within themselves an infinite variety of things intelligible only to anthropologists, or that lives, like our own, lived after an incalculable number of preceding lives and in the accumulation of what they have left behind, are socially complicated even when they appear to be socially innocent. To me, the accumulation of lives at a university has seemed to be a subject that might disclose something extraordinary. What is the residual effect of the years we spend at a university, the years of imaginative life, if ever in our lives there are such years, on the social form of our own future and on the social form of the future of the world of which we are part, when compared with the effects of our later economic and political years?

The discussion of the imagination as metaphysics has led us off a little to one side. This is justified, however, by the considerations, first, that the operation of the imagination in life is more significant than its operation in or in relation to works of art, or perhaps I should have said, from the beginning, in arts and letters; second, that the imagination penetrates life; and, finally, that its value as metaphysics is not the same as its value in arts and letters. In spite of the prevalence of the imagination in life, it is probably true that the discussion of it in that relation is incomparably less frequent and less intelligent than the discussion of it in relation to arts and letters. The constant discussion of imagination and reality is largely a discussion not for the purposes of life but for the purposes of arts and letters. I suppose that the reason for this is that few people would turn to the imagination, knowingly, in life, while few people would turn to anything else, knowingly, in arts and letters. In life what is important is the truth as it is, while in arts and letters what is important is the truth as we see it. There is a real difference here, even though people turn to the imagination without knowing it in life and to reality without knowing it in arts and letters. There are other possible variations of that theme, but the theme itself is there. Again in life the function of the imagination is so varied that it is not well defined as it is in arts and letters. In life one hesitates when one speaks of the value of the imagination. Its value in arts and letters is aesthetic. Most men's lives are thrust upon them. The exis-

tence of aesthetic value in lives that are forced on those that live them
is an improbable sort of thing. There can be lives, nevertheless, which
exist by the deliberate choice of those that live them. To use a single illustration: it may be assumed that the life of Professor Santayana is
a life in which the function of the imagination has had a function similar to its function in any deliberate work of art or letters. We have
only to think of this present phase of it, in which, in his old age, he
dwells in the head of the world, in the company of devoted women, in
their convent, and in the company of familiar saints, whose presence
does so much to make any convent an appropriate refuge for a generous
and human philosopher. To repeat, there can be lives in which the value
of the imagination is the same as its value in arts and letters, and I exclude from consideration as part of that statement any thought of
poverty or wealth, being a *Bauer* or being a king, and so on, as irrelevant.

The values of which it is common to think in relation to life are
ethical values or moral values. The Victorians thought of these values
in relation to arts and letters. It may be that the Russians mean to do
about as the Victorians did; that is to say, think of the values of life in
relation to arts and letters. A social value is simply an ethical value expressed by a member of the party. Between the wars, we lived, it may
be said, in an era when some attempt was made to apply the value of
arts and letters to life. These excursions of values beyond their spheres
are part of a process which it is unnecessary to delineate. They are like
the weather. We suffer from it and enjoy it and never quite know the
one feeling from the other. It may, also, be altogether wrong to speak
of the excursions of values beyond their spheres, since the question of
the existence of spheres and the question of what is appropriate to
them are not settled. Thus, something said the other day, that "an objective theory of value is needed in philosophy which does not depend
upon unanalyzable intuitions but relates goodness, truth, and beauty to
human needs in society," has a provocative sound. It is so easy for the
poet to say that a learned man must go on being a learned man but that
a poet respects no knowledge except his own and, again, that the poet
does not yield to the priest. What the poet has in mind, when he says
things of this sort, is that poetic value is an intrinsic value. It is not the
value of knowledge. It is not the value of faith. It is the value of the
imagination. The poet tries to exemplify it, in part, as I have tried to
exemplify it here, by identifying it with an imaginative activity that dif-

fuses itself throughout our lives. I say exemplify and not justify, because poetic value is an intuitional value and because intuitional values
cannot be justified. We cannot very well speak of spheres of value and
the transmission of a value, commonly considered appropriate to one
sphere, to another, and allude to the peculiarity of roles, as the poet's
role, without reminding ourselves that we are speaking of a thing in
continuous flux. There is no field in which this is more apparent than
painting. Again, there is no field in which it is more constantly and
more intelligently the subject of discussion than painting. The permissible reality in painting wavers with an insistence which is itself a value.
One might just as well say the permissible imagination. It is as if the
painter carried on with himself a continual argument as to whether
what delights us in the exercise of the mind is what we produce or the
exercise of a power of the mind.

A generation ago we should have said that the imagination is an
aspect of the conflict between man and nature. Today we are more
likely to say that it is an aspect of the conflict between man and organized society. It is part of our security. It enables us to live our own lives.
We have it because we do not have enough without it. This may not
be true as to each one of us, for certainly there are those for whom reality and the reason are enough. It is true of us as a race. A single, strong
imagination is like a single, strong reason in this, that the extreme
good of each is a spiritual good. It is not possible to say, as between
the two, which is paramount. For that matter, it is not always possible
to say that they are two. When does a building stop being a product of
the reason and become a product of the imagination? If we raise a building to an imaginative height, then the building becomes an imaginative
building since height in itself is imaginative. It is the moderator of life
as metempsychosis was of death. Nietzsche walked in the Alps in the
caresses of reality. We ourselves crawl out of our offices and classrooms
and become alert at the opera. Or we sit listening to music as in an
imagination in which we believe. If the imagination is the faculty by
which we import the unreal into what is real, its value is the value of
the way of thinking by which we project the idea of God into the idea
of man. It creates images that are independent of their originals, since
nothing is more certain than that the imagination is agreeable to the
imagination. When one's aunt in California writes that the geraniums
are up to her second story window, we soon have them running over
the roof. All this diversity, which I have intentionally piled up in con-

fusion in this paragraph, is typical of the imagination. It may suggest that the imagination is the ignorance of the mind. Yet the imagination changes as the mind changes. I know an Italian who was a shepherd in Italy as a boy. He described his day's work. He said that at evening he was so tired he would lie down under a tree like a dog. This image was, of course, an image of his own dog. It was easy for him to say how tired he was by using the image of his tired dog. But given another mind, given the mind of a man of strong powers, accustomed to thought, accustomed to the essays of the imagination, and the whole imaginative substance changes. It is as if one could say that the imagination lives as the mind lives. The primitivism disappears. The Platonic resolution of diversity appears. The world is no longer an extraneous object, full of other extraneous objects, but an image. In the last analysis, it is with this image of the world that we are vitally concerned. We should not say, however, that the chief object of the imagination is to produce such an image. Among so many objects, it would be the merest improvisation to say of one, even though it is one with which we are vitally concerned, that it is the chief. The next step would be to assert that a particular image was the chief image. Again, it would be the merest improvisation to say of any image of the world, even though it was an image with which a vast accumulation of imagination had been content, that it was the chief image. The imagination itself would not remain content with it nor allow us to do so. It is the irrepressible revolutionist.

In spite of the confusion of values and the diversity of aspects, one arrives eventually face to face with arts and letters. I could take advantage of the pictures from the Kaiser Friedrich Museum in Berlin, which have been exhibited throughout the country. The pictures by Poussin are not the most marvelous pictures in this collection. Yet, considered as objects of the imagination, how completely they validate Gide's "We must approach Poussin little by little"; and how firmly they sustain the statement made a few moments ago that the imagination is the only genius. There is also among these pictures a Giorgione, the portrait of a young man, head and shoulders, in a blue-purple blouse, or, if not blue-purple, then a blue of extraordinary enhancings. Vasari said of Giorgione that he painted nothing that he had not seen in nature. This portrait is an instance of a real object that is at the same time an imaginative object. It has about it an imaginative bigness of diction. We know that in poetry bigness and gaiety are precious characteristics of the diction. This portrait transfers that principle to painting. The subject is severe, but its embellishment, though no less severe, is big and gay; and one feels in the presence of this work that one is also in the presence of an abundant and joyous spirit, instantly perceptible in what may be called the diction of the portrait. I could also take advantage, so far as letters are concerned, of a few first books of poems or a few first novels. One turns to first works of the imagination with the same expectation with which one turns to last works of the reason. But I am afraid that although one is, at last, face to face with arts and letters and, therefore, in the presence of particulars beyond particularization, it is prudent to limit discussion to a single point.

My final point, then, is that the imagination is the power that enables us to perceive the normal in the abnormal, the opposite of chaos in chaos. It does this every day in arts and letters. This may seem to be a merely capricious statement, for ordinarily we regard the imagination as abnormal per se. That point of view was approached in the reference to the academic struggle between reason and the imagination, and again in the reference to the relation between the imagination and social form. The disposition toward a point of view derogatory to the imagination is an aversion to the abnormal. We see it in the common attitude toward modern arts and letters. The exploits of Rimbaud in poetry, if Rimbaud can any longer be called modern, and of Kafka in prose are deliberate exploits of the abnormal. It is natural for us to identify the imagination with those that extend its abnormality. It is like identifying liberty with those that abuse it. A literature overfull of abnormality and, certainly, present-day European literature, as one knows it, seems to be a literature full of abnormality, gives the reason an appearance of normality to which it is not, solely, entitled. The truth seems to be that we live in concepts of the imagination before the reason has established them. If this is true, then reason is simply the methodizer of the imagination. It may be that the imagination is a miracle of logic, and that its exquisite divinations are calculations beyond analysis, as the conclusions of the reason are calculations wholly within analysis. If so, one understands perfectly the remark that "in the service of love and imagination nothing can be too lavish, too sublime or too festive." In the statement that we live in concepts of the imagination before the reason has established them, the word "concepts" means concepts of normality. Further, the statement that the imagination is the power that enables us to perceive the normal in the abnormal is a form of repetition of this statement. One statement does not demonstrate the other. The two statements together imply that the instantaneous disclosures of living are disclosures of the normal. This will seem absurd to those that insist on the solitude and misery and terror of the world. They will ask of what value is the imagination to them; and if their experience is to be considered, how is it possible to deny that they live in an imagination of evil? Is evil normal or abnormal? And how do the exquisite divinations of the poets and for that matter even the "aureoles of the saints" help them? But when we speak of perceiving the normal we have in mind the instinctive integrations which are the reason for living. Of what value is anything to the solitary and those that live in misery and terror, except the imagination?

Jean Paulhan, a Frenchman and a writer, is a man of great sense. He is a native of Tarbes. Tarbes is a town in southwestern France in the High Pyrenees. Marshal Foch was born there. An equestrian statue of the Marshal stands there, high in the air, on a pedestal. In *Les Fleurs de Tarbes*, Jean Paulhan says.

One sees at the entrance of the public garden of Tarbes, this sign:
   It is forbidden
   To enter into the garden
   Carrying flowers.

He goes on to say, "One finds it, also, in our time at the portal of literature. Nevertheless, it would be agreeable to see the girls of Tarbes (and the young writers) carrying a rose, a red poppy, an armful of red poppies."

I repeat that Jean Paulhan is a man of great sense. But to be able to see the portal of literature—that is to say, the portal of the imagination—as a scene of normal love and normal beauty is of itself a feat of great imagination. It is the vista a man sees, seated in the public garden of his native town, near by some effigy of a figure celebrated in the normal world, as he considers that the chief problems of any artist, as of any man, are the problems of the normal, and that he needs, in order to solve them, everything that the imagination has to give.

I. 6

The Defense of the Illusion and the Creation of Myth[*]

Device and Symbol in the Plays of Shakespeare

LESLIE A. FIEDLER

Montana State University

THERE IS a sense, annoying I think to the more tender-minded reader or beholder, in which a work of art is a history of itself, a record of the scruples and hesitation of its maker in the course of its making, sometimes even a defense or definition of the kind to which it belongs or the conventions which it respects. The artist in most times is driven to conceal, with a wariness that becomes habitual and unconscious, this face of his work from all but the canniest of his audience, for he comes early to realize the resentment which a betrayal of this inward concern is like to arouse. "Treachery!" the reader cries. "Unfair!" For to him the *maintenance* of the illusion is what counts, though to the artist the primary thing is the *justification* of the illusion. And so their relationship has been conventionally based upon a complementary blindness and deceit.

Within the last few generations it has become possible to admit openly the aspect of self-concern in a work of art, even to flaunt it in the tradition of *épater le bourgeois*. One thinks of the classic device of Gide's *Counterfeiters*, of the novel within the novel. Gide tells us brazenly of a novelist writing a book in which he exists writing precisely

[*] Read at the Institute in 1948. Published in the *Institute Essays*, 1949.

the book in which we have met him writing the book in which, and so forth and so on.

It all opens up, or more accurately opens *inward*, toward the fake infinity of the girl on the cereal box holding a cereal box on which another girl (or perhaps the same one) holds a cereal box on which another girl holds a cereal box on which—and so on until the label blurs to a breakfast table indeterminate.

The contriving of fictive infinities is the immemorial business of the writer, but in Gide it has finally the air of an intellectual joke, a suitable fraud in a world in which we are all coiners, and the currency of the artist presumably as counterfeit as our other media of exchange: the book is not really by Uncle Edouard, but rather Uncle Edouard by the book, and the Gide who composes them both, it is inevitably suggested, was composed for just that purpose by a more ultimate Gide. Here is a general problem reduced to a special irony, stated in terms of a travesty on romantic notions of authorship, and in the context of an age that is ready to think of the artist primarily as an illusionist, a perpetrator of hoaxes (consider Joyce's key image of Shem the Penman, the forger as artist, or Mann's gamut of symbols for the writer from Felix Krull the confidence Man to the charlatan hypnotist of *Mario and the Magician*).

Yet the general problem persists outside of the chosen context; in any age a work of art is on one level about the problems of its own composition, the threat to the illusion it attempts to create; and just so far as it comments on those perils, it further endangers the basic illusion. The use in comedy from the Greeks to the Marx Brothers of the deliberate breaking of the illusion (the deprecatory aside: "That's what it says here!") tries to laugh the danger out of existence, to anticipate the audience's awareness of art's essential hokum, or at least to shock them out of feeling superior in that awareness by a defensive self-exposure; but such a method is a desperate and degrading expedient— "Anything for a laugh!"—and is, of course, quite inadequate for serious art.

But there has long existed in drama another expedient, capable at once of confessing and exorcising art's central illusion ("Now you see it, now you don't!") and of objectifying the artist's need to make his creation a record of its creating. That expedient is the "play within a play," which, though used sometimes for partial or even trivial ends, can be said to have as its essential meaning the solution of the dilemma we

have been considering. The "play within a play," like the Happy Ending or the Reversal, is an example of a technical or structural myth: a
plot configuration or a technical device with an archetypal meaning
quite independent of any individual's conscious exploitation of it.

It is an easy step from *The Counterfeiters to Hamlet,* for the
"novel within a novel" of *The Counterfeiters* is a translation of the
"play within a play" of *Hamlet* or, more precisely, a profanation, an
honorific parody, that is to say, a critical analysis of the myth. The
myth, by definition, cannot be conscious, and the moment we take
pains to know it, it is degraded, profaned—the Joseph story in Genesis
is mythic, in Thomas Mann an endless, middle-aged joke.

In *Hamlet,* however, we have rather than an analysis, the *realization* of the myth: its meaning is evident but unstated; all its ambiguities
are in solution; its mystery is intact but at rest. Add to *The Counterfeiters* and *Hamlet* the *Spanish Tragedy* of Kyd (or Shakespeare's own
A Midsummer Night's Dream) and we have a full triad: the myth imperfectly exploited, the myth realized, the myth analyzed.

Kyd and Shakespeare share certain assumptions about the role of
the artist and the relation of art to the given world which separate them
sharply from Gide: to them the type of the artist is the Man with the
Mirror, not the Swindler; the process is not forgery but imitation. "It's
all done with mirrors," we say and echo ironically the Shakespearean
"hold the mirror up to nature," with all the sad denigration of the mirror as metaphor that lies between. The Renaissance mind was convinced from one side of the "truth" of artistic representation in a context in which arithmetic, theology and rhetoric subscribed to a single
criterion of truth; just as from the other it was convinced of the
"falsity" of art in a context in which the meanings of "lie" and "fiction"
had not yet been discriminated. This impossible contradiction, like a
thousand others, the Renaissance mind ordinarily endured, with a lost
art of accommodation that we must by turns envy and despise.

To Shakespeare, however, the contradiction was apparently a lifelong vexation, a conflict which he strove at first to conceal by all the
grace of his art, but which ultimately he attempted to reconcile in a
solution that abandoned the stratagems of technique for those of metaphysics. The Shakespearean corpus is a self-justification (one remembers
the vaunt: *Non sanz droict!*), a justification of his art, of the art of the
playwright as practised in his time down to the last detail: the patching
of plays, the use of the boy actor—eventually of all art, of the lie as

truth. But that is a possible definition of myth, the lie as truth, and it is the extraordinary achievement of Shakespeare to have created the myth in defense of the illusion, to have revealed the universal symbolic relevance of those devices which persuade us to suspend disbelief.

Shakespeare seems to have felt the illusion of his art imperiled on four main fronts, and to have evolved, in response to those four threats, four essential myths that come to full flower in the last plays: the myth of the *Cosmic Drama*, the myth of the *Cosmic Dream*, the myth of the *Beardless Beloved*, and the myth of *Qualitative Immortality*.

I hope some day to treat all four of these topics in detail, but here I shall concentrate on the first, touching the others only incidentally. I should like, though, before returning to a consideration of Hamlet and my center, to indicate briefly the four threats to illusion from which Shakespeare's mythical trajectories begin.

First, that the actors are merely—actors; that is, they are today this, tomorrow that, and there persists, behind the this or that they put on and doff, a recognizable self, inevitably felt as more real, the *real* self. There was in the Elizabethan theater at least the beginnings of a star system—of all systems the one which most emphasizes the actor as existing outside of his role. Further, the Shakespearean stage seems to have been at an uneasy point between frankly conventionalized presentation and realistic production, making for a certain basic shakiness of conviction.

Second, as a special and extraordinarily difficult case under the first, the actors of women's parts were not even women, but boys never quite sure of avoiding the gauche gesture or the cracked voice that would betray utterly the possibility of acceptance. "Boy my greatness i' th' posture of a whore," Cleopatra says, foreseeing her possible presentment in Rome in terms of the actuality of the performance in which she, the actor-she, moves.

Third, that the dead live. The corpses which fall to the stage, stabbed or poisoned or asp-bitten, will rise to acknowledge the audience's applause. Even before they are carried off, the closest of the "understanders" in the pit will have seen the eyelid's betraying flutter, the heaving of the chest.

Fourth, that the play ends. The action is framed with an arbitrary beginning and close, moves its three or four hours to an inevitable concluding couplet. Jack has his Joan, or the villain his quietus, and the stage is empty; but the felt mode of lived experience, or "real life," is continuity.

The third and fourth problems demand apparently contradictory solutions and indeed seem to get them; but if we are left at last with a contradiction, it is not the elementary one with which we begin. In the simplest apprehension of life, there seems to be a continuity, an immortality of the general, though the individual dies. The show, that is to say, goes on—and on and on. The world survives our particular endings; but in the universe of play acting the individual survives his age, his world—which is to say the actor survives the play. Four hours and there's an end to Denmark, but Burbage is resurrected next night in Illyria or Bohemia or Rome.

The author's immediate problem is to deceive his audience, to leave us unshakeably convinced that the stage dead are really dead; and for the elementary reinforcement of the illusion Shakespeare is full of devices, from the expedient of *Romeo and Juliet*, in which Juliet first *appears* to Romeo within the play to have died (though we outside *know* she "really" lives), and then dies actually for *us*; or by the simulated death of the Player King in the inner play in *Hamlet*, a remove of "pretend" from which we return to find the death of the actor who plays Claudius "true."

But this device is perilous, for, though the double order of belief proposed by the play within the play on the first convolution inveigles us into belief, on second thought, or to the naturally more complicated mind, it suggests that just as the Player King has not really died, no more has *this* king, after all a Player too, and leaves us the more emphatically undeceived. But this disenchantment, Shakespeare has apparently decided by the end of his career, is precisely what he is after—nobody is dead at all, not in any ultimate sense, for all death is appearance only. And by the time we have got to the final plays, to Hermione or Imogen, the hoax of stage-death seen through by the wary has been translated into the symbolic statement that *all* death is a hoax, a seeming. The presumed failure of illusion becomes the revelation of a higher truth, and the last plays are, as Wilson Knight has so convincingly argued, myths of immortality.

In an analogous way, the poet begins by resenting the arbitrary ending, the betrayal of the play's fictional time by the inevitable close of the last act. In the young and "arty" *Love's Labour's Lost*, there is an outright refusal even to pretend that the play ends at all, but that particular stratagem only a bright young man in a work aimed at a special audience can afford. Things are just *beginning* when the play is through. But a mass audience demands other devices, less frank, more conventional. A closing marriage or a birth or coronation helps to create the sense of an open ending, a conclusion without finality—and in *Hamlet*, as we have seen, the inner play is used to create a double continuity of intension and extension, a fake circular infinity. But in *The Tempest*, Shakespeare makes his typical reaffirmation of the breach of illusion, abandons any attempt at concealing the play's limits. In the speech "Our revels now are ended . . ." he explicates the meaning of the interrupted masque, the performance arbitrarily brought to a close, as a symbol of the world's transience, collective impermanence.

"The great globe itself . . . shall dissolve." The world *does* decay, and only the individual, in his moment of discovery or passion or tragic insight, is forever. In this sense the apparent contradiction between our being immune to death ("Not a hair perished") and yet "such stuff as dreams are made on" is reconciled.

The problem of the ambiguity of sex and the stratagems demanded by the stubborn convention of the boy as girl in Elizabethan production deserve, and I hope some day to give them, a full-length examination. *Cymbeline* appears to me now to be the climactic play in the study of that problem and its mythic implications. It is probably sufficient to say here that Shakespeare begins in his customary fashion with the aim of defending the illusion of femininity against the inevitable shortcomings of the boy actor, but that, before he is through with those disguised boys who are really girls who in turn are actually boys, those master-mistresses, who win the hearts of men and women alike, often both at once, he has established the myth of an androgynous Beloved, the focus of whose attraction is neither femininity nor masculinity but the delightful ambiguity of youth—the Beardless as Beloved; and that myth enables him, without abandoning the Heroine altogether, to maintain his determining sexual attitude (clear in the Sonnets and elsewhere) which regards the blatant, the mature female (especially the mother) as a symbol of evil, blackness, lust, and so on. Connected with this syndrome, too, is the concept of the perfect Hero as the man without a female component, the child born not of a living mother but of death, that strange deliverer who breaks through the tragic circumstances of *Cymbeline* and *Macbeth* (paired plays that mark Shakespeare's escape from an obsession with unmitigated tragedy), the "man not born of woman."

All these instances except the last achieve a kind of focus in the "play within the play," and it is to that that I wish now to return.[1]

In the "Pyramus and Thisbe" of A *Midsummer Night's Dream*, we have the "play within the play" used as a stunt to maintain a precarious illusion, to reinforce the reality of the larger production. Shakespeare plays upon the inevitable audience conviction that characters shown planning a play cannot themselves be characters in a larger play; the run-of-the-mill "understander" cannot get back past the second convolution; and the few who can, who are able to *see the lie*, fulfill the poet's other wish: to have someone know the deft machinery of the illusion he manipulates, appraise his skill.

But the *Dream* with its loose structure makes no real attempt to integrate the inner play into the outer plot; rather it deliberately holds it off as mockery, as foil: bumbling tragedy versus graceful comedy—a courtly joke, all kept down among the peripheral vulgar characters, who seem to exist so often in Shakespeare, like Negroes in Hollywood films, largely to amuse the gentry.

Thomas Kyd in his *Spanish Tragedy* transfers the inner play from subplot to plot, from comedy to tragedy (or at least melodrama), from dream to nightmare. Kyd's is a considerable achievement, and is the cue, either directly or via his lost *Ur-Hamlet*, to much in Shakespeare's *Hamlet*; but he still muffs something essential to the integral, the mythic, meaning of the inner play. The relationship of Kyd's double play is concentric; the play within and the play without dissolve into each other. Hieronimo and Bel-Imperia, disguised as the Bashaw and Perseda, kill Lorenzo and Balthazar, in the roles of Erastus and Solyman. The pivot of revenge upon which the whole structure turns, the climactic action of the whole fable, falls within the inner play, so that the outer play has no true ending but trails off into supererogatory and unconvincing horrors (Hieronimo biting off his own tongue, as if to confess what the author will not admit), merely to have something more to

---

[1] Behind the "play within the play" lies the "stage within the stage." The relation of inner stage and outer is an implicit metaphor fixed in the physical structure of the Elizabethan theater. The meanings whose more explicit formulation this paper is examining are implicitly present in Shakespeare's world, even before the mounting of any individual play; they belong to the community and to the unconscious. Granted the inner stage and the accessibility of the acting platform to parts of the audience, the development of the myth of a Cosmic Drama is inevitable.

add, though there is nothing more to say. The characters are all involved, and no one remains outside to define the innerness of the play within—only the audience and its proxies, the King and the Viceroy, who are, more accurately perhaps, rather its Dr. Watsons than its proxies, for they do not know, as the audience does, that the deaths they behold are "real," but take the murders as entertainment, illusory horror performed with exceeding conviction. That irony (the audience all the time *knowing!*) is for Kyd the sufficient meaning of the inner play, and beyond that, to be sure, the irony of the irony, the esoteric irony: the characters whose deaths had first seemed "fabulously counterfeit" and who were then revealed really to have died we know, outside the illusion, are not dead at all, but prepare to take our applause, bowing, as we move toward the exits.

This is a more complex device than that of the *Dream*, ending on a third convolution, but like the simpler comedy it offers the cream of its jest only at the expense of its overall credibility. It remains a technical expedient, a dodge to protect and complicate the illusion.

In Shakespeare's *Hamlet*, however, where the ironic climax has been detached from the inner play and isolated in the duel scene, in which the Prince and Laertes "play" at swords whose real threat is known to neither Hamlet nor the Queen mother, the "play within the play" is freed for its more essential, its pure mythic, function.

With an insistence that risks the obvious, Shakespeare hammers home the artificiality, the counterfeit of the inner play: we see the entry of the professional actors (that they are *professionals* to begin with is the first turn of the screw), and we are given, at some pains, a sense of their existence as persons outside their performance (the boy has grown; there is danger of his voice cracking); we are shown them being lectured on the art of gesture and delivery so that their technique cannot fail to show through their acting; we are permitted to hear an impromptu recitation set in a context of remembering lines; and lest, listening to that recitation, we have been betrayed into a suspension of disbelief, there is Hamlet's subsequent soliloquy to remind us that the player's passion and its occasion exist only in fancy: "What's Hecuba to him or he to Hecuba?"

The fictive nature of the inner play, its play-ness, is insisted upon almost desperately, suggesting at first that Shakespeare must have doubted the credibility of his main plot, strained between its sources and its meanings; or that some imperative need for an ultimate verisimilitude moved him. What is at stake? Surely, the playwright must have sensed that such an extraordinary emphasis on the contrived nature of the play within threatened to defeat itself, increased proportionally the peril to the illusion and made more drastic the eventual shattering of belief, when the audience passed inevitably from the convolution of increased credence to that of disenchantment. But that may, after all, have been precisely Shakespeare's point.

For by a simple expedient the poet *forces* us toward the disruptive realization: just such a contrived fabric as this, is the whole tragedy in which it is set! The inner play and the outer play *are the same play.* To be sure we get that point (*Hamlet* is preeminently a work in which no chances are taken), the inner play is acted twice, first in the dumb show, in a striking departure from Elizabethan custom that either treated such pantomimes in terms of allegory or used them with a narrator to speed up the action; yet here the dumb show reenacts literally the crime later to be played with speech: "Into the porches of mine ear. . . ."

It has been a disturbing scene for actors and commentators ever since. Why, the question is asked over and over, does the King, later so rattled by precisely the same thing, not rise in fright at the pantomimic crime? To make his behavior credible, he is traditionally shown occupied in conversation with the Queen throughout the dumb show. This is what is conventionally called "the problem of the dumb show," but the ulterior, the real problem has, as far as I know, never been raised: why does Shakespeare, in the first place, fall into this difficulty which can at best be solved only by a somewhat awkward piece of stage business? Surely, because he is convinced that at any risk he must clinch in the minds of the least subtle the *identity* of the two plays. In the pantomime there is no disturbing limitation of names (indeed, even in the inner play proper the characters do not name each other; only Hamlet, a chorus and proxy for the playwright, with a foot in each world, gives mockingly their Italianate names, their locale and pretended date): these are, quite simply, the King, the Queen, the Betrayer, the very ones who, as in a nightmare at once within and without, look on or haunt the scene.

It is necessary for the prosecution of the plot that the plays be similar, of course, and on the plot level Shakespeare has explained away an improbable degree of coincidence between the inner play and the actual events at Elsinore with Hamlet's added "dozen or sixteen lines";

but consider, in terms of the mythic convention we have been tracing, the import of this coincidence. Hamlet has, with those dozen or sixteen lines, imposed a meaning upon an old playlet (and we know that this is precisely the sort of tinkering that Shakespeare himself had done with the Ur-Hamlet) in which we have just reached the point at which, had Claudius not interrupted with his terror, his ironic cry of "Give me some light!" a Hamlet-character, some melancholy sniffer out of evil, would inevitably have had to come upon the scene to contrive another play to catch the conscience of Gonzago, and in that play another Hamlet, and so on.

In that sense the play narrows inward like *The Counterfeiters* toward a vortex of infinity; but it opens outward, too, unlike the modern work, in a widening circle toward an infinity of extension. Is not the very piece we are seeing, the inner play suggests, precisely that play Hamlet has arranged before us—and are we not then a stage audience, beheld as well as beholding, at a play within some greater play, actors all in a universal drama which inevitably defines all our plays as "plays within a play"? If Hamlet is Shakespeare—and who can really deny that romantic insight?—Shakespeare in turn is Hamlet to some more ultimate Shakespeare, in whose reworking of a recalcitrant matter, we as onlookers are, according to our guilt, Ophelia or Gertrude, Polonius or the usurping King, walking shadows, poor players.

"All the world's a stage." Reality dissolves around us to that fearful metaphor, ordinarily meaningless for us who have memorized it as children. It is Shakespeare's most obsessive figure, "the conceit of this inconstant stay," spoken not only through the ambiguous mouths of characters in his plays, but confessed in the personal voice of the Sonnets: "this huge stage presenteth nought but shows / Whereon the stars in secret influence comment." In *Hamlet* the figure is never reduced to a tag, but at the focus of the inner play the whole tragedy is epiphanized as that metaphor in infinite extension. That the playwright understand the world's illusion in terms of his own craft is understandable enough, for such a conceit at once familiarizes the cosmic mutability he feels and dignifies his own despised profession; the final Maker, too, it suggests, is concerned with just such shows as devour the poet's talent and lay up a modest fortune for his old age. The playwright's very life is mythic, the limitations of his art a clue to the meanings of life.

On one level certainly *Hamlet* is (or *can* be, once we have thought of it) an account of the writer's essential experience: the tragic vision, the relapse into doubt (what ghost is true?), the shaken faith in the adequacy of his medium ("Must like a whore unpack my heart with words"), and the final restitution of belief in art as a symbolic act.

"The play's the thing," Hamlet cries in the anguished moment of recovering his faith in the efficacy of talk. For in the end, notice, he does not, for all his envy of the inarticulate soldier, cease verbally to unpack his heart, but learns to organize his words into the cunning form that gives them consequence in action. His only deliberately chosen act, his only real *success* in the course of the tragedy, is dramatic: the play within the play of passion and free will and fate—emended by some dozen or sixteen lines.

"Wherein I'll catch the conscience of the King." The phrase oddly suggests the Joycean conception of art's function: to recreate the conscience of the race; but in Shakespeare the accent is upon the sly disclosure, the revelatory trick. Art is a trap, the mousetrap, a miching mallecho that promises to amuse us with a lie—and shows in its unforeseen truth ourselves caught in the compulsive pattern of the fall. There is an apt mockery in the taunt: "Let the galled jade wince." Who is ungalled? Our consciences caught, we rise, our guilt confessed, to call out, "Give me some light!" and retire to plot our various and singular dooms.

This is a subtle and apt parable of art's genesis and role, its hesitations and its incredible victory snatched from defeat; but it is more. It is a *particular* instance, scrupulously defined; it is a singular account of itself. Perfectly circular (the two plays, we remember, are one), it comments on its own history, on the career and genesis of the very *Hamlet* at which we assist in all its particularity—the old play, the Oedipus horror, the playing style of the actors, the mystery of repetition—and thus redeems at the last minute its peculiar failure to its peculiar success.

Commentators have long though dimly felt the ambiguity of success and failure in *Hamlet* and in its protagonist, and the special difficulty of disentangling the Prince's failure from the play's. No one who has read T. S. Eliot's acute, wrongheaded discussion can doubt that in some sense the play does not quite work out, that there is an unexorcisable incoherence at its heart—and yet, when the last lines are spoken, we are somehow *satisfied,* and convinced that our satisfaction is more ultimate than the sense of incoherence. And this is precisely how we feel about Hamlet the character: he has envied the soldier's readiness, the philosopher's dispassion, but his own actions have invariably been at the mercy of both passion and circumstance—and so, at last, ineffectual. He thrusts at a King, and an old fool dies. The denouement he does not achieve, but suffers; and he dies at the almost accidental consummation of his revenge, not really convincing us that he must.

Yet we do not feel as ironic the elegiac praise of Horatio and Fortinbras, who read the wreck of feeling and the wreck of enterprise as success. Hamlet does, in some sense, succeed, as only failure can succeed where success is bound either, like Claudius, to embrace evil or, like Fortinbras and Horatio, utterly to ignore it in simplicities of commitment or self-control. To this dubious victory the Play's incomplete assimilation of its sources is a perfect objective correlative; the given plot defies the control of the poet's meaning and yet obliquely fulfills it, as the rottenness at Elsinore defies and yet fulfills in its own ways the Prince's plan to see it right.

The refusal of life ever wholly to conform to the poet's plan is one of the inevitable meanings of art, and the intrinsic sadness of the artist before that failure is the sadness of *Hamlet*. That Shakespeare inherited a genre and a tradition which defined the artist as Patcher, Emender of the recalcitrant given, and that the disparities of *Hamlet* fix formally the hopelessness and glory of his task, conspire to make *Hamlet* a play upon itself and on all plays. Hamlet is sad because he cannot write the perfect *Hamlet*; but the record of his sadness becomes his triumph, our second-best and only play. The ultimate, the real *Ur-Hamlet*, is irrecoverable, unwritten, yet for a moment glimpsed and lost again at the dizzying focus of the play within the play within the play.

Further than *Hamlet*, Shakespeare could not go in terms of tragedy; its end term, revealed through the metaphor of the play within the play, is the myth of the Cosmic Drama. "All the world's a stage, . . . the men and women merely players"; "struts and frets his hour upon the stage and then is heard no more." There is a double implication in this view: a strong determinism (the plot is given, and at best we can only amend it) and a conviction that the stage survives the player, that the universe persists and the individual perishes. In the life of the individual only his death, that is, his departing the stage, his becoming nothing, is "true." The myth of tragedy is a pagan myth, or in the current atheistic sense an "existential" one.

But the end term of Comedy, the concealed meaning of the Happy Ending, is the myth of the Cosmic Dream and of qualitative immortality, death as a dream and transformation. "These our actors . . . were all spirits." "Like this insubstantial pageant faded, leave not a rack behind." There is a contrasting twofold implication in this view: a strong emphasis upon free will and a conviction that the player survives the stage. There is no death, only the individual, the master of dreams, the magician dreaming for as long as forever is. The myth of Comedy is a Christian myth.

Hamlet is an actor who desires to become a playwright trapped inside a tragedy, at last, a patcher of an old play, an emender of a pattern given like a fate. Prospero, the artist as magician, is not within a play at all, but the play, become his dream, is within him. Not necessity but wish controls the action, and the protagonist does not die to his situation, but wakes from it.

Prospero does not have, like Hamlet, to die with the plot he sets in motion; he must, though, be abandoned with its consummation. His is the failure of success that matches the success of Hamlet's failure. Only the disinherited, or as we say now the "alienated," controls the means of art; the magic of dreams is given in exile and loneliness, a weapon for casting out the usurper, for creating the brave new world in which love is a thing of innocence and law, and death is dead—in short, for redeeming the Fall. But the perfection of the dream is the dream's ending, and the Dreamer must let fall his cloak and wand, bid the powers of air depart, stand outside illusion forever, and, naked as all men are essentially naked, learn to ask men's prayers as he has once compelled their applause.

> . . . Now I want
> Spirits to enforce, art to enchant;
> And my ending is despair,
> Unless I be relieved by prayer . . .

I. 7
Mimesis and Katharsis:
an Archetypal Consideration*

PHILIP WHEELWRIGHT

Dartmouth College

So VAST is the critical literature on Aristotle's *Poetics* that it might well be wondered, without undue cynicism, whether anything at once new and useful remains to be said. But each generation must revaluate its classics—must find out what the old wine tastes like in new bottles. Three new emphases, in particular, have become prominent in literary discussions during the past generation—two of them having their sources outside, the third within, the practice of literature and literary criticism themselves. The sciences of anthropology and what may broadly be called depth psychology have offered to the creative writer and the critic not merely a vast new fund of materials to be understood and assimilated but also to the creative writer new dimensions of consciousness to be explored and to the critic new obligations of attentiveness, as well as new possibilities of discrimination, analogy, and allusion.

The third new emphasis, which has emerged from within the practice and centripetal study of literature itself, can be stenographically spoken of as "the New Criticism." The trouble with this epithet is that to the "middle-brow mind" it connotes snobbery or worse, and denotes pretty much anything from a sleuthing after paradox to the obiter dicta of T. S. Eliot. Nevertheless, underneath the provocative label, which I for one would gladly see discarded, there lies something of

* Read at the Institute in 1951. Published in the *Institute Essays*, 1952.

first importance for intelligent and pertinent criticism—a renewed and more explicit interest in the role of thematic imagery.

A thematic image is one that somehow illumines the larger meaning of the poem, drama, or novel of which it is a part. In this sense it may be called also an illuminative image, or a depth image, or (if the adjective is taken gently) a functional image. Whatever its name, the notion is central to the kind of pursuit on which the so-called new critics are engaged: it invites us on the one hand to be alert to the presence of imagistic overtones and associations counterpointing the main lines of narrative, dramatic, or lyrical development, while at the same time it reminds us that the more important images, and ultimately the more rewarding ones, are those which bear, however obliquely, upon the total intent. The New Criticism, in short, is focally concerned with poetic meanings—with meanings in the most fully expressive and associative sense of the word—and the discipline to which it pledges itself is fundamentally a semantic discipline; for "semantics" properly means the science of meanings—any meanings at all—and need not be restricted to technologically oriented meanings as logical positivists insist.

These three elements of contemporary criticism—the anthropological, the psychological, and the semantic—are handled by Aristotle too superficially for modern critical needs. In the *Poetics* his sole reference to anthropology is found in the statement that "tragedy arose, as did comedy, from improvisation—as practiced respectively by choral leaders of the dithyramb and of phallic songs such as are still in vogue in many of our cities." He tells us nothing of the steps by which tragedy evolved out of the dithyramb, except for the bare statement that "Aeschylus first increased the number of actors from one to two, curtailed the chanting of the chorus, and gave dialogue the leading role." This scarcely slakes our curiosity; we could have deduced these operations from his original statement that tragedy arose out of the dithyramb; the second sentence throws no new light upon the heritage of tragedy except to identify Aeschylus as its inventor.

Psychology of a sort receives more attention: we may distinguish references to the psychology of the poet, of the spectators, and of the dramatic characters. The psychology of the poet is involved obliquely in Aristotle's statement of the two instincts in man's nature from which poetry takes its rise; the psychology of the spectators is involved in the mention of Katharsis: both of which topics I shall deal with presently.

Much of what Aristotle wrote under the remaining head, the psychology of the *dramatis personae*, has retained little more than antiquarian interest, as evidence of ancient Greek standards of decorum; although certain of the generalizations do express insights of perduring value—for instance, that "the poet, when representing a man who is irascible or lazy or otherwise morally defective, should set him forth with those very traits while at the same time ennobling him." This is admirable so far as it goes, but in the presence of an Orestes, an Oedipus, or a Hippolytus we feel that a subtler and profounder technique of interpretation is demanded. For such heroes, as indeed Aristotle sometimes seems on the verge of saying, have an archetypal, as well as an individual, aspect, and one of our tasks as critics is to see the archetypal and the particular in their proper balance and to understand, without excessive reliance upon any single school of psychology, what the archetypal mode of being involves.

The third concern of modern criticism—the semantic, or what I may call (to avoid misinterpretation) the poeto-semantic—is hardly to be found in Aristotle's analysis. He identifies *metaphora* (usually translated "metaphor") with *epiphora* (superimposition, in the sense that one thing stands surrogate for another, and hence implies on the subjective side "imaginative transference")—which is more appropriate to simile than to metaphor, if we distinguish the two tropes semantically, not merely by conventions of syntax. Moreover, both the definition and the three-fold classification of *metaphora*—transference from genus to species, from species to genus, and from species to analogous species—are more applicable to oratory than to poetry. Aristotle shows no understanding of the illuminative, thematic employment of metaphor and of sustained metaphoric pattern. Aeschylus, the supreme master of illuminative metaphor among the ancients, is mentioned only twice in the *Poetics*, and never in this connection.

I hope, then, that I have given you sufficient preliminary reason why a re-examination and revaluation of Aristotle's *Poetics* in the context of present-day criticism is very much needed. Broadly speaking, our attitude toward that noble, but no longer entirely serviceable, treatise should be mixed. To a degree we can accept its basic terms and extend their range of signification—recalling Butcher's apt remark that Aristotle's sayings are likely to have "a capacity for adaptation beyond what was immediately present to the mind of the writer." This somewhat positive method I shall follow now in reconsidering the terms

Mimesis and Katharsis. The other, the negative method, consists in frankly acknowledging Aristotle's inability to deal with some aspect of the problem and in pointing out what kind of critical approach has to be substituted. That is the method which I am obliged to use when considering Aristotle's treatment of poetic diction, and the elaboration of it must await a sequel to the present paper.

MIMESIS

Let us look first at the concept of mimesis and see not merely what it appears to mean explicitly in the *Poetics* but also what extensions of its meaning, latent in some of Aristotle's utterances, must be explored if the notion is to be suitably applicable to the greatest examples of tragic drama.

The simplest and for mature understanding the least adequate indication of what mimesis can mean turns up in chapter iv of the *Poetics*. There are two natural instincts in man, Aristotle declares, from which poetry has arisen. On the one hand, there is the human instinct to imitate, to mime, to represent (*mimeisthai*)—a primary factor in man's ability to learn. On the other hand, man has an instinct for form, he wants to stylize his miming into patterns. It must be admitted that this second component of man's expressive life is passed over hastily and somewhat obscurely; a defect which may have been due to faulty transcription of Aristotle's lecture or may indicate that a fuller account of the matter was to be found elsewhere in the corpus of lecture notes which belonged to the Peripatetic School. At all events, an effective combination of these two instincts, the mimetic and the stylistic, constitutes the poetic process. The former, the mimetic, Aristotle then illustrates by reference to the art of painting.

The reason why men enjoy seeing a picture is that in contemplating it they are incidentally learning and drawing logical inferences in their recognition of particulars, as when they exclaim, "Ah, that is so-and-so!" For if they happen not to have seen the original, any pleasure that they get will be due, not to the picture in its imitative capacity, but to the execution or coloring or some other such cause.

The passage lets us down rather badly, with its undue emphasis on recognition of particulars, as though mimesis were little more than the reportorial process which we nowadays call photographic realism. And please note a significant corollary. When mimesis is interpreted in so

particularistic a way, the duality of the poet's instinctual endowment
becomes sharpened into a dichotomy. That is to say, one's judgment
of artistic adequacy becomes broken into two distinct questions. On
the one hand, you can ask, "Would I recognize the object portrayed in
that picture as our old barn?" and on the other, "Do I find the lines
masses, and colors of the painting harmonious and satisfying?" Virtually the same disjunction appears again in Book II of the *Natural Science* (*Physica*), where the familiar statement in chapter ii that "Art
imitates Nature" is elaborated in chapter viii into the statement that
"Art *either* imitates nature *or else* gives the finishing touches to what
nature has perforce left incomplete"; the statement of alternatives
seems to distinguish two and only two aspects of the artistic function:
copyist fidelity, on the one hand, and aesthetic form, on the other.
So naïve a conception has comparatively small relevance to the larger
questions of dramatic art with which Aristotle is intentionally concerned. Generally he means by "mimesis" something substantially more
than quasi-photographic fidelity, but the passage I have quoted is a
reminder of the ambiguities that lurk in the word.

Now, there is good reason for admitting even such simple mimesis
as an element, though a minor element, in the conception and practice of art—of some art. Children like to mime, as we all know; and
no doubt there is a partial truth in the behaviorist thesis that the miming arises out of frustration, so that the child can play at having or
being something which he has not or is not in actuality. But the question of genesis is not very relevant to the question of how mimesis
operates in a maturing individual after it has started. To the reflective
consciousness an imitation comes to be preferred to its original, not
because it can be used, but precisely for the opposite reason: as John
Crowe Ransom has said, "not being actual it cannot be used, it can
only be known." [1]

The prizing of something precisely because it cannot be turned
to utilitarian account is surely anything but ignoble. That it is an
element in the aesthetic experience I gladly admit; its presence may be
a test of the degree to which a supposed aesthetic experience is really
aesthetic and not just a mask for something else. But there are two objections to overstressing it. In the first place, it is vulnerable to the
Platonic attack upon imitative art; for Plato, acknowledging man's

[1] "The Mimetic Principle," in *The World's Body*, New York, 1938, pp. 196–
197.

instinctive tendency to imitate, asks, "But what is to be the object, the prototype of imitation?" The imitation itself is but a shadow—the shadow of a shadow, according to the analysis given in Book X of *The Republic*—and therefore a doubly distorted version of the real. By what justification, Plato demands, can anyone prefer the distorted versions given by art to the true version, or at least the progressive approxima-tions to the true version which are attained by a properly disciplined philosophy? In the second place, the concept of imitation, taken by itself, represents only the contemplative Apollonian aspect of art—a blessed state of repose which can be enjoyed, I suspect, only by those who have subjugated their natural emotions and instincts with a per-fection that most of us cannot hope and perhaps do not wholeheartedly want to emulate. To men so far embedded in the natural world as to be witnessing a tragic drama—for this, after all, is the focal application of our present discussion—the contemplative moment has both a mean-ing and a beauty somehow emergent from, somehow opposed to, yet harmonized with, the excitement of the blood, the Dionysian dance.

Both these objections are directed against a too-simple acceptance of what I may call the "iconic" conception of mimesis—the conception which is presumably implied when the Greek word is translated as "imitation." Now I believe that the problem may be illuminated if we examine mimesis explicitly in its semantic role—that is, as a conveyor of meaning. For please note this principle, which to my mind appears virtually self-evident: that mimesis is essentially something meaningful; that it is not merely an actual process but also an intentive relation, a pointing of the semantic arrow; that where we accept B as an imita-tion or mimetic representation of A, we therein accept B as semanti-cally referring to A as its referent; that B draws its meaning from A; and that as far as we consider the meaning of B in its mimetic role we must thereby refer, however imperfectly, to the meaning of A. The cave man who imitates a bison—whether by miming the bison in a dance or by drawing it on the cave wall—thereby produces something which is a symbol of the animal prototype and of whatever it in turn may connote.

But there are different kinds of symbol—or (what it often amounts to) different aspects of a given symbol—and to distinguish them properly is the business of semantics. The semantic distinction to which I here invite your attention is the distinction between iconic symbols and what I can best designate as "threshold symbols." To imi-

tate a bison's appearance with a drawing or to imitate its movements
with a dance is to produce a symbol that is iconic. When Aristotle un-
guardedly illustrates mimesis by the sort of picture which pleases us
because we can say "Ah, that is so-and-so!" he is reducing the picture's symbolic role to the simply iconic. By a threshold symbol, on the
other hand, I mean one that participates in the object which it signifies. When primitive man imitates an animal in mimetic dance there is
plenty of evidence to suggest that he regards himself or feels himself
as actually partaking of the animal essence, actually becoming part of
that animal species for the duration of the dance. Even graphic imitation may sometimes exemplify the participative principle as supplementing the iconic: a holy icon may be felt by the worshiper to partake
of some of the qualities of its unseen object, and also to involve the
worshiper as participant in, or at least sensibly related to, those qualities. No doubt the sense of participation is likely to be more forcible in
mimetic dancing than in figure drawing; Dionysus presides over the
dance, Apollo over the visible pattern; but in every authentic work of
art there is some merging of the two attitudes, to greater or lesser degree. And that Aristotle's way of conceiving mimesis in tragic drama
carries participative, as well as iconic, connotations is evident from his
statement in the *Metaphysics* that "imperishable types are imitated
(*mimēsthai*) by things in a natural condition of change," as well as
from his familiar doctrine that poetry, unlike history, deals with universals. To imitate a universal is not so much an iconic as a participative
operation.

In short, our semantic analysis has brought us into much the same
position as that which Nietzsche, in *The Birth of Tragedy*, reached by
direct intuition: the recognition that Dionysiac frenzy and Apollonian
calm—passionate self-giving and bright security of outline—are the two
inseparable sides of all authentic art. Neither drunkenness nor dreams,
neither katharsis nor mimesis, will suffice by itself. To speak with
stricter logic, let me summarize my argument at this transitional point
in the following three propositions.

1. Mimesis functions symbolically: we envisage the mimetic representation as somehow referring to, intending, signifying a nonimmediate
original.

2. Mimetic symbolism tends to be at once iconic and participative
—though in different ratios, according to the kind of art in question.

3. Where a mimetic icon is participative, it invites and perhaps

challenges the observer to participate also. Which is to say that mimesis in its full sense involves katharsis.

This conclusion leads into the converse side of my argument, where I shall briefly examine the meaning of katharsis in order to see in what sense it, in turn, involves mimesis.

KATHARSIS

What, then, is katharsis? In the unacknowledged background of Aristotle's somewhat technical usage there are two main sets of connotations—the one medical; the other religious. I shall try to show briefly how each of these contributory notions, if interpreted in an adequate and mature way, involves, by a natural dialectic, something of the presence of mimesis as its counterpart.

Let us consider the medical aspect first. Mr. Ransom [2] interprets katharsis as a rude metaphor alluding to colonic evacuation, and he derides Aristotle for regarding the work of art as scarcely more than a cathartic pill. So openly cloacal an emphasis distorts the Greek medical idea quite out of focus. In the Hippocratic writings—which, though not altogether typical, furnish the only extant systematic account of pre-Aristotelian medicine—the word "katharsis" occurs in a general therapeutic sense: as where one of the Aphorisms speaks of "the purging (*katharsis*) of pus." To be sure, a line or two later diarrhea is also described as a purging; but the context makes plain that it is there taken as a species of therapeutic purging, not as equivalent to purging in general. From such scattered evidences as appear in the Hippocratic corpus we may reconstruct the ancient Greek medical conception of katharsis somewhat as follows. Health consists in a right proportion of elements in an organism; disease in a disproportion. So far there appears to have been agreement among all Greek medical schools; the main theoretical difference of opinion having to do with the kind of elements out of which the bodily proportions and disproportions are built—whether to be identified with the four elements, fire, air, water, and earth (as was probably the most widespread opinion, given quasi-scientific status by Empedocles), or with different pairs of qualitative opposites (as the Pythagorean school maintained), or with the four main bodily juices, afterward called "humours" (the first real attempt at empirical chemistry and espoused, perhaps as a working hypothesis, by Hippocrates

[2] *The World's Body*, pp. 175–176, 194.

himself). However they may have conceived the constituents of bodily organization, Hippocrates and his rival *sophoi* seem all to have agreed on two medico-philosophical axioms: (1) that a right ordering of the elements, a right proportion, balance, or measure, is what gives health, while a loss of such ordering gives illness; (2) that health is the natural state; disease the unnatural.

Is the second proposition tautologous? If we can see in what sense it is not a tautology to the Greek mind, we thereby take a step toward understanding the medical conception of katharsis. To say that health is the natural state and disease the unnatural had come, by the time of Hippocrates, and no doubt largely as a result of his genius and energy, to mean this: that an organism tends by its own powers to maintain the equilibrium that is health and to reattain that equilibrium when it has become disrupted by outside causes. The autonomous working is made possible by the bodily heat, which Hippocrates described as *emphytos*—which is to say, it lives and grows naturally within the body itself. To say that health is natural, then, is to say that an organic body can best attain health by itself rather than by outside manipulation provided, of course, that the material conditions are not overpoweringly malign. Accordingly, Hippocrates instructs his itinerant physicians not to try to dislodge a patient's ailment by direct operation, as though they were dislodging a stone, but to strengthen the patient by proper diet and regimen so that he can pass through the ordeal with the odds as much as possible in his favor. Every disease must follow its natural course; a physician cannot ordinarily cut it short, but with skill he can, perhaps, hurry it toward its crisis and prevent complications from setting in. To understand more exactly what both Hippocrates and Aristotle understood by the "crisis" of a disease we must consider two other related terms: "coction" (*pepsis*) and "blend" (*krasis*). Coction is the cooking process, produced by the body's natural heat, which fuses the bodily elements together in such a way that waste products are formed, ready for discharge at the proper time; "blend" is a technical term for the new healthy combination of elements that is formed after the waste products have been separated off. In is in this specific context that "katharsis" should be understood—as an evacuation of waste elements, which is at the same time a purification. The meaning of "katharsis" is continuous with the meaning of "krasis" which is its effect —the new bodily blend that is health. So much for physical katharsis.

The psychic katharsis involved in tragedy involves an analogous pattern and something more. The analogy might be stated thus. Man falls readily into a psychically unbalanced condition; for temperance, as Aristotle remarks more than once in his ethical writings, is hard to attain. The events of a tragic occurrence, striking a man into pity and fear, may, in a well-tempered character, become assimilated and digested ("cooked," according to the Hippocratic metaphor) so that a right blend of emotions—the psychic krasis—is restored and the emotional residue rejected, or "katharated." Milton's language in describing the attainment of the new krasis is well known: in the Preface to *Samson Agonistes* he ascribes to tragedy, citing Aristotle, a "power by raising pity and fear, or terror, to purge the mind of those and such like passions, that is to temper and reduce them to just measure with a kind of delight stirr'd up by reading or seeing those passions well imitated." And he, too, draws an analogy from medicine, or "physic," wherein "things of melancholic hue and quality are used against melancholy, sour against sour, salt to remove salt humours." From this standpoint the katharsis is seen as operating by the homeopathic principle —as when we accept into the blood stream a carefully measured inoculation of the very poison that we wish to dispel or guard against.

But now let us look beyond the analogy. Artistic tragedy is more readily assimilable than an actual tragic occurrence: partly because we accept it as real only within a framework and therefore are not called upon to act, but also because, being a patterned experience, it furnishes a contribution of its own to the psyche's attempt at re-equilibration, which now takes place upon a new level, as a result of experiencing the tragedy. Lessing therefore interpreted the re-equilibration, or krasis, as having ethical import in the specific Aristotelian sense that it must be governed by the principle of moderation, the law of the ethical mean.

As this Katharsis (*Reinigung*) consists in nothing else but the transformation of the passions into virtuous tendencies, and as, according to our philosopher, there is for every virtue a pair of contrary extremes between which the virtue is to be found: so tragedy, if it is to transform our pity into virtue, must be capable of purifying us from both extremes of pity [too much and too little]; and the same may be said of fear.[3]

Although Lessing has elaborated Aristotle's meaning more than the text of the *Poetics* strictly warrants, there remains a sound truth in his interpretation. For Aristotle's ethical demand is not primarily for single good acts, but for men of good character, from whom good acts flow

[3] *Hamburg Dramaturgy*, No. LXXVIII, 29 January, 1768.

forth by sustained habituation. From that standpoint the *Poetics* may be conceived as supplementing the *Ethics* and *Politics*, implementing the ideal of the virtuous man by showing how the institution of tragic drama can further that moderation of impulses which is the *sine qua non* of an ethically good character. Hence, when H. B. Garland, in his recent book on Lessing, repudiates Lessing's interpretation of Aristotle as implying "that virtue may be attained by way of the emotions whereas Aristotle held that it could only be achieved by the will," [4] he is setting up a sharper disjunction than either Aristotle or Lessing would have found acceptable. Certainly Aristotle does say that "deliberate choice" (*proairesis*) is the essential cause of moral action, its focal *aitia*, which is to say "that on which the responsibility for being moral essentially rests." But Aristotle knows the complex world too well ever to expect that a single explanation can suffice. The order or disorder of our emotional makeup can help or hinder man's quest for the good life, and the psychic krasis which may emerge from tragic experience as its best is an important element in the ethical life of both the individual and the city-state.

Now there appears an important corollary of psychic equilibration. Since the new krasis thus attained is psychic, not merely physical, it involves a new emotional perspective, and even, arising out of that, a new intellectual vision. The "cooking" (*pepsis*) of the simple emotions of pity and fear in the cauldron of authentically tragic experience produces the metaphysical emotion of awe, which is the human precondition of any genuine philosophy. A wisdom is thus distilled from tragic suffering—man is *pathei mathos*, "taught by suffering," as the chorus in the *Agamemnon* sings. The tragic katharsis and the ensuing krasis have brought the spectator to a new living awareness—an *Erlebnis*—of what the plot of the drama most essentially represents, what its action (its meaning in motion) essentially is. Through katharsis he grasps the essential mimesis.

The religious meaning of katharsis is admittedly less prominent in Aristotle than the medical, and is is not surprising that many critics have overlooked it or even denied its presence. Aristotle's philosophical bias is prevailingly naturalistic, and his doctrine of God as the Unmoved Mover is arrived at by rational deduction from the principles of cosmology and ontology laid down in his *Natural Science* and *Meta-*

[4] *Lessing, the Founder of Modern German Literature,* Cambridge (Eng.), 1937, p. 72.

physics, respectively. His occasional references to the popular mystery cults are perfunctory and unsympathetic. Nevertheless, words are likely to derive a connotative flavor from previous usage, and it is worth noting that "katharsis" and its related forms are employed by Greek writers more frequently in a religious than in a medical sense, as a glance at the entries in Lidell and Scott's unabridged Lexicon will show. Plato uses the word in its religious sense, sometimes seriously, one or twice playfully. Even his playful usage throws a bit of light. In the course of those fanciful and tiresome etymologies in the *Cratylus* he remarks that the name "Apollo" is admirably appropriate to the power of the god, deriving it from *apolouōn* (he who washes away). The derivation has no scientific standing, of course, but the important thing is that Plato argues his point via the word "Katharsis": Apollo is the washer away (*apolouōn*) because he is the god who purifies (*katharōn*) and whom we worship with a purification ceremony (*katharsis*) in order to make ourselves pure (*katharos*) in both body and soul. Plato's serious usage is found most characteristically in the *Phaedo*, where, for instance, he declares katharsis to consist "in separating, so far as possible, the soul from the body, and in teaching the soul the habit of collecting and bringing itself together from all parts of the body, and of living, so far as it can, both now and hereafter, alone by itself, freed from the body as from fetters." The thought here is largely Pythagorean and probably indicates the way in which katharsis was understood as the purpose of those religious exercises in which the Pythagorean communities at Crotona and elsewhere schooled themselves.

At the end of Aristotle's treatise *On Statecraft* (the so-called *Politics*) there is a passage of some further relevance. Having mentioned three affections of the psyche which are present in all individuals, to greater or lesser degree—pity, fear, and *enthousiasmos*, that is, religious excitement—he declares: "And we may see how some persons who are in the grip of this kind of emotion [lit., "motion," *kinēsis*], by using melodies that throw the soul into orgiastic frenzy, are calmed as though they had found healing and purgation." [5] The participle which I have translated "that throw the soul into orgiastic frenzy" is *exorgiadzōn*, whose base is the noun *orgia*, meaning secret religious rites and the frenzied excitement supposedly and perhaps actually attached to them, and applied mainly, though not exclusively, to the worship of

[5] VIII, 7: 1342a, 5 ff.

Demeter at Eleusis, as shown by the Homeric Hymn to Demeter (lines 273 and 476), and by Aristophanes' *The Frogs* (line 384). Aristotle was evidently unsympathetic to such religious phenomena as the Eleusinian Mysteries, of which, we may presume, he had only hearsay knowledge, for the inner secrets were carefully guarded.

Why, then, do I emphasize the religious aspect of katharsis, since it is evidently of such minor importance for the author we are investigating? My answer is that I do not regard the *Poetics* as an end in itself, but mainly as an instrument for the clearer and fuller understanding of Greek tragic drama. Its principles have a considerable validity when applied to Sophoclean tragedy, a subject which receives admirable commentary in the first chapter and the Appendix of Francis Fergusson's *The Idea of a Theatre*,[6] but they are strikingly inadequate when applied to the tragedies of Aeschylus. In conclusion I wish to indicate summarily why this is so, thereby indicating also certain intrinsic shortcomings of Aristotle's critical approach.

KATHARSIS AND MIMESIS IN AESCHYLEAN PERSPECTIVE

The outstanding weakness of the *Poetics*, I submit, is its inadequate treatment of poetic diction (*lexis*), more specifically of metaphor, and its failure to indicate any of the potentialities of relationship between metaphoric development and tragic design. I need only remind you that when, immediately after formulating his celebrated definition of tragedy, Aristotle enumerates the six "formative elements" (*eidos*) of which a tragedy consists—story, characters, thought, diction, staging (usually translated "spectacle"), and music—he ranks diction fourth in the scale of importance and defines it in two complementary ways: first as "the putting together (*synthesis*) of measures (*metron*)," later as "interpretation (*hermēneia*) through naming (*onomasia*)." Although these two definitions correspond respectively to the two major aspects of expressive diction—the rhythmic and what in the most inclusive sense may be called the metaphoric—it is clear that Aristotle intends them too narrowly for serviceable criticism. Obviously, expressive dramatic rhythm involves a good deal more than metrical composition; but of that I will not speak. I choose to look rather at the other aspect of diction—at what it can express by the device of metaphor.

Hardly any contemporary reader of poetry, I dare say, finds much

[6] Princeton, 1949.

enlightenment in the rather picayune treatment given to metaphor in chapter xxi of the *Poetics*. There is no glimmer of understanding shown for the role of thematic or illuminative metaphor as I have defined it above. Accordingly, Aristotle is better equipped to speak of the tragedies of Sophocles, in which the major poetic and dramatic effects are attained without much use of metaphor, than of the tragedies of Aeschylus, where the role of illuminative metaphor is indispensable for a full grasp of the significant action.

Aeschylus, like Dante and Shakespeare, has a way of writing on two or more semantic levels at once. His principal ironic effects, not unlike theirs, are achieved through a contrapuntal relation, so to speak, between direct statement and the persuasive associations of the imagery. But as Aeschylus stands closest of the three to that prelogical rituo-mythic style of envisagement in which the heritage of poetry is rooted, his imagery reflects, more strikingly than theirs, the peculiarities of certain primal rituo-mythic forms.

Now the most primal of all rituo-mythic forms has to do in some way with the cycle of death and rebirth. Some of its most direct imagery is therefore seasonal and vegetative—summer harvest after winter frost, the growth of plant from seed—and also, by extension, diurnal—the emergence of bright day out of night. Man is fully a part of and a participant in the rituo-mythic world which is his ambience; his own birth and death, therefore, and sometimes, too, his rebirth out of and beyond death become recurrent themes. There is also a concern with the restoration of health out of illness; for this is the mundane reflection, the intermittent hither side, of the restoration of life out of death. Then, as man's ethical sense becomes more acute, the rituo-mythic ideas of rebirth and bodily healing develop a new dimension of meaning and aim: there emerges that primal element of religious consciousness, the desire to be liberated from sin (however sin may be specifically conceived in a given culture) and from the morally ambiguous condition of life in a mortal body. The ritual appropriate to this stage tends to be less dependent upon sheer convention, demands more co-operation from the individual will; rituals of fasting and other forms of abstinence at once suggest themselves, but I call your attention to two forms of ritual more essential than these, because more inwardly connected with purification of the spirit—the ritual of silence and the associated ritual of watching or (exchanging eye for ear) of listening. Finally, since man does not exist only as an individual, but is a *zoön politikon*, finding and expressing his nature through the medium of organic community—through the *oikia* or household most spontaneously, and then later but more perfectly (if we believe Aristotle) through the *polis*, or small autonomous city-state—there arise rituo-mythic forms connected with the idea of governance, celebrating man's emergence from barbarian chaos to the privileges of civilized socially ordered living. And through all such rituo-mythic expressions there runs the bright actuality of dance, stylized gesture, and cadenced song.

Of course my slim account does small justice to the indescribable variety of rituo-mythic forms which have existed. But the ones I have enumerated are outstandingly archetypal in the sense of recurring under one guise or another in many cultures. And they furnish the clue to an understanding of the dominant imagistic themes of the *Oresteia*.

A number of the dominant themes are announced imagistically in that magnificently orchestrated overture to both the play and the trilogy —the Watchman's speech, which opens the *Agamemnon*. "Of the Gods I ask deliverance from my labors"—so the soliloquy opens, and two mythopoeic themes, both alive with metaphoric possibilities, are set before us: the theme of guardian Divinity and the related theme of spiritual deliverance. To trace them in all their poetically relevant associations would require a chapter apiece; my indications here must be brief. Let us look only at the second. The phrase "deliverance from labors" (*apallagē ponōn*), announced in line 1 and repeated in line 20, has the surface meaning of "Deliver me from this long year's vigil by sending the fire-signal for which I am waiting, which will announce the fall of Troy." Then there is the background reference to the curse upon the House of Atreus; Orestes will be hailed later as the deliverer, the liberator of the house from that curse, and Orestes in turn will require to be delivered from the pursuing Furies. But further, the phrase "deliverance from labors" was probably one employed in the ritual of the cult of Demeter at Eleusis, of which Aeschylus was almost certainly a member—that is, an initiate. The "labors," in Eleusinian context, would probably have meant, as with the Pythagoreans, the laborious imprisonment of the soul in the body. The phrase, on its second appearance (line 20), becomes connected with the word *euangellos*—good news, "evangel," in both a commonplace and a religious sense—and more explicitly than before with the mythopoeic theme of Light-out-of-Darkness. "Now, by good chance, let there be deliverance from these labors, when the light of the fire comes to birth out of the darkness, bringing good news."

The light imagery in the soliloquy has three stages. It appears first as the assembly of the nightly stars, no doubt actually pointed to in the sky that visibly overhung the City Dionysia. The stars wax and wane; by their cycle of rising and fading away (more literally, withering away) they bring winter storms and summer harvests to me: thus the darkness-light cycle is imagistically, as it was mythically, joined with the cycle of frost and harvest, and thereby with the cycle of death and life. Next (line 8), the light-imagery appears in the Watchman's imaginings; he describes the flash of fire, the beacon-signal which he awaits. Finally (line 22), the beacon-flash sent from Mount Ida is actually seen—by the Watchman and presumably by the audience as well; the former hails it with joy and celebrates it with dancing.

But his joy is tempered by a note of fear, suspicion, and possession of a weighty secret which he is prevented by ritual silence from revealing. "A great ox had trod upon my tongue" is not simply a colloquialism, as most interpreters appear to take it. At any rate the colloquialism most likely had a religious origin, and the religious overtones seem to me clearly present in the passage. I take the ox to be thematically connected with the consecrated "god-driven" ox to which the Chorus likens the doomed Cassandra in lines 1296/7; it probably alludes also, although lightly, to the ritual silence imposed upon the consecrated initiate in the Eleusinian and in higher forms of the Dionysian mysteries. Furthermore, as the word *bous*, here translated "ox," can be applied loosely in Greek to various members of the cattle family, there are doubtless further overtures of allusion to the bull-god Dionysus and to Agamemnon, of whom Cassandra later speaks as a doomed bull and who treads the purple carpet with ritual solemnity as though a victim consecrated for sacrifice, with Clytemnestra as the presiding priestess.

And through it all there is the watching. Dog-imagery in the *Oresteia* functions plurisignatively: not only are the Watchman and afterward Electra "treated like dogs," they are also, in different ways, watchdogs; and in the third play, *The Eumenides*, the idea of hounds on the scent has so permeated the metaphoric action that it bursts into actuality and we hear the Furies barking and whining like dogs in their sleep. Through its connection with the Furies the watching becomes associated with the snake imagery and hence with symbolic rebirth.

Time prohibits an extended pursuit of the details of Aeschylus's Oresteian symbolism. These few examples, however, have prepared the ground for my concluding thesis, although I am aware that they are inadequate to prove it. The thesis may be put baldly thus: that Aeschylus's use of thematic imagery is the focal area of coalescence between mimesis and katharsis in Greek tragic drama. Such imagery is mimetic, but in a way that quite transcends what Aristotle understood poetic mimesis to be: for the "action" which it "imitates" or represents is action with a rituo-mythic dimension. Aeschylus takes the kathartically changed imagery of certain religious cults of his place and time, especially, no doubt, the Eleusinian, and weaves it, together with other strands of imagery which I must here ignore, into the pattern of his tragedies. Thus, the ceremonies surrounding the sacred ear of corn become dramatically blasphemed by Clytemnestra when describing her murder of Agamemnon: "Sprinkled with the deadly drizzle of his bloody dew I rejoiced as does the growing ear of corn under the god-sent rain."

The holy mystery of Persephone's descent into the subterranean dark and of her annual resurrection becomes echoed in the *Choephori* in the theme of Orestes reborn from the dead, first presaged in Clytemnestra's dream of the serpent suckling at her breast and afterward epitomized in the servant's cry, "The dead are slaying the living." These themes are not irresponsibly kathartic, as an array of Gothic horrors might be; they are kathartic because they are mimetic. But how they are mimetic can never be understood in the simplicity of naturalistic perspective, whether Aristotle's or our own. Aeschylus was a religious poet. I do not allude to the fact that his Choruses frequently give voice to religious ideas and sentiments; that in itself is poetically irrelevant. Nor do I mean that he heightens an otherwise self-sufficient drama with the evocative power of religious imagery. That would be poetically superficial. I mean that the Aeschylean mimesis itself is religious: which is to say, Aeschylus's principal images, in their main hearing, are threshold symbols of a rituo-mythic reality in which he was deeply schooled.

The relation of thematic imagery to its rituo-mythic matrix is not the least of the interests that vitalize the poetic criticism of our own day. Such relationship is mimetic in the sense that the imagery symbolizes its rituo-mythic prototype. Its way of symbolizing is participative; it draws the reader-hearer-spectator into a threshold situation, where some of the great moving patterns of human living—the concrete universals, the *Urphenomene*—are apprehended dimly, ambivalently, insecurely, yet with great power. The insecurity is realized and felt as an aspect of the universal condition: it elicits our pity and fear, and we are thereby somehow purged and re-equilibrated. I conclude, then, that mimesis and katharsis are valid critical concepts—no less valid now than in fourth-century Greece—provided that they are reinterpreted with attention to all levels of meaning, all relevant overtones of allusion, which the work under scrutiny is found to contain.

I. 8

Ramus: Rhetoric and the Pre-Newtonian Mind*

WALTER J. ONG, S. J.

Harvard University

PETER RAMUS is known to the world today chiefly as a reformer, in logic an anti-Aristotelian, in rhetoric not only anti-Aristotle but anti-Quintilian and anti-Cicero too. However, Ramus thought of himself not only as a revolutionary but also as a champion of the past. Revolution was for him confusedly synonymous with return to the past, for the issue of reform with him, as with many of his contemporaries, was tied up emotionally with the notion of recuperating what had supposedly been lost since the times of antiquity. He taunts the medieval and Renaissance Aristotelians with the earlier achievements of Quintilian and Cicero, both these with the still earlier "laws of method" proposed by Aristotle, to which they do not conform, only to taunt Aristotle himself with the achievements of his master Plato.[1]

Part of the confusion in Ramus's mind was due to the economy of the revolutionary mentality itself. The professed revolutionary carries about in himself the germs of retrogression. Everyone's future grows out of his past, but for the revolutionary the past too often tyrannizes over the future. Specializing in the overthrow of the past, the revolutionary sees everything in terms of this overthrow, which is to say, everything in terms of the past itself. For this reason, the study of a revolutionary

---

* Read at the Institute in 1952 Published in the *Institute Essays*, 1954.

[1] Ramus, *Aristotelicae animadversiones*, Paris, 1543, fol. 2ᵛ ff.; "Scholae rhe-toricae," in his *Scholae in liberales artes*, Bastle, 1569, fol. [k₀] preceding col. 233, col. 344 ff.

often demands to be understood in terms of his past even more than the study of other types of persons.

Study of Ramus has been neglected because we have for centuries been deliberately inattentive to the immediate past out of which he grew. His opponent, Antonio de Gouveia, taunts Ramus, saying that everybody in Paris knows whose works he has raided for the material in his *Dialectica*:[2] But apart from Aristotle and Melanchthon, the names which Gouveia mentions—Johannes Caesarius, Hegendorphinus, Titelmannus—mean nothing to us. The chief source of Ramus's *Dialectica* and indirectly of the Tolan Ramist *Rhetorica*, and thus of the hundreds upon hundreds of editions of Ramus's own works and the hundreds of other editions of his followers, is Rudolph Agricola. But since his death, in the fifteenth century, Rudolph Agricola has never been accorded more than a monograph, and his principal claim to attention is his tendency to get himself confused with his more famous namesake George.

The scholastic logicians, in whose tradition Ramus had been trained and against whom he says his reform—and, incidentally, the whole humanist movement at Paris—was directed, are to us, with few exceptions, not even names. We have heard vaguely of Buridan, but the Belgian Dulardus, the Frenchman Pierre Tartaret (or Tataret), the tremendously influential Scot John Major, his more mysterious compatriot John Caubraith, the Spaniard Juan de Celaya, and most of their equally important confrères are sunk in oblivion. Yet theirs is the central linguistic tradition of the Western world. Out of this tradition there stares the dim figure of Ralph Strode—Chaucer's "philosophical Strode"—and of the most important personage of all, Peter of Spain. This is the unknown milieu into which Ramus's revolution was faced and in which it has its meaning.

Our knowledge of the early logical and rhetorical tradition is seriously handicapped by the specialization of our interests in the past. This specialization has taken several characteristic turns, the first of which can be indicated by taking a sharp look at so familiar an object as the *Short-Title Catalogue*. If the *Short-Title Catalogue* had attempted to list all the books by British authors published during the period it covers

[2] Antonio de Gouveia, *Opera iuridica, philologica, philosophica*, ed. by Iacobus van Vaassen, Rotterdam, 1766, pp. 787–788. See also Iacobus Schegkius (Iakob Schegk or Iakob Degen), *Hyperaspistes responsi ad quatuor epistolae Petri Rami contra se editas*, Tübingen, 1570, p. 61.

up to 1640, it would have had to be at least twice its present size. It has been kept to its present dimensions by limiting its inclusion of Latin works. However, most of the writing in the period up to 1640 was in Latin. Moreover, what was not written originally in Latin was often translated into Latin and went through more editions in Latin than in the vernacular in which it was first written. In the schools most of the teaching was not only *of* Latin and Latin literature but also actually *in* Latin—at least in principle—for the very lowest grades. Except for his "lesse Greeke," Shakespeare studied practically nothing but Latin in school. When he did study something else, he studied it, as he studied Latin, in, Latin—unless his masters were remiss, as some masters no doubt were. But remissness in this respect called for initiative, for the textbooks, even for such things as arithmetic, were in Latin, too.

The *Short-Title Catalogue* limits its inclusion of Latin works by omitting all such works published by British authors outside England, Scotland, and Ireland. This gives its listings an artificially provincial tone, for one of the advantages of writing in Latin was that it gave work first published in England a larger circulation and greater influence. Thus, it happens that in terms of the general intellectual climate the works excluded by the *Short-Title Catalogue* are often more important than the ones included. Because he wrote in Latin, Ralph Strode, Chaucer's friend from Oxford, was already appearing in Venetian editions of the incunabula period and exerting an influence on Italian thought impossible for his fellow-countryman Chaucer.

It made little difference where you published Latin works. In the early 1600s the Ramist Anglican bishop of Derry, George Downham, found Frankfort-on-the-Main a more convenient publishing center for his works than London or anywhere else in Great Britain. These Frankfort editions are quite as common today in old British libraries as are editions of the same or similar works printed less frequently in London. Whether or not we connect it with nineteenth-century jingoism, the specialization of the *Short-Title Catalogue* has given prominence in our minds to the works which were often regarded by their authors as the least important of their creations.

Specialization has taken another form in the case of our study of scholasticism. Despite the prevailing impression, scholasticism as a whole has not been studied exhaustively over the past few decades. What has been studied is a certain kind of scholasticism, the scholasticism of theologians, and of a select group of theologians at that. Very few "scholastics," if by that we mean teachers of philosophy in the period called scholastic, were theologians. Still fewer of the students of this period ever studied any theology at all. They studied mostly the scholasticism of the arts course. The scholasticism which most students knew has never appeared in modern editions.

Who, we might ask, were these students who studied arts-course scholasticism? They were not only those preparing for theology but also those preparing for law and medicine—medicine was the higher course most intimately connected with arts course scholastic philosophy. Most especially, however, those studying arts-course scholasticism were those arts-course students preparing themselves for everything or for nothing at all—just attending the university. All in all, perhaps three-fourths of the scholasticism of the Middle Ages and the Renaissance was studied in the arts faculty.

This arts scholasticism was almost entirely logic and physics. Of metaphysics there was almost none—at least as prescribed in the arts curricula and studied directly. There was much implied metaphysics, particularly in "physics," as, for instance, in the tracts *De anima*, but, as a separate discipline the arts professors seem not to have liked to handle metaphysics. Alone, it veered too close to theology, which was not their field at all. Hence they kept it rather as tangent to physics, as a genuine metaphysics—with the result that this metaphysics had a quite different tonality from even scholastic metaphysics today.

Their chariness of problems touching theology reminds us that these arts professors as a group were not by any means all priests, as we may be sometimes inclined to suppose they were. Indeed, priests were the only class of men some of whose members were positively excluded from being professors of arts, for Paris University statutes excluded from the arts faculty all members of religious orders, so that the only priests who could act as masters of arts were secular priests. The arts faculty as such had no theological interests. Its teachers were masters of arts— or, for certain courses, bachelors of arts, apprentice teachers in their mid-teens—often studying for a medical degree at the same time, or perhaps for a theology degree, rather less likely for a law degree (to undertake the study of law one did not need an M.A.). The arts-course professor could also be a master of arts who with only that degree made teaching his life work—such was Peter Ramus. These teachers of arts were people with the privileged, rather indefinable social status of Chaucer's Clerk of Oxenford.

The condition of our knowledge concerning arts-course scholasticism as this touches Ramus and the linguistic attitudes he exploits can nowhere be more strikingly seen than by looking to the case of Peter of Spain, a contemporary of St. Thomas Aquinas, but a physician rather than a theologian, whose work, the *Summulae logicales*, became probably the most influential of all medieval scholastic textbooks. At Paris, where Ramus tells us nearly one third of the philosophy course was spent studying Peter of Spain,[3] so that the word for the first-year philosophy students was *summulistae*,[4] this logician-physician ranks in university documents alongside Aristotle.[5] His influence was comparable in other universities. Scores of editions of his work appeared everywhere after the invention of printing—a count which does not pretend in any way to be complete has numbered some 160 by 1530.[6] But after 1530, near silence ensued, and by the end of the century it had become total. This situation prevailed till our own day. This is the man at the very center of the tradition against which Renaissance humanism took form. With the rest of the tradition, he dropped out of sight and memory during Ramus's lifetime with a dismaying finality. We think of the Renaissance as a revolution, but our first-hand knowledge of what the revolution took place against is close to zero and has been since the Renaissance itself.

At the risk of being a little too sweeping, we can here attempt a description of the arts-course intellectual milieu in which the Ramist dialectic and rhetoric take shape, making our description as relevant as possible to the Ramist tradition itself.[7] We must imagine a milieu in

[3] Ramus, "Pro philosophica Parisiensis academiae disciplina oratio," in his *Scholae in liberales artes,* col. 1049.

[4] This term had been in official use for at least some hundred years by Ramus's day. It occurs ("artistas, maxime Summulistas, et Logicos") in the decree of Louis XI in 1464 for the government of the College of Navarre (which was to be Ramus's college), cited in Jean de Launoy, *Regii Navarrae gymnasii Parisiensis historia,* Paris, 1677, I, 170 (Pars I, Lib. II, cap. ix). In unofficial use, the term may well go back to the early fourteenth century or even the late thirteenth.

[5] "Reformatio universitatis Parisiensis facta per Cardinalem legatum Guillelmum de Estoutevilla" (1452), in *Chartularium universitatis Parisiensis,* ed. by Henri Denifle and Emile Chatelain, IV, Paris, 1897, 728–729 ff.

[6] Joseph P. Mullally, *The Summulae logicales of Peter of Spain,* Notre Dame, Ind., 1945, pp. 132–158. Publications in Medieval Studies, University of Notre Dame.

[7] The best approach to the pre-Ramist educational tradition is still through Hastings Rashdall, *The Universities of Europe in the Middle Ages,* new ed. by F. M. Powicke and A. B. Emden, 3 vols., Oxford, 1936, and through the works cited therein.

which, of course, logic played a dominant role. This is the logic which we have been taught to call decadent, without knowing very well in what the decadence consists—understandably, since we have had no editions in which to examine the logic for some four hundred years. The decadence is often imagined to consist in a preoccupation with distinctions, but first-hand acquaintance with the logic does not give us precisely that impression. There are treatises studied, such as Boethius's *De divisione*, which treat distinctions at some length, and there is some treatment of distinction in Aristotle's *Organon* itself. But any real obsession with distinction is not easy to detect. If this logic is decadent, it is decadent in the sense in which non-Euclidean geometry or any pure mathematics is decadent or in the sense in which modern logistic is decadent. It simply goes its own way in speculation without regard for the practical use to which the speculation can perhaps be put. It evolves all sorts of complicated descriptions of complicated logical situations. In Peter of Spain's famous "Treatise on Supposition" we encounter this sort of "rule":

It is impossible for a general term, functioning as a predicate, to have simple suppositional value and to be movably or immovably indeterminate when there is a universal sign in the subject of an affirmative proposition, as in the statement: "Every man is an animal." The reason for this is, as Porphyry indicates, that everything which is predicated of something is either greater than or equal to that of which it is predicated—and he had essential predication in mind.[8]

This kind of detailed fence-running represents much the same kind of logic, recent studies have remarked,[9] as is found in the modern logistic of Carnap and others. The easiest way, perhaps, to form a notion of the high and late medieval arts course and of the intellectual climate in which it existed is to imagine a university course made up principally of a logic such as Professor Carnap taught in itself and as applied to Physics. Like many modern logicians, Peter of Spain, in a fashion which cannot be detailed here, but is connected with the way he manipulates the predicaments, or categories, develops in his logic a strong mathematical torque. The way for Newton's mathematical physics was here being prepared, not by training in mathematics—

---

[8] From the text of the "Tractatus de Suppositione," in Mullally, *The Summulae logicales of Peter of Spain*—Mullally's translation, as given in parallel with the Latin.

[9] See Philotheus Boehner, *Medieval Logic*, Manchester, 1952, pp. xii–xvi; Mullally, *The Summulae logicales of Peter of Spain*, p. v.

that was to come later—but by a kind of pretraining in forming concepts in terms of quantitative and spatial analogies. The subject and predicate, as in the passage from Peter of Spain just quoted, were sized up as being "greater" or "lesser" than one another.

In this logical tradition interest in making distinctions shows up, indeed, in a special way in the technique of disputation which before the Renaissance took the place of written exercises almost completely. In the disputation process, indeed, distinctions were exploited—but again it is hard to discover any infatuation with them. When Ramus, in one of his rare amusing passages, makes fun of disputation procedures, he makes fun of the formal way of putting objections and responses rather than of the practice of making distinctions.[10] Ramus himself was infatuated, as perhaps no one else—except one or another of his followers—has ever been, with making distinctions, and if making distinctions is a mark of scholastic decadence then Ramus, the anti-scholastic—can lay claim to being the most decadent scholastic of all times. But "decadence" is a chameleon term and often confuses issues under the guise of emotionally simplifying them. Moreover, in Ramus's case there is something far more interesting than decadence or the lack thereof—the matter of *what* Ramus is interested in distinguishing, for at this point his interests represent the very culmination of the scholastic tradition which ejects him on the world.

What, then, is Ramus interested in distinguishing? Not angels dancing on the points of needles—the average arts professor kept angels at a good arm's length. Not "entities," or *entitatulae*, in any way which would give much meaning to the often quoted, but hard to explain, razor associated with William of Ockham, *entia non sunt multiplicanda sine necessitate*. Ramus, true heir of arts-course scholasticism, is interested chiefly and primarily in distinguishing the arts and/or sciences one from another and in distinguishing within these arts and/or sciences their separate parts.

This is one of the culminating points, if not, indeed, the chief culminating point, of the medieval arts course and the point at which this arts course helps generate the modern interest in scientific method. The study of logic in the scholastic tradition had been built around Aristotle's *Organon*, and this collection of most of Aristotle's logical treatises had kept in more or less continuous agitation questions con-

10 Ramus, "Prooëmium reformandae Parisiensis academiae," in his *Scholae in liberales artes*, cols. 1087–1096.

cerning the different kinds of logic—the logic of dialectic, rhetoric, sophistic, poetic, and science—as well as questions concerning the interior structure of the various disciplines to which one or another of these logics applied. Throughout the centuries these questions were agitated, but they were not solved; that is, no generally accepted solution was arrived at which would be served up uniformly to all arts-course students by all arts-course professors. In Ramus's day, the various answers which had been generated were still proliferating. Ramus has one notion, Jacques Charpentier another, Adrien Turnèbe a third, and Melanchthon still one more.

The reasons for the lack of a universally accepted solution are manifold and rather respectable, on the whole. First, Aristotle's discussion had itself been conducted with a full awareness of the complexity of the linguistic situation, and not only his answers but also his very formulations of the questions are most often tentative, frequently downright puzzling, and almost always entirely too cagey to be open to the kind of whipping-boy interpretation which Ramus or, in our own day, Korzybski put on them—with documentation which at best is kept slender. Secondly, the philosophy program of three and one-half years, only one of which, Ramus tells us, was in his day devoted to the Organon, at Paris,[11] scarcely gave time for a really adequate treatment of this not very systematic bundle of treatises discussing complicated questions concerning the various kinds of knowledge treasured by the human mind. University professors were aware of the difficulty here and came more and more to acknowledge it openly. In the early sixteenth century Juan de Celaya begins his lectures on Porphyry's Isagoge or introduction to Aristotle's Organon by explaining that he will follow the "modern" fashion of not treating at the beginning the question whether logica is a science or not, since such a thorny question is more fit to conclude than to begin a course in logic.[12]

Thirdly, apparently genuinely profound treatment of philosophical problems in the arts course was precluded by the youth of the students, if not of the professors, throughout the whole medieval and Renaissance history of universities (or of scholasticism—for there is no practical distinction whatsoever between the two histories, the university and the

---

[11] Ramus, "Pro philosophica Parisiensis academiae disciplina," in his Scholae in liberales artes, col. 1049.

[12] Juan de Celaya, Expositio . . . in librum Predicabilium Porphyrii, Paris, 1516, fols. ii ff.

scholastic tradition being exactly the same thing). Students became masters of arts, which meant that they completed everything the uni-versity had to offer by way of courses in grammar, rhetoric, logic, and all philosophy, by the time they were approximately twenty. The University of Paris had actually been forced to have statutes on its books to forbid anyone from actually teaching, M.A. or no M.A., before he was twenty years old.[13] And Ramus himself brags that he could turn out M.A.'s at the age of fifteen at his Collège de Presles better than the average university product.[14]

If we marvel at the youth of the universities, we may marvel still more at the curious development of human intellection it manifests: the whole intellectual community which has produced the modern scientific world was fascinated with the problem of the structure and in-terrelation of the sciences before it had given many of these sciences a satisfactory content. But a historical fact is a historical fact, and this phenomenon in such a fact. It brings home to us the curious economy of human intellection, which first approaches its problems over the most abstract route—which, if often the most fruitless, is also the most direct route—doubling back only when it finds it must. At any rate, this abstract approach to the sciences, the attempt to determine their inter-relation and structure before most of them were given satisfactory con-tent, is the prelude to all our modern scientific and linguistic attitudes. It is the overture of modern scientific method. Nowhere else in the history of mankind and only after such a prelude does the symphony or the cacophony of the modern world appear.

Ramus has been arraigned for confusing logic and dialectic and for erecting the wrong kind of distinctions between both these things and rhetoric.[15] But seen in this real historical setting, Ramus shows no particular genius for confusing these things. He turns up in a confused situation, and his professed attempts to better the situation only per-petuate the confusion. He can be blamed, perhaps, for giving chaos a new lease on life. The huge problem of the regimentation of the sci-ences which swirls out of the Middle Ages and around him was too much for any professor caught in the arts-course tradition. Or at least,

13 *Chartularium universitatis Parisiensis*, 1215, I, 78.
14 Ramus, "Pro philosophica Parisiensis academiae disciplina oratio," in his *Scholae in liberales artes*, col. 1022.
15 See Norman E. Nelson, *Peter Ramus and the Confusion of Logic, Rhetoric, and Poetry*, Ann Arbor, Mich., 1947, University of Michigan Contributions in Modern Philology, No. 2.

for any we know of so far. It is true that St. Thomas Aquinas had notions on the structure and interrelation of the sciences painstakingly
thought out and matured—notions far from complete, but astute, carefully elaborated, cautious, and open to tremendous further development. However, like most of those reared in the scholastic tradition,
Ramus did not make a point of studying St. Thomas, who was a theologian and, one knows, matured his notions in the long—often twelve-
or even fifteen-year—theology courses, working out from theological
problems a metaphysics and a kind of epistemology which is scarcely a
part of the arts-course scholastic tradition at all.

Ramus's preoccupations and confusions derive, often with astonishing directness, from the arts-course scholasticism in which he was
trained. With reference to arts-course authors, not for nothing did his
contemporaries call him the *usuarius*, the usufructuary, the man living
off the income of property belonging to someone else. When he drives
trenches right and left between the sciences, taking as his motto, in a
revealing analogy, "Solon's Law" which regulated building developments in ancient Athens—a foot's margin for a wall, two feet for a
house, and so forth [16]—Ramus is only continuing the preoccupation
with assorting the sciences which began with the medieval study of the
Organon.

When he says that dialectic and logic are the same thing, he
does so not because he feels called to overthrow an old order in favor
of a new chaos, but because for more than two centuries university
students in every part of Europe, particularly at Paris, Peter of Spain's
alma mater as she was Ramus's, had found in their introduction to
logic, that is, in Peter of Spain's *Summulae logicales*, no distinction between logic and dialectic at all.[17]

Similarly, when Ramus makes no clear-cut distinction between *ars*
and *scientia*, this is not only because no clear-cut distinction is maintained in Cicero and Quintilian but more precisely because this same
Summulae logicales seems specifically to identify the two in its opening
words, which after a few Biblical phrases and a bit of St. Augustine,
form probably one of the most recurrent expressions throughout the
Middle Ages and the Renaissaice: "Dialectic is the art of arts, the
science of sciences." [18] Peter of Spain had not made clear whether he

---

[16] Ramus, "Scholae rhetorica," in his *Scholae in liberales artes*, cols. 255–256.

[17] Mullally, *The Summulae logicales of Peter of Spain*, p. xxi.

[18] "Dialectica est ars artium scientia scientiarum, ad omnium methodorum
principia viam habens."—Peter of Spain, *Summulae logicales cum Versorii Parisiensis*

meant the "science of sciences" to be a synonym for or a supplement to the "art of arts." Very likely he was uncertain himself and wanted to blur the question. Certainly art-course scholasticism as a whole had maintained the suspended state of mind, and it is a serious mistake to import a nicer terminology out of St. Thomas Aquinas or St. Albert the Great or any other author and call it "scholastic" without further ado.

It is impossible to consider Ramus's rhetoric apart from the background of scholastic dialectic and logic out of which it grew. This follows, indeed, from Ramus's own reiterated principles, which set up dialectic and rhetoric as correlatives of one another, limiting one another's possessions, since between them were distributed the "laws" or "matter" hitherto held conjointly by a jumble of ill-assorted arts. But it follows even more imperiously from the psychological bent of Ramus's own mind, which, while not that of all scholastics, is certainly that of his own scholastic predecessors of the arts course at Paris and many other universities. Melanchton, Ramus's great competitor and posthumously his enforced partner, once remarked that there was no medieval corruption of rhetoric as there had been of dialectic: the medieval authors had been relatively inactive on the rhetorical front, and "no authors are extant except the best"—that is, Quintilian and Cicero, chiefly.[19] That is true, but it meant for Melanchthon, as for Ramus, that his own handling of rhetoric, deriving necessarily from a mentality inherited from his immediate predecessors, whom he affected to despise, but whose influence he could not abdicate, was colored by the dialectical or logical tradition which was in all but complete possession of the field in the youth of Melanchthon, Ramus, and their contemporaries.

Indeed, humanism, with its program calling for a controlled

---

clarissima expositione; parvorum item logicalium eidem Petro Hispani adscriptum opus, Venetiis, F. Sansovinus, 1572, fol. 2ᵛ. Cf. Mullally, *The Summulae logicales of Peter of Spain*, pp. xxi and lxxiv, where it is pointed out that this definition is reminiscent of Cicero's *Brutus*, cap. xli–xlii. The definition is also echoed by Ockham and many others. The *Summulae logicales* have been edited by I. M. Bochenski, O. P., Turin: Marietti, 1947; Mullally, *The Summulae logicales of Peter of Spain*, gives the most significant part of the work *Tractatus Septimus*, also known as the *Parva logicalia*, in the complete Latin text with a parallel English translation.

19 "Nulli enim extant autores nisi optimi"—Melanchthon, *Elementorum rhetorices libri duo, recens recogniti ab autore* (s.l., 1572—copy in my possession). The complete passage from Melanchthon is given in translation in T. W. Baldwin, *William Shakspere's Small Latine and Lesse Greeke*, Urbana, Ill., 1944, II, 9.

vocabulary and a carefully policed classical style, is a product of scholastic scientism almost as much as a reaction against it. No one can mistake the different accent when the same ground is covered by these professed devotees of the classical rhetoricians, who foreswear scholasticism with bell, book, and candle, and the classical rhetoricians themselves. The Renaissance rhetoricians, almost to a man, have a pronounced dialectical twang which contrasts with the smoother, more random, and often inconsistent observations of Cicero.

It is true that Ramus can be quite as inconsistent as Cicero ever was. But he cries loudly and incessantly in favor of consistency, which for him is an obsession in a way it could not be for either Cicero or Quintilian. Ramus's *Brutus' Problems* (*Brutinae quaestiones*) and *Evaluations of Quintilian's Rhetoric* (*Rhetoricae distinctiones in Quintilianum*) are both nothing but long and circumstantial diatribes against the alleged inconsistencies and lack of "method" in Cicero and Quintilian.

The dominance of dialectic in setting the rhetorical climate was also guaranteed by a fact about which we sometimes do not like to think. Through the Middle Ages and the Renaissance, rhetoric was a subject for little boys. Practically speaking, it had no existence for students after they were ten or twelve (later, perhaps, fourteen) years old. It was taught as a chore often by young masters of arts who were studying other subjects themselves, or even, perhaps, by still younger bachelors, also studying. Neither the Middle Ages nor the Renaissance rhetoric courses were sophistic or Attic schools for orators, late finishing schools polishing off their prospective graduates for immediate entry into active political life. Despite the campaigning of Erasmus and others, the rhetoric course mostly remained a propaedeutic to logic, philosophy, and thereafter professional studies. After the arrival of the universities, a training capped by rhetoric was never more to be known. Even Johann Sturm's Strasbourg Gymnasium soon became a university in name, as it had been already in inclination, and the Jesuit colleges evolved very early a university structure, with philosophy, not rhetoric, at the top. Harvard, which started as a Renaissance college, followed exactly the same pattern.

This does not mean that rhetoric was not an important subject or that it did not involve very important attitudes toward language and life in general which stayed with students forever. But it does mean that Ramist and other Renaissance rhetoric must be viewed in the whole complex educational picture of which it is a part and which we find so much difficulty in piecing together.

Renaissance rhetoric is, first of all, a means of teaching boys style, that is, Latin style. It is conceived practically, even when it fails to be practical. Melanchthon's justification for his statement that "dialectic presents things unclothed, rhetoric adds elocution as clothing" is typical: "Although many object to it, I am not against this distinction," he says, "for the reason that it can be grasped by youngsters," [20] and, he adds, because it is etymologically consistent, if not with regard to the word "rhetoric,' at least with regard to the word elocutio. Intellectually, this position may make us wince, but Melanchthon's reason —"because it can be grasped by youngsters"—lies at the base of whole philosophies, from Ramus to John Dewey.

In the writings of St. Thomas there is a carefully thought out theoretical position for rhetoric as one of the probable logics directed toward a practical rather than a speculative end. That is not the kind of thing we have here. As it existed in the ancient world and as it emerged in the Middle Ages, rhetoric has no commonly accepted theoretical position. The implications of the position it actually did have, as the science which added "ornamentation" or clothing to naked thought, were not thought out by most of those who taught or studied rhetoric. Rhetoric existed as a curriculum subject, not because anyone had a clear-cut theoretical grasp of how to define it, but simply because somehow or other as a practical discipline it fitted into the reality of the curriculum. Moreover, rhetoric fitted into the curriculum at a level which did not encourage speculation about it. Youngsters who studied it were in no condition to profit from a philosophical discussion of what rhetoric was, and most of the writing about rhetoric comes to rest, directly or indirectly, at the level of these same youngsters. There is no explicitly grasped theoretical position at all, although there is an implied one, one with tremendous consequences.

To catch sight of this position it is often less profitable to spin out the philosophical implications of one or another remark made by a rhetorician than it is to cut under such remarks to the general frames of thought, the modes of conceptualization, the ways of conceiving reality,

[20] "Dialectica res nudas proponit: Rhetorica vero addit elocutionem quasi vestitum. Hoc discrimen etsi nonnulli reprehendunt, ego tamen non repudio, quia et ad captum adolescentium facit, et ostendit, quid Rhetorica maxime proprium habeat, videlicet elocutionem, a qua ipsum Rhetorices nomen factum est."— Melanchthon, *op. cit.*, p. 13.

which determine the direction taken by the rhetorician's thought when he feels he is going about his business of being a practical teacher. When we try to do this in the case of Ramus and the Ramists, we are driven back immediately to arts-course scholasticism and its own distinctive frames of thought as the machinery out of which the Ramist development, dialectical and rhetorical, is almost automatically to flow.

Arts-course scholasticism is, as has been earlier remarked here, a scholasticism of logic and physics—of a physics often erroneous and laced with too much logic, but nevertheless definitely a physics, and of a logic decidedly more oriented psychologically toward physics than toward metaphysics. This orientation of logic can be considered in Peter of Spain's *Summulae logicales*, doubtless the most important preparation for the Ramist dialectic and rhetoric. "This is the book of the *Summulae*," the influential John Major (or Mair) was telling his Paris auditors soon after the opening of the sixteenth century, when young Pierre de la Ramée came up to Paris, "[this is] the door to all logic, the usefulness of which is plain from its very definition. . . . Dialectic, which is also called logic, is ordinarily defined thus: It is the art of arts, the science of sciences." [21]

One historian of philosophy described the *Summulae logicales* as "a dialectical fencing manual," [22] but one need only read a little of it to perceive that it is scarcely this at all. This work is not concerned primarily with telling you what move to make when your opponent threatens to pink your predicate or to run through your entire major proposition from S to P. Rather than a book on practice, it is a kind of summary adaptation of Aristotle's quite theoretical *Organon*, with a new medieval development on what is known as "supposition" (*suppositio*) and associated subjects tacked on at the end. At the risk of some misunderstanding, we can describe Peter of Spain's special fashion of presentation as a kind of dephilosophizing, or demetaphysicizing of logical questions in favor of a treatment of those aspects of logic which can be summed up diagrammatically or by means of some sort of quantitative analogy.

21 "Iste est Summularum liber, totius logices inaua: cuius utilitas ex eius definitione et proxime dicendis nota evadet. Dialectica, quae et logica dicitur, sic definiri solet: est ars artium, scientia scientiarum."—John Major, *Introductorium in Aristotelicam dialecticen, totamque logicen . . . nuper . . . repositum*, Paris, 1521, fol. IIII (Libellus I, tractatus ii).

22 Maurice de Wulf, *Histoire de la philosophie médiévale*, 6th ed., Louvain: Institut Supérieur de Philosophie, 1936, II, 85.

For example, Peter of Spain not only passes over the difference between a dialectic concerned with what is merely probable and a logic of strict scientific demonstration, but he similarly disregards the crucial issue whoch forces itself on him concerning the difference between terms which are univocal and admit of classification by genus and species in categories and terms which are analogous—such as "being" or "one"—which cannot be fitted into one category rather than another. This issue is central and must be faced at least once in any theoretically grounded logic, but for Peter of Spain it does not even exist as a problem. He throws everything together higgledy-piggledy, without a pause for explanation, making "being" a genus just like "animal." [23] Similarly, the problem concerning the universal concept, which Porphyry had at least raised, is for Peter of Spain equally nonexistent. As inevitably happens when this problem is not squarely faced, the author of the *Summulae logicales* ends by saying all sorts of things, but to all intents and purposes treating the universal as a thing outside the mind just like an individual horse or dog.[24] The epistemological problems raised by the *Posterior Analytics* of Aristotle are likewise brushed quickly aside.

By contrast with this lack of interest in the basic and recurrent problems of philosophy, Peter of Spain becomes tremendously preoccupied with all possible intricacies of problems of another sort. This can be seen in his "Treatise on Suppositions," which forms the new part of the *Summulae logicales* representing a medieval development and which Ramus says formed almost the entire content of the first-year philosophy course at Paris. Here the problems in which Peter of Spain specializes reveal an intense interest in the quantitative or quantified aspects of propositions. The signification (*significatio*) of a term is the concept in the mind for which the term is a sign; but the *suppositio* is the actual individual for which the term "stands" or "supposes." In the proposition "Man is a rational animal," the "man" supposes for all the individual men in the world. This kind of consideration opens questions such as what happens to such a proposition when another individual is born or dies and, by tying up logic with such head-counting, stresses the points at which logical operations resemble the jockeying of counters on a checker board or abacus.

This tendency to specialize in spatial, quantified conceptualization

[23] See Mullally, *The Summulae logicales of Peter of Spain*, p. xxx.
[24] *Ibid.*, pp. xxxi–xxxii.

which bulks so large in the *Summulae logicales* gives a clue, if we did not have one already, as to what is forcing the particular kind of development which we find in this work, so important in the history of Western thought and the development of the modern mind. Here is being evolved a logic and by implication a whole attitude toward language which will govern rhetoric, too, which can be taught to bright little boys—for exactly the same reason that surprisingly complicated kinds of mathematical reason can be taught to bright little boys. In this kind of logical world the metaphysical depths are carefully filled in. After this the problems—or rather what is left of them—are handled legitimately, for the most part. If we disregard the falsification occasioned, if not actually caused, by omissions, there is really very little wrong with the positive development here, nothing decadent—as far as it goes. Very little more decadent, certainly, than in mathematical logic today. But there is a narrowly specialized way of considering the logical processes. The quantitative imaginative constructs which implement this specialized viewpoint are not too much for a bright fifteen-year-old, or possibly even a twelve-year-old—for the same youngster, that is, who would be completely at a loss in sighting even the problem at issue in a genuinely philosophical discussion about language.

The force at work here in shaping this logic is so elemental that we can miss it completely: the demand for a logic which can be absorbed by a youngster in his teens. Once we are aware of the imperiousness of this demand, some of the most characteristic and puzzling developments in the medieval logic which prepares the way for Ramist logic and rhetoric begin to open to us: the specialization in categorization, for example, or the tremendous interest in sophistic. These are things assimilable by boys. We recall that John of Salisbury remarked about sophistic that there was nothing easier to explain to youth.[25]

It was easy to explain to youth, so you had it in the arts of discourse. The same reason, as we have seen, accounts for Melanchthon's distinction between dialectic and rhetoric, which was practically Ramus's distinction, too, and which was not far from being the distinction of most of the educated world for centuries. The accent on youth explains even more than we might at first blush think, when we advert to the fact that before the rise of the universities in the Middle Ages the sciences had never catered to youth in the way in which they were made to do from then on.

[25] Quoted in *ibid.*, p. xcvii.

What we have called the quantification of logic went hand in hand with the emphasis on physics rather than metaphysics in the scholasticism of the arts course and the orientation of this course as a whole toward medicine. Law students did not need to complete the master of arts degree, and theologians were constantly campaigning for an abbreviated arts course so as to get more quickly to their specialized studies. The doctors of medicine took the arts course more seriously, and it is no accident that Ramus's philosophical opponents—Jacques Charpentier, Jean Riolan the elder, and Jean Quentin—were M.D.s, as many of Ramus's followers and his own star pupil Nicolas de Nancel were to be. Peter of Spain had been a physician himself.[26]

The implications of the scholastic physics, which the medical interests did so much to sustain, have been sounded a little in studies which have pointed up the connections of one or another old theory— the theory of impetus, for example—with more modern developments. But the larger psychological implications of medieval and Renaissance physics remain to be explored. These implications connect intimately with the quantified logic we have just mentioned. We know that the difference between the old arts-course scholastic physics and the far superior Newtonian physics lay largely in the explicit reliance on mathematics in the latter. The difference was not simply that the early physics was metaphysical, the later mechanical. The early physics was, if anything, too mechanical—as in the case of the impetus theory of the Parisian School of Buridan, Albert of Saxony, and Nicholas of Oresme, who seem to have conceived of the impetus as a kind of thing which lay inside the body which had acquired it. Such an objectified "impetus" was better fitted mechanically to push things along. Aristotle's theory of propulsion, which this had replaced, was in a way even more mechanistic. He seems to have conceived of the air as continually closing in behind and pushing an arrow when it had left the bow.[27] From this kind of conceptualization Newtonian theory was a movement toward at least a more refined sort of mechanics.

This all may seem a far cry from rhetorical theory, but in reality it

[26] Peter of Spain's posthumous reputation for black magic, which grew out of his great reputation as a physician, was not dimmed by the fact that he had been Pope (John XXI) for six months before he was killed by a falling roof. He had been connected with the papal court as physician to his predecessor, and while Pope he found time not only to concern himself with Nominalism at Paris but to issue documents on alchemists as well.

[27] Herbert Butterfield, *The Origins of Modern Science*, London: 1950, pp. 11 ff.

is only a fraction of an inch distant. Whether at Paris or at Oxford or at Salamanca, rhetoric was uniformly taught by masters of arts who had been put through this arts course. Peter of Spain and the arts course in which he plays such a representative role form the common background of Ramist and anti-Ramist, of semi-Ramists, of Philippo-Ramists, and of the collusionists of every stripe who plied back and forth between any and all of these camps.

The rigidity in Ramist rhetorical theory, the counterpart of the rigidity in Ramist dialectic, and the quality which helps produce the Puritan plain style have their roots here. The sources and the implication of Ramist rhetoric in the development of the Western sensibility have long been a major puzzle, and many have found it hard to believe that a theory of "ornamentation" of language could be proposed with the downrightness or crudity which seems to be found in the Ramist tradition. The puzzle has been increased by the fact that Ramism does not seem to add anything to the ingredients in the huge rhetorical and dialectical broth which the centuries had brewed, but rather to be merely some sort of rearrangement of the ingredients in the old recipes.[28]

This is, in a sense, even more true than has been generally realized, although it is likewise more true than has generally been realized that the century-old ingredients are undergoing in Ramism a real, if subtle, change corresponding to the changes in other areas of awareness in the Western world. The epistemological naïveté in the Ramist attitudes toward language, the tendency to envision concepts as clipped off neatly from all association with imagery and to relegate them as total abstractions to the field of Ramist "dialectic," where they were thereupon treated as things, to be "opened," Ramus says, like closed baskets,[29] the corresponding impoverishment of rhetorical theory which on the one hand maintained that to these abstract "arguments" rhetoric added ornament, or what Ramus's literary lieutenant Omer Talon liked to call *lumen*, but which, on the other hand, is quite unable to explain what this "ornament" can be that is added to naked truth— these things have sometimes been discussed as though the impasse arrived at here were particularly Ramist. It is not at all; it is the heritage of the scientism of the medieval arts course and of the structure of the university educational system.

[28] Rosemond Tuve, *Elizabethan and Metaphysical Imagery*, Chicago, 1947, p. 331.
[29] Ramus, *Dialecticae institutiones*, Paris, 1543, fol. 18^v.

Back of the Ramist rhetoric and the Puritan's notion of a plain style is the arts course in which logical development takes its curiously quantified form as a preparation, not for metaphysics, but for Newtonian physics. The Puritan doctrine of plain style is puzzling, not because it rests on some well-thought-out theory plunged deep in a metaphysics which escapes our blunt twentieth-century minds, but because it rests on attitudes and habits of conceptualization which its proponents did not understand very well and are not necessarily consistent, as a well-thought-out theory should be, but which are none the less subtly connected with the whole complex intellectual ferment producing the modern mind.

In the university educational system as a whole, logic and linguistics in general were occasionally given a well-thought-out treatment, but this was for the most part a peripheral treatment occasioned by work in theology or medicine. It is in the interest in symbolism in these traditions that the seeds of a mature theory of language are contained. The theologians were interested in "typology," by which the meaning of Old Testament history is seen as matured in the actual historical events of the life of Christ. The physicians were interested in the human body and in all physical reality from a physical and symbolic view simultaneously. A voluminous tradition specializes in analogies between the human body, or microcosm, and the macrocosm, or universe, as well as in the general symbolic valences of the physical world. Thomas Browne's treatise on the mysteries of the quincunx is exceptional, not because of its subject, but rather because, through some happy accident, unlike the hundreds of similar treatises, it is not written in Latin. This whole medical tradition has, of course, obvious connections—psychological, philosophical, and, I am inclined to think, also historical—with the present work of Jung and others on symbolic archetypes.

Within these two traditions, logical and rhetorical theory could retain or regain the suppleness which the mehano-scientistic bent of arts-course scholasticism was constantly tending to deny it. Here we find persistent, if not ubiquitous, exploitations of Aristotle's notion of the various kinds of logic—scientific, rhetorical, dialectic, and sophistic —which, as Peter of Spain's *Summulae* show us, the arts course tended to nullify and which Ramus makes the central objective to be destroyed by his curricular reform. But even when rhetorical theory was allowed a promising suppleness, it seldom overcame the handicap of being a subject for little boys, and, however supple, it tended to remain rudimentary.

This is the intellectual setting in which Ramism arose—I speak of the setting in terms of theory and the determinants of theory. The teaching and the practice of rhetoric, at least by the Renaissance, was another thing. But Ramism was, before everything else, a theoretical reform, and its practical effects were shaped, rather more than is usual with such things, by its theory.

All this we should have been prepared more readily to see had we entertained so many undemonstrable presuppositions concerning the past out of which grew Ramism and much in the Renaissance, that is, concerning the nature of arts scholasticism—which, considered in terms of the large number of those who studied it, was most scholasticism. Once we become aware of this background in many of its implications, we can see why Ramism—with its ideas opened like baskets, its arguments "glued" together in judgments, its methodized syllogisms, and its tropes and figures strung deftly through the whole—can often wear an expression so strangely familiar to us. The Ramist view of language exhibits the hallmarks of mechanistic views always, such as we find two centuries later in the associationist philosophers and can find all about us today: an engaging downrightness, based more or less obviously on rather crude spatial analogies which reveal themselves by a passion for charts or sometimes for more subtle schematizations, which turn out nevertheless to be little more than caricatures. In Ramus's case the characteristic symptom, although not by any means the most profound manifestation, of the real state of affairs is the dichotomized table—there are enough of these in print in Ramist works to extend, if laid end-to-end, for miles. These are the things which have their serviceableness in presenting material to youth, but which, philosophically, are so lethal, rendering unwelcome anything which cannot be so represented. For reasons which are assignable, but cannot be gone into here, undue attachment to these spatial images seems to be psychologically inevitable in any mentality which makes too much of distinctions or of "clear" ideas; in this way Ramus is the forerunner, if not exactly the cause, of Descartes.

But for all its naïveté, the quantitative manner of conceptualization is not to be neglected. It deserves serious study. Ramism alerts us to the fact that the psychological preparations for the modern specialization in quantity, in mathematical physics and all that goes with it, good and bad, has roots which are far deeper and rather more definitely assignable than we have thought. Ramist rhetoric is an event in an historical and psychological framework which we can grasp only by bettering our notions of what its antecedents really were.

I. 9

Belief and the Suspension
of Disbelief*

M. H. ABRAMS

Cornell University

NOMINALLY THE current preoccupation with the role of belief in literature goes back only some thirty-five years, to the issue as raised by I. A. Richards and debated by T. S. Eliot, Middleton Murry, and the many other critics and philosophers who took up the challenge. In fact, however, Richards's theory is a late stage in a perennial concern about the clash between what poets say and what their readers believe to be true. The problem of belief, in one or another formulation, is no less ancient than criticism, and it has always been argued in terms of "knowledge," "truth," and "reality," which are the cruxes of all philosophical disagreement. After twenty-five centuries, there seems greater weight than comfort in T. S. Eliot's weary conclusion that "the problem of belief is very complicated and probably quite insoluble." [1] But a review of the conditions of this endless debate may itself offer some possibility of headway. We have inherited from the past not only the problem, but the largely unvoiced aims and assumptions which control the way it is posed and answered, and to know how we got where we are may help us to decide where we are to go from here.

It all began, of course, with Plato. Plato's cosmos is the frame for the play of his dialectic, and cosmos and dialectic cooperate to force the consideration of poetry as a rival of philosophy for access to the

---

* Read at the *Institute in* 1957. Published in *Institute Essays: Literature and Belief*, 1958.

[1] *Selected Essays, 1917–1932* (London, 1932), p. 138.

true and the good, but under conditions—since poetry is an imitation
of an imitation of the criterion Ideas—in which it is hopelessly out of
the running. And how remarkably acquiescent the interlocutor in *The
Republic* is to this management of the question! "Yes," "Quite true,"
"Just so," "That follows," "I agree." But suppose he had interjected:
"Now look here, Socrates. I see your game. You've got me trapped in a
set of premises by which the end is foreordained. But I refuse to consider poetry in a context in which it must aim to do what philosophy
can do better. I propose instead that when we consider poetry, we consider it as poetry and not another thing."

Had the interlocutor delivered himself thus, the history of criticism
might well have been radically different. It seems quite plain now that
Aristotle's *Poetics* transferred the discussion to precisely these new
grounds, but silently, so that over the centuries Aristotle has been interpreted as refuting or correcting Plato's theory on its own terms. As
a consequence literary criticism has been maneuvered into a defensive
stance from which it has never entirely recovered. Alone among the
major disciplines the theory of literature has been mainly a branch of
apologetics; and we shall mistake the emphases of many major critical
documents, whether or not they are labeled a Defense of Poetry, if we
fail to recognize the degree to which they have constituted the rebuttal
in a persistent debate. The positions most strongly defended have
shifted, to meet the threat from one or another enterprise claiming
exclusive access to the kind of truth poetry was supposed to pretend to:
philosophy, history, Christian theology and morals, and then, in the
seventeenth century, the New Philosophy. But in every age the seemingly positive principles of criticism have been designed for the defense
of poetry, and usually, as in the Platonic dialogues, on a terrain selected
by the opposition.

Since the eighteenth century the situation has stabilized, for the
great and portentous claimant to truth has become, and has remained,
science. Consonantly, attempts to save the credit of poetry have been
directed mainly against the pretensions to universal application of
scientific standards of language, and against scientific criteria for judging the validity of all claims to knowledge and value. And quite early
the pressure of a scientific culture gave their characteristic shape to
two types of poetic theory which set the conditions under which we
still for the most part undertake to deal with the problem of belief in
literature. The first theory conceives poetry to be a special language

whose function is to express and evoke feelings, and which is therefore immune from the criteria of valid reference, as well as from the claims on our belief, appropriate to the language of science. The second theory conceives a poem to be an autonomous world all its own, and therefore immune from the requirement that it correspond to our knowledge and beliefs about the world revealed by sciience.

Early in the nineteenth century Jeremy Bentham, heir to the traditional English semantics of scientific language, charged that by the standards of "logical truth" poetic statements are false. "All poetry is misrepresentation." "Indeed, between poetry and truth there is a natural opposition: false morals, fictitious nature." [2] John Stuart Mill, a disciple of Bentham who became an ardent defender of poetry, although in terms controlled by the semantics of positivism, defined poetry as "the expression or uttering forth of feeling" and therefore what he called the "logical opposite" of "matter of fact or science." Accordingly, while science "addresses itself to belief" by "presenting a proposition to the understanding," poetry acts by "offering interesting objects of contemplation to the sensibilities"; so that the reader can accept it, without belief, for the sake of its emotional effects. Poetic illusion, he wrote, "consists in extracting from a conception known not to be true . . . the same benefit to the feelings which would be derived from it if it were a reality." [3]

By Matthew Arnold's time religion had become codefendant with poetry against the attack of positivism; and Arnold, accepting as inevitable the demise of dogmatic religion because it "has attached its emotion to the fact, and now the fact is failing it," transferred its function to poetry because (like Mill) he regarded it as emotively efficacious independently of its truth or the reader's belief. For "poetry attaches its emotion to the idea; the idea *is* the fact." And I. A. Richards, who used this pronouncement from "The Study of Poetry" as the epigraph to his *Science and Poetry,* expanded upon it in terms of a more developed form of the positivist semantics he shared with Hobbes, Bentham, and Mill. All language divides into two kinds. On the one side is "scientific statement," whose truth is ultimately a matter of correspondence "with the fact to which it points." On the other side is

[2] J. S. Mill, "Bentham," in *Early Essays by John Stuart Mill,* ed. by J. W. M. Gibbs (London, 1897), p. 208; Jeremy Bentham, *The Rationale of Reward,* in *Works,* ed. by John Bowring (Edinburgh, 1843), II, 253–54.

[3] *Early Essays,* pp. 202, 208; *Letters of John Stuart Mill,* ed. by H. S. R. Elliot (London, 1910), II, 358.

"emotive utterance," including poetry, which is composed of "pseudo-statements" whose function is not to assert truths but to organize our feelings and attitudes. And since we have learned to free the emotional efficacy of poetry from belief, poetry must take over the function of ordering our emotional life hitherto performed by the pseudo statements of religion.[4]

In our age, dominated by the odd assumption that all discourse which is not science must be of a single kind, many opponents of positivism fall in with the tendency to conflate religion with poetry in a common opposition to science. But this tactic will not do, whether we hold, with the positivists, that poetry will replace religion because it works without belief, or, with the antipositivists, that poetry and religion share access to a special kind of nonscientific truth beyond logic and the law of excluded middle. On this distinguished panel I stand as an infidel *in partibus fidelium*, but I will venture the opinion that it is equally unjust to religion to poetize it and to poetry to sanctify it. Religion is patently not science, but no more is it poetry; and it can survive only if granted its own function and processes and claims upon belief. As for poetry, I shall soon maintain that it depends for its efficacy upon evoking a great number of beliefs. Besides, it must inevitably paralyze our responsiveness and ready delight to approach a poem as a way to salvation—in Richards's words, as "capable of saving us." [5]

To the view that poetry is an emotive use of language, the most common alternative is the view that poetry is a world *sui generis*, to be experienced and valued on its own terms, independently of its correspondence to reality or of its emotive and moral effects on the reader. This concept also originated as a defensive tactic, this time against the demand that the materials of poetry be limited to the objects and possibilities of the empirical world revealed by the new science. In rebuttal eighteenth-century proponents of the mythical and marvelous in poetry developed the possibilities of the old Renaissance analogy—the most influential new concept in postclassical criticism—between the poet and the Creator. The poet, it was said, emulates God by creating a "second world" which is not an imitation of the real world, but a world of its own kind, subject only to its own laws, and exhibiting not the truth of correspondence, but only the truth of coherence, or purely internal consistency. "Poetic truth," as Richard Hurd said in 1762, is not the truth to "the known and experienced course of affairs in this

---

[4] *Science and Poetry* (London, 1926), pp. 56–61. [5] *Ibid.*, p. 82.

world" demanded by Hobbes. For "the poet has a world of his own, where experience has less to do than consistent imagination." [6]

The radical implications of the concept of a poem as an *alter mundus* were exploited most fully in Germany, especially after Baumgarten for the first time set out to construct a philosophy of the fine arts in general, for which he coined the term "aesthetics." In Baumgarten's formulation, the end of a work of art is not to reflect reality, nor to foster morality or yield pleasure; "the aesthetic end is the perfection of sensuous cognition . . . that is, beauty." Produced by a poet who is "like a maker or a creator . . . the poem ought to be a sort of world," related to the real world "by analogy." Poetic fiction is "heterocosmic," consisting of things possible in another world than the one we live in, and subject therefore not to the criterion of strict philosophic truth, but only to the criterion of "heterocosmic truth"; that is, self-consistency and the maximum internal coherence.[7] In his *Critique of Judgment* Kant added the corollary ideas that a beautiful work of art is experienced as an end in itself, by an act purely contemplative, disinterested, and free from any reference to desire, will, or the reality and utility of the object.

Now that these discoveries have become so commonplace that they seem the intuitions of common sense, it is easy to derogate the attempts of aesthetic philosophers to talk about all the arts at once. But the achievement of eighteenth-century aestheticians was immensely important: they made current a set of premises enabling the defenders of poetry to meet the charges of Plato and his successors, not on grounds that poetry can compete successfully with the philosopher, the scientist, and the moralist, but on grounds that poetry is entirely its own kind of thing, with its own laws, its own reason for being, and its particular mode of excellence. No wonder, then, that in the nineteenth century these ideas were enthusiastically seized upon and deployed (at first mainly on hearsay) by French and English theorists of art for art's sake in their strenuous counterattack against the demands for truth, morality, and utility in art by philosophical positivists, literary conservatives, and a society of Philistines. In his inaugural lecture at Oxford, "Poetry for Poetry's Sake," A. C. Bradley stripped this theory

---

[6] *Letters on Chivalry and Romance* (London, 1911), pp. 137–39.

[7] *Meditationes philosophicae* (1735), §§ 51–69; *Aesthetica* (1750, 1758), §§ 14, 441, 511–18, 585. See also Karl Philipp Moritz, *Ueber die bildende Nachahmung des Schönen* (1788).

of its curious theological and ethical adjuncts about art as a religion and life as a work of art, and gave it a classic statement. The experience of poetry, he says, "is an end in itself," and "its *poetic* value is this intrinsic worth alone." For the nature of poetry

is to be not a part, nor yet a copy, of the real world . . . but to be a world by itself, independent, complete, autonomous; and to possess it fully you must enter that world, conform to its laws, and ignore for the time the beliefs, aims, and particular conditions which belong to you in the other world of reality.

And since this poetic world is an indissoluble unity of content and form, he decries in criticism "the heresy of the separable substance." [8]

For a lecture delivered more than a half-century ago, this sounds remarkably up-to-date. It should indeed, for its primary assumptions continue to be the grounds of the most familiar contemporary criticism. We assent heartily to Eliot's dictum that poetry is "autotelic" and to be considered "as poetry and not another thing." [9] We affirm with Ransom "the autonomy of the work itself as existing for its own sake," [10] and conceive the poem to be a self-sustaining entity—variously described as "an object in itself" or an "independent poetic structure" (Brooks) or an "icon" (Wimsatt) or "a kind of world or cosmos" (Austin Warren)—although, in accordance with the modern *furor semanticus*, we tend to think of the poetic other-world as a universe of discourse rather than a universe of creatures, setting, and events. And by a tactic reminiscent of A. C. Bradley's "heresy of the separable substance," and of "the heresy of the didactic" exposed by a still earlier proponent of art for art, Edgar Allan Poe, we severely proscribe a variety of heresies and fallacies which threaten to violate the independence and integrity of the sovereign poem.

This austere dedication to the poem *per se* has produced an unprecedented and enlightening body of verbal explication. But it threatens also to commit us to the concept of a poem as a language game, or as a floating Laputa, insulated from life and essential human concerns in a way that accords poorly with our experience in reading a great work of literature. Hence, I think, the persistent struggle in recent criticism to save the autonomy of a poem, yet to anchor it again to the world beyond itself and to reengage it with the moral conscious-

---

[8] *Oxford Lectures On Poetry* (London, 1950), pp. 4–6, 17.
[9] *Selected Essays*, p. 30; *The Sacred Wood* (London, 1950), p. viii.
[10] *The World's Body* (New York, 1938), p. 343.

ness of the reader. One example is the frequent insistence that a poem is cognitive and yields valid knowledge, although in the final analysis the knowledge a poem yields turns out to be coterminous with the poem itself. The poem's value, as Allen Tate puts it, "is a cognitive one; it is sufficient that here, in the poem, we get knowledge of a whole object." [11] By a procedure which has been a constant corollary of the view that a poem is a world in itself ever since it was expounded by Baumgarten and his contemporaries, the truth of a poem is interpreted to be a truth of inner coherence, and the relation of the poetic world to the real world is conceived to be not a relation of correspondence, but of analogy. Just as A. C. Bradley declared at the beginning of this century that poetry and life "are parallel developments that nowhere meet . . . they are analogues," so John Crowe Ransom's cognitive claim for poetry comes down to the proposal that the structure and texture of a poem are an analogical reminder that the world's body is "denser and more refractory" than the "docile and virtuous" world represented by poetry's great opposite, science.[12] And if I read him correctly, W. K. Wimsatt's point about literature as "a form of knowledge" is that poetic truth is inner coherence and the relation of a poem to the world is one of analogy. In his words, "the dimension of coherence is by various techniques of implication greatly enhanced and thus generates an extra dimension of correspondence to reality, the symbolic or analogical." [13]

We are particularly uneasy today about the pressure of the doctrine of poetic autonomy toward the conclusion of art for art; with a candor that is rare in contemporary discussion of this issue, Allen Tate affirms "that poetry finds its true usefulness in its perfect inutility." [14] The attempt to break out of the sealed verbal world of the poem-as-such is, I think, one cardinal motive for the current insistence that, in all poems which are more than trivially agreeable, the structure of symbols, images, and meanings is governed by a "theme." In practise this

[11] *On the Limits of Poetry* (New York, 1948), p. 48.

[12] Bradley, *Oxford Lectures*, p. 6; Ransom, *The New Criticism* (Norfolk, Conn., 1941), pp. 43, 281.

[13] *The Verbal Icon* (Lexington, Ky., 1954), p. 241. E. M. Forster wrote, in *Anonymity* (London, 1925), p. 14: In reading a poem, "we have entered a universe that only answers to its own laws, supports itself, internally coheres, and has a new standard of truth. Information is true if it is accurate. A poem is true if it hangs together." See also Philip Leon, "Aesthetic Knowledge," in *The Problems of Aesthetics*, ed. by Eliseo Vivas and Murray Krieger (New York, 1953).

[14] *On the Limits of Poetry*, p. 113.

theme frequently turns out to be a moral or philosophical commonplace which bears a startling likeness to the "moral," or governing
proposition, once postulated by the didactic theorists of the Renaissance
and neoclassic ages. Homer, declared Dryden in his Preface to *Troilus
and Cressida*, undertook to "insinuate into the people" the moral "that
union preserves a commonwealth and discord destroys it; Sophocles, in
his *Oedipus*, that no man is to be accounted happy before his death.
'Tis the moral that directs the whole action of a play to one center."
The difference is that, according to the modern critic, the theme subsists only in the concrete embodiment of the poem, as an ownerless,
unasserted, nonreferential, uncredited, and thoroughly insulated something which serves nevertheless to inform the meanings of a poem both
with their unity and their moral "seriousness," "maturity," and "relevance." This existential oddity has been engendered by the opposing
conditions of poetic autonomy and poetic relevance under which
modern critics typically conduct their inquiry into the relations between poetry and life. As W. K. Wimsatt describes the conditions
governing his essay on "Poetry and Morals": "We inquire . . . about
the work so far as it can be considered by itself as a body of meaning.
Neither the qualities of the author's mind nor the effects of a poem
upon a reader's mind should be confused with the moral quality of the
meaning expressed by the poem itself." [15]

I confess that my own view of the matter involves something like
this divided premise, with its attendant difficulties. It seems to me that
our experience in reading serious literature, when uninhibited by theoretical prepossessions, engages the whole mind, including the complex
of common sense and moral beliefs and values deriving from our experience in this world. Yet I also think it essential to save the basic insight of aesthetic theory since the eighteenth century: that a poem is a
self-sufficient whole which is to be read for its own sake, independently
of the truths it may communicate or the moral and social effects it may
exert, and that its intrinsic value constitutes its reason for existing as a
poem and not as something else. I am also uncomfortably aware that
this looks very much like an attempt to have art for art's sake and eat it
too.

I would suggest that the apparent antinomy comes from relying
too implicitly on aesthetic ideas inherited from a polemical past. The
persistently defensive position of criticism, and its standard procedure
of combating charges against poetry by asserting their contraries, has

[15] *Verbal Icon*, p. 87.

forced it into an either-or, all-or-none choice that breeds dilemmas: either language is scientific or it is purely emotive; either a poem corresponds to ths world or it is a world entirely its own; either poetry has a moral aim or it is totally beyond judgment of good or evil; either all our beliefs are relevant to reading poetry, or all beliefs must be suspended. What we obviously need is the ability to make more distinctions and finer discriminations; and perhaps these will follow if we substitute for concepts developed mainly as polemical weapons a positive view designed specifically for poetic inquiry and analysis.

Suppose, then, that we set out from the observation that a poem is about people. Or a bit more elaborately, that a poem presents one or more persons recognizably like those in this world, but imposes its artistic differences by rendering the characters and their perceptions, thought, and actions so as to enhance their inherent interest and whatever effects the poem undertakes to achieve. This statement is not to be understood as contradicting the statements that a poem is an emotive use of language, or that a poem constitutes a verbal universe. It is offered merely as an alternative point of critical departure for inquiry into such questions as the role of belief in the appreciation of poetry. Furthermore, this viewpoint is as old as Aristotle's *Poetics*, and will produce no radical novelties. But I think the issue of morality and belief in poetry has been made to seem unnecessarily recondite because of the common tendency to define a poem as a special kind of language, or a special structure of words and meanings, and then to slip in characters and actions quietly through a back door.

I propose also not to begin with universal statements about "all poetry" or "all art," but to proceed inductively, beginning with single poetic passages and using these, in Wittgenstein's parlance, as "paradigm cases" on which to base only such generalizations as they promise to support. Convenient instances to hand are the few examples of poetic statements which have been mooted again and again in discussions of belief, although with little heed to their differences in kind and usually as illustrations for a foregone conclusion. The examples are: "Beauty is truth"; "Ripeness is all"; "In His will is our peace"; and "Thou best philosopher . . . Mighty Prophet! Seer blest!"

I

"Beauty is truth, truth beauty" is not asserted by Keats, either as a statement or as a pseudo-statement. The Grecian Urn, after remaining obdurately mute under a hail of questions, unexpectedly gives voice to this proposition near the end of the poem. In discussions of the problem of belief the significance of this obvious fact is often over-looked or minimized. Middleton Murry, for example, although he ob-serves that the speaker is the Urn, goes on immediately to reconstruct the biographical occasion Keats himself had for such a comment, and then (like so many other critics) evolves an elaborate aesthetico-onto-logical theory to demonstrate that the statement is philosophically valid, and merits assent.[16] For his part, I. A. Richards describes "Beauty is truth" as "the expression of a certain blend of feelings," and asks us to accept such emotive expressions without belief; and T. S. Eliot replies that he would be glad to do so, except that "the statement of Keats" seems to him so obtrusively meaningless that he finds the under-taking impossible.[17]

There is also a second and more important speaker in the poem. The whole of the *Ode on a Grecian Urn*, in fact, consists of the ut-terance of this unnamed character, whose situation and actions we follow as he attends first to the whole, then to the sculptured parts, and again to the whole of the Urn; and who expresses in the process not only his perceptions, but his thoughts and feelings, and thereby dis-covers to us a determinate temperament. By a standard poetic device we accept without disbelief, he attributes to the Urn a statement about beauty and truth which is actually a thought that the Urn evokes in him. How we are to take the statement, therefore, depends not only on its status as an utterance, in that place, by the particular Urn, but beyond that as the penultimate stage, dramatically rendered, in the meditation of the lyric speaker himself.

Obviously the earlier part of the *Ode* by no means gives the Urn a character that would warrant either its profundity or its reliability as a moral philosopher. In the mixed attitudes of the lyric speaker toward the Urn the playfulness and the pity, which are no less evident than the envy and the admiration, imply a position of superior understanding:

> Bold lover, never, never canst thou kiss,
> Though winning near the goal—yet, do not grieve;
> She cannot fade, though thou hast not thy bliss. . . .

The perfection represented on the Urn is the perdurability of the specious present, which escapes the "woe" of our mutable world only by

[16] "Beauty is Truth," *The Symposium*, I (1930), 466–501.
[17] Richards, *Practical Criticism* (1930), pp. 187, 278–79; Eliot, *Selected Essays*, p. 256.

surrendering any possibility of consummation and by trading grieving flesh for marble. The Urn, then, speaks from the limited perspective of a work of Grecian art; and it is from the larger viewpoint of this life, with its possibilities and its sorrows, that the lyric speaker has the last word, addressed to the figures on the Urn:

That is all
Ye know on earth, and all ye need to know.

The Urn has said, "Only the beautiful exists, and all that exists is beautiful"—but not, the speaker replies, in life, only in that sculptured Grecian world of noble simplicity where much that humanly matters is sacrificed for an enduring Now.[18]

I entirely agree, then, with Professor Brooks in his explication of the *Ode*, that "Beauty is truth" is not meant "to compete with . . . scientific and philosophical generalizations," but is to be considered as a speech "in character" and "dramatically appropriate" to the Urn. I am uneasy, however, about his final reference to "the world-view, or 'philosophy,' or 'truth' of the poem as a whole." [19] For the poem as a whole is equally an utterance by a dramatically presented speaker, and none of its statements is proffered for our endorsement as a philosophical generalization of unlimited scope. They are all, therefore, to be apprehended as histrionic elements which are "in character" and "dramatically appropriate," for their inherent interest as stages in the evolution of an artistically ordered, hence all the more emotionally effective, experience of a credible human being.

Is an appreciation of the *Ode*, then, entirely independent of the reader's beliefs? Surely not. As it evolves, the poem makes constant call on a complex of beliefs which are the product of ordinary human experiences with life, people, love, mutability, age, and art. These subsist less in propositional form than in the form of unverbalized attitudes, propensities, sentiments, and dispositions; but they stand ready to precipitate into assertions the moment they are radically challenged, whether in the ordinary course of living or in that part of living we

---

[18] For another instance in which Keats uses "truth" as equivalent to "existence," see *The Letters of John Keats*, ed. by M. B. Forman (London, 1947), p. 67. I prefer attributing "That is all / Ye know on earth . . ." to the lyric speaker rather than to the Urn, because the former reading is at least as probable in the context and makes a richer poem. But even if we take the whole of the last two lines to be asserted by the Urn, the point holds that their significance is qualified by the nature imputed to the speaker.

[19] *The Well-Wrought Urn* (New York, 1947), pp. 141–42, 151–52.

call reading poetry. Kant's claims, as I have said, seem valid, that the apprehension of a work of art, as opposed to our ordinary cognitive and practical concerns, is properly contemplative, disinterested, and free from will and desire, and that the function of presentative art is not to persuade us to beliefs or actions, but to be a terminal good. But here is where we need to make an essential discrimination. These observations are valid in so far as we are concerned to make a broad initial distinction between poetic and nonpoetic experience, and to separate specifically poetic values from effects outside the experience of the poem itself. But when applied to our apprehension of what goes on *inside* a poem, they seem to me, as often interpreted, to be not merely misleading, but directly contrary to aesthetic experience. If the poem works, our appreciation of the matters it presents is not aloofly contemplative, but actively engaged. We are not disinterested, but deeply concerned with the characters and what they say and do, and we are interested in a fashion that brings into play our entire moral economy and expresses itself continuously in attitudes of approval or disapproval, sympathy or antipathy. And though the poet is not concerned to persuade us to take up positions outside the poem, it is his constant concern to persuade us to concur with the common-sense and moral positions presupposed by the poem, to take the serious seriously and the comic comically, and to acquiesce in the probability of the thoughts, choices, and actions which are represented to follow from a given character. All these results, however distinguishable from our responses in practical life, depend in great part on beliefs and dispositions which we bring to the poem from life; and these operate not as antagonists to our aesthetic responses, but as the indispensable conditions for them, and therefore as constitutive elements in our appreciation of the poem as a poem. The skillful poet contrives which of our beliefs will be called into play, to what degree, and with what emotional effect. Given a truly impassive reader, all his beliefs suspended or anesthetized, he would be as helpless, in his attempt to endow his work with interest and power, as though he had to write for an audience from Mars.

So with Keats's *Ode*. We accept without disbelief the given situation of the speaker confronting an Urn, and we attend delightedly to the rich texture and music of his speech. But if what follows is to be more than superficially effective, we must take the lyric speaker's emotional problem seriously, as possessing dignity and importance according to the criteria of ordinary experience. By the same criteria, we must find the speaker himself credible and winning—sensitive, intelligent, warm, yet (unlike many of the profoundly solemn commentators on his utterance) able to meditate the woes of this life and the limitations of art with philosophic lucidity and a very lively sense of the irony of the human situation, and even of the humor of his dialogue with an Urn. Above all, we must so recognize ourselves and our lot in him as to consent imaginatively to his experience until it is resolved, in both artistic and human terms, in a way that is formally complete, hence beautiful, and intellectually and emotionally satisfying.

II

Whatever the case may be with the lyric, it had always seemed obvious that the words of a drama constitute speeches by determinate characters until several decades ago, when by a notable stratagem we critics succeeded in dehumanizing even Shakespeare's tragedies by converting them into patterns of thematic imagery. But I am bound by my critical premise to take "Ripeness is all" in the old-fashioned way, as a statement by a person in a given situation rather than as a moment in the dialectic of a vegetational symbol.

The statement is Edgar's, and it is not uttered in philosophical humor as a summary philosophy of life, but with sharp impatience, for an urgently practical purpose, at a desperate moment in the action. The battle has been lost, Lear and Cordelia captured, and Edgar must rally his blind father from a recurrence of his suicidal impulse, in the hopeless decision to bide and be captured:

EDGAR: Give me thy hand! Come on!
GLOUCESTER: No further, sir. A man may rot even here.
EDGAR: What, in ill thoughts again? Men must endure
        Their going hence, even as their coming hither;
        Ripeness is all. Come on.

The question of our giving or withholding assent to this statement, taken as a universal philosophic predication, has arisen only because it has been pulled out of Shakespeare's context and put in the artificial context of our own discussions of the problem of belief. In its original place we respond to the speech, in the curt perfection of its phrasing, as following from Edgar's character, appropriate both to the bitter events preceding and to the exigency of the moment, and also, it should be noted, as an element in the action of people whose fortunes we strongly favor.

A popular opinion about Shakespeare's objectivity seems to place his characters completely outside the purview of our moral beliefs and judgments. It derives ultimately from Kant's concept of disinterested aesthetic contemplation, came to England by way of Coleridge and Hazlitt, and received its best-known formulation in Keats's comment on Shakespeare's "negative capability" and his claim that the poetical character "has as much delight in conceiving an Iago as an Imogen. What shocks the virtuous philosopher delights the camelion poet," for whom all ends "in speculation." [20] Rightly understood, the concept is true and important. We apprehend Shakespeare's villains with a purity and fullness of appreciation possible only in art, where we see the characters from within, and independently of the practical effects on us of their being what they are. But the aesthetic attitude, though different from the practical attitude, is not so different as all that. In Dr. Johnson's phrase, the attitude is one of "tranquillity without indifference"; our aesthetic judgments, while not those of a participant, remain those of a partisan. We may take as great delight in Shakespeare's villain as in his hero, but we are constantly aware that the villain is a villain and the hero a hero. I. A. Richards has said in *Science and Poetry* that we must have no beliefs if we are to read *King Lear*. But *King Lear* presents a conflict of characters in which the author must make us take sides; and he is able to do so only by presupposing that we bring to the work deep-rooted moral beliefs and values which will cause us instinctively to attach our good will to some characters and ill will to others, and therefore to respond appropriately to their changing fortunes with hope and disappointment, delight and sadness, pity and terror.

Like all the greatest poets Shakespeare pays the human race the compliment of assuming that it is, in its central moral consciousness, sound. So from the opening words of the play we are invited to accept without disbelief the existence of King Lear and his three daughters, but to believe, and never for a moment to doubt—however the violence of circumstance may shake the assurance of this or that character in the play—that a king, while regal, ought to possess human understanding, moral penetration, and a modicum of humility, and that daughters should be loyal, kindly, and truthful, not treacherous, sadistic, and murderous. Shakespeare does not lay out Dante's geometrical distinc-

[20] *Letters of Keats*, pp. 72, 227–28.

tions between the utterly damnable and the merely damnable, but he does presuppose that we find good to be admirable and evil abhorrent, in the nuance of their manifestations in concrete behavior. We relish a villain like Edmund, skillfully rendered by the poet in all his unillusioned intelligence, self-insight, and vitality. But if, through some lapse in the author or some obtuseness or obliquity in ourselves, we remain indifferent, paring our fingernails, or so lose our moral bearings as to attach our sympathies to Edmund and the pelican daughters instead of to Lear and Gloucester (however flawed) and to Cordelia, Edgar, and Kent, then the play collapses into an amorphous mass without catastrophe or catharsis.

III

Far from Dante himself asserting that "In His will is our peace," he portrays Piccarda making the assertion to him, in smiling commiseration for the narrowness and pettiness of his earthly mind, and in a tone as near reproof as is possible for a spirit in felicity. For Dante has just inquired whether Piccarda is not dissatisfied with her place on the lowest of the heavenly spheres, and she replies that God draws all wills to what he wills, so that "In His will is our peace; it is that sea to which all moves." And Dante is enlightened and convinced: "Clear was it then to me how every where in heaven is Paradise."

This statement, then, like our earlier examples, is uttered in a dramatic context. There are, however, important differences in its literary conditions. The poem is not lyric or dramatic, but narrative in form; the author himself plays a role both as narrator and as one of his own characters; the total assertion this time involves a theological subproposition ("God exists"); and the passage occurs in a work of which the aim is not presentative, but didactic.

So Dante himself insists in his *Letter to Can Grande*. His work, he says there, is allegorical; its purpose "is to remove those living in this life" from misery to happiness; and its genus is ethical, "for the whole and the part are devised not for the sake of speculation but of possible action" (§§ 7–16). The *Divine Comedy*, then, like *Paradise Lost*, *Prometheus Unbound*, *A Doll's House*, and *Lady Chatterley's Lover*, is a work of literature specifically designed to dramatize and empower a set of beliefs. In it Piccarda's statement about God's will (in Dante's words) is one of the many things "that have great utility and delight" which are asked from the blessed souls in heaven "who see all the truth" (§ 33). The function of this statement is not, like that of "Ripeness is all," merely to instance character and advance the action, but to render in a dramatic, and therefore in the most efficacious possible way—as a truth achieved through error—a universal doctrine which is one aspect of the total theological truth propagated by the poem. For the first time in our discussion, accordingly, it becomes relevant to consider the relation of the reader's beliefs to his apprehension of an isolated poetic statement, offered for his assent. And the testimony of innumerable readers demonstrates that the passage can certainly be appreciated, and appreciated profoundly, independently of assent to its propositional truth. It touches sufficiently on universal experience— since all of us, whether Catholic, Protestant, or agnostic, know the heavy burden of individual decision—to enable us all to realize in imagination the relief that might come from saying to an infallible Providence, "Not my will, but Thine be done." This ability to take an assertion hypothetically, as a ground for imaginative experience, is one we in fact possess, and the business of critical theory is to recognize and confirm our reading skills, not to inhibit them by arguments from inadequate premises.

The *Divine Comedy*, however, raises other questions about the role of belief which are specific to thesis narratives. What Dante undertakes, as a poet, is so to realize his abstract theological scheme as to transform our intellectual assent, which he largely takes for granted, into emotional consent and practical action. This task sets him extraordinarily difficult artistic problems. To take one striking example, he must persuade us, against all our natural inclinations, that the Inferno, with its savage, repulsive, and exquisitely ingenious tortures protracted in perpetuity, is not only required by God's justice but (as the Gate of Hell announces) is entailed by God's "Primal Love." And the more credible and terrifying Dante, in his one function as moral monitor, makes the exemplary sufferings of the damned, the more difficult he makes his other task of winning our emotional consent to the thesis that God is Love, and Hell follows.

To this end Dante inserts himself, a mortal like us, into the poem as the experiential center through whose eyes and sensibility we invariably view Hell, as well as Purgatory and Heaven. And he exhibits with entire credibility the terror, the anguish, the incomprehension, the divided mind and emotions of the finite and temporal intelligence which is forced to look upon the universe under the aspect of eternity. He repeatedly misapplies his sympathy, feels an irrepressible admiration for the strength and dignity of some of the sinners in their ultimate adversity, weeps with such an abandon of fellow-feeling that Virgil must sternly reprimand him, and when he hears Francesca's tender story, faints with pity.

Dante's invention of himself is the supreme artistic achievement of the *Divine Comedy*. For Dante is a poet, though a didactic poet, and like any poet must endow his work with emotional power by engaging the sympathies and feelings of his readers with the matters he presents. To do so he appeals not merely to our theological beliefs (which we can yield or deny him) but also to beliefs and attitudes which are broader than any particular creed, and almost irresistibly compelling; for all of us, whatever our doctrinal differences, share the humanity of his central character and so follow and consent to his entirely human experiences, whether of the inhuman horrors of the doomed in Hell or the inhuman felicity of the Saints in Heaven.

Since he is, however, though a poet, a didactic poet, Dante relies on our prior beliefs and sentiments to involve us with the matters he shows forth, not as an end in itself, but as a means toward retroacting upon and reforming our beliefs and sentiments. If we circumvent him by stopping at the appreciation of what he shows forth, he would no doubt consider his great undertaking a failure. But for most of us the enjoyment of his didactic poem as, simply, a poem must perforce be enough.

IV

In our final example the question of belief is raised by the author himself, and in a form that makes it especially pertinent to contemporary literature. Wordsworth told Isabella Fenwick in 1843 that his *Ode: Intimations of Immortality* was based on experiences of his own childhood which he regarded "in the poem . . . as presumptive evidence of a prior state of existence." But he did not, he affirms, mean "to inculcate such a belief." "I took hold of the notion of preexistence as having sufficient foundation in humanity for authorizing me to make for my purpose the best use of it I could as a poet." [21]

[21] *The Poetical Works of William Wordsworth*, ed. by E. de Selincourt (Oxford, 1940–49), IV, 463–64.

With Wordsworth we impinge on our own age of self-consciousness about multiple choices in beliefs when, as T. S. Eliot declared, it
is impossible to say how far some poets "write their poetry because of
what they believe, and how far they believe a thing merely because they
see that they can make poetry out of it." [22] William Blake had already
created his own mythical system lest he "be enslaved by another man's,"
and thereby set the example for the spirits who came to give Yeats
"metaphors for poetry." [23] So Wordsworth tells us that he did not
mean to assert Platonic metempsychosis, but utilized it as an available
poetic premise, an as-if ground for a metaphorical structure by which to
manage what he called "the world of his own mind."

In this comment Wordsworth probably remembered what Coleridge had said about the *Ode* in the *Biographia Literaria* some twenty-
six years earlier. There Coleridge described poetic illusion as "that *negative* faith, which simply permits the images presented to work by their
own force, without either denial or affirmation of their real existence by
the judgment." In the same chapter he went on to justify Wordsworth's
use of Platonic preexistence as an uncredited poetic postulate, necessary
in order to deal with "modes of inmost being, to which . . . the attributes of time and space are inapplicable and alien, but which yet can
not be conveyed save in symbols of time and space." But Coleridge refused equal immunity from disbelief to those lines in the *Ode* hailing
a six-year-old child as "Thou best philosopher . . . Mighty Prophet!
Seer blest!" "In what sense," he demands, "can the magnificent attributes . . . be appropriated to a child, which would not make them
equally suitable to a bee, or a dog, or a field of corn?" For "the child is
equally unconscious of it as they." [24]

In his *Coleridge on Imagination*, I. A. Richards took Coleridge
severely to task for this limitation on the principle of suspended disbelief. For "we may," he said, "if we wish, take all the alleged attributes
of Wordsworth's child," and even their applicability to a field of corn,
"as fictions, as part of the myth." [25] But again, I think, we need to
make distinctions. While it is true that the poet may educe from the
myth of preexistence the conclusion that a child is the best philosopher,

22 "Poetry and Propaganda," in *Literary Opinion in America*, ed. by Morton
Dauwen Zabel (New York, 1951), p. 103.
23 Blake, *Jerusalem*, 1.10; Yeats, *A Vision* (New York, 1938), p. 8.
24 *Biographia Literaria*, ed. by J. Shawcross (Oxford, 1907), II, 107, 111–13,
120–21.
25 *Coleridge On Imagination* (London, 1934), pp. 135–37.

the myth by no means enforces this conclusion, as Plato's original use of it amply demonstrates. We must remember that Wordsworth's *Ode*, as he himself said, is not primarily about the myth; rather, the myth is auxiliary to the poetic management of events in this life to which every one, "if he would look back, could bear testimony." The lyric, we can say, presents the meditation of a man like ourselves, confronted abruptly by the need to adapt himself to a discovery which, in one or another form, is universally human: the discovery that in losing his youth he has lost the possibility of experiences on which he places the highest value. The postulate of the preexistence of the soul, realized in the great image of the rising and westering sun, affords him the spatial and temporal metaphors he needs in order to objectify, dignify, and re- solve what Coleridge called "a fact of mind." Ultimately the resolution depends on a shift in the point of view. From the vantage of the "im- perial palace" of our origin, the earth is a "prison-house" and the process of aging a cumulative loss. But from the alternate vantage of this earth this life—with its acquisitions of strength, sympathy, faith, and the philosophic mind, which spring from the very experience of human suffering—maturity is seen to have compensatory rewards; so that the metaphoric sun of the initial myth, which has risen "trailing clouds of glory," sets as the material sun we know in this world, yet takes another, if more sober, coloring from an eye "That hath kept watch o'er man's mortality."

What Coleridge queries is the credibility, in a poem which bears on our ordinary experience, and after Wordsworth has already described a very realistic six-year-old at his childish games, of the sudden apos- trophe:

> Thou best Philosopher, who yet dost keep
> Thy heritage, thou Eye among the blind,
> That, deaf and silent, read'st the eternal deep,
>
> . . . .
>   Mighty Prophet! Seer blest!

This is grandly said, but I understand and think I share Coleridge's sen- sation that, in its place and circumstances, it arouses counterbeliefs about real urchins which enforce an impression of what Coleridge called "mental bombast." If a child is a philosopher only in the sense that a field of corn is one, why the passionate and superlative encom- ium?

But this is a delicate decision, and I would not insist on it against contrary judgments by Richards, Brooks, and other expert readers. I want to insist, however, on the validity of Coleridge's implicit principle. A poet is entitled to his initial predication, or myth, or donnée, whether or not he is prepared to assert it outside the poem, and especially if, as Wordsworth said, it has "sufficient foundation in humanity" for his purpose "as a poet." But the inference is not justified that, from then on, anything goes. The poet must still win our imaginative consent to the aspects of human experience he presents, and to do so he cannot evade his responsibility to the beliefs and prepossessions of our common experience, common sense, and common moral consciousness. Even a phantasy such as the *Ancient Mariner*, Coleridge noted, requires a protagonist endowed with "a human interest and a semblance of truth sufficient to procure . . . that willing suspension of disbelief for the moment, which constitutes poetic faith"; [26] and in a more recent literary nightmare, Kafka put at the center of *The Trial* the matter-of-fact character K., to whose extraordinary experiences we acquiesce because his responses are so entirely ordinary.

The artistic cost of failure in this essential respect is demonstrated by the writings of accomplished craftsmen in which the substance is too inadequately human to engage our continuing interest, or which require our consent to positions so illiberal, or eccentric, or perverse that they incite counterbeliefs which inhibit the ungrudging "yes" that we grant to masterpieces. Blake's prophetic poems, for instance, lack what the *Divine Comedy* possesses—a human center of reference on which the imagination can rest; so that, fine isolated passages apart, and when we have exhausted their interest as symbolic puzzles, they become not a little tedious. Swinburne solicits our sympathy for modes of feeling so *outré* that a number of his lyrics remain brilliant items of literary *curiosa*, teetering on the edge of self-parody. In *The Counterfeiters* André Gide lavishes his intricate art to beguile us into taking seriously a resolution in which a nephew cohabits with his uncle, but the inherent risibility of an anomaly which is multiplied so ingeniously makes the resolution precarious. The difficulty is not in the literary material as such. Vladimir Nabokov's recent *Lolita*, which treats a somewhat parallel and even more scabrous matter, seems to me humanly right in inviting an attitude of horrified hilarity toward Humbert Humbert, on whom outrageous nature has forced the grotesque role

[26] *Biographia Literaria*, II, 6.

of parent and paramour to a bobby-soxer. Ernest Hemingway's *The Short Happy Life of Francis Macomber* is a triumph of spare artistry. The discovery, however, that all depends on the street-corner assumption that a man's physical courage, his sexual virility, and his dominance over his wife are mutually implicative, provokes a skepticism which makes the triumph a somewhat hollow one. We have been assured that D. H. Lawrence is one of the few English novelists in the Great Tradition; yet, for all the power of the individual scenes, perhaps other readers share my imperfect accord with many of his protagonists: the Aaron of *Aaron's Rod*, for example, who deserts his wife and children to give unfettered scope to his ego, only to end by delivering his will over to the writer Lilly, that peculiarly Laurentian version of the God-given Great Man.

Here we reach the twilight zone between reasoned discussion of a critical problem and the expression of idiosyncrasy, and it is important not to let disagreement about particular applications obscure the issue in question. The implicit but constant requisition of a serious literary work upon our predispositions and beliefs is not an end in itself, but a necessary means to engage our interest and feelings, in order to move them toward a resolution. Furthermore, the great writer does not merely play upon the beliefs and propensities we bring to literature from life, but sensitizes, enlarges, and even transforms them. But in order to get sufficient purchase on our moral sensibility to accommodate it to the matters he presents, any writer must first take that sensibility as he finds it. There is no escaping the circumstance that a poet must submit to the conditions of human nature in order to be their master.

I. 10

Patristic Exegesis in the Criticism of Medieval Literature: The Opposition*

E. TALBOT DONALDSON

Yale University

I AM NOT aware of any valid theoretical objection to the use of patristic exegesis in the criticism of medieval literature: if, as D. W. Robertson, Jr., says,[1] it is true that all serious poetry written by Christians during the Middle Ages promotes the doctrine of charity by using the same allegorical structure that the Fathers found in the Bible, then it follows that patristic exegesis alone will reveal the meaning of medieval poetry, and it would be sheer folly to disapprove of the fact. And even if one disbelieves, as I do, that the generality of good medieval poetry is such single-minded allegory, it would still be foolish to ignore the influence of the patristic tradition on medieval poetry, including that of the great poets Chaucer and Langland. But to admit such influence is not at all the same thing as admitting either that poetry which is nonallegorical in manner must be allegorical in meaning or that allegorical poetry which does not seem to be promoting charity must in fact be promoting it. There may be handful of such poems, but

---

* Read at the Institute in 1958. Published in *Selected Institute Papers: Critical Approaches to Medieval Literature*, 1960. In the same volume, see R. E. Kaske, *The Defense*; Charles Donahue, *Summation*.

[1] "Historical Criticism," in *English Institute Essays, 1950*, ed. by A. S. Downer (New York: Columbia University Press, 1951), p. 14.

I doubt that they are very good, or, if they are good, that they are good because they are cryptically allegorical or charity-promoting. In any case, I know of no such poems in Middle English, which is the only field in which I am competent. The patristic influence on Middle English poetry seems to me to consist in providing occasional symbols which by their rich tradition enhance the poetic contexts they appear in, but which are called into use naturally by those contexts and are given fresh meaning by them.

It is scarcely necessary to reassert the right of a poem to say what it means and mean what it says, and not what any one, before or after its composition, thinks it ought to say or mean. The existence of this right gives me, I hope, the right to test the validity of a kind of criticism which, it seems to me, imposes a categorical imperative upon the critic to operate in a certain way regardless of how the poem is telling him to operate. Since I lack a theoretical objection to patristic criticism as such, I can justify my opposition to it only by the invidious method of analyzing specific patristic critiques; but surely the burden of the proof is on the proponents of the critical method, who deny that I can understand what I read without possessing their special knowledge. To excuse my invidiousness I shall invoke a passage from the Scriptures: By their fruits ye shall know them. This I shall apply with twofold reference—though not, I trust, allegorically: that is, I shall apply it not only to those who try to prove the necessity for patristic exegesis, but also to the works in which this necessity is supposed to exist. I shall try to suggest that to give a reader a flat injunction to find one predetermined specific meaning in Middle English poetry is anything but the ideal way of preparing him to understand something old and difficult and complicated; for in his eagerness to find what must be there he will very likely miss what is there; and in so doing he may miss a meaning arising from the poem that is better than anything that exegesis is able to impose upon it. I hope I shall not offend any one if I suggest that while charity is the most important of doctrines it is not the only subject worth writing about, and that many poems may conduce to charity without mentioning it either specifically or allegorically. I may say rather ruefully that one of the natural disadvantages of the opponent of patristic criticism is that he is constantly being put in the position of seeming to deny that the Fall of Man has any dominant importance in the history of man's thought just because he denies that it has any relevance in a specific literary work. There are, indeed, moments when

I could wish that scholars in Middle English literature would remind themselves that they are not angels but anglicists.

Having gone so far, I might go on to suggest that the Fathers of the Church were less expert at devising rules for poets than they were at devising rules for Christians. I am not, however, entirely persuaded that they did devise rules for poets. The case for the generalization that medieval poets were enjoined by patristic authority to write nothing but allegories supporting charity seems rather less than crystal-clear. It was natural that the fourfold method of scriptural interpretation should exert an influence on secular poets, especially in view of its occasional extension to the great pagan poets; and of course some medieval poets were, like Dante, deeply interested in exalting Christian doctrine through their poetry and consciously used allegory—even, perhaps, multi-leveled allegory—to do so. But this does not mean that they all felt obliged to behave like Dante. I may quite well be wrong, but I cannot find that any of the patristic authorities ever clearly exhorted secular poets to write as the Bible had been written, even though the inference is pretty strong that some of them would have so exhorted if they had got round to it. But it seems to me that in order to find a definite injunction the modern critic has consciously to make a large inference.[2] Nor do I think that the case is much supported by the fact that in medieval schools reading was taught with attention to three

---

[2] See the historical treatment of the matter by Robertson in the essay cited above and in "Some Medieval Literary Terminology, with Special Reference to Chrétien de Troyes," *Studies in Philology*, XLVIII (1951), 669–92; also that by Robertson and B. F. Huppé in the first chapter of *Piers Plowman and Scriptural Tradition* (Princeton: Princeton University Press, 1951). The evidence for a genuine claim by Dante that he was writing on four levels in the *Divine Comedy* seems weakened by such recent studies as R. H. Green's "Dante's 'Allegory of Poets' and the Mediaeval Theory of Poetic Fiction," *Comparative Literature*, IX (1957), 118–28. For a clear explanation of the four-level method of reading the Scriptures, see Charles Donahue, "Patristic Exegesis: Summation," *Critical Approaches to Medieval Literature*, ed. Dorothy Bethurum (New York: Columbia University Press, 1960), pp. 78, 79, summarizing and citing St. Thomas: "Scripture has four meanings, literal or historical, allegorical, tropological or moral, and anagogical. . . . The literal or historical forms a class by itself; the others are all members of a second class, the spiritual or mystical. . . . [The spiritual senses] have nothing directly to do with words or meanings. They are derived from the things—events, persons—signified by the literal sense. 'When the things of the Old Law signify the New, there is an allegorical meaning; when things done by Christ or the *figurae* of Christ [the just who preceded Christ] are signs of what we ought to do, there is a moral [or tropological] meaning; finally, if one regards these things as pointing to eternal glory, there is an anagogical meaning'."

matters, the *littera* or text, the *sensus* or narrative statement, and the *sententia* or theme, since the identification of *sententia* with an allegory promoting charity is itself no more than an inference.[3] After all, competent poetry has always contained something more than words making a statement, something that might well be called *sententia*, and I should imagine that Greeks, Romans, Arabs, Jews, and other non-Christians might inevitably teach poetry according to the same system: does the *Iliad* have no *sententia* because it is not Christian? Finally, there is at least one dissenting vote in the roll call of theologians presumably enjoining poets to write allegory after the example of Scripture. As W. K. Wimsatt pointed out in a paper on this topic several years ago,[4] Thomas Aquinas makes the unequivocal statement that "in no intellectual activity of the human mind can there properly speaking be found anything but literal sense: only in Scripture, of which the Holy Ghost was the author, man the instrument, can there be found" the spiritual sense—that is, the three levels of allegory on top the literal.[5] While I recognize that St. Thomas is not a Father and that his statement may be idiosyncratic (as I believe some scholars regard it),[6] nevertheless I think he ought to be honestly reckoned with. To date I have seen no real discussion of his opinion by supporters of patristic exegesis. Nor will I accept as reputable the excuse that because he was a friar St. Thomas would hardly reflect the point of view of such medieval poets as favored the monks.[7]

I shall support my opposition to patristic exegesis in its extreme and most common form by examining three examples from its literature: critiques of *Piers Plowman*, of a poem by Chaucer, and of a Middle English lyric. I have naturally chosen the examples that seem to serve my purposes best, but this partiality is somewhat compensated for by the fact that these analyses have been taken as models by those

---

[3] See Robertson, "Historical Criticism," p. 13, and Huppé and Robertson, p. 1.

[4] Wimsatt, "Two Meanings of Symbolism: A Grammatical Exercise," *Catholic Renascence*, VIII (1955), 19: I am indebted to Mr. Wimsatt's excellent paper for this reference to St. Thomas.

[5] *Quaestiones Quodlibetales*, VII, Quaestio VI, Art. XVI: Unde in nulla scientia, humana industria inventa, proprie loquendo, potest inveniri nisi litteralis sensus; sed solum in ista Scriptura, cujus Spiritus sanctus est auctor, homo vero instrumentum.

[6] Green ("Dante's 'Allegory of Poets,'" p. 121) speaks of St. Thomas's *effort* "to restrict the term *allegoria* to the mode of Sacred Scripture."

[7] Huppé and Robertson (p. 10) say that they in general exclude the commentaries of friars because the poet was anti-fraternal.

who practice patristic exegesis. To the reasonable question of whether there are in existence specimens of patristic exegesis which do not arouse my opposition, I give a qualified yes; these concern poems where the Christian preoccupation is clearly a marked feature of the poem and where this sort of exegesis may help to enrich our appreciation of the poet's handiwork. My opposition begins, however, when the author of the critique tries to substitute a special meaning for the one the poem yields without exegesis, an attempt that is common enough to seem characteristic of the current school of exegetes.[8]

Christian preoccupation is certainly a marked feature of *Piers Plowman*, and on the surface of it the poem appears admirably suited to patristic exegesis. It is, in the first place, an allegory that promotes charity (though sometimes in a rather malevolent way); its author frequently cites the Fathers of the Church; it uses symbols, such as the Tree of Charity and Patience, that come from the patristic tradition; its meaning is occasionally so murky that one must invoke every sort of aid to understanding (not, I think, one of the poem's virtues); and, most important, it not only is based in large part upon biblical texts, but it frequently quotes the Scriptures, so that we should expect patristic interpretations to show up along with the passages they interpret. Here, if anywhere, is favorable soil for the plow drawn by the four oxen who ornament the title page of Huppé and Robertson's book, *Piers Plowman and Scriptural Tradition*. I am therefore the more disappointed by what the book itself contains.

Every one will recall the opening of the B-Text. On a May morning the speaker goes to sleep among the Malvern Hills and dreams that he sees before him

> . . . a towr on a toft, trieliche ymaked,
> A deep dale binethe, a dungeon therinne
> With deepe diches and derke, and dredful of sighte.
> A fair feeld ful of folk foond I therbitweene
> Of al manere of men, the mene and the riche,
> Worching and wandring as the world asketh.[9]

The critics begin their analysis of the poem with the statement, "In *Piers Plowman* the basic contrast between Jerusalem and Babylon is

---

[8] R. P. Miller, in "Chaucer's Pardoner, the Scriptural Eunuch, and the Pardoner's Tale," *Speculum*, XXX (1955), 180–99, for instance, gives an excellent account of the patristic significance of the Pardoner's condition; but when he replaces Chaucer's spiritual (and physical) eunuch with the Fathers' scriptural enunch, he seems to me to be depreciating the poem.

[9] B-Prologue, ll. 14–19, normalized spelling.

suggested at once by the dreamer's opening vision of the Tower of Truth, the Dungeon of Hell, and, in between, the Field of Folk." [10] This is certainly true, but nevertheless the phrasing of the statement causes me discomfort. Some one who had not read the poem carefully, or who had read only part of it, might very well get the idea that Langland habitually deals in terms of the compound patristic symbol Jerusalem vs. Babylon: the critics' phrasing surely suggests his easy familiarity with the patristic tradition. Yet the symbol here is the critics' and not Langland's. Indeed, while in his poem Jerusalem appears again and again with all its ancient symbolism upon it, Babylon is never hell, but just a foreign city. Instead of employing the patristic allegory of the two cities, the poet is content to give us two towers, one on a hillock, one in a dale, one fair, one ugly, but in any case towers of the kind that dotted the medieval English landscape. Since the critics fail to derive the towers from patristic sources, one might suggest that the poet had eschewed tradition for everyday reality, as poets often do: his own practical sensibility saw the great contrast as between the soaring watchtower (Watchman, tell us of the night) and the sullen keep (which is the night). And if this is going too far, one can at least, I think, say that the critics are guilty of smuggling in patristic symbolism at the very outset of their journey.

Let us proceed to their following sentences: "It is significant that the Folk are not assembled in an orderly pilgrimage toward the Tower [i.e., of Truth]: they are occupied with the world. . . . This situation represents the underlying problem in the poem. The folk of the world are preoccupied with worldly affairs, 'wandrying' in confusion." [11] Now this, I submit, is unwarranted intrusion upon the poem. It has not said or even hinted that the folk of the field are wrong in being occupied with the world; "worching and wandring" suggests that some of them are occupied with the world in the right way, some in the wrong way; but in either case, being in the world, they are necessarily concerned with it. The disapproval of this fact is not the poet's, but the critics'. St. Augustine might, in one of his more world-hating moments, have agreed with them, but he was not writing *Piers Plowman*. And indeed the critics suggest by their next sentence that in pursuing Augustine they have perhaps tripped on Langland. "But not all of them [the Folk] seem hopeless. The dreamer's attention is at once called to the hard working plowman." [12]

---

[10] Huppé and Robertson, p. 17.   [11] *Ibid.*   [12] *Ibid.*

Some putten hem to the plow, played ful selde,
In setting and in sowing swonken ful harde,
And wonnen that wastours with glutonye destroyeth.[13]

Now if I rightly understand the purport of the critics' remarks, these hard-working plowmen ought to be off on an orderly pilgrimage to the Tower of Truth, which, I take it, would make them somewhat better than merely not hopeless. And, of course, the image of life as a pilgrimage to Truth, or the Celestial City, is a time-honored one:

This world nis but a thurghfare ful of wo,
And we been pilgrimes passing to and fro.

Furthermore it is an image which Langland does, at times, invoke, but not here. For the poem is not considering just now the good man's life allegorically as a pilgrimage to Truth but literally as a life of productive work. The poem does indeed concern salvation, but it also recognizes the practical fact that salvation in the next world depends upon one's actions in this, and while it points the way to heaven it is also concerned with tidying up earth. The pilgrimage of the hard-working plowmen is their hard work. Later on in the poem Piers Plowman himself, like Huppé and Robertson, momentarily identifies the allegorical with the literal when he volunteers to leave off plowing and lead a pilgrimage to Truth; but Truth tells him in no uncertain terms to stay home and keep on plowing.[14] It is appropriate to notice here what St. Thomas repeats from St. Augustine about the fourfold interpretation of Scripture: "There is nothing darkly related in any part of Holy Writ which is not clearly revealed elsewhere." [15] In this case the critics have detected a dark pronouncement on the management of earthly affairs which the poem clearly controverts later. Plowmen by definition ought to plow.

Huppé and Robertson continue: "Unfortunately, the plowmen are accompanied by false plowmen, by persons who dress as plowmen through pride:" [16]

And some putten hem to pride, apparailed hem therafter,
In countenance of clothing comen disgised.[17]

While these lines directly follow the description of the plowmen, the only way one can turn the proud men they mention into false plowmen

---

[13] B-Prologue, ll. 20–22.   [14] See especially B-Text 7.1–5.

[15] *Quodlibetales*, VII, Quaestio VI, Art. XIV: nihil est quod occulte in aliquo loco sacrae Scripturae tradatur quod non alibi manifeste exponatur.

[16] Huppé and Robertson, p. 17.   [17] B-Prologue, ll. 23–24.

is by taking as the antecedent of the adverb *therafter* not the noun *pride*, which immediately precedes it, but the plowmen of three lines before. Now one may reasonably doubt that any one at all in the Middle Ages would, through pride, dress as a plowman, the lowest of the low; but this is as nothing to my doubt about the syntax which yields such an interpretation. It ought to be stated loudly that Middle English syntax, while it is different from that of Modern English and often far more colloquial, is wholly logical and bound by its own firm rules: it is not mere illiterate imprecision that permits one to read without regard for the niceties of correlation. Here the chances are about ninety-eight out of a hundred that *therafter* refers to pride; about one out of a hundred that it refers to *wastours*, which is the next closest antecedent; and about one out of a thousand that it refers to the plowmen. And certainly the natural sense is the best one: people filled with pride of worldly position dress up in fancy clothes. There are no false plowmen in the text: there are merely ornamental parasites contrasted with hard-working peasants.

The trouble is that the critics have been kidnapped by their preconceptions. Since they believe one of the most important themes of *Piers Plowman* to be that "the function of those in the *status praelatorum* has been usurped by certain members of the *status religiosorum*" [18]—the friars have taken over the duties of the secular clergy—they are anxious to have the poet develop this theme at once. For, as it now appears, the poem's plowmen are not just "simple peasants," [19] but represent, in the patristic tradition, "the true followers of the prelatical life." [20] Naturally, if the true plowmen are the displaced prelates, the poem ought at once to have mentioned the false plowmen—the friars—who have displaced them. We have seen how the text is made to do what it ought to have done. But the simple literal reading does not permit false plowmen. Furthermore, I am sure that the plowmen of the Prologue represent not prelates, but plowmen, men who are doing a necessary part of the dirty work exacted by this world. Having spent a good deal of time with the poem, I am aware that a plowman may be an image for a spiritual plowman, which is what Piers Plowman is or becomes in the course of the poem; but I hope that the first time I read the poem I had enough sensitivity to it to realize that the word *plowmen* was loaded, even without benefit of the Fathers. On the other hand, I do not think that I said at this point, "Hah, 'plowmen,' *id est, praelati.*" Nor do I think that any contemporary reader would

[18] Huppé and Robertson, p. 7.   [19] *Ibid.*, p. 17.   [20] *Ibid.*, p. 19.

have, though he might well have thought of all hard-working honest
men, including priests. If he had said that, one cannot help wondering
what he would have said when, a little later in the came catalogue of
folk, he encounters parish priests. What in the world (or out of it) do
they represent?

I shall pass over the remainder of Huppé and Robertson's interpretation of the catalogue of folk, merely pausing to observe that it seems
wantonly to confuse the literal and the metaphorical. There are anchorites who are said to represent anchorites, merchants who are said to
represent the whole laity, minstrels who are said to represent "those
who use the goods of the world properly for the worship of God, who
praise the Lord without desire for temporal reward" [21] (despite the fact
that they "get gold with their glee" [22]), japers and janglers who are
said to represent "those who profess the faith but do not work accordingly"; and finally beggars who are allowed to represent beggars, pardoners pardoners, priests priests, and bishops bishops. Any cryptographer who keeps forgetting his code and writing plain English is
simply incompetent; I do not think Langland was incompetent or, for
that matter, a cryptographer.

I shall conclude this part of my paper with one final analysis.
Shortly after his vision of the Field of Folk the dreamer sees a vision
of the founding of an earthly kingdom:

> Thanne cam ther a king, knighthood him ladde,
> Might of the comunes made him to regne;
> And thanne cam Kinde Wit, and clerkes he made,
> For to conseille the king and the comune save.
> The king and knighthood and clergye bothe
> Casten that the comune sholde [hir comunes] finde.
> The comune contreved of Kinde Wit craftes,
> And for profit of alle the peple plowmen ordaigned,
> To tilie and to travaile as trewe lif asketh.
> The king and the comune and Kinde Wit the thridde
> Shoop lawe and lewtee, eech [lif] to knowe his owne.[23]

I had always thought this an idealized picture of the political community. A king, supported by his knights and by the common people,

---

[21] *Ibid.*, p. 22.   [22] B-Prologue, l. 34.

[23] B-Prologue, ll. 112–22; the emendations seem obvious, though, as the following quotation from Huppé and Robertson shows, Skeat's text reads *man* for *lif* and
hemself for *hir comunes:* the reference of either pronoun—*hemself* or *hir*—is ambiguous.

counseled by clerks, assisted at every turn by Natural Intelligence, in order to serve the common profit and to fulfill the demands of a life of integrity, creates law and justice and assigns each component of the kingdom its place, so that every man should know his privileges and responsibilities. Apparently I was wrong, for the king's council

did not consist of a representative body of his subjects; it was made up of clerks appointed by Kind Wit or *scientia*. The king, his barons, and the clergy, neglecting their responsibilities, decided that the commons must take care of themselves, so that the commons, also resorting to *scientia*, found it necessary to establish "plowmen." Together, the king and his commons, guided by *scientia*, formulated law and loyalty for the protection of private property, "eche man to knowe his owne." [24]

My errors had been many. I had not realized that representative government was a patristic ideal: I had thought it the ideal of a rather anti-patristic rationalism. I had not known that Kinde Wit was *scientia* and a villainously unreliable faculty: I had rather supposed the poet approved of it, since he very frequently couples it with Conscience; and Dunning and Hort exalt it almost to the position of modern "conscience" and "reason." [25] I had not been aware that king, knights, and clergy were neglecting their responsibility for taking care of the commons: for it had not occurred to me that the defenders and administrators of the realm ought to be out producing food, which is what I thought the verb *finden* meant and which I had assumed was a function of the commons, and specifically of plowmen. Nor had it become clear to me that the creation of law was a conspiracy to protect private property: I had thought that law and justice—which is what *lewtee* seems to mean—made possible social order, and that social order was desirable in this miserable world.

But my worst mistake was in connection with the last phrase of the passage, "each man [lif] to know his own," which I had once written was "the most significant phrase for understanding [the poet's] idea of earthly government." [26] I should have said "misunderstanding." For the two critics write of it: "That this is not a proper goal is evident from

24 Huppé and Robertson, p. 27.

25 T. P. Dunning, *Piers Plowman: An Interpretation of the A-Text* (Dublin: Talbot Press, 1937), pp. 39 ff; Greta Hort, *Piers Plowman and Contemporary Religious Thought* (London: Society for Promoting Christian Knowledge, n.d.), pp. 69 ff.

26 *Piers Plowman: The C-Text and Its Poet* (New Haven: Yale University Press, 1949), pp. 109–10.

I. Cor. 10.24: *Nemo quod suum est quaerat.*" [27] Let no man seek his own. They go on, quite correctly, to define the seeking of one's own as cupidity, the opposite of charity, and hence the negative side of the principle which, according to them, is the theme of all medieval literature.

You may remember that at the end of the Rat Parliament in the B-Prologue a little mouse taunts the rats with their failure to bell the cat and offers the cold consolation that it was a bad idea in the first place. The mouse ends his speech with the line,

> Forthy eech a wis wight I warne, wite wel his owene.

Therefore I warn each wise wight to wit well his own. Needless to say, under the scrutiny of the critics this turns out to be a very wicked little rodent indeed, counseling the rats, like Belial, to slothful ease, or, like Mammon, to seeking wealth and heeding not St. Paul's injunction. But the truth is that he is no more telling the rats to seek their own than law is encouraging men to seek their own in the earlier passage. I once wrote that "without risk of error, one may add the word *place* or *part* in order to make the phrase meet the requirements of modern idiom: each man, and therefore each class, should know and keep his own place." [28] Furthermore, I remain persuaded that this is what the phrase means, and that knowledge of one's own place in the world is a cardinal point in medieval theorizing of the most idealistic kind, that it is a principle upon which all order in this world depends: I'll bet it is in the Fathers. The truth is that Huppé and Robertson have on two occasions mistranslated Middle English to make a point that is not only entirely foreign to the poem's but directly opposed to it and disproved by other passages within the poem. They have made an ideal state a wicked one; and they have made of a poet counseling forbearance a revolutionary. In order to do this, they have taken first Middle English *knowen*, then *witen*, as the equivalents of Latin *quaerere*; they have made knowing the same as seeking. Once again it is relevant to quote St. Thomas on scriptural interpretation: "The spiritual sense is always based upon the literal sense, and proceeds from it." [29] The literal sense of *to know* is "to know."

[27] Huppé and Robertson, p. 27.

[28] Donaldson, *Piers Plowman: The C-Text*, p. 110.

[29] *Quodlibetales*, VII, Quaestio VI, Art. XIV: sed sensus spiritualis semper fundatur super litteralem, et procedit ex eo.

It seems to me that the failure which the two critics suffer with regard to the literal sense in the beginning of their analysis is repeated again and again as the analysis proceeds. It is patently unfair to condemn a whole work on the basis of a few pages, but I do not consider the sample uncharacteristic. The authors seem constantly to be contorting the text to find the message they want to find. This tendency reaches a kind of open confirmation in their discussion of the meaning of the protagonist's name, Will. After pointing out, I think rather suggestively, that Will, like the human will, "moves between the opposites of willfulness and charity," they go on to observe: "Because the poet has been successful as a poet, he has created in Will so appealingly human a character that through interest in him many have lost sight of the fact that Will is merely a device by means of which the poet may set off the actual against the ideal in the poem and so develop his major theme." [30] It is fair to read this as saying that because the poet has been a good poet, he has been a poor teacher, and one might work out the proposition, the better the poet, the worse the teacher, and vice versa. Ultimately one has the poem going in one direction and its teaching going in the opposite. Under these circumstances I should prefer to follow the poem rather than outsiders who are telling me what it means to be saying.

There are, of course, good things in Huppé and Roberston's book. But curiously enough, these are in general not concerned with patristic exegesis, but are the insights of two excellent minds that have thought long and hard about the poem. The poet himself, when he is following patristic tradition, tends to explain his use of symbols in such a way that a reader ignorant of the tradition can understand them from the text —though of course knowledge of the tradition will enhance the reader's appreciation. Thus when the dreamer meets some one called Abraham representing faith, the first thing that Abraham says is, "I am Faith." [31] A character named Hope appears only to say at once that he has been given a "maundement" upon the Mount of Sinai.[32] The most heavily patristic passage in the poem, that describing the Tree of Charity,[33] is also well glossed by the poet—rather better glossed by him, I think, than by Huppé and Robertson. Scholars must, indeed, be grateful to the critics for the information they provide about the patristic background, a field in which they are enormously learned. But I can think

[30] Huppé and Robertson, p. 240.   [32] B-Text 17.2.
[31] B-Text 16.176.   [33] B-Text 16.1–89.

of little that they say on the subject which the poem does not say equally well. And when, as in the passages I have analyzed, they substitute a remote allegory for the easy sense, they are letting their desire to show patristic influence override the simple demands of Middle English.

Having shown what I think to be a failure with regard to the *littera* of a medieval poem, let me turn to what I consider a failure with regard to the *sensus*. The *Nun's Priest's Tale* has always been one of Chaucer's most popular and at the same time most elusive works: one is apt to come away from this feast feeling that one has been abundantly fed, but one is not sure on what kind of food. No simple critical formula explains the reader's delight in the poem, which has so little plot and such enormous rhetorical dilation. Since the scholarly mind naturally abhors a vacuum of this sort, it is inevitable that a number of attempts should be made to show that the little plot is weighty enough to compensate for and even to overbalance the infinite expansiveness of the narrator. Of several attempts of this sort more or less concerned with the patristic tradition, I shall choose that of Mortimer Donovan, since his is the most specifically patristic.[34]

According to Donovan, the morality of the *Nun's Priest's Tale*—or sermon, as he prefers to call it—emerges only if one understands the patristic significance of the personages concerned. The poor widow who owns Chauntecleer and his several wives is the Church;[35] the fox is either the Devil or a heretic, or rather, both;[36] the rooster, originally a symbol of alertness,[37] comes, in the course of the analysis, to represent the alert Christian, though strictly speaking he should represent an alert priest; Dame Pertelote is, of course, woman, whose counsel Chauntecleer, through lechery, has listened to "against his own superior judgment."[38] The climax of the action in which these figures share is, according to the critic,

reached as Chauntecleer rides uncomfortably on the fox's back. Since Christian hope extends to the last, the once uxorious Chauntecleer now turns for divine aid against an adversary as powerful as Daun Russell, and, with all the alertness of his celebrated nature, he begs help. He knows with Chaucer's Parson that "for as muchel as the devil fighteth agayns a man moore by queyntise and by sleighte than by strengthe, therefor men shal withstonden

---

[34] "The *Moralite* of the Nun's Priest's Sermon," *Journal of English and Germanic Philology*, LII (1953), 498–508.

[35] *Ibid.*, p. 505.   [37] *Ibid.*, pp. 501 ff.

[36] *Ibid.*, pp. 498 ff.   [38] *Ibid.*, p. 506.

hym by wit and by resoun and by discrecioun." . . . So, begging divine
help, he devises a plan which shows a return of reason.[39]

And so the alert Christian defeats the Devil-heretic in the nick of time.

There is no way of proving that the widow does not represent the
Church—unless, of course, we apply to the tale St. Augustine's and St.
Thomas's stricture that nothing is darkly said in one place is not
clearly revealed elsewhere. But I doubt that the fox represents the Devil
or that Chauntecleer represents the alert Christian, not with seven
wives. There were, if I may say so, foxes long before there were devils,
and roosters were crowing off the hours long before Christians heard
them. One might say that if there were no Devil a poultry-keeping
farmer would have invented one in order to describe a fox, so that we
hardly need Rabanus Maurus to explain the similarity between fox and
devil, any more than we need Hugh of St. Victor to tell us that the
cock in his hourly crowing makes a good natural example of attention
to duty.[40] What we have here in poetic (or barnyard) terms is a devilish
fox-villain and a conscientious, if foolish, rooster-hero. I am willing to
accept the premise that Pertelote represents woman, though I think it's
unkind of the critic to repeat the Nun's Priest's slander that Chauntecleer took her advice, something the Nun's Priest suggests in his
eagerness to blame Chauntecleer's misfortune on anything and everything except Chauntecleer. Actually, Pertelote had advised certain medi-
cines, but Chauntecleer had defied them, heroically, just as he defied
dreams: Adam Rooster was at least able to resist eating Eve Hen's
hellebore, and thereby maintained a kind of integrity, if a prideful and
lecherous one.

On first reading Donovan's criticism I though he had inadvertently
left out Chauntecleer's prayer for divine aid—which I couldn't recall—
for all he quotes is Chauntecleer's speech to the fox:

. . . Sire, if that I were as ye,
Yet sholde I sayn, *as wis God helpe me,*
'Turneth again, ye proude cherles alle!
A verray pestilence upon you falle!'

Then I realized that the words "as wis God helpe me," as surely as
God help me, were italicized,[41] and were, indeed, the prayer that
Chauntecleer uttered "with all the alertness of his celebrated nature."
But even this crumb is not really available: the prayer qualifies the

[39] *Ibid.*, pp. 506–7.   [40] *Ibid.*, p. 501.   [41] *Ibid.*, p. 507.

apodasis of a contrary-to-fact condition, in a position safely removed from the actual Chauntecleer; and it is, indeed, not a prayer at all, but an oath of which Chaucer's Parson would not have approved.

Even if one were to accept the allegorical interpretation of this tale I cannot see that much has, critically speaking, been gained. If one connects things up with a specific Christian doctrine one does, to be sure, introduce a kind of weightiness into the discussion, but in this case it seems a deadweight of which the poem were better relieved. I must say, in all seriousness, that if the *sententia* of the *Nun's Priest's Tale*, the quality which justifies our reading the tale, is that the alert Christian with God's help can thwart the Devil-heretic, then Chaucer has let us down with a thud. But I do not think he has. At the end of his critique, Donovan tells us that "the identity of the cock and fox is almost lost behind what Professor Kittredge calls this 'preacher's illustrative anecdote, enormously developed until it swallows up the sermon.'" [42] This seems a little like running out into the streets shouting "Eureka!" only to discover that one has neglected to dress; for the fact is that the little anecdote on which the exegesis depends is only one tiny grain of wheat in an intolerable deal of chaff, and if it contains Chaucer's main point then he is guilty of the most horrid misproportioning. But one ought to trust the statistics of great poetry rather than those of critics, and any interpretation of a poem that ignores the bulk of it is likely to be wrong: a medieval teacher would have warned us to heed the *sensus* before extracting the *sententia*.

The *Nun's Priest's Tale* does have a real point, a serious point, and a better point than the one I reject, and it lies where one should expect to find it, in the enormous rhetorical elaboration of the telling. For rhetoric here is regarded as the inadequate defense that mankind erects against an inscrutable reality; rhetoric enables man at best to regard himself as a being of heroic proportions—like Achilles, or like Chauntecleer—and at worst to maintain the last sad vestiges of his dignity (as a rooster Chauntecleer is carried in the fox's mouth, but as a hero he rides on his back); rhetoric enables man to find significance both in his desires and in his fate, and to pretend to himself that the universe takes him seriously. And rhetoric has a habit, too, of collapsing in the presence of simple common sense. Chauntecleer is not an alert Christian; he is mankind trying to adjust the universe to his own specifications and failing—though not, I am happy to say, fatally. Donovan

[42] *Ibid.*, p. 508.

assumes that Chauntecleer, has been cured of his uxoriousness—perhaps he is going to retire into voluntary widowhood. I am less sanguine. I fear he is going to go on behaving as the roosters and men of Western civilization have always behaved, preserving their dignity by artificial respiration and somewhat against the odds. In short, the fruit of the *Nun's Priest's Tale* is its chaff.[43]

I shall conclude with one final analysis of patristic exegesis, Robertson's interpretation of the little lyric "Maiden in the Moor." [44] In this poem we have the barest of literal statements and almost no *sensus* at all; one must proceed directly from the letter to the *sententia*. The poem is short; therefore I quote it entire:

> Maiden in the moor lay,
>   In the moor lay,
> Sevenight ful, sevenight ful;
> Maiden in the moor lay,
>   In the moor lay,
> Sevenightes ful and a day.
>
> Wel [i.e., good] was hir mete.
>   What was hir mete?
> The primerole and the—
> The primerole and the—
> Wel was hir mete.
>   What was hir mete?
> The primerole and the violet.
>
> Wel was hir dring.
>   What was hir dring?
> The chelde water of the—
> The chelde water of the—
> Wel was hir dring.
>   What was hir dring?
> The chelde water of the welle-spring.
>
> Wel was hir bowr.
>   What was hir bowr?
> The rede rose and the—
> The rede rose and the—
> Wel was hir bowr.

---

[43] For a fuller expression of this interpretation, see my *Chaucer's Poetry: An Anthology for the Modern Reader* (New York: Ronald Press, 1958), pp. 940–44.

[44] "Historical Criticism," pp. 26–27.

> What was hir bowr?
> The rede rose and the lilye flowr.[45]

Of this charming little piece Robertson writes:

> On the surface, although the poem is attractive, it cannot be said to make much sense. Why should a maiden lie on a moor for seven nights and a day? And if she did, why should she eat primroses and violets? Or again, how does it happen that she has a bower of lilies and roses on the moor? The poem makes perfectly good sense, however, if we take note of the figures and signs in it. The number seven indicates life on earth, but life in this instance went on at night, or before the Light of the World dawned. The day is this light, or Christ, who said, "I am the day." And it appears appropriately after seven nights, or, as it were, on the count of eight, for eight is also a figure of Christ. The moor is the wilderness of the world under the Old Law before Christ came. The primrose is not a Scriptural sign, but a figure of fleshly beauty. We are told three times that the primrose was the food of this maiden, and only after this suspense are we also told that she ate or embodied the violet, which is a Scriptural sign of humility. The maiden drank the cool water of God's grace, and her bower consisted of the roses of martyrdom or charity and the lilies of purity with which late medieval and early Renaissance artists sometimes adorned pictures of the Blessed Virgin Mary, and, indeed, she is the Maiden in the Moor. . . .[46]

I cannot find that the poem, as a poem, makes any more "sense" after exegesis than it did before, and I think it makes rather more sense as it stands than the critic allows it. Maidens in poetry often receive curiously privileged treatment from nature, and readers seem to find the situation agreeable. From the frequency with which it has been reprinted it seems that the "Maiden in the Moor" must have offered many readers a genuine poetic experience even though they were without benefit of the scriptural exegesis. I do not think that most of them would find it necessary to ask the questions of the poem that Robertson has asked; indeed, it seems no more legitimate to inquire what the maiden was doing in the moor than it would be to ask Wordsworth's Lucy why she did not remove to a more populous environment where she might experience a greater measure of praise and love. In each case the poetic *donnée* is highly primitive one which exposes an innocent woman to the vast, potentially hostile, presumably impersonal forces of nature; and the Middle English lyric suggests the mystery by which

---

[45] For the poem in its original form, see *Secular Lyrics of the XIVth and XVth Centuries*, ed. by R. H. Robbins (Oxford: Clarendon Press, 1947), pp. 12–13.
[46] "Historical Criticism," p. 27.

those are, at times, transmuted into something more humane, even benevolent, by their guardianship of the innocent maiden. The poetic sense is not such as necessarily to preclude allegory, and I shouldn't be surprised if medieval readers often thought of the Virgin as they read the poem, not because they knew the symbols and signs, but because the Virgin is the paramount innocent maiden of the Christian tradition: such suggestivity is one of poetry's principal functions. Robertson's hard-and-fast, this-sense-or-no-sense allegory, however, seems to me so well concealed and, when explicated, so unrevealing that it can be considered only disappointing if not entirely irrelevant. The function of allegory that is worth the literary critic's attention (as opposed to cryptography, which is not) cannot be to conceal, but is to reveal, and I simply do not believe that medieval poets veiled their poems in order to hide their pious message from heretics and unbelievers. In allegory the equation is not merely *a* equals *b*, the literal statement reanalyzed equals the suggested meaning, but is something more like *a* plus *b* equals *c*, the literal statement plus the meaning it suggests yield an ultimate meaning that is an inextricable union of both. Patristically the primrose may be a figure of fleshly beauty, but actually (and the actual is what poetry is made of) it is one of the commonest of the lovely flowers which nature in its benevolent aspects lavishes upon mankind and, in this case, all-benevolent lavishes upon the maiden of the moor. Robertson asks the question "Why should she eat primroses?" I hope that if I answer "Because she was hungry," it will not be said of me that a primrose by the river's brim a yellow primrose was to him, and it was nothing more.

I said at the beginning of this paper that I did not know of any valid theoretical objection to patristic criticism. I do, however, object to a procedure which substitutes for the art of the poet the learning or good intentions of the reader. Reading a poem intelligently is, I believe, one of the hardest things on earth to do:

Humankind cannot bear very much reality,

and I believe that great poetic art offers something very close to an ultimate reality. In order to read it well one has to put oneself into the impossible position of having all one's wits and faculties about one, ready to spring into activity at the first summons; yet, like hunting dogs, they must not spring before they are summoned; and only those that are summoned must spring; and the summons must come from the poem. To maintain oneself in this state of relaxed tension is frightfully fatiguing, and any serious reader will, I am sure, want to rest a good deal. This is fortunate for scholarship, since such activities as source study, investigation of historical context, philology, editing, and patristic exegesis are salubrious vacations from the awful business of facing a poem directly. For a good many people the interest implicit in such studies and the fun of them will become more important than the poems themselves, and this is understandable; and the activities I have mentioned and many more are as necessary and as honorable as literary criticism. I look forward myself to a year when the many incidental problems of editing *Piers Plowman* will, I hope, constantly distract me from the effort of understanding its meaning. But these activities are not the same at literary criticism, and none of them should be permitted to replace an interpretation of the poem arising from the poem. At certain periods source study, philology, historical orientation, and even some of the techniques of the new criticism have tended to obliterate the meaning of the poems with which they have associated themselves. It seems to me that patristic criticism is operating under a categorical imperative to do the same thing.

Robertson concludes his English Institute paper on patristic criticism with the remark that literature, "regarded historically"—by which he means patristically—"can provide the food of wisdom as well as more transient aesthetic satisfaction." [47] It is here that my disagreement with him becomes absolute. I do not feel that the effect that the poems of Chaucer and Langland and other poets have upon me is mere transient aesthetic satisfaction. I believe that a great work of art provides the reader with the food of wisdom because it is a great work of art. If this food is not specific Christian doctrine, I console myself that it emanates from a humane tradition that is as old as Western civilization and that Christianity has done much to preserve.

[47] *Ibid.*, p. 31.

I. 11

The Fate of Pleasure

Wordsworth to Dostoevski*

LIONEL TRILLING

Columbia University

Of all critical essays in the English language, there is none that has established itself so firmly in our minds as Wordsworth's Preface to *Lyrical Ballads*. Indeed, certain of the statements that the Preface makes about the nature of poetry have come to exist for us as something like proverbs of criticism. This is deplorable, for the famous utterances, in the form in which we hold them in memory, can only darken counsel. A large part of the literate world believes that Wordsworth defines poetry as the spontaneous overflow of powerful feelings. With such a definition we shall not get very far in our efforts to think about poetry, and in point of fact Wordsworth makes no such definition. Much less does he say, as many find it convenient to recall, that poetry is emotion recollected in tranquillity. Yet the tenacity with which we hold in mind our distortions of what Wordsworth actually does say suggests the peculiar power of the essay as a whole, its unique existence as a work of criticism. Its cogency in argument is notable, even if intermittent, but the Preface is not regarded by its readers only as an argument. By reason of its eloquence, and because of the impetuous spirit with which it engages the great questions of the nature and function of poetry, it presents itself to us not chiefly as a discourse, but rather as a dramatic action, and we are prepared to respond to its utterances less for their truth than for their happy boldness.

* Read at the Institute in 1962. Published in *Selected Papers from the Institute: Romanticism Reconsidered*, 1963. The present text is that of Lionel Trilling. *Beyond Culture* (New York: The Viking Press), 1968.

This being so, it should be a matter for surprise that one especially bold utterance of the Preface has not engaged us at all and is scarcely ever cited. I refer to the sentence in which Wordsworth speaks of what he calls "the grand elementary principle of pleasure," and says of it that it constitutes "the naked and native dignity of man," that it is the principle by which man "knows, and feels, and lives, and moves."

This is a statement which has great intrinsic interest, because, if we recognize that it is bold at all, we must also perceive that it is bold to the point of being shocking, for it echoes and controverts St. Paul's sentence which tells us that "we live, and move, and have our being" in God (Acts 17:28). And in addition to its intrinsic interest, it has great historical interest, not only because it sums up a characteristic tendency of eighteenth-century thought but also because it bears significantly upon a characteristic tendency of our contemporary culture. Its relation to that culture is chiefly a negative one—our present sense of life does not accommodate the idea of pleasure as something which constitutes the "naked and native dignity of man."

The word *pleasure* occurs frequently in the Preface. Like earlier writers on the subject, when Wordsworth undertakes to explain why we do, or should, value poetry, he bases his explanation upon the pleasure which poetry gives. Generally he uses the word in much the same sense that was intended by his predecessors. The pleasure which used commonly to be associated with poetry was morally unexceptionable and not very intense—it was generally understood that poetry might indeed sometimes excite the mind but only as a step toward composing it. But the word has, we know, two separate moral ambiences and two very different degrees of intensity. The pleasures of domestic life are virtuous; the pleasures of Imagination or Melancholy propose the idea of a cultivated delicacy of mind in those who experience them; the name of an English pipe-tobacco, "Parson's Pleasure," although derived from the place on the river at Oxford where men have traditionally bathed naked, is obviously meant to suggest that the word readily consorts with ideas of mildness. None of these point to what Byron had in mind when he wrote, "O pleasure! you're indeed a pleasant thing,/ Although one must be damn'd for you no doubt." The *Oxford English Dictionary* takes due note of what it calls an "unfavorable" sense of the word: "Sensuous enjoyment as a chief object of life, or end, in itself," and informs us that in this pejorative sense it is "sometimes personified as a female deity." The Oxford lexicographers do not stop there but go on to recognize what they call a "strictly physical" sense, which is even lower in the moral scale: "the indulgence of the appetites, sensual gratification." The "unfavorable" significations of the word are dramatized by the English career of the most usual Latin word for pleasure, *voluptas*. Although some Latin-English dictionaries, especially those of the nineteenth century, say that *voluptas* means "pleasure, enjoyment, or delight of body or mind in a good or bad sense," the word as it was used in antiquity seems to have been on the whole morally neutral and not necessarily intense. But the English words derived from *voluptas* are charged with moral judgment and are rather excited. We understand that it is not really to the minds of men that a voluptuous woman holds out the promise of pleasure, enjoyment, or delight. We do not expect a voluptuary to seek his pleasures in domesticity, or in the Imagination or Melancholy, or in smoking a pipe.

It is obvious than any badness or unfavorableness of meaning that the word *pleasure* may have relates to the primitiveness of the enjoyment that is being referred to. Scarcely any moralist will object to pleasure as what we may call a secondary state of feeling, as a charm or grace added to the solid business of life. What does arouse strong adverse judgment is pleasure in its radical aspect, as it is the object of an essential and definitive energy of man's nature. It was because Bentham's moral theory represented pleasure in this way that Carlyle called it the Pig-philosophy. He meant, of course, that it impugned man's nature to associate it so immediately with pleasure. Yet this is just how Wordsworth asks us to conceive man's nature in the sentence I have spoken of—it is precisely pleasure in its primitive or radical aspect that he has in mind. He speaks of "the grand *elementary* principle of pleasure," which is to say, pleasure not as a mere charm or amenity but as the object of an instinct, of what Freud, whose complex exposition of the part that pleasure plays in life is of course much in point here, was later to call a *drive*. How little concerned was Wordsworth, at least in this one sentence, with pleasure in its mere secondary aspect is suggested by his speaking of it as constituting the *dignity* of man, not having in mind such dignity as is conferred by society but that which is *native* and *naked*.

When Carlyle denounced Bentham's assertion that pleasure is, and must be, a first consideration of the human being, it was exactly man's dignity that he was undertaking to defend. The traditional morality to which Carlyle subscribed was certainly under no illusion about the crude force of man's impulse to self-gratification, but it did not associate man's dignity with this force—on the contrary, dignity, so far as it was personal and moral, was thought to derive from the resistance which man offers to the impulse to pleasure.

For Wordsworth, however, pleasure was the defining attribute of life itself and of nature itself—pleasure is the "impulse from the vernal wood" which teaches us more of man and his moral being "than all the sages can." And the fallen condition of humanity—"what man has made of man"—is comprised by the circumstances that man alone of natural beings does not experience the pleasure which, Wordsworth believes, moves the living world. It is of course a commonplace of Wordsworth criticism that, although the poet set the highest store by the idea of pleasure, the actual pleasures he represents are of a quite limited kind. Certainly he ruled out pleasures that are "strictly physical," those which derive from "the indulgence of the appetites" and "sensual gratification," more particularly erotic gratification. His living world of springtime is far removed from that of Lucretius: nothing in it is driven by the irresistible power of *alma Venus*. This is not to say that there is no erotic aspect to Wordsworth's mind; but the eroticism is very highly sublimated—Wordsworth's pleasure always tended toward *joy*, a purer and more nearly transcendent state. And yet our awareness of this significant limitation does not permit us to underrate the boldness of his statement in the Preface about the primacy of pleasure and the dignity which derives from the principle of pleasure, nor to ignore its intimate connection with certain radical aspects of the moral theory of the French Revolution.[1]

For an understanding of the era of the Revolution, there is, I think, much to be gained from one of the works of the German economic historian Werner Sombart, whose chief preoccupation was the origins of capitalism. In his extensive monograph, *Luxury and Capitalism*, Sombart develops the thesis that the first great accumulations of capital were achieved by the luxury trades in consequence of that ever-increasing demand for the pleasures of the world, for comfort, sumptuousness, and elegance, which is observed in Western Europe between

[1] And we ought not let go unheeded the explicit connection that Wordsworth makes between poetry and sexuality. Explaining the pleasure of metrical language, he says that it is "the pleasure which the mind derives from the perception of similitude in dissimilitude." And he goes on: "This principle is the great spring of the activity of our minds and their chief feeder. From this principle the direction of the sexual appetite, and all the passions connected with it, take their origin."

the end of the Middle Ages and the end of the eighteenth century. As a comprehensive explanation of the rise of capitalism, this theory, I gather, has been largely discredited. Yet the social and cultural data which Sombart accumulates are in themselves very interesting, and they are much to our point.

Sombart advances the view that the European preoccupation with luxury took its rise in the princely courts and in the influence of women which court life made possible; he represents luxury as being essentially an expression of eroticism, as the effort to refine and complicate the sexual life, to enhance, as it were, the quality of erotic pleasure. The courtly luxury that Sombart studies is scarcely a unique instance of the association of pleasure with power, of pleasure being thought of as one of the signs of power and therefore to be made not merely manifest but conspicuous in the objects that constitute the *décor* of the lives of powerful men—surely Egypt, Knossos, and Byzantium surpassed Renaissance Europe in elaborateness of luxury. But what would seem to be remarkable about the particular phenomenon that Sombart describes is the extent of its proliferation at a certain period—the sheer amount of luxury that got produced, its increasing availability to classes less than royal or noble, the overtness of the desire for it, and the fierceness of this desire. Sombart's data on these points are too numerous to be adduced here, but any tourist, having in mind what he has even casually seen of the secondary arts of Europe from the centuries in question, the ornaments, furniture, and garniture of certain stations of life, will know that Sombart does not exaggerate about the amount of luxury produced. And any reader of Balzac will recognize the intensity of the passions which at a somewhat later time attended the acquisition of elaborate and costly objects which were desired as the means or signs of pleasure.

What chiefly engages our interest is the influence that luxury may be discovered to have upon social and moral ideas. Such an influence is to be observed in the growing tendency of power to express itself mediately, by signs or indices, rather than directly, by the exercise of force. The richness and elaboration of the objects in a princely establishment were the indices of a power which was actual enough, but they indicated an actual power which had no need to avow itself in action. What a prince conceived of as his dignity might, more than ever before, be expressed by affluence, by the means of pleasure made overt and conspicuous.

And as the objects of luxury became more widely available, so did the dignity which luxury was meant to imply. The connection between dignity and a luxurious style of life was at first not self-evident—in France in 1670 the very phrase *bourgeois gentilhomme* was thought to be comical. In the contemporary English translation of the title of Molière's comedy, *The Cit Turned Gentleman*, it was funny too, but the English laugh was neither so loud nor so long as the French, with what good consequences for the English nation Tocqueville has made plain. Yet in France as in England, the downward spread of the idea of dignity, until it eventually became an idea that might be applied to man in general, was advanced by the increasing possibility of possessing the means or signs of pleasure. That idea, it need scarcely by said, established itself at the very heart of the radical thought of the eighteenth century. And Diderot himself, the most uncompromising of materialists, as he was the most subtle and delicate, could not have wanted a more categorical statement of his own moral and intellectual theory than Wordsworth's assertion that the grand elementary principle of pleasure constitutes the native and naked dignity of man, and that it is by this principle that man knows, and lives, and breathes, and moves.

Nothing so much connects Keats with Wordsworth as the extent of his conscious commitment to the principle of pleasure. But of course nothing so much separates Keats from his great master as his characteristic way of exemplifying the principle. In the degree that for Wordsworth pleasure is abstract and austere, for Keats it is explicit and voluptuous. No poet ever gave so much credence to the idea of pleasure in the sense of "indulgence of the appetites, sensual gratification," as Keats did, and the phenomenon that Sombart describes, the complex of pleasure-sensuality-luxury, makes the very fabric of his thought.

Keats's preoccupation with the creature-pleasures, as it manifests itself in his early work, is commonly regarded, even by some of his warmest admirers, with an amused disdain. At best, it seems to derive from the kind of elegant minuscule imagination that used to design the charming erotic scenes for the lids of enameled snuff boxes. At worst, in the explicitness of its concern with luxury, it exposes itself to the charge of downright vulgarity that some readers have made. The word *luxury* had a charm for Keats, and in his use of it he seems on the point of reviving its older meaning, which is specifically erotic and nothing but erotic; for Chaucer and Shakespeare *luxury* meant lust and its indulgence. Women present themselves to Keat's imagination as luxuries: "All that soft luxury/ that nestled in his arms." A poem is described as "a posy/ Of luxuries, bright, milky, soft and rosy." Poetry itself is defined by reference to objects of luxury, and even in its highest nobility, its function is said to be that of comforting and soothing.

Nor is the vulgarity—if we consent to call it that—confined to the early works; we find it in an extreme form in a poem of Keats's maturity. The lover in *Lamia* is generally taken to be an innocent youth, yet the most corrupt young man of Balzac's scenes of Parisian life would scarcely have spoken to his mistress or his fiancée as Lycius speaks to Lamia when he insists that she display her beauty in public for the enhancement of his prestige. Tocqueville said that envy was the characteristic emotion of plutocratic democracy, and it is envy of a particularly ugly kind that Lycius wishes to excite. "Let my foes choke," he says, "and my friends shout afar,/ While through the thronged streets your bridal car/ Wheels round its dazzling spokes." I am not sure that we should be at pains to insist that this is wholly a dramatic utterance and not a personal one, that we ought entirely to dissociate Keats from Lycius. I am inclined to think that we should suppose Keats to have been involved in all aspects of the principle of pleasure, even the ones that are vulgar and ugly. Otherwise we miss the full complication of that dialectic of pleasure which is the characteristic intellectual activity of Keats's poetry.

The movement of this dialectic is indicated in two lines from an early poem in which Keats speaks of "the pillowy silkness that rests/ Full in the speculation of the stars"—it is the movement from the sensual to the transcendent, from pleasure to knowledge, and knowledge of an ultimate kind. Keats's intellect was brought into fullest play when the intensity of his affirmation of pleasure was met by the intensity of his skepticism about pleasure. The principle of pleasure is for Keats, as it is for Wordsworth, the principle of reality—by it, as Wordsworth said, we *know*. But for Keats it is also the principle of illusion. In *The Eve of St. Agnes*, to take the most obvious example, the moment of pleasure at the center of the poem, erotic pleasure expressed in the fullest possible imagination of the luxurious, is the very essence of reality: it is all we know on earth and all we need to know. And it is the more real as reality and it is the more comprehensive as knowledge exactly because in the poem it exists surrounded by what on earth denies it, by darkness, cold, and death, which make it transitory, which make the felt and proclaimed reality mere illusion.

But we must be aware that in Keats's dialectic of pleasure it is not only external circumstances that condition pleasure and bring it into question as the principle of reality, but also the very nature of pleasure itself. If for Keats erotic enjoyment is the peak and crown of all pleasures, it is also his prime instance of the way in which the desire for pleasure denies itself and produces the very opposite of itself.

> Love in a hut, with water and a crust,
> Is—Love, forgive us—cinders, ashes, dust;
> Love in a palace is perhaps at last
> More grievous torment than a hermit's fast.

This opening statement of the second part of *Lamia* is not, as it is often said to be, merely a rather disagreeable jaunty cynicism but one of Keats's boldest expressions of his sense that there is something perverse and self-negating in the erotic life, that it is quite in the course of nature that we should feel "Pleasure . . . turning to Poison as the bee-mouths sips." He insists on the seriousness of the statement in a way that should not be hard to interpret—referring to the lines I have just quoted, he says

> That is a doubtful tale from faery land,
> Hard for the non-elect to understand.

That faery land we know very well—in the Nightingale Ode, Keats's epithet for the region is *forlorn;* it is the country of La Belle Dame sans Merci, the scene of erotic pleasure which leads to devastation, of an erotic fulfillment which implies castration.

Keats, then, may be thought of as the poet who made the boldest affirmation of the principle of pleasure and also as the poet who brought the principle of pleasure into the greatest and *sincerest* doubt. He therefore has for us a peculiar cultural interest, for it would seem to be true that at some point in modern history the principle of pleasure came to be regarded with just such ambivalence.

This divided state of feeling may be expressed in terms of a breach between politics and art. Modern societies seek to fulfill themselves in affluence, which of course implies the possibility of pleasure. Our political morality is more than acquiescent to this intention. Its simple and on the whole efficient criterion is the extent to which affluence is distributed among individuals and nations. But another morality, which we may describe as being associated with art, regards with a stern and even minatory gaze all that is implied by affluence, and it takes a dim or at best a very complicated view of the principle of pleasure. If we speak not only of the two different modes of morality, the political and the artistic, but also of the people who are responsive to them, we can say that it is quite within the bounds of possibility, if not of consistency, for the same person to respond, and intensely, to both of the two moral modes: it is by no means uncommon for an educated person to base his judgment of politics on a simple affirmation of the principle of pleasure, and to base his judgment of art, and also his judgment of personal existence, on a complex antagonism to that principle. This dichtomy makes one of the most significant circumstances of our cultural situation.

A way of testing what I have said about the modern artistic attitude to pleasure is afforded by the conception of poetry which Keats formulates in "Sleep and Poetry." This poem does not express everything that Keats thought about the nature and function of poetry, but what it does express is undeniably central to his thought, and for the modern sensibility it is inadmissible and even repulsive. It tells us that poetry is gentle, soothing, cheerful, healthful, serene, smooth, regal; that the poet, in the natural course of his development, will first devote his art to the representation of the pleasures of appetite, of things that can be bitten and tasted, such as apples, strawberries, and the white shoulders of nymphs, and that he will give his attention to the details of erotic enticement amid grateful sights and odors, and to sexual fulfillment and sleep. The poem then goes on to say that, as the poet grows older, he will write a different kind of poetry, which is called nobler; this later kind of poetry is less derived from and directed to the sensuality of youth and is more fitted to the gravity of mature years, but it still ministers to pleasure and must therefore be strict in its avoidance of ugly themes; it must not deal with those distressing matters which are referred to as "the burrs and thorns of life"; the great end of poetry, we are told, is "to soothe the cares, and lift the thoughts of man."

Such doctrine from a great poet puzzles and embarrasses us. It is, we say, the essence of Philistinism.

The conception of the nature and function of poetry which Keats propounds is, of course, by no means unique with him—it can be understood as a statement of the common assumptions about art which prevailed through the Renaissance up to some point in the nineteenth century, when they began to lose their force.[2] Especially in the eighteenth century, art is closely associated with luxury—with the pleasure or at least the comfort of the consumer, or with the quite direct flattery of his ego. The very idea of Beauty seems to imply considerations of this sort, which is perhaps why the eighteenth century was so much drawn to the idea of the Sublime, for that word would seem to indicate a kind of success in art which could not be called Beauty because it lacked the smoothness and serenity (to take two attributes from Keats's catalogue) and the immediacy of gratification which the idea of Beauty seems to propose. But the Sublime itself of course served the purposes of egoism—thus, that instance of the Sublime which was called the Grand Style, as it is described by its great English exponent in painting, Sir Joshua Reynolds, is said to be concerned with "some instance of heroic action or heroic suffering" and its proper effect, Reynolds explains, is to produce the emotion which Bouchardon reported he felt when he read Homer: "His whole frame appeared to himself to be enlarged, and all nature which surrounded him diminished to atoms." [3]

In connection with the art of the eighteenth century I used the disagreeable modern word *consumer*, meaning thus to suggest the affinity that art was thought to have with luxury, its status as a commodity which is implied by the solicitude it felt for the pleasure and the comfort of the person who was to own and experience it. Certainly

[2] One of the last significant exponents of the old assumptions was the young Yeats. He was "in all things pre-Raphaelite"—a partisan, that is, not of the early and austere pre-Raphaelite mode, but of the later sumptuous style, tinged with a sort of mystical eroticism—and he stubbornly resisted the realism of Carolus Duran and Bastien-Lepage, which was being brought back to England by the painters who had gone to study in Paris. His commitment to the "beautiful," as against truthful ugliness, was an issue of great moment between him and his father.

[3] All writers on the Sublime say in effect what Bouchardon says—that, although the sublime subject induces an overpowering emotion, even fear or terror, it does so in a way that permits us to rise superior to it and thus gives us occasion to have a good opinion of our power of intellect and of ourselves generally. The Sublime has this direct relation to comfort and luxury, that it induces us "to regard as small those things of which we are wont to be solicitous" (Kant, *Critique of Aesthetic Judgment*). A more ambitious treatment of my subject would require a much fuller exposition of the theory of the Sublime. Of this theory, which so much occupied the writers on art of the eighteenth century, it can be said that it has much more bearing upon our own literature than modern critics have recognized. The classic study in English is Samuel H. Monk's *The Sublime*, first published in 1935, recently reissued as an Ann Arbor Paperback.

Wordsworth was preeminent in the movement to change this state of affairs,[4] yet Wordsworth locates the value of metrical language as lying in its ability to protect the reader from the discomfort of certain situations that poetry may wish to represent and he compares the effect of such situations in novels with their effect in Shakespeare, his point being that in novels they are "distressful" but in Shakespeare they are not.[5] It was, we know, an explanation which did not satisfy Keats, who was left to puzzle out why it is that in *King Lear* "all disagreeables evaporate." He discovers that this effect is achieved by "intensity," and we of our day are just at the point of being comfortable with him when he disappoints our best hopes by hedging: he is constrained to say that the "disagreeables" evaporate not only by the operation of intensity but also by "their being in close connection with Beauty & Truth." But we do at last find ourselves at one with him when, in his sonnet "On Sitting Down to Read King Lear Once Again," he dismisses all thought of pleasure and prepares himself for the pain he is in duty bound to undergo:

> . . . Once again, the fierce dispute
> Betwixt damnation and impassion'd clay
> Must I burn through; once more humbly assay
> The bitter-sweet of this Shakespearian fruit.

He is by no means certain that the disagreeables really will evaporate and that he will emerge whole and sound from the experience, and he prays to Shakespeare and "the clouds of Albion" that they will guard him against wandering "in a barren dream," and that, when he is "consumed in the fire," they will contrive his Phoenix-resurrection.

[4] ". . . Men . . . who talk of Poetry as a matter of amusement and idle pleasure; who will converse with us as gravely about a *taste* for Poetry, as they express it, as if it were a thing as indifferent as a taste for rope-dancing, or Frontiniac, or Sherry."

[5] The strength of Wordsworth's impulse to suppress the "distressful" is suggested by the famous passage in *The Prelude* in which the poet explains how his childhood reading served to inure him to the terrors of actuality. He recounts the incident, which occurred when he was nine years old, of his seeing a drowned man brought up from the bottom of Esthwaite Lake. He was, he says, not overcome by fear of the "ghastly face," because his "inner eye" had seen such sights before in fairy tales and romances. And then he feels it necessary to go further, to go beyond the bounds of our ready credence, for he tells us that from his reading came "a spirit" which hallowed the awful sight

> With decoration and ideal grace
> A dignity, a smoothness, like the works
> Of Grecian Art, and purest poetry.

This we of our time can quite understand. We are repelled by the idea of an art that is consumer-directed and comfortable, let alone luxurious. Our typical experience of a work which will eventually have authority with us is to begin our relation to it at a conscious disadvantage, and to wrestle with it until it consents to bless us. We express our high esteem for such a work by supposing that it judges us. And when it no longer does seem to judge us, or when it no longer baffles and resists us, when we begin to feel that we *possess* it, we discover that its power is diminished. In our praise of it we are not likely to use the word *beauty*: we consented long ago—more than four decades ago—to the demonstration made by I. A. Richards in collaboration with Ogden and Wood that the concept of Beauty either could not be assigned any real meaning, or that it was frivolously derived from some assumed connection between works of art and our sexual preferences, quite conventional sexual preferences at that. "Beauty: it curves: curves are beauty," says Leopold Bloom, and we smile at so outmoded an aesthetic—how like him! With a similar amusement we read the language in which the young Yeats praised beauty in *The Secret Rose* (1896)—he speaks of those who are so fortunate as to be "heavy with the sleep/Men have named beauty." [6]

In short, our contemporary aesthetic culture does not set great store by the principle of pleasure in its simple and primitive meaning and it may even be said to maintain an antagonism to the principle of pleasure. Such a statement of course has its aspect of absurdity, but in logic only. There is no psychic fact more available to our modern comprehension than that there are human impulses which, in one degree or another, and sometimes in the very highest degree, repudiate pleasure and seek gratification in—to use Freud's word—unpleasure.

[6] Mr. Bloom's observation (which goes on to "shapely goddesses Venus, Juno: curves the world admires" and "lovely forms of women sculped Junonian") follows upon his lyrical recollection of his first sexual encounter with Molly; Yeats's phrase occurs in the course of a poem to Maud Gonne. I think it is true to say of Joyce (at least up through *Ulysses*) and of Yeats that they were among the last devotees of the European cult of Woman, of a Female Principle which, in one way or another, *ziegt uns hinein*, and that Molly and Maud are perhaps the last women in literature to be represented as having a transcendent and on the whole beneficent significance (although Lara in *Dr. Zhivago* should be mentioned—it is she who gives that novel much of its archaic quality). The radical change in our sexual mythos must surely be considered in any speculation about the status of pleasure in our culture. It is to the point, for example, that in Kafka's account of the spiritual life, which is touched on below, women play a part that is at best ambiguous.

The repudiation of pleasure in favor of the gratification which may be found in unpleasure is a leading theme of Dostoevski's great *nouvelle, Notes from Underground.* Of this extraordinary work Thomas Mann has said that "its painful and scornful conclusions," its "radical frankness . . . ruthlessly transcending all novelistic and literary bounds" have "long become parts of our moral culture." Mann's statement is accurate but minimal—the painful and scornful conclusions of Dostoevski's story have established themselves not only as parts of our moral culture but as its essence, at least so far as that culture makes itself explicit in literature.

Notes from Underground is an account, given in the first person, of the temperament and speculations of a miserable clerk, disadvantaged in every possible way, who responds to his unfortunate plight by every device of bitterness and resentment, by hostility toward those of mankind who are more unfortunate than he is, and also by the fiercest contempt for his more fortunate fellow beings, and for the elements of good fortune. He hates all men of purposeful life, and reasonable men, and action, and happiness, and what he refers to as "the sublime and the beautiful," and pleasure. His mind is subtle, complex, and contradictory almost beyond credibility—we never know where to have him and in our exhaustion we are likely to explain his perversity in some simple way, such as that he hates because he is envious, that he despises what he cannot have: all quite natural. But we are not permitted to lay this flattering unction to our souls—for one thing, he himself beats us to that explanation. And although it is quite true, it is only a small part of the truth. It is also true that he does not have because he does not wish to have; he has arranged his own misery—arranged it in the interests of his dignity, which is to say, of his freedom. For to want what is commonly thought to be appropriate to men, to want whatever it is, high or low, that is believed to yield pleasure, to be active about securing it, to use common sense and prudence to the end of gaining it, this is to admit and consent to the *conditioned* nature of man. What a distance we have come in the six decades since Wordsworth wrote his Preface! To know and feel and live and move at the behest of the principle of pleasure—this, for the Underground Man, so far from constituting his native and naked dignity, constitutes his humiliation in bondage. It makes him, he believes, a mechanic thing, the puppet of whoever or whatever can offer him the means of pleasure. If pleasure is indeed the principle of his being, he is as *known* as the sum of 2 and 2; he is a mere object of reason, of that rationality of the revolution which is established upon the primacy of the principle of pleasure.

At one point in his narrative, the protagonist of Notes from Underground speaks of himself as an "anti-hero." He is the eponymous ancestor of a now-numerous tribe. He stands as the antagonistic opposite to all the qualities which are represented by that statute of Sophocles which Professor Margarete Bieber tells us we are to have in mind when we try to understand the Greek conception of the hero, the grave beauty of the countenance and physique expressing the strength and order of the soul; the Underground Man traces his line of descent back to Thersites. It is in his character of anti-hero that he addresses the "gentlemen," as he calls them, the men of action and reason, the lovers of "the sublime and the beautiful," and brags to them, "I have more life in me than you have."

More life: perhaps it was this boast of the Underground Man that Nietzsche recalled when he said, "Dostoevski's Underman and my Overman are the same person clawing his way out of the pit [of modern thought and feeling] into the sunlight." One understands what Nietzsche meant, but he is mistaken in the identification, for his own imagination is bounded on one side by that word sunlight, by the Mediterranean world which he loved: by the tradition of humanism with its recognition of the value of pleasure. He is ineluctably constrained by considerations of society and culture, however much he may despise his own society and culture, but the Underground Man is not. To be sure, the terms of the latter's experience are, in the first instance, social; he is preoccupied by questions of status and dignity, and he could not, we may suppose, have come into existence if the fates of the heroes of Balzac and Stendhal had not previously demonstrated that no object of desire or of the social will is anything but an illusion and a source of corruption, society being what it is. But it is the essence of the Underground Man's position that his antagonism to society arises not in response to the deficiencies of social life, but, rather, in response to the insult society offers his freedom by aspiring to be beneficient, to embody "the sublime and the beautiful" as elements of its being. The anger Dostoevski expresses in Notes from Underground was activated not by the bad social condition of Russia in 1864 but by the avowed hope of some people that a good social condition could be brought into being. A Utopian novel of the day, Chernyshevski's What Is to Be

Done?, seemed to him an especially repugnant expression of this hope.[7] His disgust was aroused by this novel's assumption that man would be better for a rationally organized society, by which was meant, of course, a society organized in the service of pleasure. Dostoevski's reprobation of this idea, begun in *Notes from Underground*, reached its climax in Ivan Karamazov's poem of the Grand Inquisitor, in which again, but this time without the brilliant perversities of the earlier work, the disgust with the specious good of pleasure serves as the ground for the affirmation of spiritual freedom.

I have taken the phrase "specious good" from a passage in Wallace Fowlie's little book on Rimbaud, in which Mr. Fowlie discusses what he calls "the modern seizure and comprehension of spirituality." Without evasion, Mr. Fowlie identifies a chief characteristic of our culture which critics must inevitably be conscious of and yet don't like to name. If we are to be aware of the spiritual intention of modern literature, we have to get rid of certain nineteenth-century connotations of the word *spiritual*, all that they may imply to us of an overrefined and even effeminate quality, and have chiefly in mind what Mr. Fowlie refers to when he speaks of a certain type of saint and a certain type of poet and says of them that "both the saint and the poet exist through some propagation of destructive violence." And Mr. Fowlie continues: "In order to discover what is the center of themselves, the saint has to destroy the world of evil, and the poet has to destroy the world of specious good."

The destruction of what is considered to be specious good is surely one of the chief literary enterprises of our age. Whenever in modern literature we find violence, whether of represented act or of expression, and an insistence upon the sordid and the disgusting, and an insult offered

---

[7] "A Utopian novel of the day" does not, of course, give anything like an adequate notion of the book's importance in the political culture of Russia. Dostoevski chose his antagonist with the precision that was characteristic of him, for Chernyshevski, who thought of himself as the heir of the French Enlightenment, by his one novel exercised a decisive influence upon the Russian revolutionaries of the next two generations, most notably upon Lenin, who borrowed its title for one of his best-known pamphlets and whose moral style was much influenced by the character Rakhmétov. This paragon of revolutionists, although very fond of the luxury in which he was reared, embraces an extreme asceticism because, as he says, "We demand that men may have a complete enjoyment of their lives, and we must show by our example that we demand it, not to satisfy our personal passions, but for mankind in general; that what we say we say from principle and not from passion, from conviction and not from personal desire." Only one pleasure is proof against Rakhmétov's iron will—he cannot overcome his love of expensive cigars.

to the prevailing morality or habit of life, we may assume that we are in the presence of the intention to destroy specious good, that we are being confronted by that spirituality, or the aspiration toward it, which subsists upon violence against the specious good.

The most immediate specious good that a modern writer will seek to destroy is, of course, the habits, manners, and "values" of the bourgeois world, and not merely because these associate themselves with much that is bad, such as vulgarity, or the exploitation of the disadvantaged, but for other reasons as well, because they clog and hamper the movement of the individual spirit toward freedom, because they prevent the attainment of "more life." The particular systems and modes of thought of the bourgeois world are a natural first target for the modern spirituality. But it is not hard to believe that the impulse to destroy specious good would be as readily directed against the most benign socialist society, which, by modern definition, serves the principle of pleasure.

In the characteristically modern conception of the spiritual life, the influence of Dostoevski is definitive. By comparison with it, the influence of Nietzsche is marginal. The moral and personal qualities suggested by a particular class, the aristocracy, had great simple force with Nietzsche and proposed to his imagination a particular style of life. Despite the scorn he expressed for liberal democracy and socialist theory as he knew them, he was able to speak with sympathy of future democracies and possible socialisms, led to do so by that element of his thought which served to aerate his mind and keep it frank and generous —his awareness of the part played in human existence by the will to power, which, however it figures in the thought of his epigones and vulgarizers, was conceived by Nietzsche himself as comprising the whole range of the possibilities of human energy, creativity, libido. The claims of any social group to this human characteristic had weight with him. And he gave ready credence to the pleasure that attends one or another kind of power; if he was quick to judge people by the pleasures they chose—and woe to those who preferred beer to wine and *Parsifal* to *Carmen!*—the principle of pleasure presented itself to him as constituting an element of the dignity of man. It is because of this humanism of his, this naturalistic acceptance of power and pleasure, that Nietzsche is held at a distance by the modern spiritual sensibility. And the converse of what explains Nietzsche's relative marginality explains Dostoevski's position at the very heart of the modern spiritual life.

If we speak of spirituality, we must note that it is not only humanism that is negated by the Underground Man but Christianity as well, or at least Christianity as Western Europe understands it. For not only humanism but the Christianity of the West bases reason upon pleasure, upon pleasure postponed and purified but analogous in kind to worldly pleasure. Dostoevski's clerk has had his way with us: it would seem to be true that, in the degree that the promises of the spiritual life are made in terms of pleasure—of comfort, rest, and beauty—they have no power over the modern imagination. If Kafka, perhaps more than any other writer of our time, lends the color of reality to the events of the spiritual life, his power to do so lies in his characterizing these events by unpleasure, by sordidness and disorder, even when, as in *The Castle*, the spiritual struggle seems to yield a measure of success. He understood that a divinity who, like Saint Augustine's, could be spoken of as gratifying all the senses, must nowadays be deficient in reality and that a heaven which is presented to us as well ordered, commodious, beautiful—as *luxurious*—cannot be an object of hope. Yeats tells us that "Berkeley in his youth described the summum bonum and the reality of Heaven as physical pleasure, and thought this conception made both more intelligible to simple men." To simple men perhaps, but who now is a simple man? How far from our imagination is the idea of "peace" as the crown of spiritual struggle! The idea of "bliss" is even further removed. The two words propose to us a state of virtually infantile passivity which is the negation of the "more life" that we crave, the "more life" of spiritual militancy. We dread Eden, and of all Christian concepts there is none we understand so well as the *felix culpa* and the "fortunate fall"; not, certainly, because we anticipate the salvation to which these Christian paradoxes point, but because by means of the sin and the fall we managed to escape the seductions of peace and bliss.

My first intention in trying to make explicit a change in the assumptions of literature which everybody is more or less aware of has been historical and objective. But it must be obvious that my account of the change has not been wholly objective in the sense of being wholly neutral. It asks a question which is inevitably adversary in some degree, if only by reason of the irony which is implicit in the historical approach to a fact of moral culture. It suggests that the modern spirituality, with its devaluation of the principle of pleasure, because it came into being at a particular time, may be regarded as a contingent and not a necessary mode of thought. This opens the way to regarding it as a mode of thought which is "received" or "established" and which is therefore, like any other received or established mode of thought, available to critical scrutiny.

And that possibility is by no means comfortable. We set great store by the unillusioned militancy of spirit which deals violently with the specious good. Upon it we base whatever self-esteem we can lay claim to—it gives us, as one of D. H. Lawrence's characters says of it (or something very much like it), our "last distinction"; he feels that to question it is a "sort of vulgarity." [8] To what end, with what intention, is it to be questioned? Can an adversary scrutiny of it point away from it to anything else than an idiot literature, to "positive heroes" who know how to get the good out of life and who have "affirmative" emotions about their success in doing so? The energy, the consciousness, and the wit of modern literature derive from its violence against the specious good. We instinctively resent questions which suggest that there is fault to be found with the one saving force in our moral situation—that extruded "high" segment of our general culture which, with its exigent, violently subversive spirituality, has the power of arming us against, and setting us apart from, all in the general culture that we hate and fear.

Then what justification can there be for describing with any degree of adversary purpose the diminished status of the principle of pleasure which characterizes this segment of our culture?

Possibly one small justification can be brought to light by reference to a famous passage in the *Confessions* of Saint Augustine, the one in which Augustine speaks of an episode of his adolescence and asks why he entered that orchard and stole those pears. Of all the acts of his unregenerate days which he calls sinful and examines in his grim, brilliant way, there is none that he nags so persistently, none that seems to lie so far beyond the reach of his ready comprehension of sin. He did not steal the pears because he was hungry. He did not steal them because they were delicious—they were pears of rather poor quality, he had better at home. He did not steal them to win the admiration of the friends who were with him, although this comes close, for, as he says, he would not have stolen them if he had been alone. In all sin, he says, there is a patent motivating desire, some good to be

[8] Gerald Crich, in chapter XXIX of *Women in Love*.

gained, some pleasure for the sake of which the act was committed. But this sin of the stolen pears is, as it were, pure—he can discover no human reason for it. He speaks again of the presence of the companions, but although their being with him was a necessary condition of the act, it cannot be said to have motivated it. To the mature Augustine, the petty theft of his youth is horrifying not only because it seems to have been a sin committed solely for the sake of sinning, but because, in having no conceivable pleasure in view, it was a sort of negative transcendence—in effect, a negation—of his humanity. This is not strange to us—what I have called the extruded high segment of our general culture has for some time been engaged in an experiment in the negative transcendence of the human, a condition which is to be achieved by freeing the self from its thralldom to pleasure. Augustine's puzzling sin is the paradigm of the modern spiritual enterprise, and in his reprobation of it is to be found the reason why Dostoevski contemned and hated the Christianity of the West, which he denounced as, in effect, a vulgar humanism.

To be aware of this undertaking of negative transcendence is, surely, to admire the energy of its desperateness. And we can comprehend how, for the consumer of literature, for that highly developed person who must perforce live the bourgeois life in an affluent society, an aesthetic ethos based on the devaluation of pleasure can serve, and seem to save, one of the two souls which inhabit his breast. Nearly overcome as we are by the specious good, insulted as we are by being forced to acquire it, we claim the right of the Underground Man to address the "gentlemen" with our assertion, "I have more life in me than you have," which consorts better with the refinement of our sensibility than other brags that men have made, such as, "I am stronger than you," or "I am holier than thou." Our high culture invites us to transfer our energies from the bourgeois competition to the spiritual competition. We find our "distinction"—last or penultimate—in our triumph over the miserable "gentlemen," whether they are others or ourselves, whether our cry be, "I have more life in me than you have" or "I have more life in me than I have."

Now and then it must occur to us that the life of competition for spiritual status is not without its own peculiar sordidness and absurdity. But this is a matter for the novelist—for that novelist we do not yet have but must surely have one day, who will take into serious and comic account the actualities of the spiritual career of our time.

More immediately available to our awareness and more substantive and simple in itself is the effect which the devaluation of pleasure has upon the relation between our high literature and our life in politics, taking that word in its largest possible sense. There was a time when literature assumed that the best ideals of politics were naturally in accord with its own essence, when poetry celebrated the qualities of social life which had their paradigmatic existence in poetry itself. Keats's *Poems* of 1817 takes for its epigraph two lines from Spenser which are intended to point up the political overtone of the volume: "What more felicity can fall to creature/ Than to enjoy delight with liberty." Even when Wordsworth is deep in Toryism and Stoic Christianity, it is natural for him to assert the Utopian possibility.

> Paradise and groves
> Elysian, Fortunate Fields—like those of old
> Sought in the Atlantic Main—why should they be
> A history only of departed things,
> Or a mere fiction of what never was?

He goes on to say categorically that these imaginations may become, at the behest of rationality and good will, "a simple produce of the common day." But the old connection between literature and politics has been dissolved. For the typical modern literary personality, political life is likely to exist only as it makes an occasion for the disgust and rage which are essential to the state of modern spirituality, as one particular instance of the irrational, violent, and obscene fantasy which life in general is, as licensing the counter-fantasy of the poet.

In a recent essay,[9] William Phillips described in an accurate and telling way the division that has developed between modern literature and a rational and positive politics, and went on to explain why, for literature's sake, the separation must be maintained. "It now looks," Mr. Phillips said, "as though a radical literature and a radical politics must be kept apart. For radical politics of the modern variety has really served as an antidote to literature. The moral hygiene, the puritanism, the benevolence—all the virtues that sprout on the left—work like a cure for the perverse and morbid idealism of the modern writer. If writing is to be thought of as radical, it must be in a deeper sense, in the sense not simply of cutting across the grain of contemporary life but also of reaching for the connections between the real and the forbidden and the fantastic. The classic example is Dostoevski."

[9] "What Happened in the 30's," *Commentary*, September 1962.

The situation that Mr. Phillips describes will scarcely be a matter of indifference to those of us who, while responding to the force of the perverse and morbid idealism of modern literature, are habituated to think of literature and politics as naturally having affinity with each other. We cannot but feel a discomfort of mind at the idea of their hostile separation, and we are led to ask whether the breach is as complete as Mr. Phillips says it is. His description, it seems to me, so far as it bears upon the situation of the moment, upon the situation as it presents itself to the practitioner of literature, needs no modification. But if we consider the matter in a more extended perspective, in the long view of the cultural historian, it must occur to us to speculate— even at the risk of being "hygienic"—whether the perverse and morbid idealism of modern literature is not to be thought of as being precisely political, whether it does not express a demand which in its own way is rational and positive and which may have to be taken into eventual account by a rational and positive politics.

If we do ask this question, we will be ready to remind ourselves that the devaluation of the pleasure principle, or, as perhaps we ought to put it, the imagination of going *beyond the pleasure principle* is, after all, not merely an event of a particular moment in culture. It is, as Freud made plain in his famous essay, a fact of the psychic life itself. The impulse to go beyond the pleasure principle is certainly to be observed not only in modern literature but in all literature, and of course not only in literature but in the emotional economy of at least some persons in all epochs. But what we can indeed call an event in culture is that at a particular moment in history, in our moment, this fact of the psychic life became a salient and dominant theme in literature, and also that it has been made explicit as a fact in the psychic life and forced upon our consciousness by Freud's momentous foray into metapsychology. And this cultural event may indeed be understood in political terms, as likely to have eventual political consequences, just as we understood in political terms and as having had political consequences the eighteenth-century assertion that the dignity of man was to be found in the principle of pleasure.

We deal with a change in quantity. It has always been true of some men that to pleasure they have preferred unpleasure. They imposed upon themselves difficult and painful tasks, they committed themselves to strange, "unnatural" modes of life, they sought out distressing emotions, in order to know psychic energies which are not to be summoned up in felicity. These psychic energies, even when they are experienced in self-destruction, are a means of self-definition and self-affirmation. As such, they have a social reference—the election of unpleasure, however isolate and private the act may be, must refer to society if only because the choice denies the valuation which society in general puts upon pleasure; and of course it often receives social approbation in the highest degree, even if at a remove of time: it is the choice of the hero, the saint and martyr, and, in some cultures, the artist. The quantitative change which we have to take account of is: what was once a mode of experience of a few has now become an ideal of experience of many. For reasons which, at least here, must defy speculation, the ideal of pleasure has exhausted itself, almost as if it had been actually realized and had issued in satiety and ennui. In its place, or, at least, beside it, there is developing—conceivably at the behest of literature!—an ideal of the experience of those psychic energies which are linked with unpleasure and which are directed toward self-definition and self-affirmation. Such an ideal makes a demand upon society for its satisfaction: it is a political fact. It surely asks for gratification of a sort which is not within the purview of ordinary democratic progressivism.

What I have called the spirituality of modern literature can scarcely be immune to irony, and the less so as we see it advancing in the easy comprehension of increasing numbers of people, to the point of its becoming, through the medium of the stage and the cinema, the stuff of popular entertainment—how can irony be withheld from an accredited subversiveness, an established moral radicalism, a respectable violence? But although the anomalies of the culture of the educated middle class do indeed justify an adversary response, and perhaps a weightier one than that of irony, a response that is nothing but adversary will not be adequate.

We often hear it said nowadays, usually by psychoanalysts and by writers oriented toward psychoanalysis, that the very existence of civilization is threatened unless society can give credence to the principle of pleasure and learn how to implement it. We understand what is meant, that repressiveness and oppression will be lessened if the principle of pleasure is established in our social arrangements, and we readily assent. Yet secretly we know that the formula does not satisfy the condition it addresses itself to—it leaves out of account those psychic energies which press beyond the pleasure principle and even deny it.

It is possible to say that—whether for good or for bad—we confront a mutation in culture by which an old established proportion between the pleasure-seeking instincts and the ego instincts is being altered in favor of the latter.[10] If we follow Freud through the awesome paradoxes of *Beyond the Pleasure Principle*, we may understand why the indications of this change should present themselves as perverse and morbid, for the other name that Freud uses for the ego instincts is the death instincts. Freud's having made the ego instincts synonymous with the death instincts accounts, more than anything else in his dark and difficult essay, for the cloud of misunderstanding in which it exists. But before we conclude that *Beyond the Pleasure Principle* issues, as many believe, in an ultimate pessimism or "negation," and before we conclude that the tendencies in our literature which we have remarked on are nothing but perverse and morbid, let us recall that although Freud did indeed say that "the aim of all life is death," the course of his argument leads him to the statement that "the organism wishes to die only in its own fashion," only through the complex fullness of its appropriate life.

[10] See the remarks on tragedy in "On the Teaching of Modern Literature" (pp. 18 ff.) and also Lionel Abel's brilliant chapter on tragedy in *Metatheatre*. For a full and detailed account of the modern devaluation of that good fortune the destruction of which once pained us in tragedy, see Thomas Munro, "The Failure Story: A Study of Contemporary Pessimism," *The Journal of Aesthetics and Art Criticism*, vol. XVII, no. 2, December 1958.

I. 12

Ghostlier Demarcations*

GEOFFREY H. HARTMAN

University of Iowa

"The dark Religions are departed and sweet Science reigns." BLAKE

COMMENTING ON Aristotle's *Poetics*, the first systematic criticism known to us, S. H. Butcher remarks that its author is preeminently "a Greek summing up Greek experience." Northrop Frye, the latest and most ambitious exponent of a systematic criticism, can hardly be described as a Canadian summing up Canadian experience, or even as a scholar summing up the experience of English literature. His situation is so different from Aristotle's that to express it it is tempting to use Copernicus' image of the "virile man standing in the sun . . . overlooking the planets." I do not intend this image to suggest a premature deification, but to describe a new vantage point with its promise of mastery and also its enormously expanded burden of sight. Certainly no literary thinker, systematic or not, has attained so global a point of view of literature. The nearest parallels to this achievement come from other though related disciplines: there is Mircea Eliade's work in comparative mythology, or André Malraux's in his history of art.

It is the question of point of view, or of the critic's situation, I shall be initially concerned with. For although Frye has said that his system exists for the insights and not the other way around, the excitement, the liberation, the play, as well as the most serious claim he makes is the possibility of system. Frye is an overreacher, a man with hubris, but it is a methodical hubris, a heuristic and applied attitude. There is, in other words, a more-than-intellectual aspect to system-

* Read at the Institute in 1965. Published in *Selected Papers from the Institute: Northrop Frye in Modern Criticism*, 1966.

making on such a scale. Literary criticism remains an expressive act; and despite its claims to objectivity, its moral and intellectual ends mingle. If Aristotle is a Greek summing up the experience of his culture, we should be able to discern the *polis* of Northrop Frye, and what visionary politics are his.

THE SITUATION OF THE CRITIC

Literature has not always been the property or interest of the many. Some, even today, think that the *paideia* of the New Criticism, the attempt to open literature to the direct understanding of students of any background, is undesirable or doomed to failure. It may not please those who know the great differences in pedagogical method between the New Critics and Northrop Frye to have me begin by suggesting that Frye is part of a single modern movement to democratize criticism and demystify the muse. I would go further and say that Frye is our most radical demystifier of criticism even though his great achievement is the recovery of the demon, or of the intrinsic role of Romance in the human imagination. His importance to literary history proper is as a topographer of the Romance imagination in its direct and displaced forms. But his service to the ongoing need to have greater numbers of persons participate in the imaginative life, to open the covenant of education until the difference between persons is really "ghostly," only a matter of intenser or lesser partipation, in this he continues the vision of those first struck in the nineteenth century with the possibility of universal education, and who felt with Victor Hugo that the multiplication of books was comparable to the multiplying of loaves of bread.

Demystification begins in Frye with the very concept of system. This concept should be distinguished, at first, from the particular system furthered. To systematize criticism is to universalize it, to put its intellectual or spiritual techniques into the hands of every intelligent person, of every child even. To imagine children of the future performing little Anatomies as easily as they now do basic operations in mathematics may not be everyone's Utopia, but we should recall that Frye is ambitious only with respect to the possibility of system and not to his particular version of it. Yet it must be pointed out that he fuses, or confuses, two notions of universality. One is the scientific, and holds that the criticism of literature should be pursued as a coherent and systematic study, which, like mathematics, has elementary principles explainable to anyone. The other is evangelical, and holds that critics have stood like priests between literature and those desiring to participate in it, whereas even a child should be able to be instructed in the principles that make art nourishing. When Frye says "the only guarantee that a subject is theoretically coherent is its ability to have its elementary principles taught to children," [1] it is hard to tell the scientific from the evangelical notion. Frye's scientism is therefore the opposite of exclusionary: he does not seek to overdignify criticism or scholarship but to place its basic principles and their creative development in the hands of every earnest reader. "What critics now have is a mysteryreligion without a gospel . . . they are initiates who can communicate, or quarrel, only with one another." [2]

But who put the mystery Frye wants to purge into criticism? Nobody: Frye is indicating that unorganized innocence falls prey to the latest compulsions in taste—to casual, sentimental, or social valuejudgments. This is the more likely as the assumption of innocence, in literary scholarship, takes the form of an appeal to pragmatism, commonsense, or impartiality. The unsystematic critic considers his lack of system proof that he cannot possibly be prejudiced. Frye, I think, would hesitate to go further and to accuse specific groups of surrounding the study of literature with a mystique. Yet the feature of his system that has caused most protest is precisely his relegation of certain kinds of value-judgment to the history of taste and his resolute exclusion of them from criticism. If there is a mystique, it lies here, in the conviction challenged by him that literature is to be used as a training ground for the élite judgment.

Such a conviction is a carry-over from the time when Classics were at the center of humanistic studies, and English did not exist as an academic field. The Classics were studied not for themselves but as part of the proper education for the upper classes, composed of administrators, churchmen, and statesmen. When English, a mere baby among academic disciplines, won its freedom in the 1920s and 1930s (Tillyard's *The Muse Unchained* records vividly part of that emancipation), it engendered its own protective and self-dignifying mystique. It did

---

[1] "The Developing Imagination," in *Learning in Language and Literature* (Cambridge, Mass., 1963), p. 33. Cf. *Anatomy of Criticism* (Princeton, 1957), p. 14.
[2] *Anatomy*, p. 14.

this by assuming the mantle of Classical studies and claiming for English literature the same function of training the judgment. It also insisted that this training was best provided by the immediacies of vernacular literature. We may admire the careful scrutiny, the chaste inquisition brought to bear on the vernacular status of words, or on the consciousness organizing them, which now for the first time enters literary studies, and still acknowledge that the object of the new discipline was not a total or synoptic conception of literature but the training, through literature, of a specific and judicious sensibility. And it is hard not to feel the breath of a mystique in the following recommendation of the "English School," which shows how thoroughly Leavis, who wrote it, adapted and refined the Classicist emphasis on the importance of judgment:

The essential discipline of an English School is the literary-critical; it is a true discipline, also in an English School if anywhere will it be fostered, and it is irreplaceable. It trains, in a way no other discipline can, intelligence and sensibility together, cultivating a sensitiveness and precision of response and a delicate integrity of intelligence—intelligence that integrates as well as analyzes and must have pertinacity and staying power as well as delicacy.[3]

Whether or not Frye's expulsion of rationalized "taste" from the history of criticism is viable, its purpose is to cleanse that discipline of a sporadically chauvinistic cult of culture. His "categorial criticism" is a direct challenge to the English mystique of English Studies. It bypasses personalistic judgment and the tutorial approach to literature. Instead of the tutor there is the system, instead of judgments reposing on a precarious blend of moral, verbal, literary sensibility, there is the extroversion of archetypes and the free yet controlled establishment of a criticism without walls. The act of appreciating literature has its private pleasures, but it becomes criticism by becoming extramural—by interpretations that link the Classics to English literature and all literature to a total form that reveals archetypal features. Frye's concern is with a point of view determined by culture as such, rather than by a particular culture, tradition, or line.

This raises the question of what Frye means by total form, and obliges us to turn from his concept of system to the system itself. The

[3] Quoted by Fred Inglis, "Professor Northrop Frye and the Study of Literature," *Centennial Review*, IX (1965), 325–26. On the importance of the "Vernacular Matrix" for modern criticism, see W. J. Ong, s.j., *The Barbarian Within* (New York, 1962), ch. x.

intellectual problems here are very great, but ours are greater: for Frye is an eloquent man who somewhere has provided an answer to every question. What must therefore be judged is not his comprehensiveness, which is extraordinary, or his intentions, which are the best since Matthew Arnold, but how well he has dealt with problems every literary critic faces whatever his attitude toward systematic thought. These problems must center, at some point, on how the individual work is related to art's general function in consciousness or society. "No discussion of beauty," says Frye, "can confine itself to the formal relations of the isolated work of art; it must consider, too, the participation of the work of art in the vision of the goal of social effort, the idea of complete and classless civilization." [4]

If we were to apply the technique of "extracting the myth" to Frye himself, we would come on a pastoral motif: "The hungry sheep look up, and are not fed." His critical system moves in the same direction as the history of art it seeks to liberate—away from the closed culture, the closed society, the priest-interpreter, the critic's critic. Properly understood he appears as a knight in a continuing quest: that of removing the dragon from the hoard, or mystery from communion.

THE CONCEPT OF TOTAL FORM

In saying that Frye aims at a "criticism without walls," I was implicitly adapting a phrase used by André Malraux. He remarked that modern techniques of reproduction had created in the visual arts a "museum without walls," and made the world's masterpieces available to every viewer. But he also noted that this had changed profoundly our conception of the uniqueness of the artifact which is now universally distributed and no longer in a special relation to its place of origin. The more transportable the sacred objects of a culture, the more abstract our notion of art tends to be. "You do not put gods in a museum," says Malraux, "the gods there become paintings." Modern photography converts all "historical" artifacts into "free" works of art. It robs them of their original context and reveals through synopsis and juxtaposition a more coherent or self-referring entity.

Frye, whose concern is chiefly with the verbal arts, where the revolution of which Malraux is talking began with Gutenberg, does not stress the technological factor. "The revolution," he writes, "is not

[4] *Anatomy*, p. 348.

simply in technology but in spiritual productive power." [5] Yet we have seen that his very concept of system combines a technological result with an evangelical purpose. If the Bible had not been unchained by Gutenberg and the Reformers, and if this liberation had not continued until the gods sit as books in our libraries, the kind of analysis Frye calls "archetypal" might not have come about.

For there is no mystery about "archetype." The archetype is simply the typical at the highest power of literary generalization. The typical was valued in the eighteenth century for its universality within the context of polite society; and the archetypal emerges when the concept of a literary universe, made possible by technology, is substituted for that of polite society. And just as the world of the typical is society perfected, with its hieratic structure, its vertical line of authority; so the world of the archetypal is not some primitive communion but Arnold's and Malraux's "complete and classless civilization" with its intersubjective structure and its authority derived purely from a continuing vision transmitted by the arts.

Thus art contributes to a supreme fiction, an archetypal or total form, which is the forerunner of a new, demystified theory of participation. The Marxist concepts of types, the Western historians' concept of topoi, the renewal of interest in biblical typology, the attempt to see art as an especially concrete sort of universal—as well as the varieties of myth-criticism—show how deeply modern literary theory is implicated in transcending the view that art is a private or élitist enterprise.

Historically the new theory of participation was given its most radical statement by the Romantics. "Would to God that all the Lord's people were prophets," writes Blake, quoting the reply of Moses to those who wished him to restrict the divine vision.[6] Art must be freed from mystery, from the very thing Mallarmé cultivated as "le mystère dans les lettres." It is to be within the reach of all and practically a biological inheritance: "The mystery in the greatness of *King Lear* or *Macbeth* comes not from concealment but from revelation, not from something unknown or unknowable in the work, but from something unlimited in it." [7]

The emphasis on demystification also helps with the curious flatness of archetypes as Frye conceives them. Archetypes are not hidden but almost too open—if we do not easily spot them it is because we ex-

[5] *Anatomy*, p. 344.   [7] *Anatomy*, p. 88.
[6] Epigraph to *Milton*; Numbers XI:29.

pect the wrong kind of mystery. Frye does not practice depth-criticism or depth-psychology; in this he differs absolutely from Jung, and it is impossible to attach an occult or, simply, ontological virtue to the structures he derives from mythology. This flattening out of the mythic substance is like transforming a landscape into a map, but also like opening a closed book. Archetypal analysis brings art into the public domain and makes it what nature was to Sir Thomas Browne, a "manuscript expans'd unto the eyes of all."

When we recall the rejection of myths of depth in contemporary literature and phenomenology, and when we think of how Wallace Stevens tries to return to a fundamental insight of the Romantics obscured even in him by traces of Symbolist cultism, we easily perceive Frye's link to the modern movement which insists on demystification. The "virile man standing in the sun" begins to merge with Stevens's virile poet and central man who declares he has outlived the esoteric muses: "No longer do I believe that there is a mystic muse, sister of the Minotaur. This is another of the monsters I had for nurse, whom I have wasted. I am myself a part of what is real, and it is my own speech and the strength of it, this only, that I hear or ever shall." [8]

Yet archetypes, unmysterious as they are, cast a shadow. It has often been remarked that the particularity of the literary work may be obscured by too great or synoptic an angle of vision. Archetypal analysis can degenerate into an abstract thematics where the living pressure of mediations is lost and all connections are skeletonized. These faults appear clearly in the little book on T. S. Eliot and the essay on Milton's "Lycidas," inexpensive world tours of myth. Yet what we are facing here is not merely the weaker side of a method but something inherent in any response to a dilemma posed by the very promise of technology. "What we have to defend today," Marshall McLuhan has said, "is not the values developed in any particular culture or by any one mode of communication. Modern technology presumes to attempt a total transformation of man and his environment. This calls in turn for an inspection and defense of all human values." [9] The need for a global perspective is evident.

Every greater critic has recognized this situation, which demands the rejection or else redemption of technology, but in any case a total

[8] "The Figure of the Youth as Virile Poet," *The Necessary Angel* (New York, 1951).

[9] "Sight, Sound and the Fury," *The Commonweal*, LX (April 9, 1954), 11.

rather than piercemeal approach. Yet few have accepted the challenge so optimistically as Northrop Frye. Ortega y Gasset writes of the dehumanization, and not humanization, of modern art; and Walter Benjamin, "The Work of Art in the Era of Its Technical Reproduction," sees more sharply than anyone the estranging influence of technology on culture. Technology, he asserts, will transform works of art into exhibition pieces and consumer goods, and so destroy what he calls their *aura*.[10] And Erich Auerbach toward the end of *Mimesis*, a book almost the obverse in temperament to Frye's *Anatomy*, foresees the withering away of those fully individuated civilizations of which he has just written as if already their last historian. What, then, is the future of historical criticism? Can the aura of the individual work be saved? Or is Frye's totalizing approach, which looks more and more Olympian, the true alternative? The theory of literature, like literature itself, seems to have entered the crisis stage in its attempt to find the relation of the particular, the "dreadful sundry of this world," to any authentic concept of totality.

THE COURSE OF THE PARTICULAR

The possibilities of myth as a structural principle were brought to light by the practice of certain writers in the Symbolist era. Yeats and Joyce, T. S. Eliot said in a famous essay of 1923, substituted "the mythical method" for the "narrative method." Eliot had resolved the "dreadful sundry" by similar means. The new method, according to him, "is simply a way of controlling, of ordering, of giving shape and significance to the immense panorama of futility and anarchy which is contemporary history." [11] It is clear that the substitution of mythical for narrative method, in literature or criticism, expresses the difficulty of finding ideas of order within secular history.

Frye, however, does not emphasize the heuristic character of the new method. Although his system is frankly speculative, it rarely allows for counterpoint or opposition between the historical and the mythical. Supremely eclectic, Frye melts what many would consider as

---

[10] "Das Kunstwerk im Zeitalter seiner technischen Reproduzierbarkeit," *Schriften* (Frankfurt a.M., 1955), I, 366–405.

[11] "Ulysses, Order, and Myth." First published in *The Dial*. Eliot's practice may also be indebted to the rediscovery of the ritual origin of literary forms by the Cambridge anthropologists. See his somewhat condescending remarks on Jane Harrison and others in "Euripides and Professor Murray" (1920).

contraries into one system of alternative yet concordant approaches. What counterpoint exists is for the richness of the melody: he does not make us feel the problematic situation of either writer or critic, or any sign of that divided consciousness which the mythical method affirms by remaining an artifice in Yeats and Joyce.[12]

To bring out the discords between Frye's mode of criticism and a more historical one, let us consider a model of the act of interpretation furnished by biblical hermeneutics. When Donne, in his Sermons, uses the expression "the intention of the Holy Ghost *in that place*," the word "place" refers to one or more of three things: topos, or figure of speech; context; locality. These relations of words to "place" also situate secular literature in its particularity. Thus the question of verbal or internal context can be equated with that of the temporal medium of the literary work; the question of topoi or figures with that of the authenticity of myth or figures derived from myth; and the question of the relation of words to native place with the aim of conventional histories to understand the literary work *in situ* by recovering its lexical and social ambiance.

What does Frye have to say on these matters which are essential to any historically based criticism? His attitude toward the fact that literature unfolds in time rather than quasi-simultaneously in space is puzzling. It would be possible to apply his type of analysis to the visual arts as well as to the verbal, for he stands back from poem or play as from a picture. A full-fledged example of the pictorial stance is his book on the development of Shakespearean comedy (A *Natural Perspective*), where he identifies structural similarities by removing himself to a "middle distance." In fact, as is well known, Frye's concept of literary structure is consciously spatial. It depends on a disjunction between our immediate experience of literature, which is guided by the tempo of the work, and criticism, which lays out the completed pattern spatially. "When a critic," he writes, "deals with a work of literature, the most natural thing for him to do is to freeze it, to ignore its move-

---

[12] Though Mr. Fletcher has begun to study Frye as what Kierkegaard would have called a "subjective thinker," Frye's strength lies in that "grammar" of imagery, or "morphology" of myth, derived from Blake and Yeats, which has allowed literary criticism to be—for the first time—truly systematic (synchronic) rather than historical (diachronic). He is better, in other words, at respecting the identity of mythical and systemic (an identity glimpsed by Vico and elaborated by French anthropologists from Durkheim to Lévi-Strauss) than the difference between mythical-systemic and historical. He is closest to Plato, for whom, as he observes in the *Anatomy*, "the ultimate acts of apprehension were either mathematical or mythical."

ment in time and look at it as a completed pattern of words with all its parts existing simultaneously." [13] In the *Anatomy*, this disjunction is presented as fundamental to the establishment of criticism as a progressive body of knowledge.

Unfortunately it is also an evasion of the whole problem of temporality. With the related question of the unity of the literary work, this problem has been the single most important topic of poetics. It is true that systematic thought on temporality, starting with Lessing and renewed by Heidegger, is mainly German. Yet Helen Gardner expresses the identical concern when she says that "the discovery of a work's center, the source of its life in all its parts, and response to its total movement—a word I prefer to 'structure,' for time is inseparable from our apprehension of works of literature—is to me the purpose of critical activity." [14] One of the most formal differences of literature is omitted if we cannot encompass by reflection its moving power in time.

Frye's practice here is preferable to his theory. In his concern not to isolate the work of art, but to let it flow into a larger realm of discourse, he often perfects the example of G. Wilson Knight, who first applied a "spatial" analysis to Shakespeare in the *Wheel of Fire* (1930).[15] Frye on Beckett, Shakespeare, or Wallace Stevens can even be compared with the structuralist critics in Europe and America, with

[13] "Myth, Fiction, and Displacement" (1961), *Fables of Identity: Studies in Poetic Mythology* (New York, 1963), p. 21.

[14] *The Business of Criticism* (Oxford, 1959), pp. 23–24. One wonders why Frye has not made greater use of Mircea Eliade's argument that literary time remains basically mythical, because literature submerges us in a "strange" time, and it is the character of myth to cure or at least purify temporality by a ritual "going back" to the origins (anamnesis). The spatializing habit of all structuralist analysis of the imagination has been ably defended by a French work devoted to "archetypology." See Gilbert Durand, *Les Structures Anthropologiques de l'Imaginaire* (1st ed., Paris, 1960).

[15] "One must be prepared to see the whole play in space as well as in time. It is natural in analysis to pursue the steps of the tale in sequence, noticing the logic that connects them, regarding those essentials that Aristotle noted: the beginning, middle, and end. But by giving supreme attention to this temporal nature of drama we omit what, in Shakespeare, is at least of equivalent importance. A Shakespearian tragedy is set spatially as well as temporally in the mind. By this I mean that there are throughout the play a set of correspondences which relate to each other independently of the time-sequence which is the story. . . . Now if we are prepared to see the whole play laid out, so to speak, as an area, being simultaneously aware of these thickly-scattered correspondences in a single view of the whole, we possess the unique quality of the play in a new sense." From Knight's first chapter, "On the Principles of Shakespeare Interpretation."

writers like Bachelard, Poulet, Lucien Goldmann, René Girard, J. Hillis Miller, and (sui generis) Leslie Fiedler. Also in search of the "total form," they insist that the bounding lines of the individual work are to be subordinated to larger patterns revealed by decomposing those outlines. But for them this form cannot finally be expressed in literary or mythical terms: it merges with an analysis of society, consciousness, and language. Although Frye posits the goal of society, and art's drive toward it, he does not specify what has separated man from his vision or into what temporal errors the vision has fallen. The European-trained philosophical critic might therefore say that Frye looks at literature from the point of view of the Hegelian end-state. It would seem to him as if Frye were replacing mystery with obscurity—unless he knew that Frye's analysis of error is identical with Blake's, and that his book on Blake, *Fearful Symmetry*, must be read in conjunction with the *Anatomy*.

The second topic of any historical inquiry, the authenticity of myth and of poetic language, is involved with religious doctrine. All disputes, for example, concerning the use of pagan or indeed any mythology in literature belong as much to the history of religion as of art. To resolve such disputes, scriptural and secular hermeneutics may differ in approach. The former depends almost totally on the principle of accommodation for its criterion of authenticity, but criticism is free to develop other criteria. Since Frye develops his own principle of accommodation, it may be useful to recall here the gist of the original doctrine.

It states that what is said or written may be a limiting form of what is meant, the limit being determined historically by the capacity of the hearers.[16] Interpretation, therefore, is essential not only to prevent wrong conclusions arising from the limiting form but also, in the presence of more capable hearers, to translate the intended thought into its true form. Criticism, however, as distinct from exegesis, may decide that the original form in its very concreteness or obscurity is more authentic than any supposed translation of it. Thus we often say that a metaphorical expression is not really translatable.

---

16 This does not imply that the speaker himself knows what is meant—he may be inspired, or the hermeneutic paradox which Dilthey emphasized may obtain, that we understand the author better than he understands himself. The speaker can be one of his hearers, sharing their limited historical situation.

Frye's system reposes on a tacit assumption of the authenticity of myth, but we are in some difficulty if we ask how this authenticity is revealed. By what process do we accept the "Romantic" element in Shakespeare's comedies? According to Frye it is authenticated by being placed in a context of totality. The individual myth or isolated play reveals its archetypal features by the mutual association of a great number of works of art. What Fyre proposes is, in effect, a hermeneutic translation of literature into a clarified form, or "reconstructed mythology." Yet the absence of an official or dogmatic theology must always leave the authenticity of that form in doubt. Keats, for example, appreciated Romance and certainly understood the Romantic element in Shakespeare, yet felt like Wordsworth that the modern vocation was to surpass it. Myth, whether used substantively or merely as a narrative device, remains a problem for the Wordsworthian tradition. The literary counterpoint of mythical and secular in Eliot and others is a method reflecting this problematic yet insistent presence of myth.

There is, however, a concept in Frye which corresponds to the principle of accommodation and contributes to literary history because it reveals the difficult relation of poetic to ordinary discourse. I refer to what Frye calls displacement and defines as the "adaptation of myth and metaphor to canons of morality or plausibility." [17] So defined it is a restatement of the doctrine of accommodation. Frye supposes that there is such a thing as a pure myth (archetype) the displacements of which can be traced through history. The displacements have a specific direction which his first essay in the *Anatomy*, or Historical Criticism, describes. He there classifies all fiction in terms of the status of the hero who moves from a mythic or supernatural to an ironic or all-too-human mode of being. Thus Shakespeare's use of the Proserpine story shows a twofold displacement: as well as being an oblique version of the myth of death and revival, it had to be accommodated in Shakespeare's time to a "high mimetic" level of plausibility, i.e., it could no longer be a mythic story about gods, or a romantic fable, but only a tale of heroism in which the order of nature is not violated.

The concept of displacement enables us to revalue what grosser histories of literature see merely as secularization. For the movement from myth to realism does not infer the sad decline of hero into anti-hero or of an ancestor's great seal rings into Belinda's hairpin. We dis-

[17] *Anatomy*, "Glossary," and cf. p. 136.

cover that secular man is not devoid of mythical attributes.[18] Except for
Frye's hint of a cyclical return of realism to myth, the notion of displacement is empirically sound: it works; it is teachable; above all it reveals the permanence of Romance. One can no more remove the Romance element from art than natural instincts from man. It is eternal,
as Freud discovered the instincts to be eternal, and therefore gave them
the name of gods, Eros and Thanatos.

I suspect, however, that Frye has shown not that myth is displaced
but that it is historical. It is never found in that unaccommodated
state he posits when he mentions "the pure myth of death and revival"
or when he claims that literature is a reconstructed mythology. One
can make such a claim only by reducing myths to archetypes in the
strictly Platonic sense of simples rather than complexes. But anyone
who has read the *Anatomy* will agree that there are no simples in it.
Or what simples there are, are hooked simples in the sense in which
Lowe's *Road to Xanadu* explained Coleridge's fantastically assimilative
mind by memories that are "hooked atoms." We do not find myth
pure of religion or literature; it comes to us institutionalized from the
beginning, and though it may also be a body of structural principles
there is no point in underplaying the war in the members of that body.

For, historically, some structural principles seem to exclude others:
the realistic writer, as Frye notes, "finds that the requirements of
literary form and plausible content always fight against each other.
Just as the poetic metaphor is always a logical absurdity, so every inherited convention of plot in literature is more or less mad." [19] What is
true of the realist is true of any writer, as Frye's own theory of displacement has shown: reality is never more than the *plausible* artifice. But
in that case the notion of displacement becomes unnecessary except to
indicate the direction of human credibility—credibility defining that
realm in which contraries are no longer felt.

To Frye's total myth we must therefore add a historical account of
the war that myth has waged with myth. Just as the redactors of the
Book of Genesis had to reconcile several divergent formulas of the
"myth" of creation, so it is in non-oral tradition: a writer does not confront a pure pattern, archetype, or convention, but a corpus of tales or

[18] So Hawthorne's Hester Prynne, Melville's Billy Budd, Hardy's Tess, and
Mrs. Woolf's Septimus seem to assume the role of *pharmakos* or scapegoat—an observation carried into modern American fiction by Ihab Hassan's study of the "Radical Innocent."

[19] "Myth, Fiction, and Displacement," *Fables of Identity*, p. 36.

principles that are far from harmonized. The pressure bringing unity out of diversity may indeed come from a latent archetype in the competing stories, but this raises the question of artistic unity—its necessary relation to a dialectical principle, such as the reconciliation of opposites or the harmonizing of variant traditions.

Temporality and authenticity are aspects, finally, of the largest topic of historical criticism: the relation of words to place of utterance. The metaphor of "situation," used several times in this essay, suggests that there is a determinable ground of presuppositions on which a writer stands consciously or unconsciously. Even the divine word, according to Angelus Silesius, could not exist without place—the world which it creates. "Der Ort und's Wort ist eins, und wäre nicht der Ort,/ Bei ewiger Ewigkeit! es wäre nicht das Wort." (Word and place are one, and if place did not exist/ By all that is eternal, the word could not exist.) The sense that art is addressed, that it is always in dialogue, is what historical criticism furthers.

Although Frye increases significantly our knowledge of the structural presuppositions of the literary work, he neglects the one presupposition which is most affected by place or origin: the verbal. He seems relatively unconcerned with the exact dialogue or status of words in the individual consciousness and the particular society. Such apt remarks, for example, as that Emily Dickinson's poetry was a form of personal correspondence ("This is my letter to the World") remain undeveloped or linked to these on the general nature of poetry that diminish her peculiar paradox. Instead of examining "the verbal," Frye immediately subsumes it in what is called the "verbal universe." But this concept prevents a definitive description of the very element after which it is named.

For the concept of a verbal universe does not agree with what we know of the place of words in society. The opposition of science to art has always centered on the relation of words to things, which is another way of stating that words compete with conventions claiming to be better than verbal. Every writer *in* society is therefore concerned with the alternatives to the word. There has been fruitful conflict even among the arts themselves on the question of alternatives (musical, pictorial, hieroglyphic) to the verbal. This *paragone* may simply express the fact that all art aspires to the condition of totality; it remains, even so, a force in the writer's consciousness. Is there room in Frye's system —which has many chambers and not all opened—for that radical doubt, that innermost criticism which art brings to bear on itself? Or does his system circumvent the problematic character of verbal fictions?

Since the verbal, in Frye, is a larger category than the literary or the mythical, he may have intended to say that literature itself is always in dire need of being humanized. It becomes an institution easily infected by *ratio* and must be led back to its source in *oratio*. This surely is what the great work of fiction (or criticism) achieves: it recalls the origin of civilization in dialogic arts of naming, cursing, blessing, consoling, laughing, lamenting, and beseeching. These speak to us more openly than myth or archetype because they are the first-born children of the human voice. Myth and metaphor are endued with the acts, the gesta, of speech; and if there is a mediator for our experience of literature, it is something as simply with us as the human body, namely the human voice. It is here that one possibility of progress lies: in honoring the problematic relation of words to a reality they mediate rather than imitate. To envision "ghostlier demarcations" a poet must utter "keener sounds."

Thus Frye's criticism and a historical approach differ more than we are led to believe. Yet the reservations I have expressed should not be taken as a plea for conventional literary history, for that either does not face the question of the mission of art, or is content to show that art, like any cult or closed society, has a self-authenticating range of allusions to be decoded only by the priest of the cult: the historical expert.

CRITICISM AND THE ORAL TRADITION

In conclusion, I recall ruefully Aristotle's remark that unity of plot does not consist in the unity of the hero. The plot was criticism, the hero Frye; and in case my reflections have been too picaresque, I would like to end with a firm and even didactic estimate of Frye's importance to contemporary criticism. The more we read in him the more we understand how essential the Romance tradition is, both in itself and in its modern afterlife. Poetry is inconceivable without it; even Shakespearean drama and the vast majority of novels conform to a Romance poetics, or are significantly clarified by it. Frye's permanent achievement is as a theorist whose recognitions favor Romance rather than Tragedy; and had he no more than rescued for us the spiritual form of William Blake, and then the spiritual form of Romance, it would have been sufficient.

Frye will not be grateful to me for considering him as the fulfill-ment of Bishop Hurd. And indeed he is much more, as I hope to have shown; yet his claim to provide the basis for a universal criticism re-mains less convincing than his Anatomy of Romance. His discoveries reflect on unity of design rather than unity of plot, and on the unity of art rather than the unity of the work of art. Even his style, a constant pleasure, is a Romance multiplication of recognitions and its symmetry an allegorical layering of the levels of recognition.

But this revival of a Romance poetics is of more than professional literary interest. It is Romance which mediated the themes and struc-tures of the oral tradition; so that the revival of the one is linked to an interest in the other. Frye reverses the preference of Aristotle, who at-tempted to modify the predominance of oral tradition by esteeming unity of action more than the variegated energies of epic. The *Anatomy of Criticism* returns to the values implicit in the multiple design of Epic and Romance. The achetype as a structural principle resembles nothing so much as the *formula* of oral poetry, while Frye's system is in quest of a community as universal as that which oral poetry may have reached.

There is of course no question of a return to oral tradition. But there is some hope that its renewed appreciation will change our narrow concepts of originality in art, and permit us in reading a book to touch the central man and through him the life of generations. There is some hope that reading can become once more an encounter of imagination with imagination, as in Blake. But if Frye's purpose is to contribute to this encounter and to recover for literature its widest audience, his emphasis on system remains a stumbling block. Systems are the ink-horn children of bookcraft and erudition: they arise whenever human-ists warm themselves on the ashes of myth. Despite Frye's return to a criticism nourished by the values of oral tradition, he has not escaped the ethos of the printed word. That "virile man standing in the sun" belongs to the Gutenberg Galaxy and is scanning the Milky Way of Romance as if it were an alienated part of his—and our—imagination. I cannot wish he were standing anywhere else or that he should descend to that "lower flight" which Raphael in *Paradise Lost* urged on Adam.

I. 13
Sign, Sense, and Roland Barthes*

HUGH M. DAVIDSON

University of Virginia

In the fall of 1965 Raymond Picard, a professor at the Sorbonne, and well known for his exhaustive research—basically historical in conception—on Racine, published a short but explosive little book entitled *Nouvelle critique ou nouvelle imposture*.[1] While it is clear that Picard intended to question the procedures of a whole group of new critics in France (Sartre, Poulet, Richard, Mauron, Goldmann, for examples), his principal target was Roland Barthes, director of studies at the Ecole pratique des hautes études, who had published in 1963 a volume of studies on Racine done in one of the new modes. Barthes took as his main point of departure the proposition that Racine's characters form a horde or tribe of about fifty people, dominated by harsh father-figures usually at war with their sons over women and power. Picard was not at all convinced by this mixture of anthropology and psychoanalysis. By the time his rebuttal was finished, he had attacked Barthes for subjectivity, for violating the elementary rules of scientific thought (or, for that matter, of articulate thought), for cynical and obsessive preoccupation with sexuality, for unverifiability, ambiguity, contradictions, aberrant extrapolations, jargon, inaccuracy, incoherence, arbitrariness, ideological impressionism, dogmatic fantasy, ignorance of scholarship, galloping systematization, and so on.

In February of 1966 Barthes gave his riposte, entitled *Critique et*

* Read at the Institute in 1971.
[1] Utrecht, 1965.

vérité.[2] Some of his compliments, if less luxuriant, were hardly less deadly: Picard, he said, represented the interests of an intellectual caste; he spoke and defended the critical language not even of yesterday but of the day before yesterday; he was attached to phantomatic models of thinking and to a number of tautologies, linguistic myths, and stereotypes; and, as his supreme weakness, he suffered from *asymbolia*, or the inability to understand the symbolic language of literature. But there was light as well as heat in this reply, some of which deserves at least a quick review. After that introduction to the critical position of Barthes, I want to go on, in the second part of this essay, to a discussion of his latest and most remarkable book of criticism, *S/Z*.[3] I believe that *Critique et vérité* and *S/Z* taken together lead us directly into the way of thinking and some of the conclusions that have caused Roland Barthes to be generally recognized as one of the initiators of the science of semiology in France and one of the most original advocates of structuralism as a way of approach to the study of literature.[4]

In the first of these works Barthes evokes on the one hand the hostile camp of university criticism—*la critique universitaire*—with Raymond Picard, of course, as one of its most distinguished representatives, and, on the other, a different type of criticism, one that he has described with various adjectives. Perhaps the most satisfactory are contained in the phrases *critique idéologique* and *critique d'interprétation*. He marks off thus a rough grouping, composed of people who, in their discussion of literature, use one of the principal intellectual languages now being spoken, who find their vocabulary and grammar, so to say, in Marxism, psychoanalysis, structuralism, existentialism, or phenomenology. (As a matter of fact, he argues, university criticism is a *critique idéologique* without realizing it; it embodies the ideology of two or three generations ago.)

Now a particular type of this ideological or interpretative criticism is what interests Barthes. Let us begin by noting that he admires linguistics, especially the structuralist kind. We are not surprised, therefore, to find that the reality he turns to at the start of his own reflection —the logical start, I mean—is *language*. To know literature one must

----

2 Paris, 1966.   3 Paris, 1970.

4 The first section of this essay reviews briefly the main points made in a longer presentation published in *Criticism: Speculative and Analytical Essays*, ed. L. S. Dembo (Madison, 1968).

first know language, since the former grows as a sort of parasite-system on the principal system formed by the latter. The truth of this proposition has become quite clear in the last hundred years, he thinks. From Mallarmé to Blanchot, writers have constantly recognized that language is both the matter and the sphere of literature (p. 38).

Once decided upon, this step, this assimilation of literature to language, affects everything else. The literary work is not a thing, or more precisely, language transformed into a kind of object, as it is for some of the Formalists in this country. Nor is it essentially a kind of mental activity, like the aesthetic intuitions posited by Croce, or more recently, like the tight species of dialectical thinking that fascinates Georges Poulet and that he finds everywhere he looks, or, again, like the concrete workings of sense and imagination that fascinate Jean-Pierre Richard, for whom the literary work is a key to the writer's encounter with the world. I realize that the true state of affairs is quite complex; still I think it obvious that Barthes does not see in the work primarily an art-object or an act of knowing or feeling. It is significant language, signs used in a special way.

"Significant" and "sign" are very important words here. Barthes borrows from Ferdinand de Saussure the distinction of *significant-signifié-signe*, the first referring to the vehicle, the second to what is conveyed, and the third to what comes into being through the association of the other two. By a special twist given to the notion of the *signifié*, what is signified, Barthes establishes the specific order of literary language. When language is involved in *praxis*, in activity designed to modify a situation, it is transitive, aimed at something beyond itself, and, indeed, limited in what it signifies by the situation to be changed. The natural tendency of language toward ambiguity is thus checked by the circumstances. But literary language is intransitive; there is no external situation surrounding literary language and restricting its semantic possibilities. As a result, such language becomes *symbolique*, that is, plural, capable of sustaining more than one sense. It is enigmatic, like an oracle, and the critic composes, rather than recovers, the sense of it with the aid of vital elements present in *his* situation.

Where we are going can be indicated if we return for a moment to Raymond Picard. Picard once said in an interview that Barthes conceives of language as something intermediate between rubber and molasses. He (Picard) believes rather in the notion of a recoverable historical sense for a work and for the language in which it is written. He further conceives of this sense as a function of a period or moment in the history of a civilization. If, after managing this task of recovery and referral—and the effort of self-denial implied in it—the critic wishes to see the relevance of the sense to his own time, he is free to do so. But as far as Barthes is concerned, to give such emphatic attention to the historical and, for him, literal sense is to reveal that *asymbolia* that I mentioned earlier. No one sense may be set up as a canon. The work is a question or sign that has no answer or sense until a reader or critic furnishes one out of his own history, freedom, and language.

In fact, and it is essential not to miss this further point, Barthes calls upon the critic to *write* something that is consubstantial with what the author wrote. In satisfying this condition the critic must elaborate a sense that respects the symbolic character of the literary language: symbol must seek symbol (p. 73). Thus, as the work was written, so must the critic read and write. The need to harmonize the language of the work and the language of the critic is related to the recent change in the relationship of criticism to literature. Since Mallarmé, the two functions—poetic and critical—of writing have tended toward exchange, interpenetration, solidarity. The metalanguage of criticism accompanies and extends creative activity, so that now there is only one kind of writing (p. 46).

In *Critique et vérité* Barthes replies to one objection that is frequently addressed to him: that his conception of criticism leads fatally to subjectivity in interpretation. He lists three sanctions that apply to criticism as he understands it: (1) It must take everything into account; it must find a place in a system of meanings for every detail. (2) It must proceed according to definite rules; however, these will be derived, not from a model of scientific reasoning in the usual sense, but from the logic (as yet only partly developed and understood) of symbolic language. Here linguistics will be powerfully aided by psychoanalysis, which already can provide some of the formulas by which polyvalent language may be understood—either from the analysis of persons, as practiced by Freud and others, or from the analysis of substances, as exemplified in the works of Gaston Bachelard and his disciples. (3) It must move always in the same direction, assuming the same conditions accepted by the writer, and, in particular, the basic one that *language*, not the *person* speaking (and, as we might say, "expressing" himself), is the subject under consideration. If these three sanctions are observed, the critic is not by any means free to say *n'importe quoi.* Bound by the kind of rigor befitting his inquiry, he will trace out in a work long chains of transformations, developments of themes, and series of images.

The pages in which Barthes develops these points introduces us to some of the most characteristic concerns of the *nouvelle critique* in France. In one place he tells us that the movement is national in character, with little or no debt to Anglo-Saxon criticism, to Spitzerism or to Croceanism. I shall take this remark as the point of departure for a comment or two. During the last thirty-five years the nature and history of literary criticism have been widely explored here and in England. This exploration has made possible some awareness of the types and limits of literary criticism, some discernment of the patterns involved in the frequent changes of alliance and fortune that seem to be its lot, some understanding of the philosophic bases that underlie persistent differences of approach, and some appreciation of the unavoidable irony in it, since what it says in any one instance reminds us constantly of all that is being left unsaid. I think that we can assert, in the light of this experience, that controversy over the legitimacy of the *nouvelle critique,* insofar as it is a coherent, self-conscious, responsible movement, is unnecessary, in this country at least. That being true, we can turn our attention from clashes of principle to the problems of defining and situating it, of studying its results and standards of performance.

One further remark. It is impossible to miss the resemblances between this polemic in France and some of the discussions in American criticism in the period from about 1935 to 1960. There is the taste for immanent (we said "intrinsic") values in literature; there is the hostility to literary history, the tendency to oversimplify and caricature it, with the answering strong reactions from the representatives of that discipline; the decision to ask many of the important questions in terms drawn from linguistics and semantics, with some revival of interest in ancient rhetoric and poetics; the effort to distinguish literary language from other uses of language (American New Critics usually preferred negative analogies with *science,* while Barthes prefers to say that literary language has nothing to do with *praxis*); the inclination to turn to the inventors of techniques for exploring pre- or extralogical forms of thought (we had Frazer, Freud, and Jung; Barthes has Lévi-Strauss, Lacan, and Bachelard).

Well then, in 1966 Barthes thought of himself as a member of a group of new critics and in some degree as the defender of the group. Here are a few lines that sum up his position and suggest its tone at the time of *Critique et vérité*:

Certain books of criticism have, then, come into existence, offering themselves to be read in the same ways as works that are literary, properly speaking, although the authors of these books are, as to official status, only critics and not writers. If the new criticism has some reality, it is there: not in the unity of its methods, even less in the snobbism, which—it is convenient to say—sustains it, but in the solitude of the critical act, affirmed henceforth, far from the alibis of science or of institutions, as a deliberate act of *writing* in the full sense of that word (*un acte de pleine écriture*). Formerly separated by the worn-out myth of the "proud creator and the humble servant, both necessary, with each in his place, etc.," the writer and the critic now meet in the same difficult situation, facing the same object: language. (p. 46)

In 1967, one year after *Critique et vérité*, Barthes published a substantial volume called *Système de la mode*. A work of applied semiology, it is a study of fashion clothing, more specifically of language used in certain fashion magazines (*Elle, Jardin des modes, Echo de la mode,* and *Vogue*). Barthes had already noted, in his *Eléments de sémiologie* of 1964, the possibility of using the Saussurian distinction of *language-parole*, language-speech, in matters of clothing, food, automobiles, and furniture. Though not exactly light reading, *Système de la mode* has agreeable ironic and even sarcastic overtones as it applies to the clichés of fashion-writing terms like "denotation," "connotation," "syntagma," "metalanguage," "matrix," "transformation," and "simultaneous systems." In and through the technicalities of his analysis one can see distinct movement toward the method he applies in *S/Z* (1970), his most significant single work of criticism.

In an interview with Raymond Bellour (*Les Lettres françaises,* May 20, 1970), Barthes was asked: "In your view, what is represented by the experience of *S/Z*, the title of which, like a witticism, symbolizes the work of reading that you carried out on a not very well-known story by Balzac: *Sarrasine?*" Barthes replied:

I must say, in the first place, that in the year when I began to write the *Sarrasine* episode—the seminar that I gave at the Ecole pratique des hautes études, then the book that followed it—was perhaps the densest and happiest of my working life. I had the exalting impression that I was attacking something really new, in the strict sense of the term, that is, which had never been done. For a long time, in order to advance the structural analysis of narrative I had wanted to devote myself to a micro-analysis, an analysis that would be patient and progressive, but not exhaustive, because there can be no question of exhausting all (possible) senses: a perpetual analysis, as one might speak of a perpetual calendar. . . . The experience of S/Z represents for me, above everything else, a pleasure, a delight (*jouissance*) in work and writing.

He has said more specifically elsewhere that what he has attempted in S/Z is to "write a reading" (*écrire une lecture*) (*Figaro littéraire*, March 9–15, 1970). "Has it never happened to you," he asks, "to stop constantly while reading, not for lack of interest, but, on the contrary because of a flood of ideas, of stimulations, of associations? . . . It is that kind of reading, disrespectful because it cuts up the text, and fascinated, loving (*éprise*) because it returns to it and feeds on it, that I have tried to write."

Sarrasine, a sculptor with a name that sounds feminine in French, falls in love with a beautiful singer, a *castrato*, whom he believes to be a woman. When he finds out the truth, he feels degraded, tries to kill the man and to break up the statue he has made of him. Then, a *castrato* himself in a symbolic sense, Sarrasine dies by the hand of an assassin. One would expect the name Sarrasine to be spelled with a Z, a letter whose very shape, according to Barthes, connotes a "stinging, castrating whip"; the Z has disappeared from his name, censored, like his own desire for castration, but it reappears in the name of the singer, Zambinella. The bar that separates the S of Sarrasine and the Z of Zambinella signifies the unbridgeable gap between them and also, of course, the work of the psychic censor.

As one might expect, the outer shape of this written-reading is unusual. The Balzac story has been cut into 561 numbered fragments (with Arabic numerals), varying in length from one word to five or six lines. After each fragment come a few lines of commentary, printed in small type; and then, interpolated in this sequence running from 1 through 561, are 103 numbered digressions (with Roman numerals), printed in large type, and amounting in each case to a page or two of text. In an appendix the story is reprinted without interruption. In another appendix the digressions are integrated by number into an outline, a *Table raisonnée*, so that the reader can see at a glance, although it depends somewhat on how good he is at glances, how the topics of the digressions fit into a logical scheme.

Among the principles in the back of Barthes' mind as he starts to work on *Sarrasine* are three that seem to me fundamental. The first concerns the plural aspect of literary texts. The aim in interpretation is not to arrive at a simple, exclusive sense (that much we know from *Critique et vérité*), but to grasp and appreciate the plural (*le pluriel*) of which the text is composed. Here Barthes' thinking appears to have evolved considerably. He posits, as a limiting case, an ideal text that is *infinitely* plural and contrasts with it the classical text (*le texte classique*), which is characterized by a limited or, as he says, *parsimonious* plurality of sense. There is a long sentence describing the ideal text that I shall quote, translating as best I can Barthes' abundant, at times baroque, style:

Let us pose first of all the image of a triumphant plural which is not impoverished by any constraint of representation (of imitation). In this ideal text, the networks are multiple with an interplay among them, such that no network dominates the others; this text is a galaxy of signifiers, not a structure of signifieds; it has no beginning; it is reversible; one has access to it by several entries, none of which can be declared with certainty to be the principal one; the codes that it mobilizes extend their profiles as far as one can see—they are undecidable (the sense is never submitted to a decisive principle, unless it be by a throw of dice): systems of sense may take hold of this absolutely plural text, but the number of these systems is never closed, having as their measure the infinite of language. (pp. 11–12)

This ideal text has no exterior to be outlined; it has no totality: insofar as we can speak of narrative structure or of narrative grammar and logic apropos of a text, we are concerned with incomplete or parsimonious plurality. It is important to note that infinite plurality is, as mentioned above, an ideal, but also that it is part of a historical trend. As Barthes looks back over the history of French literature, he sees *textes classiques*—of limited plurality—from the seventeenth century through Romanticism, until in fact about 1850, when the modern text (*le texte moderne*), attracted by the infiite play of sense and senses, began to appear. And of course, *Sarrasine*, the Balzac story under consideration, belongs to the former category of classical texts.

The second principle follows from the fact that the objective of the reader/interpreter is the plural aspect of his text. What can he use as his prospecting instrument, his divining rod? The answer is: *connotation*. A full account of what Barthes means by that term would make a story too long to be told here. He describes it in a number of ways (the following adverbs are literal translations): "definitionally," "topically," "analytically," "topologically," "semiologically," "dynamically," "functionally," "structurally," and "ideologically." Some idea of what he means can be gathered from these lines where he writes "definitionally":

[A connotation] is a determination, a relation, an anaphora, a trait having the power to refer to earlier, later, or exterior items that have been mentioned, to other places in the text, or to some other text; we must not restrict in any way this relation, except by not confusing connotation with the association of ideas: the latter sends us back to the system or texts; or again, if you will, it is an association made by the text as subject within its own system. (pp. 14–15)

In the third place, as he prepares for the step-by-step analysis of *Sarrasine*, Barthes has in mind a special notion of the status that any particular text has. It is not to be thought of as embodying some ideal structure; it does not give access by induction to a model which then explains the example. Rather, *it is one entry into the network that is all of literature.* "La littérature elle-même n'est jamais qu'un seul texte" (p. 19), he says, and in the context he means that all of literature, past, present, and future, is no more (nor less!) than a single unbounded text. Therefore to work on *a* text is to enter *the* text; to analyze *Sarrasine* is to enter a vast perspective whose vanishing point is not and can never be fixed.

What do these principles lead to in practice? As I have pointed out, Barthes cuts the text—the line formed by the text, so to speak—into 561 segments or *lexies*. An absolutely essential notion appears after Barthes has commented on details in the first three fragments: that of *code*. Since he is observing and pondering the behavior of signs, of meanings, of connotations in his text, he needs some means of drawing them together: a code is, precisely, that which groups the separate items into sequences and configurations. Moreover, in the first three *lexies*, consisting of the title and first sentence of the story, *five* codes are visible, and since this list appears to be exhaustive, the implication is that every item to be commented on will fall under one of these headings, take its place in one of these systems of meaning. There one has, I think, the main point of the rich and ingenious analyses, always interesting, sometimes irritating, contained in *S/Z*: it is a study of the emergence and interweaving of codes, seen in and through the text.

There is a hermeneutic code, for references to the unraveling of the plot, in this case, the identity of Zambinella; a semantic code, for traits attached to persons mainly, but sometimes to places or things;

a proaïretic code (Barthes is fond of neologisms based on Greek roots), for choices and sequences of actions; a cultural code, for citations of received wisdom; a symbolic code or field, the place par excellence of multivalence and reversibility, marked in this story by the breakdown of distinctions and antitheses, by disorder in meanings, sexes, and fortunes.

These codes form a kind of network through which the text passes, or out of which it comes; without them there could be no text. Barthes deliberately does very little to systematize the codes internally or to order them with reference to each other. In fact, his purpose is much less to show a structure or structures than to begin five inventories of elements and to point to a process of structuration. The result is not an "interpretation" of *Sarrasine* (except in some very loose meaning of the word); it is not at all like Barthes' interpretation of the tragedies of Racine, which was a discursive account, an essay on Racinian anthropology, as he called it, standing in sharp opposition to other accounts or interpretations. Without mentioning his earlier work and the controversy it aroused, Barthes nonetheless seems quite clear about the difference between *an* interpretation and his present work, which offers a way of thinking about interpretation and furnishes an elaborate prelude to interpretations, in the plural. As he says:

We shall not expound the criticism of a text or a criticism of this text; we shall propose the semantic material (divided up but not distributed) of several criticisms (psychological, psychoanalytic, thematic, historical, structural); it is up to each critic then (if he so desires) to play, to make his voice heard, which is [i.e., means] listening to one of the voices of the text. What we are trying to do is to sketch the stereographic space of a writing (*une écriture*). (p. 21)

That passage suggests that we ought to pay some attention to the imagery that sustains Barthes' reflection. Each of the codes is a voice; the crossing and blending of voices is the very activity of writing; and the product of that activity is the text. From the image of voice or voices to that of music and polyphony is only a short step, and Barthes takes it. His divisions of the text, his *lexies*, correspond to measure; and using musical notation, he even makes up something like a score for the first thirteen measures or fragments, with lines for the codes and passing allusions to brasses, percussion, woodwinds, and strings. However, his most insistent image is that of plaiting and weaving, the production of fabrics, lace, woven tresses. After comparing at length the working of the hermeneutic code to the activity of the lacemaker, Barthes generalizes:

This process holds for the entire text. The codes taken together (*l'ensemble des codes*), as soon as they are drawn into the work, into the movement of reading, constitute a tress (text, tissue, and trees are all the same thing); every thread, every code is a voice; these voices, tressed or tressing, form the writing (*écriture*); alone the voice does no work, it transforms nothing: it *expresses*, but as soon as the hand intervenes to assemble and mingle the inert threads, there is working, there is transformation. (p. 166)

The concept of code and the imagery surrounding it throw a great deal of light on what seem to be some of Barthes' central intuitions. One persistent idea in his work has been the turning of culture into nature. I mean that he has seen and sought to question decisively the general human tendency to think that what is before us, what is about us, what we do and say as a matter of course—to think that all that is innocent, natural. We carelessly treat *what is by culture* as though it were *what must be by nature*. Hence the necessity to get beneath the surface of behavior and language, in order to see how that transformation occurs. The notion of sign, which allies itself easily with a distrust of surfaces and of face-values, provides him with the key. Everywhere Barthes looks he sees men making signs, attaching meaning to signifiers; the science of signs, semiology, can presumably reduce this process to rule and order, and at the same time, show the true relation between nature and culture. Moreover, there is an intellectual method that corresponds perfectly to this complex of intuitions: logistic, analysis and recombination, discovery of primitive elements and of the ways by which they enter into structures and sequences that become ever larger and longer.

In literature, to be specific, he looks below the smooth surface —apparently innocent, natural, final—and discovers signs, that is, discontinuous and primitive elements. These signifiers and signifieds call to each other and even have systematic relations to each other, and so they cluster into codes or systems like the five that underlie the voices he hears in the story by Balzac; these codes or systems, these threadlike or chainlike elements, may in turn be tressed into a text; and every text takes its place, with every other text, in the total fabric that is literature.

That sounds and is, I think, quite mechanistic, but Barthes has found a way to animate the machine. His main concern has shifted from structure to structuration, seen as an autonomous activity with a life of its own, almost independent of men, for, as he has said, man is no longer the center of structures. This shift he connects to a change in emphasis in linguistics from problems of taxonomy to problems of generation and transformation.

Again, as a means of counteracting simplistic formulas that might emerge in a theory that seems to begin and end with elements and syntax, Barthes plays still another trump card, the notion of the infinite, of the *infini du language*. I think it is the presence of this term in his argument that accounts for the slight feeling of dizziness induced occasionally by S/Z. In his famous fragment on the disproportion of man and nature, Pascal produces a similar sensation with two infinites—the infinitely large and the infinitely small, with uneasy man somewhere in between. Unless I am mistaken, Barthes confronts us with *three* infinites: one's native language, the linguistic ocean from which the signs of literature are drawn; the codes, which have no distinct boundaries or limits; and literature itself, the text with a capital *T*, which stretches without end behind and before us as an orderly process, an interlace of signs.

One way of saying to ourselves what, in general, Barthes is doing in *Critique et vérité* and *S/Z* is to trace out what happens to some critical reflexes—our own, perhaps—when they encounter this radical decision to discuss literature in the context of sign-theory. (1) If it is our bent to imagine the *author* as a unique person, full of experience and fortified by an art of expression who freely brings into being objects that otherwise would never have existed, we must be prepared for a challenge: Barthes rejects the idea of a psychological and moral subject with something to say; for him the author is empty, a paper being, inscribed in the work, but not determining it, and not having over it any right of property. (2) If we incline to the view of the literary *work* as made up in some way, simple or subtle, of two elements or levels, content and form, or if, in place of that, we opt for the work as a whole consisting of organically related parts, we are in for another shock: Barthes proposes to us not works but texts, that is, tissues of signs derived from codes, chains of signifiers and signifieds having no limits or centers that merge, in fact, into a single text held together (at least in its essential tendency) by a dreamlike logic of the intemporal, the reversible, the interchangeable. (3) If, again, we find ourselves conceiving of the *reader-critic* as a kind of consumer of literature, first passive and then reactive, either moving toward a judgment of what the author has offered or joining him in his way of seeing himself and the world, we are brought up short by Barthes' assertions: for him the reader has an extraordinarily active role to play; he is a producer, not a consumer, of meanings; he is, himself, a system of meanings and codes; by microanalysis he discovers structures and watches them move into and out of his field of views; and most important of all, he writes as well as reads, trying always to tie his mode of discourse into the circuits resonating in the original text. (4) If, finally, we adopt —on the example of some ancient and neo-clasical critics—the thesis that literary works have as their *aim* or *effect* some kind of instructing, moving, and pleasing (taken together or in some combination and preferably redefined so as to save our vocabulary from too-close association with that of oratory), we collide once again with the position of Barthes: having pulverized the work *as such*, he makes of it the means whereby we may enter a process of using and transforming signs; we shall no doubt be instructed, moved, and pleased in the peculiar way that semiology makes possible; but we must realize, by a Copernican leap, that we are not the center of this activity; we do not constitute it —we are born into it; we do not select it—it selects us; and so the effect of the *text* is finally to draw us into the infinitely permutative play of subjectless language.

Another and less paradoxical way of saying what Roland Barthes does is to speak of disciplines rather than of topics. Here we find that we cannot answer the question without defining the relationship of his enterprise to *science*. He has for a long time and in various degrees thought of himself as a *sémiologue*, a semiologist; and he has often affirmed the value of Freudian psychology (especially as continued by Jacques Lacan). But he insists on maintaining a certain distance between himself and science, while at the same time making free and inventive use of its concepts and techniques. In an interview in *Les Lettres françaises* (March 2, 1967) published when the *Système de la mode* appeared, he made the point very clearly:

The status of science constitutes a problem for me, and I am far from having on this point the same position as the other structuralists. That no doubt arises from the fact that my object of study is literature . . . I am trying to specify (*préciser*) scientific procedures, to test them more or less, but never to end them with a conclusion (*clausule*) that is typically scientific, because literary science cannot in any case or in any fashion have the last word about literature.

Later in the same interview, after saying that he now speaks less of science and its metalanguages than he used to, he adds:

When I write, it seems to me that I seek to establish a certain play (*jeu*) with science, an activity of disguised parody. I believe more and more that the profound movement of the critic is [toward] the destruction of meta-language . . . [scientific] objectivity is merely one field of images among others . . . As far as *critical* metalanguage is concerned, one can only get around it by instituting a sort of isomorphism between the language of liter-ature and discourse about literature. The science of literature is literature.

The simultaneous affirmation and denial of science and the effort to overcome the separation of literature and criticism give us two im-portant clues. *Science* does not preside over his work; at crucial mo-ments it gives way to *dialectic*. But the dialectic of Barthes is not meta-physical in scope; it always emerges against a background of *history*—Marxist history, freely interpreted—which fixes the terms in which contradictions are stated and sometimes resolved. Finally, science, dialectic, and history (which I do not intend to place here in a strict order of precedence: one of the difficulties in achieving a satisfactory approximation to Barthes' views comes from the ease with which he travels back and forth among disciplines)—these perspectives are sub-ordinated to what he likes to call *écriture*, writing, or as I think we may call it without injustice, *rhetoric*. Not rhetoric in some reduction to combative or flowery speech, of course; I mean rhetoric as eclectic cul-ture, commitment to language, operational attitude, effective force. Al-though his work is focused mainly on the interpretation of literature, he offers it in all its phases and moments as a contribution to bringing in a freer way of thinking and feeling than we now know. But we must not oversimplify. "I should like to be a writer," he said in 1970, and as the context shows, he meant by that not someone for whom language is only an instrument, but someone who accepts language as a fateful milieu in which one lives and moves; in this approach to sign and sense, insofar as a writer is a force and, indeed, is at all, *he is his language*.

I. 14

Whorf, Chomsky and the Student of Literature*

GEORGE STEINER

Churchill College, Cambridge

I

THE TWO positions we are considering can be termed "monadist" or "relativist," and "universalist." The monadist case holds that differences between languages outweigh similarities. That all men known to man use language in some form, that all languages of which we have evidence are able to name perceived objects or to signify action— these are undoubted truths. But belonging to the type "all members of the species require oxygen to sustain life," they do not illuminate except in the most abstract, "trivially deep" sense the actual workings of human speech. What matter are the fantastic diversities of grammatical form and semantic habit, what demands explanation is a complex but manifest history of centrifugal development. Our condition is, both obviously and in essence, that of mutual incomprehensibility after Babel. Between four and five thousand tongues are current on the earth. Several thousand more are known to have been spoken in the past. Any insight into the phenomenology of language must start from this enigmatic largesse and, finally, come back to it.

The universalist position asserts that the underlying structure of all languages is the same and thus common to all men. Dissimilarities between human tongues are essentially of the surface. Deep-seated structures and constraints generate and determine the forms of all grammars

---

Read at the Institute in 1971. Published in *New Literary History*, IV, 1. Autumn 1972. Reprinted by permission of *New Literary History*.

however singular or bizarre certain surface features seem to be. What is important is the understanding and formalization of these central generative elements; surface study is of primarily phonetic or historical interest.

Between these two poles of argument, there can be and there are numerous intermediary, qualified approaches. Neither position is maintained very often with absolute rigor. There are "monadic" touches and nuances of linguistic relativism in the universalist grammars of Roger Bacon, of the grammarians of Port Royal, and even in the contemporary transformational generative grammars. There are, on the other hand, universalist notions in the relativism of Humboldt, of Sapir, and even of Whorf.

In their modern guise, moreover, both great lines of argument may be traced to a common source.

In 1697, in his tract on the amelioration and correction of German, Leibniz put forward the all-important suggestion that language is not the vehicle of thought but its determining medium. Thought is language internalized and we feel and think as our particular language impels and allows us to do. Tongues differ even more profoundly than do nations. They also are monads, "perpetual living mirrors of the universe" each of which reflects or, as we would now put it, "structures" experience according to its own particular sight-lines and habits of cognition. No two languages construe the same world. Yet, at the same time, Leibniz shared many of the universalist aims and hopes which had been, since Bacon's plea for a "real character" in the *Advancement of Learning* of 1605, so typical a strain in seventeenth-century thought. To the end of his life, Leibniz made suggestions toward a universal semantic system, immediately legible to all men. Such a system would be analogous to mathematical symbolism, so efficacious precisely because the conventions of mathematics are grounded in the very fabric of human reason and are, therefore, independent of any local variation. A *characteristica universalis* would be analogous also to Chinese ideograms. Once a "world catalogue" had been agreed to, all messages could be deciphered instantaneously whatever the native speech of the recipient and the disaster at Babel would, on the graphic level at least, be mended.

A comparable co-existence of monadist and universalist concepts may be found in Vico. Philology is the key to the *Scienza nuova* because a study of the evolution of speech faculties is a study of the evolution of mind. Metaphor, especially, is a universal factor in man's acquisition of active sensibility and cultural self-awareness. All nations most probably traverse the same major phases of linguistic usage, from the immediate and sensory to the abtract. Simultaneously, however, Vico's opposition to Descartes and to the extensions of Aristotelian logic in Cartesian rationalism made of him the first true "linguistic historicist" or relativist. Though all men sought expression through "imaginative universals" (*generi fantastici*), these universals rapidly acquired very different configurations. "Almost infinite particulars" make up both the syntactic and lexical corpus of different tongues. These particulars engender and reflect the strikingly diverse world-views of races and cultures. The degree of "infinite particularity" reaches so deep that a universal "logistic" or grammar of language of the Aristotelian or Cartesian-mathematical model is fatally reductionist.

II

It is doubtful that Vico really influenced Hamann. Kabbalistic speculations and the pregnant muddle of Hamann's remarkable intellect were obviously more important. But whatever the immediate background, Hamann's *Versuch über eine akademische Frage* of 1760 marks the decisive move towards a relativistic language theory. It is of little importance that Hamann erroneously ascribed linguistic differences to imperceptible variations in the speech organs of different races. The suggestive strength of his theories lies in the axiom that each language is an "epiphany" or articulate embodiment of a specific historical-cultural landscape. Hebrew verb forms are inseparable from the intricate niceties of Jewish ritual. But Hebrew has itself shaped and determined what it reveals as being the specific genius of a community. The process is dialectical, with the formative energies of language moving both inward and outward in a civilization.

Despite their turgid, rhapsodic manner, Hamann's *Vermischte Anmerkungen* (1761) and *Philologische Einfälle und Zweifel* (1772) are, so far as I know, the first serious applications of relativist principles to the study of actual languages. Examining the differing lexical and grammatical resources of French and German, Hamann argues that neither Cartesian coordinates of general, deductive reasoning nor Kantian mentalism can account for the creative, "pre-rational" and manifold proceedings through which language—unique to the human species but exceedingly varied among nations—shapes reality (*Sprachgestaltung*) and is, in turn, shaped by local historical experience.

Though indebted to certain of Hamann's suggestions, Herder's work marks a transition to genuine comparative linguistics. Calling for "a general physiognomy of the nations from their languages," Herder asserted that national characteristics are "imprinted on speech" and, reciprocally, carry the stamp of the particular tongue. Where a language is corrupted or bastardized, there will be a corresponding decline in the temper and fortunes of the body politic. It is the pre-eminent job of the poet to ensure the vitality of his native speech.

The short years between Herder's writing and those of Wilhelm von Humboldt were among the most productive in the history of linguistic thought. Sir William Jones's celebrated *Third Anniversary Discourse on the Hindus* of 1786 initiated modern Indo-European philology. Schlegel's *Ueber die Sprache und Weisheit der Indier* (1808) helped to disseminate Jones's ideas and did much to establish the concepts of comparative grammar. In 1813, Mme de Staël's *De l'Allemagne* gave wide currency to the theory that there were crucial, formative interactions between a language (in this case, German) and the history, political institutions, and psychology of a people. All these directions of argument and conjecture seem to come together in the work of Humboldt.

Humboldt's achievement is too central and wellknown to require more than a brief summary. It includes the January 1822 lecture *Ueber das Entstehen der grammatischen Formen und ihrem Einfluss auf die Ideen Entwicklung,* and the magnum opus on which Humboldt was engaged from the 1820s until his death in 1835: *On the Differentiation of the Structure of Human Language, and its Influence on the Spiritual Evolution of the Human Race.* Language is the only verifiable and *a priori* framework of cognition. Our perceptions result from the imposition of that framework on the total, unorganized flux of sensations. "Die Sprache ist das bildende Organ des Gedankens," says Humboldt, using both *bildend* and *Bildung* in their forceful, twofold connotation of "image" and "culture." Different linguistic frames define different world-images. "Every language is a Form and carries in itself a Form-Principle. Each has a unity consequent on the inherent, particular Principle." So far as each human tongue differs from every other, the resulting shape of the world is a local selection from a total but random potentiality. In this way, Humboldt conjoins the environmentalism of Montesquieu and the nationalism of Herder with an essentially post-Kantian model of human consciousness as the active and diverse shaper of the perceived world.

Ueber die Verschiedenheit des menschlichen Sprachbaus (particularly sections xix and xx) is crowded with linguistic ideas of prophetic brilliance. It can be shown to anticipate both C. K. Ogden's theory of "opposition" and the binary structuralism of Lévi-Strauss. But the heart of the argument lies in its application to actual linguistic-cultural material.

Humboldt sets out to correlate Greek and Latin grammar with the histories and social character of the two respective civilizations. Greek syntax casts a finely woven net of relations over the currents of life. Hence the diacritical genius of Greek thought and poetry. Hence also the atomizing, divisive quality of Greek political life and its vulnerability to the tempting ambiguities of sophistry. The sobriety, the laconic idioms, the inbuilt masculinity of Latin are the active mould of the Roman way of life. And so on.

The presentation is eloquent and acute in its treatment of historical details: but it is circular. Civilization is uniquely and specifically informed by a given language; that language is the unique and specific matrix of its civilization. The one proposition is used to demonstrate the other and *vice versa*. Given the final mystery of creative relation between *Sprache* and *Geist*, it could hardly be otherwise. But this circularity will continue to be the weakest aspect of the relativist position.

There is no need here to do more than indicate the lines of continuity from Humboldt to Whorf. Via the work of Steinthal (the editor of Humboldt's fragmentary texts), linguistic relativity enters the anthropology of Franz Boas. From there it reaches the ethno-linguistics of Sapir and Whorf. A parallel movement takes place in Germany. Cassirer's doctrine of the unique "inner form" which distinguishes a particular tongue from all others, derives immediately from Humboldt's *Form-Princip*. In a series of books written between 1929 and 1950, Leo Weisgerber sought to apply the "monadic" principle to actual, detailed investigations of German syntax and of the intellectual and psychological attitudes which that syntax has generated and embodied in German history. During the 1930s, Jost Trier developed his theory of "the semantic field." Each tongue or language-monad "diffuses" and operates inside the shell of a total conceptual field (the imagistic correlations with quantum physics are obvious). In each case the linguistic feedback from experience is a particular one. Speakers of different languages thus inhabit different "mediary worlds" *Zwischenwelten*).

Edward Sapir's formulation, in an article dated 1929, summarizes the entire line of argument as it goes back to Leibniz:

The fact of the matter is that the "real world" is to a large extent unconsciously built up on the language habits of the group. No two languages are ever sufficiently similar to be considered as representing the same social reality. The worlds in which different societies live are distinct worlds, not merely the same world with different labels attached.

Our customs of speech are the outcome of a cumulative dialectic of differentiation: languages generate different social forms, these forms further divide languages.

III

The work of Benjamin Lee Whorf can be seen as an extension and refinement of Sapir's statement. Whorf's "metalinguistics" are currently under severe attack by both linguists and ethnographers. But the papers gathered in *Language, Mind and Reality* (1956) constitute a model and methodology of understanding which has extraordinary elegance and philosophic tact. They are a statement of vital possibility relevant not only to the linguist and anthropologist but also to the poet and student of literature. Whorf had something of Vico's philosophic curiosity. The years in which he, Roman Jakobson, and I. A. Richards are active simultaneously count among the key moments in the history of the formal penetration of consciousness.

Whorf's theses are well known. The native tongue of an individual determines what he perceives of the world and how he thinks/feels about it. Each language constructs its own "thought world" made up of "the microcosm which each man carries about within himself, by which he measures and understands what he can of the macrocosm." There is no "universal objective reality," only an aggregate of "segmentations" made by different language-cultures. This does *not* mean (Whorf is often misconstrued on this issue) that there are not rudimentary universal neuro-physiological apprehensions of time, space, identity, and sequence common to the human species. But these universals ramify and take on local specification as soon as the infant enters the world of his particular speech. Thus there is a distinctive Indo-European time-sense and a corresponding system of tense. Different "semantic fields" divide the total spectrum of colors, sounds, and scents in very different ways (the only universal would be that of organic limitation). Whorf sums up his vision in one of his last papers.

Actually, thinking is most mysterious, and by far the greatest light upon it that we have is thrown by the study of language. This study shows that the forms of a person's thoughts are controlled by inexorable laws of pattern of which he is unconscious. These patterns are the unperceived intricate systemizations of his own language—shown readily enough by a candid comparison and contrast with other languages, especially those of a different linguistic family. His thinking itself is in a language—in English, in Sanskrit, in Chinese. And every language is a vast pattern-system, differing from others, in which are culturally ordained the forms and categories by which the personality not only communicates, but also analyzes nature, notices or neglects types of relationship and phenomena, channels his reasoning, and builds the house of his consciousness.

To show that this thesis "stands on unimpeachable evidence" Whorf was prepared to apply comparative semantic analyses to Latin, Greek, Hebrew (there are notable links between his own work and the theosophic Kabbalism of Fabre d'Olivet), Kota, Aztec, Shawnee, Russian, Chinese, and Japanese. But it is Whorf's work on the Hopi languages of Arizona, in a series of key papers written between ca. 1935 and 1939, which counts most. It is here that the notion of interactive "pattern-systems" of life and language is argued from specific, detailed example.

Though only the expert is qualified to deal with these analyses, Whorf's conclusion is famous and arresting enough to be worth restating. The metaphysical framework imposed by Hopi grammars is far better suited than that of English to the world-picture of modern science. The Hopi treatment of events, inferential reasoning, and "action at a distance" is, according to Whorf, delicate and susceptible of provisional postures in just the way required by twentieth-century wave-particle theory or relativity physics.

Whorf was tireless in emphasizing the built-in bias, the axiomatic arrogance of any theory of language based on very few tongues or on a scarcely veiled presumption that Sanskrit, Latin, or English constitute the natural, let alone optimal typology of all human speech. A picture of langauge, mind, and reality based almost exclusively on Cartesian-Kantian logic and on the semantic conventions of SAE (Standard Average European) is, argues Whorf, a hubristic simplification. The close of "Science and Linguistics," a paper published in 1940, is worth quoting in full—especially at a time when the study of language in the United States is so largely dominated by an orthodoxy of confident generality and mathematical certitude:

A fair realization of the incredible degree of diversity of linguistic system that ranges over the globe leaves one with an inescapable feeling that the human spirit is inconceivably old; that the few thousand years of history covered by our written records are no more than the thickness of a pencil mark on the scale that measures our past experience on this planet; that the events of these recent millenniums spell nothing in any evolutionary wise, that the race has taken no sudden spurt, achieved no commanding synthesis during recent millenniums, but has only played a little with a few of the linguistic formulations and views of nature bequeathed from an inexpressibly longer past. Yet neither this feeling nor the sense of precarious dependence of all we know upon linguistic tools which are themselves largely unknown need be discouraging to science but should, rather, foster that humility which accompanies the true scientific spirit, and thus forbids that arrogance of the mind which hinders real scientific curiosity and detachment.

It is this kind of statement, added perhaps to I. A. Richards' observation that the translation of a Chinese philosophic text into English constitutes the "most complex event" yet in the history of man, which the student of literature may wish to bear in mind when he thinks of his raw material—language.

Such is the assertive reach of Whorf's position that critiques of it, *per se*, make up a fair statement of the universalist case. "There is no cogent reason to assume," writes E. H. Lenneberg, "that the gammarian's articulation of the stream of speech is coterminous with an articulation of knowledge or the intellect." Words do not embody invariant mental operations. Any operational model of the linguistic process, i.e., Wittgenstein's finding that "the meaning of a word is its use in the language," will refute Whorf's primitive and deterministic parallelism of thought and speech. Moreover, if the Sapir-Whorf hypothesis were correct, if languages were indeed monads with essentially disparate meanings of reality, how then could we communicate interlingually? How could we acquire a second language or traverse into another language-world by means of translations? Yet, manifestly, these transfers do occur.

To the twelfth-century relativism of Pierre Hélie, with his belief that the catastrophe at Babel had generated as many kinds of irreconcilable grammars as there are languages, Roger Bacon opposed his axiom of fundamental unity: "Grammatica una et eadem est secundum substantiam in omnibus linguis, licet accidentaliter varietur." Without a *grammatica universalis* there can be no hope of genuine communication among peoples, nor any rational science of language. The accidental, historically moulded differences between tongues are, no doubt, striking. But underlying these there are principles of constraint, of invariance, of articulate relation which govern the character of all human speech. All languages known and conceivable are, says Noam Chomsky, "cut from the same pattern." Thus the true job of linguistics "must be to develop an account of linguistic universals that, on the one hand, will not be falsified by the actual diversity of languages and, on the other, will be sufficiently rich and explicit to account for the rapidity and uniformity of language learning, and the remarkable complexity and range of the generative grammars that are the product of language learning."

These universals may be phonological. As Trubetskoy and Jakobson have shown, the neuro-physiological equipment with which we emit and receive sounds is reflected in the acoustic structures of all human speech forms. Grammatical universals go deeper. These bear, for instance, on the ordering of subject-verb-object combinations and suggest that "verb-object-subject" and "object-verb-subject" are so rare as to constitute an eccentric violation of a universal sequence of perception. Other grammatical universals concern points of detail: "when the adjective follows the noun, the adjective expresses all the inflectional categories of the noun. In such cases the noun may lack overt expression of one or all of these categories." Drawing on thirty languages, J. H. Greenberg has listed forty-five fundamental grammatical relations which underlie all systems of human speech and which organize an essentially unitary picture of reality.

Chomskian grammar starts from dissatisfaction with the "soft-edged" material of phonology and the superficiality of any ethno-linguistic, statistical treatment of grammatical universals. It proceeds to much greater phenomenological depths with its scheme of "deep structures" which via a set of rules generate, i.e. "bring to the surface," the sentences or "phonetic events" which we actually speak and hear. The surface aspects of all languages, however divergent they may seem from each other, obey the same ultimate constraints and transformational procedures. Located "far beyond the level of actual or even potential consciousness," these deep structures can be thought of as patterns of relation or strings of an order of abstraction far greater than even the most formal of grammatical rules. "There is no reason to expect," says Chomsky, "that reliable operational criteria for the deeper and more important theoretical notions of linguistics . . . will ever be forthcoming." Try to bring the creature to the light from the immense deeps of the sea and it will disintegrate or change form utterly. Yet some recent theories of universal grammar would go even deeper. Speaking of "deep deep structures," Prof. Emmon Bach suggests that Chomsky may be guilty of superficiality in comparing deep structures, even by analogy, with "atomic facts" of grammatical relation. What we may be dealing with at this final level of instrumental universality are "abstract kinds of pro-verbs which receive only indirect phonological representation" (in which I take "pro-verbs" to signify potentialities of order "anterior to" any conceivable rudiments of grammatical form).

But at whatever degree of depth we take it, generative grammar on the Chomskian model is universalist. It "expresses directly the idea that it is possible to convey any conceptual content in any language, even though the particular lexical items available will vary widely from one language to another—a direct denial of the Humboldt-Sapir-Whorf hypothesis in its strongest form."

IV

Which of the two hypotheses is right?

As soon as one puts the question in this way, its crudity is apparent. Yet it is a crudity inherent in a good many of the claims of total insight and definitive verification put forward by transformational generative grammarians to this time. It may be a banal move, but of some heuristic use, to suggest that no single hypothesis of origin and structure will at one go elucidate the most complex phenomenological experience known to man, which is language. The probabilities against the finality of a single approach are increased by the fact that any model of the generation of human speech necessarily involves areas of molecular biology, neuro-physiology, anthropology and, possibly, "archaeo-sociology" in which no single discipline has general competence.

Both the relativist and the universalist cases are open to serious question.

The circularity of argument, which we noted with reference to Humboldt, applies also to Whorf. What "outside" evidence would either confirm or falsify Whorf's contention that differences of cognition underlie the Apache's description of a spring as "whiteness moving downward"? There is a latent tautology in the assumption that a native speaker perceives experience differently because he talks about it differently—an assumption based on the fact that we deduce these differences of perception from those of speech. If genuine typologies of cognition and perception are involved, moreover, how is it that the Hopi or African speaker can communicate with us and is able, though with manifest strain, to adjust quite rapidly to "our world"? (Yet Whorf might ask: "do we ever really get through to each other, does he ever really adjust, or is that adjustment a psychological mask forced upon the 'primitive' by our economic and behavioral demands?")

The underlying problem is that of *translation* in the full sense. There is, I believe, no deeper problem in the theory of language nor any about which our thoughts ought to be more provisional and solicitous of dissent.

The monadist position, carried to its logical conclusion, holds that no complete acts of translation between different semantic fields are possible, that all translation is approximate and ontologically reductive of meaning. The matrix of feeling and associative context which energizes usage in any given tongue can be transferred into another idiom only partly, and by virtue of periphrastic and metaphrastic manoeuvers which inevitably downgrade the intensity, the evocative means, the formal autonomy of the original. Poets have often felt this; today, the case is put in its most bleak and fastidious form by Nabokov.

A universalist grammar will affirm the contrary. The "inter-translatability" of all languages, the fact that no "closed speech" has been found on earth, none that native informant and learner from outside cannot, albeit by long and arduous work, "externalize," make up one of the strongest universalist "proofs." But let us look closely at the argument as it is stated in Chomsky's *Aspects of the Theory of Syntax*:

> The existence of deep-seated formal universals . . . implies that all languages are cut to the same pattern, but does not imply that there is any point by point correspondence between particular languages. It does not, for example, imply that there must be some reasonable procedure for translating between languages.

It is difficult to avoid the sense of a very important hiatus or *non-sequitur*. A footnote re-enforces one's perplexity: "The possibility of a reasonable procedure for translation between arbitrary languages depends on the sufficiency of substantive universals. In fact, although there is much reason to believe that languages are to a significant extent cast in the same mould, there is little reason to suppose that reasonable procedures of translation are in general possible."

What does this mean?

"Point by point" only obscures the logical and substantive issue. The "topology" through which linguistic universals can be transferred from language to language—note the covert pressure in the phrase "between arbitrary languages"—may lie very deep, but if it operates at all, a "point by point" correspondence *at some level* must be demonstrable. In which case a "reasonable procedure of translation" must, at least, be analytically describable. If, on the contrary, there is little reason to suppose that such a procedure is "in general" possible (and what does "in general" signify?), what true evidence have we of universal structures? Could it be that the theory whereby transformational rules map semantically interpreted "deep structures" into phonetically interpreted "surface structures" is a meta-mathematical idealization of great elegance and logical reach, but not a picture of natural language?

The lacuna between the assumption of universal deep structures and any "reasonable procedure for translation" is a serious one. Quine's treatment of the indeterminacies of translation in chapter ii of *World and Object* probably comes as close as any we have to putting this immensely difficult topic into focus. Significantly, Quine's analysis has aspects that can be called Whorfian and an analytic framework which is nearer to Chomsky. And incisive as it is, Quine's discussion is far from being a solution to the problem of what it is that occurs, of what formal and existential moves are performed, when a speech act crosses from one language to another.

Obviously the critical test for the two approaches lies in their application to the study of actual languages. As Chomsky himself says, what is needed is "serious comparative work that tries to operate in the only logically appropriate way, namely, by constructing descriptive adequate grammars of a variety of languages and then proceeding to determine what universal principles constrain them, what universal principles can serve to explain the particular form that they have." He cites Hugh Matthews' grammar of Hidasta, Paul Postal's work on Mohawk, Ken Hale's studies of Papago and Walbiri, and several other studies as cases in point. Though only the ethno-linguist in the relevant field can judge, there is no reason to query Chomsky's estimate of these monographs. The difficulty arises over what is meant by the construction of a "descriptively adequate grammar." Whether we have such a grammar for Latin, let alone English, is a moot point. There are logicians and linguists who are convinced that no set of rules, however complete, is sufficient to describe the utterances possible in any living language, and that the notion of such description being made adequately by an outsider to the ethnic, cultural, historical milieu is entirely unrealistic.

At the same time, it is worth emphasizing that the issues raised by

Whorf and the methods he initiated are far from being exhausted or refuted. Lines of work first sketched at the 1953 conference on "Language in Culture" are still in progress. It is far too early to tell whether the solution to undoubted problems of differentiation between cultures and conceptual conventions lies in the fact, urged by Franklin Fearing among others, that the earth is peopled by communities at very different stages of evolution. In relation to the total number of spoken languages, our studies remain statistically almost insignificant: "it is still premature to expect," says one linguist, "that we can make any except the most elementary observations concerning linguistic universals and expect them to be permanently valid. Our knowledge of two-thirds or more of the world's languages is still too scanty (or in many instances non-existent)." As Helmut Gipper concludes, in what is the most balanced assessment made so far of Whorf's theses, these theses are, in their initial form, inadequately supported and methodologically vulnerable. But the questions posed by Whorf are of the utmost importance to the understanding of language and of culture (Helmut Gipper, *Bausteine zur Sprachinhaltsforschung* [Düsseldorf, 1963], pp. 297–366). The jury is still out.

Perhaps I may be allowed one further quotation. It sets the debate between relativists and universalists in its philosophic context: "In the light of the foregoing considerations," says Max Black in his paper on "Language and Reality," "the prospects for a universal philosophical grammar seem most unpromising. I believe the hope of finding *the* essential grammar to be as illusory as that of finding the single true co-ordinate system for the representation of space. We can pass from one systematic mode of spatial representation to another by means of rules for transforming co-ordinates and we can pass from one language to another having the same fact-stating resources by means of rules of translation. But rules for transformation of co-ordinates yield no information about space; and translation rules for sets of languages tell us nothing about the ultimate nature of reality."

V

As we step back from the immediate topic of universals, it becomes readily apparent that nothing less is involved than a view of the fundamental realities of language. At bottom, the controversy between transformational generative theories and other approaches turns on the question as to whether or not languages are well-defined or ill-defined systems. These two terms have exact mathematical and philosophic meanings and entailments. A Chomskian analysis of deep structures and re-write rules is based on the working hypothesis that language is a well-defined system. "What we scholars have learned about language in the course of a hundred and fifty years of backbreaking work," counters Hockett, "persuades me that language is an ill-defined system, and that it is part of the total physical human experience that has made it possible for man to invent well-defined systems in the first place."

It is improbable that this disagreement, rooted as it is in much more ancient epistemological conflicts over nominalism and realism, will ever be resolved by any unitary, demonstrable solution. Alternative mappings and orderings of major phenomenologies (i.e., language) do not cancel each other out. And where even the acutest of linguistic philosophers fears to tread—remember Austin's modest goal of doing no more than augmenting the "sensitivity of our awareness of ordinary language usage"—the student of literature will be doubly hesitant.

Yet, in fact, he has made his choice. This is my main point. Where-ever and whenever we are studying a literary text, we have chosen as between a Whorfian and a Chomskian methodology. Whether we trouble to define such frameworks for ourselves or not, our perceptions of language *in literature* are relativist and, if the term may be allowed, *ultra-Whorfian.*

When we investigate the history of a language, when we read a poem or piece of prose with full response, we are implicated in a matrix of inexhaustible specificity. The more we get on with the job, the more enmeshed we are in an experience of irreducibly complex, singular life-forms.

The sources of this specificity are various. The student of literature sees language diachronically. He knows that the pressures of time are incessant and intricate. A speech act is embedded in the conventions, social and philosophic inferences, contingent emphases of the moment. The armature of locution, the way in which a proposition is hinged and pressed home in, say, a poem of the 1720s differs markedly from what would be current only fifteen years later. The permanence of major literature is paradoxically time-bound. Indeed it is inside literature that linguistic change, the development of new tonalities, the transforma-tions of the semantic field, are most salient. As our antennae grow less blunt, we come to know that poetry, drama, fiction, the essay, are the calendar of language and that a year—1798, 1836, 1924—can bring on changes whose complexity and reach our best means of analysis fail to exhaust.

Another source of uniqueness is that of location. Language varies from place to place, sometimes from borough to borough. It carries the manifold impress of the social and professional milieu. There is an idiom above and below stairs, an argot in the ghetto and a *lingua franca* of the market place. The circumstantial pressures on speech are, in a strict sense, immeasurably diverse, and literature embodies that plurality.

Let me argue the point in a heightened, over-simplified way: there is not a significant literary text—it may be quite short—which does not generate its own "language-sphere," whose bare existence will not, if we choose to experience it fully, somewhat alter the matrix of recognitions, the associative fabric, of the rest of language. The apprehension of literature does not bear on universals but on "ontological particulars" (the term derives from Heidegger and from Heidegger's commentary on Hölderlin). The readiest example is that of the total work of a given writer. The performative acts by which a writer creates his recognizable "world" are linguistic. The concept of "style" is notoriously elusive but, when looked at seriously, comprises far more than an external treatment of certain aspects of language. A coherent style is a counter-statement to the collective, unexaminedly normative conventions of vision operative or, more precisely, residual and largely inert in the surrounding vulgate. It "speaks its vision of things," and where that locution has scope and a logic of internal unfolding, we enter the writer's construct as we would a climate and a landscape in its singular light. But at all points, that new and "signed" reality is generated by language, by the writer's use of a vocabulary and syntax grounded in the vulgate but refined, complicated, made new by intensity of personal statement.

Thus there is, in the strict sense, a lexicon and grammar for every serious work of literature. That we have such glossaries and grammars for, say, Dante, Shakespeare, or Balzac and not for most other writers is an accident of pre-eminence. Every writer of substance develops a "language world" whose contours, tonality, and idiosyncracies we come to recognize. And each is susceptible of lexical and grammatical investigation. Where Whorf finds that every language and the culture which that language articulates organizes (makes organic) its particular "thought world," the reader of literature will say the same of every writer and, where penetrative response is pressed home, of every major poem, play, or novel.

The difficulty lies in the bluntness, in the improvised character of what Coleridge called our "speculative intruments." It is not only that we know next to nothing about the anatomy of the inventive proceedings, about the translation of private feelings into public form, but that the elements of particularity which a work of literature offers to examination are formidably numerous, subtle, and interrelated. It is likely that they are, in the arithmetic and logical sense of the term, incommensurable.

The issue is straightforward but needs exact phrasing. The analytic modes which we can focus on a text are numerous and fairly well defined. They include the bibliographical, the philological, the historical, the psychological, the sociological, the biographic, and several more. Let us suppose that we have brought each of these "readings" to bear, that there is no linguistic, formal contextual aspect of the poem to which we have not applied the relevant discipline of elucidation. Yet invariably the sum of our understanding will fall short of the facts of meaning before us. If it were otherwise, our exegesis would produce an active tautology, a counterpart to the poem which would in every respect of significance be the equal of the original. But outside the fables of Borges there are no total meta- or para-phrases. The best reading, the best criticism will serve the poem or the play by making visible, by making analytically expressive, the distance which separates it from the object of its attention. A major exercise of understanding—Coleridge on the *Lyrical Ballads*, Mandelstam on the *Divina Commedia*—is one which circumscribes the original text with a scrupulously drawn circuit of inadequacy. It says to us: "analysis, location, interpretative echo can go so far and no further." But it says so in a manner that leaves the work itself more spacious, more autonomously lucid, and that leaves criticism stronger, more worth attempting and disagreeing over. The process is one of honestly argued distance and epistemological tact.

There is nothing mystical about the "inexhaustibility" of the literary work. In part the reasons are contingent. We can never know enough of the precise etymological values of the writer's vocabulary, of the exact interplay between general currency and personal idiom at the moment in which the poem was written, of the sensibility, itself perhaps local and intimately inferred, to which the writer addresses himself on a given occasion. In a mature poem, novel, or drama the defining context of any element—stylistic, prosodic, phonetic—is the work as a whole. It could be shown that there is not a paragraph, perhaps not a sentence in *Madame Bovary* whose semantic values do not implicate the entirety of the book. This sort of dynamic cohesion is beyond the enumerative and dissociative scope of critical re-statement. But one can go further: the context of a great work of art is the sum of its culture, of the executive means that have gone before, of the works that will follow. There are no methodologically predicated limits of relevance. The total context of potential meaning is, in the Wittgensteinian sense, "all that is the case."

But there are also ontological grounds of irreducibility. The interaction of text and interpreter is never closed. The very opaque concept of "indeterminacy" in physics, the difficulties which stem from the ways in which observation acts on that which is being observed, are a commonplace in our experience of literature. No reading is neutral. The material alters in what could be termed "the field of force" set up by the reader's demands and responses. The existentiality, the histories of the *Odyssey*, of *Lear*, of *Les Fleurs du mal* are made up, in substantial proportion, of all the readings and misreadings which these texts have elicited and will elicit in future. Our own sight-lines to the work change with different personal circumstances, with age, and in relation to the open-ended aggregate of whatever else we have read or experienced. Both halves of the equation—the text and the act of reading— are, as it were, in motion. That the classic work persists enhanced and productively complicated by the accumulation of commentaries, imitations, pastiches, parodies, and explications is one of the mysteries of major form (minor work can be diminished by insight, it can become the equivalent or even the lesser occasion of the interpretations it gives rise to).

The upshot is that the order of complexity, the order of relation between analysis and object as they occur in the study of literature are generically beyond anything that can be dealt with in linguistics. It is a matter of acute philosophical and technical controversy as to whether we have, until now, achieved a *complete* description, a complete formalization of even the most elementary speech unit ("John loves Mary"). It is, to put it modestly, less than plausible that such analysis will be applicable to the literally open-ended dynamics of even the simplest of literary texts.

VI

Does this mean that the critic and student of literature have nothing to learn from linguistics? As I have tried to show, most recently in a set of papers on the two approaches (*Extraterritorial* [New York, 1971]), precisely the contrary is the case.

The kind of collaborative study of poetics, literary composition, style and genre, advocated by the Leningrad and Moscow "Language Circles" at the start of the century, and later pursued in Prague, continues to be a vital current and necessary ideal. Simplistic, schematized as is their treatment of natural language, linguistic techniques nevertheless are of extreme interest to the "reader in depth." To a large extent, this is a matter of stance, of the quality of closeness and surprise which the linguistic analysis of syntax and semantics brings to the texture of statement. It is hardly possible to read the best of modern linguistics from, say, Saussure to Chomsky, or such linguistic philosophers as Moore, Austin, Quine, or Strawson without acquiring a more patient, critically tensed regard for the problem before one. Jakobson's famous plea that we see the grammar of poetry as a product of the "poetry of grammar," i.e., of "the poetic resources concealed in the morphological and syntactic structure of language," is no more than common sense. But the force of interrelation is, I think, heuristic and methodological: it is, in Austin's vein, a matter of keeping oneself more scrupulously off balance.

If we allow "linguistics" to include ancillary disciplines such as "ethno-linguistics" or linguistic anthropology, "socio-linguistics" and the study of speech lesions and pathologies ("psycho-linguistics"), the extent of relevance to the history and criticism of literature becomes unmistakable. Dr. Leavis' admonition that "language, in the full sense, in the full concrete reality . . . eludes the cognizance of any form of linguistic science," is, if anything, too restrictive. It is by no means clear that there is, as yet, "a linguistic science" as contrasted with a provisional aggregate of models and methodological trials. But "language in the full sense" also eludes the cognizance of all known techniques of critical, textual historical penetration. What are hoped for are local gains, clarifications of the particular case, moves toward a more resilient, productive condition of disagreement. And in that respect the profit to be derived from a collaborative linguistic-critical approach is already visible.

We *do* read differently since Jakobson and I. A. Richards. We have a new intimation of the ways in which a literary work internalizes its criteria of coherence. We deal far more warily than did Dr. Johnson or Matthew Arnold with the vexed question of "poetic truth," with the supposition that such practices as metaphor generate a system of "truth-functions," a logic, properly speaking "a symbolic logic," of their own. We benefit from a growing awareness of the interactions—cumulative, contradictory, dislocatory—between meaning and syntax in a literary style. A statistical analysis which shows that sound effects in Pope are likely to coincide with lexical meanings whereas in Donne there is a discordance, probably intentional, between phonetic effects and semantic units, is more than ingenuity. It may induce fundamental insights about the differences in the relations of feelings to expressive means as between Metaphysical and Augustan poetics. It is difficult to suppose that Austin's work on the "illocutionary force of utterance" in speech acts, and the grammatical-philosophic discussions which have arisen from it, will be of no interest to our understanding of dramatic verse, of dialogue in fiction, of vocative structures in rhetoric. Such examples can be mutiplied.

Already, there have been at least two movements in literary study that embody the stimulus and controls of linguistics. The first would include the work of Spitzer, of Curtius, and much of Jakobson. It represents a conjunction of stylistic and historical concerns with comparative philology and diachronic *Sprachwissenschaft* in the traditional sense. Via Jakobson, Richards, and Empson, these traditional comparative approaches modulate towards the new, more technically oriented language-consciousness of modern semantics, linguistic philosophy and deep-structure. The dual focus of literary-linguistic grasp which has produced Empson's *Structure of Complex Words*, Donald Davie's two incisive books on energy and structure in English verse, Tzvetan Todorov's analyses of epic narrative, Roland Barthes on Balzac, Josephine Miles's "More Semantics of Poetry," or Archibald Hill's "Poetry and Stylistics," to name a few, will not be readily ignored. Indeed, there is ground for supposing that the future of literary studies and of certain important aspects of criticism lies in a developing relation to linguistics. The latter will, I would judge, form an increasing part of the backbone of discipline and acquired competence in the university curriculum in literature.

But the relation can be fruitful only if the respective orders of concern are clearly understood. What stands in the way of this essential discrimination is the current usage of the terminology of "depth" and "surface" or, more exactly, the entailments of hierarchy which these terms carry with them.

By definition, the reader and student of literature work "at the surface." They deal with the phonetic facts, the words and sentences as we can actually see and hear them. That is the only reality available to us. Is there any other? Transformational generative grammars assure us that there is, that the articulate presence of the text is merely the external, partly contingent product of generation out of deep and primal structures. What are these structures like? Are they neurophysiological or even molecular in nature, are they in some way "imprinted" on the evolving cortex, do they constitute a kind of "presyntactic" holograph of an order of abstraction and formalization beyond anything we are able to describe? The Chomskian theory of language gives no answers. At times, Chomsky suggests that it is entirely unrealistic to believe that any answer will ever be forthcoming. At other points, as in the often acrimonious exchanges on innate ideas, he seems to hint at a more traditional, meta-Kantian scheme of mentalism and "programming."

But whatever its opaqueness and unexamined metaphoric content, the notion of "deep structure" conveys a powerful positive valuation and that of "surface" is inherently pejorative. Yet it may be that this whole axis of verticality, with its strong symbolic inferences, is spurious. As we have seen, the "surface" of language is inexhaustibly complex. Here surface has nothing qualitatively, ontologically superficial. The idiomatic, historical, contextual, personal parameters which energize spoken and written speech are diverse and changing beyond any available analytic reduction. And they have their own genuine "depths." In the actual history of a word or phrase, time has a fantastically complex life of previous echo. Deep planes of social evolution, perhaps of kinetic and neuro-psychological adjustment, underlie prosodic modes in verse and the less visible but operative stress systems of prose. Whether or not psychoanalytic investigations have offered verifiable insights into the creative process, whether their elucidations of image and symbol are valid, remains an open question. But there can be no doubt as to the realities of depth which relate the presence of the poem to the nascent purpose of the writer. These relations, like the invention of melody, are among the most complex phenomena of which we have any, albeit the most rudimentary, cognizance.

We must discriminate between uses of "deep." The tree-structure of diagrams which spangle the pages of current readers in transformational generative grammar are *not* an X-ray. They do *not* give a "picture in depth" in any empirical, independently verifiable sense. They are themselves an argumentative device, a graphic presentment of a particular hypothesis about language and mind. That hypothesis may or may not prove valid. And even if it should prove valid, the result may be a "trivial depth." That is to say: the discoveries made about grammatical structure and universals may prove to be applicable only to elementary, arbitrarily schematized units, or they may prove to be of an unexceptional but banal generality such as the proposition that all grammars include some form of quantifiers. This possibility of "trivial depth" is a key one. The inexhaustible, elegant, mentally taxing profundities of chess offer a fair analogy.

The "depths" with which we are confronted in our study of literature are, by contrast, messy, ill-defined, and individuated. But they are not trivial. There is, from the point of view of the reader, of the critic, more insight into the generation of language in the letters of Keats or in Nadezhda Mandelstam's account of her husband's methods of composition—the lips under compulsion of inchoate music before the shadowy "ascent to words"—than can be found in any linguistic treatise. Which is as it should be. Both approaches are concerned with the overriding fact of human speech. But the areas of inquiry and the degrees of precision aimed at differ significantly.

"Wanted: An Ontological Critic" advertised John Crowe Ransom in 1941. If that phoenix turns up he will, I expect, be part linguist. What I have wanted to suggest is that his linguistics—so far as they bear on the autonomous life-forms of the poem—will be, uneasily, Whorfian. Ours must remain, as Blake said, "the holiness of minute particulars."

Part II. ACT:
English Literature, 1600–1950

II. 1

Musica Mundana and Twelfth Night*

JOHN HOLLANDER

Harvard University

"As FOR the division," wrote Thomas Morley in the last decade of the sixteenth century, "music is either speculative or practical. Speculative is that kind of music which, by mathematical helps, seeketh the causes, properties and natures of sounds, by themselves and compared with others, proceeding no further, but content with the only contemplation of the art. Practical is that which teacheth all that may be known in songs, either for the understanding of other men's, or making of one's own . . ."[1] There is perhaps an echo of dispraise shown here by Morley, a most enterprising practical musician, for studies involving "the only contemplation of the art." But in his *Plain and Easy Introduction to Practical Music*, published in 1597, Morley could well choose to enforce such a distinction. His own century had inherited a rich tradition of discourse about music, both "speculative" and "practical," from the Middle Ages. It had produced a huge body of ad hoc theory occasioned by particular problems arising from contemporary musical customs. Both of these and the growing Renaissance attention to the musical uses of antiquity combined in a tradition of encyclopedic musical learning. Such a monumental work was Gioseffe Zarlino's *Institutione Armoniche*, published in 1558, which devoted as

* Read at the Institute in 1956. Published in *Institute Essays: Sound and Poetry*, 1957.

[1] Thomas Morley, *A Plain and Easy Introduction to Practical Music*, ed. R. A. Harman (New York, 1953), p. 101.

much attention to such matters as classic myths of the power of music, general speculations of the nature of mathematical proportion, correspondences obtaining among tonal configurations, the elements and the humors, and so on, as it did to the exigencies of contrapuntal writing. The production of such compendia of lore, mistakes, natural science, aesthetics, and principles of craftsmanship was continued through the seventeenth century, as evidenced by the treatises of Robert Fludd, Mersenne, Praetorius, and Athanasius Kircher. Even before 1600, however, music as a subject for systematic writing embraced many different categories of thought and experience. At a time when musical practice had varied forms, each playing its respective social role and each generating its particular stylistic conventions, a simple description of "practical music" would be complex enough. But to this has to be added the strange body of theory and doctrine, mathematical, cosmological, prosodical, mythological, ethical, and pseudo-physiological that had accumulated during the Middle Ages. The Renaissance, with its increasing requirements by both amateur and professional musicians for practical investigation, was unable to dispense with such an accumulation of authority on the subject of music's *raison d'être*.

Actually, Morley's distinction between speculation and practice was by no means a new one, having been drawn implicity by Boethius, and explicitly since the tenth century. But it had previously enjoyed the not uncommon privilege of having been drawn only that it might be obliterated. Boethius himself did not distinguish, as did later writers, between *musica activa* and *musica speculativa*. He did insist, however, that a true musician must be a man who "on reflection has taken to himself the science of singing, not by the servitude of work, but by the rule of contemplation." [2] The fifteenth-century theorist Tinctoris insisted that "*Musicorum et cantorum magna est differentia*," [3] the musician being the one who had mastered theory as well as practice. Classic sources, too, transmitted the importance of the distinction in both direct and metaphorical ways. Even more strong, perhaps, than Plato's stress on the importance of speculative music in education, was the embodiment of a distinction between reason and blind irrational action in the classic differentiation of role of the Greek *aulos*, or oboe,

[2] Boethius, *De Institutione Musica*, I, 33, tr. O. Strunk, in Oliver Strunk, *Source Readings in Music History* (New York, 1950), p. 86.
[3] Joannes Tinctoris, *Diffinitorium Musices* (ca. 1475), in E. de Coussemaker, *Oeuvres théoriques de Jean Tinctoris* (Lille, 1875), p. 489.

and *kithara,* or lyre. *Auloi* were conventionally Dionysaic, hard to play, provoking to Greek theorists because of the tuning problems they created, distasteful to the Goddess who disliked the way in which they distorted the face of the player, and, most important of all, impossible for the player to sing to. The Apollonian *kithara,* on the other hand, employed strings (the basis of Greek empirical tuning), and permitted the player to rationalize his music by identifying its significance in the words of a sung text. It is perhaps with the distinction in mind that Bacon turns the story of Orpheus and the Maenads who destroyed him into a parable of rational science and blind destructive passion.

For centuries, then, to be described as a musician entailed being a scholar. To practice the art without understanding the ways in which people were affected by musical sounds was considered irresponsible. Now the authority of Boethius on many general musical questions remained unshaken up through the Renaissance, and his famous tripartite division between *musica mundana, musica humana,* and *musica instrumentalis* helped to blur many distinctions between speculative and practical music in later writers. By *musica mundana* Boethius meant the harmony of the universe, including the cosmological order of elements, astral bodies, and seasons. By human music he meant "that which unites the incorporeal activity of the reason with the body . . . a certain mutual adaptation and as it were a tempering of high and low sounds into a single consonance." [4] This paralleled the cosmic music in causing "the blending of the body's elements." The third category is simply practical music. The first two designate what is in fact not music at all, but figurative ascriptions of a regularity to nature. The harmony of the universe and the tempering of warring elements in the human character are both metaphors from Greek thought, in which the extended sense of the term "harmony" did not preserve the same implications that it holds for us. By and large, we must understand the word *harmonia* as ordered melody, and, when extended, as the rationalized proportions of the whole numbers that were seen to generate the intervals between musical tones. Modern usage has reserved for the word "harmony" the sense of the unity that comes from the simultaneous sounding of different tones, and it is probable that it suggested this meaning (although "consonance" was the term then employed) from the tenth century on. But it is *proportion* that remains the dominant notion in the Pythagorean view of universal harmony. It

[4] Boethius, *De Institutione,* I, 2, in Strunk, *Source Readings,* p. 85.

was only with the growth of polyphonic music that the idea of harmony as the essence of universal order came to be conceived in terms of the more familiar notion of *e pluribus unum*.

But the application of the term "harmony" remained invariant with respect to the sweeping changes in musical practice that resulted in its utterly different connotations. For example, St. Augustine's *De Musica*, a treatise on prosody, defines music as *"ars bene modulandi,"* the "proper patterning of sound." Using terms such as "concord" and "discord" to refer not to tonal intervals, but to patterns of length in metrical feet, the author classifies all meters with respect to the number of short syllables in *arsis* and *thesis*, respectively. For each type of foot, numerical proportions of *arsis*-"times" to *thesis*-"times" are given and commented upon.[5] It is these proportions involving whole numbers that seem to comprise the universally "musical" character of the prosodic discussions. Over 1,200 years later, Johannes Kepler still clung in a strange way to this element of Pythagoreanism, but with a significant difference. After having pointedly denied the existence of the planetary spheres, and even the circularity of their orbits, Kepler nevertheless sought to demonstrate the "harmony of the universe" by showing how certain ratios involving the angular velocities of the planets (rather than the traditionally used ratios of the diameters of the heavenly spheres) generated musical intervals. He was eager to show that this was not an actual music, but instead, a "harmonious" set of relationships. This was clearly in opposition to the view held by most writers from Aristotle to Montaigne, which regarded the music of the spheres as actual, but unheard, either because it was beyond audible range, or because human ears were dulled to it by custom. But Kepler's concern in justifying his description of the heavenly harmony led him to try to actualize the metaphor in terms of the practical music of his own age. He consequently performed elaborate arithmetical operations on his figures to show how the little melodic fragments he had assigned to each planet could be put into conventional six-part counterpoint, on the grounds that only this could serve as the true test of harmony.[6]

The concept of the music of the spheres was a popular one, passed down from antiquity through Plato, Cicero, and Macrobius' commentary on Cicero's *Somnium Scipionis*. It is of interest not only because

[5] See W. F. Jackson Knight, *St. Augustine's De Musica: A Synopsis* (London, n.d.), pp. 11–31.

[6] Joannes Kepler, *Harmonices Mundi* (Linz, 1619), V, 6–8.

of its embodiment of universal harmony, but because of its implications of both human and actual music, Boethius' second and third categories, as well. Historically, Plato's fiction of a singing siren seated on each sphere underwent considerable refinement. In its most widely received form, the doctrine held that the music of the spheres was produced by the rubbing of the supposedly hard, glassy celestial spheres against the ether, their varying sizes and velocities producing respectively varying pitches. The following passage from Cicero might be called the *locus classicus* of the idea of the celestial music:

"What is this loud and agreeable sound that fills my ears?"

"That is produced," he replies, "by the onward rush and motion of the spheres themselves; the intervals between them though unequal, being exactly arranged in a fixed proportion, by an agreeable blending of high and low tones various harmonies are produced; for such mighty motions cannot be carried on so swiftly in silence; and Nature has provided that one extreme shall produce low tones while the other gives forth high. Therefore this uppermost sphere of heaven, which bears the stars, as it revolves more rapidly, produces a high, shrill tone, whereas the lowest revolving sphere, that of the moon, gives forth the lowest tone; for the earthly sphere, the ninth, remains ever motionless and stationary in its position in the centre of the universe. But the other eight spheres, two of which move with the same velocity, produce seven different sounds—a number which is the key of almost everything. Learned men, by imitating this harmony on stringed instruments and in song, have gained for themselves a return to this region . . ."[7]

In commenting on this last sentence, Macrobius remarks that:

Every soul in this world is allured by musical sounds so that not only those who are more refined in their habits, but all the barbarous peoples as well, have adopted songs by which they are inflamed with courage or wooed to pleasure; for the soul carries with it into the body a memory of the music which it knew in the sky, and is so captivated by its charm that there is no breast so cruel or savage as not to be gripped by the spell of such an appeal.[8]

Thus microcosmic man, imitating in his *musica instrumentalis* or practical music the ideal order of the *harmonia mundi*, can regain in some small way the *musica humana*, the ordering of his being, that characterizes the music of the spheres.

But *musica humana* had another dimension as well. The ethical

[7] Cicero, *De Re Publica*, VI, 8, tr. C. W. Keyes (Loeb Edition), pp. 271–73.
[8] Macrobius, *Commentary on the Dream of Scipio*, tr. W. H. Stahl (New York, 1952), p. 195.

implications of music, stressed so heavily by Plato, were based on an elaborately reasoned system of classification of the effects of different kinds of melody on listeners. Particular tonal constellations were held necessarily to affect all men in various ways. Long after the death of the Attic musical practices that associated certain types of melody with the singing of certain types of text on particular occasions, the notions of an *ethos* that accompanied each conventional *harmonia* or scale remained an accepted tradition. The Greek ethical doctrines passed into Renaissance thought, aided by a confusion between the classical scales and the tones or "modes" of liturgical chant. The study of *ethos*, a huge body of Biblical and Classical lore concerning the curative power of music, and the various myths of Orpheus, Arion, Amphion, and Timotheus were continually invoked as evidence of music's beneficial powers. But up through the end of the sixteenth century, the most complete explanations of the reasons for music's ability to move the passions entailed an account of the *musica mundana*, coupled with a characterization of man as the microcosm. In Zarlino's *Institutione* we find that proportion, the essence of both cosmic order and the intervals of practical music, also governed the passions by adjudicating among the conflicting humors, aided by correspondences between modes, humors, and elements. Other arguments were brought up to reinforce this kind of notion. They ranged from correspondences between the rhythm of the alternating upbeat and downbeat of music to the systole and diastole of the human heartbeat, to the somewhat unruly uses of puns on *chorda* "string" and *cor, cordis* "heart" [9] in attempting to demonstrate the effects of music on the soul through the purely physical principle of sympathetic vibration.

The final link in the chain between *musica mundana* and *musica humana* in Renaissance musical speculation is a political one. Plato in his perfect state treated music as if it were ideology, and carefully legislated its uses. Horace had depicted Orpheus and Amphion as the poet-musicians whose art established and governed states, literally, in the case of the latter, from the ground up. Aside from the purely conventional assimilation of political notions into the universal patterns of order, degree, and harmony, the political nature of ideal music enters sixteenth-century thought in peculiar ways. It has been seen that a stringed instrument tended conventionally to connote reason, but in

---

[9] The possibilities of this word-play may have been initially suggested by Cassiodorus. See *Variae*, II, 40.

the *Hieroglyphics* of Horapollo, a possibly Hellenistic work published in 1505, the lyre turns up as the symbol of a man who "binds together and unites his fellows," with the explanation that "the lyre preserves the unity of its sounds." [10] In Alciati's emblem book, so widely distributed and imitated throughout the sixteenth century, there appears the picture of a lute, labelled *"Fides"* above it and *"Foedera"* below, followed by a Latin poem in praise of the great Duke who will some day unite all of Italy. Here another apparently traditional pun on *fides* "trust" and *fides* "stringed instrument" is invoked, and here too, the adaptation of the contemporary lute to the symbolic role of the lyre of antiquity can be seen. These, along with the harp upon which David eased Saul's melancholy, seem to be completely substitutable for each other in certain iconographic contexts. A final stage of symbolic adaptation might be pointed out in the version of Alciati's emblem in Henry Peacham's *Minerva Britannia*, published in 1612. Here, a cut of a bardic harp, labelled in Latin "The Irish Republic to King James," is followed by a little poem in praise of the English monarch which concludes:

Ne'er was the musick of old *Orpheus*, such,
As that I make, by meane (Dear Lord) of thee,
From discord drawne, to sweetest unitie.[11]

The order of the heavens, political concord, and the organic unity of individual men, each a "little world, made cunningly," were all thus embraced under the extended metaphor of harmony. It was the singular accomplishment of the sixteenth century, however, to incorporate into its *musica speculativa* so much of its practical music. This had for centuries been generating its own forms and conventions independently of the almost hermetically sealed body of literary discourse that comprised musical speculation. The whole question of the great interest that the sixteenth century took in tuning and temperament, for example, cannot be accounted for by either the mathematical demands of speculative music, or the immediate necessities of the widespread uses of instrumental music. And here lies another problem. The music of instruments was, in itself, as common as singing, although the rationalized doctrines of *musica speculativa* tended to reinforce the notion that there was nothing superior to the voices of men. Plato had disapproved

10 *The Hieroglyphics of Horapollo*, tr. George Boas (New York, 1950), p. 111.
11 Reproduced in *The Mirour of Maiestie*, ed. H. Green and J. Croston (London, 1870), plate V.

of textless music; Aristotle in *De Anima* had maintained that only sounds produced by a windpipe and infused with soul could be meaningful; and Ficino's synthesis of musical doctrine had laid great stress on the importance of the sung texts in understanding the effects of music on a hearer.[12] We might say that vocal polyphony was the model for all music, even at a time when *a capella* singing was merely one of many different practical styles. But by a strange historical irony, it was an overinsistence of the importance of the text by members of the Florentine *Camerata* toward the end of the sixteenth century that led to their experiments in expressive monody, the repercussions of which helped to shape the dominant vocal and instrumental styles of Baroque music. While the quarrels that helped to bring seventeenth-century musical conventions into being were waged on the grounds of expressive textual representation, however, it was eventually the music of instruments that came to be the model for music in general. At the risk of some oversimplification, it might be said that the Renaissance treated instruments as voices, while the Baroque eventually did just the opposite. "There is not any Musicke of Instruments whatsoever, comparable to that which is made of the voyces of Men," writes William Byrd in 1588. After an intervening century of change, the tables are turned, and John Gay can praise womankind by comparing her charms to the acme of expressive effectiveness: "Like the notes of a fiddle, she sweetly, sweetly/ Raises the spirits and charms our ears." (Air XXI)

In sixteenth-century England, then, the word "music" could suggest a wealth of speculation to an informed mind. Both a variety of actual practice, and an even more complex intellectual institution were embraced in a dialectic that unified inherited Medieval traditions, more recently acquired information about Antiquity, and the bare facts of how and what people played and sang. Traditional divisions of music into practical and theoretical, or into Boethius' cosmological, psychological, and instrumental were all retained in one way or another. And any answer to the question "What is music?" would involve a confusion between an abstract institution and a concrete practice that a modern philosopher might deplore, but one that we need only consider as an intricate yet unified series of metaphors.

---

[12] See D. P. Walker, "Ficino's *Spiritus* and "Music," *Annales Musicologiques* I (1953), pp. 131–50.

When seen in the light of the richness of sixteenth-century musical thought, the modern academic question of "Shakespeare and Music" tends to be more blinding than the glittering of its generality would warrant. With the aid of the musicological studies of the past thirty years, we are better able than ever before to reconstruct the actual music performed, and referred to, in Shakespeare's plays. The growth of study in the History of Ideas has given us models for understanding how words and customs that have misleadingly retained their forms to this day reverberated differently in various historical contexts. The forays of sixteenth- and seventeenth-century poets into *musica speculativa*, consequently, can now be understood as more than either the fanciful conceits or the transmission of quaint lore that many nineteenth-century readers took them to be. But the recent critical traditions that read all of Shakespeare with the kind of attention previously devoted to other kinds of poetry has tended to create a third, queer category of symbolic music. G. Wilson Knight in particular has employed the images of tempest and music in his criticism to suggest the universal themes of disorder and resolving, reconciling order. These concepts stem largely from his invaluable early work on the last plays, in which, trivially speaking, storm and music do appear to alternate in profound and general ways. But more recently, Professor Knight has elevated his rather *symboliste* construction of the word "music" to the heights proclaimed in Verlaine's manifesto: *"De la musique avant toute chose."* One result of this has been, I feel, to credit Shakespeare's imagination with the creation of what, for hundreds of years, had been fairly widely received ideas. Worse than this, however, has been the failure to see exactly to what degree Shakespeare's poetic intelligence utilized these received ideas about music, both speculative and practical, analyzing and reinterpreting them in dramatic contexts. Finally, and perhaps worst of all, some of Shakespeare's amazingly original contributions to *musica speculativa* have been lost sight of.

Twelfth Night represents, I feel, an excellent case in point. Probably written late in 1600, its treatment of the theme of music is considerably more complex than that of the plays preceding it. By and large, the bulk of the references in all the plays is to practical music, which is cited, satirized, and praised in various contexts like any other human activity. Of particular interest to Shakespeare always was the richness of various technical vocabularies, and much of the wit in all but the later plays consists of puns and twisted tropes on technical terminology, often that of instrumental music. Two well-known passages of *musica speculativa* in the earlier plays, however, deserve some comment.

The first of these is Richard II's great speech in Pomfret castle. After likening his prison to the world and to his own body, the King hears music offstage:

> Music do I hear?
> Ha, ha! Keep time. How sour sweet music is
> When time is broke and no proportion kept!
> So is it in the music of men's lives,
> And here have I the daintiness of ear
> To check time broke in a disordered string,
> But for the concord of my state and time
> Had not an ear to hear my true time broke.   (V,v,41–48)

"Proportion" here is used in its immediate sense of time-signature, and "time broke in a disordered string" refers to the music he hears playing. But the "disordered string" is also himself, an emblem of the unruled, unruly state. "The concord of my state and time" invokes the musical connotations of "concord" as well—for centuries the word had reverberated with the old pun on "heart" and "string." What the King is saying is that now, in his broken state, he is sensitive to all the nuances of musical order, but formerly, lulled by the metaphorically musical order of his earlier reign, he had been unable to hear the tentative tempi in his own *musica humana*. In this passage an occurrence of practical music is interpreted in perfectly traditional terms, and human and worldly musics are made to coincide, both in Richard's own rhetoric and in the hierarchical imagery throughout the play. The conventional multiplicity of extensions of the term "music" are employed directly, and Richard, aside from the tireless progression of his thoughts, is talking like something out of an Old Book.

The final irony of Richard's soliloquy:

> This music mads me, let it sound no more,
> For though it have holp madmen to their wits,
> In me it seems it will make wise men mad.
> Yet blessings on his heart that gives it me!
> For 'tis a sign of love, and love to Richard
> Is a strange brooch in this all-hating world.   V,v,61–66)

is reinforced by the fragmentation of "music" into its various categories. The music is maddening because its human and universal roles have not coincided for the King, whose necessary identity with the proper order of the state has been called into question by the fact of his deposition and imprisonment. Bolingbroke, the discord, the untuner, will himself become the well-tuned regulating instrument of state. And finally, the practical music is sundered from its speculative form in Richard's gratitude for the instrumental sounds themselves, which he takes as the evidence of someone's thoughtful care.

I believe that it is this same conventional use of the emblematic stringed instrument in a political context that is at work during a moment in Brutus's tent in Act IV scene iii of *Julius Caesar*. The boy Lucius has fallen asleep over his instrument after singing for Brutus, and the latter has taken it away from him lest it drop to the ground and break. After the ominous appearance of Caesar's ghost, Brutus cries out, and the boy half-awakens, murmuring, "The strings, my lord, are false." Brutus, missing the import of this, comments, "He thinks he still is at his instrument," and shakes Lucius fully awake, inquiring after the phantom. But the meaning, I think, is clear, and the false strings are the discordant conspirators, now jangling and out of tune even among themselves. Brutus, who "in general honest thought/ And common good to all, made one" of the varying faction he led, meets the prophetic truth of the boy's half-dreamed image with a benevolently naturalistic interpretation of it.

The even better known music at Belmont in *The Merchant of Venice* shows a more dramatically sophisticated use of *musica speculativa*. In general, the dramatic structure of the whole play hinges on the relationship between Venice, the commercial city where gold is ventured for more gold, and the symbolically golden Belmont, where all is hazarded for love. Belmont is full of practical music in one of its most common sixteenth-century forms. Music used for signalling, the tuckets, flourishes, and sennets familiar to modern readers through stage directions, were not confined to the uses of dramaturgy; it was a matter of actual practice for distinguished persons to be accompanied by their private trumpeters. It is almost as a signal that the song "Tell me where is fancy bred" is employed. Like a nursery-rhyme riddle, it advises against appearances, and cryptically urges the choice of the lead. In a speech preceding the song, Portia's wit analyzes and interprets the ceremonial music she has ordered:

Let music sound while he doth make his choice,
Then, if he lose, he makes a swanlike end,
Fading in music. That the comparison
May stand more proper, my eye shall be the stream
And watery deathbed for him. He may win,
And what is music then? Then music is
Even as the flourish when true subjects bow
To a new-crowned monarch.   (III,ii,43–50)

Here Portia makes the point that the same music can play many roles, that the institution emerges from the fact as the result of an intellectual process. She selects two polar institutions, incidentally: music as signal, which plays little or no part in traditional musical speculation, and the myth of the dying swan, a stock image in romantic lyrics throughout the century. Portia reaffirms this later on, when she remarks of the music that Jessica and Lorenzo hear on the bank, "Nothing is good, I see, without respect./ Methinks it sound much sweeter than by day." Nerissa replies that "Silence bestows that virtue on it," invoking one of the dominant Belmont themes of the deception of ornament, of the paleness more moving than eloquence. It is the same theme that prefaces Lorenzo's initiation of Jessica into the silent *harmonia mundi:*

Soft stillness and the night
Become the touches of sweet harmony.
Sit, Jessica. Look how the floor of heaven
Is thick inlaid with patines of bright gold.
There's not the smallest orb which thou behold'st
But in his motion like an angel sings,
Still quiring to the young-eyed cherubins.
Such harmony is in immortal souls,
But whilst this muddy vesture of decay
Doth grossly close it in, we cannot hear it.   (V,i,56–65)

This is the vision of Plato's Er and Cicero's Scipio. It is significant that the one instance of Shakespeare's troping of the doctrine is Lorenzo's explanation of the inaudible character of the heavenly music. Neither of the traditional reasons (acclimatization, or the physical thresholds of perception) is given. Instead, the unheard music is related to immortality, and by extension, to a prelapsarian condition, a world which, like heaven, need not conceal its ultimate gold, which even Belmont must do. This approaches Milton's treatment of the subject in *At a Solemn Musick.*

Then enter the musicians, to play at Lorenzo's bidding. "I am never merry when I hear sweet music," says Jessica. She may, of course, be referring to the concentration demanded by the soft, "indoor" music of Portia's house musicians, as opposed to the more strident character of "outdoor" instruments. Lorenzo, at any rate, answers this with an instructive, though standard, disquisition on music and the affections, ending on a note of *musica humana* with all of its ethical and political connotations:

> The reason is, your spirits are attentive.
> For do but note a wild and wanton herd,
> Or race of youthful and unhandled colts,
> Fetching mad bounds, bellowing, and neighing loud,
> Which is the hot condition of their blood.
> If they but hear perchance a trumpet sound,
> Or any air of music touch their ears,
> You shall perceive them make a mutual stand,
> Their savage eyes turned to a modest gaze
> By the sweet power of music. Therefore the poet
> Did feign that Orpheus drew trees, stones, and floods,
> Since naught so stockish, hard, and full of rage
> But music for the time doth change his nature.
> The man that hath no music in himself
> Nor is not moved with concord of sweet sounds,
> Is fit for treasons, stratagems, and spoils.
> The motions of his spirit are dull as night
> And his affections dark as Erebus.
> Let no such man be trusted. Mark the music.   (V,i,70–88)

Innuendoes of *musica mundana*, golden, silent, and inaccessible, are intimated at Belmont, where actual music is heard, and where the Venetian incompatibilities of gold and love are finally reconciled, almost as much in the golden music as in the golden ring.

In *Twelfth Night*, however, the role of music is so obviously fundamental to the spirit of the play that it is momentarily surprising to find so little speculative music brought up for discussion. But I think that, on consideration of the nature of the play itself, the place of both active and intellectual music, and the relations between them, emerge as something far more complex than Shakespeare had hitherto cause to employ. *Twelfth Night* is, in very serious ways, a play about parties and what they do to people. Full of games, revels, tricks, and disguises, it is an Epiphany play, a ritualized Twelfth Night festivity in itself, but it is much more than this: the play gives us an analysis, as well as a representation, of feasting. It develops an ethic of indulgence based on the notion that the personality of any individual is a function not of the static proportions of the humors within him, but of the dynamic appetites that may more purposefully, as well as more pragmatically, be said to govern his behavior. Superficially close to the comedy of humors in the characterological extremes of its *dramatis personae*, the play nevertheless seems almost intent on destroying the whole theory of comedy and of morality entailed by the comedy of humors.

The nature of a revel is disclosed in the first scene. The materials are to be music, food and drink, and love. The basic action of both festivity in general, and of the play itself, is declared to be that of so surfeiting the appetite that it will sicken and die, leaving fulfilled the tempered, harmonious self. The movement of the whole play is that of a party, from appetite, through the direction of that appetite outward toward something, to satiation, and eventually to the condition when, as the Duke hopes for Olivia, "liver, brain and heart/ These sovereign thrones, are all supplied, and filled/ Her sweet perfections with one self king." The "one self king" is the final harmonious state to be achieved by each reveller, but it is also, in both the Duke's and Olivia's case, Cesario, who kills "the flock of all affections else" that live in them, and who is shown forth in a literal epiphany in the last act.

The Duke's opening speech describes both the action of feasting, and his own abundant, ursine, romantic temperament. But it also contains within it an emblematic representation of the action of surfeiting:

> If music be the food of love, play on.
> Give me excess of it, that, surfeiting,
> The appetite may sicken, and so die.
> That strain again! It had a dying fall.
> Oh, it came o'er my ear like the sweet sound
> That breathes upon a bank of violets,
> Stealing and giving odor! Enough, no more.
> 'Tis not so sweet now as it was before.   (I,i,1–8)

The one personage in the play who remains in a melancholy humor is the one person who is outside the revels and cannot be affected by them. Olivia's rebuke cuts to the heart of his nature: "Thou

art sick of self love, Malvolio, and taste with a distempered appetite."
Suffering from a kind of moral indigestion, Malvolio's true character is
revealed in his involuted, Puritanic sensibility that allows of no appetites directed outward. His rhetoric is full of the Devil; it is full of
humors and elements as well. No other character tends to mention
these save in jest, for it is only Malvolio who believes in them. Yet real,
exterior fluids of all kinds, wine, tears, sea-water, urine, and finally the
rain of inevitability bathe the whole world of Illyria, in constant reference throughout the play.

The general concern of *Twelfth Night*, then, is *musica humana*,
the Boethian application of abstract order and proportion to human
behavior. The literalization of the universal harmony that is accomplished in comedy of humors, however, is unequivocally rejected. "Does
not our life consist of the four elements?" catechizes Sir Toby. "Faith,
so they say," replies Sir Andrew, "but I think it rather consists of eating
and drinking." "Thou'rt a scholar," acknowledges Sir Toby. "Let us
therefore eat and drink." "Who you are and what you would are out of
my welkin—I might say 'element,' but the word is overworn," says
Feste, who, taking offense at Malvolio's characterization of him as a
"dry fool" touches off the whole proceedings against the unfortunate
steward. The plot to ridicule Malvolio is more than the frolicsome
revenge of an "allowed fool"; it serves both to put down the "party-
pooper" and to affirm the psychology of appetite and fulfillment that
governs the play. To the degree that the *musica humana of Twelfth
Night* involves the substitution of an alternative view to the fairly
standard sixteenth-century descriptions of the order of the passions, an
application of the musical metaphor would be trivial, and perhaps misleading. But the operation of practical music in the plot, the amazingly
naturalistic treatment of its various forms, and the conclusions implied
as to the nature and effects of music in both the context of celebration and in the world at large, all result in some musical speculation
that remains one of the play's unnoticed accomplishments.

The actual music in *Twelfth Night* starts and finishes the play,
occurring throughout on different occasions and in different styles. The
presumably instrumental piece in which the Duke wallows at the opening dampens his desire for it very quickly, but that desire returns before
long. Orsino's appetite at the start of the play is purportedly for Olivia,
who hungers for, and indulges herself in, her own grief. The Duke's
actual love, too, is for his own act of longing, and for his own exclama-

tions of sentiment. Both of these desires are directed outward before the play is over. But until a peculiar 'musical mechanism, which will be mentioned later on, as has been set to work, the Duke will hunt his own heart, and his desires, "like fell and cruel hounds," will continue to pursue him. The music in Act II, scene iv, is of just such a nature to appease the Duke's extreme sentimentality. Orsino makes it plain what sort of song he wants to hear:

> Now, good Cesario, but that piece of song,
> That old and antique song we heard last night.
> Methought it did relieve my passion much,
> More than light airs and recollected terms
> Of these most brisk and giddy-pacèd times.   (II,iv,2–6)

This is a familiar sentimental attitude, the desire for the Good Old Song that nudges the memory, the modern request made of the cocktail pianist, the half-ironic translation in Bert Brecht's *Happy End*, where a singer tries to recapture better days by imploring *"Joe, mach die Musik von damals nach."* Orsino's favorite song, he says,

>   is old and plain.
> The spinsters and the knitters in the sun
> And the free maids that weave their thread with bones
> Do use to chant it. It is silly sooth,
> And dallies with the innocence of love,
> Like the old age.   (II,iv,44–49)

Actually, the song that Feste sings him is a highly extravagant, almost parodic version of the theme of death from unrequited love. Its rather stilted diction and uneasy prosody are no doubt intended to suggest a song from an old miscellany. "Come away" is a banal beginning, appearing at the start of four song texts in Canon Fellowes' collection. We may also presume that the setting employed was rather more archaic than that of the well-polished lute accompaniments of the turn of the century.

It is just one of these "light airs and recollected terms," however, with which Sir Toby and Feste plague Malvolio in their big scene of carousal (II,iii). A setting of "Farewell, dear heart" appears in Robert Jones' first book of airs, published in 1600. Of the other songs in the same scene, one is a round, a more trivial form of song, certainly with respect to its text, than the sophisticated and intricate lewdness of the post-Restoration catch. The other is a "love song" sung by Feste, and preferred by Sir Toby and Sir Andrew to "a song of good life," perhaps with a pious text. It is of the finest type of Shakespearean song that catches up the spirit of overall themes and individual characters, ironically and prophetically pointing to the end of a plot or bit of action. All of "Oh mistress mine" is in one sense an invocation to Olivia to put off her self-indulgent grief, her courting of her dead brother's memory. In particular, the first stanza refers to Viola, the boy-girl true love, "that can sing both high and low."

Feste's songs to Malvolio in his madman's prison are both of an archaic cast. The first is a snatch of a song of Wyatt's, "A robyn, joly robyn" that was set to music by William Cornish during the reign of Henry VIII. The other one, a parting jibe at Malvolio's cant about the Devil, suggests the doggerel of an old Morality, invoking Malvolio as the Devil himself, and continuing the game of mocking him by appealing to his own rhetoric.

All of these occurrences of practical music function in the plot as well as with respect to the general theme of feasting and revels. The one reference to *musica speculativa* is a very interesting one, however, and leads to the most important aspect of the operation of music in *Twelfth Night*. Olivia is exhorting Viola to refrain from mentioning the Duke to her, and implying that she would rather be courted by his messenger:

> I bade you never speak again of him.
> But, would you undertake another suit,
> I had rather hear you to solicit that
> Than music from the spheres.   (III,i,118–21)

The citation of the music of the spheres here has the tone of most such references during the later seventeenth century in England. With the exception of poets like Milton and Marvell, who used metaphors from the old cosmology for intricate poetic purposes of their own, the music of the spheres became, in Cavalier and Augustan poetry, a formal compliment, empty of even the metaphorical import that the world view of the centuries preceding had given to it. Just as the word "heavenly," used in exclamations of praise, long ago became completely divorced from its substantive root, the music of the spheres gradually came to designate the acme of effective charm in a performer. It was often employed in compliments to ladies, for example, whose skill at singing made the spheres sound dissonant, abashed the singing angels, and so forth.

As in the case of Dryden's music that would "untune¹the sky," references to the heavenly harmony had nothing to do with received ideas of music's importance during the later seventeenth century, which were more and more becoming confined to a rhetorical ability to elicit passion, on the one hand, and to provide ornament to the cognitive import of a text, on the other. Purcell likens music and poetry to beauty and wit, respectively; the former can unite to produce the same wondrous effects in song that the latter can in a human being, although the virtues of each are independent. The differences between music and poetry also tended to cluster about the celebrated rift between thought and feeling. Most important of all, traditional *musica speculativa* gradually ceased being a model of universal order, and was replaced by a notion of music as a model of rhetoric, whose importance lay in its ability to move the passions, rather than in its older role of the microcosmic copy of universal harmony. The Apollonian lute-harp-lyre constellation, once an emblem of reason and order, became an instrument of passion in the hands of Caravaggio's leering boys, and in the hands of Crashaw's musician who slew the nightingale by musically ravishing her, as even her avatar Philomela was never so ravished, to death.

With these considerations in mind, the crucial role of Viola as an instrument of such a rhetorical music becomes quite clear. It is unfortunate that we have no precise indication of an earlier version of the play, presumably rewritten when the superior singer Robert Armin entered Shakespeare's company, in which some of the songs may have been assigned to Viola. She declares herself at the outset:

> I'll serve this Duke.
> Thou shalt present me as a eunuch to him.
> It may be worth thy pains, for I can sing,
> And speak to him in many sorts of music,
> That will allow me very worth his service.   (I,ii,55–59)

She will be the Duke's instrument, although she turns out to be an instrument that turns in his hand, charming both Olivia and himself in unexpected fashion. Orsino is given an excess of music in Viola. As Cesario, she wins Olivia for her alter ego Sebastian who is himself, in his few scenes, rhetorically effective almost to the point of preciosity, and who is likened to the musician Arion who charmed his way to safety. Viola is the affective, instrumental, prematurely Baroque music in *Twelfth Night*, and it is she whose charm kills off the gourmandizing sentimentality in both Orsino and Olivia, directing their appetites of love outward, in fact, towards herself. Among the characters to whom Malvolio refers as "the lighter people," it is Feste, the singer and prankster, whose pipe and tabor serve as a travesty of Viola's vocal chords. The operation of Viola's "music" involves charming by the use of appearances; the effects of the trickery instigated by Feste are to make Malvolio appear, until he is undeceived, to be Olivia's ridiculously amorous swain. (It is, of course, the phrase "To be Count Malvolio" that appears on his lips after reading the forged letter.) Through the mechanism of fooling, the travesty of music below stairs, Sir Andrew is chastened, Sir Toby is soberly married to Maria, Malvolio is made to act out the madness of which he falsely accused Feste, and "the whirligig of time brings in his revenges."

The music that brings about the conclusion of the revels is thus a figurative music. It pervades the symbolic enactment of indulgence and surfeit in the plot as the actual music, relegated to its several uses and forms with considerable eye to details of practice in Shakespeare's own day, pervades the spectacle of *Twelfth Night*. The play is about revelry, and, in itself, a revels; so too, there is music in it, and a working out of a theme in speculative music that strangely coincides with later views on the subject. The *Ursprung* of Viola's music is certainly in the action of the play; it is not to be implied that *Twelfth Night* is anything of a formal treatise, and the music in Illyria all serves its immediately dramatic purposes. Within the context of the play's anti-Puritan, anti-Jonsonian treatment of moral physiology, the role of music seems to have become inexorably defined for Shakespeare. Set in a framework of what, at this point, might be almost coy to call a study in *musica humana*, practical music becomes justified in itself. Free of even the scraps of traditional musical ideology that had been put to use in the plays preceding it, *Twelfth Night* represents a high point in one phase of Shakespeare's musical dramaturgy. It is not until *Antony and Cleopatra* and the last romances that the use of an almost supernatural music, perhaps imported to some degree from the musical *données* of the masque, comes to be associated with the late, great themes of reconciliation and transformation.

II. 2

On the Value of *Hamlet*[*]

STEPHEN BOOTH

University of California, Berkeley

IT IS a truth universally acknowledged that *Hamlet* as we have it—usually in a conservative conflation of the second quarto and first folio texts—is not really *Hamlet*. The very fact that the *Hamlet* we know is an editor-made text has furnished an illusion of firm ground for leaping conclusions that discrepancies between the probable and actual actions, statements, tone, and diction of *Hamlet* are accidents of its transmission. Thus, in much the spirit of editors correcting printer's errors, critics have proposed stage directions by which, for example, Hamlet can overhear the plot to test Polonius' diagnosis of Hamlet's affliction, or by which Hamlet can glimpse Polonius and Claudius actually spying on his interview with Ophelia. Either of these will make sense of Hamlet's improbable raging at Ophelia in III,i. The difficulty with such presumably corrective emendation is not only in knowing where to stop, but also in knowing whether to start. I hope to demonstrate that almost everything else in the play has, in its particular kind and scale, an improbability comparable to the improbability of the discrepancy between Hamlet's real and expected behavior to Ophelia; for the moment, I mean only to suggest that those of the elements of the text of *Hamlet* that are incontrovertibly accidental may by their presence have led critics to overestimate the distance between the *Hamlet* we have and the prelapsarian *Hamlet* to which they long to return.

I think also that the history of criticism shows us too ready to indulge a not wholly explicable fancy that in *Hamlet* we behold the

[*] Published in *Institute Papers: Reinterpretation of Elizabethan Drama*, 1969.

frustrated and inarticulate Shakespeare furiously wagging his tail in an effort to tell us something, but, as I said before, the accidents of our texts of *Hamlet* and the alluring analogies they father render *Hamlet* more liable to interpretive assistance than even the other plays of Shakespeare. Moreover, *Hamlet* was of course born into the culture of Western Europe, our culture, whose every thought—literary or non-literary—is shaped by the Platonic presumption that the reality of any-thing is other than its apparent self. In such a culture it is no wonder that critics prefer the word *meaning* (which implies effort rather than success) to *saying*, and that in turn they would rather talk about what a work *says* or *shows* (both of which suggest the hidden essence bared of the dross of physicality) than talk about what it *does*. Even stylistic critics are most comfortable and acceptable when they reveal that rhythm, syntax, diction, or (and above all) imagery are vehicles for meaning. Among people to whom "It means a lot to me" says "I value it," in a language where *significant* and *valuable* are synonyms, it was all but inevitable that a work with the peculiarities of *Hamlet* should have been treated as a distinguished and yearning failure.

Perhaps the value of *Hamlet* is where it is most measurable, in the degree to which it fulfills one or another of the fixable identities it suggests for itself or that are suggested for it, but I think that before we choose and argue for one of the ideal forms toward which *Hamlet* seems to be moving, and before we attribute its value to an exaggera-tion of the degree to which it gets there, it is reasonable to talk about what the play *does* do, and to test the suggestion that in a valued play what it does do is what we value. I propose to look at *Hamlet* for what it undeniably is: a succession of actions upon the understanding of an audience. I set my hypothetical audience to watch *Hamlet* in the text edited by Willard Farnham in The Pelican *Shakespeare* (Baltimore, 1957), a text presumably too long to have fitted into the daylight avail-able to a two o'clock performance, but still an approximation of what Shakespeare's company played.

I

The action that the first scene of *Hamlet* takes upon the understand-ing of its audience is like the action of the whole, and most of the in-dividual actions that make up the whole. The first scene is insistently incoherent and just as insistently coherent. It frustrates and fulfills expectations simultaneously. The challenge and response in the first lines are perfectly predictable sentry-talk, but—as has been well and often observed—the challenger is the wrong man, the relieving sentry and not the one on duty. A similarly faint intellectual uneasiness is provoked when the first personal note in the play sets up expectations that the play then ignores. Francisco says, "For this relief much thanks. 'Tis bitter cold,/ And I am sick at heart" (II,i,8-9). We want to know why he is sick at heart. Several lines later Francisco leaves the stage and is forgotten. The scene continues smoothly as if the audience had never focused on Francisco's heartsickness. Twice in the space of less than a minute the audience has an opportunity to concern itself with a trouble that vanishes from consciousness almost before it is there. The wrong sentry challenges, and the other corrects the oddity instantly. Francisco is sick at heart, but neither he nor Bernardo gives any sign that further comment might be in order. The routine of sentry-go, its special diction, and its commonplaces continue across the audience's momentary tangential journey; the audience returns as if *it* and not the play had wandered. The audience's sensation of being unexpectedly and very slightly out of step is repeated regularly in *Hamlet*.

The first thing an audience in a theater wants to know is why it is in the theater. Even one that, like Shakespeare's audiences for *Richard II* or *Julius Caesar* or *Hamlet*, knows the story being dramatized wants to hear out the familiar terms of the situation and the terms of the particular new dramatization. Audiences want their bearings and expect them to be given. The first thing we see in *Hamlet* is a pair of sentries. The sight of sentries in real life is insignificant, but, when a work of art focuses on sentries, it is usually a sign that what they are guarding is going to be attacked. Thus, the first answer we have to the question "what is this play about?" is "military threat to a castle and a king," and that leads to our first specific question: "what is that threat?" Horatio's first question ("What, has this thing appeared again to-night?" I,i,21) is to some extent an answer to the audience's question; its terms are not military, but their implications are appropriately threatening. Bernardo then begins elaborate preparations to tell Horatio what the audience must hear if it is ever to be intellectually comfortable in the play. The audience has slightly adjusted its expectations to accord with a threat that is vaguely supernatural rather than military, but the metaphor of assault in which Bernardo prepares to

carry the audience further along its new path of inquiry is pertinent to
the one from which it has just deviated:

> Sit down awhile,
> And let us once again assail your ears,
> That are so fortified against our story,
> What we two nights have seen.   (I,i,30–33)

We are led toward increased knowledge of the new object—the ghost
—in terms appropriate to the one we assumed and have just abandoned
—military assault. Bernardo's metaphor is obviously pertinent to his occupation as sentinel, but in the metaphor he is not the defender but
the assailant of ears fortified against his story. As the audience listens,
its understanding shifts from one system of pertinence to another; but
each perceptible change in the direction of our concern or the terms of
our thinking is balanced by the repetition of some continuing factor in
the scene; the mind of the audience is in constant but gentle flux, always shifting but never completely leaving familiar ground.

Everyone onstage sits down to hear Bernardo speak of the events
of the past two nights. The audience is invited to settle its mind for a
long and desired explanation. The construction of Bernardo's speech
suggests that it will go on for a long time; he takes three lines (I,i,35–
38) to arrive at the grammatical subject of his sentence, and then, as
he begins another parenthetical delay in his long journey toward a
verb, "the bell then beating one," *Enter Ghost.* The interrupting action
is not a simple interruption. The description is interrupted by a repetition of the action described. The entrance of the ghost duplicates on a
larger scale the kind of mental experience we have had before. It both
fulfills and frustrates our expectations: it is what we expect and desire,
an action to account for our attention to sentinels; it is unexpected and
unwanted, an interruption in the syntactical routine of the exposition
that was on its way to fulfilling the same function. While the ghost is
on the stage and during the speculation that immediately follows its
departure, the futile efforts of Horatio and the sentries (who, as
watchers and waiters, have resembled the audience from the start)
are like those of the audience in its quest for information. Marcellus'
statement about the ghost is a fair comment on the whole scene: " 'Tis
gone and will not answer" (I,i,52), and Horatio's "In what particular
thought to work I know not" (I,i,67) describes the mental condition
evoked in an audience by this particular dramatic presentation of events

as well as it does that evoked in the character by the events of the fiction.

Horatio continues from there into the first statement in the play that is responsive to an audience's requirement of an opening scene, an indication of the nature and direction of the play to follow: "But, in the gross and scope of my opinion,/ This bodes some strange eruption to our state" (I,i,68–69). That vague summary of the significance of the ghost is political, but only incidentally so because the audience, which was earlier attuned to political/military considerations, has now given its attention to the ghost. Then, with only the casual preamble of the word *state*, Marcellus asks a question irrelevant to the audience's newly primary concerns, precisely the question that no one asked when the audience first wanted to know why it was watching the sentries, the question about the fictional situation whose answer would have satisfied the audience's earlier question about its own situation: Marcellus asks "Why this same strict and most observant watch/ So nightly toils the subject of the land" (I,i,71–72). Again what we are given is and is not pertinent to our concerns and expectations. This particular variety among the manifestations of simultaneous and equal propriety and impropriety in *Hamlet* occurs over and over again. Throughout the play, the audience gets information or sees action it once wanted only after a new interest has superseded the old. For one example, when Horatio, Bernardo, and Marcellus arrive in the second scene (I,ii,159), they come to do what they promise to do at the end of scene one, where they tell the audience that the way to information about the ghost is through young Hamlet. By the time they arrive "where we shall find him most conveniently," the audience has a new concern—the relation of Claudius to Gertrude and of Hamlet to both. Of course interruptions of one train of thought by the introduction of another are not only common in *Hamlet* but a commonplace of literature in general. However, although the audience's frustrations and the celerity with which it transfers its concern are similar to those of audiences of, say, Dickens, there is the important difference in *Hamlet* that there are no sharp lines of demarcation. In *Hamlet* the audience does not so much shift its focus as come to find its focus shifted.

Again the first scene provides a type of the whole. When Marcellus asks why the guard is so strict, his question is rather more violent than not in its divergence from our concern for the boding of the ghost. The answer to Marcellus' question, however, quickly pertains to the subject

of ours: Horatio's explanation of the political situation depends from
actions of "Our last king,/ Whose image even but now appeared to us"
(I,i,80–81), and his description of the activities of young Fortinbras as
"The source of this our watch" is harnessed to our concern about the
ghost by Bernardo, who says directly, if vaguely, that the political
situation is pertinent to the walking of the ghost:

> I think it be no other but e'en so.
> Well may it sort that this portentous figure
> Comes armèd through our watch so like the king
> That was and is the question of these wars.   (I,i,108–11)

Horatio reinforces the relevance of politics to ghosts in a long speech
about supernatural events on the eve of Julius Caesar's murder. Both
these speeches establishing pertinence are good examples of the sort
of thing I mean: both seem impertinent digressions, sufficiently so to
have been omitted from the folios.

Now for the second time, *Enter Ghost.* The reentrance after a
long and wandering digression is in itself an assertion of the continuity,
constancy, and unity of the scene. Moreover, the situation into which
the ghost reenters is a careful echo of the one into which it first entered,
with the difference that the promised length of the earlier exposition is
fulfilled in the second. These are the lines surrounding the first entrance; the italics are mine and indicate words, sounds, and substance
echoed later:

HORATIO: *Well, sit we down,*
> And let us hear Bernardo speak of this.
BERNARDO: Last night of all,
> *When yond same star* that's *westward* from the pole
> Had made his course t' illume that part of heaven
> Where now it burns, Marcellus and myself,
> The bell then beating one—   *Enter Ghost.*
MARCELLUS: *Peace, break thee* off. *Look where it comes again.* (I,i,33–40)

Two or three minutes later a similar situation takes shape in words
that echo, and in some cases repeat, those at the earlier entrance:

MARCELLUS: *Good now, sit down,* and tell me he that knows,
> *Why this same* strict and most observant watch,
> So nightly toils the subject of the land . . .   *Enter Ghost*
> *But soft, behold, lo where it comes again!*   (I,i,70–72, 126)

After the ghost departs on the crowing of the cock, the conversation, already extravagant and erring before the second apparition when it ranged from Danish history into Roman, meanders into a seemingly gratuitous preoccupation with the demonology of cocks (I,i,148–65). Then—into a scene that has from the irregularly regular entrance of the two sentinels been a succession of simultaneously expected and unexpected entrances—enters "the morn in russet mantle clad," bringing a great change from darkness to light, from the unknown and unnatural to the known and natural, but also presenting itself personified as another walker, one obviously relevant to the situation and to the discussion of crowing cocks, and one described in subdued but manifold echoes of the two entrances of the ghost. Notice particularly the multitude of different kinds of relationship in which "yon high eastward hill" echoes "yond same star that's westward from the pole":

> But look, the morn in russet mantle clad
> Walks o'er the dew of yon high eastward hill.
> Break we our watch up. . . .   (I,i,166–68)

The three speeches (I,i,148–73—Horatio's on the behavior of ghosts at cockcrow, Marcellus' on cocks at Christmas time, and Horatio's on the dawn) have four major elements running through them: cocks, spirits, sunrise, and the presence or absence of speech. All four are not present all the time, but the speeches have a sound of interconnection and relevance to one another. This at the same time that the substance of Marcellus' speech on Christmas is just as urgently irrelevant to the concerns of the scene. As a gratuitous discussion of Christianity, apparently linked to its context only by an accident of poulterer's lore, it is particularly irrelevant to the moral limits usual to revenge tragedy. The sequence of these last speeches is like the whole scene and the play in being both coherent and incoherent. Watching and comprehending the scene is an intellectual triumph for its audience. From sentence to sentence, from event to event, as the scene goes on it makes the mind of its audience capable of containing materials that seem always about to fly apart. The scene gives its audience a temporary and modest but real experience of being a superhumanly capable mental athlete. The whole play is like that.

During the first scene of Hamlet two things are threatened, one in the play, and one by the play. Throughout the scene the characters look at all threats as threats to the state, and specifically to the reigning

king. As the king is threatened *in* scene one, so is the audience's understanding threatened *by* scene one. The audience wants some solid information about what is going on in this play. Scene one is set in the
dark, and it leaves the audience in the dark. The first things the play
teaches us to value are the order embodied in the king and the rational
sureness, purpose, and order that the play as a play lacks in its first
scene. Scene two presents both the desired orders at once and in one—
the king, whose name even in scene one was not only synonymous with
order but was the regular sign by which order was reasserted: the
first confusion—who should challenge whom—was resolved in line
three by "Long live the king"; and at the entrance of Horatio and
Marcellus, rightness and regularity were vouched for by "Friends to
this ground. And liegemen to the Dane." As scene two begins it is
everything the audience wanted most in scene one. Here it is daylight,
everything is clear, everything is systematic. Unlike scene one, this
scene is physically orderly; it begins with a royal procession, business-
like and unmistakable in its identity. Unlike the first scene, the second
gives the audience all the information it could desire, and gives it
neatly. The direct source of both information and orderliness is
Claudius, who addresses himself one by one to the groups on the stage
and to the problems of the realm, punctuating the units both with
little statements of conclusion like "For all, our thanks" and "So much
for him" (I,ii,16, 25), and with the word "now" (I,ii,17, 26, 42, 64), by
which he signals each remove to a new listener and topic. Denmark
and the play are both now orderly, and are so because of the king. In
its specifics, scene two is the opposite of scene one. Moreover, where
scene one presented an incoherent surface whose underlying coherence
is only faintly felt, this scene is the opposite. In scene one the action
taken *by* the scene—it makes its audience perceive diffusion and fusion,
division and unification, difference and likeness at once—is only an
incidental element in the action taken or discussed *in* the scene—the
guards have trouble recognizing each other; the defense preparation
"does not divide the Sunday from the week," and makes "the night
joint-laborer with the day" (I,i,76, 78). In scene two the first subject
taken up by Claudius, and the subject of first importance to Hamlet, is
itself an instance of improbable unification—the unnatural natural
union of Claudius and Gertrude. Where scene one brought its audience
to feel coherence in incoherence by response to systems of organization
other than those of logical or narrative sequence, scene two brings its

audience to think of actions and characters alternately and sometimes nearly simultaneously in systems of value whose contradictory judgments rarely collide in the mind of an audience. From an uneasiness prompted by a sense of lack of order, unity, coherence, and continuity, we have progressed to an uneasiness prompted by a sense of their excess.

Claudius is everything the audience most valued in scene one, but he is also and at once contemptible. His first sentences are unifications in which his discretion overwhelms things whose natures are oppugnant. The simple but contorted statement, "therefore our . . . sister . . . have we . . . taken to wife," takes Claudius more than six lines to say; it is plastered together with a succession of subordinate unnatural unions made smooth by rhythm, alliteration, assonance, and syntactical balance:

> Therefore our sometime sister, now our queen,
> Th' imperial jointress to this warlike state,
> Have we, as 'twere with a defeated joy,
> With an auspicious and a dropping eye,
> With mirth in funeral and with dirge in marriage,
> In equal scale weighing delight and dole,
> Taken to wife.   (I,ii,8–14)

What he says is overly orderly. The rhythms and rhetoric by which he connects any contraries, moral or otherwise, are too smooth. Look at the complex phonetic equation that gives a sound of decorousness to the moral indecorum of "With mirth in funeral and with dirge in marriage." Claudius uses syntactical and rhetorical devices for equation by balance—as one would a particularly heavy and greasy cosmetic —to smooth over any inconsistencies whatsoever. Even his incidental diction is of joining: "jointress," "disjoint," "Colleaguèd" (I,ii,9, 20, 21). The excessively lubricated rhetoric by which Claudius makes unnatural connections between moral contraries is as gross and sweaty as the incestuous marriage itself. The audience has double and contrary responses to Claudius, the unifier of contraries.

Scene two presents still another kind of double understanding in double frames of reference. Claudius is the primary figure in the hierarchy depicted—he is the king; he is also the character upon whom all the other characters focus their attention; he does most of the talking. An audience focuses its attention on him. On the other hand,

one of the members of the royal procession was dressed all in black—
a revenger to go with the presumably vengeful ghost in scene one.
Moreover, the man in black is probably also the most famous actor in
England (or at least of the company). The particulars of the scene
make Claudius the focal figure, the genre and the particulars of a given
performance focus the audience's attention on Hamlet.

When the two focuses come together ("But now, my cousin
Hamlet, and my son—") Hamlet's reply (I,ii,65) is spoken not to
the king but to the audience. "A little more than kin, and less than
kind" is the first thing spoken by Hamlet and the first thing spoken
aside to the audience. With that line Hamlet takes the audience for
his own, and gives himself to the audience as its agent on the stage.
Hamlet and the audience are from this point in the play more firmly
united than any other such pair in Shakespeare, and perhaps in dramatic literature.

Claudius' "my cousin Hamlet, and my son" is typical of his stylistic
unifications of mutually exclusive contrary ideas (cousin, son). Hamlet's
reply does not unify ideas, but disunifies them (more than kin, less
than kind). However, the style in which Hamlet distinguishes is a
caricature of Claudius' equations by rhetorical balance; here again,
what interrupts the order, threatens coherence, and is strikingly at odds
with its preamble is also a continuation by echo of what went before.
Hamlet's parody of Claudius and his refusal to be folded into Claudius'
rhetorical blanket is satisfying to an audience in need of assurance that
it is not alone in its uneasiness at Claudius' rhetoric. On the other hand,
the orderliness that the audience valued in scene two is abruptly destroyed by Hamlet's reply. At the moment Hamlet speaks his first line,
the audience finds itself the champion of order in Denmark and in the
play, and at the same time irrevocably allied to Hamlet—the one
present threat to the order of both.

II

The play persists in taking its audience to the brink of intellectual
terror. The mind of the audience is rarely far from the intellectual des-
peration of Claudius in the prayer scene when the systems in which
he values his crown and queen collide with those in which he values
his soul and peace of mind. For the duration of *Hamlet* the mind of
the audience is as it might be if it could take on, or dared to try to

take on, its experience whole, if it dared drop the humanly necessary intellectual crutches of compartmentalization, point of view, definition, and the idea of relevance, if it dared admit any subject for evaluation into any and all the systems of value to which at different times one human mind subscribes. The constant occupation of a sane mind is to choose, establish, and maintain frames of reference for the things of its experience; as the high value placed on artistic unity attests, one of the attractions of art is that it offers a degree of holiday from that occupation. As the creation of a human mind, art comes to its audience ready-fitted to the human mind; it has physical limits or limits of duration; its details are subordinated to one another in a hierarchy of importance. A play guarantees us that we will not have to select a direction for our attention; it offers us isolation from matter and considerations irrelevant to a particular focus or a particular subject. *Hamlet* is more nearly an exception to those rules than other satisfying and bearable works of art. That, perhaps, is the reason so much effort has gone into interpretations that presume that *Hamlet*, as it is, is not and was not satisfying and bearable. The subject of literature is often conflict, often conflict of values; but, though the agonies of decision, knowing, and valuing are often the objects of an audience's concern, an audience rarely undergoes or even approaches such agonies itself. That it should enjoy doing so seems unlikely, but in *Hamlet* the problems the audience thinks about and the intellectual action of thinking about them are very similar. *Hamlet* is the tragedy of an audience that cannot make up its mind.

One of the most efficient, reliable, and usual guarantees of isolation is genre. The appearance of a ghost in scene one suggests that the play will be a revenge tragedy. *Hamlet* does indeed turn out to be a revenge tragedy, but here genre does not provide the limited frame of reference that the revenge genre and genres in general usually establish. The archetypal revenge play is *The Spanish Tragedy*. In the first scene of that, a ghost and a personification, Revenge, walk out on the stage and spend a whole scene saying who they are, where they are, why they are there, what has happened, and what will happen. The ghost in *The Spanish Tragedy* gives more information in the first five lines of the play than there is in the whole first scene of *Hamlet*. In *The Spanish Tragedy* the ghost and Revenge act as a chorus for the play. They keep the doubt and turmoil of the characters from ever transferring themselves to the audience. They keep audience safe from doubt, safely outside the action, looking on. In *The Spanish Tragedy* the act of revenge is presented as a moral necessity, just as, say shooting the villain may be in a Western. Revenge plays were written by Christians and played to Christian audiences. Similarly, traditional American Westerns were written by and for believers faithful to the principles of the Constitution of the United States. The possibility that an audience's Christian belief that vengeance belongs only to God will color its understanding of revenge in *The Spanish Tragedy* is as unlikely as a modern film audience's consideration of a villain's civil rights when somebody shouts, "Head him off at the pass." The tension between revenge morality and the audience's own Christian morality was a source of vitality always *available* to Kyd and his followers, but one that they did not avail themselves of. Where they did not ignore moralities foreign to the vaguely Senecan ethic of the genre, they took steps to take the life out of conflicts between contrary systems of value.

When Christian morality invades a revenge play, as it does in III,xiii of *The Spanish Tragedy* when Hieronimo says *Vindicta Mihi* and then further echoes St. Paul's "Vengeance is mine; I will repay, saith the Lord," the quickly watered-down Christian position and the contrary position for which Hieronimo rejects it are presented as isolated categories between which the *character* must and does choose. The conflict is restricted to the stage and removed from the mind of the audience. The effect is not to make the contrariety of values a part of the audience's experience but to dispel the value system foreign to the genre, to file it away as, for the duration of the play, a dead issue. In its operations upon an audience of *The Spanish Tragedy*, the introduction and rejection of the Christian view of vengeance is roughly comparable to the hundreds of exchanges in hundreds of Westerns where the new schoolmarm says that the hero should go to the sheriff rather than try to outdraw the villain. The hero rarely gives an intellectually satisfying reason for taking the law into his own hands, but the mere fact that the pertinent moral alternative has been mentioned and rejected is ordinarily sufficient to allow the audience to join the hero in his morality without fear of further interruption from its own.

The audience of *Hamlet* is not allowed the intellectual comfort of isolation in the one system of values appropriate to the genre. In *Hamlet* the Christian context for valuing is persistently present. In I,v the ghost makes a standard revenge-tragedy statement of Hamlet's moral obligation to kill Claudius. The audience is quite ready to think in that frame of reference and does so. The ghost then—in the same breath—opens the audience's mind to the frame of reference least compatible with the genre. When he forbids vengeance upon Gertrude, he does so in specifically Christian terms: "Taint not thy mind, nor let thy soul contrive/ Against thy mother aught. Leave her to heaven . . ." (I,v,85–86). Moreover, this ghost is at least as concerned that he lost the chance to confess before he died as he is that he lost his life at all.

Most of the time contradictory values do not collide in the audience's consciousness, but the topic of revenge is far from the only instance in which they live anxiously close to one another, so close to one another that, although the audience is not shaken in its faith in either of a pair of conflicting values, its mind remains in the uneasy state common in nonartistic experience but unusual for audiences of plays. The best example is the audience's thinking about suicide during *Hamlet*. The first mention of suicide comes already set into a Christian frame of reference by the clause in which self-slaughter is mentioned: "Or that the Everlasting had not fixed/ His canon 'gainst self-slaughter" (I,ii,131–32). In the course of the play, however, an audience evaluates suicide in all the different systems available to minds outside the comfortable limitations of art; from time to time in the play the audience thinks of suicide variously as (1) cause for damnation, (2) a heroic and generous action, (3) a cowardly action, and (4) a last sure way to peace. The audience moves from one to another system of values with a rapidity that human faith in the rational constancy of the human mind makes seem impossible. Look, for example, at the travels of the mind that listens to and understands what goes on between the specifically Christian death of Laertes (*Laertes:* " . . . Mine and my father's death come not upon thee,/ Nor thine on me."— *Hamlet:* "Heaven makes thee free of it V,ii,319–21) and the specifically Christian death of Hamlet (*Horatio:* ". . . Good night, sweet prince,/ And flights of angels sing thee to thy rest . . ." V,ii,348–49). During the intervening thirty lines the audience and the characters move from the Christian context in which Laertes' soul departs, into the familiar literary context where they can take Horatio's attempted suicide as the generous and heroic act it is (V,ii,324–31). Audience and characters have likewise no difficulty at all in understanding and accepting the label "felicity" for the destination of the suicide—even though Hamlet, the speaker of "Absent thee from felicity awhile" (V,i,336), prefaces the statement with an incidental "By heaven" (V,ii,332), and even though Hamlet and the audience have spent a lot of time during the preceding three hours actively considering the extent to which a suicide's journey to "the undiscovered country" can be called "felicity" or predicted at all. When "Good night, sweet prince" is spoken by the antique Roman of twenty lines before, both he and the audience return to thinking in a Christian frame of reference, as if they had never been away.

The audience is undisturbed by a nearly endless supply of similar inconstancies in itself and the play; these are a few instances:

The same audience that scorned pretense when Hamlet knew not "seems" in I,ii admires his skill at pretense and detection in the next two acts.

The audience joins Hamlet both in admiration for the self-control by which the player "could force his soul so to his own conceit" that he could cry for Hecuba (II,ii,537), and in admiration for the very different self-control of Horatio (III,ii,51–71).

The audience, which presumably could not bear to see a literary hero stab an unarmed man at prayer, sees the justice of Hamlet's self-accusations of delay. The audience also agrees with the ghost when both have a full view of the corpse of Polonius, and when the ghost's diction is an active reminder of the weapon by which Hamlet has just attempted the acting of the dread command: "Do not forget. This visitation/ Is but to whet thy almost blunted purpose" (III,iv,111–12).

The audience that sees the ghost and hears about its prison house in I,v also accepts the just as obvious truth of "the undiscovered country from whose bourn no traveller returns. . . ."

What have come to be recognized as the problems of *Hamlet* arise at points where an audience's contrary responses come to consciousness. They are made bearable in performance (though not in recollection) by means similar to those by which the audience is carried across the quieter crises of scene one. In performance, at least, the play gives its audience strength and courage not only to flirt with the frailty of its own understanding but actually to survive conscious experiences of the Polonian foolishness of faith that things will follow only the rules of the particular logic in which we expect to see them. The best example of the audience's endurance of self-knowledge is its experiences of Hamlet's madness. In the last moments of Act I Hamlet makes Horatio, Marcellus, and the audience privy to his intention to pretend madness: ". . . How strange or odd some'er I bear myself/ (As I per-

chance hereafter shall think meet/ To put an antic disposition
on) . . ." (I,v,170–73). The audience sets out into Act II knowing
what Hamlet knows, knowing Hamlet's plans, and secure in its superiority to the characters who do not. (Usually an audience is superior to
the central characters: it knows that Desdemona is innocent, Othello
does not; it knows what it would do when Lear foolishly divides his
kingdom; it knows how Birnam Wood came to come to Dunsinane.
In *Hamlet*, however, the audience never knows what it would have
done in Hamlet's situation; in fact, since the King's successful plot in
the duel with Laertes changes Hamlet's situation so that he becomes
as much the avenger of his own death as of his father's, the audience
never knows what Hamlet would have done. Except for brief periods
near the end of the play, the audience never has insight or knowledge
superior to Hamlet's or, indeed, different from Hamlet's. Instead of
having superiority *to* Hamlet, the audience goes into the second act to
share the superiority *of* Hamlet.) The audience knows that Hamlet will
play mad, and its expectations are quickly confirmed. Just seventy-five
lines into Act II, Ophelia comes in and describes a kind of behavior in
Hamlet that sounds like the behavior of a young man of limited
theatrical ability who is pretending to be mad (II,i,77–84). Our confidence that this behavior so puzzling to others is well within our grasp
is strengthened by the reminder of the ghost, the immediate cause of
the promised pretense, in Ophelia's comparison of Hamlet to a creature
"loosèd out of hell/ To speak of horrors."

     Before Ophelia's entrance, II,i has presented an example of the
baseness and foolishness of Polonius, the character upon whom both
the audience and Hamlet exercise their superiority throughout Act II.
Polonius seems base because he is arranging to spy on Laertes. He instructs his spy in ways to use the "bait of falsehood"—to find out directions by indirections (II,i,1–74). He is so sure that he knows everything,
and so sure that his petty scheme is not only foolproof but brilliant,
that he is as contemptible mentally as he is morally. The audience
laughs at him because he loses his train of thought in pompous byways,
so that, eventually, he forgets what he set out to say: "What was I
about to say? . . . I was about to say something! Where did I leave?"
(II,i,50–51). When Ophelia reports Hamlet's behavior, Polonius takes
what is apparently Hamlet's bait: "Mad for thy love?" (II,i,85). He
also thinks of (and then spends the rest of the act finding evidence for)
a specific cause for Hamlet's madness: he is mad for love of Ophelia.

The audience knows (1) Hamlet will pretend madness, (2) Polonius is a fool, and (3) what is actually bothering Hamlet. Through the rest of the act, the audience laughs at Polonius for being fooled by Hamlet. It continues to laugh at Polonius' inability to keep his mind on a track (II,ii,85–130); it also laughs at him for the opposite fault—he has a one-track mind and sees anything and everything as evidence that Hamlet is mad for love (II,ii,173–212, 394–402). Hamlet, whom the audience knows and understands, spends a good part of the rest of the scene making Polonius demonstrate his foolishness.

Then, in Act III, scene one, the wise audience and the foolish Polonius both become lawful espials of Hamlet's meeting with Ophelia. Ophelia says that Hamlet made her believe he loved her. Hamlet's reply might just as well be delivered by the play to the audience: "You should not have believed me . . ." (III,i,117). In his next speech Hamlet appears suddenly, inexplicably, violently, and really mad—this before an audience whose chief identity for the last hour has consisted in its knowledge that Hamlet is only pretending. The audience finds itself guilty of Polonius' foolish confidence in predictable trains of events. It is presented with evidence for thinking just what it has considered other minds foolish for thinking—that Hamlet is mad, mad for love of an inconstant girl who has betrayed him. Polonius and the audience are the self-conscious and prideful knowers and understanders in the play. They both overestimate the degree of safety they have as innocent onlookers.

When Hamlet seems suddenly mad, the audience is likely for a minute to think that it is mad or that the play is mad. That happens several times in the course of the play; and the play helps audiences toward the decision that the trouble is in themselves. Each time the play seems insane, it also is obviously ordered, orderly, all of a piece. For example, in the case of Hamlet's truly odd behavior with Ophelia in III,i some of the stuff of his speeches to her has been otherwise applied but nonetheless present in the play before (fickleness, cosmetics). Furthermore, after the fact, the play often tells us how we should have reacted; here the King sums up the results of the Ophelia experiment as if they were exactly what the audience expected they would be (which is exactly what they were not): "Love? his affections do not that way tend,/ . . . what he spoke . . ./ Was not like madness" (III,i,162–64). In the next scene, Hamlet enters perfectly sane, and lecturing, oddly enough, on what a play should be (III,ii,1–42). Whenever the play seems mad it drifts back into focus as if nothing odd had happened. The audience is encouraged to agree with the play that nothing did, to assume (as perhaps for other reasons it should) that its own intellect is inadequate. The audience pulls itself together, and goes on to another crisis of its understanding. Indeed, it had to do so in order to arrive at the crisis of the nunnery speech. At exactly the point where the audience receives the information that makes it so vulnerable to Hamlet's inexplicable behavior in the nunnery scene, the lines about the antic disposition (I,v,170–73) act as a much needed explanation—*after the fact of the audience's discomfort*—or jocular behavior by Hamlet ("Art thou there, true-penny?" "You hear this fellow in the cellerage," "Well said, old mole!" I,v,150–51, 162) that is foreign to his tone and attitude earlier in the scene, and that jars with the expectations aroused by the manner in which he and the play have been treating the ghost. For a moment, the play seems to be the work of a madman. Then Hamlet explains what he *will* do, and the audience is invited to feel lonely in foolishly failing to understand that that was what he was doing before.

III

The kind of experience an audience has of *Hamlet* in its large movements is duplicated—and more easily demonstrated—in the microcosm of its responses to brief passages. For example, the act of following the exchange initiated by Polonius' "What do you read, my Lord?" in II,ii is similar to the larger experience of coping with the whole career of Hamlet's madness:

POLONIUS: . . . What do you read, my lord?
HAMLET: Words, words, words.
POLONIUS: What is the matter, my lord?
HAMLET: Between who?
POLONIUS: I mean the matter that you read, my lord.
HAMLET: Slanders, sir, for the satirical rogue says here that old men have grey beards, that their faces are wrinkled, their eyes purging thick amber and plum-tree gum, and that they have a plentiful lack of wit, together with most weak hams. All which, sir, though I most powerfully and potently believe, yet I hold it not honesty to have it thus set down, for you yourself, sir, should be old as I am if, like a crab, you could go backward.
POLONIUS: [aside] Though this be madness, yet there is method in't. . . .
(II,ii,190–204)

The audience is full partner in the first two of Hamlet's comically absolute answers. The first answer is not what the questioner expects, and we laugh at the mental inflexibility that makes Polonius prey to frustration in an answer that takes the question literally rather than as it is customarily meant in similar contexts. In his first question Polonius assumes that what he says will have meaning only within the range appropriate to the context in which he speaks. In his second he acts to limit the frame of reference of the question, but, because "What is the matter?" is a standard idiom in another context, it further widens the range of reasonable but unexpected understanding. On his third try Polonius achieves a question whose range is as limited as his meaning. The audience—composed of smug initiates in Hamlet's masquerade and companions in his cleverness—expects to revel further in the comic revelation of Polonius' limitations. Hamlet's answer begins by letting us laugh at the discomfiture inherent for Polonius in a list of "slanders" of old men. Because of its usual applications, the word "slander" suggests that what is so labeled is not only painful but untrue. Part of the joke here is that these slanders are true. When Hamlet finishes his list, he seems about to continue in the same vein and to demonstrate his madness by saying something like "All which, sir, though . . . , yet are lies." Instead, a syntactical machine ("though . . . yet"), rhetorical emphasis ("powerfully and potently"), and diction ("believe") suitable for the expected denial are used to admit the truth of the slanders: "All which, sir, though I most powerfully and potently believe, yet I hold it not honesty to have it thus set down, for you yourself, sir . . ." The speech seems to have given up comic play on objection to slanders on grounds of untruth, and to be about to play from an understanding of "slander" as injurious whether true or not. The syntax of "I hold it not honesty . . . , for" signals that a reason for Hamlet's objections will follow, and—in a context where the relevance of the slanders to Polonius gives pain enough to justify suppression of geriatric commonplaces—"for you yourself, sir" signals the probable general direction of the explanation. So far the audience has followed Hamlet's wit without difficulty from one focus to another, but now the bottom falls out from under the audience's own Polonian assumption, in this case the assumption that Hamlet will pretend madness according to pattern: "for you yourself, sir, should be old as I am if, like a crab, you could go backward." This last is exactly the opposite of what Polonius calls it, this is madness without method.

The audience finds itself trying to hear sense in madness; it suddenly undergoes experience of the fact that Polonius' assumptions about cause and effect in life and language are no more arbitrary and vulnerable than its own. The audience has been where it has known that the idea of sanity is insane, but it is there very briefly; it feels momentarily lonely and lost—as it feels when it has failed to get a joke or when a joke has failed to be funny. The play continues blandly across the gulf. Polonius' comment reflects comically on the effects on him of the general subject of old age; the banter between Hamlet and Polonius picks up again; and Polonius continues his self-confident diagnostic asides to the audience. Moreover, the discussion of Hamlet's reading is enclosed by two passages that have strong nonlogical, nonsignificant likeness to one another in the incidental materials they share —breeding, childbearing, death, and walking:

HAMLET: For if the sun breed maggots in a dead dog, being a good kissing carrion—Have you a daughter?
POLONIUS: I have, my lord.
HAMLET: Let her not walk i' th' sun. Conception is a blessing, but as your daughter may conceive, friend, look to't.
POLONIUS: [aside] How say you by that? Still harping on my daughter. Yet he knew me not at first. 'A said I was a fishmonger. 'A is far gone, far gone. And truly in my youth I suffered much extremity for love, very near this. I'll speak to him again.—What do you read, my lord?
                                                                                        (II,ii,181–90)

POLONIUS: [aside] Though this be madness, yet there is method in't.— Will you walk out of the air, my lord?
HAMLET: Into my grave?
POLONIUS: Indeed, that's out of the air. [aside] How pregnant sometimes his replies are! a happiness that often madness hits on, which reason and sanity could not so prosperously be delivered of. . . .   (II,ii,203–9)

From beginning to end, in all sizes and kinds of materials, the play offers its audience an actual and continuing experience of perceiving a multitude of intense relationships in an equal multitude of different systems of coherence, systems not subordinated to one another in a hierarchy of relative power. The way to an answer to "What is so good about *Hamlet?*" may be in answer to the same question about its most famous part, the "To be or not to be" soliloquy.

    The soliloquy sets out with ostentatious deliberation, rationality, and precision. Hamlet fixes and limits his subject with authority and— considering that his carefully defined subject takes in everything humanly conceivable—with remarkable confidence: "To be, or not to be —that is the question." He then restates and further defines the question in four lines that echo the physical proportions of "To be or not to be" (two lines on the positive, two on the negative) and also echo the previous grammatical construction ("to suffer . . . or to take arms"):

> Whether 'tis nobler in the mind to suffer
> The slings and arrows of outrageous fortune
> Or to take arms against a sea of troubles
> And by opposing end them.   (III,i,57–60)

The speech is determinedly methodical about defining a pair of alternatives that should be as easily distinguishable as any pair imaginable; surely being and not being are distinct from one another. The next sentence continues the pattern of infinitives, but it develops the idea of "not to be" instead of continuing the positive-negative alternation followed before:

> To die, to sleep—
> No more—and by a sleep to say we end
> The heartache, and the thousand natural shocks
> That flesh is heir to. 'Tis a consummation
> Devoutly to be wished.   (III,i,60–64)

As an audience listens to and comprehends the three units "To die," "to sleep," and "No more," some intellectual uneasiness should impinge upon it. "To sleep" is in apposition to "to die," and their equation is usual and perfectly reasonable. However, death and sleep are also a tradition type of unlikeness; they could as well restate "to be or not to be" (to sleep or to die) as "not to be" alone. Moreover, since to die is to sleep, and is also to sleep no more, no vocal emphasis or no amount of editorial punctuation will limit the relationship between "to sleep" and "no more." Thus, when "and by a sleep to say we end . . ." reasserts the metaphoric equation of death and sleep, the listener feels a sudden and belated need to have heard "no more" as the isolated summary statement attempted by the punctuation of modern texts. What is happening here is that the apparently sure distinction between "to be" and "not to be" is becoming less and less easy to maintain. The process began even in the methodically precise first sentence where passivity to death-dealing slings and arrows described "to be," and the positive aggressive action of taking arms described the negative state, "not to be." Even earlier, the listener experienced a substantially irrelevant instability of relationship when "in the mind" attached first to "nobler," indicating the sphere of the nobility, and then to "suffer," indicating the sphere of the suffering: "nobler in the mind to suffer."

"The thousand natural shocks/ That flesh is heir to" further denies the simplicity of the initial alternatives by opening the mind of the listener to considerations excluded by the isolated question whether it is more pleasant to live or to die; the substance of the phrase is a summary of the pains of life, but its particulars introduce the idea of duty. "Heir" is particularly relevant to the relationship and duty of Hamlet to his father; it also implies a continuation of conditions from generation to generation that is generally antithetical to any assumption of finality in death. The diction of the phrase also carries with it a suggestion of the Christian context in which flesh is heir to the punishment of Adam; the specifically religious word "devoutly" in the next sentence opens the idea of suicide to the Christian ethic from which the narrowed limits of the first sentences had briefly freed it.

While the logical limits and controls of the speech are falling away, its illogical patterns are giving it their own coherence. For example, the constancy of the infinitive construction maintains an impression that the speech is proceeding as methodically as it began; the word "to," in its infinitive use and otherwise, appears thirteen times among the eighty-five words in the first ten lines of the soliloquy. At the same time that the listener is having trouble comprehending the successive contradictions of "to die, to sleep—/ No more—and by a sleep to say we end . . . ," he also hears at the moment of crisis a confirming echo of the first three syllables and the word "end" from "*and by op*posing *end* them" in the first three syllables and word "end" in "*and by a* sleep to say we *end*." As the speech goes on, as it loses more and more of its rational precision, and as "to be" and "not to be" become less and less distinguishable, rhetorical coherence continues in force. The next movement of the speech begins with a direct repetition, in the same metrical position in the line, of the words with which the previous movement began: "To die, to sleep." The new movement seems, as each new movement has seemed, to introduce a restatement of what has gone before; the rhetorical construction of the speech insists that all the speech does is make the distinct natures of "to be" and "not to be" clearer and clearer:

To die, to sleep—
To sleep—perchance to dream: ay, there's the rub,
For in that sleep of death what dreams may come
When we have shuffled off this mortal coil,
Must give us pause. There's the respect
That makes calamity of so long life.   (III,i,64–69)

As Hamlet describes his increasing difficulty in seeing death as the simple opposite of life, the manner of his description gives his listener an actual experience of that difficulty; "shuffled off this mortal coil" says "cast off the turmoil of this life," but "shuffled off" and "coil" both suggest the rejuvenation of a snake which, having once thrown her enamelled skin, reveals another just like it underneath. The listener also continues to have difficulty with the simple action of understanding; like the nature of the things discussed, the natures of the sentences change as they are perceived: "what dreams may come" is a common construction for a question, and the line that follows sounds like a subordinate continuation of the question; it is not until we hear "must give us pause" that we discover that "what dreams may come" is a noun phrase, the subject of a declarative sentence that only comes into being with the late appearance of an unexpected verb. In the next sentence ("There's the respect/ That makes calamity of so long life"), logic requires that we understand "makes calamity so long-lived," but our habitual understanding of *makes* . . . *of* constructions and our recent indoctrination in the pains of life make us likely to hear the contradictory, illogical, and yet appropriate "makes a long life a calamity."

Again, however, the lines sound ordered and reasonable. The rejected first impressions I have just described are immediately followed by a real question, and one that is largely an insistently long list of things that make life a monotonously painful series of calamities. Moreover, nonlogical coherence is provided by the quiet and intricate harmony of "to dream," "of death," and "shuffled off" in the metrical centers of three successive lines; by the echo of the solidly metaphoric "there's the rub" in the vague "there's the respect"; and by the repetition of "for" from "For in that sleep" to begin the next section of the speech.

For who would bear the whips and scorns of time,
Th' oppressor's wrong, the proud man's contumely,
The pangs of despised love, the law's delay,
The insolence of office, and the spurns

That patient merit of th' unworthy takes,
When he himself might his quietus make
With a bare bodkin? Who would fardels bear,
To grunt and sweat under a weary life,
But that the dread of something after death,
The undiscovered country, from whose bourn
No traveller returns, puzzles the will,
And makes us rather bear those ills we have
Than fly to others that we know not of?   (III,i,70–82)

Although the list in the first question is disjointed and rhythmically frantic, the impression of disorder is countered by the regularity of the definite article, and by the inherently conjunctive action of six possessives. The possessives in 's, the possessives in of, and the several nonpossessive of constructions are themelves an underlying pattern of simultaneous likeness and difference. So is the illogical pattern present in the idea of burdens, the word "bear," and the word "bare." The line in which the first of these questions ends and the second begins is an epitome of the construction and action of the speech: "With a bare bodkin? Who would fardels bear, ..." The two precisely equal halves of a single rhythmic unit hold together two separate syntactical units. The beginning of the new sentence, "Who would fardels bear," echoes both the beginning, "For who would bear," and the sound of one word, "bare," from the end of the old. Moreover, "bare" and "bear," two words that are both the same and different, participate here in statements of the two undistinguishable alternatives: "to be, or not to be"—to bear fardels, or to kill oneself with a bare bodkin.

The end of the speech sounds like the rationally achieved conclusion of just such a rational investigation as Hamlet began. It begins with thus, the sign of logical conclusion, and it gains a sound of inevitable truth and triumphant clarity from the incremental repetition of and at the beginning of every other line. The last lines are relevant to Hamlet's behavior in the play at large and therefore have an additional sound of rightness here. Not only are the lines broadly appropriate to the play, the audience's understanding of them is typical of its understanding throughout the play and of its understanding of the previous particulars of this speech: Hamlet has hesitated to kill Claudius. Consideration of suicide has seemed a symptom of that hesitancy. Here the particular from which Hamlet's conclusions about his inability to act derive in his hesitancy to commit suicide. The audience hears those conclusions in the context of his failure to take the action that suicide would avoid.

Thus conscience does make cowards of us all,
And thus the native hue of resolution
Is sicklied o'er with the pale cast of thought,
And enterprises of great pitch and moment
With this regard their currents turn awry
And lose the name of action.   (III,i,83–88)

These last lines are accidentally a compendium of phrases descriptive of the action of the speech and the process of hearing it. The
speech puzzles the will, but it makes us capable of facing and bearing
puzzlement. The "To be or not to be" soliloquy is a type of the overall
action of *Hamlet*. In addition, a soliloquy in which being and its opposite are indistinguishable is peculiarly appropriate to a play otherwise
full of easily distinguishable pairs that are not easily distinguished from
one another by characters or audience or both: Rosencrantz and
Guildenstern; the pictures of Gertrude's two husbands (III,iv,54–68);
the hawk and the handsaw (II,ii,370); and father and mother who are
one flesh and so undistinguished in Hamlet's farewell to Claudius
(IV,iii,48–51). The soliloquy is above all typical of a play whose last
moments enable its audience to look unblinking upon a situation in
which Hamlet, the finally successful revenger, is the object of Laertes'
revenge; a situation in which Laertes, Hamlet's victim, victimizes Hamlet; a situation in which Fortinbras, the threat to Denmark's future in
scene one, is its hope for political salvation; in short, a situation in
which any identity can be indistinguishable from its opposite. The
soliloquy, the last scene, the first scene, the play—each and together—
make an impossible coherence of truths that are both undeniably in-
compatible and undeniably coexistent.

IV

The kind of criticism I am doing here may be offensive to readers conditioned to think of revelation as the value of literature and the purpose
of criticism. The things I have said about *Hamlet* may be made more
easily palatable by the memory that illogical coherence—coherent madness—is a regular topic of various characters who listen to Hamlet and
Ophelia. In the Reynaldo scene (II,i) and Hamlet's first talk with
Rosencrantz and Guildenstern the power of rhetoric and context to
make a particular either good or bad at will is also a topic in the play.
So too is the perception of clouds which may in a moment look "like a

camel indeed," and "like a weasel" and be "very like a whale" (III,ii, 361–67).

What I am doing may seem antipoetical; it should not. On the contrary, the effects I have described in *Hamlet* are of the same general kind as the nonsignificant coherences made by rhythm, rhyme, alliteration, and other of the standard devices of prosody. For example, the physics of the relationship among Hamlet, Laertes, Fortinbras, and Pyrrhus, the four avenging sons in *Hamlet*, are in their own scale and substance the same as those of the relationship among *cat, rat, bat,* and *chat.* The theme of suicide, for all the inconstancy of its fluid moral and emotional value, is a constant and unifying factor in the play. So too is the theme of appearance and reality, deceit, pretense, disguise, acting, seeming, and cosmetics which gives the play coherence even though its values are as many as its guises and labels. The analogy of rhyme or of a pair of like-metered lines applies profitably to the non-signifying relationship between Hamlet's two interviews with women. Both the nunnery scene with Ophelia and the closet scene with Gertrude are stage-managed and overlooked by Polonius; neither lady understands Hamlet; both are amazed by his intensity; in both scenes Hamlet makes a series of abortive departures before his final exit. There is a similar kind of insignificant likeness in numerous repeated patterns of scenes and situations like that of Hamlet's entrance reading in II,ii and its echo in Ophelia's show of devotional reading in III,i. Indeed, the same sort of things can be said about any of the themes and images whose value critics have tried to convert to significance.

The tools of prosody and the phenomena I have talked about show their similarity well when they cooperate in Hamlet's little poem on perception and truth, a poem that is a model of the experience of the whole play. Polonius reads it to the king and queen.

> Doubt thou the stars are fire;
>> Doubt that the sun doth move;
> Doubt truth to be a liar;
> But never doubt I love.   (II,ii,116–19)

I suggest that the pleasure of intellectual possession evoked by perception of the likeness and difference of "fire" and "liar" and of "move" and "love," or among the four metrically like and unlike lines, or between the three positive clauses and the one negative one, or between "stars" and "sun" or "truth" and "liar" is of the same kind as the greater achievement of intellectual mastery of the greater challenge presented by "doubt" in the first three lines. The first two *doubts* demand disbelief of two things that common sense cannot but believe. The third, whose likeness to the first two is insisted upon by anaphora, is made unlike them by the words that follow it: disbelief that truth is a liar is a logical necessity; therefore, "doubt" here must mean "believe" or "incline to believe" as it does earlier in this sense (l. 56) and several other times in the play. To be consistent with the pair of hyperbolic impossibilities to which it is coupled, and to fit the standard rhetorical formula (Doubt what cannot be doubted, but do not doubt . . .) in which it appears, "Doubt truth to be a liar" must be understood in a way inconsistent with another pattern of the poem, the previously established meaning of "doubt." Even the first two lines, which seem to fit the hyperbolic formula so well, may make the poem additionally dizzying because their subject matter could remain a Renaissance listener (once disturbed by the reversal of the meaning of the third "doubt") of doubts cast upon common-sense impressions by still recent astronomical discoveries, notably that the diurnal motion of the sun is an illusion.

The urgent rhetorical coherence of the poem is like that of the play. As the multitude of insistent and overlapping systems of coherence in the poem allows its listener to hold the two contradictory meanings of "doubt" in colloid-like suspension and to experience both the actions "doubt" describes, so in the play at large an alliteration of subjects—a sort of rhythm of ideas whose substance may or may not inform the situation dramatized—gives shape and identity, nonphysical substance, to the play that *contains* the situation. Such a container allows Shakespeare to replace *conclusion* with *inclusion;* it provides a particular and temporary context that overcomes the intellectual terror ordinarily inherent in looking at an action in all the value systems it invades. Such a container provides a sense of order and limitation sufficient to replace the comforting boundaries of carefully isolated frames of reference; it makes its audience capable of contemplating more truth than the mind should be able to bear.

In summary I would say that the thing about *Hamlet* that has put Western man into a panic to explain it is not that the play is incoherent, but that it is coherent. There are plenty of incoherent plays; nobody ever looks at them twice. This one, because it obviously makes sense and because it just as obviously cannot be made sense of, threatens our inevitable working assumption that there are no "more things in earth" than can be understood in our philosophy. People see *Hamlet* and tolerate inconsistencies that it does not seem they could bear. Students of the play have explained that such people do not, in fact, find the play bearable at all. They therefore whittle the play down for us to the size of one of its terms, and deny the others. Truth is bigger than any one system for knowing it, and *Hamlet* is bigger than any of the frames of reference it inhabits. *Hamlet* allows us to comprehend—hold on to —all the contradictions it contains. *Hamlet* refuses to cradle its audience's mind in a closed generic framework, or otherwise limit the ideological context of its actions. In *Hamlet* the mind is cradled in nothing more than the fabric of the play. The superior strength and value of that fabric is in the sense it gives that it is unlimited in its range, and that its audience is not only sufficient to comprehend but is in the act of achieving total comprehension of all the perceptions to which its mind can open. The source of the strength is in a rhetorical economy that allows the audience to perform both of the basic actions of the mind upon almost every conjunction of elements in the course of the play: it perceives strong likeness, and it perceives strong difference. Every intellectual conjunction is also a disjunction, and any two things that pull apart contain qualities that are simultaneously the means of uniting them.

II. 3

Shakespeare's Texts and Modern Productions*

DANIEL SELTZER

Princeton University

IT USED to be necessary to speak with some energy to the point that any play considered only as a text could not help one toward a complete apprehension of it; and of course it is quite correct to remind students of Shakespeare that performance is needed for full understanding. Unhappily this does not cover the matter at all thoroughly, if one is really involved in the nature of performance and what can happen to a play when it is staged. Certainly one cannot object to the advisability of performance, nor to the simple fact that performance can make vivid many ideas and feelings in the texts; but I think this sort of observation no longer requires much discussion. The real problem is simply that performance, while by nature unlike an act of literary criticism, always has one of the same results: *it cannot avoid implying a point of view.* In other words, I think it is impossible to "do Shakespeare straight," a goal espoused very often by those who teach. This paper will be concerned, then, with the reasons why I feel this to be true, and with alternative goals, or modified ones, and with examples of Shakespearean production that seem to me to elucidate different approaches to the problem.

One such approach is stated succinctly and usefully by Stanley Wells, a scholar and historian of the theater with much experience in observing production work: "The greater Globe itself," writes Wells,

---

* Read at the Institute in 1968. Published in *Institute Papers: Reinterpretations of Elizabethan Drama,* 1969.

"has vanished into air; so have its audiences. But the texts of the plays remain, and the effort must be made to present them in a manner that will reproduce for a modern audience the effect they may be supposed to have had upon their original audiences. It is a task in which personal opinion plays an enormous part." [1] The statement suggests—correctly—that much surrounding the original productions of Shakespeare's plays—including, perhaps, many of Shakespeare's intentions in writing them—is lost; and it suggests as well—probably as correctly—that at one time (the span of years of the plays' early performances) these intentions could be known and that the first audiences of the plays did in fact perceive them. It is Wells's opinion that the responsibility of our directors and actors is to try to discover those intentions—the way toward this goal being the texts of the plays—and then to articulate them to a contemporary audience so as to produce an effect comparable to that made upon their first audiences.

Our problem, however, is in knowing how to deal with these effects, and to admit candidly that sometimes the right effect—or *a* right one—has varying relevance to Shakespeare's intention, if we can discover it; that at times a conceptual emphasis which in the days of the Globe and Blackfriars may have been mirrored with parallel *effectiveness* in stage terms can be rendered no longer in this way—either because the original intention is now obscure or because, even if we can detect it, it no longer affects the emotions as it may have done once. In any case, intellectual understanding does not always contribute to a rich theatrical moment. There can be no question that Shakespeare's audiences grasped—really *heard*—more of the plays than we do, because as art objects they were conceived within patterns of perception and response that Shakespeare and his audiences had in common, and which were of course in many ways quite different from ours. But once we have granted that discovering Shakespeare's intentions can sometimes inform the way we produce his plays, and even if we grant that his original audiences inferred those intentions more readily than we do, I am not at all sure that it is those intentions that modern actors and directors ought to seek out and try to render in stage terms, but, in Wells's phrase, "the effect they may be supposed to have had."

[1] Stanley Wells, "Shakespeare's Text on the Modern Stage," *Deutsche Shakespeare-Gesellschaft West Jahrbuch* (1967), p. 180. My debt to Dr. Wells's thoughts on Shakespearean production is greater than can be acknowledged in a single note. While this paper takes a different point of view than does his article, he has provided for me a basic approach to this subject matter for which I am most grateful.

Sometimes these effects—the special theatrical impact of a moment of stage action—are easily within an imaginative circuit between the Elizabethans and us, and when they are we have the rare opportunity to observe something of Shakespeare's stage methods, a subject much more difficult to discuss than his thematic concerns.

Let us examine one such moment in *Richard II*. I choose it because it is such a useful one in teaching the play and because, considered textually, it is also a dynamic example of clearly articulated "thematic" concern. It is that sort of moment in the theater when the playwright's intention is contained very clearly within a stage effect, the stage effect itself implicit in the text. Richard stands facing the usurper Bolingbroke, holding the most important stage property of the Elizabethan theater.

> Here, cousin, seize the crown. Here, cousin,
> On this side my hand, and on that side yours.
> Now is this golden crown like a deep well
> That owes two buckets, filling one another,
> The emptier ever dancing in the air,
> The other down, unseen, and full of water.
> That bucket down and full of tears am I,
> Drinking my griefs,

(and here Richard would probably have removed his hand)

> whilst you mount up on high.   (IV,i,181–88)

Obviously this moment represented for the Elizabethans, as to an extent it can for us, a living emblem of abdication and usurpation of the English crown; Richard himself sees to it that the act is dramatized and not simply described. The moment provides an easy approach to Tudor conceptions of kingship behind all of Shakespeare's histories, as well as many of his other plays, and of course such theory in this instance vividly informs the staging. *But the scene is not "about" that theory,* and a modern director anxious to find the effectiveness of the text for a modern audience would do better to turn to the character of his hero rather than to the emblematic prop in his hands. In this lucky instance when Shakespeare's theatrical emphasis is charged with psychological material as accessible to us as it was to the Elizabethans, our director will discover, we hope, that *Richard II* as a play is much more concerned with the way in which its hero gives up his crown than with the way Henry Bolingbroke usurps it. The great danger in assuming that one can act or direct Shakespeare "straight" is not only in the mistaken notion that we can always perceive as his original audiences may have perceived, but in the erroneous idea that if we could do so we should find the clues to production in a philosophical energy and not in a theatrical—and hence a human and personal—one. Shakespeare's *Richard II* is about a king who gives up his crown in a fascinating, self-dramatizing, often perverse way, and then, in some terms, finds his manhood. Tudor views of kingship inform the action of this play, but the play is not about them. Similarly, an awareness of Renaissance Christianity's understanding of the sin of despair, an awareness of the theological description of the inevitable damnation that follows it, and an awareness of the Elizabethans' feelings about necromancy and of the misuses of nature and intellect—all explain much that is absolutely basic to *Dr. Faustus*; but Marlowe's play is no more "about" these matters than *Richard II* is "about" the responsibilities of kingship and the dangers of usurpation, or *Lear* "about" the great hierarchies of society and nature—no matter how vitally such materials of intellectual history may relate to these texts. Richard's crown is not so important a symbol for modern audiences, American or English, as it must have been for Shakespeare's; and modern audiences know both less and more about science—and perhaps about black magic!—then did Marlowe's. But this does not mean that the behavior of King Richard and Faustus can never be theatrically vivid for us, although the degree to which we feel their motivations and responses explicable in terms of our own is relative. Faustus' great cry, "See, see, where Christ's blood streams in the firmament!/ One drop would save my soul, half a drop . . ." refers to a belief to which we may or may not respond "feelingly," but what is certain is that we can grasp his anguish as deeply as any Elizabethan could.

It is in reproducing the effect of such moments that modern productions find their greatest challenge, and only rarely do an actor's lines, a stage property, and an explicit intention on the part of the playwright meet so conveniently as they do in the abdication scene of *Richard II*. Some modern productions, however, have found correlatives of theatrical impact within many of the plays, and these suggest an approach to those vast stretches of the texts where total recall, so to speak, is impossible. The life of a play may be articulated in a manner that varies considerably from what we know of original production conditions and methods, yet remain nevertheless in the largest sense

"Shakespearean." Such methods of production are very hard to describe, but I will try to give some examples of them. Obviously, it is the degree to which any modern production varies from what we know, or think we know, of Elizabethan methods that provides most ground for debate—perhaps especially among members of the academic profession who attend Shakespearean productions with some frequency.[2] Some directors—mainly those attracted to studies of stage history—prefer to stage Shakespeare under conditions as close as possible (in their view) to the Elizabethan way; others, in Wells's words, "believe that the plays can make their true effect only when they are rewritten, recostumed, recomposed, restaged, reset, and generally reconstituted. . . . There is moreover a third class . . . made up of those whose prime concern in staging a play of Shakespeare's is not to put across the body or the idea of the original . . . but rather to construct a theatrical event which will work in its independent way." [3] These are very categorical descriptions of the preferences of our directors (and audiences), and I have overgeneralized Wells's presentation of them; but the categories may be useful for our own discussion.

I suggest that the first way—to attempt a staging as close as possible to the Elizabethan procedure, so far as we know it—is essentially untheatrical and pointless. Even though the physical nature of Shakespeare's theaters and the styles of his actors are to some extent discoverable, to rerender them would result only in a rather dull form of

[2] Peter Brook's description of scholars at the theater should make most of us wince, but the shoe fits too perfectly not to quote him, and, as he has borne in the past few years perhaps more often than he has deserved the attacks of scholars (particularly in this country), to quote him at length. He is speaking of a sort of theater he finds "Deadly," as containing no potential either for growth or immediate theatrical excitement: "The Deadly Theater takes easily to Shakespeare. We see his plays done by good actors in what seems to be the proper way—they look lively and colorful, there is music and everyone is all dressed up, just as they are supposed to be in the best of classical theaters. Yet secretly we find it excruciatingly boring—and in our hearts we either blame Shakespeare, or theater as such, or even ourselves. To make matters worse there is always a deadly spectator, who for special reasons enjoys a lack of intensity and even a lack of entertainment, such as the scholar who emerges from routine performances of the classics smiling because nothing has distracted him from trying over and confirming his pet theories to himself, whilst reciting his favorite lines under his breath. In his heart he sincerely wants a theater that is nobler-than-life and he confuses a sort of intellectual satisfaction with the true experience for which he craves. Unfortunately, he lends the weight of his authority to dullness and so the Deadly Theater goes on its way" (*The Empty Space* [New York, 1968], p. 10).

[3] Wells, *Deutsche Shakespeare-Gesellschaft West Jahrbuch*, p. 181.

archeology—and never in vivid theatrical action. As Professor E. H. Gombrich has observed in his great study of the graphic arts and human understanding of them,[4] successful art reminds us of reality simply because art mirrors not nature but the artist's perceptions of nature. When we recognize common ground between an artist's way of seeing reality and our own, we can see nature—or human nature—in his work. Sometimes his way of seeing is typical enough of his time that we come to recognize it as a part of a nameable style, and we call it a convention. The history of style is therefore the history of human perception itself. The phenomenon of drama is exhilarating because it is intensely pleasurable to see people on a stage who seem to be *real*—and this apparent reality can encompass a wide range of styles of production. If what is happening onstage does not seem to be realistic human behavior, if we are unable to feel, even if we cannot say, *why* a character does or says a certain thing, then something essentially undramatic is taking place. A production set in the Elizabethan mode—accurately, if that were possible, or approximately, to the limits of our ability—would set forth human behavior realistic only to Elizabethans, except in those rare instances when their "vocabulary of motif" (in Gombrich's phrase) has not been lost in the flux of time, and we recognize it. Shakespeare was performed "straight" only during Shakespeare's lifetime, and not for very long after it, and teachers and scholars should not complain if a production of Shakespeare attempts to be "modern" in some way —what else can it aim to be, if we are to find understandable human behavior in it? A commitment to the achievements of the past and its relevance to the present must never be allowed to obscure the fact that it cannot be relived. Members of the academy are perhaps particularly protective of the past, but its literal resuscitation in drama can never be more than an empty gesture. It can never be directly relevant, never deeply involving, never truly exciting—and most important and, for historical scholars, perhaps, most ironic—it can never really achieve the noble purpose of understanding Shakespeare's intentions. If Shakespeare is to continue to be as theatrically valid as most of us tend to claim he is without giving much thought to a matter that seems so obvious, then we must be alert to those phenomena of the theater that really *do* involve and exhilarate us, which help us perceive performance

---

[4] E. H. Gombrich, *Art and Illusion* (Bollingen Series XXXV.5, A. W. Mellon Lectures in the Fine Arts, 1956) (New York, 1960). See especially pp. 63–66, 85, 90, 131, 175, 356.

of the great texts realistically. We should never forget that the revolutionary productions by Poel and Granville-Barker in the first of this century would seem now very dated to us, and in any case hardly accurate renderings either of the texts or of the staging of Shakespeare's time; they were as typical in their way of their years as Garrick's Shakespeare was of his, or Kean's, Macready's, Tree's, or, for that matter, Gielgud's, were of theirs.

I prefer a kind of "reconstituted" Shakespeare, to use Wells's adjective, but with the qualification that such productions be based, so far as it is possible, on those clues within the texts that help us grasp the *theatrical effects* of the originals—and it is in recognizing these when they appear that historical scholarship is most helpful. It is delightful and reassuring, by the way, to observe how many great actors and directors at times come intuitively in the course of their work to decisions and choices that corroborate, or are corroborated by, some conclusions of criticism and scholarship, reached after detailed research and years of thought and reconsideration. For me, two examples of Shakespeare so reconstituted were the performances of Sir Laurence Olivier as Othello (in 1964) and of Paul Scofield as Macbeth (in 1967). Although I cannot describe each performance in detail, let me try to indicate why each of them seemed to me to answer the theatrical requirements of modern productions of Shakespeare.

In a way, actors of Othello and Macbeth are challenged by a similar problem—a problem relating, as it happens, to a point about both of these characters made clear for us by a historical and scholarly understanding of the Elizabethans' view of evil and its potential strength. Both plays are made richer when we remember that they contain much more than those rubrics suggest by which they were described—at least to me—in secondary school: as a tragedy "of jealousy" and a tragedy "of ambition." Jealous Othello surely is, and Macbeth is ambitious—but the modern actor must ask, interestingly enough, the same questions asked by the inquisitive student: where do the jealousy and the ambition come from, and why are they so overwhelmingly *personal*, so clearly typical in scope of everything else in the lives of these two men? The Elizabethans' awareness that neither Iago nor the witches could have succeeded had not Othello and Macbeth somehow been prepared for their visitations greatly helps the modern actor and his director who may have come by intuition or research to the same conclusion—a conclusion perfectly suited to current acting techniques and role preparation: that the horror is first conceived *inside* Othello and Macbeth, and not outside them, and that just as Mephistophiles could not succeed had Faustus not called him in the first place, so the sexual ego and possessiveness that eventually prepare Othello to succumb to Iago and "the swelling act/ Of the imperial theme" that already corrupts Macbeth's imagination are rooted deeply in the consciousness—or subconsciousness—of each hero before the evil appears on stage in external shape. One could say simply that they are men psychologically ready for what is to happen, and this readiness was manifest in the performances of Olivier as Othello and Scofield as Macbeth, thus making the behavior of the characters perceivable, acceptable, human.

The work of both actors in preparing their roles was extensive and detailed; from the results of this work, one can choose only a few. There was Olivier's brilliant physical presentation of Othello, amazingly convincing for a man who stands actually only a bit over five feet ten inches—onstage, in this production, because of his charismatic presence, apparently well over six feet; the sensuous roll of his gait, the easy turns, the carriage of a man obviously in battle trim yet whose energies could be totally luxurious and specifically sexual, suggesting a dangerous narcissism; the vocal preparation that allowed an extra octave of bass range when it was wanted; the careful choice and use of properties—the long-stemmed, blood-red rose, for example, with which he played, lightly, absent-mindedly, in his first scene, or the heavy cross suspended from his neck, reminding us—and him?—that Othello has been a Christian warrior in the employ of a Christian state, yet torn loose and thrown to the winds with the force of gigantic agony, as he knelt to his old pagan and exotic gods, the marble heavens and the tides of the Pontic, the Propontic, and the Hellespont, the gesture following Iago's "Your mind may change," on his "Never, Iago!" (III.iii.449–50). Throughout the vocalizations *filled* the character: the subtle yet audible emphases given all the personal pronouns, for example, in those speeches to the senate in which Othello defines so eloquently what he is and—a consideration of immense importance to the actor— how emphatically he believes in himself; and, later in the play, the vocal placement, emphasis, and pacing given, for example, those lines in which Othello identifies himself with those so great that they are born to be betrayed, self-confidence merging with his huge self-pity through an infinitely subtle trick of the voice, a nuance of phrasing:

> Haply for I am black
> And have not those soft parts of conversation
> That chamberers have, or for I am declined
> Into the vale of years—yet that's not much—
> She's gone. I am abused, and my relief
> Must be to loathe her. O curse of marriage,
> That we can call these delicate creatures ours,
> And not their appetites! I had rather be a toad
> And live upon the vapor of a dungeon
> Than keep a corner in the thing I love
> For others' uses. Yet 'tis the plague to great ones;
> Prerogatived are they less than the base.
> 'Tis destiny unshunnable, like death.
> Even then this forkèd plague is fated to us
> When we do quicken. . . .   (III,iii,262–76) [5]

For the actor playing Macbeth, the problem is at once simpler and harder; his lines suggest, but do not make explicit, the inner readiness for corruption I tried to describe earlier. This is in any case a matter of the degree of emphasis found by the actor in rehearsal and private thought. The hero's rendering of any speech can be made to affect the audience's apprehension of his inner state in many subtle ways—specifically, the nature of the surprise or shock he feels when confronted by the witches, or, later in the play, by the vision of the dagger. Scofield's reaction was prepared brilliantly by Macbeth's very first line in the play, the delivery of which I can describe only as charged with an awareness of surrounding time and place, both in terms of the military victories just achieved and in terms of whatever the physical context of the action was conceived to be. We had seen, in more or less traditional terms (yet set forth with staggering theatrical power), the personifications of the witches, the armies of Duncan, their leather and furred clothing crusted with blood, only the King himself in clean and shining white, absolutely saint-like, "clear in his great office," the bleeding Captain, one horrid scar of battle, collapsing finally to the earth—earth made of a huge shaggy ruglike material that covered the

[5] Happily, Sir Laurence's performance has been preserved on phonograph records; the recording (RCA Victor album VDS-100) was taped at a special performance, and not in a studio-reading, and is therefore a much more accurate archive of the production. The phrasing and specific nuances to which I refer may be heard throughout, of course, but perhaps best in the speeches on Sides 1, 4, and 5 (containing 1.iii and 111.iii).

whole stage, capable of assuming in different lights the texture of a realistic heath or an open wound, ranging in color from a deep rust to crimson to black; then the witches again, then the drum, and then—a stroke of genius, I think, on the part of the director, Peter Hall—Macbeth's entrance alone, not with Banquo, who came on after the hero's first line. Here Scofield walked, a tall man to begin with, huge against the smoky red of the stage, his battle sword across the shoulder, held with the easy grace of a soldier familiar with his weapon, his eyes cast up and out, beyond his own path, all the way from upstage center to the very lip of the narrow protruding apron, all in that utter silence of anticipation and attention that can be commanded by the simple presence of a great actor, and, finally, conveying somehow the sense of a man who knows and feels too much that hasn't yet a name, in his deep Sussex twang, pacing the sounds and silences of the line with the intuitive understanding that came from long rehearsals full of trial and error, "So foul and fair a day I have not seen." Then on came Banquo, businesslike with his question about the distance to Forres, then seeing suddenly those crouching shapes in the shadows; but even as Banquo exclaimed, we paid less attention to him than to Macbeth, whose gaze had now swung toward them, his eyes clouded, no movement or gesture signifying shock, but only a feeling that the whole man, mind and body, had assimilated what he saw and felt a deep reverberation in his memory by the time he too addressed them: "Speak, if you can: what are you?" We have all of us felt evil within us (whatever name we have given it), and Scofield let us understand how a great man had felt it greatly, had not yet succumbed to it, yet had at his fingertips, so to speak, dangerously ready in his memory that "horrid image" of the witches' "suggestion." Later, of course, the great and so often clichéd soliloquy on the dagger became part of the texture of everything that had gone before in Macbeth's mind: it did indeed "[marshal him] the way that [he] was going."

I grant that these two examples of "reconstituted" Shakespeare deal with material for which modern rendering could find good correlatives in Elizabethan psychology; methods of work are different, but the stage *effect* is where Shakespeare put it: in the composition of human character productive of behavioral responses. Reconstitution, it must be stated clearly, does not always retain so much of the original in its literal form. I should like to turn to another modern production which, while deeply illuminating the text at hand, to a great extent remolded and reshaped it while retaining at base the implicit force and theatricality of Shakespeare's work—Orson Welles's film of the *Henry IV* plays called *Chimes at Midnight* (in this country, simply *Falstaff*). The fact that we are dealing with a different art form does not alter, I think, some of the principles we have been discussing.

Welles's movie is essentially a kaleidoscopic revisualization of Shakespeare's two plays. Scenes are set in new sequences, many of them cut entirely, others formed of the original text intact but with lines from elsewhere in the plays inserted for conceptual emphasis—either ironic or corroborative, some of the characters eliminated, but those remaining never destructively oversimplified. Amazingly, into two and a half hours of film time, Welles has set forth the psychological reality of these plays, taking as his dynamic center the same core of deep human emotion that energizes Shakespeare's texts—the struggle within Prince Hal simultaneously to love, to resist, and to survive two parents, one his father and the other a surrogate, and to choose from among several life styles one that is uniquely and triumphantly his. As is the case with *Richard II*, a historical understanding of Tudor views of kingship can enrich our understanding of the Shakespeare chronicles; more directly informative at times about the major characters of the *Henry IV* plays are those lumpy yet somehow attractive moral interludes of the sixteenth century. Shakespeare's drama, once again, is filled with living stage emblems of the personal and political conflicts that form their narrative content. To speak only of one such moment, Hal, after Shrewsbury, stands lonely and triumphant between the dead body of Hotspur and the apparently dead Falstaff; one thinks of many parallel moments in the old interludes when Youth—call him Lusty Juventus, even Mankind—triumphs over the temptations of Pride on the one hand and Revelry on the other, and no doubt the line of descent to that moment at the end of 1 *Henry IV* is a direct one. But the history of this dramaturgy will not make the behavior of Shakespeare's characters closer to our grasp, and it is perhaps particularly true of the histories that this behavior—in terms of motive and response—most frequently eludes us, whether we attempt to teach these plays or to produce them. What Welles has achieved in *Falstaff* is to find a way to make this action absolutely realistic in psychological terms not far, if at all, removed from Shakespeare's. He has placed his emphasis where it is in Shakespeare, and so often is not in modern productions—upon the Prince himself. The King, Falstaff, and Hot-

spur move about him, come tangent to him, but never do we forget
what these scenes are *about*.

Welles himself, of course, portrays Fallstaff—and although I was
almost invariably irritated by his underenergized line readings, his intention was clear, and it supported the plan of the overall project (an
amazing achievement for this great director and actor, who has not in
the past so successfully suppressed his own ego!); jovial he can be, but
predominantly he is sad. A man with the depth of emotion and intellect to be witty in himself while evoking wit in other men will not
necessarily be—nor is he likely to be—the clean and happy, pink-
cheeked master of the revels we so often find in our Falstaffs. This is a
fat old man more often than not quiet and introspective, yet the embodiment of personal license, shown to be dying of drink and, in all
probability, tertiary syphillis, who does not tempt the Prince because
he is descended from the Vice, nor boast because he is related to the
Miles gloriosus, but does both because he is desperately attracted to,
loves, and requires Prince Hal's youth and promise, and because he
knows that Hal—far from being only superficially amused with him—
loves him and understands him, even if that understanding clearly
carries with it an element of contempt. King Henry IV is played by
Sir John Gielgud, a brilliant casting decision. He too is dying, and although the Jerusalem Chamber is not made much of in the film, the
process of death is supported by constant references to the King's guilt
—shown to be as much a cause of death as old age. He feels little if
any warmth for his son, but his political consciousness is razor-sharp,
and the actor's major intention is to show the politician's consuming
desire for an heir equal to his understanding of kingship. Henry Mon-
mouth, between these two old and dying men, is only beginning to live,
and must choose not only between them but between two views of
the world, both of which, with Hotspur's, he is to reject.

It was easier for Shakespeare to write Prince Hal into the center
of his plays than it is for any modern actor or director to keep him
there; not only do Falstaff or Hotspur threaten to swamp him, but his
own stage life exists often in terms of stage conventions we no longer
perceive as conveying reality. The most important, and the most difficult, of these is that component of stage narrative in Elizabethan plays
in which a character seems (to us) to step outside the action, comment
upon it, even anticipate it, such as Hal does at the end of the second
scene of 1 *Henry IV*. Not only the device itself, but the subject matter

of Hal's soliloquy, is difficult. Even if we discount as uninformed or as insensitive those readers who would infer the Prince priggish or Machiavellian or both, as he anticipates his own kingship, his useful playing holidays, and the way he will appear to men when he banishes his tavern companions, the speech remains a remarkably hard one for any modern actor. In Shakespeare's stage terms, it was essentially theatrical and engaging; in ours, it is potentially untheatrical and even dull. To whom is it addressed? Although it is partially apostrophic, how are those sections and phrases that are purely introspective to be rendered so as to be felt by a modern audience as expressions of a warm and generous young man? Welles's answer not only suits the requirement of the modern director—who would demand of the text a reason for the Prince to speak the lines in the first place—but is actually a more "Shakespearean" solution than I have seen in most productions following the apparently straighter and narrower line. He moves the speech from its place in the text to one where it is much clearer, for both Hal and the audience watching him, that Falstaff has offended and irritated him; the talk of the robbery, which precedes the speech in the text, is in the film augmented by a full tavern scene that allows the Prince to set his personal objective against exactly that social context of revelry that opposes it—just as Falstaff opposes any king who would hang thieves. Although the speech is a soliloquy in the text, Welles does not leave Hal alone, but makes the camera track Falstaff, following Hal as he leaves the tavern door, watching him eagerly for any sign of anger or affection, the old man almost constantly in the background of the frame, slightly out of focus, while close up we see the Prince's face as he speaks softly aloud—in very realistic reaction to his situation—his feelings about his companions, his role, and his future. Keith Baxter, who played Hal for Welles, speaks the speech with great honesty, as well as with a good sense of the verse, and powerfully projects the irony in his perception that one day he will in fact "pay the debt [he] never promisèd"—not only to become King of England and to cleanse the land, but to succeed his father, to become his own man. Such moments as these give richness to the life of such a son, who must remind us of any son who realizes in pain and grief that, actually or metaphorically, he must replace his father. If today all roads lead to Vienna as in Shakespeare's day they led to Jerusalem, it remains true that a psychological depth of character here can reconstitute with validity the shape of Shakespeare's text. Just as the man,

Richard II, is at the center of his play, and the crown itself a meaningful object only because of human uses of it, so in his direction of Baxter as Prince Henry Welles reminds us that the agony of father and son informs the *Henry IV* plays, and, indeed, makes much more meaningful the political significance that stands beyond the paternal theme.

Throughout the film, quick, almost frenetic, alternation of camera shots emphasizes alternation between youth and age in the characters.[6] The repeated image-motif of Shallow and Falstaff as they move painfully through heavy snow silently falling upon the English countryside is a beautiful emblem of the end of life, of the exhausted, dying elements in the nation. The social consciousness of the movie is as alert as Shakespeare's, and thematically pertinent in Shakespearean terms too: vast, forbidding castle walls dominate the dirty stucco of the tavern, and the footage of the Battle of Shrewsbury itself must be some of the finest, truest, ugliest scenes of warfare ever shot and edited for a movie. Throughout, small directorial touches make direct and accessible the thematic center Welles has chosen for his reconstitution of the plays. As the King angrily dismisses Northumberland from council, for example, he emphasizes with both pace and stress the one word that reminds us of the conflict and jealousy in his mind as he compares his own Henry with that other one: "My lord Northumberland, we license your departure with your . . . *son*" (my punctuation and italics); later, Bolingbroke's breath freezes with every word into small puffs of vapor as he berates his own son in the cold sunlight of the castle hall, and, with the petulance of the old and self-pitying, he ignores Hal's oath to defeat Hotspur in battle. This is an omission that emphasizes, perhaps overpurifies, an ironic rivalry of viewpoint—just as, during the battle scenes, Welles omits Hal's rescue of his father from Douglas. Shakespeare's method is richer and more varied in texture, here and elsewhere, but the omissions, for example, do not make the King seem a less detailed personality in the movie than he does in the plays—simply because, I think, the movie finds the dynamic impulse for action under the text. Welles's film is a *reimaging* of the texts. In cutting the text, much is lost, but the director's rearrangement is not irresponsible, for it emphasizes an underlying statement in Shakespeare's text itself: the *effect*, theatrically, may be supposed to be close to the

---

[6] I am indebted to one of my former students at Harvard, Mr. Peter Jaszi, for his perceptive comments about Welles's film.

one intended. One might almost speak, in fact, of Welles's dramatization of the plays' *subtext*. "Subtext" is a term often misused in post-Stanislavsky acting schools, but it has a very useful meaning for the study of any drama, even drama in which the verbal element is as powerful as it is in Shakespeare. Stanislavsky meant by "subtext" simply that line of intention, of motivation, that might exist beneath the actual words of a script. The implications of subtextual investigation in rehearsals are perhaps more obvious for plays in the modern repertory than for those of Shakespeare. Characters in contemporary drama, for one reason or another, do not at times say what they really mean—most often because the playwright wants our ironic awareness to become part of his total effect. Shakespeare's characters, as Stoll observed long ago, almost always say what they mean—or, one might say, what they want to mean—unless they are consciously lying, and when this happens we know it, too. Nevertheless, the technique of finding a character's intention in a Shakespearean speech or scene—the technique of discussing, at least, the possibility of a subtextual element—can serve a valuable purpose in modern productions, provided the technique is carried forward with common sense. It can be most useful to the modern director or actor when there exists in the text a conventional gesture—a speech, an action, the use of a property—that we sense, or which research tells us, would have been immediately understood by an Elizabethan audience, but the significance of which is lost for us. At times such as these it may well serve a genuine purpose to try to ask ourselves what it is, quite simply, the character wants to do, to what he may be reacting, what he hopes may happen. When these questions are asked, we may discover—as in Welles's direction of Prince Hal's soliloquy—that human psychology provides a behavioral answer that is not so distant from the Shakespearean intention, so far as we can know it.

This leads directly to that third class of current productions described by Stanley Wells—those that are directed so as to become "theatrical [events] which will work in [their] independent way"; or which, one might add, are so thoroughly "reconstituted" as to appear a different play, a new work for the stage. One should make a firm distinction between these, by the way, and a simple "jollying-up" of a text, as in some of the brilliantly wrongheaded, happily irresponsible productions of Tyrone Guthrie. The best example of this form of re-imaged Shakespeare in recent years is probably Peter Brook's production of *King Lear*, with, as it happens, Paul Scofield again in the title role.[7] Fortunately, this production was seen by so many either in this country or in England, and has been so thoroughly described in various reviews and articles, has been attacked or defended in such detail, that I need do no more, I think, than summarize what I take to be its intention and its special effectiveness.

The production was conceived in terms of a universe much as Samuel Beckett might describe it—or at least as Beckett might as interpreted by Jan Kott, whose essay about the play strongly influenced Brook's direction and rehearsal procedures. It depicted, in short, a dead or dying universe, in which the evil or blindness of individual men and women, or their frustrated attempts to communicate with each other, inevitably cause their extinction in a mood more of catatonic grief and dullness than of protest or verbalized agony. Setting, costumes, and vocal levels all emphasized this mood and tone. Yet no production in modern theater proves so clearly, I think, that cutting alone is not the most important factor in altered staging of Shakespeare today: the promptbook for this production, filed in the Shakespeare Center at Stratford-upon-Avon, accessible for easy comparison with the promptbooks for all other Royal Shakespeare Company productions, reveals that Brook's cuts were fewer and much more conservative than those for many other stagings of *Lear*—productions we might willingly call Shakespeare served up "straight." His most important cuts were Folio cuts in any case. It is what happened onstage that made the production, however brilliant, essentially un-Shakespearean. After Gloucester's blinding, he was painfully tormented by Cornwall's servants, and the kindness shown toward him by one of them was eliminated; Goneril and Regan were given loud and extended cause for their complaints against the knights in Lear's train, and the evil intentions of these daughters were mitigated, an important distortion of the text; the repentance of Edmund at the end of the play was cut, and, as the great deaths in the last scene occurred, they were made unimportant in

----

[7] Brook's production of *A Midsummer Night's Dream* is a more recent example of this great director's development of his art, and deserves in fact a retrospective examination too long to include in a reprint of the present essay. In fact it represents less accurately the sort of "reconstituted" Shakespeare being discussed than does Brook's *Lear*, for a case could be made that in his production of *A Midsummer Night's Dream* he achieved a textual felicity and a projection of the playwright's intentions greater than in any other production of Shakespeare in recent years. In any case, the *Dream* elicited as much controversy as did the *Lear*, and it is impossible to discuss the production here.

this production by others' monotonic observation of them. Finally, Edgar lugged the guts of his dead brother off into the dusty haze upstage, the other characters left on unmoved and unmoving—the dead and the near-dead only so many rocks in a dead landscape, all of them bearing only the most distant resemblance to human beings. The effect of all this was, for me, very powerful; but it had nothing to do with Shakespeare, who intended to show—no matter how difficult it may be many times to know his purpose—that men are at least not blind to the inner resources of love, that suffering can dignify even if ultimately it obliterates, that the tolerance of the world is oriented more favorably toward good men than toward evil men, and that if good men die, their importance, if they can achieve the insight implcit in a tragic action, is rather clear to the society in which they have lived, and is not obscured from it.

But let me suggest that to argue these points is in some sense a waste of time. Brook's irresponsibility, if one can call it that, is that of an important creative artist engaged in a part of his craft, and I do not think he should be attacked; his major offense, if offense it be, was to compose a paraphrase in a new mode on an old text and not to call our attention to the fact that he had done so. Beyond this, it is important to see what Brook and others like him have done rather than to slap their wrists petulantly. The act of theater is not like an act of scholarship, nor is the performance of a play remotely like editing one, for living drama must view a text as a starting point for further creativity. The major problem in works of criticism such as those by Kott and works for the theater such as those by Brook is that, unlike the works of Shakespeare, they are philosophical. Shakespeare's world, however one may wish to describe it, or whichever part of it is chosen for detailed analysis, is ultimately imponderable and may not be reduced to an abstract statement, whereas the work of such directors as Peter Brook often seeks to make a statement *about* the world—Shakespeare's and our own. As it happens, the world of Beckett does not really illuminate Shakespeare's, but it does help to make a statement about ours. In some way, Brook has written an essay about *Lear* much as Brecht wrote one about *Coriolanus,* and he has done so by altering, by reconstituting, the very molecular structure of the original, by paraphrasing the text in a new medium of theater.

Remember that we do not condemn as irresponsible Boito and Verdi on *Othello,* Liszt on *Don Giovanni,* Picasso on the portraits of

Rembrandt, or Busoni or Schoenberg on Bach. We recognize some paraphrases as new and different works, and to argue that their vaguely parallel movement is not "accurate" is a waste of critical energy. They may be in themselves bad works or good works; they may teach us something new about the original; most likely, they will tell us something about the age in which they were conceived. Brook on the text of Shakespeare is, I think, an analogous phenomenon. An achievement of scholarship in this century has been to affirm the "integrity" of Shakespeare's text: the modes of the language, the sequence of scenes, the overall structures of the plays. All has been investigated, it seems, and we know, or think we know, that very little in a play by Shakespeare is there by accident. It is true, of course, that any director who chooses to disturb this texture of action usually does so to his own peril. But that does not mean that he *must* not alter it. The director's job is a relatively new one in theater history; it is not likely, for example, that anything like his function as we know it existed in Shakespeare's theater. In these years he has become an increasingly powerful figure, and is currently more important than any leading actor in most produc-tions. Mainly because of such a phenomenon as Brook's productions represent, a director is thought to be responsible for a conceptual state-ment as well as a theatrical one. I do not think this is necessarily a dangerous development; any strong and cumulative effect onstage must be the result of one man's vision of Shakespeare's art. But its virtues or shortcomings depend on the man at work, and must be described in terms of individual productions. Brook himself has produced some very "straight" and very pallid Shakespeare. Nominally, the director of the Olivier *Othello* was John Dexter, but I doubt very much that he had more to say about Olivier's readings than Olivier himself, or, perhaps, than Mr. Kenneth Tynan.

A director must work today with the living personalities of his actors. He really has no other option, except to refuse to acknowledge the events of his own times. A sense of ensemble onstage—that most highly regarded achievement among the great repertory companies of the past—remains an achievement possible only in terms of work with human behavior and not with critical theory. This method of work has parallel results in production style. If Orson Welles almost out-rageously altered the texts of 1, 2 *Henry IV*, there is still no denying that in this instance (the same cannot be said, I think, for his other film versions of Shakespeare) he clarified a pattern of character and behavior that rings true to the energy that informs the original texts. To remain aware of new ways to perceive reality in human action: that must be the goal of any responsible director of Shakespeare today. To do this is to evoke, surely, a richer sense of history than to attempt (what is in any case impossible) a derivative reproduction of the old style. This can only result in mannerism. One thinks of those very pretty productions of Shakespeare in the prewar years, resumed, happily only for a short time, in the late forties, usually designed by Motley and featuring some astounding elocution, but very little that we could recognize *now* as absorbing action. I grant this a drastic attitude. It involves the opinion that in other areas of drama, and in other art forms, too, some works no longer pertain to our lives in any important way. For my money, Shaw's Caesar's views on war, love, and honorable empire are almost as empty as Respighi's on Roman festivals. One must be grateful for the energy of the practicing artist, for although he may seem to call attention only to himself—and, indeed, may have intended nothing more than that!—he actually turns our attention to the work itself, to the processes of creativity in Shakespeare. The mysteries of those processes invite experimentation and innovation. If they did not, they would no longer be mysteries and we should have discovered long ago their dull and lifeless answers.

II. 4

EXCURSUS: The Example of Cervantes: The Novel as Parody*

HARRY LEVIN

Harvard University

To CROWN him with an adjective of his own choosing, Cervantes continues to be the exemplary novelist. It is a truism, of course, that he set the example for all other novelists to follow. The paradox is that, by exemplifying the effects of fantasy on the mind, he pointed the one way for fiction to attain the effect of truth. We state his achievement somewhat more concretely when we say that he created a new form by criticizing the old forms. *Don Quixote*, in terms of its intention and impact, constituted an overt act of criticism. Through its many varieties of two-sided observation, there runs a single pattern: the pattern of art embarrassed by confrontation with nature. This is the substance of the critical comment that every chapter makes in a differing context. We can test it by considering the implications of two such passages, taken from familiar and typical episodes, widely separated yet closely related.[1]

Our first passage occurs in Chapter XXII of the First Part, which is entitled "Of the liberty Don Quixote gave to many wretches, who were a-carrying perforce to a place they desired not." Let us pause for a

---

* Read at the Institute in 1955. Published in *Institute Essays: Society and Self in the Novel*, 1956.

[1] With some cross reference to the original Spanish in the interests of semantics, and a good deal of paraphrase in the interests of condensation, I shall be quoting Cervantes from the contemporaneous English translation of Thomas Shelton. Spelling will be modernized, and parenthetical numbers will refer to any standard text.

moment over this heading. It turns into a characteristically dry under-statement as soon as we realize that "the place they desired not" was the galleys. But the emphasis falls on the two common nouns in the main clause, "liberty" and "wretches." *Libertad:* The very word, which was to reverberate with such easy sonority for Walt Whitman, carried a poignant overtone for Cervantes. After the famous battle of Lepanto in which he lost the use of his hand, as he never tires of retelling, he had been captured by pirates and sold as a slave, and had perforce spent five long years in Algerian captivity. That enslavement, in a place Cervantes desired not, must have lent special meaning to Don Quixote's gesture of liberation. The tale later told by the Captive—the Spanish Captain enslaved at Algiers who recovers his greatest joy, lost liberty— is highly romanticized but it hints that the actual truth was stranger than the incidental fiction when it mentions a certain Cervantes ("tal de Saavedra") and the deeds he did—and all to achieve liberty ("y todas por alcanzar libertad," I,xl).

Hence the wretches are more to be pitied than scorned; and here the key word, *desdichados*, is not so much a term of contempt as an ironic expression of fellow-feeling. It may not be irrelevant to recall that *El Desdichado* is also the title Gérard de Nerval gives to his melan-choly sonnet on the romantic hero. A similar ambiguity characterizes the French *les misérables* or the Russian *neshchastnenki*. The under-tones of humanitarian sympathy, implied when Don Quixote liberates the convicts, come to the surface when he finally reaches Barcelona, and we are brought face to face with galley-slaves. Again we cannot help thinking of the author—not because his book is, in any sense, auto-biographical; but because it is, like most great books, the unique distilla-tion of mature experience. Behind the book stands a soldier of misfor-tune who had encountered many setbacks on his personal journey to Parnassus. Having tried his one good hand at virtually all the flowery forms of the artificial literature of that baroque period, he had addressed himself to the hazards of the road in the uncongenial guise of tax collector. And again it is of himself that he speaks with rueful humor, when the Priest and the Barber hold their inquisition over the books in Don Quixote's library. Among those which are set aside from the burning is the pastoral romance of *Galatea* by Miguel de Cervantes Saavedra. The Priest mitigates his criticism with a pun: this author is "más versado en desdichas que en versos"—better versed in misfortunes than in verses (I, vi).

Don Quixote's ideal of humanistic perfection is to be equally well versed in arms and letters. It might be opined that he fails because his military training has lagged so far behind his literary preparation. Something like the contrary might be maintained about his creator. At all events, after all he had been through, Cervantes would have been the very last man to cherish romantic illusions on the subject of adventure. He was therefore just the man to dramatize a distinction which has since become an axiom, which has indeed become so axiomatic that it might well be called Cervantes's formula. This is nothing more nor less than a recognition of the difference between verses and reverses, between words and deeds, *palabras* and *hechos*—in short, between literary artifice and that real thing which is life itself. But literary artifice is the only means that a writer has at his disposal. How else can he convey his impression of life? Precisely by discrediting those means, by repudiating that air of bookishness in which any book is inevitably wrapped. When Pascal observed that true eloquence makes fun of eloquence—"La vraie éloquence se moque de l'éloquence"—he succinctly formulated the principle that could look to Cervantes as its recent and striking exemplar. It remained for La Rochefoucauld to restate the other side of the paradox: some people would never have loved if they had not heard of love.

The chapter that sees the convicts liberated is rather exceptional in its direct approach to reality. The preceding chapter has been a more devious and characteristic excursion into the domain of romance. Its theme, which has come to be a byword for the transmuting power of imagination, as well as for Don Quixote's peculiar habit of imposing his obsession upon the world, is the barber's basin he takes for the fabulous helmet of Mambrino, stolen from Rinaldo by Sacripante in the *Orlando Furioso*. If the recovery of this knightly symbol is effected without undue incident, it is because the barber has no wish to fight; subsequently, when he returns to claim his property, he allows himself to be persuaded that it is really a helmet which has been enchanted to look like a basin. Such is the enchantment Don Quixote invokes to rationalize his defeats and embarrassments. Delusions of grandeur, conveniently enough, are sustained by phobias of persecution; somehow hostile enchanters always manage to get between him and the fulfillment of his ideals. Cervantes borrowed his plot from an interlude about a peasant bemused by popular ballads; though that *donnée* is elaborated through an infinite series of variations, it remains almost repetitiously simple. Each episode is a kind of skit in which the protagonist, attempting to put his heroic ideals into action, is discomfited by realities in the shape of slapstick comedy.

Thus deeds, with a vengeance, comment on words; and Cervantes's formula is demonstrated again and again. Afterward there are more words, pleasant discussions, "graciosos razonamientos"—which naturally require the presence of an amusing companion, an interlocutor, a *gracioso*. The hero of cape-and-sword drama is squired by such a buffoon; the courtier is often burlesqued by the zany who serves him; Don Quixote's servant—like Figaro or Jeeves—is cleverer, in some vital respects, than his master. Much, possibly too much, has already been written on the dualism of Don Quixote and Sancho Panza as a symbolic representation of soul and body, past and present, poetry and prose, the inner dilemmas of psychology, or the all-embracing antitheses of metaphysics. We need only remind ourselves in passing that, within this eternal comedy team, Sancho Panza's role is to assert a sense of reality. The incident of the windmills provides him with his usual cue and his classical response. When the knight beholds these machines in the distance, and asks the squire whether he too does not behold those monstrous giants, it is Sancho's function to reply with another question: "What giants?" In his person the challenging voice of empiricism does its best and its worst to refute the aprioristic frame of mind, which has become so closely identified with the Don that we sometimes term it "Quixotry."

Now on the comic stage, Sancho would have the final word. In the pictorial vision of Daumier, the pair coexist within the same frame of reference as the bourgeoisie and the caricatured intellectuals. Yet in a book, where words are the only medium, Don Quixote enjoys a decided advantage; the very weakness of his position in life lends strength, as it were, to his position in literature; in the field of action he may encounter discomfiture, but in the verbal sphere he soon resumes his imaginary career. When Sancho is skeptical about the basin and goes on to doubt the rewards of knighthood, the Don simply lapses into his autistic fantasies of wish-fulfillment; and his conversation during the next few pages spins out another romance in miniature. The most elaborate of the many little romances that run through his head and through the novel figures in his argument with the Canon of Toledo at the end of the First Part, and offers Cervantes occasion to develop his theory of the comic epic in prose. The Canon, on his side, is a more erudite humanist than Sancho Panza; but he casts the weight of his learning in favor of what the critics have labeled "probability"; and he pertinently distinguishes between fictitious and truthful histories (*historia imaginada, historia verdadera*).

Don Quixote's answer is a powerful statement of the appeal of romance. Freud would have diagnosed it as the purest indulgence in the pleasure-principle, the sheerest escape from the reality-principle. It is the daydream of a golden world of gardens and castles where art improves upon nature, where blandishing damsels await the errant adventurer and every misadventure leads toward a happy ending. It is a heady and concentrated restatement of the ever appealing myth that, in Cervantes's day, incarnated its bland archetype in Amadís of Gaul. Amadís, like every true cavalier, was by definition a paragon who surpassed all other cavaliers; his invulnerable prowess was as unparalleled as the peerless beauty of his lady, Oriana, or the perfect faithfulness of his squire, Gandalín. He was predestined to triumph over an all but endless sequence of rivals and obstacles, and to be united with his heroine in an enchanted chamber which only the bravest and fairest could enter, somewhere out of this world on an uncharted island misleadingly named Terra Firma. Meanwhile the chronicle of his adventures and those of his progeny, prolonged through five generations and twenty-four volumes, furnished the primary source of inspiration for Don Quixote, whose pattern of behavior is—to speak it profanely—a kind of *imitatio Amadís*.

Imitation is the test that Cervantes proposes, knowing full well that when nature imitates art, art reveals its innate artificiality. Literally his hero reenacts episodes from the life cycle of his own hero, as when he assumes the name of Beltenebros and undergoes penance in the Sierra Morena. But since he aspires to combine the virtues of other heroes—the Nine Worthies, the Twelve Paladins, the aggregate musterroll of knight errantry—he must likewise emulate Ariosto's Orlando. And since Orlando went mad for love of the fair Angelica, Don Quixote must rage in order to prove his devotion to the fair Dulcinea del Toboso. The place name he attaches to his kitchen-maid heroine is less aristocratic than anticlimactic, particularly when it is left to dangle as the refrain of one of the poems addressed to her. The process of emulation, dedicated to a whole set of models at once, going through their motions so pedantically and overstating their claims so fanatically, tends to reduce them all to absurdity. Because this tendency is deliberate, the prevailing method is that of parody: a marvelous gift, according to Ben

Jonson, which makes a work "absurder than it was." But *Amadís de Gaula* could hardly have been absurder than it was; its innumerable sequels might almost have been parodies; while *Don Quixote* might be no more than another sequel, if it had no objective vantage-point from which to chart the deviations of its subjective course.

Its protagonist sallies forth at the outset, talking to himself—as will be his wont—about the historian who will have the honor of recording the exploits he is about to accomplish (I,ii). With a dizzying shift of the time sense, he looks back from the future upon events which have yet to take place. From first to last the narration is colored by his own self-consciousness. A much later sally is introduced by this mock-heroic sentence: "Scarce had the silver morn given bright Phoebus leave with the ardor of his burning rays to dry the liquid pearls on his golden locks, when Don Quixote, shaking off sloth from his drowsy members, rose up and called Sancho his squire, that still lay snorting (II,xxx)" Here, with the calculated anticlimax of the last word, all the mythological ornamentation sinks into bathos. Actuality, suddenly intervening, restores our perspective to a more firmly grounded base of observation. The highflown monologue becomes a pedestrian dialogue, which in turn restates the dialectical issue of the book. Sancho Panza, the principal dialectician, is quite aware of that variance which makes his fall into a mere hole so utterly different from Don Quixote's exploration of the Cave of Montesinos: "There saw he goodly and pleasant visions and here, I believe, I shall see nothing but snakes and toads (II,lv)." The pleasant visions are abstract and remote; the snakes and toads are concrete and immediate; the variance is all in the point of view.

The psychological contrast is reflected in the stylistic texture from the opening page, where the first paragraph is straight factual exposition, while the second echoes two florid sentences from Don Quixote's reading. Diction shows the increasing influence of Sancho's viewpoint when —amid bouquets of poetic conceit and parades of learned authority, the regular mental context of Don Quixote—Cervantes apologizes for using the homely substantive *puercos*, and thereby calling a pig a pig. Once this sort of interplay has been established, Don Quixote himself can take the metaphorical step from the sublime to the ridiculous. When Sancho reports that Dulcinea's visage is slightly blemished by a mole, he can respond with an inappropriate amplification—"Though she had a hundred moles as well as that one thou sawest in her, they were not moles but moons and bright stars"—a pretty picture which outdoes even

Shakespeare's hyperbolic gibes against the Petrarchan sonneteers (II,x). The gravity of his demeanor is matched by the grandiosity of his rhetoric, a manner of speaking broadly connoted by the rhetorical term *prosopopeya*. His dead-pan humor would not be humorous were someone else not there to see the joke, to watch the imitation becoming a parody by failing to meet the challenge at hand. As his purple passages are juxtaposed with Sancho's vernacular proverbs, the bookish and sluggish flow of his consciousness is freshened and quickened; flat assertion is rounded out and soliloquy is colloquialized.

Cervantes, whose *Colloquy of the Dogs* we must not forget, was well schooled in those mixed modes of Erasmus and Lucian which—linking the early modern spirit to the late Greco-Roman—seem to express the self-questionings of a traditional culture during an epoch of rapid and far-reaching change. The literature of the Ranaissance, which moves from one extreme to the other so readily, is the register of a violent effort to catch up with the expanding conditions of life. With its realization that certain themes are still untreated goes the feeling that certain techniques are becoming outmoded. The needed renewal and the strategic enlargement begin by adapting, experimenting, cross fertilizing, and incidentally producing giants and dwarfs whose incongruous qualities merely bear witness to the overplus of creativity. Extraordinary combinations of langauge, such as macaronics, waver between Latinity and the vulgar tongues. Poetry, evoking the legendary past, varies its tone from nostalgia to facetiousness. Prose impinges, entirely unaware of its possibilities as an imaginative medium. A transitional sense of disproportion makes itself felt, not only in mannerist painting, but in complementary literary genres: mock epic, which magnifies vulgarity, applying the grand manner to commonplace matters; and travesty, which minimizes greatness, reclothing noble figures in base attire.

It will easily be seen, from page to page, how Cervantes ranges between these two reductive extremes. One of his own descriptions of his style, at the beginning of the chapter before us, oscillates from high-sounding (*altisonante*) to trivial (*minima*). This oscillation puzzled Shelton so much that he translated the latter word by one more congruent to the former: "divine" (*divina*). However, Cervantes encompasses many such disparities, bridging the gap between style and subject by the continual play of his irony. Rabelais could revel in the *mélange des genres*, parodying the quest for the Holy Grail in the cult of the

Holy Bottle. A lesser writer, Robert Greene, could live between two worlds and keep them apart: first-hand journalistic accounts of the London underworld and mannered pastoral romances set in some escapist Arcadia, with very little intermixture of styles. The immeasurable contribution of Cervantes was to broaden the province of prose fiction by bringing both realms together, not in a synthesis perhaps, but in the most durable antithesis that literature has known; by opening a colloquy between the romance and the picaresque, so to speak, between *Amadís de Gaula* and *Lazarillo de Tormes*. Spain, with its strongly marked chiaroscuro of contrasts, social as well as cultural, presented the pertinent matter of fact along with the far-fetched matter of fiction. The first-person narrative of the little beggar, Lazarillo, whose harsh masters taught him to cheat or be cheated, gave Cervantes the fructifying example for an exemplary novel to which *Don Quixote* refers, *Rinconete and Cortadillo*—a tale endearing to American readers as a Sevillian adumbration of *Tom Sawyer* and *Huckleberry Finn*.

Having proceeded discursively, after the fashion of Rocinante, we have come back to our starting point and are ready to set out once again. Our preliminary amble has not been wasted if it has confirmed our awareness of the "disorderly order" that regulates the imaginary gardens of Cervantes, and that may emerge from the passage to which we now return. After the gang of unfortunates bound for the galleys is released through the officiousness of Don Quixote, he is confounded by reality in the shifty person of their ringleader: a rogue indeed, the authentic picaroon, Ginés de Pasamonte. Ginés, among his other dubious traits, harbors pretensions as a man of letters; to beguile the time in prison, he declares, he has made a book out of the story of his life. This may strengthen the bonds of affinity that connect the present chapter with the life of Cervantes; for we know that the author was imprisoned, through some bureaucratic complication, during the period when he was writing *Don Quixote*; and he may be referring to that circumstance, with his genius for rising above a situation, when his prologue alludes to "some dark and noisome prison." In any case, Don Quixote is curious about this particular product of incarcerated endeavors.

"Is it so good a work?" said Don Quixote.

"It is so good," replied Ginés, "that it quite 'puts down *Lazarillo de*

Tormes and as many others as are written or shall write of that kind: for that which I dare affirm to you is that it treats of true accidents, and those so delightful that no like invention can be compared to them."
"And how is the book entitled?" quoth Don Quixote.
"It is called," said he, "*The Life of Ginés of Pasamonte.*"
"And is it yet ended?" said the knight.
"How can it be finished," replied he, "my life being not yet ended?"
                                                                    (I,xxii)

To mention a work of fiction in the course of another work of fiction can be a two-edged device. It can show up the book that is mentioned, thereby sharpening the realism of the book that does the mentioning. This is what Ginés does for his own work at the expense of Lazarillo, and what Cervantes is doing for *Don Quixote* at the expense of *Amadís de Gaula*, expressly invoked by his own commendatory verses. Conversely, the invidious comparison can glance in the other direction, as in the case of many a derivative academic novel today: the pale reflection of a dream of the shadow of Henry James. But that is unmitigated imitation, and it produces a conventional literature, circumscribing novelists to the point where even their titles must be quotations from other books. The method of Cervantes utilized literary means to break through literary conventions and, in the very process, invented a form substantial and flexible enough to set forth the vicissitudes of modern society. Parody, explicitly criticizing a mode of literature, developed into satire, implicitly criticizing a way of life. Developing out of the debris of feudalism, the novel has waxed and waned with the middle class. Yet in the twentieth century, according to Thomas Mann's contemporary Faust, the arts tend more than ever to parody themselves. The writer's problem, as André Gide has rephrased Cervantes's formula, is still the rivalry between the real world and the representation we make of it—"la rivalité entre le monde réel et la représentation que nous en faisons."

It is significant that Gide's most serious novel, which likewise probes the theme of how novels come to be written, is called *The Counterfeiters*; and that Mann's last fragment—begun forty years before and completed only, in the peculiar sense of Ginés, by the author's death—is a reversion to the picaresque cycle, *Confessions of Felix Krull*. For trickery is inherent, as artists recognize, in their business of dealing with illusion. We do well then to scrutinize some of their tricks rather closely; and Cervantes is well justified in conveying this caveat, or insight, through the mouth of an incorrigible charlatan. After all, no one can express what is by nature inexpressible. Life itself is infinitely larger than any artistic medium. However, by revealing the limitations of their medium, writers like Cervantes heighten our consciousness of what existence means. The real story of Ginés de Pasamonte, comparatively more real than the imagined *Life of Lazarillo de Tormes*, is bound to be incomplete because life is endless. It lasts forever, as Tolstoy's peasant says before he dies in *War and Peace*. In all sincerity, therefore, we cannot say *finis*; we can only write "to be continued." And so with Cervantes, like Ginés writing in prison, and breaking off his First Part with a provisory ending and a cautionary moral: Beware of fiction! It is fictitious; that is to say, it is false! Don't let it mislead you!

The ironic consequence of his warning was the creation of an archetype, a fictional personage destined to be far more influential than Amadís of Gaul. The remarkable success of the First Part was the precondition of the Second, which is consequently more deliberate in its artistry. By that time, the latter volume announces, the fame of its predecessor has spread so widely that any lean horse would be hailed as Rocinante. The earlier conclusion, in which so little was concluded, clearly invited some continuation. Before Cervantes could take up his own tale again, the interloper who signed himself "Avellaneda" brought out his notorious sequel: an imitation of a parody. Because the impersonation had to be imitative, it could not be organic; it could not live and grow as Cervantes's original would do in his Second Part. The mysterious Avellaneda, when Cervantes finally caught up with him, all but took the place of Amadís as a satirical target, and as a measure of the distance between echoed phrases and lived experiences. Adding insult to injury, he had not only plagiarized; he had also criticized his victim for not keeping his own brain-children in character, and—even more significantly—for introducing Ginés. That scoundrel had shown a comparable ingratitude when he rewarded his liberator with a shower of stones, absconding with Don Quixote's sword and—temporarily— Sancho Panza's ass. But the Second Part arranges a further encounter and, for the knight, an opportune revenge.

This involves our second illustration, a rather more extended example which need not be cited at length, since it figures so prominently in the celebrated episode of Master Peter's puppet show. Poetic drama —another genre which Cervantes had practiced with indifferent results—is here reduced to its most elementary level, just as prose fiction was in the instance we have been discussing. The link between these two passages, as we learn from the next chapter, is Maese Pedro himself, who turns out to be none other than Don Quixote's old enemy, Ginés. Always the escape artist, he is now an itinerant showman and more of a dealer in deception than ever. One of his other exhibits happens to be a fortunetelling ape, whose roguish trick is subsequently exposed. Now Cervantes was obviously fond of animals; a dog lover and a master of the beast fable, he satirizes war in a parable about braying asses and courtly love in a serenade of cats; the *dramatis personae* of his book include a traveling menagerie; but the ape, above all, is the parodistic animal. When the lovelorn Dorothea joins the friendly conspiracy to bring the knight to his senses, she poses as the Infanta Micomica of Micomicón ("Princess Monkey-Monkey of Monkeyland"). Actually a damsel in distress, she acts the part of a damsel in distress; and the make-believe story she recounts to Don Quixote is the parody of a parody, her own story.

This monkey-business, if it may be so designated, accelerates to its climax through a sequence of scenes at the inn. There the incidental stories accumulate, and there the actual personages who tell or figure in them are interrelated through the fiat of romantic coincidence. Viktor Shklovsky has aptly described this meeting place as "a literary inn," though another emphasis would interpret it as a social microcosm. On the one hand, the relationship between letters and arts is the appropriate topic of Don Quixote's discourse; on the other, the crude farce of the wineskins and the stern intervention of the Holy Brotherhood, searching for the importunate busybody who freed the convicts, underline the romance with a touch of reality. The central interpolation is a tale which comes out of the same bag of manuscripts as some of Cervantes's *Exemplary Novels*—or so the literary host very plausibly informs his guests. It is the tale of the so-called Curious Impertinent, an almost Proustian study in point of view, wherein Anselmo's universal suspicion functions as a sort of mirror-opposite for Don Quixote's ubiquitous credulity. Characterization of the protagonist gains in depth as he passes through the levels of the characters who surround him, in their assumed roles, with their recounted adventures—sometimes tales within tales. As in Chaucer's *Canterbury Tales*, the storytellers take on an extra dimension against the formal backdrop of their stories.

The First Part situates these episodes, within the tradition of the frame-story, at an extra remove from the reader. In the Second Part, as the narrator proudly explains, they are unified by the divagations of a single plot. Where the First Part centered upon an inn, which the hero insisted on taking for a castle, the Second Part leads to a long sojourn at a genuine castle, where the conversation is less inspired and the horseplay heavier than at any other juncture of the book. Castles in Spain, for non-Spaniards, have proverbially symbolized the veritable fabric of romance. "Castle-building," in the library at Waverley Honour, was the state of mind that engendered the latter-day romances of Sir Walter Scott. The terrain of Don Quixote, the arid region of La Mancha, overlaps Castille, which is quite literally the land of castles. But Cervantes's castle seems to mark an anticlimactic turning point, a release from mental imprisonment, the beginning of an undeception for the knight; while it bewitches the squire, offering him a brief chance to go his own way and to impose the rough justice of the common man on the neighboring dependency of Barataria. Overshadowed by that glimpse of a democratic community, or the disillusioning city of Barcelona just ahead, chivalric entertainment may well pall. Not that the Duke and Duchess have spared any courtesy; they have humored their fantastic guest with such labored vivacity that they are accused of being madder than he; there has been more manipulation and masquerading, more play-acting and practical joking, at the castle than at the inn.

The effectiveness of the play-within-the-play lies in making the main drama more convincing: when the king interrupts the players in *Hamlet*, we feel that at last we have come to grips with reality. One way of attaining this effect is to make the theatrical figures unconvincing; and when these are puppets rather than actors, wooden dolls imitating human beings, everything undergoes a reduction of scale; their performance becomes a mode of ridicule, as Bergson has suggested in his essay on laughter. Hence, among the many stratagems that Cervantes employs against the romance, none is more sharply conceived nor more skilfully executed than the puppet play. His description of it commences in epic style, with the spectators—Tyrians and Trojans— falling silent, and the youthful reciter appealing to the authority of old French chronicles and Spanish ballads (II,xxvi). The setting is a city whose ancient name, Sansueña, suffuses a dreamy atmosphere. The plot concerns the Princess Melisendra, imprisoned by the Moors even as Cervantes himself has been, and her knightly rescuer, Gaiféros, who must accomplish his task by fighting the Moors as Cervantes has done

—but with a difference, that crucial difference between fantasy and actuality which it is his constant purpose to emphasize.

For once Don Quixote has no need to superimpose his fancies; he need only take the presentation literally. As a matter of fact, he starts by criticizing certain details of Moorish local color. Gradually he suspends his disbelief—which has never been too strong—and enters into the spirit of the occasion so actively that, before others can stop him, he has begun "to rain strokes upon the puppetish Moorism." The puppeteer, Ginés alias Pedro, cries: "Hold, Señor Don Quixote, hold! and know that these you hurl down, destroy, and kill, are not real Moors but shapes made of pasteboard." And reality is restored no less abruptly than it is when Alice cries out to the creatures of Wonderland: "You're nothing but a pack of cards!" Pedro–Ginés, the arch-manipulator, the ever versatile illusionist, laments his loss for an operatic moment or two, and then shrewdly reckons it up: so much for Charlemagne split down the middle, so much for Melisendra without a nose, and so on down to the last marivedi, paid in full by Don Quixote in coin of the realm. Such mercenary language contrasts with another aspect of the show: the puppets were knocked down, we are told, "in less than two credos." This is rather a figure of speech than an article of belief; and the wax candles probably have no ritual significance; yet it is worth remembering that the word *retablo*, applied to the puppet show, signifies primarily an altarpiece. I do not want to place undue stress on symbols which prove so brittle; but we cannot altogether ignore the iconoclasm of Cervantes, since the Inquisition did not.

In the next chapter, when the narrator swears to his own veracity as a Catholic Christian, the author himself feels obliged to point out that this protestation comes from an unbelieving Moor (II,xxvii). Elsewhere he repeatedly warns us that Moors are not to be trusted: they are "cheaters, impostors, and chemists" (II,iii). Cervantes's fictional narrator is one of these elusive infidels: an "Arabical and Manchegan historiographer" named the Cide Hamete Benengeli, who does not appear in the opening pages of the book. Don Quixote completes his first sally, saunters forth again, challenges the Biscayan, and is left sword in air by the break between the seventh and eighth chapters. In a digression, Cervantes tells us that his documentation has run out, and that we might well have been left in suspense forever; again, as in the later colloquy between Don Quixote and Ginés, life is conceived as an unfinished book. Happily, in a bazaar at Toledo, Cervantes has chanced upon an Arabic manuscript which will supply the rest of the story; and from now on the Cide Hamete will be responsible for it, even as Captain Clutterbuck or Jedediah Cleishbotham would be responsible for Scott's narrations, and other pseudonymous narrators for Stendhal's and Manzoni's. Since the author presents himself as editor, assuming the intervention of a Spanish translator from the Arabic, the text stands at three removes from ourselves, enriched with afterthoughts like a palimpsest. This procedure has the advantages of enabling the author to disgress more freely, to blame his source for indiscreet remarks, and to cultivate an air of authenticity.

But authenticity is deeply called into question on one problematic occasion, when the whole trend of the book is reversed, turning back from pragmatic demonstration to metaphysical speculation, or—in the more incisive phrase of Américo Castro—from a critique of fiction to a critique of reality. Can men's lives be so sharply differentiated from their dreams, when all is said and done? Can we live without illusion? we are asked. Don Quixote may be right, the rest of us wrong. Many of the philosophers, most of the poets, would take his side. Spanish imagination is not unique in having been fascinated by Calderón's refrain: "La vida es sueño," life is a dream. Even Shakespeare conceded the possibility: "We are such stuff/ As dreams are made on. . . ." Who are we, in that event, to look down upon puppets imprisoned within the dream-city of Sansueña? May it not be that the images of ourselves created by writers, as Pirandello would urge, are more real than we are? For example, *Don Quixote*. The chapter that explores such ultimate doubts is admittedly apocryphal; it may be an intermixture of truth and falsehood, as pantomimed by Maese Pedro's ape. We are tempted to believe that Don Quixote's descent into the Cave of Montesinos is a return to the deep well of the past, the unconscious memory of the race, and that the mythical heroes sleeping there personify the ideals he struggled to practice, the ideology of the Golden Age. Yet the simple and brutal alternative persists that he may have been caught in a lie and have become a party to the general imposture.

In the absence of other witnesses, certainty continues to elude us. The best advice Don Quixote can report is the gambler's maxim spoken, curiously enough, by the flower and mirror of chivalry, Durandarte: "Paciencia y barajar," patience and shuffle, go on with the game (II,xxiii). After the underground interview with the dead heroes, the next stage is the fable about the asses, and then the puppetry of Pedro-Ginés; and each successive chapter is a station on the pilgrimage of disenchantment. Disarmed, dismounted, and finally discomfited, the former knight is on his way homeward, when the sight of shepherds rouses his flagging impulses to their last wish-dream. Sancho, of course, has an important part in it:

"I'll buy sheep and all things fit for our pastoral vocation; and calling myself by the name of shepherd Quixotiz and thou the shepherd Pansino, we will walk up and down the hills, through the woods and meadows, singing and versifying and drinking the liquid crystal of the fountains, sometimes out of the clear springs and then out of the swift-running rivers." (II,lxvii)

But Don Quixote has come to the end of his life and, accordingly, of his book. It remained for other books to parody the pastoral romances, as his had parodied the romances of chivalry: notably a French disciple of Cervantes, Charles Sorel, who wrote a novel entitled *Anti-Romance*, and subtitled *The Wayward Shepherd* (*L'Anti-roman, ou le berger extravagant*). That would be another story; but perhaps the term "anti-romance" might be usefully borrowed to generalize a major premise of the modern novel, from Fielding, who began as Cervantes's professed imitator by lampooning Richardson, to Jane Austen, who sharpened her acute discriminations on Gothic romances and novels of sensibility:

Charming as were all of Mrs. Radcliffe's works, and charming even as were the works of all her imitators, it was not in them perhaps that human nature, at least in the midland counties of England, was to be looked for.

The time, the place, and the style of *Northanger Abbey* have little in common with Cervantes; but his protean formula has held, as it has been readjusted to varying situations through the lengthy record of Don Quixote's posthumous adventures. One of the many female Quixotes has been Madame Bovary; one of the many Russian Quixotes has been Prince Myshkin. Heinrich Heine summed up the Romantic Movement as a school of Quixotry when he exclaimed: "Jean-Jacques Rousseau was my Amadís of Gaul!" In a parallel vein, it might be argued that Voltaire's Amadís of Gaul was Leibniz, that Tolstoy's was Napoleon, or Mark Twain's Baedeker. The number of specific instances would seem to indicate some broader principle, such as André Malraux has recently formulated in his illustrated treatise on the creative imagination. His dictum—that every artist begins with *pastiche*—is highly illuminating, so far as it goes; it has to be qualified only by recognizing that *pastiche* implies both activities which we have associated and distinguished, imitation and parody. The novelist must begin by playing the sedulous ape, assimilating the craft of his predecessors; but he does not master his own form until he has somehow exposed and surpassed them, passing from the imitation of art through parody to the imitation of nature.

II. 5

Unifying Symbols in the Comedy of Ben Jonson*

RAY L. HEFFNER, JR.

Indiana University

CRITICS SINCE the seventeenth century have agreed that Ben Jonson is a master of comic structure, but there has been serious disagreement as to just what kind of structure it is in which he excels. To Dryden, Jonson was preeminent among English dramatists because he obeyed the neoclassic rules of unity of time, place, and action. Of the three, unity of action is fundamental, and it is Jonson's plotting that Dryden found most praiseworthy. He preferred *The Silent Woman* above all other plays because he found it an ideal combination of the scope, variety, and naturalness of the English drama with the control and careful organization of the French. And the *examen* of that play in the *Essay of Dramatic Poesy* emphasizes that there is immense variety of character and incident but that the action is "entirely one." [1] Critics in recent years, however, have disputed Dryden's picture of a regular, neoclassic Jonson, especially in the matter of plot structure. Freda L. Townsend, for example, argues persuasively that none of Jonson's great comedies has the unified action characteristic of Terentian comedy and enjoined by neoclassic precept. [2] She compares Jonson's art with that of Ariosto and the baroque painters, and she sees

---

* Read at the Institute in 1954. Published in *Institute Essays: English Stage Comedy,* 1955.

[1] *Essays of John Dryden,* ed. by W. P. Ker (Oxford, 1926), 1, 83.

[2] *Apologie for Bartholmew Fayre: the Art of Jonson's Comedies* (New York, Modern Language Association, 1947), *passim,* especially pp. 91–97.

Bartholomew Fair rather than *The Silent Woman* as the culmination of his development away from a simply unified comedy towards one which involves the intricate interweaving of as many different interests as possible. T. S. Eliot perhaps best sums up this "modern" view of Jonson's technique when he says that his "immense dramatic constructive skill" is not so much in plot as in "doing without a plot," and adds:

The plot does not hold the play together; what holds the play together is a unity of inspiration that radiates into plot and personages alike.[3]

The views of Eliot and Miss Townsend seem to me substantially more correct than that of Dryden on this matter. In this paper I shall try to define more precisely the "unity of inspiration" which Eliot and others have found in Jonson's comedy and to describe the dramatic devices by which it is expressed. Briefly, I believe that the essential unity of Jonson's comedy is thematic. In each of his major plays he explores an idea or a cluster of related ideas through a variety of characters and actions. And the central expression of the unifying idea is usually not in a fully developed plot but in a fantastic comic conceit, an extravagant exaggeration of human folly, to which all of the more realistically conceived characters and incidents have reference.

For such an investigation the crucial cases are *The Silent Woman* and *Bartholomew Fair*, Dryden's ideal "regular" comedy and Miss Townsend's ideal "baroque" comedy. If I can show that, despite the very evident differences in superficial structure, a similar kind of thematic unity underlies each of these and that it is expressed in similar symbolic devices, my analysis may have some claim to inclusiveness.

In the case of *The Silent Woman*, I must first undertake to show that it is not, even at the level of action, held together by the "noble intrigue" as Dryden analyzes it. Dryden's spokesman Neander, accepting the definition of unity of action given earlier in the debate by Crites, tries to show that at least one English comedy adheres to the rule. Crites's principles are those derived by Renaissance and neoclassic criticism mainly from the practice of Terence. The emphasis is on the single, clearly defined aim of the action, which should be announced in the *protasis* or beginning of the play, delayed by all sorts of complications and counter-intrigues in the *epitasis* or middle, and finally

---

[3] "Ben Jonson," *Elizabethan Essays* (London, 1934), p. 77.

brought to completion by the *catastrophe* or denouement. Neander discusses *The Silent Woman* as if it follows exactly this formula. "The action of the play is entirely one," he says, "the end or aim of which is the settling of Morose's estate on Dauphine." And he continues:

You see, till the very last scene, new difficulties arising to obstruct the action of the play; and when the audience is brought into despair that the business can naturally be effected, then, and not before, the discovery is made.[4]

If we consider the play in retrospect, after we have seen or read the last scene, we may agree with Neander that the securing of Morose's estate is the central aim of the whole. Dauphine's sensational revelation of the true sex of Epicoene does indeed finally and irrevocably secure for him the estate, and after the play is over we can see that all the intrigues of Truewit and Clerimont, no matter what their intended purpose, have aided Dauphine's scheme by exhausting his uncle's patience and thus making the old man desperate enough to sign the settlement. But the fact that the true nature of Dauphine's scheme is concealed until the very end makes a great difference in the kind of unity which can be perceived by the audience during the course of the play. The settling of Morose's esate on Dauphine is not the ostensible aim of the action after Act III, for the audience as well as the other characters have been led to believe that Dauphine's purposes have been fully accomplished by the marriage of Morose and Epicoene. No new difficulties arise to obstruct this action in Acts IV and V: we assume it has already been settled and our attention has turned to other matters. Even in the early acts the course of Dauphine's intrigue is remarkably smooth, and little suspense of the kind Dryden describes is generated. By the last scene, far from being brought into despair that the business of the estate can naturally be effected, we have forgotten all about it and are surprised to see it reintroduced.

As the play unfolds, the settling of Morose's estate upon Dauphine is but one among several aims which give rise to action, and it is dominant only in Act II. It is much more accurate to consider *The Silent Woman* as consisting not of a Terentian plot depending upon the delayed completion of a single, well-defined objective but of a number of separable though related actions which are initiated and brought to completion at various points in the play and which are skillfully arranged to overlap and interlock. Each of these actions is essentially

4 Ker, *Essays of Dryden*, 1, 88.

a trick played on a dupe or a group of dupes, and each has four fairly well-defined stages: (1) the exposition of background material, including the characterization of the dupe; (2) the planning of the trick by the intriguer; (3) the actual execution of the trick; and (4) the reminiscence of the trick as a source of continued laughter. The general plan is that a different major action occupies the center of attention in each act except the first, which consists of exposition of material for all the actions to follow. Act II is thus centered on Dauphine's scheme to marry his uncle to Epicoene, Act III on Truewit's scheme to torment Morose by moving Sir Amorous La Foole's dinner party to Morose's house, Act IV on the double scheme to discredit the foolish knights and make all the Collegiate Ladies fall in love with Dauphine, and Act v on the tormenting of Morose through the mock discussion of marriage annulment by the pretended canon lawyer and divine.

This basic plan is complicated by the introduction of several minor actions, notably the one precipitating the disgrace of Captain Tom Otter, and by the overlapping previously mentioned. At almost every point at least three actions are under simultaneous consideration: one is at the peak of fulfillment, a second has passed its climax but is still producing laughter, and the groundwork for a third is being carefully prepared.

These sundry intrigues are connected in a number of different ways. The peculiarities of the various dupes which make them fit objects of ridicule are all described in the course of an apparently aimless conversation in Act I, so that the jokes played on them later in the play, though they seem to arise spontaneously out of particular situations, nevertheless are not unexpected. All the tricks are planned by the same group of witty companions, most of them by Truewit, and every character has some part in more than one intrigue. Often one intrigue depends on the completion of another, as the transferring of the banquet on the completion of the marriage. And the final revelation of Epicoene's sex, as Miss Townsend points out, has some relevance to all the major actions;[5] it not only accomplishes Morose's divorce and gains the estate for Dauphine, it also shows the foolish knights to be liars and discomfits the Collegiate Ladies, who have had to depend on a despised male for the vindication of their honors.

Such an elaborate intertwining of episodes demonstrates great

[5] Townsend, *Bartholmew Fayre*, p. 64.

technical skill in what Renaissance criticism called *disposition* and *economy*.[6] But we are still entitled to ask, is this the only kind of structure the play possesses? Are there no more fundamental relationships among these various characters and actions, of which the mechanical interconnections we have been discussing are but the external evidences? The thematic structure of the play will be clearer if we consider that its real center is not in any of the tricks or schemes but in the ridiculous situation in which Morose finds himself. My argument is not genetic, but a brief look at the probable sources of the play may help to confirm this impression. The sources of the separable parts are extremely varied. Passages of dialogue come from Juvenal and Ovid, many of the characters belong in the series of satiric portraits stretching back through Jonson's early plays and through contemporary nondramatic satire; the aborted duel between the two knights seems to come from *Twelfth Night*, the conflict between Dauphine and his uncle bears some resemblance to *A Trick to Catch the Old One*, and the device of trickery through concealed sex may come from Aretino's comedy *Il Marescalco*.[7] But the center around which all this material is arranged is clearly the comic conceit which Jonson took from a declamation of Libanius—the ludicrous plight of a noise-hating man married by fraud to a noisy woman.

Herford and Simpson observe that, "The amusing oration of Libanius offered but slender stuff for drama." [8] This is true enough, in that it contained only a situation and not a complete plot, and the implications of that situation were but little developed. The Morosus of Libanius merely describes the horrors of his noise-ridden existence and pleads with the judges for permission to commit suicide. The oration could not simply be translated to the stage without the addition of much extra material. But it is, nevertheless, an admirable idea for a

6 In his *Discoveries* (lines 1815–20 in the Herford and Simpson edition) Jonson speaks slightingly of Terence's skill in these matters, though it was much praised by most Renaissance critics. For the meaning of the terms, see Marvin T. Herrick, *Comic Theory in the Sixteenth Century* ("Illinois Studies in Language and Literature," Vol. xxxiv, Nos. 1–2 [Urbana, 1950]), pp. 94–106.

7 For these and other sources see C. H. Herford and Others, *Ben Jonson* (Oxford, 1925–52), II, 72–79 (1925), and the notes in Vol. x (1950); also the edition by Julia Ward Henry ("Yale Studies in English," No. xxxi [New York 1906]), pp. xxviii–lvi, and O. J. Campbell, "The Relation of *Epicoene* to Aretino's *Il Marescalco*," PMLA, xlvi (1931), 752–62.

8 *Ben Jonson*, II, 76 (1925).

comedy. For one thing, it epitomizes the eternal battle of the sexes for supremacy, including the hypocrisies of courtship and the wrangling after marriage. And then also, in its opposition of noisy people to noise haters, it suggests another eternal theme, the debate between the active and the quiet life. In constructing a play around the conceit of Libanius, Jonson greatly complicates both these latent themes, through his interpretation of the Morose-Epicoene relationship and through the addition of other characters and actions.

Jonson's interpretation of the central situation is summarized in the scene in which Morose interrogates his intended bride. (II,v.) There we learn that the old man's hatred of noise is the outward manifestation of two allied character traits. First, he has been at court and has recoiled in horror from all forms of courtliness. He tests his bride-to-be by pointing out to her that if she forbear the use of her tongue she will be unable to trade "pretty girds, scoffes, and daliance" with her admirers; she cannot, like the ladies in court, "affect . . . to seeme learn'd, to seeme judicious, to seeme sharpe, and conceited"; and she will be manifestly unable to "have her counsell of taylors, lineners, lace-women, embroyderers, and sit with 'hem sometimes twise a day, upon *French* intelligences" so as "to be the first and principall in all fashions." The meaning of the play's central symbol of noise is thus considerably developed in this scene; a noisy woman is a woman given over to all the vanity, hypocrisy, and affectation to which her sex and the courtly society of her age are prone. Morose can concentrate his hatred of all these things by hating the inclusive and concrete symbol, noise itself.

The second important aspect of Morose's idiosyncrasy is his passion for having his own way in all things. In his first soliloquy he admits that "all discourses, but mine owne, afflict mee." (II,i.) He admires the absolute obedience which oriental potentates command from members of their households; and the silence of his own servants indicates their complete subservience to his will, for they can answer perfectly well by signs so long as their judgments "jump" with his. Epicoene thus throws him into ecstasies of happiness when she answers to all his questions, "Judge you, forsooth," and "I leave it to wisdome, and you sir."

Morose's attitude towards his nephew illustrates both these aspects of his character. After putting his intended bride successfully through the test, he breaks into a scornful tirade at the notion of Sir Dauphine's knighthood:

He would be knighted, forsooth, and thought by that meanes to raigne over me, his title must doe it: no kinsman, I will now make you bring mee the tenth lords, and the sixteenth ladies letter, kinsman; and it shall doe you no good kinsman. Your knighthood it selfe shall come on its knees, and it shall be rejected. (II,v.)

By the coup of his marriage, Morose hopes to express his contempt for all the world of lords, ladies, and courtly society, as well as his complete dominance over all members of his family. The comic irony in his situation is that he inevitably brings all his troubles on himself, because his two desires, to command and to live apart, though so closely related, cannot both be fulfilled on his terms. An ascetic hermit might live apart and rail against the court; a great lord might command absolute obedience from all around him. But Morose will make no sacrifice; he will be the ultimate of both at once. In seeking to extend his circle of dominance beyond his servant and his barber to include a wife, he brings in upon himself the torrent of courtly commotion from which he has fled. In seeking to make his power over his nephew aboslute, he loses all. When Dauphine says to him at the end of the play, "Now you may goe in and rest, be as private as you will, sir," his sarcastic words may seem more than a little cruel, but it is the logic of the world that decrees Morose's sentence. He can be "private" only when he gives up all pretense of being an absolute autocrat, and this he has just done by submitting himself humbly to his nephew's will and judgment.

The other material in the play consists largely of a set of mirrors which, by reflecting various aspects of this central situation, extend its significance. The Collegiate Ladies, for example, are embodiments of all the courtly vices and affectations which Morose lumps under the heading of "female noise." The most prominent feature of their composite portrait is, in Morose's words, that they "affect to seem judicious." As Truewit says in the first act,

[They are] an order betweene courtiers, and country-madames, that live from their husbands; and give entertainement to all the Wits, and Braveries o' the time, as they call 'hem: crie downe, or up, what they like, or dislike in a braine, or a fashion, with most masculine, or rather hermaphroditicall authoritie. (I,i.)

The Collegiates are thus an appropriate part of the flood of noise that pours in upon Morose after the wedding through which he had hoped to assert his masculine dominance and to declare his independence from all courtliness. The ladies' pretense to authority is just as absurd as Morose's. This is demonstrated in Act IV by the disgrace of the two knights whom they had cried up as wits and braveries, and especially by the ease with which the ladies can be turned from one opinion to its exact opposite, from idolizing the two knights to despising them, from despising Dauphine to being infatuated with him. As Truewit says, his tricks prove that

all their actions are governed by crude opinion, without reason or cause; they know not why they doe any thing: but as they are inform'd, beleeve, judge, praise, condemne, love, hate, and in aemulation one of another, doe all these things alike. (IV,vi).

Sir John Daw and Sir Amorous La Foole are the male representatives of the affected courtliness which Morose despises. In contrast to the three ladies, these two have separate identities at the beginning, though they are merged into a composite portrait as the action progresses. Sir John is the "wit" or fool intellectual, Sir Amorous the "bravery" or fool social. Jonson had treated varieties of both in earlier plays, but he fits these into his present scheme by emphasizing in both cases the noisiness of their folly. Sir John is the "onely talking sir i'th' towne" whom Truewit dares not visit for the danger to his ears. His conversation is noise not only because it is verbose but also because it is inopportune and disorderly. He insists upon reading his wretched verses, whether or not the company desires to hear them; he pours out the names of authors in an undisciplined stream. The garrulity of Sir Amorous has similar characteristics though different subject matter. Clerimont emphasizes that this knight's pretentious courtesy respects neither place, person, nor season:

He will salute a Judge upon the bench, and a Bishop in the pulpit, a Lawyer when hee is pleading at the barre, and a Lady when shee is dauncing in a masque, and put her out. He do's give playes, and suppers, and invites his guests to 'hem, aloud, out of his windore, as they ride by in coaches. (I,iii.)

When Sir Amorous appears on the scene, he does, as Clerimont has predicted, "tell us his pedigree, now; and what meat he has to dinner; and, who are his guests; and, the whole course of his fortunes," all in one breath.

The two knights thus give a wider meaning to the notion of a

noisy man in much the same way as the Collegiates and Morose's inter-
rogation of Epicoene widen the meaning of a noisy woman. Noise
is ungentlemanly boasting about one's poetic and critical powers, about
one's family, friends, and hospitality, and, towards the end of the play,
about one's sexual powers and conquests. The one gentlemanly attribute
to which the two do not conspicuously pretend is courage on the field
of battle. We may therefore be somewhat puzzled when the main trick
against them seems to turn on their cowardice, and we sympathize
with Mrs. Doll Mavis when she defends her judgment of them by saying, "I commended but their wits, madame, and their braveries. I never
look'd toward their valours." (IV,vi.) But what has been exposed in the
mock duel is not only cowardice but pliability. Like the ladies who
admire them, the knights have no real standards for judging either
books or men, but are governed entirely by rumor and fashion. Therefore it is ridiculously easy for Truewit to persuade each knight that
the other, whose pacific disposition he should know well, is a raging
lion thirsting for his blood. If either knight had been made more on the
model of the swaggering *miles gloriosus,* the point about how easy it is
to make a fool believe the exact opposite of the obvious truth would
have been blunted.

The themes of courtly behavior, the battle between the sexes, and
the pretense to authority are intertwined with that of noise versus silence wherever one looks in the play, even in the foolish madrigals of
modesty and silence written by Sir John Daw. In the action involving
Captain and Mrs. Tom Otter, all these subjects are invested with an
atmosphere of comedy lower than that of the rest of the play. For
the salient fact about the Otters is that they are of a lower social class
than any of the other main characters. Mrs. Otter is a rich China
woman struggling for admission to the exclusive Ladies' College; Captain Tom is at home among the bulls and bears but unsure of himself
in the company of knights and wits. Here again the citizen-couple
who welcome instruction in the courtly follies are familiar figures from
Jonson's early comical satire, but the portraits are modified to fit the
thematic pattern of this play. The Collegiate Ladies may pretend to a
nice discernment in brains and fashions, but Mrs. Otter comprehends
fashionable feminism rather differently and expresses her "masculine, or
rather *hermaphroditicall* authority" more elementally by pummeling
her husband. And Captain Tom's noises are his boisterous but rather
pathetic drinking bouts, accompanied by drum and trumpet, by which

he hopes to gain a reputation among the gentry and to assert his independence from his wife. This is the comic realm of Maggie and Jiggs, the hen-pecked husband sneaking out to the corner saloon to escape his social-climbing wife, but the relationships between this farcical situation and the central one of Morose and Epicoene are clear and are emphasized at every turn. Like the characters in most Elizabethan comic sub-plots, the Otters burlesque the main action while at the same time extending its meaning toward the universal.

As the clumsy, middle-class Otters contrast with the more assured aristocrats, so all the pliable pretenders to courtliness contrast with the true gentlemen and scholars, Truewit, Clerimont, and Dauphine. Within this group of intriguers, however, there is a further important contrast. Clerimont is relatively undeveloped as a character, but the differences between Truewit and Dauphine are stressed. Truewit is boisterous and boastful about the jokes he contrives. He must have the widest possible audience; as Dauphine tells him, "This is thy extreme vanitie, now: thou think'st thou wert undone, if every jest thou mak'st were not publish'd (IV,v) Dauphine, on the other hand, moves quietly about his purposes and keeps his own counsel. Truewit characteristically invents his fun on the spur of the moment, out of the materials at hand, and is apt to promise to do something (like making all the Collegiates fall in love with Dauphine) before he has the slightest idea how it can be brought about. Dauphine's plans have been months in preparation, and he betrays little hint of his puposes until they actually have been accomplished.

The rivalry of these two for the title of master plotter runs as a subdued motive through all the action. It is most prominent in the first two acts, when Truewit's rash and suddenly conceived scheme to dissuade Morose from marrying almost upsets Dauphine's carefully laid plot. It might seem that the contrast is all in favor of the quiet, modest, but in the end more effective Dauphine. Truewit assumes too readily that he can read the entire situation at first glance, and that he can easily manipulate the stubborn Morose. He becomes almost a comic butt himself when he ridiculously tries to pretend that he has foreseen from the first the really quite unexpected consequence of his action. The denouement especially would seem to prove that Dauphine is the real master at playing chess with characters and humors, and Truewit just the bungling amateur. But Jonson is not writing a treatise after the manner of Plutarch on the virtue of silence and the folly of garrulity.

Dauphine and Truewit share the honors in the closing scene, and there is more than a little to be said throughout the play for Truewit's engaging love of good fun for its own sake as against Dauphine's colder, more practical scheming. Instead of arguing a simple thesis, Jonson is investigating another aspect of his central symbol of noise. Just as he holds a brief neither for the noise of courtly affectation nor for Morose's extreme hatred of it, so he argues neither for the noisy wit nor for the quiet wit but is content to explore the differences between them.

The essential movement of *The Silent Woman*, then, is the exploration of themes implicit in the central comic conceit of a noise-hating man married to a noisy woman. Noise and the hatred of noise take on the proportion of symbols as they are given ever-widening means by the various particulars of social satire. The play's realism and its fantastic caricature can hardly be disentangled, for they are held together firmly in the same comic structure.

Much the same things can be said of *Bartholomew Fair*, despite its even greater complexity and its different kind of surface plan. In this play, characters, actions, interests are all multiplied. If in *The Silent Woman* there are usually three separable intrigues in motion at the same time, they all have a similar pattern of development and are under the control of no more than three intriguers. But in *Bartholomew Fair* five or six actions seem always to be ripening simultaneously, there are more than a dozen intriguers, and no single pattern of development will fit all the kinds of action which the fair breeds. Jonson, however, adheres to a firm if complicated plan in devising the apparent chaos of his fair, and this play has a thematic structure much like that of *The Silent Woman*. Here again Jonson is not arguing a thesis but is investigating diverse aspects of a central problem; here again the various parts of his play are used to mirror each other; and here again the "unity of inspiration" is best expressed by a character who is a fantastic caricature, in an extremely absurd situation which is reflected by all the more "realistic" figures in the play.

The central theme is the problem of what "warrant" men have or pretend to have for their actions. The problem touches both epistemology and ethics—the questions of how we know what we think we know, and why we behave as we do. Stated thus, it is very broad indeed, but it is brought into focus by several concrete symbols of legal sanction. The Induction, for example, is built on the device of a formal contract between the playwright and the audience, giving the customers license to judge the play, but only within specified limits. The play itself opens with Proctor John Littlewit discussing a marriage license taken out by Bartholomew Cokes and Grace Wellborn, and the possession of this document becomes of centural importance not only in gulling the testy "governor" Humphrey Wasp but also in the "romantic" plot involving Grace, the two witty gallants, and Dame Purecraft.

The most important symbol of this basic theme, however, is the "warrant" which the madman Troubleall demands of almost all the characters in the fourth act. This demented former officer of the Court of Pie-Powders, who has neither appeared nor been mentioned earlier in the play. is obsessed with the necessity of documentary sanction for even the slightest action. As the watchman Bristle explains, Troubleall will do nothing unless he has first obtained a scrap of paper with Justice Overdo's name signed to it:

He will not eate a crust, nor drinke a little, nor make him in his apparell, ready. His wife, Sirreverence, cannot get him make his water, or shift his shirt, without his warrant. (IV,i.)

In Troubleall's absurd humor we have the same kind of grand, extravagant comic conceit as that provided by Morose's hatred of all noise. It is the ultimate extreme, the fantastic caricature of the widespread and not unnatural human craving for clearly defined authority, and it serves as the most significant unifying device in the play. Troubleall intervenes crucially in several of the threads of plot, settling the dispute between Grace's lovers, freeing Overdo and Busy from the stocks, and enabling Quarlous to cheat Justice Overdo and marry the rich widow Purecraft. But beyond his service as a catalyst of action, Troubleall's main function is, as his name suggests to trouble everybody as he darts suddenly on and off the stage with his embarrassing question, "Have you a warrant for what you do?" This leads to a reexamination of the motives of all the characters, a new scrutiny of what warrant they really have and what they pretend to have for their beliefs and their deeds.

Neither the outright fools nor the outright knaves are much troubled by the great question. The booby Cokes, who has never sought a reason for anything he did, exclaims scornfully, "As if a man need a warrant to lose any thing with!" And Wasp, who pretends to "judgment and knowledge of matters" but who really is just as much

motivated by irrational whim as his foolish pupil, cries out during the
game of vapours, "I have no reason, nor I will heare of no reason, nor
I will looke for no reason, and he is an Asse, that either knowes any,
or lookes for't from me." (IV,iv.) Among the knaves, Edgeworth the
cutpurse is jolted for a moment by Troubleall's question, thinking that
his villainy has been found out, but he quickly returns to planning his
next robbery. Most resolute of all is the pimp Knockem, who immediately sits down and *forges* Troubleall a warrant for whatever he
may want. As Cokes is motivated by sheer whim, so the sharpers of the
fair are motivated by sheer desire for gain, and neither feels the need
for further justification.

The watchmen Haggis and Bristle, however, who are on the fringes
of the fair's knavery, are led to reflect that Justice Overdo is "a very
parantory person" who can get very angry indeed when he has a mind
to, "and when hee is angry, be it right or wrong; hee has the Law
on's side, ever." (IV,i.) In other words, "warrant" for the watchmen is
contained entirely in the unpredictable personality of the judge whom
they serve; they have no concern with the guilt or innocence of those
whom they incarcerate, and if there is ethics behind the law, they do
not comprehend it.

Justice Overdo himself has a double function in the play. For the
watchmen and for Troubleall, his name stands as a symbol for the ultimate authority which requires no rational understanding. But as a
character in the action, Overdo has his own "warrants" for his conduct,
and they are neither irrational nor hypocritical. His motives—to protect
the innocent and reprehend the guilty—are beyond reproach; nor is his
reliance for his general ethics upon Stoic philosophy as expounded by
the Roman poets in itself anything but admirable. And he has the further laudable desire to base his judicial decisions on exact information; he will trust no spies, foolish constables, or sleepy watchmen,
but will visit the fair in disguise, to search out enormities for himself at
first hand. But for all this the Justice is completely ineffectual, because
he cannot interpret correctly what he sees, and because he fails to
differentiate between the minor vanities and major iniquities of the fair.
Many are the yearly enormities of the place, as he says, but he concentrates on the evils of bottle-ale, tobacco, and puppet shows and fails
to see the robbery and seduction going on under his nose. Even when
he taxes the right knaves, it is for the wrong crimes. Through the
characterization of Justice Overdo, Jonson seems to me to add the
warning that even the best of warrants is not in itself sufficient to insure

right action; Overdo is reminded at the end that his first name is Adam and he is but flesh and blood, subject to error like the rest of us. Even such admirable principles as reverence for the classics and reliance upon the facts of evidence can, if adhered to blindly, become fetishes almost as ludicrous as Troubleall's trust in a signature.

The application of the theme of warrant to Rabbi Zeal-of-the-Land Busy, who pretends to find authority for everything he does in the words of scripture but who really is motivated by the most elemental greed and gluttony, and whose ingenious discovery of theological reasons for the consumption of roast big by the faithful is perhaps the funniest scene in the entire play, need not be further elaborated. The most interesting *effects* of Troubleall's persistent questioning are those upon Dame Purecraft and upon Quarlous. The Puritan widow is seized with a frenzied desire to reform; the witty gentleman comes close to becoming an outright knave.

For Dame Purecraft, Troubleall's madness seems the only possible alternative to the life of double dealing she has been leading. She exclaims:

Mad doe they call him! the world is mad in error, but hee is mad in truth. . . . O, that I might be this yoake-fellow, and be mad with him, what a many should wee draw to madnesse in truth, with us! (IV,vi.)

"Madness in error" in the specific case of Dame Purecraft means reliance upon the Puritan interpretation of Biblical authority. In the first scene of Act iv she replied confidently to Troubleall's question, "Yes, I have a warrant out of the word." But now she admits freely that her adherence to scriptural authority was but subterfuge for wicked self-seeking, and she wants to exchange her hypocritical Puritanism for the absolute and ingenuous madness which Troubleall represents. The final irony is that she gains for a husband not a real madman but a gentleman-rogue disguised as a lunatic, Quarlous tricked out for his own selfish purposes in the clothes of Troubleall. Even the search for pure irrationality thus turns out to be futile; Dame Purecraft is yoked with the image of her former self, and her glorious repentance and conversion have been in vain.

Quarlous comes to a similar conclusion that the only choice is between knavery and madness, but he has little hesitation in choosing knavery. As he stands aside to deliberate Dame Purecraft's proposal, he reasons thus:

It is money that I want, why should I not marry the money, when 'tis offer'd mee? I have a *License* and all, it is but razing out one name, and putting in another. There's no playing with a man's fortune! I am resolv'd! I were truly mad, an' I would not! (V,ii.)

And so he proceeds not only to marry the rich widow but also to extract money by fraud from Justice Overdo, from his erstwhile friend Winwife, and from Grace, the girl for whom he has so recently declared his love. The warrant which Quarlous abandons is the code of a gentleman, including the chivalric ideals of loyalty to one's friend and undying devotion to one's mistress. But the movement of the play here as elsewhere is towards the discovery of true motives rather than towards change of character, for though Quarlous has loudly protested both love and friendship, he has never really been governed by either.

Quarlous's mode of thinking and of acting approaches more and more closely that of those absolute rogues, the inhabitants of the fair. And Quarlous is just as loud in protesting his difference from the fair people as Humphrey Wasp is in protesting his difference from his foolish pupil. Quarlous resents being greeted familiarly by such rascals as Knockem and Whit, and in a very revealing passage he first lashes out at the cutpurse Edgeworth for treating him like one of "your companions in beastlinesse." He then proceeds to find excuses for having been accessory before and after the fact to a robbery:

Goe your wayes, talke not to me, the hangman is onely fit to discourse with you. . . . I am sorry I employ'd this fellow; for he thinks me such: *Facinus quos inquinat, aequst.* But, it was for sport. And would I make it serious, the getting of this Licence is nothing to me, without other circumstances concurre. (IV, vi.)

This is a piece of rationalization worthy of the master, Rabbi Busy; and we observe with some amusement that Quarlous immediately starts taking steps to *make* the other circumstances concur through fraud.

The emphasis in *Bartholomew Fair* is thus on the narrow range of motives that actually govern men's actions, in contrast to the wide variety of warrants which they pretend to have. Notable prominence is given to primitive motivations: Busy scents after pork like a hound, both Mrs. Littlewit and Mrs. Overdo are drawn into the clutches of the pimps by the necessity for relieving themselves, and the longing of a pregnant woman is the ostensible reason which sets the whole Littlewit party in motion towards the fair. As the many hypocrisies are revealed, the only distinction which seems to hold up is that between fools and knaves, between Cokes and the rogues who prey on him. The other characters are seen as approaching more and more closely to these extremes, until all search for warrant seems as absurb as Troubleall's, since all authority is either as corrupt as the watchmen or as irrational as Wasp or as blind as Justice Overdo. Whim, animal appetite, and sordid greed have complete sway over men's actions without as well as within the fair; the fair merely provides the heightened conditions under which disguises fall off and the elemental motivations become manifest.

In both the plays we have been considering then, fantastic exaggerations like Morose's hatred of noise and Troubleall's search for a warrant provide the lenses through which the behavior of more realistically conceived characters can be observed and brought into focus. It is chiefly in his grand comic conceits that Jonson's "unity of inspiration" resides, for in them the interplay of realistic satire and fantastic caricature is most highly concentrated, and from them it does truly "radiate into plot and personages alike."

It is this interplay between realism and fantasy which seems to me the very essence of Jonson's comedy. To decry, as Herford and Simpson do, the prominence of the "farcical horror-of-noise-motive" in *The Silent Woman*, and to regret the "deep-seated contrarieties in Jonson's own artistic nature, where the bent of a great realist for truth and nature never overcame the satirist's and humorist's weakness for fantastic caricature" [9] is, I believe, seriously to misunderstand Jonson's art. His purpose was always to hold the mirror up to nature, but not simply to present the world of common experience, uncriticized and unstructured. Without the extravagant caricatures which he develops into organizing symbols, Jonson's comedy would lack not only the unity but also the universality of great art.

If Jonson's comedy is of the sort here suggested, then a comparison with Aristophanes may not be amiss. Here again we have a mingling of fantasy and realism, and here again we have a comic structure centered not on a plot but on the exploration of an extravagant conceit. Jonson has almost always been discussed as if he belonged in the tradition of Menander, Plautus, and Terence—of New Comedy. I believe that we might gain more insight into his art if we considered him instead in the quite different tradition of Old Comedy. Perhaps Jonson meant more than we have given him credit for meaning when he said of the comedy he was working to develop that it was not bound by Terentian rules but was "of a particular kind by itself, somewhat like *Vetus Comoedia*." [10]

---

[9] *Ben Jonson*, II, 76–78 (1925).
[10] Induction to *Every Man out of His Humour*.

II. 6

The Re-invented Poem: George Herbert's Alternatives[*]

HELEN VENDLER

Boston University

ONE OF the particular virtues of Herbert's poetry is its extremely provisional quality. His poems are ready at any moment to change direction or to modify attitudes. Even between the title and the first line, Herbert may rethink his position. There are lines in which the nominal experiences or subjects have suffered a sea-change, so that the poem we think we are reading turns into something quite other. The more extreme cases occur, of course, in Herbert's "surprise endings," what Valentina Poggi calls his "final twist," [1] where, as Arnold Stein says, Herbert "dismisses the structure, issues and method" of the entire poem, "rejecting the established terms" on which the poem has been constructed, as he does in "Clasping of Hands," which ends, after playing for nineteen lines on the notions of "thine" and "mine," with the exclamation, "Or rather make no Thine and Mine!" [2] In cases less abrupt, Herbert's fluid music lulls our questions: we scarcely see his oddities, or if we see them, they cease to seem odd, robed as they are in the seamless garment of his cadence. When in "Virtue," he breathes, "Sweet rose," we echo, "sweet rose," and never stop to think that nothing in the description he gives us of the rose—that it is angry in hue, that it pricks the eye of the rash beholder, that its root is ever in the

---

[*] Read at the Institute in 1969. Published in *Institute Papers: Forms of Lyric*, 1970.

[1] Valentina Poggi, *George Herbert* (Bologna, 1967), pp. 203 ff.

[2] Arnold Stein, *George Herbert's Lyrics* (Baltimore, 1968), pp. 150, 151.

grave—bears out the epithet "sweet." Is the stanza about a sweet rose, as the epithet would have us believe, or about a bitter rose? This is a minor example of Herbert's immediate critique of his own clichés ("The Collar" may serve us as a major example) and poses, in little, the problem of this essay: how can we give an accurate description of Herbert's constantly self-critical poems, which so often reject premises as soon as they are established?

Herbert's willingness to abolish his primary terms of reference or his primary emotion at the last possible moment speaks for his continually provisional conduct of the poem. After begging, for twenty lines, for God's grace to drop from above, Herbert suddenly reflects that there is, after all, another solution, equally good: if God will not descend to him, he may be brought to ascend to God:

> O come! for thou dost know the way:
> Or if to me thou wilt not move,
> Remove me, where I need not say,
> *Drop from above.*   ("Grace")

In part, this is simply the cleverness of finding a way out of a dilemma; but more truly, in Herbert's case, the ever-present alternative springs from his conviction that God's ways are not his ways—"I cannot skill of these thy wayes." If man insists on one way—that his God, for instance, drop grace on him—it is almost self-evident that God may have a different way in store to grant the request, and Herbert bends his mind to imagining what it might be—in this case, that God, instead of moving himself, should *re*move Herbert. The pun in the "solution" shows verbally the pairing of alternatives to accomplish the same object. Precision is all, and when Herbert catches himself in careless speech, he turns on himself with a vengeance. In "Giddinesse," human beings are reproved for fickleness, and God is asked, first, to "mend" us; but no, we are beyond mending, and so Herbert must ask God to "make" us anew; but no, one creation will not suffice—God will have to "remake" us daily, since we sin daily:

> Lord, *mend*
> or rather *make* us; one creation/ Will not suffice our turn;
> Except thou *make us dayly*, we shall spurn
>   Our own salvation.

Equally, when Herbert finds himself lapsing into frigid pulpit oratory, he pulls himself up sharply from his clichés about "Man" and in the

last breath turns inward, "My God, I mean myself." These second
thoughts are everywhere in Herbert. The wanton lover, he says, can
expend himself ceaselessly in praising his beloved; why does not the
poet do the same for God? "Lord, cleare thy gift," he asks in "Dulnesse," "that with a constant wit/ I may—" May what? we ask, and if
we continue the analogy we would say, "That I may love and praise
thee as lovers their mistresses." Something like this must have passed
through Herbert's mind, and have been rejected as overweening, so that
instead he writes:

> Lord, cleare thy gift, that with a constant wit
> I may but look towards thee:
> Look only; for to love thee, who can be,
>   What angel fit?

The italics on "look" and "love" show Herbert, as it were, doing the
revision of his poem in public, substituting the tentative alternative
for the complacent one. He takes into account our expectation,
prompted by his analogy with lovers, of the word "love," and rebukes
himself and us for daring to ask such a divine gift. The proper reading
of the poem must realize both the silent expectation and the rebuke,
as Herbert changes his mind at the last moment.

Some of Herbert's most marked and beautiful effects come from
this constant re-invention of his way. One of the most spectacular of
these occurs in "A True Hymne": Herbert has been praising the
faithful heart over the instructed wit, and says:

> The fineness which a hymne or psalme affords,
> Is, when the soul unto the lines accords.
>
> . . . If th'heart be moved,
> Although the verse be somewhat scant,
>   God doth supply the want.

He then gives us an example of God's supplying the want:

> As, when th'heart sayes (sighing to be approved)
> O, could I love! and stops: God writeth—

Logically, what God should write to reassure the soul, is Thou dost love.
To wish to love is to love; but to love God, Herbert bethinks himself,
is first to have been loved by God (as he tells us in the first "Affliction")
and so God, instead of ratifying the soul's wish, O could I love! by

changing it from the optative to the declarative, changes instead the soul from subject to object, and writes *Loved*. If we do not intuit, as in "Dulnesse," the "logical" ending *Thou dost love*, we cannot see how Herbert has refused a banal logic in favor of a truer metaphysical illogic, conceived of at the last possible utterance of the poem. He stops in his course, veers round, writes *Loved*, and ends the poem in what is at once a better pride and a better humility.

What does this mean about Herbert's mind, this rethinking of the poem at every moment? It means that he allows his moods free play and knows that logic is fallible: one may want one thing today and quite another on the Last Day, for instance. When Herbert is tormented in turn by the jeering of worldly Beauty, Money, Glory, and Wit, he remains silent, but says in his heart that on the Last Day he will be revenged, when his God will answer his tormentors for him: "But thou shalt answer, Lord, for me." And yet, as soon as he truly thinks of that scene on the Last Day, he re-invents it: the last stanza of "The Quip" shows Herbert's God, not vindicating at large the now-triumphant soul, not administering an anathema to the defeated worldly glories, but engaging in an almost silent colloquy alone with the faithful soul:

> Yet when the houre of thy designe
> To answer these fine things shall come;
> Speak not at large; say, I am thine:
> And then they have their answer home.

When we hear, in "Love Unknown," of God's wishes for Herbert (which of course amount to Herbert's best wishes for himself) we learn that "Each day, each houre, each moment of the week,/ [He] fain would have [him] be new, tender, quick." Nothing is to be taken for granted, nothing should be habitual, nothing should be predictable: every day, every hour, every moment things have to be thought through again, and the surface of the heart must be renewed, quickened, mended, suppled.

An accurate description of Herbert's work implies a recognition of where his true originality lies. A few years ago this was the subject of some debate between William Empson and Rosemond Tuve, when Empson claimed as "original" images which Miss Tuve proved traditional in iconographic usage. Empson retorted that traditional images could nevertheless bear a significant unconscious meaning, and that choice of image in itself was indicative, a statement which deserves more attention. The attic of "tradition" is plundered differently by different poets, and each poet decides what décor he will choose from the Christian storehouse in order to deck his stanzas. Though every single image in a poem may be "traditional," the choice of emphasis and exclusion is individual and revealing. Herbert, of course, often begins poems with, or bases poems upon, a traditional image or scene or prayer or liturgical act or biblical quotation; and our knowledge of these bases has been deepened by Miss Tuve's book. But a question crying out to be answered is what he makes of the traditional base. A similar question would ask what he does with the experiential *donnée*, personal rather than "traditional," of an autobiographical poem. In short, what are some of Herbert's characteristic ways of "conducting" a poem? My answer, in general, appears in my title, and in the examples I have so far offered: Herbert "re-invents" the poem afresh as he goes along; he is constantly criticizing what he has already written down, and finding the original conception inadequate, whether the original conception be the Church's, the Bible's, or his own. Nothing is exempt from his critical eye, when he is at his best, and there is almost no cliché of religious expression or personal experience that he does not reject after being tempted into expressing it. A poem by Herbert is often "written" three times over, with several different, successive, and self-contradictory versions co-existing. A different sort of poet would have written one version, have felt dissatisfied with the truth or accuracy of the account, would then have written a second, more satisfactory version, have rethought that stage, and have produced at last a "truthful" poem. Herbert prefers to let his successive "rethinkings" and re-inventions follow one another, but without warning us of the discrepancies among his several accounts, just as he followed his original qualification of the rose as sweet with a long description of the rose as bitter, without any of the usual "buts" or "yets" of semantic contradiction. (I should add that the evidence we have in the Williams manuscript, which gives Herbert's revisions of some poems, supports these conjectures on Herbert's rethinking of his lines, but what I wish to emphasize is not his revisions before he reached a final version but rather the re-invention of the poem as it unfolds itself.)

The rest of this essay will be concerned with larger examples of Herbert's re-inventing of different sorts; and I begin with a combination of the liturgical, the ethical, and the biblical, in the poem called "The Invitation." In this poem, Herbert the priest is inviting sinners to the sacraments. He is probably remembering, in the beginning, St. Paul's statement (in Romans 14:21) that it is good neither to eat flesh nor to drink wine, and he begins his invitation with the Pauline view of sinners as prodigal gluttons and winebibbers, whose taste is their waste, and who are defined by wine:

> Come ye hither All, whose taste
>   Is your waste;
> Save your cost, and mend your fare.
>   . . .
> Come ye hither All, whom wine
>   Doth define,
> Naming you not to your good.

For Herbert, though, St. Paul's revulsion is not congenial; Herbert, who "knows the ways of pleasure" and knows as well the pains of remorse, begins to alter his portrait of swinish and sensual sinners in a remarkable way. In the third stanza, the sinners become "All, whom pain/ Doth arraigne"; in the fourth stanza they are people who are misled by their delight to graze outside their bounds; and by the astonishing fifth stanza the sinners are positively seraphic:

> Come hither All, whose love
>   Is your dove,
> And exalts you to the skie:
> Here is love, which having breath
>   Ev'n in death,
> After death can never die.

Sinners, in fact, are finally seen in the poem as people with all the right instincts—they want joy, delight, exaltation, and love; and that, Herbert implies, is what the redeemed want too. The sinners, misled in their desires, seek the carnal and the temporary, Venus's doves instead of the Holy Spirit, sky instead of heaven. The equation of wants in saints and sinners permits Herbert's final startling stanza:

> Lord, I have invited all . . .
> For it seems but just and right
>   In my sight,
> Where is All, there All should be.

The liturgical "dignum et justum est" and the verbally indistinguishable "All"'s (both capitalized) give the sinners a final redeemed and almost divine place at the banquet. The poem amounts, though implicitly, to a total critique of the usual scorn toward sinners, a scorn which Herbert himself began with, but which in the course of the poem he silently rejects. He makes no announcement of his rejection as he changes his view, and therefore we are likely to miss it, as we miss other changes of mind in his poems. Nevertheless, over and over, Herbert re-invents what he has received and embraced, correcting it to suit his own corrected notions of reality.[3]

Our received notion of Doomsday, for instance, is a severe one, the Dies Irae when the whole world, as Herbert says elsewhere, will turn to coal. That day is sometimes thought of from God's point of view, as when we say, "He shall come to judge the living and the dead," or from the human point of view (as when St. Paul says, "We shall be changed, be raised incorruptible"), but Herbert chooses to think of it via the fanciful construct of the emotions felt by the bodies already-dead-but-not-yet-raised, unhappy in their posthumous insensibility, imprisonment, noisomeness, fragmentation, and decay. The "fancy" behind the poem is that it is not so much God who awaits the Last Day, nor is it those on earth who wish to put on immortality, nor is it the disembodied souls in heaven, but rather it is those poor soulless corrupting bodies confined in their graves. It is they who really yearn after a lively and sociable Judgment Day, when they can each "jog the other, each one whispring, *Live you, brother?*" A poem like this begins with a poet thinking not "What are the traditions about Doomsday?" but rather, "I know what is usually said about Doomsday, but what would it really be like, and who really longs for it?" Herbert's poem is very different from Donne's more conventional "At the round earth's imagined corners, blow/ Your trumpets, Angels, and arise, arise/ From death, you numberless infinities/ Of souls," a poem in which we at once recognize the Doomsday conventions at work.

Herbert's corrections extend, of course, to himself as well as to his liturgical or biblical sources, and these self-corrections are his most interesting re-inventions. Some of them do not at first sight seem per-

---

[3] When John Wesley rewrote "The Invitation" for hymn-singing, he did far more than adapt the meter. (An adaptation faithful to Herbert's meaning had been made in 1697, reprinted now in *Select Hymns Taken out of Mr. Herbert's Temple* [1697], Augustan Reprint Society No. 98 [Los Angeles, 1962], pp. 31–32.) Wesley's adaptation insists on the wickedness and carnality of the sinners, intensifying in every case Herbert's description, and showing none of Herbert's changes of attitude. Wesley's version may be found in the *Collected Poetical Works of John and Charles Wesley*, ed. G. Osborn (London, 1868–69), I, 111–13.

sonal, and since these are rather deceptive, I should like to begin with one of them—his self-correction in the sonnet "Prayer." This famous poem is impersonally phrased, and is, as everyone knows, a definition poem consisting of a chain of metaphors describing prayer. "Rethinking" is in fact most likely to occur in ordinary life in just this sort of definition-attempt, but whereas in life this rethinking and refining is generally an exercise in intellectual precision, in Herbert it is an exercise in the affections. Herbert's images cannot be said to be ambiguous; they are, though sometimes recondite, in general perfectly clear. It is the whole which is complex, a something (prayer, in this instance) which can be any number of things, not only at different times, but even at once. This tolerance of several notions at once appeals to us in Herbert nowadays, just as his profusion of images appeals. As Rosemond Tuve pointed out in *Elizabethan and Metaphysical Imagery*, an attempt to make clear the logical actions or passions of a subject will all by itself engender images, as it does in "Prayer." These twenty-six or so images of prayer tell us several things. To begin with the easiest, we know the sort of prayer which is an engine against the Almighty, which reverses the Jovian thunderbolt and hurls it back at its source. It is not too much to call this the prayer of resentment uttered by the wounded soul; it is the sinner's tower (with overtones of Babel) raised against a seemingly unjust God. We have any number of these "rebellious" prayers in the Herbert canon. To pray in this indignant warlike way is scarcely a sign of perfection; it is an emanation of the lowest possible state above the outright rebellion of sin. The next easiest group of images in the poem, by all odds, is the group toward the end—the Milkie Way, the Bird of Paradise, the Land of Spices. When prayer seems like this to the soul, the soul is clearly experiencing an unearthly level of feeling quite without aggressive elements. The poem, then, arrives at this state of joy from an earlier state of anger and rebellion; so much is clear as soon as we assume a single consciousness behind the metaphors of the poem. But what, then, are we to make of the beginning of the poem, which seems neither aggressive nor exalted?

> Prayer, the Churches banquet, Angels age,
>> God's breath in man returning to his birth,
>> The soul in paraphrase, heart in pilgrimage,
> The Christian plummet sounding heav'n and earth.

In what state is the soul when it speaks these lines? It must be a state which precedes the sudden rise of injured "virtue" in the use of engines and thunderbolts and spears against God; it is certainly not the heavenly state of the sestet. These lines which begin the sonnet are, in fact, without affect; they are the lines of the man who sets himself to pray frigidly, out of duty, drawing his metaphors not from feeling but from doctrine. What has he been taught, theologically, in dogma, about prayer? That it is the banquet of the church, that angels determine their age by how long they have been praying, that it engages both the heart and the soul, that it is "the Christian plummet" connecting the church militant to the church triumphant. When, from these artificialities, the speaker turns to his own feelings and takes stock of his own state and lapses into his own resentment, the poem takes on human reality: what, thinks Herbert, aside from these stock phrases, is prayer really? to me? now? A weapon, a spear, against the God who cripples my projects and cross-biasses me; and the aggressive images multiply. But that weapon (in the traditional image on which the entire poem hinges), by piercing Christ's side, initiates a countermovement, not of Jovian thunder this time but of grace, an infusion transforming the workaday world into the Sabbath (or rather, a transposing not a transforming, says Herbert with his usual precision; we are not changed but glorified). Whereas earlier the man praying had been active, launching engines, building towers, piercing with spears, he now relaxes in an ecstasy of passivity; prayer becomes a constellation of experienced essences, "softness and peace and joy and love and bliss." But Herbert cannot rest in that passivity of sensation; with a remarkable energy he introduces, again just as the poem is about to end in its celestial geography, the hitherto neglected intellect. Prayer, he says, correcting his delighted repose, is in the last analysis not simply a *datum,* something given, but a *comprehensum,* something understood. This phrase is at once the least and the most explicit in the poem. Finally the poet understands, and is no longer the frigid reciter of theological clichés, the resentful beggar, the aggressive hurler of thunderbolts, the grateful receiver of Manna, nor the seeker of a Land of Spices. As a final definition, "something understood" abolishes or expunges the need for explanatory metaphors. Metaphor, Herbert seems to say, is after all only an approximation; once something is understood, we can fall silent; once the successive rethinkings of the definition have been made, and the truth has been arrived at, the poem is over.

To arrive at that truth, to be able to end the poem, is often difficult. "The Temper" (I) has to try three different endings before it succeeds in ending itself satisfactorily, or at least to Herbert's satisfaction. He has complained that God is stretching him too hard, subjecting him to exaltations succeeded by depressions:

> O rack me not to such a vast extent!
> Those distances belong to thee.

God's stretching and then contracting him suggests to Herbert another image, not this time the rack but another image of equal tension, introduced with a characteristic concessive "yet"—

> Yet take thy way; for sure thy way is best:
> Stretch or contract me, thy poore debter:
> This is but tuning of my breast,
> To make the musick better.

If Herbert had been content (as he sometimes could be) with resolution on an easy level, there it was. Herbert's pain does not diminish, but he has found a new vision of God to explain it by: God is no longer the inquisitor torturing his victim on the rack; he is rather the temperer, the tuner of Herbert's heartstrings. The ending is adequate enough, and in fact Herbert's unknown adapter of 1697 stopped here, deleting Herbert's final stanza: to him the poem was finished, since Herbert had rediscovered the true "corrective" meaning of suffering.[4] But for Herbert the poem was not finished. The image of tuning still adhered to the poem's original primitive and anthropocentric notion of being stretched, of being first lifted by God to heaven and then dashed to earth. From a more celestial point of view, of course, heaven and earth are equally in God's presence and of his making, so Herbert repents of his short-sightedness, and invents a brilliant coda to his poem, expunging all its former terms of spatial reference:

> Whether I flie with angels, fall with dust,
> Thy hands made both, and I am there.

The compact use of the one adverb—"there"—to stand for two places, heaven and earth, because both were made by God's hands, seems yet another final resolution of the distances in the poem. Still, Herbert is not satisfied. He continues with what seems at first to be a reiteration; we expect him to say that God's power makes everywhere, heaven and earth alike, one place. Instead, he says the reverse:

[4] *Select Hymns*, p. 13.

Thy power and love, my love and trust,
Make one place everywhere.

In short, Herbert first rewrote racking as tuning, then he rewrote
distance as unity ("there"), and then he rewrote unity ("one place")
as immensity ("everywhere"). We should not forget that he was re-
writing at the same time the cause of this transformation: at first everything was his God's doing, but at the penultimate line the change becomes a cooperative act in which two loves intersect, and God's power
is conjoined with man's trust.

In addition to correcting himself, whether in the impersonal terms
of "Prayer" or in the terms of repeated experience in "The Temper,"
Herbert corrects his autobiography, as usual not flaunting his re-inventions. They are for us usually the discoveries of a second reading, since
at first we take them wholly for granted. The blandness of most critical
paraphrase of Herbert indicates that readers have been misled by the
perfect grace of the finished poem, and have concluded that an uninterrupted cadence means an uninterrupted ripple of thought. Herbert
knew better: he said his thoughts were all a case of knives. The wounds
of those knives are clearest in the autobiographical poems, those three
great statements—"Affliction" (I), "The Flower," and "The Forerunners." In "The Forerunners," the simplest of the three, Herbert complains that in age he is losing his poetic powers, and he offers several
alternative explanations of the loss, which a more anxious poet would
be at pains to reconcile with each other. Herbert simply lets them
stand; truth, not coherence, is his object. First, the harbingers of age
come and evict his "sparkling notions," who are of course guiltless since
they are forcibly "disparked." They and Herbert suffer together. Next
it seems as though the "sweet phrases, lovely metaphors," are not being
evicted but are leaving of their own free will; echoing Wyatt, Herbert
asks reproachfully, "But will ye leave me thus?" accusing them of ingratitude after all his care of them. Next, they are no longer ungrateful
children leaving home but rather fully of age, seduced virgins: "Has
some fond lover tic'd thee to thy bane?" Finally, they are debased,
willingly prostituting themselves in the service of the lover who loves
dung, and, in Herbert's last bitterness, even their essence and power are
denied them. They are no longer creative "enchanting" forces but only
"embellishments" of meaning. There is no resolution to these successive
metaphors of loss—no comprehensive view is taken at the end, and we
suffer with Herbert the final pretended repudiation of those servants

who have in fact deserted him. His powerful love of his "beauteous words" has its own independent force within the poem, but so does his gloomy denial of value to those words at the end. The only true critical description of poems such as this must be a successive one; a global description is bound to be misleading.

"Affliction" (I) is too long a poem to be taken up in detail here, but it, like "The Forerunners," depends on a series of inconsistent metaphors for a single phenomenon, God's treatment of his creature. Herbert's ingenuity is matched only by his frankness. His God is at first a seducer, "enticing" Herbert's heart; next he is a sovereign distributing "gracious benefits," then an enchanter "bewitching" Herbert into his family; he is an honest wage-paying master; he is a king dispensing hope of high pleasure; he is a mother, indulgent:

> At first thou gav'st me milk and sweetnesses;
> I had my wish and way.

But then God becomes one who inflicts sickness, and the poet groans with the psalmist, "Sicknesses cleave my bones." Worse, God becomes a murderer—"Thou took'st away my life"—and an unfair murderer at that, leaving his creature with no means of suitably vengeful retaliation —"A blunted knife/ Was of more use than I." God sends famine, and Herbert becomes one of Pharaoh's lean kine: "Thus thinne and lean without a fence or friend,/ I was blown through with ev'ry storm and winde." In two lines of sinister genius, God is said to "betray" Herbert to paralysis (a "lingring" book) and death (he "wraps" Herbert in an unmistakably shroudlike gown). Next, God becomes a physician, deluding Herbert with his "sweetned pill," but then cruelly undoing his own healing, he "throws" Herbert into more sicknesses. God's last action seems his wickedest, surpassing all his previous enticements and tortures; he "clean forgets" his poet, and the abandonment is worse than the attention. These indictments of God are only one strain in this complaint, with its personal hesitations, accusations, self-justifications, and remorse, but they show Herbert's care and accuracy in describing his own notions of God as they changed from episode to episode. There is a remarkable lack of censorship; even with the Psalms as precedent, Herbert shows his absolute willingness to say how things were, to choose the accurate verb, to follow the truth of feeling. We can only guess at Herbert's inconsistencies of self-esteem which underlie the inconsistencies in this portrait of God. This God, changeable as the skies, first lightning then love and then lightning again, is reflected from a self first proud then craven and then proud again, a self which does not know whether it is a child or a victim or a dupe, a self for whom all self-assertion provoked a backwash of guilt.

With that guilt came a sense of God's absence, and that experience, habitual with Herbert, is the central topic of the third of these autobiographical poems, "The Flower." Just as the sonnet "Prayer" had redefined, over and over, with increasing approximation to the truth, what prayer is, so "The Flower" redefines, over and over, with increasing approximation to the truth, what has in fact been happening to Herbert. We are told that he has suffered a period of God's disfavor, during which he drooped, but that God has now returned to him and so he flourishes once again. This simple two-stage event could have been told, presumably, in a simple chronological account; but no, we are given several versions of the experience undergone. It is this repetitiveness, incidentally, here and elsewhere in Herbert, which caused George Herbert Palmer to class this poem together with others as redundant, lacking that fineness of structure he saw in Herbert's simpler two-part and three-part poems.[5] The redundancy is apparent, but not real; each time the experience is redescribed, it is altered, and each retelling is a critique of the one before.

The first version of Herbert's experience is a syntactically impersonal one, told without the "I": Herbert could be meditating on some universally known phenomenon:

> How fresh, O Lord, how sweet and clean
> Are thy returns! ev'n as the flowers in spring;
>   To which, besides their own demean,
> The late-past frosts tributes of pleasure being.
>   Grief melts away
>   Like snow in May
>   As if there were no such cold thing.

Now these last three lines say something not strictly true. We do keep a memory of grief. But in the first flush of reconciliation, Herbert generously says that God has obliterated all past grief in the soul. This version of the incident also says that God has been absent and has now returned, just as spring absents itself and then returns, in a natural cyclical process. We, and Herbert, shall discover in the course of the poem how

5 George Herbert Palmer, ed., *The Works of George Herbert* (Boston, 1905), I, 144.

untrue these statements, about the cyclical absence of God and the obliteration of grief, are.

The second stanza gives us yet another, and almost equally rosy, view of Herbert's experience, this time in the first person:

> Who would have thought my shrivel'd heart
> Could have recover'd greennesse? It was gone
>   Quite under ground; as flowers depart
> To see their mother-root, when they have blown;
>   Where they together,
>   All the hard weather
> Dead to the world, keep house unknown.

Here the period of grief is represented as, after all, not so difficult; it was not God who went away, really, but rather Herbert; and his absence was on the whole cosy, like the winter hibernation of bulbs, where the flowers, in comfortable company, visiting their mother the root, keep house together with her, while the weather is harsh aboveground. This certainly does not sound like a description of grief, but like a situation of sociable comfort; the only ominous word here, keeping us in touch with the truth, is "shrivel'd," which sorts very ill with the familial underground housekeeping.

So far, a cloak of palliation lies over the truth. But when Herbert has to summarize what this experience of grief followed by joy has taught him, he admits that he finds the God who lies behind such alternations of emotion an arbitrary and incomprehensible one, who one day kills (a far cry from absenting himself) and another day quickens, all by a word, an absolute fiat. We are helpless to predict God's actions or to describe his intent; we await, defenseless, his unintelligible decisions, his arbitrary power:

> These are thy wonders, Lord of power,
> Killing and quickning, bringing down to hell
>   And up to heaven in an houre;
> Making a chiming of a passing-bell.
>   We say amisse,
>   This or that is:
> Thy word is all, if we could spell.

An early anthologist of Herbert cut off the poem here; [6] for him, and we may suspect for George Herbert Palmer, too, the poem might just

---

[6] James Montgomery, *The Christian Poet* (Glasgow, 1827), pp. 243–44.

as well have ended with this summarizing stanza. For Herbert, it could not; he has presented us with too many contradictions. Does God absent himself cyclically, like the spring, or arbitrarily and unpredictably? Is God only benevolent, or in fact a malevolent killer as well? Was it he that was absent, or Herbert? Was the period of absence one of hellish grief or one of sociable retirement? The poem had begun in earthly joy, but now, with the admission that we cannot spell and that God's word is arbitrary and incomprehensible, Herbert's resentment of his earthly condition has gained the ascendancy, and he repudiates wholly the endless emotional cycles of mortal life:

> O that I once past changing were,
> Fast in thy Paradise, where no flower can wither!

Not God's changeableness, but his own, is now the issue; the "withering" and "shriveling" are now uppermost in his mind, as his past grief, tenacious in memory and not at all melted away, comes once again to his mind.

Yet once more, for the fourth time, he recapitulates his experience. This time he does it in the habitual mode, the present tense of habit, emphasizing its deadly repetitiveness:

> Many a spring I shoot up fair,
> Offring at heav'n, growing and groning thither. . . .

> But while I grow in a straight line,
> Still upwards bent, as if heav'n were mine own,
> Thy anger comes, and I decline.

This habitual recapitulation leads Herbert to realize that his God's actions are in fact not arbitrary, as he had earlier proposed, but that his punishments come for a reason: Herbert has been presumptuous in growing upwards as if Heaven were his own, and therefore he has drawn God's terrible cold wrath upon him. We must stop to ask whether this confession of guilt on Herbert's part is in fact a realization or an invention. The intolerable notion of an arbitrary and occasionally malevolent God almost necessitates the invention of a human fault to explain these punishments. That is Herbert's dilemma; either he is guilty, and therefore deservedly punished, or he is innocent, and God is arbitrary. Faced with such a choice, he decides for his own guilt. We cannot miss the tentative sexuality of his "budding" and "shooting up" and later "swelling"—one question the poem puts is whether such self-assertion can ever be guiltless, or whether every swelling is followed by a punishing shriveling. The answer of the poem is equivocal; his present "budding" seems innocent enough, but the inevitable alternation of spring and winter in the poem, of spring showers and icy frowns, tells us that we may always expect God's wrath. When that wrath directs itself upon the sinner,

> What frost to that? What pole is not the zone
>> Where all things burn,
>> When thou dost turn,
> And the least frown of thine is shown?

There is no more talk about keeping house snugly underground through all the hard weather. Herbert, on the contrary, has been nakedly exposed to the hard weather, has felt the freezing cold, has felt the tempests of God. The truth is out; he *has* suffered, and he still remembers his grief. Oddly, once the truth is out, Herbert has no more wish to reproach his God; he feels happier considering himself as guilty than indicting God. It is not God, he says, who is arbitrary and capricious, but we; his actions only follow ours; he is changeless, and we are the changeable ones. Herbert, having put off the old man, scarcely recognizes himself in the new man he has become:

> And now in age I bud again;
> After so many deaths I live and write;
> I once more smell the dew and rain,
> And relish versing: O my only light,
>> It cannot be
>> That I am he
> On whom thy tempests fell all night.

In the unearthly relief of this stanza, Herbert returns to the human norm. His two constant temptations are to be an angel or a plant, but the second half of "The Flower," like the second half of "Prayer," is the discovery of human truth after the self-deceptive first half. With the unforced expression of relief, Herbert can acknowledge that in truth he was not comfortably visiting underground, but was in fact being beaten by tempests. The paradisal experience of "budding again," like any paradisal experience in life, is in fact forfeit if the reality of past grief is denied: the sharpened senses that once more smell the dew and rain are those of a Lazarus newly emerged from the sepulchre; to deny the cerements is to deny the resurrection. At this point, Herbert can engage in genuine "wonder." The previous "These are thy wonders, Lord of power," may be translated "These are thy tyrannies," but now that Herbert has assuaged his anxiety by deciding that power is not arbitrary and perverse but rather solicitous and redemptive, he can say, "These are thy wonders, Lord of love." The poem is one of perfect symmetry, marked by the two poles of "wonder"; it is redundant, if one wishes to call it that, in circling back again and again to the same experience, but each time it puts that experience differently.

The end of the poem embodies yet another self-reproof on Herbert's part, put this time as a warning to all who, like himself, may have been presumptuous in thinking heaven their own:

> These are thy wonders, Lord of love,
> To make us see we are but flowers that glide:
> Which, when we once can finde and prove,
> Thou hast a garden for us, where to bide.
>   Who would be more,
>   Swelling through store,
> Forfeit their Paradise by their pride.

This homiletic neatness is probably a flaw in the poem, and the very harsh judgment which Herbert passes, in this impersonal and universal way, on his earlier presumption makes this one of the comparatively rare Herbert poems with an "unhappy" ending. Since the fundamental experience of the poem is one of resurrection, and since the best lines of the poem express that sense of renewal, we may reasonably ask why these last lines are so grim. They are so, I think, because of the two truths of experience at war in the poem. One is the immediate truth of renewal and rebirth; the other is the remoter, but larger, truth of repeated self-assertion, repeated guilt, repeated punishment. Until we are "fast in Paradise," the poem tells us, we are caught in the variability of mortal life, in which, however intense renewal may be when it comes, it comes uncertainly and not for long. Intellectually, the prospect is depressing, with innocence and relish spoiled by guilt and punishment. The hell of life may continue into a hell after life. But this, since it is an intellectual conclusion, cannot fundamentally damage the wonderful sense of restored life which has made this poem famous. It speaks, however, for Herbert's grim fidelity to fact that he will not submerge the gloomy truth in the springlike experience.

The inveterate human tendency to misrepresent what has happened is nowhere more strongly criticized than in Herbert. Under his repetitive and unsparing review, all the truths finally become clear. Herbert knows that to appear pious is not to be pious; to pay formal tribute is not to love; to servilely acknowledge power is not to wonder; to utter grievances is not to pray. His readers, often mistaking the language of piety for the thing itself, are hampered by dealing with an unfamiliar discourse. We have a very rich sense of social deception in human society and can detect a note of social falseness in a novel almost before it appears; but it sometimes does not occur to us that the same equivocations, falsenesses, self-justifications, evasions, skirtings, and defensive reactions can occur in a poet's colloquies with his God. We recognize defiance when it is overt, as in "The Collar" or the first "Affliction," but other poems where the presentation is more subtle elicit bland readings and token nods to Herbert's sweetness or humility. Herbert spoke of himself as "a wonder tortur'd" and his own estimate of himself can be a guide in reading his poems.

Even in that last and most quietly worded poem, "Love," which is spoken in retrospect by the regenerate soul from the vantage point of the something understood, the old false modesty lingers. There is, as Herbert says elsewhere, no articling with God, but in this poem the soul is still refusing, in William James's words, to give up the assertion of the "little private convulsive self." [7] When Herbert catches glimpses of God's order, which we may if we wish call the best order he can imagine for himself, he finds it almost unnatural, odd—even comic. His impulse is to deny that he has any connection with such a disturbing reordering of the universe, to feel a sense of strain in attempting to accommodate himself to it, and at best, he prays that his God will remake him to fit in with that scheme, if he please: "Lord, mend or rather make us." But sometimes Herbert rejects this claim on God's indulgence. At his best, and at our best, says Herbert, God refuses to indulge the view we like to take of ourselves as hopelessly and irremediably marred and ignorant creatures. Herbert's protests that he is not capable of glory are not catered to; instead of a gentle solicitude by God, he is confronted by an equally gentle but irreducible immobility. Each of his claims to imperfection is firmly, lovingly, and even wittily put aside, and he is forced to accept God's image of him as a guest worthy of his table. What Herbert wants is to linger in the antechambers, to serve, to adopt any guise except the demanding glory of the wedding garment, but Love is inflexible, and the initial "humility" of the Guest is revealed as a delusive

---

[7] William James, *Varieties of Religious Experience* (Boston, 1902), Ch. IV.

fond clinging to his mortal dust and sin. Herbert's God asks that he be more than what he conceives himself to be. Herbert invented this sort of God, we may say, to embody the demands that his own conscience put upon him, a conscience formed by that "severa parens" his mother. But even in such a brief poem as "Love," Herbert's originality in transforming his sources, in re-inventing his topic, strikes us forcibly. We know that the poem depends on St. Luke's description of Jesus' making his disciples sit while he served them, and on the words of the centurion transferred to the Anglican communion service, "Lord, I am not worthy that thou shouldst enter under my roof," and on Southwell's "S. Peter's Complaint" (cxviii), in which St. Peter knocks on sorrow's door and announces himself as "one, unworthy to be knowne." We also know, from Joseph Summers, that Herbert's actual topic is the entrance of the redeemed soul into Paradise. Now, so far as I know, this entrance has been thought of as an unhesitating and joyful passage, from "Come, ye blessed of my father," to "The Saints go marching in." The link between St. Peter knocking at a door and a soul knocking at St. Peter's door is clear, but it is Herbert's brilliance to have the soul give St. Peter's abject response, and stand hesitant and guilty on the threshold, just as it is a mark of his genius to have the soul, instead of being the unworthy host at communion, be the unworthy guest in heaven. When we first read "Love," it strikes us as exquisitely natural and humanly plausible; it is only later that the originality of conception takes us aback. As in "Doomsday," Herbert looks at the event as it *really* would be, not as tradition has always told us it would be. If the redeemed soul could speak posthumously to us and tell us what its entrance into heaven was really like, what would it say? and so the process of re-invention begins.

Herbert's restless criticizing tendency coexists with an extreme readiness to begin with the cliché—roses are sweet, redeemed souls flock willingly to a heavenly banquet, sinners are swinish, Doomsday is awesome, past grief was really not too painful. On the cliché is appliquéd the critique—roses are bitter and smarting, the soul would in reality draw back from Love's table, sinners are, in desire, indistinguishable from saints, Doomsday would in fact be agreeably social, past grief was, if truth be told, intolerable. It makes very little difference to Herbert where he finds his *donnée*—in the clichés of courtly poetry, in the Bible, in his personal experience. The artless borrowed beginning becomes very soon the scrutinized personal statement. The anxiety which must have made Herbert want to begin with the safe, the bland, the familiar, and the taken-for-granted coexists permanently with the aggression which impels him almost immediately to criticize the received idea. He seems to have existed in a permanent reversible equilibrium between the two extremes of tradition and originality, diffidence and protest, the filial and the egotistic. His poems do not "resolve" these extremes into one attitude; rather they permit successive, and often mutually contradictory, expressions of the self as it explores the truth of feeling. At any moment, a poem by Herbert can repudiate itself, correct itself, rephrase itself, rethink its experience, re-invent its topic, and it is in this free play of ideas that at least part of Herbert's true originality lies.[8]

[8] I am grateful to the American Philosophical Society for a Grant-in-Aid which assisted the research for this essay.

II. 7

A Mask Presented at Ludlow Castle: The Masque as a Masque*

C. L. BARBER

Indiana University

TWO QUESTIONS have confronted me in reading Milton's Ludlow *Mask*. How does Milton succeed—and I feel he does succeed—in making a happy work which centers, seemingly, on the denial of impulse, when typically in the Renaissance such works involve, in some fashion or other, release from restraint? Second, what is the form of the piece? how does it relate to Renaissance comedy and allied traditions? The answer to the question about its form, with which I shall begin, will I hope provide means for understanding how it orders and satisfies feeling.

I. THE FORM OF THE MASQUE AS A NOBLE ENTERTAINMENT

The *work* of criticism, as against the pleasure, is in good part the altering of expectations to suit the thing in hand. My experience with *A Mask Presented at Ludlow Castle* has been a case in point: it has involved giving up expectations of drama for expectations appropriate to the masque. Invited to consider Milton's masque as comedy, I report back after six months that Milton's masque is a masque! This shift in expectation has permitted me, I think, to get past difficulties which were fundamentally the same as those which Johnson expressed with his usual candor. "A work more truly poetical is rarely found," he said, but went on to object that it is not dramatic:

* Read at the Institute in 1964. Published in *Institute Papers: The Lyric and Dramatic Milton*, 1965.

The discourse of the Spirit is too long—an objection that may be made to almost all of the following speeches; they have not the sprightliness of a dialogue animated by reciprocal contention, but seem rather declamations deliberately composed, and formally repeated, on a moral question. The auditor therefore listens to a lecture, without passion, without anxiety.

. . . At last the Brothers enter, with too much tranquility; and when they have feared lest their sister should be in danger, and hoped she is not in danger, the Elder makes a speech in praise of chastity, and the Younger finds how fine it is to be a philosopher.

Then descends the Spirit in the form of a shepherd, and the Brother, instead of being in haste to ask his help, praises his singing, and inquires his business in that place. It is remarkable, that at this interview the Brother is taken with a short fit of rhyming. The Spirit relates that the Lady is in the power of Comus; the brother moralises again; and the Spirit makes a long narration, of no use because it is false, and therefore unsuitable for a good being.[1]

I decided to quote Johnson when it struck me that his mocking summary of the plot is just like the fun people make of operas when they do not understand how opera works, or are sick of it. All they have to do is recite the plot. "The Brother, instead of being in haste to ask [the shepherd's] help, praises his singing. . . . It is remarkable, that at this interview the Brother is taken with a short fit of rhyming." It is indeed remarkable—the rhyme has a formal, musical function to which Johnson is turning a deaf ear:

> 2 BRO. O brother, 'tis my father's shepherd sure.
> EL. BRO. Thyrsis? Whose artful strains have oft delaid
> The huddling brook to hear his madrigal,
> And sweeten'd every muskrose of the dale,
> How cam'st thou here good swain? hath any ram
> Slip't from the fold, or young kid lost his dam? [2]

Mr. Hardy, in the Brooks and Hardy study, finds this moment of recognition "one of exquisite dramatic irony," and goes after the Elder Brother, who he says "greets his father's hired man with easy condescension," while ironically "the Spirit plays his assumed role dutifully." [3] Throughout his elaborate treatment, Mr. Hardy is intent on

[1] *Lives of the English Poets* (Everyman's Library; New York, n.d.), pp. 98–99.

[2] Quotations are from *Milton's Poems 1645* (Type-facsimile; Oxford, 1924). I have corrected obvious misprints, such as the omission of the possessive in the first line here, which reads "my father Shepherd"; and I have omitted the capitalized first letters of such words as "shepherd."

[3] *Poems of Mr. John Milton: The 1645 Edition with Essays in Analysis*, by Cleanth Brooks and John Edward Hardy (New York, 1951), p. 209.

finding dramatic irony between or behind the lines. His assumption is that, to save the piece from being silly or flat in the way that Johnson thought it, we must find character, drama, irony. There *is* irony and drama in it, certainly. But these are not what makes it work as a whole, as I see it; it works as a whole as a masque. So in the greeting of the Elder Brother to Thyrsis, it seems to me that Mr. Hardy sees a kind of action that isn't there, ignoring the action that is taking place. What is taking place is the creation and relishing of a pastoral setting, by means of a poetry of heightened formal lyricism. The Brother's question serves to set moving in the direction of the lost lady the conventional pastoral metaphor of the strayed sheep; Thyrsis develops it by antithesis:

> I came not here on such a trivial toy
> As a stray'd ewe . . .

> But O my virgin Lady, where is she?

Dr. Johnson's high praise of the masque's poetry "as a series of lines" combines strangely with his complaint that almost all the speeches are too long—" 'Tis a very excellent piece of work, madam lady: would 'twere done!"

To consider how the masque form operates, let me begin by laying out what is almost self-evident. As drama is shaped by its changing environment, the theater, so the masque form was shaped by its extinct environment, the noble entertainment. The masque, indeed, is only one specialized form of a whole species of entertainment literature or pastime. The basic function of it all was to contribute meaning and beauty to noble persons, noble places, noble occasions. A masque was *presented*, not performed. Its basic method was to extend actuality by fiction, fictions developed out of the circumstances of the occasion and pointing back to realities. At its best, the make-believe was not merely added; it served to find or express meaning which was already essentially present, or ideally might be, should be, present. When Elizabeth visited a noble household, a distressed nymph from Ovid might rive an oak and implore the aid of Diana—in actuality Elizabeth was quite a fierce Diana in governing her ladies in waiting. The idealization tended to become flattery; the elaboration merely decorative. But the masquing could also be revelatory, exemplary, and persuasive, inviting nobility to realize an ideal in miming it.

The action common to almost all entertainments is greeting or encountering, with explanation which describes the occasion of the meeting so as to redefine the place and persons in terms of pastoral mythology and local lore. Visits or embassages were such fine opportunities that the formal court masque developed as a way of arranging for a visit where no actual visit was involved. The masquers tell of their origins and of their journey to the magnetic royal presence, present themselves in dance, are greeted in dance by undisguised lords or ladies, make their obeisance, and depart. In the Jacobean court, Inigo Jones's settings made visible the fabulous places from which and through which the visitors came. The masque became a way of environing a court ball, or "revel," with the pleasures of light opera and ballet. Jonson brought in the antimasque at court, drawing on the tradition at country entertainments of presenting pastimes of the common folk and on the satirical burlesque of the popular stage. The antimasquers are visitors too, or intruders, common and grotesque; they were usually played by professional entertainers who were proof against the obloquy of such miming, and skilled for it; the noble participants mimed beauty, virtue, deity, and the like, which is easy if one has the clothes. Their real skill, and it was a skill, was in dancing.

So majesty visited itself to realize majesty. The court masque was only possible so long as there was majesty to realize, or, in the great households, nobility. If James as a person was scarcely majestic, Jonson and Jones could make him so. Indeed the Stuart elaboration of the masque can be regarded as a compensation: Elizabeth would not have needed it all, and certainly would not have paid for it all! Under James, as Miss Welsford's fine book shows,[4] the masque was an important if precarious means of upholding the sense of a collective life consummated in magnificence at court—even while outside its charmed circle powerful elements in society were finding it irrelevant, or worse.

During the uneasy Caroline calm, Milton was, fortunately, enough a man of the age to enjoy the virtues of aristocratic courtesy and the courteous art of the masque. But, of course, he also felt responsible to a wider frame. In *Arcades* he wrote "part of an entertainment presented to the Countess Dowager of Darby at Harefield."

Look, nymphs, and shepherds, look,
What sudden blaze of majesty

[4] Enid Welsford, *The Court Masque: A Study in the Relationship between Poetry and the Revels* (Cambridge, 1927), especially Part Three.

Is that which we from hence descry
Too divine to be mistook:
  This this is she
To whom our vows and wishes bend,
Heer our solemn search hath end.

The Presenter, the Genius of the Wood, explains that the masquers have come from "famous Arcady" and arrived at a still better place: "Such a rural queen/ All Arcadia hath not seen." This simple redefinition of Harefield and its household is perfectly conventional and perfectly done: Milton does not withhold himself from compliment.

But the speech of the Genius contains lines which describe a setting beyond Arcady:

in deep of night when drowsines
Hath lockt up mortal sense, then listen I
To the celestial Sirens' harmony,
That sit upon the nine enfolded sphears,
And sing to those that hold the vital shears,
And turn the adamantine spindle round,
On which the fate of gods and men is wound.

Milton's mind flies up beyond festive song to a permanent music, sublimely Orphic.

Such sweet compulsion doth in musick ly,
To lull the daughters of necessity,
And keep unsteady nature to her law,
And the low world in measur'd motion draw
After the heavenly tune, which none can hear
Of human mould with grosse unpurged ear.

What can be the relevance of such music at a great household's entertainment? At a religious concert or in church, "at a solemn music," sacred music imitates divine, as Milton's poem about such an occasion beautifully says, marking as it does so the sad jar of sin that comes between. Here in *Arcades* all he can do with the music of the spheres is use it in compliment. If we *could* hear it, the Genius says,

such musick worthiest were to blaze
The peerless height of her immortal praise,
Whose lustre leads us, and for her most fit,
If my inferior hand or voice could hit
Inimitable sounds . . .

If we pause over this transition, we can feel the difficulty involved in the masque form as a vehicle for Milton's full sensibility. For would such music really be appropriate "to blaze/ The peerless height of [the] immortal praise" of the Dowager Countess of Derby, however sublimed? The word "immortal," when we pause over the use of it in compliment, wavers unsteadily under the weight of the previous immense conception.

II. MILTON'S STRATEGY IN USING THE MASQUE FORM

At Ludlow, Milton did, astonishingly enough, convert the masque to his high purposes. His second masque leaves out all but a decent measure of compliment, converting the approach to the presence, normally a climax of adulation, into a family reunion, with children honoring parents. There was an element of this already at Harefield, where members of the Duchess' family were the masquers. There was doubtless at Harefield an account of their journey to her presence: "Here our solemn search hath end." Milton either did not write that part or did not preserve it—there is nothing in the finale to indicate what sort of difficulties the journey involved. At Ludlow the journey becomes central. One side of our interest is centered in the trial of the Lady in her passage through a Spenserian dark wood. The leading masquer becomes a dramatic protagonist, and the spokesman for the antimasque becomes an antagonist, a vile enchanter who, so far as his attributes are concerned, might have stepped out from the pages of *The Faerie Queene.*

It is often assumed that, in making a drama centering on the Lady, Milton leaves the masque form behind. But this drama develops by the masque's kind of unfolding of the situation in which the drama takes place. And this situation is not simple fiction, as in drama, but rather transformation or translation of the actual, in keeping with the masque form and occasion. Milton was familiar with dramatic works which present a self-contained action shaped by traditions of the noble entertainment, notably *A Midsummer Night's Dream* and *The Tempest,* probably also Fletcher's relatively trivial teen-age pastoral romp, *The Faithful Shepherdess.* Shakespeare's habits as a professional dramatist, and his natural concern to add to the repertory of his company, led him to produce entertainments which could be reused as public stage plays. Milton, working with Henry Lawes at his elbow, for Lawes's patron, had no such further theatrical purpose. When Lawes in 1637 published A *Maske Presented at Ludlow Castle, 1634: On Michael-masse Night, before the Right Honorable John Earle of Bridgewater,* etc., the title and the dedication invite the reader to share in retrospect the occasion of its presentation. So, in reading, we must reanimate not only the work's fictions but also the literal circumstances which those fictions extended.

To look at what was regularly being done with the masque's resources for transforming or redefining the situation at an entertainment makes one realize what an emphatic thing Milton did with it. In *Coelum Britannicum,* performed on Shrove Tuesday of the same year as Milton's masque, Thomas Carew and Inigo Jones undertook to transform Charles and his chaste court into the stars of heaven, replacing the lewd constellations with which the sky had been cluttered by Jove's lusts! [5] The Edgerton brothers played the part of lesser stars, torchbearers to the masquers. The animal heads used at Ludlow for Comus' rout may well have been the same which served at court for a dance of bestial constellations, on their way to oblivion. *Coelum Britannicum* was clearly a very successful occasion. The thing worked by combining a light touch about the mythology with truly effective spectacle, song, and dance—a combination very like that which brings off our better musical comedies. To be subjected to Inigo Jones's settings must have been rather like the 3-D experience of cinerama: for Carew's masque, lights on a great globe of the heavens progressively went out, later to come on again in a blaze, "expressing the stellifying of our British Heroes." In the interval, a huge mountain rose; clouds caromed, with singers on them. Another of Jones's great resources, not used in this particular masque, was the sudden opening up of vista beyond vista. His goal was not simply to present a scene but to alter the situation of the observer by manipulating perspective, as baroque painters

[5] *The Poems of Thomas Carew, with His Masque "Coelum Britannicum,"* ed. Rhodes Dunlap (Oxford, 1949), p. 183. The masque was presented by the king to the queen in return for a Twelfth Night performance of *The Faithful Shepherdess.* Dunlap quotes from a letter of Garrard to Stafford: "There are two Masques in Hand, . . . High Expences . . . Oh that they would once give over these Things, or lay them aside for a Time, and bend all their Endeavours to make the King Rich! For it gives me no Satisfaction, who am but a looker on, to see a rich Commonwealth, a rich People, and the Crown poor. God direct them to remedy this quickly" (p. 273). Sir Henry Herbert, however, recorded his satisfaction that "the Q. was pleased to tell mee before the king, 'Pour les habits, elle n'avoit jamais rien vue de si brave'" (*ibid.*).

sought to do when, for example, they painted domes to make the observer seem to look straight up a column of air in which angels were descending, some high, others almost on top of him.

What Milton did in his Ludlow masque was to use the masque's altering and extending of situation with his own kind of seriousness. The form sanctioned reaching out to far and high things, "stellifying." As Professor William R. Parker points out,[6] Milton and posterity benefited from the fact that at Ludlow physical scenery was necessarily minimal; this was to be a masque where poetry, rather than Inigo Jones, would present the descents from above and open out the vistas. Milton did not use directly Christian iconography in redefining the entertainment situation as a Christian situation. To have done so would have been discourteous, indecorous in a social sense. In the masque form there was no distinction between social decorum and artistic decorum. Mr. Martz's essay brings out how, in the 1645 volume as a whole, Milton's concern with decorum is social, the conscious development of roles or attitudes of the poet in society. A masque was an occasion for "antique fables" and "fairy toys," classical mythology and native folklore; Milton accordingly puts these in the foreground. He provides the masque's characteristic pleasures of animating familiar reading and fusing creatures from it with shadowy presences of the local countryside. But beyond these pleasures, he provides Christian reference by pursuing in a masque the serious concern of Renaissance humanists to reunderstand ancient myth in Christian terms. As an artist and entertainer, he begins with tangibles and opens out meaning through them. The environment of Ludlow Castle is extended in this way to reveal or express a Christian situation. By a daring coup, he uses for his purpose the custom of noble persons masquerading in ideal, exemplary roles: the fifteen-year-old daughter of the house will mime the virtue proper to her stage of life, Chastity; her brothers, the defense of chastity, the role Milton found so enthralling when as a boy he read romances. As the children "present" these parts, their own identities are to be extended, drawn out, educated. If their spiritual situation is understood, Milton's masque says, they are what they masquerade—even if they did not know it before Milton's project for them.

The finding of valid, Christian spiritual realities in classical myth

[6] In his discussion of the Ludlow occasion in his forthcoming biography of John Milton, which he kindly lent me in manuscript.

was a great Renaissance enterprise; the high excitement of it is expressed by Thyrsis as he sets out to enlarge the Brothers' awareness of
their situation:

Ile tell ye, 'tis not vain, or fabulous
(Though so esteem'd by shallow ignorance)
What the sage poets taught by th' heav'nly Muse,
Storied of old in high immortal vers
Of dire Chimeras and inchanted iles,
And rifted rocks whose entrance leads to hell,
For such there be, but unbelief is blind.
        Within the navil of this hideous wood
Immur'd in cypress shades a sorcerer dwels.

To understand Milton's masque, we must be aware of the kind of moral
and spiritual meaning which Christian humanism had been finding in
classical myth for more than a century. Spenser's mythopoeia was in the
foreground for Milton and his audience; but Spenser was part of a wide
and complex tradition. Miss Tuve has beautifully exhibited the meanings which variations on the Circe myth were carrying; [7] she and Professor Woodhouse make clear how positive a virtue Milton was celebrating in presenting Chastity as an obligation of the natural order
which could find sublime fulfillment in the order of Grace.[8]

But my concern here is to consider how, by the masque form,
Milton brings such meanings into view. Dr. Johnson exhibited just the
inappropriate assumption when he objected strongly against "the prologue spoken in the wild wood by the attendant Spirit" because it is
addressed to the audience: "a mode of communication so contrary to
the nature of dramatic representation, that no precedent could support
it." [9] This astonishing lapse, which forgets so many instances in Shakespeare, results not only from Johnson's ignoring the masque form but
also from the assumptions that go with a stage seen beyond a prosce-
nium arch. The audience, he insists, cannot be in the wild wood! A
similar assumption which relates to the whole problem of interpretation appears in a recent extremely suggestive article by Professor Sears

[7] Rosemond Tuve, *Images and Themes in Five Poems by Milton* (Cambridge,
1957), pp. 112–61.
[8] A. S. P. Woodhouse, "The Argument of Milton's *Comus*," *University of
Toronto Quarterly*, XI (1941–42), 46–71, and "*Comus* Once More," *University of
Toronto Quarterly*, XIX (1949–50), 218–23.
[9] *Lives*, p. 98.

Jayne, in which he proposes that Milton's machinery be understood in terms of Ficino's Neoplatonism. Mr. Jayne sets out by saying, "The *Mask* begins with a speech of the Attendant Spirit in which he explains the setting, the world in which the action of the masque is to take place." [10] He then argues that Jove refers not to God but to the Neoplatonic World Soul, and develops Ficino's systematic conception of the individual soul's descent and return, a structure of thought which proves to have fascinating parallels or potential parallels in Milton's masque. What concerns me is not judgment among such possible meanings but the status they have in the work, the way the masque reaches toward them. The Prologue does not once for all "explain the setting, the world"; it only begins a process of opening up which continues, dynamic and fluctuating, until the last lines of the Epilogue. In the Prologue's first five lines we are made aware that where we are is "this dim spot,/ Which men call earth," that far above it are "regions milde of calm and serene ayr," and beyond these, "the starry threshold of Joves court." What are we to understand by Jove? At one moment less, at another more, as the reach of the poetry moves through one suggestion to another. We will be unaware of important meanings if we are not conscious of the systematic grids of Renaissance thinkers. But the masque keeps moving in and out of them. A slight hint that Milton was consciously concerned to keep clear of too explicit Christian reference appears in one of his minor revisions. In the Cambridge draft, the Lady, speaking of Chastity, said

> I see ye visibly; and while I see ye,
> This dusky hollow is a Paradise,
> And heaven gates o'er my head.

This seems to have been rejected as too explicit, short-circuiting a tension. In the way it advances through other symbols *toward* the Christian, the masque is, surprisingly, not unlike *The Waste Land*. The circumstances are vastly different; but both poets are concerned to move through "secular" materials to mystery and spiritual discovery.

Speeches seem too long when nothing seems to be happening. Since in many of the speeches what is happening is the *creation* of the situation, if we attend to that, instead of looking for the forwarding of event, there is high excitement and delight. As an example, consider the

---

[10] Sears Jayne, "The Subject of Milton's Ludlow Masque," *PMLA*, LXXIV (1959), 535.

lines in which Comus tells the Lady that he has seen her brothers, lines where the act of imaginative creation is emphasized by the whole thing's being a downright lie:

> Two such I saw, what time the labour'd oxe
> In his loose traces from the furrow came,
> And the swink't hedger at his supper sate;
> I saw them under a green mantling vine
> That crawls along the side of yon small hill,
> Plucking ripe clusters from the tender shoots,
> Their port was more than human, as they stood;
> I took it for a faëry vision
> Of some gay creatures of the element
> That in the colours of the rainbow live
> And play i'th plighted clouds. I was awe-strook,
> And as I past, I worshipt; if those you seek
> It were a journey like the path to Heav'n,
> To help you find them.

Comus' fabrication opens an exquisite vista, exactly in the manner of the masque. It is his supreme moment as a tempter, because a sight of her brothers is just what the Lady, prisoned from them in darkness, most desires. The "faëry vision" of "gay creatures" who can "play i'th plighted clouds" embodies the delight of perfect imaginative freedom, as in Shakespeare's Ariel. It is as though Comus gave the Lady a subliminal dose of his potion—and then he hypocritically steps into a posture of religious awe! Her response is to accept him as a guide.

III. Discovering the Resources of Chastity

To present a trial of chastity, the masque's way of moving by successive extensions of situation and awareness serves Milton perfectly. For preserving chastity involves keeping a relation with what is not present: the chaste person is internally related to what is to be loved, even in its absence. The experience of being cut off is wonderfully rendered by the poetry which creates the initial setting in the dark wood. The Lady's lines convey the disorientation that darkness can bring about, the thronging fantasies, and the soul's reaching out for objects of sight or sound through which to recover a relation to community. Her brothers, when they enter, express the same experience. "In double night of darkness and of shades," the Elder Brother longs for the sight of "som gentle taper":

Though a rush candle from the wicker hole
Of som clay habitation, visit us
With thy long levell'd rule of streaming light.

In this situation, the young people's first resources are internal. The Lady reflects that she has with her still "a strong siding champion Conscience," and welcomes to her inward eye Faith, Hope, and "thou unblemish't form of Chastity"—"I see ye visibly, and now beleave."

The Elder Brother argues the power of Virtue with the Younger Brother in the "declamations" which irritated Dr. Johnson (and many a reader since):

Vertue could see to do what vertue would
By her own radiant light . . .

It is difficult not to hear Juliet's "Lovers can see to do their amorous rites/ By their own beauties"—and difficult to sympathize with the Elder Brother once we hear the echo. Certainly the least satisfactory part of the masque is this presentation, through the Elder Brother, of the resources which "divine philosophy" can provide for the defense of chastity. His speeches do tend to become dogmatic argument: in insisting on the autonomy of the individual will and spirit, he verges on a kind of hubris, so that we sympathize with the Younger Brother's practical concern about external dangers. To try to save the lines by making the presentation of the Elder Brother heavily ironic, as Mr. Hardy does, surely does not square with the fact that he expresses convictions Milton himself held. We are intended, I think, to feel a youthful absolutism, not unlike Milton's own as a boy reading romances. It seems to me that the response called for is not ironic rejection but tutelary approval blended with the sad amusement of experience watching innocence—the response of Thyrsis to the Elder Brother's fighting words about Comus:

Alas good ventrous youth,
I love thy courage yet, and bold emprise,
But here thy sword can do thee little stead.

The Elder Brother's tone is less priggish if we keep his lines in context, feeling them as a reaching out for resources against the tensions of uncertain isolation. Frequently, dogmatism turns into something like invocation, the realization of imaginative realities:

Do ye beleeve me yet, or shall I call
Antiquity from the old schools of Greece

To testifie the arms of Chastity?
Hence had the huntress Dian her dred bow
Fair silver-shafted queen for ever chaste.

Milton's marvelous power to slow down a line and dwell on its object brings Diana home as a presence, "Fair silver-shafted queen for ever chaste."

The outreaching gesture around which the first scene pivots is the invocation of Echo; Milton uses dramatically a standard feature of entertainments. The Lady's song "moves the vocal air/ To testifie his hidd'n residence"—it brings that physical resource into play. Nothing in the masque is more beautiful than the epiphany of the Lady's quality conveyed by the song and the descriptions of it. Comus acknowledges that

> such a sacred and home-felt delight,
> Such sober certainty of waking bliss,
> I never heard till now.

The nymph Echo does not answer the Lady; instead it is Comus who comes forward. But Thyrsis, high on "the hilly crofts/ That brow this bottom glade," also hears the song. And the Lady has the strength of assuming that her need *has* an Echo. One of the stunning things about the moment when she sings her song is that at such a moment she should sing such a song; she shows she is a Lady by presuming that she is in a world inhabited by "courteous" Presences:

> my severed company
> Compell'd me to awake the courteous Echo
> To give me answer from her mossie couch.

The act of singing is an exercise of the Lady's integrity; she is internally related, beyond the darkness, to what she looks to and realizes in the song. In the song is exquisite maidenliness—"sweetest nymph, that liv'st unseen/ Within thy airy shell"—along with a rich capacity for sensuous enjoyment and sympathy with passion: the Lady envisages Echo

> in the violet embroider'd vale
> Where the love-lorn nightingale
> Nightly to thee her sad song mourneth well.
> Canst thou not tell me of a gentle pair
> That likest thy Narcissus are?

O if you have
Hid them in some flowry cave,
Tell me but where.

The contribution to Milton's sensibility of Renaissance aristocratic poetic traditions appropriate to the masque appears in the contrast between the Lady's song and the more ungracious moments of the Elder Brother's exposition. The Lady's song does not condemn amorous feeling in lines of moral firmness, addressed perhaps to "thou unblemish't form of Chastity"; instead, its stanza so interwoven and complete holds a vision of delicate eros. The Lady's shy capacity for love, attached at this moment to her brothers, is expressed in Echo's living unseen within her airy shell and yet perhaps hiding the brothers "in some flowry cave." The result is dramatic rather than didactic composition; for the Lady's vulnerability as well as her innocence is given to the air by the song. Its strains

float upon the wings
Of silence, through the empty-vaulted night,
At every fall smoothing the raven doune
Of darknes till it smil'd.

Milton presents chastity not as a negative virtue but as an intact disposition to love.

The preservation of chastity accordingly depends, his masque shows, not only on inner resources, crucial as these are, but on a world beyond the isolated individual and appropriate to the Lady's reserved ardor: there must be an actual echo. Comus provides a false echo, at first beautifully camouflaged, as we have seen, to fit the Lady's sensibility, later manifestly false in the enticements of his palace. Her security is partly in the strength of her will and the freedom of her mind. But more deeply it rests on the fact of there being other, worthy objects of love as alternatives to Comus' release. The ultimate object of love, the masque repeatedly hints, is heavenly—as in the song's final lines about Echo "translated to the skies," to "give resounding grace to all heav'ns harmonies." But on this side of heaven there is Thyrsis, at once a "glistring guardian" sent by "the Supreme good" and, in human terms, "my father's shepherd."

Here we should notice again what Milton does *not* do with the Christian supernatural. The role of the Attendant Spirit suggests at first affinities with those comedies where the action is overseen by a benevolent, omniscient figure who stage-manages it all: the Duke in *Measure for Measure*, Prospero in *The Tempest*, Reilly in *The Cocktail Party*. In such plays, the presiding figure tends to suggest Providence, and a special kind of humor arises from the contrast of his knowledge, which we share, with the ignorance in which the rest of the persons flounder about in the human condition. The perspective provided initially by Milton's Spirit serves in a somewhat similar fashion to give a background reassurance, furnishing perimeters within which the trial will take place. But it is striking that, once the action is started, the Spirit does *not* preside: he neither foretells what will happen nor speaks from behind his disguise to assure us that all will be well, as does such a figure as the Duke in *Measure for Measure*. The nearest he comes to this is in the narration telling of haemony to which Johnson objected "because it is false"! But here too there is no direct relation made to heaven or Jove's court: haemony is made the highest fruit of pastoral learning, the knowledge of simples. In the immediate context, this would include understanding of "dire chimeras," how they are and how they are not real. More simply, the herb serves as the embodiment of the resource which the presence of Thyrsis has given to the Brothers, and so completes the episode. Should we take it as Reason, or as Grace? There are associations with both, it looks *toward* both. That for the Brothers it does not entirely work fits with their incompleteness, and also with the further resource which the masque's progress will discover in Sabrina.

That the Attendant Spirit can become Thyrsis reflects the contribution of pastoral and the masque to Milton's art, an art here as elsewhere ultimately religious. The secular traditions provide mediating presences and objects between the human and the divine. One ground of this fortunate mingling of world and spirit was the aristocratic assumption of hierarchy, to which the masque was committed by its very nature as a genre devoted to compliment. A favorite pastime of the masque was "teaching difference," with moral superiority regularly linked—often factitiously enough—to social superiority. Frequently in court masques the antimasque was abruptly stopped by the arrival of some noble presence radiating awe, who would dismiss the antics from the hall with moral and aristocratic contempt. In *Pleasure Reconciled to Virtue*, Atlas dismisses in this fashion Ben Jonson's Comus, a simple god of gluttony, Shrove Tuesday style, with bottle-shaped followers.[11]

---

[11] *Ben Jonson*, ed. C. H. Herford, Percy and Evelyn Simpson (Oxford, 1941), VII, 482.

Milton uses such a break, with rich complication, when his Comus, at the approach of the Lady, abruptly ends the dance of his followers (described as "a wild, rude and wanton antic" in the Cambridge manuscript).

The essence of this encounter of masquer with antimasque, translated by Milton's poetic and dramatic elaboration into a spiritual confrontation, is distilled in the recapitulation of the event which Thyrsis communicates to the Brothers in the second episode of the first scene. This second episode is beautifully designed: it repeats the movement the Lady has been through from isolation in darkness to an encounter opening out the situation toward a world of pastoral generosity; but the succor offered the Brothers is real, not Comus' "glozing courtesy." We reexperience the threat of intemperance from the perspective of the high lawns, in language which cues an active response. "Night by night/ He and his monstrous rout are heard to howl."

> And O poor hapless nightingale, thought I
> How sweet thou singst, how near the deadly snare!

What Milton made of the masque's movement, of the choreographic commonplace of a noble presence suddenly arresting the motion of the antimasque, is concentrated for me in a single remarkable line of Thyrsis' narrative, "Till an unusual stop of sudden silence." He tells how, his labors done, he sat down

> To meditate my rural minstrelsie,
> Till fancy had her fill, but ere a close
> The wonted roar was up amidst the woods,
> And fill'd the air with barbarous dissonance,
> At which I ceas't, and listen'd them a while,
> Till an unusual stop of sudden silence . . .
>
> At last a soft and solemn breathing sound
> Rose like a steam of rich distill'd perfumes,
> And stole upon the air, that even Silence
> Was took e're she was ware . . .

Of course the power or magic of such a line is implemented by cadence, consonants, vowels: "Till" with "*stop*" and "*sudden*"; the undulations, between the stops, of "an unusual" and, after them, of "silence." Without the form and pressure of the poetry, the choreography would not carry; but the poetry is expressing or implying choreography, a moment in a dance. One can imagine (though of course one does not need to) that a hand goes up at "stop," a single dancer erect in warning above massed, subsiding figures.

IV. The Masque as a Defense and Resource

We are now in a position to consider how Milton's use of the masque form permitted him to order and satisfy feeling in an entertainment presenting Chastity. In electing to make a Masque of Chastity and put Revel in the role of villain, Milton undertook a particularly difficult task. Nobody but Milton would have tried it! His sense of life prevented his using wholeheartedly one of the great resources of entertainment literature, the release sanctioned by seasonal or periodic holiday. On a tide of such mirth, Shakespeare could move out into magic woods with an implicit confidence in a return, after the holiday moment, with humanity intact. It comes as a shock to hear the Lady speak of country pleasures as "ill manag'd merriment." But what she has actually heard is Comus' rout, who "night by night . . . are heard to howl." Milton has deliberately presented a figure of Revel who under the guise of refreshment tempts to dissolution from which there is no coming back. The whole historical development of English life, regret it though we may, was giving ground for Milton's new vantage toward the pleasures of Merry England. The old agrarian housekeeping society, based on the land and its seasons, was giving way to a dominant culture based on urban conditions, where a leisure class would try to find, and others to furnish, holiday pleasures every day:

when night
Darkens the streets, then wander forth the sons
Of Belial, flown with insolence and wine.

The first response which the attitudes of our own time suggest is that Milton's project of celebrating Chastity is impossible. For we not only have no cult of chastity, we have a cult of defloration. Crazy Jane, "Learned in bodily lowliness," tells the Bishop that "nothing can be sole or whole/ That has not first been rent." Much contemporary fiction is devoted to a mystique that spiritual exploration requires accepting one kind or another of rape by the world—or it laments the failure of this mystique. When we look at Milton in our psychological perspectives, we cannot help feeling that he was vulnerable, and that in his idealization of chastity we have, clearly, a mechanism of defense. And yet, along with this sense of the artist and his subject, most of us find his masque wonderfully beautiful and satisfying.

One necessary way to understanding the poem's success is to consider what a positive conception chastity was in Milton's thought and in that of his time, as Mr. Woodhouse, Miss Tuve, and others have done. Through the ideal of chastity, Milton could reach to vital resources of his culture and religion. If Milton was vulnerable sexually, we should recognize that sexual vulnerability is just what his masque presents. If it is a defense, it is simultaneously a resource, a gathering of resources from a civilization which did not assume sexual invulnerability as an ideal. Milton fully recognized that unintegrated passion might destroy his particular complex sensibility, with its astonishing range of relation to psychic objects through which he achieved his sense of himself and of his relation to society and deity.

In *A Mask Presented at Ludlow Castle* he presents the possibility of destructive release, and meets it by another sort of release, the release of imagination carried by rhythm out and up to other objects of love. This alternative release is in its way physical, and so can work to counter that which Comus offers. For poetry and song *are* physical, the whole body engaged in the rhythms of articulation, envisagement centered in physical utterance. It is notable that the images which suggest a benign sexual release refer to song: "Silence/ Was took ere she was ware." In so far as the masque fails, it fails by a failure of rhythm. Where instead of poetry we get mere vehemence, mere assertion, and where our imagination is allowed to rest on the merely literal or merely intellectual contest, the defense of chastity lacks the final cogency of pleasure.

I feel a different sort of failure of rhythm in the speeches of Comus: much of his part seems too shallow rhythmically for the impact it should have, too stilted, as though Milton's auditory imagination could not risk getting more deeply involved. Milton certainly had a genuine artistic problem here; his whole design would not admit of Comus' capturing our imagination fully. His solution, so far as he does solve the difficulty, is to allow his god to revel, to begin each speech strongly, often beautifully, with appeals to the traditional sanctions, youth, feast, and nature's vital dance. Then he spoils it. Professor Joseph Summers, commenting on this difficulty I feel about Comus' part, writes that "I had always assumed that Milton *meant* us to have difficulty there—that the problem is not that Milton's auditory imagi-

nation could not risk getting more deeply involved but that he was trying to imitate precisely the failure of Comus' imagination—the mechanical movement and vulgar assumptions that his speech betrays." One
can grant, as I do, that Milton's purpose required him to limit Comus
in this way, yet a limitation still remains—a necessary limitation, but to
be regretted nevertheless, as we regret Merry England. Autolycus can
sing heart-whole of a liberty Milton's masque cannot include, a liberty
which did not threaten Perdita's exquisite, passionate chastity.

Agreeing with Professor Summers, I find myself clear about *dis*-
agreeing with the many critics who have read Comus' part with uninhibited delight, as though he were a more cultivated Autolycus. To take
him without reserve, as though the release of the masque centered in
his part, throws the whole out of balance. For if Comus persuades to a
full release, there is nothing to resist him but with will, morality,
principles.

The furthest reach of feeling, going out to the objects whose superior attraction defeats Comus, is in the Epilogue, where in the final
version the imagination is carried beyond young Adonis and the As-
syrian queen to celestial Cupid and "his dear Psyche, sweet entranced."
The end of Chastity is love fulfilled, "Two blissful twins . . . Youth
and Joy." Closer to the Lady's actual condition, and crucial in her
rescue, is the figure of Sabrina, perhaps the most remarkable inspiration
or revelation of the whole masque. Sabrina is, of course, exactly the
sort of local genius looked for in noble entertainments; but Milton's
astonishing mythopoeic power created almost all her particular qualities, qualities that are exactly, deeply right. The Lady is in a state of
shock, following the attempted seduction. She cannot move, cannot go
out to anything. What sort of figure can release her? Some presence identified with her father's power, the boundary of Wales. Some presence
moist and cool—if the danger of seduction is melting heat, the danger
of chastity is fevered desiccation. She cannot come out to her brothers,
they cannot seize Comus' wand, because they are not men, and anyway they are brothers. A knight might take over from Comus, or, al-
ternatively, a Vocation to the high mystery of virginity wedded to
Christ. But a knight, or a Vocation, would take the Lady beyond the
stage of life where she *is*. So the Sabrina who is invoked is a virgin who,
threatened once, as the Lady has been, "still retains/ Her maiden gentleness." In the story of Sabrina's coming back to life, and the poetry
and song which create her, we encounter, along with suggestions of the

healing and renewing powers of water, the innocent cherishing of femininity by femininity, waiting and yet not waiting for another destiny, which is the proper resource of the Lady's stage of life:

> Sabrina fair
>   Listen where thou art sitting
> Under the glassie, cool, transparent wave,
>   In twisted braids of lillies knitting
> The loose train of thy amber-dropping hair.

Such is the power of the masque, in Milton's hands, to reach out and find, transformed, what, if embraced, is already there.

II. 8

The Rising Poet, 1645 *

LOUIS L. MARTZ

Yale University

. . . as true a Birth, as the Muses have brought forth since our famous Spencer wrote; whose Poems in these English ones are as rarely imitated, as sweetly excell'd.
HUMPHREY MOSELY, *"The Stationer to the Reader"*

IT IS hard to maintain a clear view of Milton's volume of 1645, since the annotated editions that we are most likely to be using have broken up Milton's generic groupings and have rearranged these poems in chronological order, interspersed with other poems that Milton did not choose to publish here. I do not mean to quarrel with these rearrangements, which have the advantage of allowing one to trace accurately the development of Milton's early poetical career. And indeed Milton himself has taken the lead in making such a view of his career possible, since his volume of 1645 takes care to date many of the poems and arranges them in rough chronological order, within the various genres represented. Yet Milton's attention to genre makes an immense difference, for it asks us to view the poet's development according to the principles of poetry: it asks us to look upon the writer in a special aspect. Milton's original arrangement creates the growing awareness of a guiding, central purpose that in turn gives the volume an impressive and peculiar sense of wholeness. In order to regain the significant integrity of the volume one must, now and then, go back to the original.

Perhaps the best way into the volume is to follow Milton's own description of it, in the Latin ode that he sent in January, 1646–

* Read at the Institute in 1964. Published in *Institute Papers: The Lyric and Dramatic Milton*, 1965.

47, to John Rouse, Bodley's Librarian, with a copy of the book. This is
a mock-heroic poem of remarkably high spirits, written in an unprecedented form that MacKellar calls a "metrical experiment or jest." [1]
The manner is one of learned wit that makes translation almost impossible; I give here a composite version drawn from Hughes and
McCrea,[2] with intermittent comments:

"Books in twin parts, rejoicing in a single cover, yet with a double
leaf" [that is, as the general title page says, these are "Poems of Mr.
John Milton, both English and Latin," with a separate title page for
the Latin poems and separate pagination for the English and the Latin
parts; the "double leaf," however, not only alludes to the two title
pages, or the two parts, but at the same time suggests the double wreath
of laurel that the poet has won for his performance in two languages],
"and shining with unlabored elegance which a hand once young im-
parted—a careful hand, but hardly that of one who was too much a
poet—" [that is, not yet a master-poet] "while he played, footloose"
[*vagus*, "wandering"], "now in the forest-shades of Ausonia and now
on the lawns of England" [*Ausonias umbras*: the phrase may be taken
to include a reference to his own Italian journey, to the poems in the
Italian language, to the Latin poems, and to the pervasive atmosphere
of Greek and Roman pastoral that plays throughout the volume:
Ausonia includes Magna Graecia], "aloof from the people, and forsaking the common paths, he indulged his native lute, and presently in
like fashion with Daunian quill called forth for his neighbors a melody
from far away, his foot scarcely touching the ground" [*pectine Daunio*:
the song and instrument of ancient Italy].

Here is the picture of a youthful poet, free from adult cares, sometimes wandering alone, amusing himself, sometimes making music for
his friends or acquaintances, sometimes writing in his native vein,
sometimes evoking a strain from idealized antiquity—but with a light
and dancing posture that we do not usually associate with John Milton:
et humum vix tetigit pede. It is clear, from many indications, that Milton has designed his book with great care to create this impression.

The entire volume strives to create a tribute to a youthful era now
past—not only the poet's own youth, but a state of mind, a point of

---

[1] *The Latin Poems of John Milton*, ed. Walter MacKellar (New Haven, 1930),
p. 358.
[2] *John Milton: Complete Poems and Major Prose*, ed. Merritt Y. Hughes (New
York, 1957), p. 146. See the translations of the Latin poems by Nelson G. McCrea
in *The Student's Milton*, ed. Frank Allen Patterson (New York, 1930), p. 109.

4 LOUIS L. MARTZ

view, ways of writing, ways of living, an old culture and outlook now
shattered by the pressures of maturity and by the actions of political
man. Even the frontispiece, by William Marshall, attempts to set this
theme. The aim of the engraving is clearly to present the youthful poet
surrounded by the Muses, with a curtain in the background lifted to
reveal a pastoral landscape of meadow and trees, where a shepherd
is piping in the shade, while a shepherd and a shepherdess are dancing
on the lawn. The legend around the portrait identifies it as a picture
of the poet in his twenty-first year—but in fact the portrait presents the
harsh and crabbed image of a man who might be forty or fifty! Marshall could do better than this, as his engraving of the youthful Donne
testifies; one almost suspects deliberate sabotage here.[3] If so, Milton
performed slyly an appropriate revenge. For under the portrait, neatly
engraved in Greek—engraved no doubt by Marshall himself—we have
the following comment by Milton:

> That an unskilful hand had carved this print
> You'd say at once, seeing the living face;
> But, finding here no jot of me, my friends,
> Laugh at the botching artist's mis-attempt.

With this learned practical joke, the volume begins in high spirits;
how can we doubt, after this, that Milton had a considerable sense of
humor?

Meanwhile, the facing title page prepares us for a volume that
will contain songs of unlabored elegance, in the recent courtly style:
"The Songs were set in Musick by Mr. Henry Lawes Gentleman of
the Kings Chappel, and one of His Maiesties Private Musick"—a
notice quite in line with Moseley's preface, which associates Milton's
volume with the poems of Waller that Moseley had published a year
before. Waller, as everyone knew, had been exiled for his plot against
the Parliament on the King's behalf; nevertheless Moseley insists on
saying: "that incouragement I have already received from the most
ingenious men in their clear and courteous entertainment of Mr. *Wal-
lers* late choice Peeces, hath once more made me adventure into the
World, presenting it with these ever-green, and not to be blasted
Laurels." This bland ignoring, or bold confronting, of the political situation, with its emphasis upon the transcendent values of art, is main-

[3] See the amusing account in David Masson's *Life of Milton* (7 vols., London,
1859–94), III, 456–59; Masson sees in a passage of *Tetrachordon* a pun on Marshall's name. The translation of the Greek verses below is that of Masson, III, 459.

tained by reprinting here, from the 1637 edition, Henry Lawes's eloquent dedication of Milton's *Mask* to a young nobleman with strong Royalist associations; by the Latin poems in memory of the bishops of Winchester and Ely; by the complimentary writings prefixed to the Latin poems, showing the high regard that Milton had won in Catholic Italy; by Milton's admiration for Manso, the fine old Catholic patron of Tasso; and by other aspects of the volume, notably the sonnet beginning: "Captain or Colonel, or Knight in Arms,/ Whose chance on these defenceless dores may sease." This is not a poem of presumptuous naïveté but of mature awareness, in which the poet, as Brooks and Hardy say, with a "wry humor . . . contemplates, a little ruefully but still with a fine inner confidence, the place of the poet in a jostling world of men at arms." [4]

> Lift not thy spear against the Muses Bowre,
>   The great *Emathian* Conqueror bid spare
>   The house of *Pindarus*, when Temple and Towre
> Went to the ground: And the repeated air
> Of sad *Electra's* Poet had the power
> To save th' *Athenian* Walls from ruine bare.

But will the King's Captain do the same for one who is not yet "too much a poet"? There is room for doubt, and hence the plea; but no doubt at all about the power of poetry and this poet's hopes to achieve the immortality of Fame. He has told us this through the motto on the title page, there identified as coming from Vergil's seventh eclogue:

> ————Baccare frontem
> Cingite, ne vati noceat mala lingua futuro,

The whole context is essential: the lines occur as Thyrsis opens his answer in the singing match with Corydon, *Arcades ambo:*

Bring ivy-leaves to decorate your rising poet, shepherds of Arcady, and so make Codrus burst his sides with envy. Or, if he tries to harm me with excessive praise, twine foxglove round my brows, to stop his evil tongue from hurting your predestined bard.[5]

---

[4] *Poems of Mr. John Milton: The 1645 Edition with Essays in Analysis,* by Cleanth Brooks and John Edward Hardy (New York, 1951), p. 157. This valuable edition includes only the English poems, with a very helpful commentary on each poem.

[5] In the translation of the *Eclogues* by E. V. Rieu (Penguin Books, London, 1949; Latin text included in third impression, 1954). Other translations here from the *Eclogues* are also by Rieu. My quotations from the Latin text are given according to Vergil's *Opera,* ed. F. A. Hirtzel (Oxford, 1900).

That epigraph, summoning up the world of Vergil's *Eclogues*, prepares the way for the many Vergilian characters and scenes to be encountered in the English poems here: Corydon and Thyrsis, Phillis and Thestylis, in *L'Allegro*; Thrysis and Meliboeus in the *Mask*; Lycidas, Amaryllis, and Damoetas, with the setting of Vergil's seventh eclogue, "where the Mincius embroiders his banks with a green fringe of bending rushes"; and the shepherds of the Arcadian Entertainment at Harefield. The epigraph prepares us too for the echoes of Vergil's Messianic eclogue that occur in the volume's opening poem, the Nativity Ode; and, above all, it prepares us to watch, as we read the Latin poems, the poet's growth away from the light elegy toward the Vergilian mode in which Milton wrote the most mature and the finest of all the Latin verses in this volume: *Ad Patrem, Mansus,* and *Epitaphium Damonis,* all three of which confirm the "rising poet's" place as a "predestined bard."

In particular, the *Epitaphium Damonis,* spoken by Thyrsis, becomes appropriately the final poem of the entire volume, for with all its echoes of Greek pastoral it is the most deliberately Vergilian poem in the book. Here, clustered together, are those pastoral names that Vergil drew together in his *Eclogues:* Thyrsis and Damon, Daphnis, Tityrus, Alphesiboeus, Aegon, Amyntas, Mopsus, Aegle, and Menalcas; the use of the refrain reminds us of Vergil's eighth eclogue, the singing match between Damon and Alphesiboeus, while the words of Milton's refrain are modeled upon a line from the seventh eclogue (7,44) and also upon the final line of the last eclogue; the account of the two cups which Manso gave the poet is bound to recall the pairs of cups carved by Alcimedon, as described in Vergil's third eclogue; and verbal echoes of Vergil are so frequent that the poem seems to grow within a Vergilian matrix.[6]

The unity of Milton's volume, from title page to final poem, is further suggested by the fact that the *Epitaphium Damonis* laments the death of the very friend to whom the first Latin poem in the book had been written—*Elegia prima,* that gay and thoroughly Ovidian elegy composed by the arrogantly clever and quite unrepentant sophomore during his rustication. At the same time, the reader is bound to recall that *Elegia sexta* and the fourth sonnet have also been explicitly addressed to this same friend, Charles Diodati. The final poem, then,

---

[6] The verbal echoes are explicit, not only from the *Eclogues,* but also from the *Georgics* and the *Aeneid:* see MacKellar's admirable notes to this poem.

in paying tribute to a friend of youth, becomes a farewell to the pleasures and attitudes of youth, including the pleasures of pastoral poetry and the imitative pleasures of writing such Latin verse—a farewell that Milton appropriately gives with unmistakable echoes of Vergil's *Eclogues:*

And I—for I know not what my pipe was grandly sounding—it is now eleven nights and a day—and then perhaps I had put my lips to new pipes, but they burst asunder, broken at the fastening, and could no more bear the deep tones—I hesitate too lest I seem puffed up, yet I will tell the tale— give place then, O forests.[7]

Milton's *vos cedite silvae* is a clear echo of the *concedite silvae* with which Gallus bids farewell to Arcadian pleasures in Vergil's last eclogue (10,63); while Milton's following farewell to Latin poetry and Latin themes is based explicitly on the wording of Vergil's seventh eclogue:

> aut, si non possumus omnes,
> hic arguta sacra pendebit fistula pinu. (7.23–24)

Thus, after the famous passage in which Milton tells of his resolve to write an epic on British themes, he cries:

> O mihi tum si vita supersit,
> Tu procul annosa pendebis fistula pinu
> Multùm oblita mihi, aut patriis mutata camoenis
> Brittonicum strides, quid enim? omnia non licet uni
> Non sperasse uni licet omnia.

Ah! then if life remain, you, my pipe, shall hang on some aged pine far off and forgotten, unless forsaking your native songs you shrilly sound a British theme. Why not a British theme? One man cannot do all things, cannot hope to do all things.

MacKellar's version of these lines helps to bring out the complexity of the state of mind here expressed. The poet is resolved to leave behind the *fistula*, the reed pipe of his pastoral muse, and he will turn instead to write of those deeper themes which have already on one occasion proved to be stronger than that youthful pipe could bear. At the same time the *fistula* may represent Latin poetry, as MacKellar argues (p. 347), and the *patriis camoenis* may thus suggest the Latin language itself. That is to say, the poet is contemplating deeper themes, British

[7] This and the following translation are from MacKellar, ed., *Latin Poems*, p. 169.

themes, and themes composed in English. The power of poetry represented by these early compositions on the *fistula* will not be developed unless the poet can commit himself to English. Perhaps he has already tried those deeper themes in Latin, but without success: the rising poet knows, as Vergil says in the eighth eclogue, *non omnia possumus omnes* (8,63); and he foresees that his future fame must be entrusted to his native tongue.

The *Epitaphium* thus marks the end of an era that the whole volume serves to celebrate and commemorate, while the whole volume has been arranged to convey a sense of the predestined bard's rising powers.

II

In two important studies W. R. Parker has shown how, within carefully arranged groupings, the poems of this volume tend to follow the chronological order of their composition.[8] This is particularly clear in the Latin poems, most of which, as the Latin title page points out, were written *intra Annum aetatis Vigesimum*: that is, before his twentieth year had ended. In keeping with this emphasis, Milton has taken unusual care in dating his Latin poems, so as to make clear their youthfulness and the rising poet's precociousness. This atmosphere is borne out, in the elegies, by their heading *Liber primus*—a first book, a primer, for which no second book follows; and also by the retractation which ends the sequence of the seven numbered elegies. There is no need to suspect a misprint in the dating of the seventh, which comes out of chronological order, for the placing of this elegy seems to be dictated by the presence of the retractation, evidently written for the seventh elegy alone, and not for this whole set of elegies; yet placed here as it is, the retractation covers any similar materials in the preceding poems and puts last the latest piece of composition, the retractation itself. This palinode creates the impression of having been composed for some special occasion (such as, perhaps, a recitation of the seventh elegy before one of those "privat Academies in *Italy*," where Milton tells us that he presented "some trifles . . . compos'd at under twenty

[8] William Riley Parker, "Some Problems in the Chronology of Milton's Early Poems," *Review of English Studies*, XI (1935), 276–83, and "Notes on the Chronology of Milton's Latin Poems," in *A Tribute to George Coffin Taylor* (Chapel Hill, N.C., 1952), pp. 113–31.

or thereabout"),[9] when it was appropriate for the poet to speak of this youthful love poem with a tone of humorous exaggeration and a touch of mock-heroic banter:

These are the monuments to my wantonness that with a perverse spirit and a trifling purpose I once erected. Obviously, mischievous error led me astray and my undisciplined youth was a vicious teacher until the shady Academy offered its Socratic streams and taught me how to escape from the yoke to which I had submitted. From that hour those flames were extinct and thenceforward my breast has been rigid under a thick case of ice, of which the boy himself fears the frost for his arrows, and Venus herself is afraid of my Diomedean strength.[10]

When we turn to the English poems, we find the dating less explicit in most cases, but the mode of arrangement equally clear. The group headed "Sonnets," for example, opens with the English love sonnet that echoes Italian addresses to the Nightingale, but basically follows the medieval and pseudo-Chaucerian tradition of the Cuckoo and the Nightingale. Then follow the five sonnets in Italian, with their *Canzone*, paying tribute to the Petrarchans by using, as Milton says, "the language of which Love makes his boast." [11] These are all poems written in the youthful atmosphere suggested by the opening line of Sonnet VI ("Giovane piano, e semplicetto amante"), and dramatized in the *Canzone*, where the poet shows himself surrounded by "Amorous young men and maidens . . . jesting." [12] After these playful exercises in a fading, once-popular mode, the stern lines on the flight of his three-and-twentieth year come with the shock of a sudden recognition, setting a severe Calvinist view of life against these early trifles:

All is, if I have grace to use it so,
As ever in my great task Masters eye.

The meaning of these much-discussed lines, I think, is clarified if we take the word "grace" in a strict Calvinist sense: the speaker's future lies completely in the hands of God. Though Time has stolen away his youth, all his hopes remain as valid as they ever were; nothing has really changed, for the use of his life depends upon the timeless will

[9] See *The Reason of Church-government*, prologue to Book 2, in *Complete Prose Works of John Milton*, ed. Don M. Wolfe (New Haven, 1953—), I, 809.
[10] Hughes, ed., *John Milton*, p. 61.
[11] From the last line of the *Canzone*: "Questa è lingua di cui si vanta Amore." *Ibid.*, p. 55.
[12] *Ibid.*, p. 54.

and eye and grace of God. Nothing could form a sharper contrast with the preceding sonnets; and yet the sternness of the doctrine itself may suggest a veering from one youthful extreme to another—especially since the movement of the sonnet still maintains a conventional, end-stopped, balanced manner. The succeeding sonnet on the military threat to London shows, as we have seen, a greater maturity, reflected in the graceful sentence that winds its sinewy length over the last five lines.

Then the group closes with two more sonnets addressed to women, both sonnets forming a tacit contrast with the Petrarchan mode, in theme and in technique. Recalling the "Donna" of Milton's Italian sonnets, we are alert to appreciate the growth and change represented in the strongly suspended opening of Sonnet IX:

> Lady that in the prime of earliest youth,
>   Wisely hast shun'd the broad way and the green,
>   And with those few art eminently seen,
>   That labour up the Hill of heav'nly Truth,
> The better part with *Mary*, and [with] *Ruth*,
>   Chosen thou hast . . .

Lastly, Sonnet X, with an even greater suspension and involution, addresses a married lady who in herself maintains the virtues that once ruled in England, before the turmoil of the present age began:

> Daughter to that good Earl, once President
>   Of *Englands* Counsel, and her Treasury,
>   Who liv'd in both, unstain'd with gold or fee,
>   And left them both, more in himself content,
> Till the sad breaking of that Parlament
>   Broke him, as that dishonest victory
>   At *Chaeronéa*, fatal to liberty
>   Kil'd with report that Old man eloquent,
> Though later born, then to have known the dayes
>   Wherin your Father flourisht, yet by you
>   Madam, me thinks I see him living yet;
> So well your words his noble vertues praise,
>   That all both judge you to relate them true,
>   And to possess them, Honour'd *Margaret*.

Thus the syntax involves the troubled, more inclusive vision of maturity, while the *disio amoroso* of the Italian sonnets lies far in the past.

Similarly, it is helpful to read *L'Allegro* and *Il Penseroso* in the context of Milton's chosen arrangement; for these two poems come at the end of a group that might best be described as Jonsonian: poems in the mode of the "terse" couplet characteristic of Jonson and his Sons. First, the "witty" *Epitaph on the Marchioness of Winchester*; next, that perfect distillation of the Elizabethan madrigal, the *Song On May morning*; then the rather labored epigram on Shakespeare, dated 1630, and marked as early by the archaic "Star-ypointing"; and then the two jocular epitaphs for the University Carrier. Out of these experiments arise the two great companion poems, or twin poems, or the double poem, as we have come to call them. Reading these two poems in their original context may guide us toward a slight modification or qualification of these descriptive phrases. They are companion poems, certainly, but, as Don Cameron Allen has contended, they are not of equal strength and stature.[13] Their relation is rather that of Younger Brother to Elder Brother. The parallels between them, so familiar to everyone, should not lead us to read the poems in parallel, as though they were two sides of a coin, or two sides of an academic debate. For the poems develop a linear, sequential effect, moving from youthful hedonism toward the philosophic, contemplative mind.[14]

L'Allegro's dismissal of "loathed Melancholy" is extreme and violent, too violent to be taken seriously; while *Il Penseroso's* dismissal of "vain deluding joyes" is by comparison thoroughly under control, judicious, and temperate. The first poem sums up a youthful Elizabethan world of poetry now past: the tone is set by the opening archaism, "In Heav'n ycleap'd *Euphrosyne*." It is full of all the maying and the pastoral joys celebrated in hundreds of Elizabethan songs and madrigals, including the famous "Come live with me," strongly echoed near the beginning (l. 39) and at the end; and it remembers too those popular legends about Mab and the drudging Goblin, celebrated by Shakespeare and Drayton. One notes that, in Leishman's fine study of the literary echoes in these poems, most of the parallels with

---

[13] See D. C. Allen's essay on these poems in *The Harmonious Vision* (Baltimore, 1954), pp. 3–23.

[14] See the important brief essay by Kester Svendsen in *Explicator*, Vol. VIII (May, 1950), Item 49; here Svendsen deals with "the dynamics of the twin poem," showing "the progressive emphasis in both parts on images of sound and music." He notes how, in the finale of *Il Penseroso*, "the many references to sound and in particular to music build toward this conclusion, so that structurally it is the end of a progressive development within both poems."

Elizabethan, Shakespearean, and seventeenth-century poetry are found in *L'Allegro*.[15] Then there are the overt allusions to the "high triumphs" of archaic chivalry, to the courtly "Ladies, whose bright eies/ Rain influence" in Petarchan fashion, to "mask, and antique Pageantry," to Jonson's comedies, and to Shakespeare in his comic and pastoral vein. It is a joyous celebration and re-creation of an era, a state of mind, now past; but we note that it ends with hints of imperfection in this mode of harmony. As every Platonist knew, Plato had condemned the "soft *Lydian* Aires," and Milton subtly recalls the condemnation, while seeming to ignore it:

> With wanton heed, and giddy cunning,
> The melting voice through mazes running;
> Untwisting all the chains that ty
> The hidden soul of harmony.

But the words "wanton," "giddy," and "melting" recall the implications of the *Republic*:

> Again, drunkenness, effeminacy, and inactivity are most unsuitable in Guardians. Which are the modes expressing softness and the ones used at drinking-parties?
> There are the Ionian and certain Lydian modes which are called "slack."
> You will not use them in the training of your warriors?
> Certainly not.[16]

And does one really produce harmony by untwisting *all* the chains that tie? The final picture of Orpheus heaving up his head "From golden slumber on a bed/ Of heapt *Elysian* flowres" carries on, however beautifully, the "softness" of the Lydian mode. We note, by contrast, how the second poem invokes Orpheus in a potent, active role, singing

> Such notes as warbled to the string,
> Drew Iron tears down *Pluto's* cheek,
> And made Hell grant what Love did seek.

Furthermore, this second reference to Orpheus is subsumed within the middle of *Il Penseroso*, where he is only one of many great poets and thinkers: Hermes, Plato, the Greek tragedians, Musaeus, Chaucer,

---

[15] J. B. Leishman, "*L'Allegro* and *Il Penseroso* in Their Relation to Seventeenth-Century Poetry," *Essays and Studies*, N.S., IV (1951), 1–36.

[16] *Republic*, III, 398c–400c; in the translation by F. M. Cornford (New York, 1945), pp. 86–87.

Spenser. The spirit of Plato's "shady Academy" dominates *Il Penseroso*, from the opening salutation of the Goddess "sage and holy" to the grand musical close which extends this poem two dozen lines beyond the length of *L'Allegro*, to present a movement toward the "extasies" of Neoplatonic mysticism. All is, however, moderated and controlled by the quiet, detached tone of the poet, as at the very end he presents a picture that is too obviously archaic and sentimental to be taken solemnly: its excess tells us that Melancholy too needs tempering:

> And may at last my weary age
> Find out the peacefull hermitage,
> The Hairy Gown and Mossy Cell,
> Where I may sit and rightly spell,
> Of every Star that Heav'n doth shew,
> And every Herb that sips the dew;
> Till old experience do attain
> To something like Prophetic strain.
> These pleasures *Melancholy* give,
> And I with thee will choose to live.

That echo of "Come live with me" is phased more positively than the closing couplet of *L'Allegro:*

> These delights, if thou canst give,
> Mirth with thee, I mean to live.

Yet the echo reminds us that either choice involves a limitation.

Thus the two poems move from youth to age—the word "youthfull" is invoked twice in *L'Allegro*, and not at all in *Il Penseroso*—while in their movement these two unequal but compatible companions suggest the growth toward maturity that constitutes this volume's dominant theme.

III

Beyond the developments observable within these various subgroupings, each part of the volume displays a larger movement. As the Latin part begins with a youthful elegy and ends with a farewell to youth, so the English part begins with poems of youth and ends with *Lycidas* and the Ludlow *Mask:* two poems that in themselves enact a movement toward the broader visions of maturity. The essays following will, I think, suggest the integral relation of these two great poems to the dominant theme implied by Milton's arrangement of his volume. Here, by way of prelude and conclusion, I should like to consider the ways in which the development of this central theme is foreshadowed in the group of religious poems that Milton has chosen to open his volume of 1645.

Milton has carefully stressed the youthfulness of the four opening poems. First, out of strict chronological order, we have the poem headed: *On the morning of Christs Nativity. Compos'd 1629.*—with the date thus given prominence as part of the title. Then come the two Psalms, "don by the Author at fifteen years old," as the headnote tells us. Then the unfinished poem on the Passion, with the famous note at the end: "This Subject the Author finding to be above the yeers he had, when he wrote it, and nothing satisfi'd with what was begun, left it unfinisht." One may wonder why Milton bothered to include this acknowledged failure and fragment, when he did not include the more interesting and at least completed English poems that he added in 1673: the poem *On the Death of a fair Infant,* and the lines from the Vacation Exercise. But the inclusion of the fragment has a clear function: to stress the immaturity of these opening pieces, to suggest the ambitious young man outreaching his powers, and achieving poetical success only when he can subject his muse to some deliberate limitation. What he can accomplish is then demonstrated in the three short pieces that follow: *On Time, Upon the Circumcision,* and *At a solemn Musick;* these are undated, and thus, we assume, not quite so youthful. *Upon the Circumcision,* in particular, suggests a new beginning, in a less venturous mode, after the false start of *The Passion;* here the poet creates, within two madrigal-like stanzas, a carefully designed and reasoned meditation on the love of the suffering Infant. The other two lyrics are experiments in the handling of the canzone, anticipating the flexible verse form of *Lycidas.*

But all these brief experiments are insignificant when set beside the remarkable success of the long poem which is rightly placed first, as prologue to the rising poet's achievement. Its dating, "Compos'd 1629," accords with the poem's relation to an age and mode of English poetry now outgrown, both by the nation and by the poet. In understanding this poetical mode, one may gain important clues from Milton's description of the Nativity Ode in his sixth Latin elegy— especially when we read this elegy in Milton's chosen context, between the pagan celebration of Spring in Elegy Five and the mildly Ovidian eroticism of Elegy Seven. Read thus, Elegy Six does not lend itself easily to the widely held interpretation expressed, for example, by Woodhouse:

The Ode teaches us to read the contrast of the elegiac and the heroic vein as a repudiation of the former, to transliterate the description of the heroic poet into Christian terms as the account of a dedicated spirit divinely inspired, and to see in the ascetic discipline referred to, a turning towards that moral and religious preparation for his life-work on which Milton finally entered at Horton.[17]

This elegy begins with a broad joke about Diodati's feasting at the Christmas season: "With a stomach anything but full, I send you a prayer for sound health, of which, perhaps, you, with your stomach stretched to its uttermost, may be in sore need." [18] Then follows lively praise of the "light elegy," in a passage twice as long as the subsequent praise of epic: wine, feasting, maidens, and dancing inspire, says Milton, an excellent kind of poetry, blessed by many gods. Of course, he adds, if a poet wants to write on grand epic themes, then he must live quite differently; and Milton proceeds to write a hyperbolical account of the ascetic life required for such a bard: "let herbs furnish his innocent diet. Let the purest water stand beside him in a bowl of beech and let him drink sober draughts from the pure spring." He goes on to express his belief in the exalted power of this kind of bard, but he does not wholly lay aside the tone of "Ovidian banter" that Rand has found in the earlier part.[19] Milton no doubt hopes to reach that higher vein himself; but he does not appear to be saying so here. When he turns to discuss himself at the end of the poem, he makes a clean break with the previous discussion of elegy and epic; both are excellent in their kinds, the poet implies, but he is not writing in either vein at the moment. One must stress the *At tu si quid agam, scitabere*: "But if you will know what I am doing (if only you think it of any impor-

---

[17] A. S. P. Woodhouse, "Notes on Milton's Early Development," *University of Toronto Quarterly*, XIII (1943), 66–101; see p. 75. W. R. Parker, in a review (*Modern Language Notes*, LV [1940], 216–17), has strongly disagreed with this interpretation of Elegy Six as given by E. M. W. Tillyard in *The Miltonic Setting* (Cambridge, 1938); see, for example, p. 179 of Tillyard's book: "The neophytic and ascetic tone of *Elegia Sexta* fits well enough with his self-dedication to heroic poetry."

[18] From the translation by Charles Knapp in the Columbia edition of *The Works of John Milton* (New York, 1931–38), I, 207. The other passages translated from this poem are taken from Hughes, ed., *John Milton*, pp. 52–53.

[19] E. K. Rand, "Milton in Rustication," *Studies in Philolgy*, XIX (1922), 109–35; see pages 110, 124.

tance to know whether I am doing anything)"—note how he maintains the familiar tone with which the poem has opened—"I am singing the heaven-descended King, the bringer of peace, and the blessed times promised in the sacred books—the infant cries of our God" [which in fact are not mentioned in the Nativity poem as we have it; but Milton is emphasizing the poem's allegiance to the naïve tradition of the Christmas carol, as his next words further indicate] "and his stabling under a mean roof who, with his Father, governs the realms above. I am singing the starry sky and the hosts that sang high in air, and the gods that were suddenly destroyed in their own shrines. These are my gifts for the birthday of Christ—gifts which the first light of its dawn brought to me." In that last clause Milton seems to be saying only that the thought of writing such a poem came to him at dawn; there seems to be no indication of some special experience of religious conversion.

In this elegy's final couplet the opening *Te quoque* has allowed various interpretations:

> Te quoque pressa manent patriis meditata cicutis,
> Tu mihi, cui recitem, judicis instar eris.

In some versions (as in that of the Columbia edition) it appears that Milton is referring to certain *other* English poems that he has also written; but the *quoque* modifies *te*; or, rather, it is pleonastic and is best omitted, as in the revised translation of Hughes, which makes it plain that the passage is still alluding to the Nativity poem: "For you these simple strains that have been meditated on my native pipes are waiting; and you, when I recite them to you, shall be my judge." *Patriis meditata cicutis*: meditated on the native hemlock pipes of the humble shepherd. Milton has suggested here the poem's basic decorum.

It is, first of all, a poem that declares, in many ways, this poet's indebtedness to his predecessors in the line of English poetry. The four prefatory stanzas, written in a variation of rhyme royal, suggest the use of this ancient stanza form by Chaucer and the Chaucerians, by Spenser, in *The Ruines of Time* and the *Fowre Hymnes*, and by Shakespeare, in *Lucrece*; while the modification into hexameter in the final line declares a further allegiance to Spenser and the Spenserians. The stanza of the Hymn proper is even more significant, for its first six lines suggest the movement of a popular song or carol:

It was the Winter wilde,
While the Heav'n-born-childe,
　All meanly wrapt in the rude manger lies;
Nature in aw to him
Had doff't her gawdy trim,
　With her great Master as to sympathize.

The use of three-foot and five-foot lines, in various combinations, is found in many Elizabethan songs: thus among Thomas Morley's canzonets we find this stanza running 335335335, though the rhyme differs from Milton's:

I follow, lo, the footing
Still of my lovely cruel,
Proud of herself that she is beauty's jewel.
　And fast away she flieth,
　Love's sweet delight deriding,
In woods and groves sweet Nature's treasure hiding.
　Yet cease I not pursuing,
　But since I thus have sought her,
Will run me out of breath till I have caught her.[20]

But the first six lines of Milton's stanza also suggest another pattern: the combination of two- and three-foot lines, with Milton's rhyme scheme, found in some of the ancient Christmas carols:

The God Almyght
And Kyng of Lyght,
　Whose powr is ouer all,
Gyue vs of grace
For to purchas
　Hys realme celestyall.

Wher hys aungels
And archangels
　Do syng incessantly,
Hys princypates
And potestates
　Maketh gret armony.

The cherubyns
And seraphyns

20 *English Madrigal Verse*, 1588–1632, ed. E. H. Fellowes (2d ed., Oxford, 1929), p. 141.

With ther tvnykes mery,
The trones al,
Most musycall,
Syng the heuenly Kery.[21]

Then, by allowing his last line to swell out into a Spenserian Alexan-
drine, Milton draws his poem out of the realm of the popular song
into the larger area of this poet's predestined goals. In stanza after
stanza we may feel this change from the simple language and steady
beat of the ballad into the realms of a more ambitious art:

But wisest Fate sayes no,
This must not yet be so,
    The Babe lies yet in smiling Infancy,
That on the bitter cross
Must redeem our loss;
    So both himself and us to glorifie:
Yet first to those ychain'd in sleep,
The wakeful trump of doom must thunder through the deep.

Yet with all the poem's lofty expansions in rhythm, in language,
and in rich allusion, the poet's chosen method of control never falters:
he clings to the central mode of the ancient naïve, the mode of the
nativity ballad, the mode that Milton points to when he calls his
poem a "humble ode" that he seeks to lay "lowly at his blessed feet."
The touches of archaic, Spenserian language sprinkled throughout,
very lightly, are all adjusted to maintain this effect, as in the "ychain'd"
of the stanza just quoted, the "lusty Paramour" of the Hymn's opening
stanza, the "silly thoughts" of the shepherds, or the "dusky eyn" of
the doomed god Osiris. At the same time touches of old-fashioned
heavy alliteration recall the style, not only of Spenser, but of all those
lesser writers whom Sidney mocked for their "rimes, running in ratling
rowes."

This decorum of an ancient and traditional simplicity pervades
every aspect of the poem, versification, language, scene painting, imagery, and theme. The scenes and images are given in broad and simplified terms, as in some old tapestry or pageant. The original line in
which Truth and Justice wear "Th'enameld *Arras* of the Rainbow" is
more closely in accord with the poem than Milton's more sophisticated
revision: "Orb'd in a Rain-bow." Thus Nature seeks to hide her "guilty

---

[21] *The Early English Carols*, ed. Richard Leighton Greene (Oxford, 1935),
p. 58. I have omitted the editor's brackets and italics.

front" with "The Saintly Vail of Maiden white"; and "the meek-eyd
Peace . . . crown'd with Olive green, came softly sliding/ Down
through the turning sphear." "The Shepherds on the Lawn . . . Sate
simply chatting in a rustick row"; then

> At last surrounds their sight
> A Globe of circular light,
>   That with long beams the shame-fac't night array'd,
> The helmed Cherubim
> And sworded Seraphim,
>   Are seen in glittering ranks with wings displaid.

One should note, too, in these quotations, the curious mixture of
past and present tense, which Lowry Nelson has ably interpreted to
indicate the poem's sense of a timeless world; [22] this is so, yet Milton's
manner of thus mixing past and present also adds to the effect of the
naïve, as though the poet were artlessly following the instinct of a
momentary mood or were using past and present tense as the needs of
rhythm and rhyme might, for a moment, require.

Then, in the latter half of the poem, this effect is strongly heightened by Milton's treatment of the various characters that here are
shown in action. The Dragon of Revelation is presented in the guise
of a dragon out of folklore:

> And wrath to see his Kingdom fail,
> Swindges the scaly Horrour of his foulded tail.

And his antagonist, the blessed Babe, is likewise shown in the manner
of some ancient folk-hero, some infant Hercules:

> Our Babe to shew his Godhead true,
> Can in his swadling bands controul the damned crew.

Meanwhile, in the superb rendition of the fall of the pagan deities, it
is helpful, while we recognize the foreshadowing of *Paradise Lost*, to
notice also how utterly lacking in sophistication this account is, when
compared with Milton's later roll call of the fallen angels. In *Paradise
Lost* it is made plain that these are devils adored as deities, and the
horror of the deception is brought home by showing in detail the effect
of these devils upon mankind:

> First *Moloch*, horrid King besmear'd with blood
> Of human sacrifice, and parents tears,

[22] Lowry Nelson, Jr., *Baroque Lyric Poetry* (New Haven, 1961), pp. 41–52.

Though for the noyse of Drums and Timbrels loud
Their childrens cries unheard, that past through fire
To his grim Idol. Him the *Ammonite*
Worshipt in *Rabba* and her watry Plain,   (I,392–97)

and so on for eight more lines of particular detail, showing the ravages
wrought by Moloch on the earth.

But here in the Nativity poem Moloch is simply mentioned as
a totally defeated character, while the scene of his idolatry is represented in elementary colors and sounds:

And sullen *Moloch* fled,
Hath left in shadows dred,
    His burning Idol all of blackest hue,
In vain with Cymbals ring,
They call the grisly king,
    In dismall dance about the furnace blue.

These vanquished gods are not devils in disguise; they are the supernatural beings of antique folklore, who exist in their own right as a
part of nature, a part of man's primitive consciousness of forces that
lie beyond his control:

The lonely mountains o're,
And the resounding shore,
    A voice of weeping heard, and loud lament;
From haunted spring, and dale
Edg'd with poplar pale,
    The parting Genius is with sighing sent,
With flowre-inwov'n tresses torn
The Nimphs in twilight shade of tangled thickets mourn.

Finally, bringing to a brilliant close this basic effect of the simple
and naïve, Milton ends with two stanzas that sum up the basic techniques and attitudes of the poem. First we have the poem's most
extravagantly naïve image—one that would have offended at the outset
—but, now, with our minds attuned to the poem's peculiar decorum,
we can perhaps accept it as a youthful excess:

So when the Sun in bed,
Curtain'd with cloudy red,
    Pillows his chin upon an Orient wave.

Then come the ghosts and fairies of folklore, treated with sympathy
and even affection:

The flocking shadows pale,
Troop to th'infernal jail,
    Each fetter'd Ghost slips to his severall grave,
And the yellow-skirted *Fayes*,
Fly after the Night-steeds, leaving their Moon-lov'd maze.

And lastly, we return to the traditional scene, ten thousand times represented in ancient poetry and painting: the manger scene upon which
this technique of the naïve has been based:

But see the Virgin blest,
Hath laid her Babe to rest.
    Time is our tedious Song should here have ending.

Here, still, is the simple, humble singer, who is well aware of his
defects, but nevertheless has been led by gratitude to sing this song
of praise:

Heav'ns youngest teemed Star,
Hath fixt her polisht Car,
    Her sleeping Lord with Handmaid Lamp attending.

All Heaven, whether physical or spiritual, stands fixed in a service of
unlabored elegance:

And all about the Courtly Stable,
Bright-harnest Angels sit in order serviceable.

The last rhyme seems to call attention to the way in which Milton
has contrived, within his chosen mode, to make even the poem's defects appear as virtues, contributing to the total effect of the youthful
singer writing as well as he can in an ancient, traditional manner of
tribute. The poem is a total success because Milton has chosen and
maintained a mode of writing that does not tempt him beyond the
range of his precocious powers.

That is not to say that the poem is simpleminded in the range of
its implications, but that the chosen mode of simplicity creates a
world in which theological problems are pushed beyond the fringe of
our vision; there is no sense of struggling with theological issues, no
sense that we need to consult the church fathers, no sense of attempting
to enforce anything but the most easily grasped and broadly acceptable
truths. This, says the poet, is the happy morn when, as everyone knows,

> the Son of Heav'ns eternal King,
> Of wedded Maid, and Virgin Mother born,
> Our great redemption from above did bring.

Everyone shares the story, how the Son laid aside the majesty that was his due as part of Trinal Unity,

> and here with us to be,
> Forsook the Courts of everlasting Day,
> And chose with us a darksom House of mortal Clay.

How can we express our gratitude for this gift of the Almighty? By a song of praise for the peace and harmony that the divine child has brought to earth, not only on the day of his birth, and in the long-range future, but, in some measure, now: it "now begins," as this poet can best testify by writing a song that in itself represents a simple and unworried harmony.

But—"Compos'd 1629." More difficult and much more complex harmonies lie ahead for the rising poet, the predestined bard.

II. 9

Literary Criticism: Marvell's "Horatian Ode"*

CLEANTH BROOKS

Louisiana State University

THE EASIEST error into which we may fall in defining the relationship between historical and critical studies is illustrated by the preface of Maurice Kelley's interesting book on Milton, *This Great Argument*. For Kelley, the problem of exegesis is almost amusingly simple: we will read Milton's *Christian Doctrine* to find out what Milton's ideas are, and then we shall be able to understand his *Paradise Lost*, explaining the tangled and difficult poetic document by means of the explicit prose statement. But Kelley's argument rests not only upon the assumption that the Milton who wrote the *Christian Doctrine* was precisely and at all points the same man who composed *Paradise Lost*—a matter which, for all practical purposes, may well be true; it rests upon the further and much more dangerous assumption that Milton was able to *say* in *Paradise Lost* exactly what he intended to say; and that what he supposed he had put into that poem is actually to be found there. In short, Mr. Kelley tends to make the assumption about poetry which most of us constantly make; namely, that a poem is essentially a decorated and beautified piece of prose.

But I propose to deal here with a more modest example than Milton's epic. I propose to illustrate from Marvell's "Horatian Ode." If we follow the orthodox procedure, the obvious way to understand the "Ode"

* Read at the Institute in 1946. Published in *Institute Essays*, 1947; republished in *Institute Papers: Explication as Criticism*, 1963, from which the present text is taken.

is to ascertain by historical evidence—by letters and documents of all kinds—what Marvell really thought of Cromwell, or, since Marvell apparently thought different things of Cromwell at different times, to ascertain the date of the "Ode," and then neatly fit it into the particular stage of Marvell's developing opinion of Cromwell. But this is at best a relatively coarse method which can hope to give no more than a rough approximation of the poem; and there lurk in it some positive perils. For to ascertain what Marvell the man thought of Cromwell, and even to ascertain what Marvell as poet consciously intended to say in his poem, will not prove that the poem actually says this, or all this, or merely this. This last remark, in my opinion, does not imply too metaphysical a notion of the structure of a poem. There is surely a sense in which any one must agree that a poem has a life of its own, and a sense in which it provides in itself the only criterion by which what it says can be judged. It is a commonplace that the poet sometimes writes better than he knows, and, alas, on occasion, writes worse than he knows. The history of English literature will furnish plenty of examples of both cases.

As a matter of fact, Marvell's "Ode" is not a shockingly special case. Indeed, I have chosen it for my example, not because it is special— not because I hope to reveal triumphantly that what it really says is something quite opposed to what we have supposed it to be saying— but because it seems to me a good instance of the normal state of affairs. Yet, even so, the "Ode" will provide us with problems enough. To the scholar who relies upon the conventional approach, the problems become rather distressingly complicated.

Let us review the situation briefly. Hard upon his composition of the "Ode" in 1650, Marvell had published in 1649 a poem "To his Noble Friend, Mr. Richard Lovelace, and a poem "Upon the Death of the Lord Hastings." Both Margoliouth and Legouis find these poems rather pro-Royalist in sentiment and certainly it is difficult to read them otherwise. If we add to these poems the "Elegy upon the Death of My Lord Francis Villiers," a Cavalier who was killed fighting for the King in 1649, the Royalist bias becomes perfectly explicit. As Margoliouth puts it: "If [the elegy on Villiers] is Marvell's, it is his one unequivocal royalist utterance; it throws into strong relief the transitional character of *An Horatian Ode* where royalist principles and admiration for Cromwell the Great Man exist side by side. . . ."

A transition in views there must have been, but the transition certainly cannot be graphed as a steadily rising curve when we take into account Marvell's next poem, "Tom May's Death." May died in November, 1650. Thus we have the "Horatian Ode," which was almost certainly written in the summer of 1650, preceding by only a few months a poem in which Marvell seems to slur at the Commander of the Parliamentary armies—either Essex or Fairfax—as "Spartacus," and to reprehend May himself as a renegade poet who has prostituted the mystery of the true poets. The curve of Marvell's political development shows still another surprising quirk when we recall that only a few months after his attack on May, Marvell was to be living under Spartacus Fairfax's roof, acting as tutor to his little daughter Mary.

Let me interrupt this summary to say that I am not forcing the evidence so as to crowd the historian into the narrowest and most uncomfortable corner possible. On the contrary, whatever forcing of the evidence has been done has been done by the editors and the historians. If we limit ourselves to historical evidence, it is possible to suppose that "Tom May's Death" was actually written on the Hill at Billborrow; and Margoliouth chooses early 1651 as the probable date for Marvell's arrival at Appleton House only because, as he says, " 'Tom May's Death' is not the sort of poem Marvell would have written under Fairfax's roof."

There is no need, in view of our purposes, to extend the review of Marvell's political development through the late 1650s with their Cromwellian poems or through the Restoration period with its vexed problems concerning which of the anti-court satires are truly, and which are falsely, ascribed to Marvell. The problem of Marvell's attitude through the years 1649–51 will provide sufficient scope for this examination of some of the relations and interrelations of the historical approach and the critical approach. For there is still another complication, which has received less attention than it deserves. It is the curious fact that the "Horatian Ode" in which Marvell seems to affirm the ancient rights of the monarchy—

> Though Justice against Fate complain,
> And plead the antient Rights in vain—

is full of echoes of the poetry of Tom May, the poet whom Marvell was, a few months later, to denounce for having failed poetry in the hour of crisis:

> When the Sword glitters ore the Judges head,
> And fear the Coward Churchmen silenced,

Then is the Poets time, 'tis then he drawes,
And single fights forsaken Vertues cause.
He, when the wheel of Empire, whirleth back,
And though the World's disjointed Axel crack,
Sings still of *antient Rights* and better Times,
Seeks wretched good, arraigns successful Crimes.

The echoes of May's poetry, of course, may well have been unconscious: to me it is significant that they are from May's translation of Lucan's poem on the Roman civil wars. (The relevant passage from Margoliouth's notes will be found on pp. 129–30.) I must say that I find the parallels quite convincing and that I am a little surprised at Margoliouth's restraint in not pushing his commentary further. For one is tempted to suppose that in the year or so that followed the execution of Charles, Marvell was obsessed with the problem of the poet's function in such a crisis; that the poet May was frequently in his mind through a double connection—through the parallels between the English and the Roman civil war, Lucan's poem on which May had translated, and through May's conduct as a partisan of the Commonwealth; and that the "Horatian Ode" and "Tom May's Death," though so different in tone, are closely related and come out of the same general state of mind. But to hazard all this is to guess at the circumstances of Marvell's composition of these poems. It can be only a guess, and, in any case, it takes us into a consideration of what must finally be a distinct problem: how the poem came to be; whereas our elected problem is rather: what the poem is. I am, by the way, in entire sympathy with the essay "The Intentional Fallacy," by W. K. Wimsatt and M. C. Beardsley, recently published in the *The Sewanee Review*. We had best not try to telescope the separate problems of "the psychology of composition" and that of "objective evaluation." I have no intention of trying to collapse them here.

Well, what is "said" in the "Horatian Ode"? What is the speaker's attitude toward Cromwell and toward Charles? M. Legouis sees in the "Ode" a complete impartiality, an impartiality which is the product of Marvell's nonparticipation in the wars. Legouis can even speak of the poem as "ce monument d'indifférence en matière de régime politique." But the "Ode," though it may be a monument of impartiality, is not a monument of indifference. To read it in this fashion is to miss what seems to me to be a passionate interest in the issues, an interest which is manifested everywhere in the poem. It is true that we have no evidence that Marvell ever served in the civil war, but we had better not leap to conclusions of his indifference from that. My own guess is that some young Cavaliers who shed their blood for the King thought and felt less deeply about the issues than does the speaker of this poem. The tone is not that of a "plague o' both your houses" nor is it that of "the conflict provided glory enough to be shared by both sides."

Mr. Margoliouth comes much closer to the point. He sums up as follows: "The ode is the utterance of a constitutional monarchist, whose sympathies have been with the King, but who yet believes more in men than in parties or principles, and whose hopes are fixed now on Cromwell, seeing in him both the civic ideal of a ruler without personal ambition, and the man of destiny moved by and yet himself driving a power which is above justice." This statement is plausible, and for its purposes, perhaps just. But does it take us very far—even on the level of understanding Marvell the man? What sort of constitutional monarchist is it who "believes more in men than in . . . principles"? Or who can accept a "power which is above justice"? I do not say that such a monarchist cannot exist. My point is that Margoliouth's statement raises more problems than it solves. Furthermore, in what sense are the speaker's hopes "fixed . . . on Cromwell"? And how confident is he that Cromwell is "without personal ambition"? I have quoted earlier Margoliouth's characterization of the "Ode" as a poem "where royalist principles and admiration for Cromwell the Great Man exist side by side." I think that they do exist side by side, but if so, how are they related? Do they exist in separate layers, or are they somehow unified? Unified, in some sense, they must be if the "Ode" is a poem and not a heap of fragments.

I hope that my last statement indicates the kind of question which we finally have to face and answer. It is a problem of poetic organization. As such, it addresses itself properly to the critic. The historical scholars have not answered it, for it is a question which cannot be answered in terms of historical evidence. (This is not to say, of course, that the same man may not be both historical scholar and critic.) Moreover, I have already taken some pains to indicate how heavily the critic, on his part, may need to lean upon the historian. To put the matter into its simplest terms: the critic obviously must know what the words of the poem mean, something which immediately puts him in debt to the linguist; and since many of the words in this poem are proper nouns, in debt to the historian as well. I am not concerned to exalt the critic at the expense of specialists in other disciplines: on the contrary, I am only concerned to show that he has a significant function, and to indicate what the nature of that function is.

But I am not so presumptuous as to promise a solution to the problem. Instead, the reader will have to be content with suggestions— as to what the "Ode" is not saying, as to what the "Ode" may be saying —in short, with explorations of further problems. Many critical problems, of course, I shall have to pass over and some important ones I shall only touch upon. To illustrate: there is the general Roman cast given to the "Ode." Marvell has taken care to make no specifically Christian references in the poem. Charles is Caesar; Cromwell is a Hannibal; on the scaffold, Charles refuses to call with "vulgar spight," not on God, but on "the Gods," and so on. Or to point to another problem, metaphors drawn from hunting pervade the poem. Charles chases himself to Carisbrooke; Cromwell is like the falcon; Cromwell will soon put his dogs in "near/The *Caledonian* Deer." Or, to take up the general organization of the poem: Marvell seems to have used the celebrated stanzas on Charles's execution to divide the poem into two rather distinct parts: first, Cromwell's rise to power; and second, Cromwell's wielding of the supreme power. This scheme of division, by the way, I intend to make use of in the discussion that follows. But I shall try, in general, to limit it to the specific problem of the speaker's attitude toward Cromwell, subordinating other critical problems to this one, which is, I maintain, essentially a critical problem too.

From historical evidence alone we would suppose that the attitude toward Cromwell in his poem would have to be a complex one. And this complexity is reflected in the ambiguity of the compliments paid to him. The ambiguity reveals itself as early as the second word of the poem. It is the "forward" youth whose attention the speaker directs to the example of Cromwell. "Forward" may mean no more than "highspirited," "ardent," "properly ambitious"; but the *New English Dictionary* sanctions the possibility that there lurks in the word the sense of "presumptuous," "pushing." The forward youth can no longer now

> in the Shadows sing
> His Numbers languishing.

In the light of Cromwell's career, he must forsake the shadows and his "Muses dear" and become the man of action.

The speaker, one observes, does not identify Cromwell himself as the "forward youth," or say directly that Cromwell's career has been motivated by a striving for fame. But the implications of the first two stanzas do carry over to him. There is, for example, the important word "so" to relate Cromwell to these stanzas:

> So restless *Cromwel* could not cease. . . .

And "restless" is as ambiguous in its meanings as "forward," and in its darker connotations even more damning. For, though "restless" can mean "scorning indolence," "willing to forego ease," it can also suggest the man with a maggot in the brain. "To cease," used intransitively, is "to take rest, to be or remain at rest," and the *New English Dictionary* gives instances as late as 1701. Cromwell's "courage high" will not allow him to rest "in the inglorious Arts of Peace." And this thirst for glory, merely hinted at here by negatives, is developed further in the ninth stanza:

> Could by industrious Valour climbe
> To ruine the great Work of Time.

"Climb" certainly connotes a kind of aggressiveness. In saying this we need not be afraid that we are reading into the word some smack of such modern phrases as "social climber." Marvell's translation of the second chorus of Seneca's *Thyestes* sufficiently attests that the word could have such associations for him:

> Climb at *Court* for me that will
> Tottering favors Pinacle;
> All I seek is to lye still.

Cromwell, on the other hand, does not seek to lie still—has sought something quite other than this. His valor is called—strange collocation —an "industrious valour," and his courage is too high to brook a rival:

> For 'tis all one to Courage high
> The Emulous or Enemy;
>   And with such to inclose,
> Is more then to oppose.

The implied metaphor is that of some explosive which does more violence to that which encloses it, the powder to its magazine, for instance, than to some wall which merely opposes it—against which the charge is fired.

But the speaker has been careful to indicate that Cromwell's motivation has to be conceived of as more complex than any mere thirst for glory. He has even pointed this up. The forward youth is referred to as one who "would appear"—that is, as one who wills to leave the shadows of obscurity. But restless Cromwell "could not cease"—for Cromwell it is not a question of will at all, but of a deeper compulsion. Restless Cromwell could not cease, if he would.

Indeed, the lines that follow extend the suggestion that Cromwell is like an elemental force—with as little will as the lightning bolt, and with as little conscience:

And, like the three-fork'd Lightning, first
Breaking the Clouds where it was nurst,
　　Did thorough his own Side
　　His fiery way divide.

We are told that the last two lines refer to Cromwell's struggle after Marston Moor with the leaders of the Parliamentary party. Doubtless they do, and the point is important for our knowledge of the poem. But what is more important is that we be fully alive to the force of the metaphor. The clouds have bred the lightning bolt, but the bolt tears its way through the clouds, and goes on to blast the head of Caesar himself. As Margoliouth puts it: "The lightning is conceived as tearing through the side of his own body the cloud." In terms of the metaphor, then, Cromwell has not spared his own body: there is no reason therefore to be surprised that he has not spared the body of Charles.

I do not believe that I overemphasized the speaker's implication that Cromwell is a natural force. A few lines later the point is reinforced with another naturalistic figure, an analogy taken from physics:

Nature that hateth emptiness,
Allows of penetration less:
　　And therefore must make room
　　Where greater Spirits come . . .

The question of right, the imagery insists, is beside the point. If nature will not tolerate a power vacuum, no more will it allow two bodies to occupy the same space. (It is amusing, by the way, that Marvell has boldly introduced into his analogy borrowed from physics the nonphysical term "Spirits"; yet I do not think that the clash destroys the figure. Since twenty thousand angels can dance on the point of a needle, two spirits, even though one of them is a greater spirit, ought to be able to occupy the same room. But two spirits, as Marvell conceives of spirits here, will jostle one another, and one must give way. True, the greater spirit is immaterial, but he is no pale abstraction—he is all air and fire, the "force of angry Heavens flame." The metaphor ought to give less trouble to the reader of our day than it conceivably gave to readers bred up on Newtonian physics.)

What are the implications for Charles? Does the poet mean to imply that Charles has angered heaven—that he has merited his destruction? There is no suggestion that Cromwell is a thunderbolt hurled by an angry Jehovah—or even by an angry Jove. The general emphasis on Cromwell as an elemental force is thoroughly relevant here to counter this possible misreading. Certainly, in the lines that follow there is nothing to suggest that Charles has angered heaven, or that the Justice which complains against his fate is anything less than justice.

I began this examination of the imagery with the question, "What is the speaker's attitude toward Cromwell?" We have seen that the speaker more than once hints at his thirst for glory:

So restless *Cromwel* could not cease . . .
Could by industrious Valour climbe . . .

But we have also seen that the imagery tends to view Cromwell as a natural phenomenon, the bolt bred in the cloud. Is there a contradiction? I think not. Cromwell's is no vulgar ambition. If his valor is an "industrious Valour," it contains plain valor too of a kind perfectly capable of being recognized by any Cavalier:

What Field of all the Civil Wars,
Where his were not the deepest Scars?

If the driving force has been a desire for glory, it is a glory of that kind which allows a man to become dedicated and, in a sense, even selfless in his pursuit of it. Moreover, the desire for such glory can become so much a compulsive force that the man does not appear to act by an exercise of his personal will but seems to become the very will of something else. There is in the poem, it seems to me, at least one specific suggestion of this sort:

But through adventrous War
Urged his active Star. . . .

Cromwell is the marked man, the man of destiny, but he is not merely the man governed by his star. Active though it be, he cannot remain passive, even in relation to it: he is not merely urged by it, but himself urges it on.

Yet, if thus far Cromwell has been treated as naked force, something almost too awesome to be considered as a man, the poet does not forget that after all he is a man too—that "the force of angry Heavens flame" is embodied in a human being:

> And, if we would speak true,
> Much to the Man is due.

The stanzas that follow proceed to define and praise that manliness—the strength, the industrious valor, the cunning. (You will notice that I reject the interpretation which would paraphrase "Much to the Man is due" as "After all, Cromwell has accomplished much that is good." Such an interpretation could sort well enough with Legouis's picture of Marvell as the cold and detached honest broker between the factions: unfortunately it will not survive a close scrutiny of the grammar and the general context in which the passage is placed.)

One notices that among the virtues composing Cromwell's manliness, the speaker mentions his possession of the "wiser art":

> Where, twining subtile fears with hope,
> He wove a Net of such a scope,
> That *Charles* himselfe might chase
> To *Caresbrooks* narrow case.

On this point Cromwell has been cleared by all the modern historians (except perhaps Mr. Hilaire Belloc). Charles's flight to Carisbrooke Castle, as it turned out, aided Cromwell, but Cromwell could have hardly known that it would; and there is no evidence that he cunningly induced the King to flee to Carisbrooke. Royalist pamphleteers, of course, believed that Cromwell did, and used the item in their general bill of damnation against Cromwell. How does the speaker use it here—to damn or to praise? We tend to answer, "To praise." But then it behooves us to notice what is being praised. The things praised are Cromwell's talents as such—the tremendous disciplined powers which Cromwell brought to bear against the King.

For the end served by those powers, the speaker has no praise at all. Rather he has gone out of his way to insist that Cromwell was deaf to the complaint of Justice and its pleading of the "antient Rights." The power achieved by Cromwell is a "forced Pow'r"—a usurped power. On this point the speaker is unequivocal. I must question therefore Margoliouth's statement that Marvell sees in Cromwell "the man of destiny moved by . . . a power that is above justice." Above justice, yes, in the sense that power is power and justice is not power. The one does not insure the presence of the other. Charles has no way to vindicate his "helpless Right," but it is no less Right because it is helpless. But the speaker, though he is not a cynic, is a realist. A kingdom cannot be held by mere pleading of the "antient Rights":

> But those do hold or break
> As Men are strong or weak.

In short, the more closely we look at the "Ode," the more clearly apparent it becomes that the speaker has chosen to emphasize Cromwell's virtues as a man, and likewise, those of Charles as a man. The poem does not debate which of the two was right, for that issue is not even in question. In his treatment of Charles, then, the speaker no more than Charles himself attempts to vindicate his "helpless Right." Instead, he emphasizes his dignity, his fortitude, and what has finally to be called his consummate good taste. The portraits of the two men beautifully supplement each other. Cromwell is—to use Aristotle's distinction—the man of character, the man of action, who "does both act and know." Charles, on the other hand, is the man of passion, the man who is acted upon, the man who knows how to suffer. The contrast is pointed up in half a dozen different ways.

Cromwell, acted upon by his star, is not passive but actually urges his star. Charles in "acting"—in chasing away to Carisbrooke—actually is passive—performs the part assigned to him by Cromwell. True, we can read "chase" as an intransitive verb (the *New English Dictionary* sanctions this use for the period): "that Charles himself might hurry to Carisbrooke." But the primary meaning asserts itself in the context: "that Charles might chase himself to Carisbrooke's narrow case." For this hunter, now preparing to lay his dogs in "near/The *Caledonian Deer*," the royal quarry has dutifully chased itself.

Even in the celebrated stanzas on the execution, there is ironic realism as well as admiration. In this fullest presentation of Charles as king, he is the player king, the king acting in a play. He is the "Royal Actor" who knows his assigned part and performs it with dignity. He truly adorned the "Tragick Scaffold"

> While round the armed Bands
> Did clap their bloody hands.

The generally received account is that the soldiers clapped their hands so as to make it impossible for Charles's speech to be heard. But in the context this reference to hand-clapping supports the stage metaphor. What is being applauded? Cromwell's resolution in bringing the King to a deserved death? Or Charles's resolution on the scaffold as he suffered that death? Marvell was too good a poet to resolve the ambiguity. It is enough that he makes the armed bands applaud.

It has not been pointed out, I believe, that Robert Wild, in his poem on "The Death of Mr. Christopher Love," has echoed a pair of Marvell's finest lines. Love was beheaded by Cromwell on August 22, 1651. In Wild's poem, Marvell's lines

> But with his keener Eye
> The Axes edge did try

become: "His keener words did their sharp Ax exceed." The point is of no especial importance except that it indicates, since Wild's poem was evidently written shortly after Love's execution, that in 1651 the "Horatian Ode" was being handed about among the Royalists. For Wild was that strange combination, an English Presbyterian Royalist.

I have pointed out earlier that the second half of the poem begins here with the reference to

> that memorable Hour
> Which first assur'd the forced Pow'r.

Cromwell is now the *de facto* head of the state, and the speaker, as a realist, recognizes that fact. Cromwell is seen henceforth, not primarily in his character as the destroyer of the monarchy, but as the agent of the new state that has been erected upon the dead body of the King. The thunderbolt simile, of the first part of the poem, gives way here to the falcon simile in this second part of the poem. The latter figure revises and qualifies the former: it repeats the suggestion of ruthless energy and power, but Cromwell falls from the sky now, not as the thunderbolt, but as the hunting hawk. The trained falcon is not a wanton destroyer, nor an irresponsible one. It knows its master: it is perfectly disciplined:

> She, having kill'd, no more does search,
> But on the next green Bow to pearch . . .

The speaker's admiration for Cromwell the man culminates, it seems to me, here. Cromwell might make the Fame his own; he *need* not present kingdoms to the state. He might assume the crown rather than crowning each year. Yet he forbears:

> Nor yet grown stiffer with Command,
> But still in the *Republick's* hand . . .

Does the emphasis on "still" mean that the speaker is surprised that Cromwell has continued to pay homage to the republic? Does he imply that Cromwell may not always do so? Perhaps not: the emphasis is upon the fact that he need not obey and yet does. Yet the compliment derives its full force from the fact that the homage is not forced, but voluntary and even somewhat unexpected. And a recognition of this point implies the recognition of the possibility that Cromwell will not always so defer to the commonwealth.

And now what of the republic which Cromwell so ruthlessly and efficiently serves? What is the speaker's attitude toward it? To begin with, the speaker recognizes that its foundations rest upon the bleeding head of Charles. The speaker is aware, it is true, of the Roman analogy, and the English state is allowed the benefit of that analogy. But it is well to notice that the speaker does not commit himself to the opinion that the bleeding head is a happy augury:

> And yet in that the *State*
> Foresaw it's happy Fate.

The Roman state was able to take it as a favorable omen, and was justified by the event. With regard to the speaker himself, it seems to me more to the point to notice what prophecy he is willing to commit himself to. He does not prophesy peace. He is willing to predict that England, under Cromwell's leadership, will be powerful in war, and will strike fear into the surrounding states:

> What may not then our *Isle* presume
> While Victory his Crest does plume!
> What may not others fear
> If thus he crown each year!

Specifically, he predicts a smashing victory over the Scots.

But what of the compliments to Cromwell on his ruthlessly effective campaign against the Irish? Does not the speaker succumb, for once, to a bitter and biased patriotism, and does this not constitute a blemish upon the poem?

And now the *Irish* are asham'd
To see themselves in one Year tam'd:
So much one Man can do,
That does both act and know.

They can affirm his Praises best,
And have, though overcome, confest
How good he is, how just. . . .

Margoliouth glosses the word "confessed" as follows: "Irish testimony in favor of Cromwell at this moment is highly improbable. Possibly there is a reference to the voluntary submission of part of Munster with its English colony." But surely Margoliouth indulges in understatement. The most intense partisan of Cromwell would have had some difficulty in taking the lines without some inflection of grim irony. The final appeal in this matter, however, is not to what Marvell the Englishman must have thought, or even to what Marvell the author must have intended, but rather to the full context of the poem itself. In that context, the lines in question can be read ironically, and the earlier stanzas sanction that reading. Cromwell's energy, activity, bravery, resolution—even what may be called his efficiency—are the qualities that have come in for praise, not his gentleness or his mercy. The Irish, indeed, are best able to affirm such praise as has been accorded to Cromwell; and they know from experience "how good he is, how just," for they have been blasted by the force of angry Heaven's flame, even as Charles has been. But I do not mean to turn the passage into sarcasm. The third quality which the speaker couples with goodness and justice is fitness "for highest Trust," and the goodness and justice of Cromwell culminate in this fitness. But the recommendation to trust has reference not to the Irish, but to the English state. The Irish are quite proper authorities on Cromwell's trustworthiness in this regard, for they have come to know him as the completely dedicated instrument of that state whose devotion to the purpose in hand is unrelenting and unswerving.

To say all this is not to suggest that Marvell shed any unnecessary tears over the plight of the Irish, or even to imply that he was not happy, as one assumes most Englishmen were, to have the Irish rebellion crushed promptly and efficiently. It is to say that the passage fits into the poem—a poem which reveals itself to be no panegyric on Cromwell but an unflinching analysis of the Cromwellian character.

The wild Irish have been tamed, and now the Pict will no longer be able to shelter under his particolored mind. It is the hour of decision, and the particolored mind affords no protection against the man who "does both act and know." In Cromwell's mind there are no conflicts, no teasing mixture of judgments. Cromwell's is not only an "industrious valour," but a "sad valour." Margoliouth glosses "sad" as "steadfast," and no doubt he is right. But sad can mean "sober" also, and I suspect that in this context, with its implied references to Scottish plaids, it means also drab of hue. It is also possible that the poet here glances at one of Virgil's transferred epithets, *maestum timorem*, sad fear, the fear that made the Trojans sad. Cromwell's valor is *sad* in that the Scots will have occasion to rue it.

Thus far the speaker has been content to view Cromwell from a distance, as it were, against the background of recent history. He has referred to him consistently in the third person. But in the last two stanzas, he addresses Cromwell directly. He salutes him as "the Wars and Fortunes Son." It is a great compliment: Cromwell is the son of the wars in that he is the master of battle, and he seems fortune's own son in the success that has contantly waited upon him. But we do not wrench the lines if we take them to say also that Cromwell is the creature of the wars and the product of fortune. The imagery of the early stanzas which treats Cromwell as a natural phenomenon certainly lends support to this reading. Cromwell can claim no sanction for his power in "antient Rights." His power has come out of the wars and the troubled times. I call attention to the fact that we do not have to choose between readings: the readings do not mutually exclude each other: they support each other, and this double interpretation has the whole poem behind it.

Cromwell is urged to march "indefatigably on." The advice is good advice; but it is good advice because any other course of action is positively unthinkable. Indeed, to call it advice at all is perhaps to distort it: thought addressed to Cromwell, it partakes of quiet commentary as much as of exhortation. After all, it is restless Cromwell who is being addressed. If he could not cease "in the inglorious Arts of Peace" when his "highest plot" was "to plant the Bergamot," one cannot conceive of his ceasing now in the hour of danger.

> And for the last effect
> Still keep thy Sword erect.

Once more the advice (or commentary) is seriously intended, but it carries with it as much of warning as it does of approval. Those who take up the sword shall perish by the sword: those who have achieved their power on contravention of ancient rights by the sword can only expect to maintain their power by the sword.

What kind of sword is it that is able to "fright the spirits of the shady night"? Margoliouth writes: "The cross hilt of the sword would avert the spirits. . . ." But the speaker makes it quite plain that it is not merely the spirits of the shady night that Cromwell will have to fight as he marches indefatigably on. It will not be enough to hold the sword aloft as a ritual sword, an emblematic sword. The naked steel will still have to be used against bodies less diaphanous than spirits. If there is any doubt as to this last point, Marvell's concluding lines put it as powerfully and explicitly as it can be put:

> The same *Arts* that did *gain*
> A *Pow'r* must it *maintain*.

But, I can imagine someone asking, What is the final attitude toward Cromwell? Is it ultimately one of approval or disapproval? Does admiration overbalance condemnation? Or, is the "Ode," after all, merely a varied Scottish plaid, the reflection of Marvell's own particolored mind—a mind which had not been finally "made up" with regard to Cromwell? I think that enough has been said to make it plain that there is no easy, pat answer to such questions. There is a unified total attitude, it seems to me; but it is so complex that we may oversimplify and distort its complexity by the way in which we put the question. The request for some kind of summing up is a natural one, and I have no wish to try to evade it. For a really full answer, of course, one must refer the questioner to the poem itself; but one can at least try to suggest some aspects of the total attitude.

I would begin by reemphasizing the dramatic character of the poem. It is not a statement—an essay on "Why I cannot support Cromwell" or on "Why I am now ready to support Cromwell." It is a poem essentially dramatic in its presentation, which means that it is diagnostic rather than remedial, and eventuates, not in a course of action, but in contemplation. Perhaps the best way therefore in which to approach it is to conceive of it as, say, one conceives of a Shakespearean tragedy. Cromwell is the usurper who demands and commands admiration. What, for example, is our attitude toward Macbeth? We assume his guilt, but there are qualities which emerge from his guilt which properly excite admiration. I do not mean that the qualities palliate his guilt or that they compensate for his guilt. They actually come into being through his guilt, but they force us to exalt him even as we condemn him. I have chosen an extreme example. I certainly do not mean to imply that in writing the "Ode" Marvell had Shakespeare's tragedy in mind. What I am trying to point to is this: that the kind of honesty and insight and whole-mindedness which we associate with tragedy is to be found to some degree in all great poetry and is to be found in this poem.

R. P. Warren once remarked to me that Marvell has constantly behind him in his poetry the achievement of Elizabethan drama with its treatment of the human will as seen in the perspective of history. He had in mind some of the lyrics, but the remark certainly applies fully to the "Ode." The poet is thoroughly conscious of the drama, and consciously makes use of dramatic perspective. Charles, as we have seen, becomes the "Royal Actor," playing his part on the "Tragick Scaffold." But the tragedy of Charles is merely glanced at. The poem is Cromwell's—Cromwell's tragedy, the first three acts of it, as it were, which is not a tragedy of failure but of success.

Cromwell is the truly kingly man who is *not* king—whose very virtues conduce to kingly power and almost force kingly power upon him. It is not any fumbling on the poet's part which causes him to call Cromwell "a Caesar" before the poem ends, even though he has earlier appropriated that name to Charles. *Both* men are Caesar, Charles the wearer of the purple, and Cromwell, the invincible general, the inveterate campaigner, the man "that does both act and know." Cromwell is the Caesar who must refuse the crown—whose glory it is that he is willing to refuse the crown—but who cannot enjoy the reward and the security that a crown affords. The tension between the speaker's admiration for the kingliness which has won Cromwell the power and his awareness that the power can be maintained only by a continual exertion of these talents for kingship—this tension is never relaxed. Cromwell is not of royal blood—he boasts a higher and a baser pedigree: he is the "Wars and Fortunes Son." He cannot rest because he is restless Cromwell. He must march indefatigably on, for he cannot afford to become fatigued. These implications enrich and qualify an insight into Cromwell which is as heavily freighted with admiration as it is with a great condemnation. But the admiration and the condemnation do not cancel each other. They define each other; and because there is responsible definition, they reinforce each other.

Was this, then, the attitude of Andrew Marvell, born 1621, some-time student at Cambridge returned traveler and prospective tutor, toward Oliver Cromwell in the summer of 1650? The honest answer must be: I do not know. I have tried to read the poem, the "Horatian Ode," not Andrew Marvell's mind. That seems sensible to me in view of the fact that we have the poem, whereas the attitude held by Marvell at any particular time must be a matter of inference—even though I grant that the poem may be put in as part of the evidence from which we draw inferences. True, we do know that Marvell was capable of composing the "Ode" and I must concede that that fact may tell us a great deal about Marvell's attitude toward Cromwell. I think it probably does. I am not sure, for reasons given earlier in this paper, that it tells us everything: there is the problem of the role of the unconscious in the process of composition, there is the possibility of the poet's having written better than he knew, there is even the matter of the happy accident. I do not mean to overemphasize these matters. I do think, however, that it is wise to maintain the distinction between what total attitude is manifested in the poem and the attitude of the author as citizen.

Yet, though I wish to maintain this distinction, I do not mean to hide behind it. The total attitude realized in the "Ode" does not seem to me monstrously inhuman in its complexity. It could be held by human beings, in my opinion. Something very like it apparently was. Listen, for example, to the Earl of Clarendon's judgment on Cromwell:

He was one of those men, quos vituperare ne inimici quidem possunt, nisi ut simul laudent [whom not even their enemies can inveigh against without at the same time praising them], for he could never have done halfe that mischieve, without great partes of courage and industry and judgement, and he must have had a wonderful understandinge in the nature and humours of men, and as greate a dexterity in the applyinge them, who from a private and obscure birth (though of a good family), without interest of estate, allyance or frenshippes, could rayse himselfe to such a height, and compounde and kneade such opposite and contradictory humours and interests, into a consistence, that contributed to his designes and to ther owne distruction, whilst himselfe grew insensibly powerfull enough, to cutt off those by whom he had climed, in the instant, that they projected to demolish ther owne buildinge. . . .

He was not a man of bloode, and totally declined Machiavells methode . . . it was more then once proposed, that ther might be a generall massacre of all the royall party, as the only expedient to secure the government, but Crumwell would never consent to it, it may be out of to much contempt of his enimyes; In a worde, as he had all the wikednesses against which damnation is denounced and for which Hell fyre is praepared, so he had some virtues, which have caused the memory of some men in all ages to be celebrated, and he will be looked upon by posterity, as a brave, badd man.

The resemblance between Clarendon's judgment and that reflected in the "Ode" is at some points so remarkable that one wonders whether Clarendon had not seen and been impressed by some now lost manuscript of the "Ode": "Who from a private and obscure birth"—"Who, from his private Gardens, where/He liv'd reserved and austere"—"could rayse himself to such a height . . . by whome he had climed"—"Could by industrious Valour climbe," and so on and so forth. But I do not want to press the suggestion of influence of Marvell on Clarendon. Indeed, it makes for my general point to discount the possibility. For what I am anxious to emphasize is that the attitude of the "Ode" is not inhuman in its Olympian detachment, that something like it could be held by a human being, and by a human being of pronounced Royalist sympathies.

I have argued that the critic needs the help of the historian—all the help that he can get—but I have insisted that the poem has to be read as a poem—that what it "says" is a question for the critic to answer, and that no amount of historical evidence as such can finally determine what the poem says. But if we do read the poem successfully, the critic may on occasion be able to make a return on his debt to the historian. If we have read the "Ode" successfully—*if*, I say, for I am far from confident—it may be easier for us to understand how the man capable of writing the "Ode" was also able to write "Tom May's Death" and "On Appleton House" and indeed, years later, after the Restoration, the statement: "Men ought to have trusted God; they ought and might have trusted the King."

Since completing this essay, I have come upon a further (see p. 434) item which would suggest that the "Horatian Ode" was circulating among Royalists—not Puritans—in the early 1650s. The stanza form of the "Horatian Ode" was used only once by Marvell (in this poem) and does not seem to occur in English poetry prior to Marvell. Margoliouth and Legouis think it probable that this stanza was Marvell's own invention. Perhaps it was. But in Sir Richard Fanshawe's translation of Horace's Odes (*Selected Parts of Horace . . . Now newly put into English*, London, 1652) the "Horatian Ode" stanza is used several times.

If Marvell invented the stanza in the summer of 1650, he must have been in close association with Fanshawe for Fanshawe to have borrowed and made use of the stanza so frequently in poems which were to be in print two years later. I suspect that Marvell borrowed the stanza from Fanshawe. Fanshawe had begun to publish translations of Horace (though none in this stanza pattern) as early as 1648 in the volume which contained his translation of *Il Pastor Fido*. But in either case a Royalist connection for Marvell is implied, for Fanshawe (1608–66) was a fervent and active Royalist throughout the war, and after the Restoration was a trusted servant of Charles II.

The following notes appear in H. M. Margoliouth's edition of *The Poems and Letters of Andrew Marvell* (Oxford: Clarendon Press, 1927), I, 237–38:

> A correspondent in *The Times Literary Supplement* (29 January 1920) compares with ll. 9–16 of this Ode Lucan, *Pharsalia*, i. 144 *et seq.* . . .
>
> Marvelle perhaps had in mind both the Latin (cf. successus urgere suos and "Urg'd his active Star") and Tom May's translation, which here reads as follows (2nd edition, 1631):

> But restlesse valour, and in warre a shame
> Not to be Conquerour; fierce, not curb'd at all,
> Ready to fight, where hope, or anger call,
> His forward Sword; confident of successe,
> And bold the favour of the gods to presse:
> Orethrowing all that his ambition stay,
> And loves that ruine should enforce his way;
> As lightning by the wind forc'd from a cloude
> Breakes through the wounded aire with thunder loud,
> Disturbes the Day, the people terrifyes,
> And by a light oblique dazels our eyes,
> Not *Joves* owne Temple spares it; when no force,
> No barre can hinder his prevailing course,
> Great waste, as foorth it sallyes and retires,
> It makes and gathers his dispersed fires.

Note the verbal resemblances, "restlesse valour" and "industrious Valour," "forward Sword" and "The forward Youth," "lightning . . . from a cloude Breakes" and "Lightning . . . Breaking the Clouds." Further I suggest with diffidence that the striking phrase "active Star" owes something to the chance neighbourhood of the two words in another passage in the same book of May's translation (*Pharsalia*, i. 229–32):

> . . . the active Generall
> Swifter than Parthian back-shot shaft, or stone

From Balearick Slinger, marches on
T' invade Ariminum; when every star
Fled from th' approaching Sunne but Lucifer . . .

Caesar is up betimes, marching when only the morning star is in the sky: Cromwell urges *his* "active star."

Sir Edward Ridley, carrying on the correspondence in *The Times Literary Supplement* (5 February 1920), points out further a likeness between Marvell's account of the death of Charles I and *Pharsalia*, viii. 613–17 (the death of Pompey):

> ut vidit comminus ensem
> involvit vultus atque indignatus apertum
> fortunae praestare caput, tunc lumina pressit
> continuitque animam, ne quas effundere voces
> posset et aeternam fletu corrumpere famam . . .

II. 10

Restoration Comedy and Later*

MARVIN MUDRICK

University of California, Santa Barbara

THE HIGH reputation of Restoration comedy has been sustained on surprisingly slight critical authority. It is true that the squeamishness of the two centuries following *The Way of the World* prevented more than an occasional outraged dismissal, or defensive impressionistic survey, of what was taken (except, disingenuously, by Lamb) for the accurate reflection of a debauched society. Critics during the past several decades have had no such excuse. The inhibition removed, we expect due and favorable examination of the age of Wycherley and Congreve. The most persuasive recent examination, however, is an attack, by L. C. Knights; and Mr. Knights is not squeamish, but bored: "The criticism . . . [their] defenders . . . need to answer is not that the comedies are 'immoral,' but that they are trivial, gross and dull." [1]

It may be said for the defenders that they, at least, are not bored with this "finely polished art of the intellect that gives us amply in return for the vulgarity." [2] They find the novel virtue of the Restoration comic dramatist in his "desire to try new ways of living"; [3] they explore his preoccupation with "life . . . accepted and observed—not

---

* Read at the Institute in 1954. Published in *Institute Essays: English Stage Comedy*, 1955.

[1] *Explorations* (New York, 1947), "Restoration Comedy: The Reality and the Myth," p. 168.

[2] A. Nicoll, *Restoration Drama* (4th ed., Cambridge, 1952), p. 201.

[3] B. Dobrée, *Restoration Comedy* (Oxford, 1926), p. 22.

as a problem, but a pageant"; [4] they single out his invention of "personalities" of "unfailing grace and distinction," to which the "thoroughly conventionalized social mode" of the court of Charles II "could not give complete expression"; [5] they confide that in the contemplation of his plays "we become for the moment pagan, without a thought of the morrow, existing solely for the joy of the hour." [6] They can also penetrate, through a modish generalization by Congreve's Angelica on the pleasures of the sex-chase ("Uncertainty and expectation are the joys of life," etc.), to the heart and *Weltschmerz* of Restoration comedy:

This is not the observation of a jilt, of a baggage without sensibility, but of a woman who has known and suffered, who has been disappointed in her early estimate of things. It is the weary cry of the knower who realizes that happiness may not be sought for or grasped, and that joy must be snatched as it flies. These were not mere puppets, but breathing, living, desiring men and women.[7]

From such throbbing appreciation it is salutary to turn back to the plays themselves and to agree with Mr. Knights. Certainly Restoration comedy lacks the "quality and variety," the vigor and scope, of interest and idiom that the Elizabethan playwrights, for example, could draw upon. In Restoration wit "the verbal pattern appears at times to be completely unrelated to a mode of perceiving," the words "have an air of preening themselves on their acute discriminations," though "the antitheses are mechanical, and the pattern is monotonously repeated." "In the matter of sexual relations Restoration comedy is entirely dominated by a narrow set of conventions," and even these conventions the dramatist does not, characteristically, examine in order to trace and predict the directions they may give to human impulses. Rather, he exploits them in order to gratify "the constant need for titillation" of an inanely artificial society "lacking the real sophistication and self-knowledge that might, in some measure, have redeemed it." [8]

Still, the indictment may not be so damaging as it seems. Mr. Knights's least disputable charge, concerning the inferiority of Restoration to Elizabethan drama, reminds us that, whatever their relative

[4] J. Palmer, *The Comedy of Manners* (London, 1913), p. 191.
[5] K. M. Lynch, *The Social Mode of Restoration Comedy* (New York, 1926), pp. 181, 216.
[6] Nicoll, *Restoration Drama*, p. 200.   [8] Knights, *Explorations, passim.*
[7] Dobrée, *Restoration Comedy*, p. 137.

merits, each of them was authoritative enough to define its age as an age of drama—the rarest kind of literary age—during which a number of playwrights, united by a community of conventions and interests and identifiable by common qualities of idiom and style, not only hold the stage but dominate the writing of their time. Aside from the century of Shakespeare and Congreve, there is indeed no English literary period with a surviving, not to mention dominating, drama. Mr. Knights's comparison may imply, then, more odium than it should: the fact that the Restoration theater is, by the standard of the Elizabethan, unresourceful and limited must be seen in the light of the equally unarguable fact that, though the English stage has had other names and other entertainments, it has had no other theater at all.

As for the superiority of Elizabethan *comedy* to Wycherley and Congreve, that is altogether arguable. "The fault . . . of Shakespeare's comic Muse," remarked Hazlitt, "is . . . that it is too good-natured and magnanimous." It is scarcely unorthodox to suggest that Shakespeare's comic figures are for the most part either casually witty observers or the merest butts, and that his "comedies" are good-natured mélanges always ready to sacrifice any dramatic pattern—including the comic patterns of mechanism and vitality, plausibility and substance, deceit and exposure—in order to examine the margin of humanness, the strong (and at times dramatically fatal) pathos discoverable by Shakespeare in Malvolio and Shylock as well as in Shallow and Falstaff. The so-called problem comedies—*Measure for Measure* and *Troilus and Cressida*, especially—are in fact Shakespeare's solution of his comic problem: they are irreducible tragicomedies, in which Shakespeare creates a form hospitable to the pathos and self-exhausting complexity of motive that he constantly discovers in protagonists not quite grand or lucky enough to be tragic.

The claim of Elizabethan comedy must rest, eventually, with Jonson, who lacked Shakespeare's talent for pathos and Fletcher's weakness for it and was therefore unimpelled to make new genres or to corrupt old ones. The contribution of Jonson's audience was the Elizabethan delight in roguery—we have the testimony of the pamphleteers and "true-history" writers as well as the dramatists—and nothing is more susceptible to the logic of comedy than the cycle of deception and self-deception, exposure and mortification between rogue and gull or between rogue and rogue, the innocent dishonest dream of something for nothing, the most enduring symbol of which is Jonson's own

Alchemist. What Jonson himself contributed was the virtue of his defect: incapable of pathos, he is supremely capable of reducing motive to monomania and so diverting attention from the players to the gusto and intricate strategy of the game itself—the game, that is, of comedy, in which there are the manipulated and the manipulators, dupedom and the triumphant or foiled ingenuity of conscious appetite.

Jonson's power is dramatic; it affirms itself primarily, not in scene-shifting or stage-business, but in language. Even the live precision and tension of his plot grow out of the sardonic precision of his verse, as if everything—in *this* comic world at least—can be said directly, as if every purpose proclaims itself. It is a language of perfect transparency in which self-recognition is offered to all, as when Mosca flatters the lawyer, one of Volpone's would-be heirs:

> I oft have heard him say how he admir'd
> Men of your large profession, that could speak
> To every cause, and things mere contraries,
> Till they were hoarse again, yet all be law;
> That, with most quick agility, could turn
> And return; make knots, and undo them;
> Give forked counsel; take provoking gold
> On either hand, and put it up; these men,
> He knew, would thrive with their humility.
> And, for his part, he thought he should be blest
> To have his heir of such a suffering spirit,
> So wise, so grave, of so perplex'd a tongue,
> And loud withal, that would not wag, nor scarce
> Lie still, without a fee. . . .

It is a language in which man can even take the measure of his own desires, as when Sir Epicure, awaiting from the Alchemist the promised philosopher's stone, prophesies his own creatable paradise:

> I will have all my beds blown up, not stuff'd:
> Down is too hard; and then, mine oval room
> Fill'd with such pictures as Tiberius took
> From Elephantis, and dull Aretine
> But coldly imitated. Then, my glasses
> Cut in more subtle angles, to disperse
> And multiply the figures, as I walk
> Naked between my succubae. My mists
> I'll have of perfume, vapour'd 'bout the room,

> To lose our selves in; and my baths, like pits
> To fall into; from whence we will come forth,
> And roll us dry in gossamer and roses. . . .

It is a language, like Chaucer's or Swift's, rooted in an idiom rich with particular moral values—the ground of agreement between author and audience—and freely expressive of any moral deviations that human impulse contrives. It may be, indeed, the very freedom and particularity of the idiom that tempt Jonson—even in *Volpone* and *The Alchemist*—to scatter his shots with conversational exuberance, to indulge at times a strenuous self-righteousness (as through the straw figures of purity that he sets up against his energetic Vices), to stray out of comedy into topical satire, to aim at easy irrelevant targets like Sir Politic Would-Be. The Elizabethan tendency to this sort of logorrhea (so feelingly pointed out in Shakespeare by Jonson himself) is a tendency that makes even the best of Jonson's comedies blur at the edges. Wycherley—in *The Country Wife* at least—attending to similar comic deceits and disclosures, taking off from a device very similar to the initiatory device in *Volpone,* and working for the most part with characters obviously conceived as Jonsonian humors, manages to achieve a tough precision comparable to Jonson's; the achievement is on a smaller scale doubtless, but without Jonson's waste and misfire; and the conventions, however narrow, of the Restoration theater and the Restoration audience may be in part responsible.

In *Volpone* and *The Alchemist,* the two principal themes are avarice and lust, which are for Jonson—and his audience—moral deviations not only grave but almost inseparable, as though one inevitably implies the other; and if this mingling of sins seems to draw on the strength of the Christian-ethical tradition (which after all concerns itself with men and not comic figures), it also divides the attention and weakens Jonson's central comic effect: the clutter of single obsessions maneuvering and colliding. Like many other Elizabethan dramatists, Jonson suffers from a surplus of themes, a superabundance of interests that he share with his audience.

By the time of the Restoration, however, the popular audience of Jonson (and Shakespeare), already dwindling with the spread of Puritan sympathies during the Caroline period, had vanished entirely. Wycherley's spectators were "the courtiers and their satellites," [9] and

9 "The noblemen in the pit and boxes, the fops and beaux and wits or would-be-wits who hung on to their society, the women of the court, depraved and licen-

for such an idle and fashionable group, certain of Jonson's themes would have appeared barbarous and dull. For the Restoration audience, lust was, fashionably, little more than a casuistical Puritan distinction; and avarice was a tiresome trait hardly worth discussing among gentlemen or representing on a civilized stage—a trait of shopkeepers. (The latter, regarding the theaters as no better than brothels, never paid the price of admission and so did not have to be appeased.) For such an audience—without occupation, consciously straining toward an ideal of heroically casual debauchery, setting out to make up for the lost years under the Commonwealth—perhaps the only possible theme and motive was sex, that neutral stuff which the Elizabethans had graded into love and lust but which might now subside into unity again.

A dramatist is far more likely, in any case, to be numbed than invigorated by the prescriptions of theme and motive that his audience imposes and anticipates. Certainly, just as Elizabethan tragedy is in its mass a hodgepodge of butchery and tattered passions, so Restoration comedy is, in its overwhelming mass, a hodgepodge of premature sophistications, of inert, self-admiring wit and resolutely impertinent reversals of established sexual morality. We need look for verification no further than the comedies of Dryden, that most illustrious of hack playwrights, whose characters, as Mr. Knights remarks of Etherege's Dorimant, are engaged in "intrigues of no more human significance than those of a barn-yard cock." [10] There are, nevertheless, exceptions in both periods; and an age—of drama or of any other genre—is to be judged, ultimately, by its masterpieces. *The Country Wife* is, as Mr. Knights says of Restoration comedy generally, "in the matter of sexual relations . . . entirely dominated by a narrow set of conventions." We have in it the fixed focus on the sex-pursuit, the wits and would-be wits exercising themselves on the pleasures of variety and the pains of marriage, the neglected and yearning wives, the jealous husband fearing cuckoldry and the foolish one inviting it, but no marriage—in this view of wives as damageable possessions—proof against it. The question whether Wycherley yields to and exploits these conventions, or examines and substantiates them, is left to be considered.

---

tious as the men, the courtesans with whom these women of quality moved and conversed as on equal terms, made up at least four-fifths of the entire audience. Add a sprinkling of footmen in the upper gallery, a stray country cousin or two scattered throughout the theatre, and the picture of the audience is complete." (Nicoll, *Restoration Drama*, p. 8.)

[10] Knights, *Explorations*, p. 158.

Volpone's pretense of mortal illness, which alerts every acquaintance persuaded of being his sole heir, is Jonson's device for drawing out and illuminating the unity of avarice, the reduction and dehumanizing of appetite, in the specious diversity of a society for which money has become its own justification.[11] Wycherley's device, within the conventions of his own stage and society, is equally brilliant: the rake Horner, to lull the suspicion of husbands and to secure in time the devotion of wives whose only coyness is for reputation's sake, pretends to have been made a eunuch and to be therefore no longer dangerous to either. Jonson's speaking rapacities, drawn out by his device, are obsessed by money, Wycherley's by sex; and Wycherley is no more the defender or dupe of the obsession he treats than is Jonson of his. As in Jonson, everything is expressed directly, in a transparent idiom, through which communication is both easy and impossible: Horner and Harcourt—the two manipulators—say what they mean and take care, when necessary, to be misunderstood; their dupes—Sparkish, Sir Jasper and his "ladies"—give themselves away in every phrase with no such intention at all; Alithea, saying what she means and intending to be taken at her word, is not believed especially when she is most earnest; Pinchwife, the cuckold in spite of himself, says what he means and, since his words mean more than he guesses, is understood in ways that must at last confirm his ferocious cynicism; only the country wife, like a judgment on this murk of rutting deceptions, says what she means with such country candor and naïveté as to clear the air from time to time, until she learns, having lost her lover, to lie habitually and for the sake of comfort with her husband: "And I must be a country wife still too, I find; for I can't, like a city one, be rid of my husband, and do what I list."

Standards become private and narcissistic, masquerading behind words once susceptible to public definition: honor, for example. For Pinchwife, honor is the patrolling of his "freehold," the banner of anticuckoldism. For Sparkish, it is the modish reflex against such insults as he is competent to unriddle. For Lady Fidget, it is a vacuum, the absence of scandal—"'tis not an injury to a husband, till it be an injury to our honours; so that a woman of honour loses no honour with a private person." For her husband it is the proper filling of social rôles in savorless private lives, as when he tells his wife to "go to your

[11] The society Jonson writes about is documented at length in Knights, *Drama and Society in the Age of Jonson* (London, 1937).

business, I say, pleasure, whilst I go to my pleasure, business," and sends her off to play games with that unscandalous shadow of a man, Horner. For Alithea, honor is stubbornness of fidelity to a detestable commitment, the sort of honor that sentimental comedy will take in dead earnest during Wycherley's own lifetime. Only for Horner, the sardonic privileged observer, like Shakespeare's Diomede making his opportunities in a corrupt age without giving up a certain hard clarity of vision, is honor significantly honorable, the saving (for his own honorless aims) of his mistresses' reputations, which is all they wish saved, until, forced to choose between the "honor" of a concealed mistress and harmless Alithea's, he chooses his pleasure and must submit to Alithea's wistful reproach: "I always took you for a man of honour."

The dialogue is, throughout, a great web of ambiguities and unexpected, symbolic relevances: firecracker strings of *double-entendre* as in the china scene, intentions and words at cross-purposes and exposing each other, unconscious prophecies by gulls of their inevitable gulling, the insidious slipperiness of language in a society alerted to sex only. And the ambiguities are never merely stock comic devices in set-piece scenes and episodes, they are the confusions to which mind makes itself liable by reducing itself to caricature, by converting language into an unintentionally rich symbolism of aborted single impulse, such as flows over in the grotesque drinking scene between Horner and the ladies: "The filthy toads," says Mrs. Dainty—she is talking about men— "choose mistresses now as they do stuffs, for having been fancied and worn by others"; "For being common and cheap," adds Mrs. Squeamish; "Whilst women of quality," concludes Lady Fidget, "like the richest stuffs, lie untumbled, and unasked for."

This is the age of Nell Gwyn and the Duchess of Cleveland. "Is it not a frank age?" Sparkish the ape of fashion asks rhetorically, having just misinterpreted to his own satisfaction—as civility, as wit, as up-to-dateness or upside-downness—a rival's insults to him and declarations of love, over her protest, to the girl he is to marry. "Blame 'em not, they must follow their copy, the age," says one of Horner's friends about poets who create fashionable fools. Frankness, somehow, is not enough. Nor is monomaniacal vigilance: "What a swarm of cuckolds and cuckold-makers!" cries Pinchwife, preparing to assist with tenacious (if unintended) complaisance at his own cuckolding; and, having dictated to his wife her letter of disavowal for which she substitutes her own breathless solicitation, directs her to "write on the backside, 'For

Mr. Horner,' " and delivers it up—wife and all—himself. Heroism is not enough: "I will not be a cuckold," says Pinchwife, "there will be danger in making me a cuckold"; and Horner punctures that bubble, "Why, wert thou not well cured of thy last clap?"

Wycherley's toughmindedness, like Jonson's, is likely to repel tender critics. "There can be no question," remarks one of the recent admirers of Restoration comedy, "but Wycherley is indescribably vulgar." [12] Another will not admit him to the suave and truly comic company of Etherege and Congreve because

Social folly and hypocrisy are much closer realities to . . . [him] than the social poise and integrity which make amends. . . . When other writers of Restoration comedy ridicule folly and vice, it is more lightheartedly and rarely with corrective emphasis. . . . On some occasions, Wycherley assails some of the most cherished ideals of the age. . . . At such times . . . [he] is playing false to the tradition of Restoration comedy of manners; he confirms our suspicion that he was not 'born' a Restoration gentleman.[13]

The view that comedy is necessarily "lighthearted," gentlemanly, and careful of the "ideals of the age" would of course have startled comic dramatists from Aristophanes to Jonson; chiefly responsible, perhaps, for a view so vapidly genteel and, since Meredith, so nearly axiomatic are the false example of Shakespeare and the sentimental comedy that has dominated the English stage since 1700. Nor does the term "comedy of manners" brighten and rarefy the comic atmosphere so much as all that. A comic dramatist must use the materials his audience affords him: the period during which the surface and finish of life, wit and social adeptness monopolized the audience's image of life produced as its characteristic genre the comedy of manners; just as in a period of more diversified interests Jonson, concentrating on a single possible Elizabethan image of life—life as energy and appetite—produced the comedy of humors. But to treat an image of life is not necessarily to defend or suppress its defects. Wycherley merely had less faith than his audience in the durability of manners and in their power to withstand the pressure of impulse or self-interest. The author has his rights also.

Still, to wince at Wycherley is more reasonable than to find in Congreve a prevailing "joyousness" and the portarit of a "*beau monde*

[12] Nicoll, *British Drama* (4th ed., London, 1947), p. 252.
[13] Lynch, *The Social Mode*, pp. 173 ff.

. . . indulgently idealized"; [14] and this traditional view of *The Way of the World* particularly, as the prop and casual glory of Restoration society (or rather of its ghost), as an elegantly falsified testament dedicated by the age to itself, has long served both addicts and detractors of Restoration comedy, who unite in affirming that the comedy of manners can breathe only in an "air of modish triviality." [15]

Congreve, it is true, presents a society of superficies, in which manners are second nature and, therefore, distinctions of a primary nature—moral and psychological—are difficult to make. In the great world Fainall is scarcely distinguishable from Mirabell, and the false wits—snappers-up of considered trifles—scarcely distinguishable from the true ones. Both Fainall and Mirabell are witty and languidly polite, and the false wits can learn patterns of politeness and patterns of wit from such formal and artificial instructors. Manners are, or appear to be, opaque and durable, a common film of plausibility over the variety of impulse and motive.

Taken by itself, the entire first act of *The Way of the World* is a surface of ease and plausibility, barely ruffled even by the need to appear witty and detached. One is untempted, for example, to pentrate, so long as it occupies the stage, the rehearsed, serpentine elegance with which Fainall and Mirabell discuss women, courtship and marriage:

She once used me with that insolence [says Mirabell, remembering Millamant] that in revenge I took her to pieces, sifted her, and separated her failings; I studied 'em, and got 'em by rote. The catalogue was so large that I was not without hopes one day or other to hate her heartily; to which end I so used myself to think of 'em at length, contrary to my design and expectation, they gave me every hour less and less disturbance; till in a few days it became habitual to me to remember 'em without being displeased. They are now grown as familiar to me as my own frailties; and in all probability, in a little time longer I shall like 'em as well.

"Marry her, marry her!" says Fainall. "Be half as well acquainted with her charms as you are with her defects, and my life on't, you are your own man again. . . . I have experience; I have a wife, and so forth." Later, Witwoud stumbles into these verbal dexterities with a compliment: "No man in town lives well with a wife but Fainall. Your judgment, Mirabell? And Mirabell replies: "You had better step and ask his wife, if you would be credibly informed."

Manners—assembling themselves in the phrases so neatly pieced

[14] *Ibid.*, p. 213.   [15] Nicoll, *British Drama*, p. 255.

and developed, seeming to repel attention except to themselves—will very shortly, however, clear into a disquieting transparency: Mirabell *is* anxiously in love and incapable of rationalizing his way out of it; Fainall *has* learned from his own calculatedly loveless marriage and his secret affair that experience is a murderer of illusions; Mrs. Fainall, when she is asked, offers a great deal of personal information, if only later the fact that her lover, as well as the pander for her hateful marriage, was Mirabell himself.

Men are ever in extremes, either doting or averse. While they are lovers, if they have fire and sense, their jealousies are insupportable. And when they cease to love, (we ought to think at least) they loathe; they look upon us with horror and distaste, they meet us like the ghosts of what we were, and as from such, fly from us.

"You hate mankind?" asks Mrs. Marwood. "Heartily, inveterately." "Your husband?" asks Mrs. Marwood. "Most transcendently; aye, though I say it, meritoriously." Mrs. Marwood, loving Mirabell without hope, trapped by Fainall in an affair from which she has long since withdrawn any love of her own, can at least amuse herself while she awaits the next occasion to cripple Mirabell's hope of love and dowry both—inventing this bitter catechism for rejected ladies to live by.

The astonishing fact about the dialogue of *The Way of the World* is not that it gives an immoral voice to the transience of manners—as indeed it does—but that it expresses, with its own imperturbable logic, a pervasive sophistication stifling all vitality except fury, jealousy, cunning, affectation, contempt, and perhaps the dignified uneasiness that occasionally breaks through Mirabell's façade. Manners have tortured the characters, and their language, into the substance as well as the style of self-baffling intricacy. There is never even the sense—as there always is in *The Country Wife*—of imminent sexual explosion: impulse and motive have suffered alchemical changes; personality has been, for the aims of the drawing-room, subtilized into a sleek, complacent uniformity; sex and self-interest and the need to sustain a perilous façade are all dissolved into one another. Charm at its best is the carefully poised, self-protective affectation of Millamant, scoring off Mrs. Marwood who has just insisted that she hates Mirabell:

O madam, why so do I. And yet the creature loves me, ha! ha! ha! How can one forbear laughing to think of it! I am a sibyl if I am not amazed to think what he can see in me. I'll take my death, I think you are handsomer and, within a year or two as young; if you could but stay for me, I should overtake you, but that cannot be. . . .

In such a world, affectation may be the only armor. Cuckoldry and cozening, and the rigors of labyrinthine intrigue, are the way of this world, which is Fainall's world and Mrs. Marwood's; and Fainall is ultimately privileged to describe himself, in a corrosive shower of wit, as the blindest and most emblematic dupe of all:

And I, it seems, am a husband, a rank husband; and my wife a very errant, rank wife, all in *the way of the world.* 'Sdeath, to be a cuckold by anticipation, a cuckold in embryo! Sure I was born with budding antlers, like a young satyr, or a citizen's child. 'Sdeath! to be out-witted, to be out-jilted, out-matrimonied! If I had kept my speed like a stag, 'twere somewhat; but to crawl after, with my horns, like a snail, and be outstripped by my wife, 'tis scurvy wedlock.

The comedy of manners does not necessarily trifle; it is hospitable to serious issues. It has for its subjects, after all, the cult of manners that grandly offers to regulate a whole society, and the Arnoldian predisposition of Mr. Knights ought to have led him to scrutinize more patiently that cultivated appearance of triviality which Congreve, for one, accepts from his audience, and which he polishes into an ironic gloss not quite dazzling enough to conceal the moral turbulence beneath.

It is by now safe to assert that Sheridan, on the other hand, had a passive audience and no cult of manners; that this audience, bottle-fed on sermons and sentimental comedy, refused to recognize entire continents of vitality; that sex was inadmissible and irony incomprehensible; that good nature—which tended to be defined, dramatically, as an incapacity for thought—had replaced good manners; that Sheridan, the presumptive inheritor of the tradition of Congreve, found his inheritance dissipated before he could lay his hands on it, and was in fact writing, not comedies of manners, but—patched out with hasty reconstructions of Jonsonian and Restoration types—good-natured sentimental dramas of comic intrigue and situation, which Fielding had acclimated to fiction, in the guise of anti-sentimentalism, a generation before.

It may be that *The School for Scandal* is a better play than *The Rivals;* but both are miscellanies of stagey, actable situations incorporating sentimental and stock-comic types, and the former is, characteristically, indifferent enough toward motive and design to leave the scandalmongers of the title without function or effect in the play.

The Rivals, in any case, is not much worse; and it is a more candid and melancholy epithaph on the comedy of manners, indeed on the English comic drama.

The most obvious quality of *The Rivals* is its literariness: its remoteness from live situations seen and live conversations recorded; its dependence on formula, contrivance, tips to the audience, plot summaries, scene-shifting and stage-business, playable circumstances and playable characters at the expense of consistency and subtlety, the comfortable simplifying echo of dead authors' perceptions—all the paraphernalia of the well-made popular play of any age.

Sheridan falls back on formula even while he affects to attack it. The sitting duck of the play is the Julia-Faulkland relationship; but its embarrassing woodenness will exceed the expectations of the most ill-disposed critic. Faulkland is ostensibly a satire on the sentimental hero of the novels Lydia borrows from the lending libraries—all nerves, doubt, sophistry, and remorse. Unluckily, however, he is presented at such length and with such abundant self-justification that Sheridan seems to be soliciting sympathy, or at least fatiguing our attention, on behalf of as windy a bore as any sentimental novel offers. And Julia, whom Sheridan exerts himself to contrast approvingly with her lover, is as smug and dreary a copybook of eighteenth-century posies as might be culled from the collected works of Charlotte Lennox:

My heart has long known no other guardian—I now entrust my person to your honour—we will fly together. When safe from pursuit, my father's will may be fulfilled—and I receive a legal claim to be the partner of your sorrows and tenderest comforter. Then on the bosom of your wedded Julia, you may lull your keen regret to slumbering, while virtuous love, with a cherub's hand, shall smooth the brow of upbraiding thought, and pluck the thorn from compunction.

To return from this preening flaccidity to any remark, however casual, by any of the women in *The Way of the World* is to measure interplanetary distances. Nor is Sheridan more successful when he attempts to manufacture—as a foil to Julia, that sober and responsible heroine—an up-to-date Millamant, her head turned by the reading of novels. The affectation of Congreve's Millamant has a purpose and is subordinated to her wit; the best Sheridan can do by way of expressing Lydia's affectation is to preface her otherwise characterless remarks with a "Heigh-ho!" and to feed the audience on curiously mixed, interminable catalogues of lending-library fiction, in which Smollett is equated with Sterne and both with the true-romance writers of the time—as if Sheridan, acquiescing in the eighteenth-century snobbery toward the novel, is himself incapable of making the distinctions. (One is reduced to looking for signs of the *author's* personality when he gives us no impression of personality, motive, or value in his characters.)

Even Sheridan's theatrical machinery makes alarming noises. In the opening scene two servants labor, during an implausibly crammed and hearty chat, to identify in detail all the characters and relationships of the play. The audience, as it doubtless deserves, is occasionally treated like an idiot with an ear trumpet: "Ye powers of imprudence, befriend me:" says Absolute in an aside, preparing to be imprudent, or, preparing to act repentant, "Now for a penitential face"; and, fearful that we may not deduce the magnitude of Lydia's silliness from the incompetence of its presentation, he nudges us with bogus good humor—"Ha! ha! ha! one would think now that I might throw off all disguise at once, and seize my prize with security; but such is Lydia's caprice, that to undeceive were probably to lose her."

Conventions are not to be trusted, either. Setting up his recognition scene, in which Lydia looks forward to the prompt exposure of a deception that has in fact been practised only on her, Sheridan has Lydia turn her face from the door and keep it turned away through half the scene, while she wonders why "I han't heard my aunt exclaim yet! . . . perhaps their regimentals are alike, and she is something blind," and later, "How strangely blind my aunt must be!" The suspense is not in the dramatic use of a frankly theatrical device—to throw light, for example, on the cumulative extravagance of self-deception—but simply in waiting for Lydia, whose turning away has made the scene possible if not credible, to turn round and see what is there. Sheridan is working, here as elsewhere, not with live conventions but with stage tricks only.

The only figures Sheridan enjoys are his bullies and blusterers: Sir Anthony, the comic-tyrannical father; Acres, the good-natured, swearing country squire with an aversion to dying; Sir Lucius, the obsessed and doctrinaire duelist—"Pray, sir be easy; the quarrel is a very pretty quarrel as it stands; we should only spoil it by trying to explain it." They are the only characters who speak with an approximation of personality, and they do their amusing vaudeville stunts with a verve that recalls to us, by unhappy contrast, the nullities in the leading rôles.

If Mrs. Malaprop is less consistently amusing (and she does have one Miltonic simile: "as headstrong as an allegory on the banks of

Nile"), it is because her "nice derangement of epitaphs" is an unfunctional, isolated humor, usually a rambling collection of improbable errors interrupted by plain sense whenever Sheridan is anxious to advance the plot, and not at all a determined flood of self-revelation as with her great predecessor, Fielding's Mrs. Slipslop. Again, though, the shattering comparison is with Congreve, with the impressionable virago of an aunt that Sheridan found in *The Way of the World*: Lady Wishfort and her fishwife eloquence as, for example, when she casts off her scheming maid:

Away! out! out! Go set up for yourself again! Do, drive a trade, do, with your three-pennyworth of small ware flaunting upon a packthread, under a brandy-seller's bulk, or against a dead wall by a balad-monger! Go, hang out an old frisoneer-gorget, with a yard of yellow colberteen again. Do; an old gnawed mask, two rows of pins, and a child's fiddle; a glass necklace with the beads broken, and a quilted nightcap with one ear. Go, go, drive a trade! These were your commodities, you treacherous trull! . . .

It is not merely that Lady Wishfort is here speaking with a freedom rather indecorus for Sheridan's stage, but that she speaks always as a character involved in the action, and with an energy and particularity of vision beyond Sheridan's powers entirely.

We must pay our respects, eventually, to talent, for literary history cannot quite conjure it away. There is little enough talent in any age: the run of Restoration comic dramatists, working unimpeded before the same audience and in the same tradition as Wycherley, produced libraries of triviality, dullness, and smut. On the other hand, less satisfactory traditions—the Wordsworthian ruminative blank verse of the nineteenth century, for example—if they inhibit, do not necessarily prevent the operation of talent. Sheridan—after one has deplored his audience and the sentimental tradition it venerates and imposes—remains a second-rate and second-hand playwright: that there is no great playwright in his time may be the fault of the time, but Sheridan himself will have to bear some of the responsibility for being no better than he is.

Without a satisfactory tradition, the dramatist is, indeed, liable to be—of all artists—the most personal and most exhibitionistic failure, to overlook even such exploitable types and situations as Sheridan salvaged, to make unguided excursions into bathos, to mistake self-indulgence for originality and nose-thumbing for wit. Wilde, like Sheridan, is vaguely credited with having revived, for his time, the comedy of manners; but Wilde's *fin de siècle* was too remote from any comic tradition at all to allow him even such tag-ends of tradition as Sheridan's. In one sense, it is true, Wilde is far more than Sheridan a dramatist of manners: he does treat—in *The Importance of Being Earnest*, at least —a uniform and polished social surface. But it is a surface that he invents without the collusion of his audience, a fable of a society; and he is not enough of a fabulist to discover or invent the values that must prop or undermine it.

The best Wilde can do is put his trust in the patterns and moral implications of epigram, or rather of a very limited and identifiable trick of epigram. He can do much worse, also; as in *Lady Windermere's Fan*, that incredible spectacle in which Wilde indecently embraces, in the presence of epigram, every Victorian cliché about wicked men, virtuous young women, self-sacrifice, and mother-love. When Cecil Graham ("lighting a cigarette") remarks, "I never seem to meet any but good women. The world is perfectly packed with good women. To know them is a middle-class education," Lord Darlington retorts, "This woman has purity and innocence. She has everything we men have lost": and before we are finished we have been lathered with Wilde's drama-school stage directions (*"Hiding her feelings with a trivial laugh,"* or *"Tears letter open and reads it, then sinks down into a chair with a gesture of anguish,"* or *"In her accents there is a note of deep tragedy. For a moment she reveals herself"*); we have been agitated by imminent disclosures to a young wife whose lackwit idealism is vulnerable, apparently, only to fact; we have been squeezed through wringers of remorse ("Why do I remember now the one moment of my life I most wish to forget? Does life repeat its tragedies? . . . Oh, how terrible! The same words that twenty years ago I wrote to her father! . . ."); and, having been purified in the self-immolation of a not quite unregenerate female heart, we rest in the stainlessness of Lady Windermere, fortifying herself with the "miniature she kisses every night before she prays" because—as she tells Mrs. Erlynne, who, though Lady Windermere must never know, is really her mother!—"We all have ideals in life. At least we all should have. Mine is my mother." Mrs. Erlynne departs at last with the fan, a photo of her daughter and grandson, and a new husband; and Lady Windermere, saved, says to Lord Windermere: "I will trust you absolutely. Let us go to Selby. In the Rose Garden at Selby, the roses are white and red."

So automatic and superficial an epigrammatist as Wilde is, of course, mortally susceptible to the most pervasive sentimental currents of his time, since these flow at a level—in his audience, and in the cynicism he himself affects—to which his wit never penetrates. Beneath the epigrams in melodrama; and we must be grateful that, in *The Importance of Being Earnest*, Wilde never breaks the skin of artifice, of manners and wit in a fabulously idle society.

The Importance of Being Earnest is a formed play: in plot, characterization, relationship, incident, and language, it is as consistently and deliberately artificial as drama can be without forfeiting all human relevance. The outrageous formality gravely imposes itself, like a clown's top hat and spats, on the inconsequence of the fable. Everything is automatically classified in terms of everything else: an apparent jumble of names and haphazard connections that will fly accurately into predetermined position at the touch of a button; impartial attention to town life and country life so that both may be seen to take place, essentially, in drawing-rooms and full-dress; a pair of heroines who are twins of innocuous forthright response (to proposals, for instance: "What wonderfully blue eyes you have, Ernest! They are quite, quite blue," says Gwendolen; and "You dear romantic boy," says Cecily, "I hope your hair curls naturally, does it?"); two heroes, one making epigrams and the other pained by them, the latter turning out to be not only the brother but the older brother of the former; a social dragon whose guardianship of caste will not permit her to accept, socially, at least one sort of family background ("To be born, or at any rate bred, in a hand-bag, whether it had handles or not, seems to me to display a contempt for the ordinary decencies of family life that reminds one of the worst excesses of the French Revolution"); a celibate rector exchanging metaphors with a spinster governess—"Were I fortunate enough to be Miss Prism's pupil, I would hang upon her lips. (MISS PRISM *glares*.) I spoke metaphorically.—My metaphor was drawn from bees"; and Miss Prism's retaliation: "Ripeness can be trusted. Young women are green. (DR. CHASUBLE *starts*.) I spoke horticulturally. My metaphor was drawn from fruits."

Sex is admissible only through an inadvertence of imagery, and only then in small talk between an old maid and a parson. Manners can no longer be anything but trivial because the motives that could insist on their vitality have been banished from polite society; and Wilde is bold enough to make a virtue of triviality. Algernon begins the play with a considerable fuss about cucumber sandwiches; Lady Bracknell, having visited her recently widowed friend, observes that she has had "some crumpets with Lady Harbury, who seems to me to be living entirely for pleasure now"; Algernon is always hungry, and closes the second act eating muffins (". . . when I am in really great trouble, as anyone who knows me intimately will tell you, I refuse everything except food and drink"): the only mentionable impulse is tea-party hunger, and the greatest mentionable pleasure—which becomes the greatest imaginable—is tea-party eating.

The Importance of Being Earnest is, in any case, a sport—triviality is a limited subject—and, admiring Wilde's achievement, we are likely to be unduly impressed by its almost parthenogenetic isolation as well as by its unrepeatability. The real trouble is that Wilde, on his own, performing before an audience of cucumber sandwiches, unassisted by even Sheridan's eighteenth-century rummage of sure-fire scenes and stereotypes, must rely exclusively on his own wit to keep things together and moving; and it will not stand the strain.

The trick of Wilde's epigram is, of course, to invert or distort commonplace; and occasionally it works. Lady Bracknell, after her call on Lady Harbury for the first time "since her poor husband's death," remarks, "I never saw a woman so altered; she looks quite twenty years younger." Cecily says with her most disarming pedantry: "It is always painful to part from people whom one has known for a very brief space of time." But Wilde's wit tends to exhaust itself in the manufacture of detachable epigrams, which—so he must hope, at least—will somehow, by standing with such conspicuous unanimity on their heads, arrange themselves into formations of impudent comment on the manners and morals of upright society. Wilde's characteristic epigram, and not only in *The Importance of Being Earnest,* is a puerile tripping-up and dislocation of truism, especially about marriage: "Girls never marry the men they flirt with"; "Divorces are made in heaven"; "In marriage three is company and two is none"; "No married man is ever attractive except to his wife." Eventually Wilde himself becomes sufficiently aware of the porousness of his wit to deny openly, in self-defense, the solid ground of genuine wit. "All women become like their mothers," says Algernon. "That is their tragedy. No man does. That's his." "Is that clever?" asks Jack; and Algernon makes a point of his pointlessness: "It is perfectly phrased! and quite as true as any observation in civilized life should be." One can even deny, finally, the utility of language. "I love scrapes," says Algernon. "They are the only things that are never serious." "Oh, that's nonsense, Algy," says straight-man Jack. "You never talk anything but nonsense." Algernon has an answer for that too, and it sounds like Wilde's own desperate answer: "Nobody ever does."

The Restoration comic dramatists had the advantage of the last English audience; and it was an accomplished audience, for whom manners were graces, and wit an exercise of the mind upon things in the world. Talking into the dark, one learns—as Wilde learned—to talk to oneself, and at length ceases to believe in talk altogether except as a kind of cheerless whistling. Laughter becomes more and more improbable, because there is no longer anything substantial to laugh at; and the comic dramatist—deprived of audience, deprived of subject and motive, deprived of any acceptable ideal of manners and decorum, deprived of everything but his own wit whirling in a void—has gone as far as possible toward writing for nobody about nothing at all.

II. 11

Imitation as Freedom: 1717–1798 *

W. K. WIMSATT

Yale University

THE PERIOD 1717 to 1798 in England (I have chosen the dates only somewhat arbitrarily) produces poems by Pope, by Swift, by Blake, by Wordsworth and Coleridge. But many of these, and among them the most exceptional poems of the century, occur near the beginning and near the end. The critical imagination in quest of the poetical essence of this century very readily, I believe, contracts, at least momentarily, to some shorter inside period—for the sake of neatness and convenience, say, from 1744, the death of Pope, to 1784, the death of Johnson. Here in fact are found most of the characteristic lyrics of the century. This was a relatively weak or dim inner period, a poetic valley of a shadow. It is shot through, nevertheless, with many interesting flashes; it is a time full of somewhat fatigued and straining traditions, transitions, retrospective creations, hard-won, even unconscious, freedoms. One motif intrinsic to the poetry of the whole century may be observed in peculiar concentration here—the method, the bondage, and the main freedom of all English neo-classic and pre-romantic poetry—the principle of imitation or free-running parallel. Imitation not only of the full, ancient, and classical models, Homer or Pindar, Horace or Juvenal, but also, increasingly, as the classical models became, or may have seemed to become, used up, imitation of the whole British tradition and notably of the English poets who had already best imi-

* Read at the Institute in 1968. Published in *Institute Papers: Forms of Lyric*, 1970.

tated or paralleled the ancients—Spenser and Milton especially and, though he was still very near, Pope. Such names remind us immediately that imitation had for some decades past been enacted for the most part on a very large scale. Translated epics, georgics, or pastorals were one conspicuous, if relatively unoriginal, sort. There was more obvious originality and fun in either high or low burlesque, the various shades of mock-heroic and parody, and in the kind of free translation most often and no doubt most properly called "imitation," the satiric London paralleled to Horace or Juvenal. These large-scale poems, dominantly narrative or discursive, do not of themselves tell us very much about our own specific object, the lyric. They do, however, mark out perspectives. The idea that burlesque and imitation were Augustan avenues of departure from the solemn models and constricting genre norms of the tradition, and thus of escape into a large, free realm of poetic creation, was expounded about twenty years ago by Austin Warren. I assume it as a demonstrated or at least as a persuasively argued and now more or less commonly received principle, which we can invoke to advantage—if only we keep reiterating the compensating principle that the escape from models *was* freedom, *was* expression, *was* fun, only so long as the models were preserved and were present as fields of reference for the realization of the new meanings. An imitation of a classic model is always a reference *to* and only thus a departure *from* the model. When does this mesothesis of likeness and difference succeed in being a free, original, interesting, genuine, and poetic expression? The ironies of Pope's Epistle to a blockhead Augustus give us one example of true freedom, and hence of brillance, in the imitative mode. Some of the pieces in Dryden's collection of Juvenal translations might be adduced to illustrate the average drabness of a more literal kind of transfer.

II

The title of my paper will perhaps already have suggested the fact that I have chosen, not the method of intensive local poetic analysis, but rather that of a wider survey, with somewhat cursory allusion to select examples. June 3, 1717, is the date of Pope's first collected edition of poems—the handsome volume (in both quarto and folio) with the foldout frontispiece engraving of Pope as the straight and slender young cavalier, which along with *Eloisa to Abelard* and the "Verses to

the Memory of an Unfortunate Lady" made R. K. Root say that had
Pope died then, he would be remembered today as a prematurely cut-
off Shelley of the Augustan age. July 13, 1717, is the date of another
publication by Pope, the anonymously edited miscellany *Poems on
Several Occasions*, containing a number of his own minor pieces. One
of these, a poem which he was ultimately to polish into one of the few
finest lyrics of the age, is a short classical imitation, the "Ode on Solitude." Later he claimed to have drafted this when he was twelve
years old. "Happy the man whose wish and care/ A few paternal acres
bound." The imitative virtues of this poem are not of the parodistic
sort, but consist rather in its plenary, if synoptic, realization of a theme
classically enshrined in Virgilian georgic, Horatian ode and epode, and
Senecan chorus, in epigrams of Martial, and in Claudian's portrait of an
aged farmer. The well-established medley of "retirement" images, the
rural felicity and innocence, the hardihood and piety, had been rendered
too by Ben Jonson, by Marvell, by Dryden, and especially by Cowley
in the garland of translations with which he adorned his essays on such
topics as "Obscurity," "Agriculture," and "The Dangers of an Honest
Man in Much Company." Cowley's verses were favorite reading and
quoting for Pope, and in the grotto and garden of his later years Pope,
as we have recently been instructed in several opulent essays by Maynard Mack, was bringing off an elaborate reenactment of the ancient
ideal of georgic wisdom. In what way did the stanzas of Pope, matured
from his boyhood until he was nearly fifty, succeed in being free, different from, or more genuine and successful than the English translations of his predecessors? One might say, of course, that he did not
translate, but made his own poem, a distillate of a whole tradition and
spirit. There would be no way of refuting the assertion that almost any
feature of this poem, especially any that we find subtle, novel, or pleasing, is a part of its freedom and its secret. It is with a sense of some
arbitrariness, then, but perhaps not too much, that I select for comment
the extraordinary freedom and éclat with which Pope has managed with
the aid of meter and rhyme and phrasal parallels to tame English
syntax and word order into something very much like the effects of
juncture, momentary contrast, pivoting, sorting, suspension, closure,
and completeness which are characteristic of Augustan Latin poetry.
Such management was a tact and power of the Augustan Latin literary
language. Other English poets, notably Milton throughout *Paradise*

Lost, give us varied anthologies in the torment of the English language
into curiously Latinate patterns. The essential refractoriness of English
word order in submitting to this discipline may be illustrated in these
lines from Cowley's translation of the second chorus in Seneca's
Thyestes:

> *Me,* O ye Gods, on Earth, or else so near
> That I no Fall to Earth may fear,
> And, O ye Gods, at a good Distance *seat*
> From the long Ruins of the Great.

Pope does something different. Taking advantage of the strong points
of his tiny stanza and the metrical parallels, he proceeds more smoothly,
calmly, and coolly, more efficiently, in his Latinate accomplishment. A
few *hints* of the Latin syntactic models are all that we need.

> *Beatus ille qui* procul negotiis,
>   ut prisca gens mortalium,
> paterna rura bobus exercet suis
>   *solutus* omni faenore
> neque excitatur classico *miles* truci . . .
>
>   Horace, *Epode* II, 1–5
>
> Felix, *qui* propriis aevum transegit in arvis,
> *ipsa* domus *puerum quem* vidit, *ipsa senem.*
>
>   Claudian, *De Sene Veronensi,* 1–2

Or, to strengthen the syntactic illustration a little, the following from a
different context in Horace, but one also very well known to Pope and
actually translated by him in another poem.

> vos exemplaria Graeca
> nocturna versate manu, versate diurna.
>
>   *Epistle to the Pisos,* 268–69

And thus:

> Happy the man whose wish and care
>   A few paternal acres bound,
> Content to breathe his native air,
>   In his own ground.
> Whose herds with milk, whose fields with bread,
>   Whose flocks supply him with attire,
> Whose trees in summer yield him shade,
>   In winter fire.

III

The date of Pope's final revision of "Happy the Man," 1736, brings this poem within a few years of the time when Gray probably wrote a first version of his "Elegy in a Country Churchyard," and when Collins was meditating or writing his *Odes*. Gray's "Elegy" is a poem which shares very much in imagery and tone with a poem of Pope's 1717 *Works*, the "Verses [later "Elegy"] to the Memory of an Unfortunate Lady." Not only did Gray continue the Augustan line of wit, as F. R. Leavis, I believe, was the first to insist, but he was so close in time to Pope that we ought not to be surprised. The generation of Gray and Collins, the Wartons, Shenstone, Lyttelton, Akenside, Mason—in short, of the gentlemen whose poems made up Dodsley's *Collection of Poems* (1748–58)—was a generation deeply sunk in a nostalgia for the age and presence of the Augustans, and above all for Pope. Collins indeed is more patently an early romantic than Gray. Nowadays the trend is to stress his allegiance to the *Popular Superstitions*, and hence to the kind of imagination represented by fairies, witches, and hobgoblins, and to discover in his "Ode on the Poetical Character" a sort of pansexual narcissism or mythopoeic movement of identically divine and human creation. But he was recognizably a classicist too, psychologically Aeschylean and Aristotelian in his allegorical odes on the passions, and metrically both Pindaric and Horatian.

The three tetrameters and the closing dimeter of Pope's little "Ode on Solitude" were an imitation of a Horatian lyric stanza ("Ode. Sapphick," he entitled it in 1726). Collins too, in the quietest and best and best-known of his poems, the "Ode to Evening," was thinking of an ode in the Horatian sense. He chose a different, perhaps a bolder, way of approximating a Latin stanza, the Fourth Asclepiadean. Take three iambic pentameter lines, add two syllables (one foot) to the third line, and make sure that the sixth syllable (the end of the third foot) is always accented and is always the end of a word. Five, five, three, three—without rhyme. As with Horace, the stanzaic effect inheres in the varied numbers and the phrasing against the numbers. True, this kind of thing had been done in English before. It had been done first by Milton in a youthful translation, straight from Horace: "The Fifth Ode of Horace, Lib. 1. *Quis multa gracilis te puer in Rosa*, rendered almost word for word without Rhyme according to the Latin Measure, as near as the Language will permit.

What slender Youth bedew'd with liquid odours
Courts thee on Roses in some pleasant Cave,
Pyrrha? for whom bind'st thou
In wreaths thy golden Hair . . . ?

After Milton the stanza was used not only by Collins but somewhat stiffly by all three of the Wartons, who wrote it, as Oliver Elton says, almost like the badge of a group. "Only Collins," he says, "brought out its music." The greater freedom, the finer tone, of Collins's stanzas to the "nymph reserved," "chaste Eve" ("Now teach me, maid compos'd,/ To breathe some soften'd strain") come in part through his novel extension of a classic form to enclose or shape the stuff of a newly intensified landscape melancholy—a mood, as Yvor Winters argues, that subsists purely in its symbols, with no real motives. (Perhaps not so new at that, but a subtly modulated old, Miltonic stuff.) This poem is a deepened version of the retirement theme. One free formal feature to be noted about it is surely that, whereas the dim landscape images and pensive mood are minor Miltonic, the movement of the phrases through the tiny stanzas is not cut or segmented, as in "Penseroso" couplets, but is like the actual movement of Horatian odes and at the same time like Milton's *Paradise Lost* style and his sonnet style too, continuous from line to line, and even from stanza to stanza.

. . . some soften'd Strain,
Whose Numbers stealing thro' thy darkning Vale,
May not unseemly with its Stillness suit,
        As musing slow, I hail
        Thy genial lov'd Return!

We can see an instructive sort of contrast to Collins's well-known verses in another "Ode to Evening," included in the twin small volume of odes published simultaneously in December, 1746, by his Winchester and Oxford friend, Joseph Warton.

Hail, meek-eyed maiden, clad in sober gray,
Whose soft approach the weary woodman loves
As, homeward bent to kiss his prattling babes,
He jocund whistles through the twilight groves.

Content with forgoing the rhyme of the first and third lines, the pentameter quatrain insists, nevertheless, on a square enough parallel, balanced halving of lines, and stanzaic closure to illustrate a minor poetic strain that was tuning quietly during the decade toward its sudden and plenary fulfillment in Gray's "Elegy." The "Colin Clout" or "Nosce Teipsum" quatrain of alternating rhymes had been employed by D'Avenant and Dryden at the middle of the preceding century as a counterpart of classical heroic hexameters, somewhat ampler than the English couplet. It was a relatively obscure and very weak poet, James Hammond, who about 1732, in a sequence of expurgated Tibullan adaptations, seems first to have conceived this quatrain as a counterpart of the Latin hexameter and pentameter, or elegiac couplet—fit metrical emblem for the pensive melancholy of frustrated love. William Shenstone, who alluded to the stanza as "Hammond's meter," wrote more of the same sort of watery elegies, twenty-six in number, and an introductory theoretical essay upon the genre. How did Gray succeed at one leap in carrying this slender tradition so far beyond the "necessities" or timidities which had hitherto seemed to constrain it? Geoffrey Tillotson suggests that one of Gray's inventions is the landscape picture laid down in separate strips, line by line.

> The lowing herd winds slowly o'er the lea,
> The plowman homeward plods his weary way.

True, we have noted the same thing in Warton's relatively tame "Ode to Evening." Still, it may be that these landscape strips, as Gray manages them, are a notable part of his unique quality. Gray's "Elegy" shares with Pope's a preservative technique in blending the softness of elegiac feeling with the tartness of satiric commentary. Cleanth Brooks has observed the ironic reciprocation between country churchyard and the funerary emblems of the great abbey church. Perhaps we shall be tempted to say that Gray transcends and outdoes Hammond and Shenstone simply because he writes a more poetic line, richer, fuller, more resonant and memorable in all the ways in which we are accustomed to analyze the poetic quality. There may be no other way of describing his poetic freedom. I would not debate long against that. Let me, however, add one more observation (I note it too in Brooks's essay and in a more recent essay by Bertrand Bronson), that the resonance and fullness of this poem in the memory come in good part from the concluding personal complement to, and affirmation of, the marmoreally impersonal main statement. The universalized meditation comes home, as Johnson said, to the reader's business and bosom through the final focus and intensification in the heart of the speaker himself, who sees (and, as Brooks argues, *chooses*) his own grave and epitaph. ("For thee, who mindful of th' unhonour'd Dead/ Dost in these lines their artless tale relate . . ." not Gray in any special personal sense, of course not West, and not a village stonecutter—but the melancholy, sensitive unkown poet meditator and speaker—and hence you, I, we, anybody who happens to be reading the poem.) One reason why I come to rest on this idea is that it affords, I believe, a very instructive moment of comparison with one of Gray's two Pindaric odes, "The Progress of Poesy."

The Pindaric ode in English was one of the straightest or most serious ways of imitating the classical model. The sublimity of the models almost precluded the kind of freedom and significant parodic fun that was invited by satire and epic. Or if parody was attempted, as by Bonnell Thornton in his burlesque St. Cecilia's Day ode set to music by Dr. Arne for Ranelagh in 1763, and by Lloyd and Colman in Two Odes (1760) ridiculing Gray and Mason, it almost necessarily fell to an extreme of contrast; it was low travesty. Dryden, improving on the neo-classic "free verse" of Cowley, had demonstrated a kind of bravura of musical mimesis, a wildly recitative ring, in two irregular St. Cecilia's Day odes. Pope, despite his admiration for Dryden's feat in the Essay on Criticism, had done less than his best in an attempt at the same genre, published in 1713. Edward Young contrived weak adaptations of Dryden's style, in sublime celebration of the British navy (1728–34).[1] Congreve had earlier (1706) come in to assert briefly that the Pindaric ode ought in fact to be a very regular three-phase construct—strophe, antistrophe, and epode (turn, counterturn, and stand, as Ben Jonson had put it), precisely repeated in successive triads. The lesson had been not much noticed for another thirty years. But with the Odes of Collins and Warton and the even more recent translation of Pindar by Gilbert West (1749), Gray was in a position to go all out in a highly intricate (countable and testable though probably never really audible) triadic pattern, precisely repeated, and to add to this formidably classic quality a range and depth of allusiveness which in the collected Poems of 1768 he permitted himself to cover with a panoply of footnotes such as American students of the present age are likely to associate with the Waste Land of Eliot. There was a kind of freedom in all this, a bold originality—to which we find the most thun-

[1] The episode is described by E. E. Reimer in his unpublished Yale doctoral dissertation of 1968, "The Paradoxical Sublime: Edward Young's Early Works," Ch. V.

derous testimony in the outrage vented by Samuel Johnson: ". . . glittering accumulations of ungraceful ornaments; they strike, rather than please; . . . the language is laboured into harshness. . . . 'Double, double, toil and trouble.' He has a kind of strutting dignity, and is tall by walking on tiptoe."

But to return to the connection with the "Elegy" which I began by hinting: the boldest, by far the most striking and shocking thing about "The Progress of Poesy" seems to me to be the closing stanza, the epode of the third triad, bringing to a conclusion, or up to the latest date, the progress of poesy from Greece through Italy to England, Shakespeare, Milton, Dryden. Thus far have the "paths of glory" led. At the end of the "Elegy," the humble poet-speaker, the melancholy "youth to fortune and to fame unknown," was lying flat, in his grave, his "head upon the lap of earth," his "frailties" sunk in "the bosom of his Father and his God." (So far as obscurity is a choice, it is a choice which Nature cooperates all too readily in helping us to make.) But the "youth pined away with desire," as a later vision will instruct us, does "arise from [his] grave and aspire,/ Where [the] sunflower wishes to go." The end of "The Progress of Poesy" is another ending of one poet's recital, but the end of a far bigger story also. No "mute inglorious" Miltons have appeared in the cast of characters, but "he" himself "that rode sublime/ Upon the seraph-wings of Extasy." And now, today, in 1754?

> Oh! Lyre divine, what daring Spirit
> Wakes thee now? Tho' he inherit
> Nor the pride, nor ample pinion,
> That the Theban Eagle bear . . .
> Yet oft before his infant eyes would run
> Such forms, as glitter in the Muse's ray
> With orient hues, unborrow'd of the Sun:
> Yet shall he mount, and keep his distant way
> Beyond the limits of a vulgar fate,
> Beneath the Good how far—but far above the Great.

The epitaph which concludes the churchyard "Elegy," I have argued, transcends or envelops the merely individual. It is the individual focus of the universal. Can the same be said for the galvanic resurrection which concludes the daring third epode of "The Progress of Poesy"? I think not. For, after all, it is our common fate to be dead and to lie flat in the ground. It is a very special and eminent experience to mount and soar, even though a little lower than the Theban eagle, yet "beyond the limits of a vulgar fate." Gray, one might plead, is not thinking of himself, but just of the sublime English poet of the moment, whoever he may be. But who else could he be at this moment, as this triumphant epode is penned? The stanza to my mind is rampant with the individuality, and the vanity, of the Cambridge scholar! In this it displays a very unusual degree of correctly wild Pindaric energy. Nevertheless, it may seem, and be, like the rest of the ode, cold enough for us, even repellent. Freedom, we may wonder, but as in many a political issue, freedom to do what?

Gray's second Pindaric ode, "The Bard," equally intricate and regular, is another celebration of the power and progress of poesy, urged with an even more intense degree of rhapsodic energy. The frenzied Welsh bard, joined in the dreadful harmony by a chorus of ghostly colleagues, pronounces a doom upon the royal line of Edward I but adds a prophecy of long poetic glories for England under the Tudors. "Robed in a sable garb of woe,/ With haggard eyes the Poet stood;/ Loose his beard, and hoary hair . . ." Every schoolboy knows, or once knew, that he punctuates his tirade by a leap from the side of Snowdon into the Conway's foaming flood. The visionary bardic afflatus, a form of wit to madness near allied, was appropriate matter for the throb of the wild Pindaric strophe. If one way to freedom was the irresponsibility of parody and burlesque, another way, known or hinted at since classic times, was madness. It was good, at any rate, as a literary device.[2] Perhaps it was even better in actuality. The date of Horace Walpole's inaugural of the printing press at Strawberry Hill with Gray's two odes, 1757, was also the approximate date when another Cambridge scholar, a prolific London hack writer, went really mad, or at any rate entered a period of confinement in several madhouses. Christopher Smart's antiphonal logbook, *Jubilate Agno* (*Rejoice in the Lamb*), written during this time, recovered and published long after, bears the marks of a genuinely mad mind. It bears also the unmistakable marks of poetic genius.

> For I will consider my Cat Jeoffry.
> For he is a servant of the Living God duly and daily serving him.
> For at the first glance of the glory of God in the East he worships in his way.

[2] Cf. Raymond D. Havens, "Assumed Personality, Insanity, and Poetry," *RES*, New Series, IV (January, 1953), 26–36.

For when his day's work is done his business more properly begins.

For he keeps the Lord's watch in the night against the adversary.

For he counteracts the powers of darkness by his electrical skin & glaring eyes.

For he has the subtlety and hissing of a serpent, which in goodness he suppresses.

For he will not do destruction, if he is well-fed, neither will he spit without provocation.

For he purrs in thankfulness, when God tells him he's a good Cat.

To my mind there is more poetic life in these disjunct antiphons than in either of Gray's intricately labored odes. What makes the poetic freedom and success of this passage? To speak roughly: loving and amused observation of a household animal is coupled with sacramental view of the universe and the prayerful form of Scripture and liturgy. The freedom arises in a reverently irreverent parody of Scripture and the Prayer Book. Madness was the interior dynamic that issued the license for this kind of parody.

IV

With Gray's Pindaric odes and Samuel Johnson's imitation of the Tenth Satire of Juvenal a few years earlier, we arrive at an approximate climax and end to the direct and straight imitation of the classics in the English neo-classical movement. To carry our narration of freedom through imitation any further, we need now a new rubric, a new term or two—none the less valid because they may be our own favorite terms, rather than those the age would most readily have applied to itself. I am thinking of some such terms as *antiquarianism* [3] *and primitivism.*

Percy's *Reliques of Ancient English Poetry* (1756) will immediately come to mind, and in connection with this it is worth our while to notice in passing one kind of native or folk freedom which flourished in that enlightened age but which an age of modern scholars seems hardly to have suspected until Bertrand Bronson brought it to light about twenty-three years ago in his account of Mrs. Brown of Falkland, who was a ballad informant of Sir Walter Scott's informants William Tytler and Alexander Fraser Tytler, Lord Woodhouselee. Daughter of

---

[3] "A mere Antiquarian is a rugged being" (Samuel Johnson in Boswell's *Life*, 1778).

a professor at Aberdeen and wife of a clergyman, this lady carried in her head, from singing heard in childhood, no fixed or bookish text of a ballad, but just the ballad itself, a narrative line or story poem (a "fluid entity") which she felt free to cast and recast in numerous rhetorical and prosodic variations.[4] In this instance, the freedom seems to have produced no important creative results. But it may help us to appreciate the fact that we are indebted to free sources of the same kind for those sharply trimmed essential versions of "Edward" and "Sir Patrick Spens" which an earlier Scottish collector, Boswell's friend Lord Hailes, had given to Percy. There is no reason to think these were any more ancient or more genuine than any of the numerous inferior versions of the same ballads which may be found in Child and Sharp. They were the work of living eighteenth-century Scottish reciters. The vital energy of the age in traditional song, as Bronson says, put forth natural "flowers—proper to the season, not exacavated fossils." The eighteenth century no less than the fifteenth was "a golden age" of Scottish balladry.

But in naming Percy I have in mind mainly another kind of freedom —one very effective way in which even the bookish poet could escape the rigors of the prevailing civilized norms of elegance and good sense. This was somewhat like the way of imitation and burlesque. I mean the escape which Percy enjoyed by the simple, half-apologetic act of electing to put before the public the rude rhymes of an earlier uncouth age. He and his readers could thus innocently disport themselves in all this raciness and vigor. The harshness and uncouthness were not their responsibility. True, some of the pieces had to be touched up a little by Percy and made more presentable. But this too was a form of connivance and participation, of fiction, and hence of freedom.

Percy's first edition of the *Reliques*, let us recall, was closely contemporary with the Gaelic pseudo-documents of another Scottish antiquary, James Macpherson, and the rhythmic English prose translations which he produced in three volumes as the poems of the ancient Fenian poet Ossian.[5] "We gave the song to the kings. A hundred harps mixed their sound with our voice." The plushy green headlands, the blue bays, the wind groaning in the pines and oaks, the ships, halls, caves,

---

[4] "Mrs. Brown and the Ballad," *California Folklore Quarterly*, IV (April, 1945), 129–40.
[5] The date of the sixteen *Fragments* is 1760, that of the epic poem *Fingal*, in six books, 1762, that of *Temora*, in eight books, 1763.

tombs, and campfires, the running deer and boars, the thrusting and the bleeding warriors, the spears, swords, harps, armor, and gems—the whole bardic idiom of Homeric and Miltonic imitation—constituted a distant poetic invention on the part of Macpherson, if no very subtle one. He gained the freedom to indulge in this invention through the removal and protection of his fictive plunge of fifteen centuries.

A very similar element of freedom in forgery appears in the more sympathetic fraud committed not much later by Thomas Chatterton, the sad and marvelous Bristol boy. The three post-humous editions of his *Rowley Poems,* by the eminent Chaucerian Thomas Tyrwhitt, the third containing the solid philological exposure, appeared in 1777 and 1778. Chatterton's Rowley poems were an orphan's flight from present reality into an archaic world of fine fabling and of plangent filial yearning.

> Sprytes of the bleste, on goulden trones astedde
> Poure oute yer pleasaunce own mie fadres hedde.

More important for the formal side of our inquiry, Chatterton used the sanction of a mock antique vocabulary and grammar to create a new kind of free poetic idiom. Like the Spenser of Ben Jonson's phrase, Chatterton-Rowley "writ no language." And yet, like Spenser, he did write a language, and marvelously well. He wrote his own expressionistic fusion of contemporary English and certain freely mingled echoes of the past. The elements, the phonemes and the morphemes, as we might say today, were all pure English. The way they were run together was the oddity and the achievement, something legitimized by the supposed antiquity, but in large part determined by a rhythmic and expressive tact which, if it has to be explained in brief, we may attempt to explain by an appeal to a principle expounded, in humorous fantasy a hundred years later, as "Jabberwocky." The effects are only in part orthographic and ocular.

> Whanne Englonde, smeethynge from her lethal wounde,
> From her gall'd necke dyd twytte the chayne awaie,
> Kennynge her legeful sonnes fall all arounde,
> (Myghtie theie fell, 'Twas Honoure ledde the fraie,)
> Thanne inne a dale, bie eve's dark surcote graie,
> Twayne lonelie shepsterres dyd abrodden flie,
> (The rostlyng liff doth theyr whytte hartes affraie,)
> And wythe the owlette trembled and dyd crie . . .
>
> Eclogue I, Stanza I

The featherd songster chaunticleer
Han wounde hys bugle horne,
And told the earlie villager
The commynge of the morne.

"Bristowe Tragedie: Or the Dethe
of Syr Charles Bawdin," Stanza I.

A great nineteenth-century scholar, the Reverend W. W. Skeat, tried to get at the essence of Chatterton's Rowley poems—"the exact amount of merit" to which Chatterton had attained"—by translating them into correct modern English. "Han" is a plural verb in Chaucerian English, not singular. And thus we get:

The feathered songster chanticleer
Has wound his bugle horn.

And thus in the interest of grammar is obliterated whatever charm the tiny alliterative clarion of the line may have had.

It may seem too big a leap (in poetic idiom even if not in chronology) from Chatterton to the publication in 1786 at Kilmarnock in Ayrshire of Robert Burns's *Poems, Chiefly in the Scottish Dialect*. But I believe there are good reasons for mentioning Burns immediately after Chatterton. Whatever we may wish to say about the racy and earthy peasant freedom of Burns's poems and his free lyric lilt and gusto, the language in which he wrote (when he was not writing like James Thomson, in the Spenserian stanzas of "The Cotter's Saturday Night"), the Lowland Scots dialect, whatever precisely that is, is of great importance for understanding the free expressive power which Burns enjoyed. The eighteenth century, we know, was full of humble and uneducated poets—in Pope's time Stephen Duck, the Poetical Thresher; later Henry Jones, the Poetical Bricklayer; Mrs. Ann Yearsley, of Bristol, the Poetical Milk-Woman, Luctilla; James Woodhouse, the Poetical Shoemaker. And others too. The marvelous thing about all these poets was that, although of lowly origin and meager opportunity, they wrote the standard style of high varnish and poetic diction, like all the other bad and mediocre poets of the era. That was their achievement. The marvelous thing about Burns, on the contrary, was that, being a peasant, he managed to write in what was apparently the language of a peasant. But just how precisely or literally he wrote in such a language, or, so far as he did, what were its peculiar capacities for poetic expression, is a difficult question. Is such a language an initial opaque obstacle to understanding, which the English reader, by historical linguistic research, penetrates, in order to get at a hidden rich meaning? Or is it not possible that in some way such a language is in fact a specially and immediately expressive medium, a contrivance for a much more direct, if inexplicit, presentation, than the civilized literary language permits? Let me suggest the nature of this problem by quoting first a few lines from an early Scottish contemporary of Burns, Robert Fergusson, who died young in 1774, a university and city man and a satirical poet of the city, Edinburgh. Still he wrote also of the country, as in the following lines from his poem entitled "The Farmer's Ingle."

> Niest the gude wife her hireling damsels bids
>   Glowr thro' the byre, and see the hawkies bound,
> Take tent case Crummy tak her wonted tids,
>   And ca' the leglen's treasure on the ground,
>   Whilk spills a kebbuck nice, or yellow pound.

A student, even a serious college student, would have trouble understanding those lines, written in a very genuine, unquestionable eighteenth-century Scots. *Hawkies, Crummy, tids, leglen, kebbuck?* The passage is about a farm wife, her milk-maids, and her cows. And now, by contrast, a few lines from Burns. From "Tam o' Shanter" (1791):

> O Tam had'st thou but been sae wise,
> As taen thy ain wife Kate's advice!
> She tauld the well thou wast a skellum
> A blethering, blustering, drunken blellum.

From a poetical epistle to a friend, in the 1786 volume:

> O, sweet are Coila's haughs an' woods,
> When lintwhites chant amang the buds,
> And jinkin hares, in amorous whids,
>   Their loves enjoy;
> While thro' the braes the cushat croods
>   With wailfu's cry!

Here again the words may be strange to us, but I dare say they will scarcely seem an obstacle to our getting a strong impression of what the passages are saying. The country Scots chosen by Burns and mixed with literary Scots and with straight English is for the most part not an opaque language to us, nor was it to Wordsworth or Keats, who in 1803 and 1818 wrote poems at Burns's grave. Nor do I think it could have been to Burns's English contemporaries, nor to the Edinburgh literati (despite a gesture of glossing in Mackenzie's review). The glossary prefixed to the Kilmarnock volume by Burns himself may be taken as a part of the act. Burns's dialect in his best-known poems—his vocabulary of the wee, the sleekit, timorous, cowrin, and generally comic and sympathetic diminutive, or at an opposite pole, of the braw, fou, blethering, blustering, blellum and skellum—is very largely transparent to an educated English reader. (Some of the pleasure which we get from it is very similar to that which we get on recognizing slapstick and indecent jokes in Shakespeare.) Let us remember again the principle of Jabberwocky. "How high browse thou, brown cow?" [6]

V

Imitation or burlesque of the Greek and Roman classic models. Imitation or forgery of the British archaic past or the primitive present. A third strain of imitation, as we noticed at the start, was imitation of the English classics, from Chaucer to Pope, or in a broader sense, imitation of the classic tradition. Sometimes free and expressive, sometimes a mere nostalgic exercise! At this point, if we had space for a longer narrative, William Shenstone's picturesque and humorous Spenserian *Schoolmistress* (in three versions, 1737 and after) might be praised at the expense of William Mason's more simply nostalgic Chaucerian, Spenserian, and Miltonic parodies in his *Monody on the Death of Pope*. An unobtrusive pastoral strain, imitative and classical, might be traced from Pope and Gay through Collins, Churchill, Goldsmith, and Chatterton, to Crabbe's anti-pastoral *Village* of 1783. And we might dwell for a little upon the curiously half-conscious debt of William Cowper to Pope in his satiric *Table Talk* (1782) and (after John Philips and Thomson) his debt to Milton in his georgic *Task* (1785). Such a detour away from the lyric, if we could afford it, would deepen, but is perhaps not needed to define, the context of imitative and parodistic assumptions which enveloped the production of the next volume of lyrics that I want to notice. It is a fact I believe not often dwelt on that George Crabbe's sourly antitraditional yet conservatively fashioned poem *The Village* appeared in the same year, 1783, as the small volume of juvenile poems, *Poetical Sketches*, printed and distributed to a few

---

[6] The matters on which I touch briefly here are in the course of being treated at length by Mr. James McArdle in a dissertation on the poetic language of Burns.

friends by the young London engraver William Blake. These were written, according to the Advertisement, between his twelfth and his twentieth year. The earliest of them, that is, may have been written about 1769, the year before the death of Chatterton. The latest must have been written a little later than Blake's twentieth year, for there would seem to be debts to Chatterton's *Rowley Poems* (1777), and to his *Miscellanies* (1778).[7] These poems, we remember, are miscellaneous, odd, rough-seeming, ragged, bold ("full of irregularities and defects," says the Advertisement)—a wider range of imitative experiments than anything we have so far consulted. They include rhythmic prose in the manner of Ossian (or of Chatterton's imitations of Ossian) and of the King James Bible; a nightmare pseudo-Gothic ballad, a mad song, and a song of frustrated love, all these in the manner more or less of Percy's *Reliques*; a large fragment of a Shakespearean history play, *Edward III*; a Miltonic prologue; a mythological poem in a sequence of variously approximate Spenserian stanzas; and, perhaps most impressive of all, opening the volume, a set of apostrophes to the four seasons, blended in a new and strangely lyric way from James Thomson, Milton, the Song of Solomon, and no doubt other sources. It is difficult to imagine what Dr. Johnson would have said of this volume of subcultural expressions if a copy had chanced to come into his hands. Blake took his liberties, right and left. One of the most obvious formal, if superficial examples is that of the successive deviations in the Spenserian stanzas.[8] Here I should say the expressive effect is nearly zero. But it is not difficult to find, though it may require some tact to analyze, examples near the opposite end of the value scale. About twenty years ago Cleanth Brooks published in the *CEA Critic*[9] an essay showing how the song of frustrated love, "My silks and fine array," is a job of sweet-sad ritual cunning performed in variations upon Elizabethan lyrics of the Walsingham type which Blake's copy of Percy's *Reliques* at Wellesley College suggests that he knew very well. At about the same time, I myself made the observation, which has been, I believe, well enough received by the guardians of the field, that one deeply and

---

[7] F. W. Bateson, *Selected Poems of William Blake* (New York, 1957), pp. 93–100.

[8] The imitative manner of *Poetical Sketches* was first extensively studied, with a strong accent on detection of sources, by Margaret Ruth Lowery in her Yale doctoral dissertation, directed by C. B. Tinker, *Windows of the Morning* (New Haven, 1940).

[9] XII, No. 9 (October, 1950), 1–6.

freely romantic feature of the apostrophe "To Spring" is the remarkable fusion yet division of the imagery whereby the biblical lover descends into and is blended with a native landscape, which also bears
the image of his waiting bride. In a curious variant of the method, the
fiery Apollonian tyrant King Summer descends upon the land, only to
be invited to seek relief in a nap under an oak or a swim in a river.

The happy manner in which such mythic fusions join Miltonic
meter and syntax to make the freedom and originality of Blake the
youthful experimenter can, as it happens, be suggested *ab extra* by contrast with a little-known poem which Blake's "To Spring" seems in
part to have inspired. William Stanley Roscoe was the son of a Liver-
pool banker who in his spare moments was an editor of Pope, a patron
of the arts, and a friend of friends of William Blake. The younger
Roscoe's poem "To Spring, on the Banks of the Cam," written presumably in his youth, about 1800, though published only in his *Poems*
of 1834, combines the stanza of Collins's "Ode to Evening" with
Blake's abruptly orotund apostrophic opening.

> O thou that from the green vales of the West
> Comst in thy tender robes with bashful feet,
> And to the gathering clouds
> Liftest thy soft blue eye:
> I woo thee, Spring!

I do not undertake to prove or even adequately to illustrate the thesis
that Roscoe's poem is not a very good one. But it is not. It can be consulted in Brooks and Warren's *Understanding Poetry*, or in the *Oxford
Book of Victorian Verse*. It deserves, I believe, special notice as perhaps
the only instance of direct, exemplary influence which can be claimed
for Blake's half-suppressed *Sketches*.[10]

More recently, Harold Bloom, in probably the most sustained
critical gaze yet directed upon Blake's *Sketches*, has observed the "small
. . . humanizing" scale of the two Spenserian epithalamic apostrophes
"To the Evening Star" and "To Morning"; the "sexual paradise and
trap" of the garden in the Song: "How sweet I roam'd"; conventional
poetic diction turned on itself in the "gently mocking" "To the Muses";
Shakespearean winter pastoral joined with the genial manner of Goldsmith in "Blind Man's Buff."

[10] Arnold Goldman, "Blake and the Roscoes," *Notes and Queries*, CCX (May,
1965), 178–82.

Blake's *Poetical Sketches* is a volume saturated with the English poetic tradition from the Elizabethan age through the mid-eighteenth century, brimming with imitative exuberance, and thus wildly and torrentially free. We might almost be tempted to think in a careless moment that it is only accidentally, crudely, and boyishly free. It would be difficult to think of a single small volume more happily illustrative of the half-genetic, half-critical argument I have been trying to push: that the expressive freedom of eighteenth-century English poetry is born only in virtue of the mimetic and repetitive tradition under which the poets labored. This volume is surely, as Harold Bloom would say, "premonitory" of the two strikingly original yet imitative lyric collections which would follow before the end of the century. Blake's *Songs of Innocence and of Experience* is perhaps most readily located by a new reader in its superficially traditional and formal aspects, the meters and the language of childish songs, the "hymns unbidden." Its radical and explosive originality lies at difficult depths. The emblematic character of the form, as John Hollander says, is used to cover a shift in the character of the content. The poems of Coleridge and Wordsworth in *Lyrical Ballads*, and especially those of Wordsworth, seemed from the start, or were said from the start, and mainly by Wordsworth himself, to be a conspicuous departure from all that was expected of poems by a reader tamed in the eighteenth-century popular tradition. "Every author, as far as he is great and at the same time *original*," Wordsworth would later say, "has had the task of *creating* the taste by which he is to be enjoyed." [11] But Coleridge would qualify that. In the *Biographia* he argued that a clamor of protest over *Lyrical Ballads* had been aroused more by Wordsworth's extreme theoretical statements than by the poems themselves. Within recent years an American scholar, Robert Mayo, has demonstrated, I think, that in all the superficials of both form and content, *Lyrical Ballads* was representative of what had already grown to be a "persistent" minority segment of the magazine verse of the 1790s. Bereaved, deserted, and vagrant females, mendicants of both sexes, old soldiers, convicts, unfortunate rustics of every sort, are frequent protagonists in those pages. Insanity and simplicity, picturesque scenery, topographical meditation, humanitarianism, and sentimental morality are dominant motifs in poems which as-

---

[11] *Essay Supplementary to the Preface,* 1815, seventh paragraph from the end. The letter to Lady Beaumont of May 21, 1807, last paragraph, attributes the same idea to Coleridge, in nearly the same words.

sume the forms of ballad, "lyric," complaint, fragment, sketch, anecdote, expostulation and reply, occasional inscription.[12]

> Old Sarah lov'd her helpless child,
>   Whom helplessness made dear,
> And life was happiness to him,
>   Who had no hope or fear.
> She knew his wants, she understood
>   Each half artic'late call,
> And he was everything to her,
>   And she to him was all.

Not a rejected Wordsworthian fragment from *Lyrical Ballads*—but part of a poem entitled "The Idiot" in the *Sporting Magazine* for October, 1798.[13] When compared with earlier eighteenth-century primitives, Stephen Duck, Henry Jones, Ann Yearsley, or even Robert Burns, Wordsworth may seem to achieve his originalitiy, as he claims, by the simple expedient of using a selection of the language of ordinary men— a plain, prosy middle sort of standard English—albeit informed by some special excitement. When he is compared with some of his more immediate contemporaries, however, this kind of originality largely disappears. Wordsworth's freedom and originality, whether in a poem of poetic diction, such as "Tintern Abbey," or in his plainest ballad narrations, will be found ultimately to consist in the fact that he is a better poet than most of his contemporaries at most moments. He has "the original gift of spreading the tone." He writes with more force and interest, even with more "wit," if I dare use such a term. This is the essence of poetic freedom.

[12] Robert Mayo, "The Contemporaneity of the *Lyrical Ballads*," PMLA, LXIX (June, 1954), 480–522.
[13] *Ibid.*, p. 499.

II. 12

The Satiric Blake:
Apprenticeship at the
Haymarket?*

MARTHA W. ENGLAND

Queens College

My PURPOSE is to compare William Blake's *jeu d'esprit* which we call *An Island in the Moon* with *Tea in the Haymarket*, a generic name for a variable product of the satiric personality and dramatic genius of the actor Samuel Foote.

The actual evidence that Blake ever heard of Samuel Foote can be quickly stated. *An Island in the Moon* was written in 1784. Many years later, in his letter "To the Deists" which opens chapter III of *Jerusalem*, he wrote: "Foote in calling Whitefield, Hypocrite: was himself one: for Whitefield pretended not to be holier than others: but confessed his Sins before all the World." By the time he wrote this subtle and complicated discussion of hypocrisy, Blake must have seen, read, or at least

* Read at the Institute in 1968. Printed in the *Bulletin of the New York Public Library* LXII (Sept.–Oct. 1969) 440–464, 531–550; and in *Blake's Visionary Forms Dramatic*, eds. David V. Erdman and John E. Grant (Princeton University Press, 1970), 3–29. The printing in BNYPL includes extensive footnotes and nine appendices: "Sources of Information about Samuel Foote," "William Hayley's Theatrical Writings," "Language—Blake's and Foote's," "Handel and Milton—and Blake," "*Daphnis and Amaryllis*," "Blake's Street Cries," "Good English Hospitality," "Blake and Handel," "London Theatrical Season 1782–1784." Reprinted here by permission of both The New York Public Library and Princeton University Press.

heard about Foote's most famous character, Squintum, in *The Minor*.
From this statement on, all is conjecture, and all is qualified by
varying degrees of probability. My hypothesis is that Blake knew of
Haymarket procedures and wrote a Haymarket piece of his own modeled
on *Tea*. The evidence, such as it is, is in the piece itself.

The comic dramatic topicality of this early work suggests that Blake
was aware of many Londons: the world of high fashion, the competitive
world of painters and engravers, the world of passionate preachers and
flamboyant pseudo-scientists, the public and private entertainment
worlds of trained monkeys and meditating philosophers and performing
bluestockings, the world of antiquarian absurdities and solemnities, the
world of the streets in his neighborhood with its street song and burlesque and hawked sideshows. On the stage of the Little Theater in
the Haymarket, all these impinging worlds met their distorted image in
the theatrical artifice of Samuel Foote, the master parodist of the illegitimate theater. *Tea in the Haymarket* was never published, and was
indeed unpublishable in its wild improvisation, but there are sober
records of its mood and method in Foote's published plays, in various
books, literary and theatrical reviews, and periodicals.[1] Foote died in
1777. It is possible that Blake saw not Foote himself but stage offerings
of the seasons immediately preceding his writing of *An Island in the*

[1] Some sources of information about Samuel Foote: twenty published plays fill
two volumes (*Works*, 1799). There are several studies of the man and his work;
memoirs and biographies supply anecdotes; theatrical memoirs show Foote's pervasive influence throughout the world of the stage, and stage histories place him in
it. W. K. Wimsatt's essay on *The Nabob*, MLN (May 1942) 325–355, not only
deals with one of Foote's plays which I use as exemplary but is itself exemplary,
showing how lives of men not directly associated with the stage can shed light on
Foote's involvement in the pettiest of private affairs and the largest affairs of empire.

My knowledge of Foote, is based primarily, however, on the periodicals of his
day. I have read what is available covering Foote's lifetime in the holdings of Harvard
University, Yale University, Folger Shakespeare Library, and the archives of the
Shakespeare Birthplace Trust in Stratford-upon-Avon. There are 43 titles, although
the files are by no means complete in all cases. *The Public Advertiser*, very nearly
the official organ of theatrical news, is the most important, but in Scottish, Irish,
provincial publications as well as the London periodicals one gets a vivid sense of
Foote's reality. Amidst battles foreign and domestic, gossip, scientific discoveries,
obituary notices, advertisements for horse liniment, reviews of Great Books and
miniscule pamphlets, fashion notes, and accounts of bankruptcies and social events
—this is where he belongs. Here the British Aristophanes is alive and kicking. One
comes to understand what prompted the outrageous opinion that Foote was "the
writer of the day most like Shakespeare, because he so faithfully mirrored his own
age." Foote did not mirror his age "in depth," and his mirror was intended to
distort; but he was truly amazing in his range, detail, sweep, comprehensive coverage.

Moon, when Foote's plays were on stage, his roles played by Bannister and other long-time associates. Also on stage were plays by Foote's imitators and dramatic sketches using as characters Foote and actors trained by him. If Blake saw none of this, he may have read the theatrical reviews. He may have listened to gossip about Foote and his exploits. Dead or alive, on stage or off, Foote was much talked about.

But Blake may have seen Foote himself. He was twenty years old when Foote was buried in Westminster Abbey—a signal honor for a "mere clown." Blake always had unusal freedom. His father was as indulgent as his means allowed, and *Tea* was not expensive. Young Blake need not even have been out at night to see *Tea,* for it was usually performed at noon, and thus Samuel Foote is credited with having instituted the first theatrical matinees in English stage history.

Samuel Foote's stage career was approximately contemporaneous with that of David Garrick, his rival and friend. At his first attempt, Foote discovered that he was unable to sustain a role on stage, either in tragedy or comedy. With the intrepidity that was always his, he made a virtue of necessity, success of failure, a career of his faults, and advantages of all his handicaps. Thenceforth he refused to "act." He was a mimic, and he was eternally himself. Whatever role he was playing, whatever costume he wore, he would turn to the audience (as Blake does in *An Island in the Moon*) and address it in his own person and voice. He made a life and made a living by deriding those who took language seriously—actors, singers, orators, preachers, and teachers of rhetoric.

After the Licensing Act of 1737 (recently revoked with appropriate celebration on the London stage) there were two Theaters Royal in London, Drury Lane and Covent Garden. In the Haymarket there were two houses, one called the King's Theater, where opera was performed, the other called the Little Theater. From 1747 on, Foote was often in occupancy in the Little Theater with a company of about twelve actors, plus singers, dancers, and instrumentalists. When he was abroad or otherwise engaged, Christopher Smart took over. During the 1750s Smart drew large crowds with a vaudeville, *Mrs. Midnight's Entertainments,* which was performed at taverns when Foote had the Little Theater, just as Foote might at times perform in taverns or fair booths. Foote, unlike Smart, had close associations with the major houses. He acted his own plays and many other roles at Drury Lane and Covent Garden. His plays were popular there, with or without him in the cast.

In 1767 he had an accident while riding and one leg had to be amputated. The Duke of York was present at the hunting party and felt himself to be in part responsible. He made such restitution as he could. Through his influence Foote was given a patent to perform during the summer months when the two major houses were closed, and the Little Theater, rebuilt and refurbished, became a Theater Royal, where Foote had a company of about fifty.

This new dignity did not cause his work to lose its raffish flavor. He had borne with jesting courage the pain of amputation without anesthesia, and thereafter he wrote his roles so as to emphasize what Doctor Johnson called his depeditation. His lusty old characters were all the funnier because of puns on his name. The young heroines whom he pursued queried, "Why should I marry a man with one foot in the grave?" Coarse—but a coarse courage which extended his license, as it were, to comment on the defects of others. Although he was fully licensed during the last ten years of his career for the summer months, and although during his entire career he performed often at the major houses, for twenty years it had been illegal to stage plays in the Haymarket, and he had consistently made that legal handicap into a peculiar strength. Those subterfuges by which he was enabled to perform there remained always his best jokes.

The contrast between his own unlicensed stage and the "license to perform" granted to various others was the foundation of his standing jokes. One result was that his work seemed to be a direct reflection of life going on around the theater door. In the Haymarket were held auctions of pictures and antiquities. Foote would announce such auctions, sometimes with elaborate catalogues and parodies of ancient and modern art. One name for him was "the Auctioneer." When he was translated to the higher world of Drury Lane, far from relinquishing his low ways, he emphasized them. *Taste* was his first success as a playwright. Garrick wrote and spoke the prologue in the guise of one of those Haymarket auctioneers. Thirty years later, Foote acted *Taste* by royal command for the King and Queen, who greatly enjoyed seeing him play Lady Pentweazle.

Opera could be performed. Members of the company came and went around his theater door, and his operatic neighbors were the butt of his constant ridicule. One part of *Tea at the Haymarket* often was *The Cat's Opera*. Foote advertised that he desired the yowling to be authentic, so he had imported a brace of cats from Italy (just as many of the favorite singers were Italian). One of his "Italian cats" came to be known as "Cat" Harris. The other was Edward Shuter, who had been marker in a billiard room when Foote took him under his tutelage. Shuter was in the very first performance of *Tea*, and became a very popular comedian. At mid-century, the most popular comic turn was Shuter's *Cries of London*, sometimes billed as a "roratorio."

In Panton Street near by, the puppets were licensed to perform. Foote carried on sparring matches with these neighbors also. His puppets at times were ordinary little wooden figures, at times life-sized; at times like his cats, they were human. At times they were merely metaphors of man's ageless silliness, man's eternal playing with toys, man's illusion that he is free, when he is actually pulled by the strings of his own fads and fancies and vanities. Or they might be any combination of these things. His puppets partook of his other standing jokes, such as his twitting of Garrick about his small stature. "Will your puppets in this play be life-sized?" "Oh no, madam; only about as large as Garrick."

Philanthropical organizations enjoyed certain privileges in the performing arts. Foote persistently pilloried all philanthropies, especially the Foundling Hospital and Magdalen Hospital. He would announce his performances as being "For the Relief of the Sufferers by a Late Calamity." These tricks were not meant to deceive; he collected no money under such false pretenses. It was his premise that those who promoted such charities were hypocritically imposing upon the public.

The hypocrisy of the Methodists was his constant target, and this subject found its way into many of his published plays. Here again, part of the satire was based on their "license to perform." It was charged against him that the Establishment in some obscure way subsidized and encouraged his attacks, so that he derided the Methodists "upon authority." He answered:

> Under authority! What! Do you suppose I play, as you preach, upon my own authority? No, sir. Religion turned farce is by the constitution of this country the only species of drama that many be exhibited for money without permission.

"I am within the law," was the Haymarket stance. The first matinee in English stage history opened in 1747 under the title *The Diversions of the Morning*; legal authorities objected, and Foote quickly advertised that his friends should come and have *A Dish of Chocolate* with him at noon. The generic title became *Tea at the Haymarket*, which properly should be served at half past six (and sometimes was), but whether auction, lecture, concert, opera, cat's opera, chocolate, it was *Tea*. Modified forms took place at the major houses, but *Tea at the Haymarket* was its general name. He mimicked other actors without mercy (it has been said the whole idea grew out of *The Rehearsal*), they were eager to retaliate, and the public loved this battle of mimes. How the composite titles were used can be seen from an advertisement published by Harry Woodward, a Harlequin second only to John Rich. "As the Auctioneer gives *Tea* tomorrow at Covent Garden, Mr. Woodward (by particular desire) on Saturday next will present him with a dish of his own chocolate, with an addition of one Mew at his Cats." Of all evasions of the Licensing Act, *Tea* was the most famous. The public paid for tea; whether or not it ever got any tea was immaterial. The performance was gratis. Since by law the performance could not be a play, *Tea* was Foote's free form at its freest.

His oldest jokes were new every day. Major disasters and minor foibles were his provender. Often he pretended to read his lines from a newspaper, but he had sources of information other than the daily press. He was familiar with levels of society lower than might seem prudent for a man in public life, and higher than might seem possible for a mere clown.

He was no mere clown. He was called "the British Aristophanes." Not his writing, but his miming deserved the title. His pen could never carry his full power. Great satire occurs when its contrary is present in the world. Aristophanes wrote in the presence of great tragic playwrights. *The Rehearsal* was evoked by John Dryden. *The Beggar's Opera* came when Handel's pastoral music drew forth a "Newgate pastoral" to match it. The greatest acting the world has ever seen evoked Foote's mimicry of acting. David Garrick made Foote possible, confronted and challenged him at very turn; and Foote in his own way was great also. He was wildly, irresistibly funny.

An Island in the Moon: The Libretto

The first general similarity between *An Island in the Moon* and *Tea at the Haymarket*, then, is that they are not plays but antiplays. Foote's plays have plots. Blake set up *King Edward the Third* in the form of a play. In contrast, *An Island* and *Tea* do not have plots as frameworks, but both are framed on social occasions. The whole point is: We are only drinking tea or rum & water. Despite the fact that *An Island* contains virtually nothing but lines, acting directions, descriptions of sets and placement of properties; despite the fact that it is more stageworthy than *King Edward the Third,* one can tell at a glance that it is "not a play."

The second general similarity is that Blake's characters are accepted as grotesque portraits of himself, his brother, and people known to him —or possibly combinations of their traits which have been distorted for the purposes of comedy. Blake's fifteen characters, ten male and five female, meet upon seven occasions, drifting in with no stated pretext. They are inhabitants of the moon, who fortunately speak English. They meet at four homes, which may be satiric reproductions of houses known to Blake's social circle, giving opportunity for amusing changes of sets chosen to represent philosophy, law, mathematics, and science. The first, third, and fifth meetings are in the home of the three Philosophers, where, in happy lunacy, dwell Quid the Cynic (Blake), Suction the Epicurean (Robert, his brother), and Sipsop the Pythagorean (a young medical student who has a cat). The fourth and seventh meetings are with Steelyard the Lawgiver (John Flaxman). The second meeting is in the home of Obtuse Angle the Mathematician, and the sixth is an explosive episode in the house of Inflammable Gass the Windfinder. Obtuse and Inflammable have been variously identified as members of Blake's circle of friends.

The third similarity is the variety and importance of Blake's offstage characters, those figures which never appear on stage in their own persons but are described and mimed by one or another of the fifteen members of the cast.

The fourth similarity is that Blake's offstage characters as well as his cast are modeled on real people. His "Jack Tearguts" is identified in his manuscript as Dr. John Hunter. His text makes almost as clear the identity of Richard and Maria Cosway among these offstage characters, and others have been conjecturally identified.

In presenting offstage characters, it was Foote's technique to layer role on top of role. He quoted himself in contrasting mood. He told about eccentrics who in recounting their own experiences would subdivide into several characters or traits. He represented real people on stage, sometimes with no effort at disguising their identity. These might be in the *dramatis personae;* but some of his most celebrated representations were offstage characters only. This is true of Sir Penurious Trifle, and as a rule it was true of his most famous role, Squintum. I have checked cast lists and find in the 1770s some few instances when Squintum was an actual member of the cast, played by Bannister or Weston or Wilkinson, while Foote played Mrs. Cole. But almost always Foote kept this "double role" for himself alone; he played Mother Cole, and, as Mother Cole, told about Squintum. Foote slid from character to character before one's eyes with startling speed and clarity. Those actors whom he trained, such as Shuter and Weston, could almost equal his dexterity. Blake demands this ability of most of his cast of fifteen.

Fifth: Blake mirrors the Man in the Street. His folk allude to Jerome, Goethe, Voltaire, Plutarch, and Pliny in a great show of erudition, but *An Island in the Moon* is geared to the urgencies of daily life. This is an especially good framework within which to stage moments of nostalgia and sentiment later in the program.

Sixth: Foote attempted on stage to join two irreconcilable elements: the maximum of "identification" and the maximum of grotesquerie. London afterpieces impressed foreign visitors because of the close relationship between the stage and the daily lives of the audience. This quality was general, but Foote was preeminent for establishing such relations. No one (certainly not Blake) had quite Foote's finesse, but Blake used the same methods and made a fair success.

Seventh: Blake used Foote's own formulaic jokes, and used them as Foote used them on stage. They were dropped quickly, like nods and winks for the delectation of the cognoscenti. As Mozart in *Don Giovanni* quoted *The Marriage of Figaro* with feigned boredom at his own popularity, so Foote in one role alluded to his other roles. Mozart's joke is not very funny if you do not know "Non più andrai," but everyone knows "Non più andrai," and in 1784 everyone knew Foote. When he was on stage, he made all his roles build on one another. It was part of his basic premise that he was always himself. The method kept his jokes alive for decades. Any audience Blake may have had in mind in 1784 would have recognized unerringly those jests of reverend ancestry. It was not necessary to play them out, just as it is not necessary for Jack Benny to play *The Bee* complete on his violin. A hint is enough, and in both cases part of your pleasure arises from recalling how your grandfather laughed at that joke.

For example: Blake gives us right away a character named Etruscan Column the Antiquarian. His name suggests those modern and native "imported antiquities" staged for many years by Foote and auctioned off by Garrick. The name suggests about as awkward and obvious a fake as one can imagine. Phoebus Apollo, when he is "brought on stage" in a song by Quid, talks like an auctioneer. The old jokes are established in their familiar ambience.

The Antiquarian "seems to be talking of virtuous cats." Why should an antiquarian ponder this particular subject? Any London theatergoer would answer, "Don't they always?" For, according to Foote, the chief preoccupation of antiquarians was precisely that creature known for feline virtue, Whittington's cat. For years *The Nabob* had been showing the public a meeting of the Society of Antiquarians with this cat as the chief item on the agenda. So deeply was the British mind impressed with the staging that even today the article on Whittington in the *Dictionary of National Biography* prudently assures the reader that Foote's interpretation of the cat was only Foote's joke. It may have been known to Blake, however, as it was known to many, that Foote's joke was based on fact.

At times there appeared in the newspapers, not an invitation to tea, but this announcement: "The Members of the Robin Hood are summoned to the Jury." Complete audience participation was solicited. The Robin Hood was a debating society, famous in its own right, and over the years made more so by Foote's stage parodies. At meetings of the Robin Hood, difficult questions were assigned for impromptu discussion so that the debaters might develop quick wit in controversy and familiarity with correct procedures. When Foote put the Robin Hood on stage, either the subject would be carried to ridiculous lengths, or the question would be left pending in mid-air. Blake demonstrates both tricks. He turns his lunatics loose on subjects which were to be his own lifelong concerns. One is the relation of classic myth to the Bible.

After Quid has sung of Apollo's physical degeneration and mercantile preoccupations, the company goes into a disquisition on "Phebus," raising the following "material points" in good Robin Hood style:

1. Who was he?
2. Did he understand engraving?
3. Was he as great as Chatterton?
4. Is he in the Bible?
5. Is he identical with Pharaoh?
6. (The moral issue properly comes last.) Is it profane to speak lightly of him and/or Pharaoh in general conversation?

The discussion is an extended one, in the course of which Phebus becomes inextricably mixed up with Chatterton.

The second topic raised is one always near the surface of Blake's mind: How is poetry related to the visual arts? A profound problem in this area is broached: "Is Pindar a better poet than Ghiotto was a painter?" The Jury gives no definitive answer, but this time leaves the question hanging.

One technique of relating a text to the visual arts had been brought to a high degree of excellence in the London theaters: the use of the stage set to reinforce drama. Loutherbourgh was at Drury Lane. Published stage pieces acknowledged the contribution of Richards and Dahl to the success of the total production. George Lambert, in whose workrooms the Beefsteak Club was organized, was another set designer and scene painter of note. Actual houses and gardens were parodied or portrayed in stage scenes. Blake's four sets—the Philosophers' House, the Mathematician's Study, the Lawgiver's Library, the Scientist's Laboratory—represent merely as setting much of the farcical nature of the piece, and the most satirical parts of the show take place against the most satirical of the settings, the Philosophers' House.

We are, of course, on the moon. The room opens out on an Oriental garden, some lunar-lit monstrosity, with the inappropriate cynosure of a statue of a fat-bellied Apollo. The two contrasting elements represent visually the clash between the neo-Palladian landscaping of "Capability" Brown and Sir William Chambers' taste for Oriental gardening. Blake may have had an immediate inspiration direct from the Haymarket of 1784 in *The Mogul Tale: or, the Descent of the Balloon*, by Mrs. Elizabeth Inchbald.

Certain of the plays on stage in 1784 may have suggested to Blake such details as names of characters, but in language, characterization, and structure *An Island in the Moon* is closer to Foote's own work than to that of Foote's imitators. Foote's imitators used his linguistic tricks but simplified them. Blake's language has greater density than Pilon's or Sheridan's or Murphy's.

Blake's characters, at the opening of his piece, are dramatizing an alienation that is deeper than that of Mrs. Inchbald's folk, or Sheridan's, or Murphy's.

Even more strongly, one is reminded of the violent and reasonless fluctuation of mood which characterizes Foote's stage work. Chaos and order alternate. Bitter words give way to fraternity and sorority. Quarrels as well as restorations of amity seem causeless. The cause, indeed, is not primarily logical or psychological, but is based in dramaturgy. The actors are thus given pretext for dazzling displays of quick-change artistry. This trait gives the structure and the dramatic nature to Foote's work and Blake's.

Offstage characters are chosen to give gross, not subtle, contrast with the person who tells about them. Sipsop, a timid soul whose name suggests milksop, mimes Jack Tearguts, the domineering surgeon. Tilly Lally, the la-de-da of assumed elegance, mimes low characters, one-eyed Joe in the sugar house and some rough-and-ready brats whose conduct of a cricket game is deplorable. Etruscan Column, towering in perpendicular antiquity, describes "a little outre fellow" who obtrudes himself rudely into his valuable meditations on Pliny and the migration of birds. Even animals are offstage characters. "Do you think I have a goat's face?" a character asks, and presumably distorts himself into a goat—or a tyger. Some of these secondary characters have direct ancestry in Foote. He often mimed the one-eyed actor Delane.

When Blake's scientist gives a slide lecture, he has the example of Foote's Doctor Hellebore, who represented to the very garments and eyeglasses Sir William Browne, President of the Royal College of Surgeons. As Blake's Inflammable Gass shows us a flea, a louse, and other unsavory exhibits, so Doctor Hellebore magnified for his auditors slides showing those yellow insects that hatch out in the blood and cause jaundice, and the standard cure: spiders must be introduced into the blood stream. The spiders eat all the flies, thus curing the jaundice, then obligingly starve to death.

One popular candidate for the original of Blake's Inflammable Gass is Joseph Priestley. In case you have been assuming that Priestley would have been inconsolably offended, I suggest, on the contrary, that Blake probably meant him to play the role himself. Sir William Browne was so delighted with his prototype that he sent Foote his own muff after the opening night of The Devil upon Two Sticks, so that Doctor Hellebore might gesticulate with it as Sir William did when he lectured, and might be even more unmistakably Sir William instructing the Royal College in the cause and cure of jaundice. If Blake had asked Priestley to play Gass and lecture on phlogiston, I have no doubt all would have been Gass and gaiters. Certainly there is no bigger fool on stage than Quid. And all who feel affection for Blake like to think that Robert Blake laughed with him when he penned the lines of Suction, while time was given for that noble Epicurean to laugh and sing and enjoy his rum.

Not all Foote's victims were as amused as Sir William. The stage representation of George Whitefield drew many protests, one from John Wesley and one, as we have seen, from Blake himself years later. Charles Churchill, in *The Rosciad*, took this play as exemplary of all Foote's stage work.

> By turns transformed into all kinds of shapes,
> Constant to none, Foote laughs, cries, struts, and scrapes:
> Now in the centre, now in van or rear,
> The Proteus shifts, bawd, parson, auctioneer.
> His strokes of humour, and his bursts of sport
> Are all contained in this one word: *Distort*.

In *The Minor*, Shift is a professional mimic. The auctioneer is on stage only because Shift is paid to pretend to be an auctioneer. The bawd, Mother Cole, is an actual member of the cast. The parson is Squintum, George Whitefield, who had a defective eye, hence the name. In some stagings (as Churchill indicates) Foote played all four roles. The audience felt no difference in the "levels of reality" of the four characters. Assuredly Squintum was "real" to the audiences, although Foote, dressed in women's clothes, described and mimed him as seen through the eyes of Mother Cole.

In like manner Blake shows us Mr. Huffcap, his enthusiastic preacher, through the eyes of one of his female admirers, Mrs. Sigtagatist. Like Mother Cole, she plays for us a series of roles in rapid succession: her defense of religion, her helpless state without it, her younger and more enthusiastic self, and a brisk quarrel in which she champions the clergy. It seems that Blake may have considered giving her yet another role, a hypocritical confession, for at times in his manuscript the name is written "Mrs. Sinagain." Foote's Mother Cole (whose original, Mother Douglas, was drawn three times by Hogarth) is a procuress who has joined the Methodists for business reasons and for the consolation of Squintum's doctrine, which (whatever Whitefield's was) is gross antinomianism. Mrs. Cole, under Squintum's tutelage, has no difficulty in reconciling her old calling with the New Call. "Salvation is not the work of a day," he has taught her, and so she will have another drink, thank you, and take the bottle when she leaves. Parson Squintum has said, "A woman is not worth saving that won't be guilty of a swinging sin; for they have no matter to repent upon." A Mrs.

Sinagain would not thus be graveled for lack of matter. But Blake rejected the name. His representation of enthusiasm, while it is very like Foote's in dramatic method, differs from it in essence.

The close of this incident demonstrates another similarity between Foote's work and Blake's. Foote, even in the more formal structure of his published plays, was notorious for the casual way in which he extricated his characters from difficulties. Blake at this point sets up an impossible situation. Mrs. Sigtagatists has described Mr. Huffcap in the pulpit, setting his wig afire and throwing it at his congregation for the good of their souls. Blake now has Inflammable set his hair afire and run about the room—a fine effect, with stage fire and utter confusion. How is Inflammable to be extricated? Easily enough. Draw the curtain, and tell the audience it never happened. Our master of ceremonies, Blake, speaks in his own person. "No No he did not. I was only making a fool of you."

This is an example of Blake's means of establishing those close relations to his audience for which London afterpieces (and Foote's supremely) were remarkable. The direct address by the one man who is completely in charge of the whole show—the totally unrealistic intervention which was Foote's policy. Blake intervenes, as shown above, in the action, and intervenes between cast and audience, as when he says directly to his house: "If I have not presented you with every character in the piece call me ass."

The use of current events in the afterpieces deeply impressed foreign visitors, and Foote was past master of blending the newest news with his oldest jokes. Three events of 1784 which had extensive coverage in the newspapers served Blake particularly well. Two of these will be discussed later (the Handel Festival and the death of Samuel Johnson), but the Great Balloon Ascension seems to have been his point of departure for lunar regions, and will be briefly outlined here.

Englishmen, after more than a year of reading about the triumphs in France of the aerostatic machines, saw their first balloon ascension on September 15, 1784. Filled with the dreadful inflammable gas, the balloon rose from Moorfields in the sight of 150,000 Londoners. The *Gentleman's Magazine* jocularly compared this space travel to Foote's *Devil upon Two Sticks*, the Bottle Imp borrowed from Le Sage, who had power to transport people through space. This periodical reviewed at length a novel, *The Man in the Moon*, mentioning the use made there of the Bottle Imp and Swift's Laputa. By fortuitous circumstance, the pilot was named Lunardi. Many were gripped with an impulse to rhyme moon with balloon and make puns about Lunardi and lunatics. On the Continent, and in England, stage farces made use of ballooning. Mrs. Inchbald's play *The Mogul Tale: or the Descent of the Balloon* opened in July at the Haymarket, set in an Oriental garden; and Frederick Pilon's *Aerostation: or the Templar's Stratagem* opened at Covent Garden in October, with a bookseller named Quarto in the cast who possibly prompted Blake to use a bookseller called "the Dean of Morocco," hinting at the mysterious East as well as the leather of fine bindings.

But these were not musical pieces. Blake's is. Albert Friedman has shown its relation to the ballad revival,[2] and it has relations with the ballad opera, as can be seen from the history of that form.[3] And it also has relation to the songs set within Foote's more formal plays. But Blake's use of music is in every way closer to Foote's use of music in *Tea at the Haymarket* than to ballad opera or a play with incidental music. We turn now to a consideration of his songs, a more important matter than his libretto.

AN ISLAND IN THE MOON:
The Songs, Suggested Divisions

ACT I

The Philosophers' House (chapters 1–4)
1. Trumpet Voluntary—Suction and Sipsop (tenor and bass)
2. To Phebus—Quid (baritone)
3. Honour & Genius—Quid, with Suction and Sipsop
   The Mathematician's Study (chapter 5)
   The Philosophers' House (chapters 6–7)
4. Old Corruption—Quid
   The Lawgiver's Library (chapter 8)
5. Phebe and Jellicoe—Miss Gittipin (soprano)

ACT II

The Philosophers' House (chapter 9)

6. Lo the Bat—Quid and Suction
7. Want Matches?—Quid and Suction with entire company

2 *The Ballad Revival: Studies in the Influence of Popular on Sophisticated Poetry* (Chicago), 1961, 264–267.

3 Edmund Gagey, *Ballad Opera* (New York, 1937). Earlier "moon" pieces are described, their staging, their association with Harlequin.

8. I cry my matches—Mrs. Nannicantipot (contralto)
9. As I walked forth—Steelyard (baritone)
10. This frog he would a wooing ride—Miss Gittipin
11. Solfeggio—Sipsop
12. Hail Matrimony—Quid
13. The Ballad of Sutton—Obtuse Angle (tenor)
14. Good English Hospitality—Steelyard and entire company

INTERLUDE
The Scientist's Laboratory (chapter 10)

ACT III
The Lawgiver's Library (chapter 11)

15. Holy Thursday—Obtuse Angle
16. When the tongues of the children are heard—Mrs. Nan.
17. O father father—Quid (baritone)
18. Joe and Bill—Tilly Lally (buffo)
19. Leave o leave me—Miss Gittipin
20. Doctor Clash—Little Scopprell (countertenor or falsetto)
21. William of Orange—Sipsop and entire company

At the Haymarket, business was better if room were made within satire for sentiment. In Foote's plays, he usually treated the young lovers quite without satire, and some parent-child relationships were also thus treated. In *Tea at the Haymarket*, music and dance took the place of sentiment in plot. Foote wrote no songs, but used whatever was most popular. At his theatrical discretion, he would use the material straight or satirically. His chief source was the pastoral as it came down from Milton and Handel by a sharp and devious descent through the theaters, public gardens, and fair booths of the eighteenth century. He hired the best singers, dancers, and instrumentalists he could afford, and he had great skill in presenting his performers on stage. The show was under his control at every moment. He knew when to give a performer the stage, and knew as well when to interrupt "Consider, Fond Shepherd," or "The Amorous Swain." He would stop his performers, parody, deride, criticize—thus giving them opportunity to play a role within a role: comic subservience, rage, chagrin, pique. Then when he asked for another song, perhaps a favorite of his, no one was better equipped to lead the applause. For if the British Aristophanes found a song touching, what red-blooded Englishman but should dissolve in tears? Foote prided himself on the sweep of emotions he could inflict on an audience. From the depths of laughing at something so low they ought not to be amused (but were), he jerked them to higher planes of patriotism and sentiment.

Blake thus deploys the twenty-one songs in his musical score, all but one of which he wrote. The songs are wept over, interrupted, criticized, so as to control audience reaction and shape a unified whole.

The singing begins as soon as the entire company is on stage, and it begins under the auspices of Phebus, though we well may ask what the sun god is doing on the moon and why he presides over an Oriental garden. "In the Moon as Phebus stood over his oriental Gardening   O ay come Ill sing you a song said the Cynic." Quid the Cynic is Blake. He does more singing than anyone else. The other two hosts halt him long enough to give him the correct formal introduction of a trumpet fanfare, scatological in words, but rendered with straight faces. Suction's tenor voice moves up the trumpet's tonic chord, Sipsop's bass moves downward on the same notes.

"Ill begin again said the Cynic," and he sings of Phebus, launching the wandering minds of the moon-dwellers on a discussion of Phebus, Chatterton, and Pharaoh.

The three Philosophers led by Quid sing:

Honour & Genius is all I ask
And I ask the Gods no more.

This is a parody of a song from *Daphnis and Amaryllis* by James Harris, staged at Drury Lane during Garrick's regime. Harris, along with his many attainments, was an excellent amateur musician, trained in the music of Handel, who was his friend. Most of the music in this pastiche is from Handel, most of the words are adapted from Milton, but the words of this song are Harris's own. Later in Blake's piece the song is repeated when spirits are high and music has induced a mood of utter contentment: "I ask the gods no more."

The fourth song is "Old Corruption," sung by Quid. The stage background of the song is the satire of the medical profession and especially of the conduct of hospitals in *The Devil upon Two Sticks*, which play was then on stage, and was part of the jesting about the balloon ascensions. The literary background is Book II *Paradise Lost*, the genealogy of Sin, Death, and the hell hounds. Its future lay ahead; it is a Blakean fable of the ancestry of disease, and the first of many grotesque births Blake would contribute to literature.

The fifth and last song of Act I has its background in James Harris's pastoral—or, to be more precise, it pokes fun at the many, many stage songs derived from *L'Allegro*. It was almost required that someone sing about the light fantastic toe, and Miss Gittipin does so. The company is gratified. The song is jocund in mood, mildly satirizing the *L'Allegro* tradition, but not much sillier than some of the genuine songs in the tradition. It provides a minor musical climax needed at this point.

Act II opens with the sociable suggestion, "Let's all get drunk." The Blake brothers sing first: an anthem to Doctor Johnson. The text was inspired by Collins' *Ode to Evening*: "Now air is hushed, save where the weak-eyed bat,/With short shrill shriek, flits by on leathern wing." The anthem opens:

Lo the Bat with Leathern Wing
Winking & blinking
Winking & blinking
Winking & blinking
Like Doctor Johnson

The music might be an "animal imitation" such as Purcell's "Lo, hear the gentle lark," or Handel's nightingales in *Solomon*, or Haydn's snakes in *The Creation*. The "short shrill shrieks" could be voiced *ad libitum*.

Blake is never more like Foote than at this point. One would need to cite all references to Foote in Boswell's *Life of Johnson* to present an argument that the anthem, with its duetto miming Johnson and Scipio Africanus greeting one another among the shades, was an appropriate tribute at the time of Johnson's death. In an age of wits, the acknowledged wits were Johnson, Quin, Garrick, and Foote. In the long battle of wits between Johnson and Foote, jests were rough on both sides. Johnson said of him, "For loud obstreperous broad-faced mirth, I know not his equal." In precisely these terms Blake pays his tribute—and we remember that it was entirely a private and unpublished tribute.

So far I have said nothing about a member of the cast called Little Scopprell. I think he was a countertenor, or had a high and effective falsetto at his command. Any actor who can laugh on stage as he does will earn his pay in a company of comedians. The loud obstreperous broad-faced mirth of the anthem leaves Little Scopprell quite undone. For some time the whole company can only echo it.

Then, led by Quid and Suction, they sing a part-song, "Want

matches?" in "Great confusion & disorder." This song brings us into a stage tradition for which Foote's pupil Shuter was famous. The most popular specialty act of the mid-century was Edward Shuter's *Cries of London*. Blake wanted a song of this type. No good stage director lets confusion reign on stage very long, and the next three songs are calming.

Mrs. Nannicantipot sings another street cry, a contrasting song of the children who sell matches on the street. It is Blake's own; so far as I can discover, there is nothing like it in the records of street cries of the period. If Mrs. Nan's original is Mrs. Anna Barbauld, then Blake gave her music to an expert in children's songs, but the words are pure Blake, not "Anna Barbauld." I think "I cry my matches" is the first really lovely musical effect of the program. Certainly I myself would stage it for such an effect. I know what Adelaide Van Wey could do on stage with New Orleans street cries. One of these, "Tant sirop est doux," speaks to me as this one does, of the pathos of a child's uncomprehending acceptance of the human condition. Blake's little match vendor moves from us toward the distant Guild Hall, and this first Song of Innocence fades as the child blesses those who sit in authority therein.

In the hush that follows, Steelyard sings a pastoral about a young maid among the violets. Critics have spoken slightingly of the words, but I have heard Leonard Warren accomplish wonders in recital with a very similar song, "Early one morning just as the sun was rising." Steelyard's baritone as it followed and contrasted with the contralto may be supposed to have made it very sweet to the ears. In fact, Tilly Lally's reaction indicates this. The key word is *sweet*; he times his lines so as to allow the song to have its full effect before he breaks the mood, but when he does, he uses the suggestion of "too much sweatness" for a transition to low comedy. He mimes one-eyed Joe Bradley licking up much too much sweetness in the sugar-house.

Miss Gittipin then sings the only song not tampered with at all by Blake. This version of "Frog went a-wooing" was active in London then, and is still active in America.[4]

Little Scopprell praises her voice by saying it is like a harpsichord. At this date, the harpsichord represented the good old days of Handel et al., in contrast with that shocking innovation, the pianoforte, which

---

[4] Cecil J. Sharp, ed., *Nursery Songs from the Appalachian Mountains*, 2nd series, London, 1923. The refrain there is "Collum a carey"; Blake's is "cock I cary."

Friedman, *The Ballad Revival* (p. 265), says Blake's is "the broadside version of the traditional 'Marriage of the Frog and the Mouse.'" An active version, then, in Blake's London when he wrote.

Johann Christian Bach had made popular in London to the dismay of all conservative souls.

Sipsop is getting restive. He has been silenced in his solo work since his trumpet voluntary at the opening. Perhaps mindful of the florid bass tricks of "And the trumpet shall sound," he begins singing a bass solfeggio. Quid stops him. He wants no Italian nonsense. (The Haymarket was one of the headquarters for this battle throughout the century.) He prefers "English Genius," and anyway he himself wants to sing a solo. He sings a satiric tribute to matrimony and the combined English genius of Milton, Handel, and the "English Blake." Scopprell interrupts "Hail Matrimony" just as Blake is alluding to his own publication of the year before, "How sweet I roam'd," having taken a swipe at "Hail wedded love," *L'Allegro*, and Handelian pastiches. Scopprell is the self-appointed music critic for the evening, and seems to have his eye on Miss Gittipin; so he professes to be outraged at Quid's cynical view of wedlock. But the rest of the company is as amused as the audience is supposed to be. Obtuse Angle has to wipe away his tears of laughter before he can sing the next song, a ballad of Old England. Blake knew well the real ballads and the imitation ones, and wrote a good imitation of the casual rhyming of folk ballad. One of the hits of the century had been *Shakespeare's Garland*, Garrick's imitations of Percy's collection of old ballads, written for the Shakespeare Jubilee. Blake's ballad uses a Shakespearean tag as Garrick used them. Obtuse Angle's song is a tribute to Thomas Sutton, who by building a hospital did more for humanity than Locke, Newton, South, Sherlock, and other Hamletlike souls who sat around wondering whether to be or not to be.

Blake, since he is making an *omnium gatherum* of all the most popular turns, could hardly neglect "The Roast Beef of Old England," from *The Grub Street Opera* by Henry Fielding, that great Haymarket emeritus. The closing song of Act II is, like that beloved song, addressed to the inward parts of Common Man, and, like it, attributes national virtue to England's careful concern for eating and drinking. Steelyard's baritone leads, and the whole company joins in the fine, noisy closing.

Between Act II and Act III is an interlude without song, a scientific demonstration given at the home of Inflammable Gass, when the deadly gas phlogiston is accidentally released all over the house to kill us with a plague.

The seven songs of Act III are placed with care. Since no such program can end with sentimental songs, the beginning of the last act is the place for them. Blake opens with three marvelous songs of child-hood. The tenor first sings *Holy Thursday*. This song and the next were used in *Songs of Innocence*. Critics use *Holy Thursday* to demonstrate the degree of irony in that book. Critical opinion covers a wide spectrum, from equating Blake with Foote's own derision of the Foundling Hospital, Magdalen, and all philanthropic endeavors, to the other end of the spectrum, Handel's attitude. Handel, in a gesture which has a place in the history of public charity as well as in the history of music, gave *Messiah* to the foundlings. It has been estimated that minimum royalties would have put the foundlings in a position to buy out some respectable segment of the city. Their chapel was the only consecrated place where Handel's oratorios could be performed during his lifetime, and the chapel was associated with "He shall feed his flock like a shepherd and gather the lambs in his bosom." Thus the foundlings came to be linked with song, and singing was an important part of the children's lives. From here the singing spread to Magdalen Hospital and other institutions for orphaned and abandoned children, until it became a custom to unite them annually at St. Paul's. The singing of the children came to be a feature of London life, drawing the general public to the hospital chapels as well as to the annual service at St. Paul's. There is fairly good evidence that Blake heard the children sing, and the poem itself evinces his knowledge of the custom. When he speaks of the children, the "multitude of lambs" who "raise to heaven the voice of song," what his attitude is seems to be anybody's guess.

Mrs. Nannicantipot then sings "When the tongues of children are heard on the green." Once again, the critics are widely divided as to how Blake meant us to hear her song.

The third song is "O father father," rather like Goethe's *Der Erlkönig*. At this point the manuscript shows Blake's hesitation. First he assigned the song to Miss Gittipin; that is wrong, for the song needs a deep voice. Then he considered the buffo Tilly Lally. But that is wrong. So he gave it to himself, trusting it to Quid's baritone. That is the right choice. A child's lone voice calls in the dark for his father, but we hear it through the father's consciousness. Schubert set *Der Erlkönig* for the baritone Johann Vogel, who sang it into his first big success in 1821, and the song is Opus 1 in Schubert's published works.

In Blake's three songs, the three voices, tenor, contralto, baritone, should move as the songs move, step by step from full morning light to twilight to dark. They move from public ceremony to social play to secret fear of some Erlking who may steal a child away from his father.

In each song, the threat to innocence is more explicit. They stop the show, as well they might.

Now we can see the rationale of the ponderings of Maestro Blake. He knew the audience ought to hear the soprano and the buffo, and now we do. Tilly Lally moves us out of this mood with another song of childhood, sung with verve and good humor, his ditty of the two urchins (lost souls by English standards) who fail to observe the niceties in the game of cricket.

Then the soprano with the harpsichord voice gives us a pre-Romantic song about one of those girls who is determined to die of thwarted love and haunt her faithless lover in the breeze. (Betty in *The Cozeners* by Foote sings such a song, but there were many others floating around to serve as models.) It is not a bad song, and gives a needed contrast between two broadly comic numbers.

Little Scopprell has served the other performers well all evening by his applause and laughter. It is only fair that he be given the last and best of the comedy turns. He has his day in the sun. His song is based on the best of all stage jokes, *The Rehearsal*. Long ago it had been made into a musical rehearsal on stage. Such a skit as *Bayes in Chromatics*, done while Garrick was at Drury Lane, was even at that date a joke with decades of stage history behind it. Blake's character Doctor Clash has a progenitor in Foote's character Doctor Catgut in *The Commissary*, one of Foote's plays that was on stage. The original of Foote's Catgut was Dr. Thomas Arne. Blake's Doctor Clash, played by Scopprell, is having a hard time rehearsing his orchestra and an Italian castrato. He yells, pounds on the podium, and (as all conductors will do) sings for his singer.

Steelyard complains about the song. He says he wants something better than Doctor Clash, and asks for the best—the most popular single piece of stage music of the era, Handel's "Water Music." The line would get a laugh, for the "Water Music" is not written for singing.

Something Handelian is needed for the closing number, and something in Handel's "big bow-wow tone." So the bass leads the company in singing a masterpiece of utter irrelevancy, "Victory! twas William the Prince of Orange." Well, hooray for him, whoever he may be and whatever he may have to do with anything! The chorus is indiscriminately patriotic. Trumpets sound. Banners wave. The hero on a white horse fights his way through the smoke of some undesignated battle while thousands cheer. I think it is one of the funniest things Blake wrote. Certainly it is very loud, and at this point in the proceedings, this is the necessary quality. What more could any Haymarket audience desire? At the finale, we are an inner circle, loyal Englishmen, castigators of folly, but rather chivalric in a vague way, and not ashamed of a bit of honest sentiment.

How aware of stage work Blake was is an unanswerable question, but there is value in asking unanswerable questions.

Was he ever present when the greatest of all Lady Macbeths chilled the air of London with her sleepwalking? Mrs. Siddons was at her most powerful as Lady Macbeth and as Queen Katherine, and accounts by those who saw the two roles border on the incredible. So does W. Moelwyn Merchant's assessment of Blake's *Queen Katherine's Dream* border on the incredible; yet both judgments do persuade the reader: "the richest, most penetrating comment by any artist on the work of Shakespeare." [5] If any actress influenced Blake's *Jane Shore*, it was Mrs. Yates, not Mrs. Siddons, for that tidal wave had not struck the London stage when his picture was made. Before he illustrated Stedman's *Narrative*, had his nerves ever been harassed by Garrick's or Kemble's overwhelming portrayals of slavery in Surinam in *Oroonoko?* Did his *Mad Song* owe anything to any Ophelia or Belvidera of the boards? Did he see Tom King's Touchstone? It there anything in Blake's *Samson* that he owed to Handel's *Samson?* When Blake's metrics moved from simple song forms to the rolling baroque rhythms of prophecy, did he owe to Handel some sense of a vast yet symmetrical shape of sound waiting to be filled up with syllables?

David Erdman, reading again Blake's letters to Hayley, dropped me a note quoting Blake on the child actor Master Betty, and commented, "Sounds like an old theatergoer. Yes?" Yes. And at the very least, it is evident that Blake wrote all his life as if the theater were a part of life to be taken into consideration.

Such knowledge as he needed to write *An Island in the Moon* could have been had elsewhere; it is simpler to conclude that he saw Foote himself in the Haymarket. The text as it stands is essentially complete, a unified whole, the parts arranged with tact, the style appropriate to the intention. The sense of a show under the complete control of one man is present. The stock jokes are there, and are handled so as to come through with novelty and freshness. We could

[5] W. Moelwyn Merchant, "Blake's Shakespeare," *Apollo* (April 1964), 318–325, referring (p. 325) to Blake's six drawings in an extra-illustrated Second Folio.

wish for more: more stage directions to tell how the Blake brothers planned to bring down the house with their weak-eyed bat, any sketches for stage sets, and, most of all, any sketches for those lecture slides. Think what the man who drew *The Ghost of a Flea* could have done with those slides! Still, the shape and substance of a Haymarket show is there.

For all that, it is imitation Foote. Blake dramatizes at the beginning the breakdown of communication between the characters. This alienation does not resolve itself on any basis of reason. It yields to song, and finally all the characters are one in their singing. This is a Blakean belief set in a Haymarket formula.

Blake did not have the "single vision" necessary for Foote's type of allegory. He was unable to deal with characters or even with institutions as Foote did. It is always possible to make the College of Surgeons the object of satire. But all Foote's doctors are quacks, idle, aimlessly cruel. Jack Tearguts is no quack. He works hard, and the pain he gives is not aimless. Almost any medical student, given enough rum & water, may refer to Old So-and-So in derision and fear. But Sipsop, when he did so, was aware that a surgeon whose duty it was to operate on cancer patients nerved himself for his day's work as best he could. Even today, with anesthetics at command, it is not an easy life. And Sipsop, lunatic though he is, cannot forget the pain he has seen. Even on the moon, Blake could not dismiss compassion. To call anything human "Sir Penurious Trifle" or "Mrs. Sinagain" and really follow through in his characterization was not William Blake's dish of tea.

We are lucky to have this "failure" left unpublished in a notebook. We can watch a great metrist and a born parodist searching for his tunes, trying out dramatic systems and metrical systems, none of which were to enslave him. Here he cheerfully takes under his examining eye song and satire, operas and plagues, surgery and pastoral song, Chatterton and science, enthusiasm and myth, philanthropy and Handelian anthem, the Man in the Street and those children whose nursery is the street—while he is making up his mind what William Blake shall take seriously. Our chief interest in the work is and properly will always be in those songs of childhood and what grew out of them. The work may also raise the question: Are those "visionary forms dramatic" more *dramatic* than we had thought? At any rate, here a master ironist flexes his vocal cords with a wide range of tone. It is good to know that this ironist (unlike some others) enjoyed a joke.

II. 13

Coleridge: The Anxiety of Influence*

HAROLD BLOOM

Yale University

COLERIDGE observed that "psychologically, Consciousness is the problem," and he added somberly: "almost all is yet to be achieved." How much he achieved, Kathleen Coburn and others are showing us. My concern here is the sadder one of speculating yet again why he did not achieve more as a poet. Walter Jackson Bate has meditated, persuasively and recently, upon Coleridge's human and literary anxieties, particularly in regard to the burden of the past and its inhibiting poetic splendors. I swerve away from Mr. Bate to center the critical meditation upon what might be called the poetics of anxiety, the process of misprision by which any latecomer strong poet attempts to clear an imaginative space for himself. Coleridge could have been a strong poet, as strong as Blake or Wordsworth. He could have been another mighty antagonist for the Great Spectre Milton to engage and, yes, to overcome, but not without contests as titanic as *The Four Zoas* and *The Excursion*, and parental victories as equivocal as *Jerusalem* and *The Prelude*. But we have no such poems by Coleridge. When my path winds home at the end of this essay, I will speculate as to what these poems should have been. As critical fathers for my quest I invoke first, Oscar Wilde, with his glorious principle that the highest criticism sees the object as in itself it really is not, and second, Wilde's critical father, Walter Pater, whose essay of 1886 on "Coleridge's Writ-

* Read at the Institute in 1971. Published in *Institute Papers: New Perspectives on Coleridge and Wordsworth*, 1972.

ings" seems to me still the best short treatment of Coleridge, and this after a century of commentary. Pater, who knew his debt to Coleridge, knew also the anxiety Coleridge caused him, and Pater therefore came to a further and subtler knowing. In the Organic Analogue, against which the entire soul of the great Epicurean critic rebelled, Pater recognized the product of Coleridge's profound anxieties as a creator. I begin therefore with Pater on Coleridge, and then will move immediately deep into the Coleridgean interior, to look upon Coleridge's fierce refusal to take on the ferocity of the strong poet.

This ferocity, as both Coleridge and Pater well knew, expresses itself as a near-solipsism, an Egotistical Sublime, or Miltonic godlike stance. From 1795 on, Coleridge knew, loved, envied, was both cheered and darkened by the largest instance of that Sublime since Milton himself. He studied constantly, almost involuntarily, the glories of the truly modern strong poet, Wordsworth. Whether he gave Wordsworth rather more than he received, we cannot be certain; we know only that he wanted more from Wordsworth than he received, but then it was his endearing though exasperating weakness that he always needed more love than he could get, no matter how much he got: "To be beloved is all I need,/ And whom I love, I love indeed."

Pater understood what he called Coleridge's "peculiar charm," but he resisted it in the sacred name of what he called the "relative" spirit against Coleridge's archaizing "absolute" spirit. In gracious but equivocal tribute to Coleridge he observed:

The literary life of Coleridge was a disinterested struggle against the application of the relative spirit to moral and religious questions. Everywhere he is restlessly scheming to apprehend the absolute; to affirm it effectively; to get it acknowledged. Coleridge failed in that attempt, happily even for him, for it was a struggle against the increasing life of the mind itself. . . . How did his choice of a controversial interest, his determination to affirm the absolute, weaken or modify his poetic gift?

To affirm the absolute, Pater says, or as we might say, to reject all dualisms except those sanctioned by orthodox Christian thought; this is not *materia poetica* for the start of the nineteenth century, and if we think of a poem like the "Hymn before Sunrise in the Vale of Chamouni," then we are likely to agree with Pater. We will agree also when he contrasts Wordsworth favorably with Coleridge, and even with Goethe, commending Wordsworth for "that flawless temperament . . . which keeps his conviction of a latent intelligence in nature within the limits of sentiment or instinct, and confines it to those delicate and subdued shades of expression which perfect art allows." Pater goes on to say that Coleridge's version of Wordsworth's instinct is a philosophical idea, which means that Coleridge's poetry had to be "more dramatic, more self-conscious" than Wordsworth's. But this in turn, Pater insists, means that for aesthetic success ideas must be held loosely, in the relative spirit. One idea that Coleridge did not hold loosely was the Organic Analogue, and it becomes clearer as we proceed in Pater's essay that the aesthetic critic is building toward a passionate assault upon the Organic principle. He quotes Coleridge's description of Shakespeare as "a nature humanized, a genial understanding, directing self-consciously a power and an implicit wisdom deeper even than our consciousness." "There," Pater comments, with bitter eloquence, " 'the absolute' has been affirmed in the sphere of art; and thought begins to congeal." With great dignity Pater adds that Coleridge has "obscured the true interest of art." By likening the work of art to a living organism, Coleridge does justice to the impression the work may give us, but he "does not express the process by which that work was produced."

M. H. Abrams, in his *The Mirror and the Lamp*, defends Coleridge against Pater by insisting that Coleridge knew his central problem: "was to use analogy with organic growth to account for the spontaneous, the inspired, and the self-evolving in the psychology of invention, yet not to commit himself as far to the elected figure as to minimize the supervention of the antithetic qualities of foresight and choice." Though Abrams called Pater "short-sighted," I am afraid the critical palms remain with the relative spirit, for Pater's point was not that Coleridge had no awareness of the dangers of using the Organic Analogue, but rather that awareness, here as elsewhere, was no salvation for Coleridge. The issue is whether Coleridge, not Shakespeare, was able to direct "self-consciously a power and an implicit wisdom deeper than consciousness." Pater's complaint is valid because Coleridge, in describing Shakespeare, Dante, Milton, keeps repeating his absolute formula that poems grow from within themselves, that their "wholeness is not in vision or conception, but in an inner feeling of totality and absolute being." As Pater says, "that exaggerated inwardness is barren" because it "withdraws us too far from what we can see, hear, and feel," because it cheats the senses and the emotions of their triumph. I urge Pater's wisdom here not only against Coleridge, though I share Pater's love for Coleridge, but against the formalist criticism that continued in Coleridge's absolute spirit.

What is the imaginative source of Coleridge's disabling hunger for the Absolute? On August 9, 1831, about three years before he died, he wrote in his Notebook: "From my earliest recollection I have had a consciousness of Power without Strength—a perception, an experience, of more than ordinary power with an inward sense of Weakness. . . . More than ever do I feel this now, when all my fancies still in their integrity are, as it were, drawn *inward* and by their suppression and compression rendered a mock substitute for Strength." Here again is Pater's barren and exaggerated inwardness, but in a darker context than the Organic principle provided.

This context is Milton's "universe of death," where Coleridge apprehended death-in-life as being "the wretchedness of *division.*" If we stand in that universe, then "we think of ourselves as separated beings, and place nature in antithesis to the mind, as object to subject, thing to thought, death to life." To be so separated is to become, Coleridge says, "a soul-less fixed star, receiving no rays nor influences into my Being, *a Solitude which I so tremble at, that I cannot attribute it even to the Divine Nature.*" This, we can say, is Coleridge's Counter-Sublime, his answer to the anxiety of influence, in strong poets. The fear of solipsism is greater in him than the fear of not individuating his own imagination.

As with every other major Romantic, the prime precursor poet for Coleridge was Milton. There is a *proviso* to be entered here; for all these poets—Blake, Wordsworth, Shelley, Coleridge (only Keats is an exception)—there is a greater Sublime poetry behind Milton, but as its author is a people and not a single poet, and as it is far removed in time, its greatness does not inhibit a new imagination, not unless it is taken as the work of the Prime Precursor Himself, to whom all creation belongs. Only Coleridge acquired a doubly Sublime anxiety of influence, among these poets. Beyond the beauty that has terror in it of Milton was beauty more terrible. In a letter to Thelwall, December 17, 1796, Coleridge wrote: "Is not Milton a *sublimer* poet than Homer or Virgil? Are not his Personages more sublimely cloathed? And do you not know, that there is not perhaps *one* page in Milton's Paradise Lost, in which he has not borrowed his imagery from the *Scriptures?*—I allow, and rejoice that *Christ* appealed only to the understanding & the affections; but I affirm that, after reading Isaiah, or St. Paul's Epistle to the Hebrews, Homer & Virgil are disgustingly *tame* to me, & Milton himself barely tolerable." Yet these statements are rare in Coleridge. Frequently, Milton seems to blend with the ultimate Influ-

ence, which I think is a normal enough procedure. In 1796, Coleridge
also says, in his review of Burke's *Letter to a Noble Lord:* "It is lucky
for poetry, that Milton did not live in our days." Here Coleridge moves
toward the center of his concern, and we should remember his formula:
"Shakespeare was all men, potentially, except Milton." This leads to a
more ambiguous formula, reported to us of a lecture that Coleridge
gave on November 28, 1811: "Shakespeare became all things well into
which he infused himself, while all forms, all things became Milton—
the poet ever present to our minds and more than gratifying us for the
loss of the distinct individuality of what he represents." Though Coleridge truly professes himself more than gratified, he admits loss. Milton's greatness is purchased at the cost of something dear to Coleridge,
a principle of difference he knows may be flooded out by his monistic
yearnings. For Milton, to Coleridge, is a mythic monad in himself.
Commenting upon the apostrophe to light at the commencement of the
third book of *Paradise Lost,* Coleridge notes: "in all modern poetry
in Christendom there is an under consciousness of a sinful nature, a
fleeting away of external things, the mind or subject greater than the
object, the reflective character predominant. In the Paradise Lost the
sublimest parts are the revelations of Milton's own mind, producing itself and evolving its own greatness; and this is so truly so, that when
that which is merely entertaining for its objective beauty is introduced,
it at first seems a discord." This might be summarized as: where Milton
is not, nature is barren, and its significance is that Milton is permitted
just such a solitude as Coleridge trembles to imagine for the Divine
Being.

Humphry House observed that "Coleridge was quite unbelievably
modest about his own poems; and the modesty was of a curious kind,
sometimes rather humble and over-elaborate." As House adds, Coleridge
"dreaded publication" of his poetry, and until 1828, when he was fifty-
six, there was nothing like an adequate gathering of his verse. Wordsworth's attitude was no help, of course, and the Hutchinson girls and
Dorothy no doubt followed Wordsworth in his judgments. There was
Wordsworth, and before him there had been Milton. Coleridge presumably knew what "Tintern Abbey" owed to "Frost at Midnight," but this
knowledge nowhere found expression. Must we resort to psychological
speculation in order to see what inhibited Coleridge, or are there more
reliable aids available?

In the *Biographia Literaria* Coleridge is not very kind to his pre-

Wordsworthian poetry, and particularly to the "Religious Musings."
Yet this is where we must seek what went wrong with Coleridge's
ambitions, here, and if there were space, in "The Destiny of Nations"
fragments (not its arbitrarily yoked-together form of 1817), and in
the "Ode to the Departing Year" and "Monody on the Death of
Chatterton" in its earlier versions. After Wordsworth had descended
upon Coleridge, supposedly as a "know-thyself" admonition from
heaven, but really rather more like a new form of the Miltonic blight,
then Coleridge's poetic ambitions sustained another kind of inhibition.
The Miltonic shadow needs to be studied first in early Coleridge, before a view can be obtained of his maturer struggles with influence.

With characteristic self-destructiveness, Coleridge gave "Religious
Musings" the definitive subtitle: "A Desultory Poem, Written on the
Christmas Eve of 1794." The root-meaning of "desultory" is "vaulting," and though Coleridge consciously meant that his poem skipped
about and wavered, his imagination meant "vaulting," for "Religious
Musings" is a wildly ambitious poem. "This is the time," it begins,
in direct recall of Milton's "Nativity" Hymn, yet it follows not the
Hymn but the most sublime moments of *Paradise Lost*, particularly the
invocation to Book III. As with the 1802 "Hymn before Sunrise," its
great fault as a poem is that it never stops whooping; in its final
version I count well over one hundred exclamation-points in just over
four hundred lines. Whether one finds this habit in Coleridge distressing or endearing hardly matters; he just never could stop doing it. He
whoops because he vaults; he is a high-jumper of the Sublime, and
psychologically he could not avoid this. I quote the poem's final passage,
with relish and with puzzlement, for I am uncertain as to how good
after all it may not be, though it does seem palpably awful. Yet its awfulness is at least Sublime; it is not the drab, flat awfulness of Wordsworth at *his* common worst in *The Excursion* or even (heresy to admit
this!) in so many passages of *The Prelude* that we hastily skip by, with
our zeal and relief in getting at the great moments. Having just shouted
out his odd version of Berkeley, that "Life is a vision shadowy of
truth," Coleridge sees "the veiling clouds retire" and God appears
in a blaze upon His Throne. Raised to a pitch of delirium by this
vision, Coleridge soars aloft to join it:

Contemplant Spirits! ye that hover o'er
With untired gaze the immeasurable fount
Ebullient with creative Deity!

And ye of plastic power, that interfused
Roll through the grosser and material mass
In organizing surge! Holies of God!
(And what if Monads of the infinite mind?)
I haply journeying my immortal course
Shall sometime join your mystic choir! Till then
I discipline my young and novice thought
In ministeries of heart-stirring song,
And aye on Meditation's heaven-ward wing
Soaring aloft I breathe the empyreal air
Of Love, omnific, omnipresent Love,
Whose day-spring rises glorious in my soul
As the great Sun, when he his influence
Sheds on the frost-bound waters—The glad stream
Flows to the ray and warbles as it flows.

Scholars agree that this not terribly pellucid passage somehow combines an early Unitarianism with a later orthodox overlay, as well as quantities of Berkeley, Hartley, Newton, Neo-Platonism, and possibly more esoteric matter. A mere reader will be reminded primarily of Milton, and will be in the right, for Milton counts here and the rest do not. The Spirits Coleridge invokes are Miltonic Angels, though their functions seem to be more complicated. Coleridge confidently assures himself and us that his course is immortal, that he may end up as a Miltonic angel, and so perhaps also a Monad of the infinite mind. In the meantime, he will study Milton's "heart-stirring song." Otherwise, all he needs is Love, which is literally the air he breathes, the sunrise radiating out of his soul in a stream of song, and the natural Sun toward which he flows, a Sun that is not distinct from God. If we reflect on how palpably sincere this is, how wholehearted, and consider what was to be Coleridge's actual poetic course, then we will be moved. Moved to what? Well, perhaps to remember a remark of Coleridge's: "There are many men, especially at the outset of life, who, in their too eager desire for the end, overlook the difficulties in the way; there is another class, who see nothing else. The first class *may* sometimes fail; the latter rarely succeed." Whatever the truth of this for other men, no man becomes a strong poet unless he starts out with a certain obliviousness of the difficulties in the way. But soon enough he will meet those difficulties, and one of them will be that his precursor and inspirer threatens to subsume him, as Coleridge is subsumed by Milton in "Religious Musings" and his other pre-Wordsworthian poems. And here,

I shall digress massively, before returning to Coleridge's poetry, for I enter now upon the enchanted and baleful ground of poetic influence, through which I am learning to find my way by a singular light, which will bear a little explanation.

I do not believe that poetic influence is simply something that happens, that it is just the process by which ideas and images are transmitted from earlier to later poets. On that view, whether or not influence causes anxiety in the later poet is a matter of temperament and circumstance. Poetic influence thus reduces to source-study, of the kind performed upon Coleridge by Lowes and later scholars. Coleridge was properly scornful of such study, and I think most critics learn how barren an enterprise it turns out to be. I myself have no use for it as such, and what I mean by the study of poetic influence turns source-study inside out. The first principle of the proper study of poetic influence, as I conceive it, is that no strong poem has sources and no strong poem merely alludes to another poem. The meaning of a strong poem *is* another strong poem, a precursor's poem which is being misinterpreted, revised, corrected, evaded, twisted askew, made to suffer an inclination or bias which is the property of the later and not the earlier poet. Poetic influence, in this sense, is actually poetic misprision, a poet's taking or doing amiss of a parent-poem that keeps *finding* him, to use a Coleridgean turn-of-phrase. Yet even this misprision is only the first step that a new poet takes when he advances from the early phase where his precursor floods him, to a more Promethean phase where he quests for his own fire, which nevertheless must be stolen from his precursor.

I count some half-dozen steps in the life-cycle of the strong poet, as he attempts to convert his inheritance into what will aid him without inhibiting him by the anxiety of a failure in priority, a failure to have begotten himself. These steps are revisionary ratios, and for the convenience of shorthand, I find myself giving them arbitrary names, which are proving useful to me, and perhaps can be of use to others. I list them herewith, with descriptions but not examples, as this can only be a brief sketch, and I must get back to Coleridge's poetry, but I hope, with this list helpfully in hand, to find my examples in Coleridge.

1. *Clinamen*, which is poetic misprision proper; I take the word from Lucretius, where it means a "swerve" of the atoms so as to make change possible in the universe. The later poet swerves away from the precursor, by so reading the parent-poem as to execute a *clinamen* in

relation to it. This appears as the corrective movement of his own poem, which implies that the precursor poem went accurately up to a certain point, but then should have swerved, precisely in the direction that the new poem moves.

2. *Tessera*, which is completion and antithesis; I take the word not from mosaic-making, where it is still used, but from the ancient Mystery-cults, where it meant a token of recognition, the fragment, say, of a small pot which with the other fragments would reconstitute the vessel. The later poet antithetically "completes" the precursor, by so reading the parent-poem as to retain its terms but to mean them in an opposite sense, as though the precursor had failed to go far enough.

3. *Kenosis*, which is a breaking-device similar to the defense mechanisms our psyches employ against repetition-compulsions; *kenosis*, then, is a movement toward discontinuity with the precursor. I take the word from St. Paul, where it means the humbling or emptying-out of Jesus by himself, when he accepts reduction from Divine to human status. The later poet, apparently emptying himself of his own afflatus, his imaginative godhood, seems to humble himself as though he ceased to be a poet, but this ebbing is so performed in relation to a precursor's poem-of-ebbing that the precursor is emptied out also, and so the later poem of deflation is not as absolute as it seems.

4. *Daemonization*, or a movement toward a personalized Counter-Sublime, in reaction to the precursor's Sublime; I take the term from general Neo-Platonic usage, where an intermediary being, neither Divine nor human, enters into the adept to aid him. The later poet opens himself to what he believes to be a power in the parent-poem that does not belong to the parent proper, but to a range of being just beyond that precursor. He does this, in his poem, by so stationing its relation to the parent-poem as to generalize away the uniqueness of the earlier work.

5. *Askesis*, or a movement of self-purgation which intends the attainment of a state of solitude; I take the term, general as it is, particularly from the practice of pre-Socratic shamans like Empedocles. The later poet does not, as in *kenosis*, undergo a revisionary movement of emptying, but of curtailing; yields up part of his own human and imaginative endowment, so as to separate himself from others, including the precursor, and he does this in his poem by so stationing it in regard to the parent-poem as to make that poem undergo an *askesis* also; the precursor's endowment is also truncated.

6. *Apophrades,* or the return of the dead; I take the word from the Athenian dismal or unlucky days upon which the dead returned to reinhabit the houses in which they had lived. The later poet, in his own final phase, already burdened by an imaginative solitude that is almost a solipsism, holds his own poem so open again to the precursor's work that at first we might believe the wheel has come full circle, and that we are back in the later poet's flooded apprenticeship, before his strength began to assert itself in the revisionary ratios of *clinamen* and the others. But the poem is now *held* open to the precursor, where once it *was* open, and the uncanny effect is that the new poem's achievement makes it seem to us, not as though the precursor were writing it, but as though the later poet himself had written the precursor's characteristic work.

These then are six revisionary ratios, and I think they can be observed, usually in cyclic appearance, in the life's work of every post-Enlightenment strong poet, which in English means, for practical purposes, every post-Miltonic strong poet. Coleridge, to return now where I began, had the potential of the strong poet, but declined the full process of developing into one, unlike Blake, Wordsworth, and the major poets after them down to Yeats and Stevens in our time. Yet his work, even in its fragmentary state, demonstrates this revisionary cycle in spite of himself. My ulterior purpose in this discussion is to use Coleridge as an instance because he is apparently so poor an example of the cycle I have sketched. But that makes him a sterner test for my theory of influence than any other poet I could have chosen.

I return to Coleridge's first mature poetry, and to its *clinamen* away from Milton, the Cowperizing turn that gave Coleridge the Conversation Poems, particularly "Frost at Midnight." Hazlitt quotes Coleridge as having said to him in the spring of 1798 that Cowper was the best modern poet, meaning the best since Milton, which was also Blake's judgment. Humphry House demonstrated the relation between "Frost at Midnight" and *The Task,* which is the happy one, causing no anxieties, where a stronger poet appropriates from a weaker one. Coleridge used Cowper as he used Bowles, Akenside, and Collins, finding in all of them hints that could help him escape the Miltonic influx that had drowned out "Religious Musings." "Frost at Midnight," like *The Task,* swerves away from Milton by softening him, by domesticating his style in a context that excludes all Sublime terrors. When Coleridge rises to his blessing of his infant son at the poem's conclusion he is in some sense poetically "misinterpreting" the beautiful declaration of Adam to Eve: "With thee conversing I forget all time," gentling the darker overtones of the infatuated Adam's declaration of love. Or, more simply, like Cowper he is not so much humanizing Milton—that will take the strenuous, head-on struggles of Blake, Wordsworth, Shelley, Keats—as he is making Milton more childlike, or perhaps better, reading Milton as though Milton loved in a more child-like way.

The revisionary step beyond this, an antithetical completion or *tessera*, is ventured by Coleridge only in a few pantheistic passages that sneaked past his orthodox censor, like the later additions to "The Eolian Harp," or the veiled vision at the end of the second verse paragraph of "This Lime-Tree Bower My Prison." With his horror of division, his endless quest for unity, Coleridge could not sustain any revisionary impulse which involved his reversing Milton, or daring to complete that sacred father.

But the next revisionary ratio, the *kenosis* or self-emptying, seems to me almost obsessive in Coleridge's poetry, for what is the total situation of the Ancient Mariner but a repetition-compulsion, which his poet breaks for himself only by the writing of the poem, and then breaks only momentarily. Coleridge had contemplated an Epic on the Origin of Evil, but we may ask: where would Coleridge, if pressed, have located the origin of evil in himself? His Mariner is neither depraved in will nor even disobedient, but is merely ignorant, and the spiritual machinery his crime sets into motion is so ambiguously presented as to be finally beyond analysis. I would ask the question: what was Coleridge trying (not necessarily consciously) to do for himself by writing the poem? and by this question I do not mean Kenneth Burke's notion of trying to do something for oneself as a person. Rather, what was Coleridge the poet trying to do for himself as poet? To which I would answer: trying to free himself from the inhibitions of Miltonic influence, by humbling his poetic self, and so humbling the Miltonic in the process. The Mariner does not empty himself out; he starts empty and acquires a Primary Imagination through his suffering. But, for Coleridge, the poem is a *kenosis*, and what is being humbled is the Miltonic Sublime's account of the Origin of Evil. There is a reduction from disobedience to ignorance, from the self-aggrandizing consciousness of Eve to the painful awakening of a minimal consciousness in the Mariner.

The next revisionary step in clearing an imaginative space for a maturing strong poet is the Counter-Sublime, the attaining of which I have termed *daemonization*, and this I take to be the relation of "Kubla Khan" and "Christabel" to *Paradise Lost*. Far more than "The Rime of the Ancient Mariner," these poems demonstrate a trafficking by Coleridge with powers that are daemonic, even though the "Rime" explicitly invokes Neo-Platonic daemons in its marginal glosses. Opium was the avenging daemon or alastor of Coleridge's life, his Dark or Fallen Angel, his experiential acquaintance with Milton's Satan. Opium was for him what wandering and moral taletelling became for the Mariner—the personal shape of repetition-compulsion. The lust for paradise in "Kubla Khan," Geraldine's lust for Christabel; these are manifestations of Coleridge's revisionary daemonization of Milton, these are Coleridge's Counter-Sublime. Poetic Genius, the genial spirit itself, Coleridge must see as daemonic when it is his own, rather than when it is Milton's.

It is at this point in the revisionary cycle that Coleridge begins to back away decisively from the ferocity necessary for the strong poet. He does not sustain his daemonization, closes his eyes in holy dread, stands outside the circumference of the daemonic agent, and is startled by his own sexual daring out of finishing "Christabel." He moved on to the revisionary ratio I have called *askesis*, or the purgation into solitude, the curtailing of some imaginative powers in the name of others. In doing so, he prophesied the pattern for Keats in *The Fall of Hyperion*, since in his *askesis* he struggles against the influence of a composite poetic father, Milton-Wordsworth. The great poems of this *askesis* are "Dejection: An Ode" and "To William Wordsworth," where criticism has demonstrated to us how acute the revision of Wordsworth's stance is, and how much of himself Coleridge purges away to make this revision justified. I would add only that both poems misread Milton as sensitively and desperately as they do Wordsworth; the meaning of "Dejection" is in its relation to "Lycidas" as much as in its relation to the "Intimations" Ode, even as the poem "To William Wordsworth" assimilates *The Prelude* to *Paradise Lost*. Trapped in his own involuntary dualisms, longing for a monistic wholeness such as he believes he is found by in Milton and Wordsworth, Coleridge in his *askesis* declines to see how much his composite parent-poet has purged away also.

After that, sadly enough, we have only a very few occasional poems of any quality by Coleridge, and they are mostly not the poems of a strong poet, that is, of a man vaulting into the Sublime. Having refused the full exercise of a strong poet's misprisions, Coleridge ceased to have poetic ambitions. But there is a significant exception, the late manuscript fragment "Limbo" and the evidently still-later fragment "Ne Plus Ultra." Here, and I think here only, Coleridge experiences the particular reward of the strong poet in his last phase, what I have called the *apophrades* or return of the dead, not a Counter-Sublime but a negative Sublime, like the *Last Poems* of Yeats or *The Rock* of Stevens. Indeed, negative sublimity is the mode of these Coleridgean fragments, and indicates to us what Coleridge might have become had he permitted himself enough of the perverse zeal that the great poet must exhibit in malforming his great precursor. "Limbo" and "Ne Plus Ultra" show that Coleridge could have become, at last, the poet of the Miltonic abyss, the bard of Demogorgon. Even as they stand, these fragments make us read Book II of *Paradise Lost* a little differently; they enable Coleridge to claim a corner of Milton's Chaos as his own.

Pater thought that Coleridge had succumbed to the Organic Analogue, because he hungered too intensely for eternity, as Lamb had said of his old school-friend. Pater also quoted De Quincey's summary of Coleridge: "he wanted better bread than can be made with wheat." I would add that Coleridge hungered also for an eternity of generosity between poets, as between people, a generosity that is not allowed in a world where each poet must struggle to individuate his own breath, and this at the expense of his forebears as much as his contemporaries. Perhaps also, to modify De Quincey, Coleridge wanted better poems than can be made without misprision.

I suggest then that the Organic Analogue, with all its pragmatic neglect of the processes by which poems have to be produced, appealed so overwhelmingly to Coleridge because it seemed to preclude the anxiety of influence, and to obviate the poet's necessity not just to unfold like a natural growth but to develop at the expense of others. Whatever the values of the Organic Analogue for literary criticism— and I believe, with Pater, that it does more harm than good—it provided Coleridge with a rationale for a dangerous evasion of inner steps he had to take for his own poetic development. As Blake might have said, Coleridge's imagination insisted upon slaying itself on the stems of generation, or to invoke another Blakean image, Coleridge lay down to sleep upon the Organic Analogue as though it were a Beulah-couch of soft, moony repose.

What was our loss in this? What poems might a stronger Coleridge have composed? The Notebooks list *The Origin of Evil, an Epic Poem, Hymns to the Sun, the Moon, and the Elements*—six hymns, and more fascinating even than these, a scheme for an epic on "the destruction of Jerusalem" by the Romans. Still more compelling is a March, 1802, entry in the Notebooks: "Milton, a Monody in the metres of Samson's Choruses—only with more rhymes / —poetical influences—political-moral-Dr. Johnson/" Consider the date of this entry, only a month before the first draft of "Dejection," and some sense of what *Milton, a Monody* might have been begins to be generated. In March, 1802, William Blake, in the midst of his sojourn at Hayley's Felpham, was deep in the composition of *Milton: A Poem in 2 Books, to Justify the Ways of God to Men*. In the brief, enigmatic notes for *Milton, a Monody*, Coleridge sets down "—poetical influences—political-moral-Dr. Johnson," the last being, we can assume, a refutation of Johnson's vision of Milton in *The Lives of the Poets*, a refutation that Cowper and Blake would have endorsed. "Poetical influences" Coleridge says, and we may recall that this is one of the themes of Blake's *Milton*, where the Shadow of the Poet Milton is one with the Covering Cherub, the great blocking-agent who inhibits fresh human creativity by embodying in himself all the sinister beauty of tradition. Blake's *Milton* is a kind of monody in places, not as a mourning for Milton, but as Milton's own, solitary utterance, as he goes down from a premature Eternity (where he is unhappy) to struggle again in fallen time and space. I take it though that *Milton, a Monody* would be modeled upon Coleridge's early "Monody on the Death of Chatterton," and so would have been Coleridge's lamentation for his Great Original. Whether, as Blake was doing at precisely the same time, Coleridge would have dared to identify Milton as the Covering Cherub, as the angel or daemon blocking Coleridge himself out from the poet's paradise, I cannot surmise. I wish deeply that Coleridge had written the poem.

It is ungrateful, I suppose, as the best of Coleridge's recent scholars keep telling us, to feel that Coleridge did not give us the poems he had it in him to write. Yet we have, all apology aside, only a double handful of marvelous poems by him. I close therefore by attempting a description of the kind of poem I believe Coleridge's genius owed us, and which we badly need, and always will need. I would maintain that the finest achievement of the High Romantic poets of England was their humanization of the Miltonic Sublime. But when we attend deeply to the works where this humanization is most strenuously accomplished—

Blake's *Milton* and *Jerusalem*, *The Prelude*, *Prometheus Unbound*, the two *Hyperions*, even in a way *Don Juan*—we sense at last a quality lacking, in which Milton abounds, for all his severity. This quality, though not in itself a tenderness, made Milton's Eve possible, and we miss such a figure in all her Romantic descendants. More than the other five great Romantic poets, Coleridge was able, by temperament and by subtly shaded intellect, to have given us a High Romantic Eve, a total humanization of the tenderest and most appealing element in the Miltonic Sublime. Many anxieties blocked Coleridge from that rare accomplishment, and of these the anxiety of influence was not the least.

II. 14
The Irrelevant Detail and the Emergence of Form*

MARTIN PRICE

Yale University

THE PROBLEM with which to start is the irrelevant detail. Every realistic novel gives us innumerable details: how people look, what they wear, where they live. We generally accept these details as what Henry James called "solidity of specification." [1] They give us the air of reality, the illusion of life, without which the novel can hardly survive. Elizabeth Bowen puts this another way: "The novel lies, in saying something happened that did not. It must, therefore, contain uncontradictable truth, to warrant the original lie." [2] Yet clearly there can be no end to such specification if we allow it full range. At what point do we set limits and by what means? Can there be pure irrelevance? And, if not, what degrees of irrelevance can we admit?

When we read a novel, we adjust more or less insensibly to the kind of relevance it establishes. We may prepare for an expansive exploration of the setting, for a solid evocation of the virtual past. Or we may settle instead for a deep descent into a consciousness, only surmising from rumination and memory the world that surrounds it. Or we may adapt to an undefined locale, perhaps one with strange, game-like rules of probability, where encounters obey laws we can only

* Read at the Institute in 1970. Published in *Institute Papers: Aspects of Narrative*, 1971.

[1] "The Art of Fiction" (1884), reprinted in F. O. Matthiessen, *The James Family* (New York, 1947), p. 360.

[2] "Notes on Writing a Novel," in *Collected Impressions* (London, 1950), p. 249.

puzzle our way into grasping. The reader is apt to find the right key, to frame appropriate expectations, and to give himself up to the terms of the fictional contract the author has established. To discover such canons of relevance may require little effort in a conventional work; it may be a major source of interest in the experimental novel, where the experiment is performed upon the reader as well as upon the material.

In the realistic novel we expect the principal characters to have a broad range of attributes, and we assume that the more attributes they have, the less important some must be. What of the color of the heroine's hair? In archetypal romance blond hair all but commands a state of innocence, gentility, and moral earnestness, whereas dark hair promises commanding will, adroitness, and a strong instinctive life. That is, the typology of romance is such that attributes are comparatively few and are tightly coordinated. In realistic novels the color of hair need not imply moral attributes; there is a lower degree of relevance imposed, and some attributes seem to be given only to create a convincingly full portrait. Yet even there we are inclined to seek significance, to expect a higher degree of relevance than the writer seems to claim. This may reflect the tendency we have in our own experience to create patterns, to relate elements, to simplify, to classify. Our first impressions are often based upon stereotypes, upon conventional categories by which we assimilate the unfamiliar or bewildering. It is only with closer knowledge and extended interest that we begin to differentiate, to specify distinctive patterns or telling peculiarities, to construct an individual.

Let us consider briefly the introduction of Mary and Henry Crawford into Jane Austen's *Mansfield Park*. Mary Crawford has lost her London home and is seeking, with some misgivings, "to hazard herself among her other relations." The first meeting is auspicious:

Miss Crawford found a sister without preciseness or rusticity—a sister's husband who looked a gentleman, and a house commodious and well fitted up; and Mrs. Grant received in those whom she hoped to love better than ever, a young man and woman of very prepossessing appearance. Mary Crawford was remarkably pretty; Henry, though not handsome, had air and countenance; the manners of both were lively and pleasant, and Mrs. Grant immediately gave them credit for everything else.[3]

Mr. Grant, although a parson, looks a gentleman; the Crawfords have a "very prepossessing appearance." The only attributes of Mrs. Grant

[3] *Mansfield Park*, Vol. I, Ch. 4.

that are noted are her manners and her facilities for entertainment; and the Crawfords, too, are surveyed for their promise as diverting visitors.

In the next chapter, the Crawfords are studied more closely by Maria and Julia Bertram, the two willful and self-absorbed daughters of Sir Thomas:

> Miss Crawford's beauty did her no disservice with the Miss Bertrams. They were too handsome themselves to dislike any woman for being so too, and were almost as much charmed as their brothers, with her lively dark eye, clear brown complexion, and general prettiness. Had she been tall, full formed, and fair, it might have been more of a trial; but as it was there could be no comparison, and she was most allowably a sweet pretty girl, while they were the finest young women in the country.[4]

We notice that Mary Crawford's "clear brown complexion" is admitted in contrast to the Miss Bertrams' fairness; but it is only one element in the image of a "sweet pretty girl," that self-comforting category under which Maria and Julia can accept her presence. To go on:

> Her brother was not handsome; no, when they first saw him, he was absolutely plain, black and plain; but still he was the gentleman, with a very pleasing address. The second meeting proved him not so very plain; he was plain, to be sure, but then he had so much countenance, and his teeth were so good, and he was so well made, that one soon forgot he was plain; and after a third interview, after dining in company with him at the parsonage, he was no longer to be called so by anybody. He was, in fact, the most agreeable young man the sisters had ever known, and they were equally delighted with him. Miss Bertram's engagement made him in equity the property of Julia, of which Julia was fully aware, and before he had been at Mansfield a week, she was quite ready to be fallen in love with.

Jane Austen uses *style indirect libre,* indirect discourse that catches the idiom of a character but may compress his reasoning, as a speeded-up film mechanizes motion. Through it she catches the rapid, almost mechanical process of rationalization by which a marriageable gentleman is found to have extraordinary charms. Henry's somewhat undistinguished appearance is searched for graces that will accord with his manner: his teeth emerge, glistening with assimilated wit and sexual vitality. In Tolstoy's *Anna Karenina* Vronsky is another man with fine teeth, and they are part of that splendid animal, so much in love with his own body, that Vronsky even at best largely remains. They are an aspect of Vronsky's limiting, if radiant, physicality, related to his love of the regiment, of St. Petersburg society, of social as well as athletic games. For Henry Crawford the teeth are of less import; they are part

[4] *Ibid.,* I, 5.

of the hastily devised blazon of masculine charms the sisters require to adapt him to their narcissistic version of the future.

What this encounter, like every other, reveals is the movement toward specification. E. H. Gombrich has described brilliantly, through the analogy of the hobby-horse, the way in which a sense of relevance governs our search for attributes, in fact constitutes the forms we ascribe to things or people. The hobby-horse begins as a broomstick that a child uses as a substitute for a horse. Having found that he can use it for riding, he may project into it other attributes of horsiness— give it a tail, ears, a mane, perhaps a saddle. The child has begun with what we might call the generalized form of a horse; he specifies it more and more as its functions are called forth in play. Is this a representation of a horse? Or rather a substitute for one? The moral of Gombrich's fable is that "substitution may precede portrayal, and creation communication." [5] We work out from needs and we use substitute objects to satisfy them; we project upon those objects the attributes that new needs require.

What does Gombrich's hobby-horse tell us about the novel? First, it reminds us that the representation of fictional reality may grow out of conventional or archetypal forms, whether we see them as projections, as forms of play, or as models for control. They may acquire more and more differentiation as the images become actors in myths and the myths are adapted to our local anxieties or desires. Even more, Gombrich's analogy can show us that the elaborate forms of realism are generated less by the desire to represent the actual than by the pressure of conventions reaching outward for more complex differentiation. George Eliot, in the famous seventeenth chapter of *Adam Bede*, renounces the easy fictions of romance for the more difficult truths of realism. By this she means an extension of the conventions of romance into a realm where plots are bent to absorb the actualities of historic life, where the traditional characters are bleached and thickened until they become our colorless and undistinguished neighbors. George Eliot is not offering to give us a literal picture of social reality but to "give a faithful account of men and things as they have mirrored themselves in my mind." [6] This in fact becomes an extension of high forms to

---

[5] Ernst H. Gombrich, *Meditations on a Hobby Horse and Other Essays on the Theory of Art* (London, 1963), p. 5.

[6] Cf. Darrel Mansell, Jr., "Ruskin and George Eliot's 'Realism,'" *Criticism*, VII (1965), 203–16.

include the subliterary, even the antiliterary, details of a "monotonous homely existence." The "exact likeness" is the limiting point of the entire process whereby the generalized form is differentiated so sharply as to direct our feeling where it does not normally flow, so that it does not need to "wait for beauty" but "flows with resistless force and brings beauty with it." She sacrifices proportion and the "divine beauty of form" so as to extend art, as the Dutch painters had, to "those rounded backs and stupid weatherbeaten faces that have bent over the spade and done the rough work of the world." The point I would stress is the deliberate—even militant—extension of forms rather than the effort at literal representation or record.

So in the encounter I have cited from Jane Austen there is a generalized image, cast in social terms, then specified in various ways by observers. How far this specification is carried will depend on the character who observes or on the governing themes of the novelist. There are certain attributes that Jane Austen requires for her conception of reality, others that would distract or confuse us in following her kind of action. As Gombrich says, "If the hobby-horse became too lifelike, it might gallop away on its own." [7] To take this view of the novel is to see relevance itself expanding to require new detail, and the irrelevant detail becomes the boundary at the limit of expansion.

In *The Sense of an Ending*, Frank Kermode draws a sharp distinction between the simplicity of myths and the complexity of fictions, between wishful pattern and the skeptical testing of that pattern against the contingencies of the actual. Only in such testing can myths be disconfirmed, and the result of such disconfirmation will be those reversals or peripeties Aristotle finds in complex plots. The need to readjust expectations earns the mature fiction that incorporates contingencies without despairing of form. The myths of which Mr. Kermode writes—and there are some who would call them by a less cherished name—have often been adapted wishfully and conventionally to the more familiar situations of contemporary life, converting archetype into stereotype. It is these generalized forms with which the realistic novel always quarrels, breaking their limits by extension and insisting upon the stubbornness of the actual.[8]

7 Gombrich, *Meditations*, p. 8.

8 *The Sense of an Ending* (New York, 1966). For criticism of Kermode's use of the term "myth," see Warner Berthoff, "Fiction, History, Myth: Notes toward the Discrimination of Narrative Form," in *The Interpretation of Narrative: Theory and*

In *Anna Karenina*, Tolstoy gives an account of the artistic process that confirms this view. Mikhailov, the painter, is making a "sketch of a figure of a man in a fit of anger." The paper on which he is working is spotted with candle grease, and the grease spot suggests a new pose for the figure:

He was drawing this new pose when he suddenly remembered the energetic face, with a jutting-out chin, of a shopkeeper from whom he bought cigars, and he gave the man he was drawing that shopkeeper's face and chin. He laughed with delight. The figure he was drawing, instead of being dead and artificial, had sprung to life and could not possibly be altered. It was alive and was clearly and unmistakeably defined. The drawing could be corrected in accordance with the requirements of the figure; one could, and indeed one should, find a different position for the legs, change completely the position of the left arm, and throw back the hair. But in making these changes he did not alter the figure, but merely removed what concealed it. He merely removed, as it were, the coverings which made it impossible to see it; each new stroke revealed more and more the whole figure in all its force and vigor as it had suddenly appeared to him by the action of the grease spot.[9]

We may notice the stress first on the generalized form of an angry man, then the arbitrary suggestion in the form of the grease spot, the outward drive of an inner content or vision that seizes upon actual details of any sort to find specification, most of all the "force and vigor" of the conception that must be adequately embodied. Most interesting is the simultaneous sense of embodiment and of revelation. Once the artist finds, through contingency, a necessary outward form, that form must in turn be protected from, stripped free of, the merely habitual or trivial irrelevancy. This double aspect of the concrete detail—at once a condition of revelation and a threat of irrelevancy—is crucial.

At what point does the covering achieve full opacity? Virginia Woolf, in her famous essay "Mr. Bennett and Mrs. Brown," warns against the reliance on mere social convention. She imagines the English public speaking:

Old women have houses. They have fathers. They have incomes. They have servants. They have hot-water bottles. That is how we know that they are old women. Mr. Wells and Mr. Bennett and Mr. Galsworthy have always taught us that this is the way to recognize them.

Practice, Harvard English Studies I, ed. Morton W. Bloomfield (Cambridge, Mass., 1970), pp. 263–87.

[9] *Anna Karenina*, Part V, Ch. 10, trans. David Magarshack (New York, 1961), pp. 472–73.

The Georgian novelists "have given us a house in the hope that we may be able to deduce the human beings who live there." In contrast, Mrs. Woolf defends "an old lady of unlimited capacity and infinite variety; capable of appearing in any place; wearing any dress; saying anything and doing heaven knows what." [10]

Any dress? Why then should we learn that Emma Bovary, when she first appears to Charles, wears a dress of blue merino wool with flounces? [11] Emma's dress is no more a thing than a statement, no more a covering than a revelation. The fine wool, the romantic blue of Emma's fantasies, the flounces that contrast with the farmhouse but accord with its self-indulgent luxuries—all these are intimations of Emma's nature and also, for Charles Bovary, intimations of a life of the senses such as he has never known. The details of Emma's dress are not mere social forms, although they include them. They mark the convergence of several themes, not all of them fully established as yet in the narrative. Their meaning catches at once something of Emma's temperament and Charles's, something of the economic pattern that will mark her career, something of the incongruity Flaubert will exploit so elaborately in the scenes of the agricultural fair. The details avoid the telltale simplification of the smart novelist with a so-called eye for detail, where the detail tends to make a strong and simple sociological assertion. Emma's dress is full of implication, some of it only retrospectively clear; but there is no suspension of narrative movement to permit it, as it were, to make its assertion, nor is there that discontinuity of literal narrative that marks the intervention of a symbol.

How, then, does the novelist prevent these objects, the conditions of plausible actuality, from becoming mere covering? How does he preserve the function of the actual as a language, that is, as relevance? This may be done in part by the presence of a narrator, commenting upon events as George Eliot does, generalizing their import, serving as a reminder and model of the whole process of translation of object into statement. Without such a narrator, there is the effect of ordonnance, of clear artifice of arrangement, of cumulative repetition. Of *Anna Karenina* Tolstoy wrote in a letter:

. . . if the shortsighted critics think that I merely wanted to describe what appealed to me, such as the sort of dinner Oblonsky has or what Anna's shoulders are like, then they are mistaken. In everything . . . I wrote I was

---

[10] "Mr. Bennett and Mrs. Brown" (1924), in *Collected Essays* (London, 1966), I, 333, 336–37.
[11] *Madame Bovary*, I, ii ("en robe de mérinos bleu garnie de trois volants").

guided by the need of collecting ideas which, linked together, would be the expression of myself, though each individual idea, expressed separately in words, loses its meaning; is horribly debased when only one of the links, of which it forms a part, is taken by itself. But the interlinking of these ideas is not, I think, an intellectual process, but something else, and it is impossible to express the source of this interlinking directly in words; it can only be done indirectly by describing images, actions, and situations in words.[12]

Those linkages reveal, as fully as the most eloquent narrator, the control of the author and the bold use of pattern. We can see one instance when Levin comes to visit his old friend Stiva Oblonsky. Levin has come to propose to Kitty; Stiva and Kitty's older sister Dolly are estranged since she has discovered his affair with a French governess. Levin calls on Oblonsky at his office, where we see Oblonsky's remarkable tact and charm as a bureaucrat, and they meet again for dinner. As they enter the restaurant there is a "sort of suppressed radiance" on Oblonsky's face; he gives his order to the Tartar waiter, he jokes with the painted French woman at the cashier's desk. Levin tries to guard his own idealized vision of Kitty in this place of unclean sensuality.

They are greeted by a "particularly obsequious white-headed old Tartar [waiter] so broad across the hips that the tails of his coat did not meet." The waiter allows Oblonsky to order in Russian but repeats the name of each dish in French, hurries off with coattails flying, and "five minutes later rushes in again with a dish of oysters, their pearly shells open, and a bottle between his fingers." Once he has poured the wine, the fat old waiter looks at Oblonsky "with a smile of undisguised pleasure." For Levin, "this continuous bustle of running about, these bronzes, mirrors, gaslights, Tartars—all this seemed an affront. . . . He was afraid of besmirching that which filled his soul." But Levin can only remark aloud on the difference from meals in the country, got over as quickly as possible so as to return to work—whereas here, in Moscow, "you and I are doing our best to make our dinner last as long as possible and for that reason have oysters." When Oblonsky replies, "That's the whole aim of civilization: to make everything a source of enjoyment,"

[12] Letter to N. N. Strakhov, April 23 and 26, 1876 (original in Jubilee Edition, *Polnoe Sobranie Sochinenii* [Moscow, 1928–58], LXII, 268–70), here cited from the Foreword to David Margarshack's translation of *Anna Karenina* (cited above), pp. xii–xiii. For an alternative translation of a portion and a discussion of *svyazi* (links, ties) or *stsepleniya* (couplings, connections), see R. F. Christian, *Tolstoy's "War and Peace": A Study* (Oxford, 1962), pp. 123–24.

Levin's response is simply, "Well, if that is so, I'd rather be a savage." [13]

Somewhat later they discuss Oblonsky's affair with the governess. Levin is incredulous and unsympathetic; he refuses Oblonsky the comfortable pathos of seeing love as a tragic dilemma. And Oblonsky replies coolly:

> . . . you are a thoroughly earnest and sincere man. That is your strength and your limitation. You are thoroughly earnest and sincere and you want all life to be earnest and sincere too, but it never is. You despise public service because you think its practice ought to be as singleminded as its aims, but that never happens. You want the activity of every single man always to have an aim, and love and family life always to be one and the same thing. But that doesn't happen either. All the diversity, all the charm, all the beauty of life are made up of light and shade.

Then Tolstoy gives us one of his moments of ironic omniscience:

> And suddenly both felt that, though they were friends and had dined and wined together; which should have brought them closer, each was thinking only of his own affairs and was not really concerned with the other.

Tolstoy has made the dinner, which occurs early in the novel, the basis of many of the linkages that will run through the book—most essentially the linkages of those who, with varying degrees of awareness and self-acceptance, take an aesthetic view of life and those who, with all the strain and quixotic intensity it may involve, take an ethical view. In Oblonsky's grace and tact, his contentment in the shallow waters that are secure and comfortably warm, we see aspects of Vronsky as well. In Levin's intransigent need to commit himself totally and to exact a meaning for his life we see the heroic possibilities, so cruelly unrealized, of Anna herself. The fat and obsequious old Tartar waiter fills out the scene of such a restaurant as Oblonsky would frequent, but he is also a striking statement of the irreducible hedonism that underlies the aesthetic vision of the beauty of life made up of light and shade.

There is a border area where details are pulled between the demands of structure and the consistent texture of a plausible fictional world. Their nature is not unlike those details of our own lives that are jointly to be explained by outward circumstance and inward motive. Each of us is thrown into a world he never made, and yet each of us

[13] *Anna Karenina*, Part I, Ch. 10.

makes of it what he must. At some level of conscious or unconscious action we choose ourselves and our world. One of the dazzling and perhaps terrifying aspects of Freud's vision is that it seems everywhere to supplant chance by choice, to shackle accidents in the tracing of purposiveness. It does not preclude contingencies, for it cannot determine what will enter into our experience, but it can show the way we use and shape that experience.

The analogy for the novel is the measure of relevance it may confer upon the most peripheral and accidental detail. Yet to live in a state of unrelieved and intense relevance is something like paranoia, a condition of lucid and overdeterminate design. Such a vision imposes its design at every point, obsessively and repetitiously. The design is everywhere present and everywhere visible. The novel gives us instead the complex awareness of seeing the tough opacity of the actual and at the same time seeing it as a radiant construction of meaning. To get at how this is done requires that we consider for a moment the famous gestalt figure of the duck-rabbit. The same drawing accommodates either image and can be read as either, but it cannot be read simultaneously as both. It is related to those subtler ambiguities of form that we see in puzzles of figure and ground. The figure, if it is given sharp enough definition, will always seek to constitute itself against the interruption of another form; it will seem to thrust the other form back into third-dimensional space as a ground. So long as there is greater definition or familiarity in one form, it will prevail in our perception as figure. These puzzles of perception give us a hint about the structure of novels.[14]

The openings of novels serve to set the rules of the game to be played by the reader. The degree of specification in setting, the presence or absence of a persona behind the narrative voice, the verbal density of the style—its metaphorical elaboration or cultivated innocence—all these are ways of indicating the nature of the game, of educating the responses and guiding the collaboration of the reader. If a novel moves through disjunct sets of characters in successive chapters, we are teased with the problem of how they shall be connected—by the working of the plot (like Esther Summerson and Lady Dedlock) or by thematic

---

[14] On figure and ground, see Rudolf Arnheim, *Art and Visual Perception* (Berkeley and Los Angeles, 1954), pp. 177–85, 198–203. The analogy introduces spatial terms that may be misleading, but it catches better than any other I know the shifting structure of the field of our attention, and, by implication, the shifting function of elements of the novel.

analogy (like Clarissa Dalloway and Septimus Smith). But once the novel enters into full narrative movement, the problem of how it shall be read becomes a matter of less immediate concern or full attention. Once its premises are given, the world of the novel becomes the scene of an action, and our commitment to the narrative movement tends to absorb our attention. Narrative may be said to depress the metaphorical status of character and setting; it gives a coherence to all the elements on the level of action that deflects attention from their meaningfulness and from their position in the structure. One can see something very much like this in pictorial representation. The use of perspective makes us read each detail of a painting as it might relate in space to every other detail in a three-dimensional "virtual world." It will require a very strong linear pattern or color relationship to win our attention once more to the flat surface from which we have imaginatively departed.

The narrative movement, with its strong temporal flow and its stress upon causal sequence, may compel full attention to itself. The setting becomes the necessary ground of the action, the characters the necessary agent. But shifts from figure to ground may be instantaneous and, where both figure and ground are more complex, far less dramatic than in the didactic example of the duck-rabbit. At moments the causal sequence moves entirely within the consciousness of the principal character, and the external action becomes the ground against which character is displayed.

Let us consider a sequence of such moments in *Anna Karenina*. First there is the instance of the mowers. Levin has been troubled by the difficulty of persuading the peasants to accept his agricultural programs. He is more immediately oppressed by the skeptical condescension of his half-brother, the intellectual Koznyshev, who always has the power to shake or completely undo Levin's convictions. Levin decides to join the peasants in order to escape from thought and from the frustrations of self-consciousness.

The longer Levin went on mowing, the oftener he experienced those moments of oblivion when it was not that his arms swung the scythe, but that the scythe itself made his whole body, full of life and conscious of itself, move after it, and as though by magic the work did itself, of its own accord and without a thought being given to it, with the utmost precision and regularity. Those were the most blessed moments.[15]

15 *Anna Karenina*, Part III, Ch. 5.

As he joins the workers at dinner time, all constraint between them vanishes, but when Levin returns home, his brother's condescension resumes. Koznyshev is filled with the well-being of having solved two chess problems, and Levin must find a pretext for escape so that he can guard his own memory of communion and of blissful self-transcendence. These moments of oblivion recur in the novel; they accompany the death of Levin's brother and the birth of his son:

But both that sorrow and this joy were equally beyond the ordinary conditions of life. In this ordinary life they were like openings through which something higher became visible. And what was happening now was equally hard and agonizing to bear and equally incomprehensible, and one's soul, when contemplating it, soared to a height such as one did not think possible before and where reason could not keep up with it.[16]

It is at these moments that the events of Levin's life, his long quixotic career of experiment and debate, come to their fullest intensity. These are moments where all the action passes into the shaping of a self and the outward action gives way to internal dialectic. As it does at the very close.

I shall still get angry with my coachman Ivan, I shall still argue and express my thoughts inopportunely; there will still be a wall between the holy of holies of my soul and other people, even my wife, and I shall still blame her for my own fears and shall regret it; I shall still be unable to understand with my reason why I am praying, and I shall continue to pray—but my life, my whole life, independently of anything that may happen to me, every moment of it, is no longer meaningless as it was before, but has an incontestable meaning of goodness, with which I have the power to invest it.[17]

At the close of the novel Levin at last achieves a fusion of temporal movement with the sense of meaningfulness that has marked these moments of oblivion, of temporal arrest. For it is meaningfulness more than timelessness that matters; the arrest of time is the intimation of meaning, a sudden ascent above the stream of events and the uncertainties that beset him so long as he remains immersed in that stream. For Levin these moments are a freedom from the conditional, the determined, the horizontal flow of time.

This slipping in and out of time, from surges of doubt and perplexity to moments of arresting meaningfulness, is comparable to shifts in our process of reading the novel. We move from the temporal action to moments where character subsumes action, where ground shifts to

[16] *Ibid.*, Part VII, Ch. 14.   [17] *Ibid.*, Part VIII, Ch. 19.

figure. So too we move, in a more general way, from the flow of temporal succession to a pattern that might be called spatial, where the recognition of relevance leaps to the center of attention and displaces the narrative sequence or the imagined world. The very repetition of this pattern of moments of oblivion and transcendence is one way in which Tolstoy's novel calls attention to the full dimensions of Levin's being, to the elements of his character that are absent from Oblonsky's. The intensity with which Levin encounters these moments is placed in contrast with Oblonsky's equable and conscienceless hedonism. To say "placed in contrast" is perhaps to beg the question, but a spatial metaphor is hard to avoid.

As critics have often observed, to speak of temporal and spatial forms is at best to use imperfect analogies. "Temporal form" stresses the ongoing movement and irreversible direction of narrative; "spatial form," the simultaneity of presentation that a painting allows. We study the painting through time and apprehend its various relationships of line and color successively, but we can see them presented before us at once. Some have preferred the metaphor of musicalization to spatialization. It does justice to temporal movement, and it stresses, as does the spatial metaphor, a structural pattern that can be schematically represented. What is at stake, clearly, is neither space nor time but the awareness of structure that relates elements in all parts of the book. One may confuse matters by evoking a new metaphor. I derive it from Roger Fry's account of a Sung bowl, written out of no concern with literary analogy and therefore all the more useful:

. . . we apprehend gradually the shape of the outside contour, the perfect sequence of the curves, and the subtle modifications of a certain type of curve which it shows; we also feel the relation of the concave curves of the inside to the outside contour; we realize that the precise thickness of the walls is consistent with the particular kind of matter of which it is made, its appearance of density and resistance; and finally we recognize, perhaps, how satisfactory for the display of all these plastic qualities are the color and the dull luster of the glaze. Now while we are thus occupied there comes to us, I think, a feeling of purpose; we feel that all these sensually logical conformities are the outcome of a particular feeling, or of what, for want of a better word, we call an idea; and we may even say that the pot is the expression of an idea in the artist's mind. Whether we are right or not in making this deduction, I believe it nearly always occurs in such esthetic apprehension of an object of art.[18]

[18] Roger Fry, "The Artist's Vision" (1919), in *Vision and Design* (London, 1920), pp. 32 f.

Fry's bowl has its various aspects, each of them apprehended in itself and yet all related by an idea, a purposiveness that can account for the simultaneous accommodation of diverse elements and functions in a single structure. We can attend to the glaze of the bowl quite apart from its form; we can see the exterior outline without relating it to the inner curve; we can see the bowl as a structure without much concern for its function. And yet we cannot quite do any of these things in isolation. Each may become momentarily the center of our attention, but there is always some latent awareness of the interrelatedness of all these aspects.

It is through this analogy that I would return to the irrelevant detail. It is not, of course, irrelevant, but it has so attenuated and complex a relevance as to confirm rather than directly to assert a meaning. Its meaningfulness, in fact, may become fully apparent only as the total structure emerges. It serves meanwhile a sufficient function in sustaining the virtual world in which the structure is embodied. One can say that its particularity is all that we are required to observe in its immediate configuration; yet only so much particularity is created as is consonant with that conceptual force the detail acquires in the large structure. The local configuration, then, has the potential lucidity of a model and the actual density of an event.

Roland Barthes has tried to isolate the detail which has no conceivable relevance, which seems mere arbitrary fact or event, "neither incongruous nor significant." He takes such a detail to have as its function the very assertion that it is the real; what it signifies is the category of the real itself.[19] This is ingenious but hardly satisfactory. Even if we

---

[19] "L'Effet du Réel," *Communications*, No. 11 (1969), pp. 84–89. M. Barthes cites as one illustration the description of Mme. Aubain's household in *Un Coeur Simple:* "un vieux piano supportait, sous un baromètre, un tas pyramidal de boîtes et de cartons." The piano, he suggests, may imply middle-class standing, the heap of boxes the disorder of the household. But the barometer has no such function, however indirect, to account for it.

If M. Barthes means, most generally, that realism involves a superfluity of detail, that is, some details which exceed any structural pattern of meaning and therefore any possible relevance, I should question the point. The effect of the real does not depend upon superfluity of detail but rather upon the kind of detail that is provided. The barometer is an object of a certain kind: practical, useful, prosaic. But so are the boxes heaped on the piano, and, whatever they suggest of disorder, they serve no less than the barometer to assert the real. So, too, with the Tartar waiter cited above from *Anna Karenina:* he acquires significance through linkages, but he is at the same time a portion of a circumstantial world presented in terms that do not insist upon its significance.

take it as a theoretical distinction which need not occur to us in the process of reading, it still seems to rest upon an ambiguous and sliding use of "signification." If one imagines a family reunion where all degrees of kinship are represented and one or two people attend whose kinship cannot be clearly established at all, shall we say of the one or two that they represent the human family or the community of mankind? This is to extend the idea of kinship to a point where it becomes an equivocation, and something of the sort occurs in Barthes's treatment of the irrelevant detail. We may claim that these limiting cases— of kinship or of relevance—awaken our consciousness of what it is that relates all these elements. But the limiting case does so through its very incongruity. It does not signify as other instances signify; it violates the rules of a language game and makes us aware of the game itself. Yet Barthes does not claim so much for the details he cites, nor is this our experience in reading the works he cites.

It is not a flounce or a barometer that alone asserts the real; all the details together make that assertion, and all are potentially significant as well. Details do not offer themselves as clearly relevant or irrelevant. It is only the special case where the detail insists upon its relevance or, as it may in some versions of surrealism or of the absurd, upon its irrelevance. Even if, in retrospective analysis, we see certain details as limiting cases of relevance, we can hardly separate them from that dense tissue of events out of which the structure emerges. For that emergence is always imperfect and incomplete. The full import of any detail remains a problem at best, just as does the structural form itself. We may achieve approximations in either case, but we may easily force meanings by distortion of emphasis or failure of tact. The elements of a novel shift in function, I have tried to show, as the work unfolds and as new linkages are revealed. For this reason we can never with confidence ascribe a single purpose or meaning to a detail, nor can we give an exhaustive reading of the structure.

Let me illustrate this with a final example, one drawn from Dickens's *Bleak House*. In the neighborhood of Chancery we encounter the deaths of Captain Hawdon, the lover of Lady Dedlock and the father of Esther Summerson, and of his drunken landlord, Krook. On both occasions we study the responses in Chancery Lane and especially in the nearby pub, the Sol's Arms:

. . . where the sound of the piano through the partly-opened windows jingles out into the court, and where Little Swills, after keeping the lovers of harmony in a roar like a very Yorick, may now be heard taking the gruff line in a concerted piece, and sentimentally adjuring his friends and patrons to Listen, listen, listen, Tew the wa-ter-Fall! Mrs. Perkins and Mrs. Piper compare opinions on the subject of the young lady of professional celebrity who assists at the Harmonic Meetings, and who has a space to herself in the manuscript announcement in the window; Mrs. Perkins possessing information that she has been married a year and a half, though announced as Miss M. Melvilleson, the noted syren, and that her baby is clandestinely conveyed to the Sol's Arms every night to receive its natural nourishment during the entertainments. "Sooner than which, myself," says Mrs. Perkins, "I would get my living by selling lucifers." Mrs. Piper, as in duty bound, is of the same opinion; holding that a private station is better than public applause, and thanking Heaven for her own (and, by implication, Mrs. Perkins's) respectability. By this time, the potboy of the Sol's Arms appearing with her supperpint well frothed, Mrs. Piper accepts that tankard and retires in-doors, first giving a fair good-night to Mrs. Perkins, who has had her own pint in her hand ever since it was fetched from the same hostelry by young Perkins before he was sent to bed.[20]

Little Swills, Mrs. Perkins, Mrs. Piper, and the suspect Miss M. Melvilleson have no conceivable relation to Dickens's plot, and this alone is a distinction in a book so elaborately contrived. Yet there they are, enormously lively and entertaining, insisting on the stability of a world that may also contain the outrageous and terrible. They are there and, being there, they demand a share in the structure of the book. To call them ground is not to absolve them of meaning, for ground and figure interlock at least through significant contrast. They may be reminiscent of that rougher texture at the lower part of the statue or the building, at once an element of the design and yet a vestige of the resistant materials from which the work was fashioned. They are not to be put by entirely; if they contribute to the condition of illusion or testify to the real, they also budge somewhat the inner meaning or structure of the work. It must be extended, however slightly, to admit their presence. So long as they have this power, the meaning remains always in process, the form always emerging.

[20] *Bleak House*, Ch. 32.

II. 15

Dickens and the Comedy of Humors[*]

NORTHROP FRYE

Victoria College, University of Toronto

DICKENS PRESENTS special problems to any critic who approaches him in the context of a "Victorian novelist." In general, the serious Victorian fiction writers are realistic and the less serious ones are romancers. We expect George Eliot or Trollope to give us a solid and well-rounded realization of the social life, attitudes, and intellectual issues of their time: we expect Disraeli and Bulwer-Lytton, because they are more "romantic," to give us the same kind of thing in a more flighty and dilettantish way; from the cheaper brands, Marie Corelli or Ouida, we expect nothing but the standard romance formulas. This alignment of the serious and the realistic, the commercial and the romantic, where realism has a moral dignity that romance lacks, intensified after Dickens's death, survived through the first half of the tweneith century, and still lingers vestigially. But in such an alignment Dickens is hard to place. What he writes, if I may use my own terminology for once, are not realistic novels but fairy tales in the low mimetic displacement. Hence there has grown up an assumption that, if we are to take Dickens seriously, we must emphasize the lifelikeness of his characters or the shrewdness of his social observation; if we emphasize his violently unplausible plots and his playing up of popular sentiment, we are emphasizing only his concessions to an undeveloped public taste. This was a contemporary view of him, expressed very lucidly by Trollope in *The Warden*, and it is still a natural one to take.

[*] Read at the Institute in 1967. Published in *Institute Papers: Experience in the Novel*, 1968.

A refinement of the same view sees the real story in Dickens's novels as a rather simple set of movements within a large group of characters. To this a mechanical plot seems to have been attached like an outboard motor to a rowboat, just to get things moving faster and more noisily. Thus our main interest, in reading *Little Dorrit*, is in the straightforward and quite touching story of Clennam's love for the heroine, of their separation through her suddenly acquired wealth, and of their eventual reunion through her loss of it. Along with this goes a preposterous melodrama about forged wills, identical twins, a mother who is not a mother, skulking foreigners, and dark mysteries of death and birth which seems almost detachable from the central story. Similarly, we finish *Our Mutual Friend* with a clear memory of a vast panoramic pageant of Victorian society, from the nouveau-riche Veneerings to Hexham living on the refuse of the Thames. But the creaky Griselda plot, in which John Harmon pretends to be dead in order to test the stability of his future wife, is something that we can hardly take in even when reading the book, much less remember afterwards.

Some works of fiction present a clearly designed or projected plot, where each episode seems to us to be logically the sequel to the previous episode. In others we feel that the episode that comes next does so only because the author has decided that it will come next. In stories with a projected plot we explain the episode from its context in the plot; in stories lacking such a plot, we are often thrown back on some other explanation, often one that originates in the author's wish to tell us something besides the story. This last is particularly true of thematic sequences like the "Dream Play" of Strindberg, where the succession of episodes is not like that of a projected plot, nor particularly like a dream either, but has to be accounted for in different terms. In Dickens we often notice that when he is most actively pursuing his plot he is careless, to the verge of being contemptuous, of the inner logic of the story. In *Little Dorrit*, the mysterious rumblings and creakings in the Clennam house, referred to at intervals throughout, mean that it is about to fall down. What this in turn means is that Dickens is going to push it over at a moment when the villain is inside and the hero outside. Similarly, Clennam, after a good deal of detective work, manages to discover where Miss Wade is living on the Continent. She did not expect him to ferret out her address, nor had she anything to say to him when he arrived; but, just in case he did come, she had written out the story of her life and had kept it in a drawer ready to hand to him. The outrage on probability seems almost deliberate, as does the burning up of Krook in *Bleak House* by spontaneous combustion as soon as the author is through with him, despite Dickens's protests about the authenticity of his device. Dickens's daughter, Mrs. Pellegrini, remarked shrewdly that there was no reason to suppose that *The Mystery of Edwin Drood* would have been any more of an impeccable plot-structure than the novels that Dickens had already completed. But, because it is unfinished, the plot has been the main focus of critical attention in that story, usually on the assumption that this once Dickens was working with a plot which was not, like a fictional Briareus, equipped with a hundred arms of coincidence.

T. S. Eliot, in his essay on Dickens and Wilkie Collins, remarks on the "spurious fatality" of Collins's detective-story plots. This is no place to raise the question of why the sense of fatality in *The Moonstone* should be more spurious than in *The Family Reunion*, but we notice in Dickens how strong the impulse is to reject a logicality inherent in the story in favor of impressing on the reader an impatient sense of absolutism: of saying, in short, *la fatalité, c'est moi*. This disregard of plausibility is worth noticing, because everyone realizes that Dickens is a great genius of the absurd in his characterization, and it is possible that his plots are also absurd in the same sense, not from incompetence or bad taste, but from a genuinely creative instinct. If so, they are likely to be more relevant to the entire conception of the novel than is generally thought. I proceed to explore a little the sources of absurdity in Dickens, to see if that will lead us to a clearer idea of his total structure.

The structure that Dickens uses for his novels is the New Comedy structure, which has come down to us from Plautus and Terence through Ben Jonson, an author we know Dickens admired, and Molière. The main action is a collision of two societies which we may call for convenience the obstructing and the congenial society. The congenial society is usually centered on the love of hero and heroine, the obstructing society on the characters, often parental, who try to thwart this love. For most of the action the thwarting characters are in the ascendant, but toward the end a twist in the plot reverses the situation and the congenial society dominates the happy ending. A frequent form of plot-reversal was the discovery that one of the central characters, usually the heroine, was of better social origin than previously thought.

This theme of mysterious parentage is greatly expanded in the late Greek romances, which closely resemble some of the plots of Menander. Here an infant of noble birth may be stolen or exposed and brought up by humble foster-parents, being restored to his original status at the end. In drama such a theme involves expounding a complicated ante-cedent action, and however skillfully done not all audiences have the patience to follow the unraveling, as Ben Jonson discovered to his cost at the opening of his *New Inn*. But in narrative forms, of course, it can have room to expand. Shakespeare gets away with it in *The Winter's Tale* by adopting a narrative-paced form of drama, where sixteen years are encompassed by the action.

Dickens is, throughout his career, very conventional in his handling of the New Comedy plot structure. All the stock devices, listed in Greek times as laws, oaths, compacts, witnesses, and ordeals, can be found in him. *Oliver Twist* and *Edwin Drood* are full of oaths, vows, councils of war, and conspiracies, on both benevolent and sinister sides. Witnesses include eavesdroppers like the Newmann Noggs of *Nicholas Nickleby* or Morfin the cello-player in *Dombey and Son*. Ordeals are of various kinds: near-fatal illnesses are common, and we may compare the way that information is extracted from Rob the Grinder by Mrs. Brown in *Dombey and Son* with the maltreating of the tricky slave in Menander and Plautus. Many thrillers (perhaps a majority) use a stock episode of having the hero entrapped by the villain, who instead of killing him at once imparts an essential piece of information about the plot to him, after which the hero escapes, gaining his wisdom at the price of an ordeal of facing death. This type of episode occurs in *Great Expectations* in the encounter with Orlick.

Every novel of Dickens is a comedy (N.B.: such words as "comedy" are not essence words but context words, hence this means: "for every novel of Dickens the obvious context is comedy"). The death of a central character does not make a story tragic, any more than a similar device does in *The King and I* or *The Yeomen of the Guard*. Sydney Carton is a man without a social function who achieves that function by sacrificing himself for the congenial society; Little Nell's death is so emotionally luxurious that it provides a kind of muted festivity for the conclusion, or what *Finnegans Wake* calls a "funferall." The emphasis at the end of a comedy is sometimes thrown, not on the forming of a new society around the marriage of hero and heroine, but on the matur-ing or enlightening of the hero, a process which may detach him from marriage or full participation in the congenial group. We find this type of conclusion in Shaw's *Candida*: Dickens's contribution to it is *Great Expectations*. Again, there is usually a mystery in Dickens's stories, and this mystery is nearly always the traditional mystery of birth, in sharp contrast to the mystery of death on which the modern whodunit is based. In Dickens, when a character is murdered, we usually see it done, and if not the suspense is still perfunctory. A detective appears in *Bleak House* to investigate the murder of Tulkinghorn, but his task is easy: Lady Dedlock keeps a French maid, and French maids, being foreign, are emotionally unpredictable and morally insensitive. The problem is less interesting than the problem of Lady Dedlock's guilty secret, which involves a birth. Unless Edwin Drood was very unlike Dickens's other heroes, the mystery about him is much more likely to have been a mystery of how he got into the world than of how he disappeared from it.

The emergence of the congenial society at the conclusion of the story is presented in the traditional New Comedy terms of festivity. It usually holds several marriages; it dispenses money if it has money, and it dispenses a good deal of food. Such features have remained unchanged in the New Comedy tradition since Greek times. Dickens's predilection for feasting scenes needs no laboring: it may be significant that his last written words are "falls to with an appetite." This feature accounts for his relentless plugging of Christmas, always for him the central symbol of the congenial family feast. The famous sentimentality of Dickens is largely confined to demonstrations of family affection, and is particularly evident in certain set scenes that immediately precede the dénouement, where the affection of brother and sister, of father and daughter, or more rarely of mother and son, is the main theme. Examples are the housekeeping of Tom and Ruth Pinch in *Martin Chuzzlewit*, the dinner of Kit and his mother in *The Old Curiosity Shop*, the meetings of Bella Wilfer with her father in *Our Mutual Friend*. Such relationships, though occasionally described as marriages, are "innocent" in the technical Victorian sense of not involving sexual intercourse, and if they seem to post-Freudian readers to be emotionally somewhat overcharged, it is because they contribute to, and anticipate, the final triumph of Eros at the end of the story. The disregard of plausibility, already mentioned, is another traditional feature, being part of the violent manipulation of the story in the direction of a happy ending. Those who object to such endings on the grounds of probability are often put in the position of questioning the ways of divine providence, which uses the author as its agent for vindicating virtue and baffling vice.

Most of the people who move across the pages of Dickens are neither realistic portraits, like the characters of Trollope, nor "caricatures," so far as that term implies only a slightly different approach to realistic portraiture. They are humors, like the characters in Ben Jonson, who formulated the principle that humors were the appropriate characters for a New Comedy plot. The humor is a character identified with a characteristic, like the miser, the hypochondriac, the braggart, the parasite, or the pedant. He is obsessed by whatever it is that makes him a humor, and the sense of our superiority to an obsessed person, someone bound to an invariable ritual habit, is, according to Bergson, one of the chief sources of laughter. But it is not because he is incidentally funny that the humor is important in New Comedy: he is important because his obsession is the feature that creates the conditions of the action, and the opposition of the two societies. In *The Silent Woman,* everything depends on Morose's hatred of noise; covetousness and gullibility set everything going in *Volpone* and *The Alchemist* respectively. Thus it is only the obstructing society which is "humorous," in the Jonsonian sense, as a society. In Dickens we find humors on both sides of the social conflict, genial, generous, and lovable humors as well as absurd or sinister ones. But the humors in the congenial society merely diversify it with amiable and harmless eccentricities; the humors of the obstructing society help to build up that society, with all its false standards and values.

Most of the standard types of humor are conspicuous in Dickens, and could be illustrated from *Bleak House* alone: the miser in Smallweed; the hypocrite in Chadband; the parasite in Skimpole and Turveydrop; the pedant in Mrs. Jellyby. The braggart soldier is not much favored: Major Bagstock in *Dombey and Son* is more of a parasite. Agreeably to the conditions of Victorian life, the braggart soldier is replaced by a braggart merchant or politician. An example, treated in a thoroughly traditional manner, is Bounderby in *Hard Times*. Another Victorian commonplace of the braggart-soldier family, the duffer sportsman, whose pretensions are far beyond his performance, is represented by Winkle in *The Pickwick Papers*. There are, however, two Winkles in *The Pickwick Papers*, the duffer sportsman and the pleasant young man who breaks down family opposition on both sides to acquire a pleasant young woman. The duality reflects the curious and instructive way that *The Pickwick Papers* came into being. The original scheme proposed to Dickens was a comedy of humors in its most primitive and superficial form: a situation comedy in which various stock types, including an incautious amorist (Tupman), a melancholy poet (Snodgrass), and a pedant (Pickwick), as well as Winkle, get into one farcical predicament after another. This form is frequent in stories for children, and was represented in my childhood by now obsolete types of comic strip and silent movie comedies. It must have left some descendants in television, but my impression is that contemporary children are deficient in this vitamin. But although traces of the original scheme persist throughout *The Pickwick Papers*, it quickly turns inside out into a regular New Comedy story, which leads up in the regular way to a recognition scene and a reversal of direction in the plot at its most serious point, in the debtors' prison. The pedant becomes a man of principle, and the humor of pedantry is transferred to the law which entraps him. Thus the comedy of humors takes root in society, as Dickens sees society, instead of merely extending from one incident to another.

The simplest form of humor is the tagged humor, who is associated with the repetition of a set phrase. Thus we have Mrs. Micawber, whose tag is that she will never desert Mr. Micawber, and Major Bagnet in *Bleak House*, who admires his wife but asserts that he never tells her so because "discipline must be maintained." We notice that our sense of superiority to such characters is edged with antagonism: when the repeated trait is intended to be endearing we are more likely to find it irritating, as E. M. Forster does Mrs. Micawber's. Jarndyce with his "east wind" tag and Esther Summerson's constant bewilderment that other people should find her charming do not stick in our minds in the way that Chadband and Mrs. Jellyby do. The humor is, almost by definition, a bore, and the technical skills in handling him consists in seeing that we get just enough but not too much of him. The more unpleasant he is, the easier this problem is to solve. Repetition which is excessive even by Dickensian standards, like the emphasis on Carker's teeth in *Dombey and Son*, is appropriate for a villain, as its effect is to dehumanize and cut off sympathy. We cannot feel much concern over the fate of a character who is presented to us mainly as a set of teeth, like Berenice in Poe. The "lifelikeness" of a humor depends on two things: on the fact that we are all very largely creatures of ritual habit, and on the strength of a perverse tendency in most of us to live up to our own caricatures. Pecksniff may be a humbug, but that can hardly be the whole of our feeling about him when he begins to sound like a member of my own profession attempting to extract a discussion from a group of clammed-up freshmen:

"The name of those fabulous animals (pagan, I regret to say) who used to sing in the water, has quite escaped me."

Mr. George Chuzzlewit suggested "Swans."

"No," said Mr. Pecksniff. "Not swans. Very like swans, too. Thank you."

The nephew with the outline of a countenance, speaking for the first and last time on that occasion, propounded "Oysters."

"No," said Mr. Pecksniff, with his own peculiar urbanity, "nor oysters. But by no means unlike oysters: a very excellent idea; thank you, my dear sir, very much. Wait! Sirens. Dear me! sirens, of course."

Humors are, at least dramatically, "good" if they are on the side of the congenial society, "bad" or ridiculous if on the side of the obstructing one. Thus the humor comedy has an easy and natural connection with the morality play. We notice this in the allegorical names that Dickens often gives some of his minor characters, like the "Pyke" and "Pluck" who are the satellites of Sir Mulberry Hawk in *Nicholas Nickleby,* or the "Bar," "Bishop," and "Physician" who turn up at Merdle's dinners in *Little Dorrit.* We notice it also in Dickens's tendency to arrange his humors in moral pairs, whether both are in the same novel or not. As just indicated, we have a "good" major in *Bleak House* and a "bad" one with a very similar name in *Dombey and Son;* we have a villainous Jew in *Oliver Twist* and a saintly Jew in *Our Mutual Friend,* and so on. Within *Dombey and Son* itself the "bad" major is paired against a "good" navy man, Captain Cuttle. If characters change sides, there may be a metamorphosis of character, which is not difficult in the humor technique, because it simply means putting on a different mask. Thus the generous Boffin pretends to be a miser for a while; Scrooge goes through the reverse process; Mercy Pecksniff changes roles from the feather-head to the faithful ill-used wife, and so on. Many humors are really chorus characters, who cannot do anything in the plot unless they step out of their roles: an example is Lord Frederick Verisopht in *Nicholas Nickleby,* who has to harden up a good deal to make his tragic end appropriate. The commonest form of this metamorphosis, and the most traditional one, is the release of the humor from his obsession at the end of the story: through the experience gained in the story, he is able to break through his besetting fault. At the end of *Martin Chuzzlewit* there is a whole series of these changes: the hero escapes from his selfishness, Mark Tapley from his compulsion to search for difficult situations in order to "come out strong," and Tom Pinch from an innocence that Dickens recognizes to be more obsessive than genuine innocence, and which we should now think of as a streak of masochism.

The rhetoric of the tagged humor consists mainly of variations of the stock identifying phrase or phrases. Some humors acquire a personal rhetorical rhythm of a strongly associative kind, which because it is associative gives the effect of being obsessive. The disjointed phrases of Jingle and the asyntactic babble of Mrs. Nickleby and Flora Finching are perhaps the most consistently successful examples. Closer to the single identifying phrase are Uriah Heep's insistence on his "'umble" qualities, which reminds us a little of Iago's "honest" tag, and the repetitions that betray the hypocrisy of Casby, the squeezing landlord in *Little Dorrit*. Others develop parodies of standard types of oratory, like Chadband with his parsonical beggar's whine or Micawber with his Parliamentary flourishes.

More significant, for a reason that will meet us in a moment, is the humor of stock response, that is, the humor whose obsession it is to insist that what he or she has been conditioned to think proper and acceptable is in fact reality. This attitude gives us the Bouvard-et-Pécuchet type of humor, whose mind is confined within a dictionary of accepted ideas. Such humors, it is obvious, readily expand into cultural allegories, representatives of the kind of anxiety that caricatures an age. Thus our stereotypes about "Victorian prudery" are represented by Podsnap in *Our Mutual Friend* and Mrs. General (the prunes-and-prisms woman) in *Little Dorrit*. Martin Chuzzlewit finds that America is full of such humors: American shysters are no better and no worse than their British counterparts, but there is a more theoretical element in their lying, and bluster about their enlightened political institutions is much more used as a cover for swindling. In America, in other words, the complacent Podsnap and the rascally Lammle are more likely to be associated in the same person. The implication, which Dickens is not slow to press, is that American life is more vulnerable than British life to character assassination, personal attacks, charges of being un-American, and mob violence. A humor of this stock-response type is comic on Freudian principles: he often says what more cautious people would not say, but show by their actions that they believe. Thus

Bumble's remarks about "them wicious paupers" are funny, not as typical of a Victorian beadle, but as revealing the hatred and contempt for the poor that official charity attempts to disguise.

Sometimes a humor's obsessed behavior and repetitive speech suggest a puppet or mechanical doll, whose response is invariable whatever the stimulus. We may feel with some of these characters that the mechanical quality is simply the result of Dickens's not having worked hard enough on them, but occasionally we realize that Dickens himself is encouraging us to see them as inanimate objects. Wemmick the postbox in *Great Expectations*, Pancks the "tug" in *Little Dorrit*, and several characters who are figuratively and to some extent literally wooden, like Silas Wegg, are examples. The Captain Cuttle of *Dombey and Son*, in particular, impresses us as an animated version of the Wooden Midshipman over the shop he so often inhabits. In *The Old Curiosity Shop*, after we have been introduced to Quilp, Little Nell and her granfather set out on their travels and see a Punch and Judy show. It occurs to us that Quilp, who is described as a "grotesque puppet," who lies, cheats, beats his wife, gets into fistfights, drinks like a salamander, and comes to a sticky end in a bog, *is* Punch, brought to life as a character. Wyndham Lewis, in an essay on Joyce (another admirer of Ben Jonson), notes the Dickensian ancestry of Bloom's interior monologue in the speech of Jingle. He might have noted a similar connection between Flora Finching's unpunctuated harangues in *Little Dorrit* and the reverie of Molly Bloom. Lewis in his turn developed, mainly out of Bergson, a theory of satire as a vision of human behavior in mechanical terms, where his main predecessor, if not one he recognized, was Dickens. We notice also the reappearance of the Punch figure in the center of *The Human Age*.

We noted that, while there are humors on both sides of the social conflict in Dickens, it is only the obstructing society which is humorous as a society. This takes us back to the feature I mentioned at the beginning which distinguishes Dickens from his major contemporaries in fiction. In most of the best Victorian novels, apart from Dickens, the society described is organized by its institutions: the church, the government, the professions, the rural squirearchy, business, and the trade unions. It is a highly structured society, and the characters function from within those structures. But in Dickens we get a much more freewheeling and anarchistic social outlook. For him the structures of society, as structures, belong almost entirely to the absurd, obsessed, sinister aspect of it, the aspect that is overcome or evaded by the comic action. The comic action itself moves toward the regrouping of society around the only social unit that Dickens really regards as genuine, the family. In other Victorian novelists characters are regrouped within their social structures; in Dickens the comic action leads to a sense of having broken down or through those structures. Naturally there are limits to this: the same social functions have to continue; but the sense that social institutions have to reverse their relationship to human beings before society really becomes congenial is very strong.

The law, for instance, as represented by the Chancery suit in *Bleak House* and the Circumlocution Office in *Little Dorrit*, is a kind of social vampire, sucking out family secrets or draining off money through endless shifts and evasions. It is explicitly said in both novels that the legal establishment is not designed to be an instrument of society, but to be a self-perpetuating social parasite. Education, again, is usually presented in Dickens as a racket, a brutal and malignant racket with Squeers and Creakle, a force-feeding racket in the "fact" school of *Hard Times* and the Classical cram school of Dr. Blimber in *Dombey and Son*. Dickens's view of the liberalizing quality of the Victorian Classical training is perhaps symbolized in the grotesque scenes of Silas Wegg stumbling through Gibbon's *Decline and Fall* to the admiration of the illiterate Boffins: an unskillful performance which nobody understands. As for religion, even the respectable churches have little to do except marry the hero and heroine, and the spokesmen of the chapel, Chadband and Stiggins, are the same type of greasy lout as their ancestor in Ben Jonson, Zeal-of-the-Land Busy. Politics, from the Eatanswill election in *Pickwick* to the Parliamentary career of Veneering in *Our Mutual Friend*, is a farce, only tolerable when an amusing one. Industry is equally repulsive whether its spokesman is Bounderby or the labor organizer Slackbridge. The amassing of a fortune in the City, by Dombey, Ralph Nickleby, or Merdle in *Little Dorrit*, is an extension of miserliness: it is closely associated with usury; the debtor's prison is clearly the inseparable other side of it, and it usually blows up a bubble of credit speculation with no secured assets, ending in an appalling financial crash and endless misery. *Martin Chuzzlewit* carefully balances the swindling of American real estate speculators with the precisely similar activities of Montague's Anglo-Bengalee Company in London. In several of the novels there are two obstructing societies, one a social establishment and the other a criminal anti-establishment. When this occurs there is

little if anything morally to choose between them. We find the Artful
Dodger no worse than the respectable Bumble in his beadle's uniform,
and Pip discovers a human companionship with the hunted convict on
the marshes that the Wopsles and Pumblechooks of his Christmas
dinner exclude him from.

It is perhaps in *Little Dorrit* that we get the most complete view
of the obstructing society, a society which is shown to be a self-
imprisoning society, locking itself in to the invariable responses of its
own compulsions. At the beginning we are introduced to various types
of prison: the Marseilles prison with Blandois, the quarantine prison
with the discontented Tattycoram and her Lesbian familiar Miss Wade,
the prison-house of the paralyzed Mrs. Clennam, and finally the Mar-
shalsea. As the story goes on these external prisons give place to internal ones. With the Circumlocution Office the prison image modu-
lates to a maze or labyrinth, a very frequent sinister image in Dickens,
and gradually a unified vision of the obstructing society takes shape.
This society is symbolized by the Barnacles, who, as their name indicates, represent a social parasitism inherent in the aristocracy, and
operating through the political and legal establishment. They are a family, but not a genuine family: their loyalties are class or tribal loyalties
cutting across the real structure of society. One of their members, Mrs.
Gowan, even goes so far as to speak of marriage as "accidental," and
stresses the primary necessity of defending the position of her class, or
rather of her private myth about her class. The fact that her son becomes the husband of the only child of the Meagles family gives a most
ambiguous twist to the happy ending of the novel. We may compare
the disaster wrought by Steerforth in *David Copperfield*, whose mother
is similarly obsessed with making her son into a symbol of class arrogance. We begin to understand how consistent the pitiful pretense of
aristocracy that old Dorrit tries to maintain, first in the prison, then
in prosperity, is with the general scheme of the story. Miss Wade's
autobiography, headed "The History of a Self-Tormentor," however
arbitrarily introduced in the story, has a genuine symbolic relevance to
it, and one of the most sharply observed passages in the novel is the
moment of self-awareness when Fanny Dorrit realizes that her own
selfishness is implacably driving her into an endless, pointless, pleasure-
less game of one-upmanship with Mrs. Merdle. Similarly in *Great
Expectations* the "gentleman's" world which entraps Pip is symbolized
by the decaying prison-house where all the clocks have been stopped

at the moment of Miss Havisham's humiliation, the rest of her life consisting only of brooding on that moment.

The obstructing society in Dickens has two main characteristics: it is parasitic and it is pedantic. It is parasitic in the sense of setting up false values and loyalties which destroy the freedom of all those who accept them, as well as tyrannizing over many of those who do not. Dickens's implicit social vision is also radical, to an extent he hardly realized himself, in dividing society between workers and idlers, and in seeing in much of the leisure class a social sanctioning of parasitism. As for its pedantry, it is traditional in New Comedy to set up a pragmatic standard, based on experience, as a norm, and contrast it with the theoretical approaches to life typical of humors who cannot escape from their reflex responses. Like Blake, like every writer with any genuine radicalism in him, Dickens finds the really dangerous social evils in those which have achieved some acceptance by being rationalized. Already in *Oliver Twist* the word "experience" stands as a contrast to the words "experimental" and "philosophical," which are invariably pejorative. This contrast comes into Bumble's famous "the law is a ass" speech. In *Hard Times* the pedantry of the obstructing society is associated with a utilitarian philosophy and an infantile trust in facts, statistics, and all impersonal and generalized forms of knowledge. We may wonder why Dickens denounces this philosophy so earnestly and caricatures it so crudely, instead of letting its absurdities speak for themselves. But it is clear that *Hard Times*, of all Dickens's stories, comes nearest to being what in our day is sometimes called the dystopia, the book which, like *Brave New World* or *1984*, shows us the nightmare world that results from certain perverse tendencies inherent in society getting free play. The most effective dystopias are likely to be those in which the author isolates certain features in his society that most directly threaten his own social function as a writer. Dickens sees in the cult of facts and statistics a threat, not to the realistic novelist, and not only to a life based on concrete and personal relations, but to the unfettered imagination, the mind that can respond to fairy tales and fantasy and understand their relevance to reality. The insistence on the importance of fairy tales, nursery rhymes, and similar genres in education often meets us in Dickens, and implies that Dickens's fairy-tale plots are regarded by Dickens himself as an essential part of his novels.

The action of a comedy moves toward an identity which is usually a social identity. In Dickens the family, or a group analogous to a family, is the key to social identity. Hence his recognition scenes are usually genealogical, concerned with discovering unknown fathers and mothers or articulating the correct family relationships. There are often three sets of parental figures attached to a central character, with several doubles of each. First are the actual parents. These are often dead before the story begins, like the fathers of Nicholas Nickleby and David Copperfield, or stagger on weakly for a few pages, like David Copperfield's mother, or are mysterious and emerge at the end, sometimes as bare names unrelated to the story, like Oliver Twist's father or the parents of Little Nell. The father of Sissy Jupe in *Hard Times* deserts her without ever appearing in the novel; the first things we see in *Great Expectations* are the tombstones of Pip's parents. Pip himself is brought up by a sister who is twenty years older and (as we learn on practically the last page of the book) has the same name as his mother. Next come the parental figures of the obstructing society, generally cruel or foolish, and often descended from the harsh step-parents of folktale. Murdstone and his sister, Pip's sister, the pseudo-mothers of Esther Summerson and Clennam, belong to this group. One very frequent device which combines these two types of relationship is that of the preternaturally loving and hard-working daughter who is the sole support of a weak or foolish father. We have, among others, Little Dorrit, Little Nell, whose grandfather is a compulsive gambler, Jenny Wren in *Our Mutual Friend* with her drunken "child," Madeline Bray in *Nicholas Nickleby*, and, in a different way, Florence Dombey. Naturally the marriage of such a heroine, following on the death of the parent, transfers her to the more congenial society. Finally we have the parental or avuncular figures of the congenial society itself, those who take on a protective relation to the central characters as the story approaches its conclusion. Brownlow in *Oliver Twist*, who adopts the hero, Jarndyce in *Bleak House*, Abel Magwitch in *Great Expectations*, the Cheeryble brothers in *Nicholas Nickleby*, the Boffins in *Our Mutual Friend*, are examples. Abel Magwitch, besides being the ultimate father of Pip, is also the actual father of Estella, which makes Estella in a sense Pip's sister: this was doubtless one reason why Dickens so resisted the conventional ending of marriage for these two. The more realistic developments of New Comedy tend to eliminate this genealogical apparatus. When one of the girls in *Les Précieuses Ridicules* announces that being so interesting a girl she is quite sure that her real parents are much more interesting people than the ones she appears to have, we do not take her very seriously. But Dickens is always ready to cooperate with the lonely child's fantasies about lost congenial parents, and this marks his affinity with the romantic side of the tradition, the side related to Classical romance.

I have used the word "anarchistic" in connection with Dickens's view of society, but it is clear that, so far as his comic structure leads to any sort of vision of a social ideal, that ideal would have to be an intensely paternalistic society, an expanded family. We get a somewhat naïve glimpse of this with the Cheeryble brothers in *Nicholas Nickleby*, giving a party where the faithful servitors are brought in at the end for a drink of champagne, expressing undying loyalty and enthusiasm for the patronizing social arrangements. The reader gets the uneasy feeling that he is listening to the commercial. When in *Little Dorrit* Tattycoram runs away from the suffocating geniality of the Meagles family she has to be brought back repentant, though she may well have had much more of the reader's sympathy than Dickens intended her to have. Even the Dedlock ménage in *Bleak House*, hopeless social anachronism as Dickens clearly recognizes it to be, is still close enough to a family to gather a fair amount of the society of the novel around it at the end. In contrast, social parasites often assume the role of a false father. Examples include the Marquis in *A Tale of Two Cities* whose assassin is technically guilty of parricide, Sir Joseph Bowley, the Urizenic friend and father of the poor in *The Chimes*, and the elder Chester in *Barnaby Rudge*.

In New Comedy the obstructing humors absorb most of the character interest: the heroes and heroines are seldom individualized. Such characters as Bonario in *Volpone* or Valère in *Tartuffe* are only pleasant young men. In Dickens too the heroes and heroines resemble humors only in the fact that their responses are predictable, but they are predictable in terms of a norm, and they seldom if ever appear in the ridiculous or selfbinding role of the humor. Such characters, who encourage the reader to identify with them, and who might be called norm-figures, could not exist in serious twentieth-century fiction, which belongs to the ironic mode, and sees all its characters as affected in some degree by hampering social forces. But they have some validity in nineteenth-century low mimetic conventions, which present only what is conventionally presentable, and whose heroes and heroines may therefore logically be models of presentability.

Comedy usually depicts the triumph of the young over the old, but Dickens is unusual among comic writers in that so many of his heroes and heroines are children, or are described in ways that associate them with childhood. Nobody has described more vividly than Dickens the reactions of a sensitive child in a Brobdingnagian world dominated by noisome and blundering adults. And because nearly all these children are predestined to belong to the congenial society, they can only be hurt, not corrupted, by the obstructing society. The one striking exception is Pip, whose detachment from the false standards of the obstructing group forms the main theme of *Great Expectations* But David Copperfield is only superficially affected by his environment, and Oliver Twist escapes from the activities of the Fagin gang as miraculously as Marina does from the brothel in Shakespeare's *Pericles*. Usually this predestined child-figure is a girl. Many of the heroines, even when grown women, are described as "little" or are compared to fairies. A frequent central theme in Dickens is the theme of *Alice in Wonderland:* the descent of the invulnerable girl-child into a grotesque world. In the preface to *The Old Curiosity Shop* Dickens speaks of his interest in the beauty-and-beast archetype, of the girl-child surrounded by monsters, some of them amiable like Kit, others sinister like Quilp. Little Nell descends to this grotesque world and then rejoins the angels; the other heroines marry into the congenial society. The girl-child among grotesques recurs in Florence Dombey's protection by Captain Cuttle, in Little Dorrit's mothering of Maggie, and in many similar scenes. Sometimes an amiable grotesque, Toots or Kit or Smike or Chivery, will attach himself to such a girl-child figure, not good enough to marry her but protesting eternal devotion nonetheless, a kind of late farcical vestige of the Courtly Love convention. Nobody turns up in *The Old Curiosity Shop* good enough to marry Little Nell, which is doubtless one reason why she dies. We may also notice the role of the old curiosity shop itself: it plays little part in the story, but is a kind of threshold symbol of the entrance into the grotesque world, like the rabbit-hole and mirror in the Alice books. Its counterparts appear in the Wooden Midshipman shop in *Dombey and Son*, the Peggotty cottage in *David Copperfield*, the bone-shop of Venus in *Our Mutual Friend*, and elsewhere.

Many of the traditional features of romantic New Comedy reached their highest point of development in nineteenth-century Britain, making it the obvious time and place for a great genius in that form to emerge. One of these, already glanced at, is the domination of narrative genres, along with a moribund drama. Dickens had many dramatic interests, but his genius was for serial romance and not for the stage. Another is the Victorian assumption of moral standards shared between author and reader. This feature makes for melodrama, where the reader emotionally participates in the moral conflict of hero and villain, or of virtue and temptation. The rigidity, or assumed rigidity, of Victorian sexual mores is a great help in a nineteenth-century plot, as it enables an author, not only to make a Wagnerian noise about a woman's extramarital escapade, but to make the most frenzied activity on her part plausible as an effort to conceal the results of it. But the relation of melodrama to the foreground action is far more important than this.

A realistic writer in the New Comedy tradition tends to work out his action on one plane: young and old, hero and humor, struggle for power within the same social group. The more romantic the writer, the more he tends to set over against his humorous world another kind of world, with which the romantic side of his story is associated. In a paper presented to the English Institute nearly twenty years ago, I spoke of the action of romantic Shakespearean comedy as divided between a foreground world of humors and a background "green world," associated with magic, sleep and dreams, and enchanted forests or houses, from which the comic resolution comes. Dickens has no green world, except for a glint or two here and there (e.g., the pastoral retreats in which Smike and Little Nell end their days, Jenny Wren's paradisal dreams, the "beanstalk" abode of Tartar in *Edwin Drood*, and the like), but he does have his own way of dividing his action. I have spoken of the nineteenth-century emphasis on the presentable, on the world of public appearance to which the nineteenth-century novelist is almost entirely confined. Behind this world lies a vast secret world, the world of privacy, where there is little or no communication. For Dickens this world is associated mainly with dreams, memories, and death. He describes it very eloquently at the opening of the third "Quarter" of *The Chimes*, and again in the first paragraph of the third chapter of *A Tale of Two Cities*, besides referring frequently to it throughout his work.

Few can read Dickens without catching the infection of his intense curiosity about the life that lies in the dark houses behind the lights of his loved and hated London. We recognize it even at second hand: when Dylan Thomas's *Under Milk Wood* opens on a night of private dreams we can see an unmistakably Dickensian influence. For most of the ironic fiction of the twentieth century, this secret world is essentially the bedroom and bathroom world of ordinary privacy, as well as the world of sexual drives, perversion, repressions, and infantile fixations that not only complements the public world but conditions one's behavior in it at every point. Characters in twentieth-century fiction have no privacy: there is no dinstinction between dressingroom and stage. Dickens is by no means unaware of the importance of this aspect of the hidden world, but it is of little use to him as a novelist, and he shows no restiveness about being obliged to exclude it. This is because he is not primarily an ironic writer, like Joyce or Flaubert. What he is really curious about is a hidden world of *romantic* interest, not a world even more squalid and commonplace than the visible one. His detective interest in hidden life is comparable to other aspects of Victorian culture: one thinks of the pre-Raphaelite paintings where we are challenged to guess what kind of story is being told by the picture and its enigmatic title, or of all the poems of Browning that appeal to us to deduce the reality behind what is presented.

In following the main action of a Dickens novel we are frequently aware of a second form of experience being held up to it like a mirror. Sometimes this is explicitly the world of the stage. The kind of entertainment afforded by the Vincent Crummles troop in *Nicholas Nickleby* parallels the uninhibited melodrama of the main story: the dance of the savage and the Infant Phenomenon, in particular, mirrors the Dickensian theme of the girl-child in the monster-world. In *Hard Times*, where the relation is one of contrast, a circus company symbolizes an approach to experience that Gradgrind has missed out on. The Punch and Judy show in *The Old Curiosity Shop*, one of several popular dramatic entertainments in that book, has been mentioned, and in *Great Expectations* Pip, haunted by the ghost of a father, goes to see Mr. Wopsle in *Hamlet*. Then again, Dickens makes considerable use of the curious convention in New Comedy of the doubled character, who is often literally a twin. In *The Comedy of Errors* the foreground Ephesus and the background Syracuse, in *Twelfth Night* the melancholy courts of Orsino and Olivia, are brought into alignment by twins. Similarly, the foreground action of *Little Dorrit* is related to the background action partly through the concealed twin brother of Flintwinch. In *A Tale of Two Cities*, where the twin theme is at its most complicated, the resemblance of Darnay and

Carton brings the two cities themselves into alignment. In *Dombey and Son* the purse-proud world of Dombey and the other social world that it tries to ignore are aligned by the parallel, explicitly alluded to, between Edith Dombey and Alice Brown. There are many other forms of doubling, both of characters and of action, that I have no space here to examine.

The basis for such a dividing of the action might be generalized as follows. There is a hidden and private world of dream and death, out of which all the energy of human life comes. The primary manifestation of this world, in experience, is in acts of destructive violence and passion. It is the source of war, cruelty, arrogance, lust, and grinding the faces of the poor. It produces the haughty lady with her guilty secret, like Lady Dedlock or Edith Dombey or Mrs. Clennam, the lynching mobs that hunt Bill Sikes to death or proclaim the charity of the Protestant religion in *Barnaby Rudge*, the flogging schoolmasters and the hanging judges. It also produces the courage to fight against these things, and the instinctive virtue that repudiates them. In short, the hidden world expresses itself most directly in melodramatic action and rhetoric. It is not so much better or worse than the ordinary world of experience, as a world in which good and evil appear as much stronger and less disguised forces. We may protest that its moods are exaggerated, its actions unlikely, its rhetoric stilted and unconvincing. But if it were not there nothing else in Dickens would be there. We notice that the mainspring of melodramatic action is, like that of humorous action, mainly obsession. We notice too that Dickens's hair-raising descriptions, like that of Marseilles at the opening of *Little Dorrit* with its repetition of "stare," are based on the same kind of associative rhetoric as the speech of the humors.

From this point of view we can look at the foreground action of the humors in a new light. Humors are, so to speak, petrified by-products of the kind of energy that melodrama expresses more directly. Even the most contemptible humors, the miserly Fledgeby or the hypocritical Heep, are exuberantly miserly and hypocritical: their vices express an energy that possesses them because they cannot possess it. The world they operate in, so far as it is a peaceable and law-abiding world, is a world of very imperfectly suppressed violence. They never escape from the shadow of a power which is at once Eros and Thanatos, and are bound to a passion that is never satisfied by its rationalized objects, but is ultimately self-destructive. In the earlier novels the emotional focus of this self-destroying passion is usually a miser, or a person in some way obsessed with money, like Ralph Nickleby, Dombey, Little Nell's grandfather, or Jonas Chuzzlewit. The folktale association of money and excrement, which points to the psychological origin of miserliness, appears in the "Golden Dustman" theme of *Our Mutual Friend*, and is perhaps echoed in the names Murdstone and Merdle. In the later novels a more explicitly erotic drive gives us the victim-villain figures of Bradley Headstone and Jasper Drood. Food and animals are other images that Dickens often uses in sexual contexts, especially when a miser aspires to a heroine. Arthur Gride in *Nicholas Nickleby* speaks of Madeline Bray as a tasty morsel, and Uriah Heep is compared to a whole zoo of unpleasant animals: the effect is to give an Andromeda pattern to the heroine's situation, and suggest a demonic ferocity behind the domestic foreground. The same principle of construction causes the stock-response humors like Podsnap or Gradgrind to take on a peculiar importance. They represent the fact that an entire society can become mechanized like a humor, or fossilized into its institutions. This could happen to Victorian England, according to *Hard Times*, if it takes the gospel of facts and statistics too literally, and did happen to prerevolutionary France, as described in *A Tale of Two Cities*, dying of what Dickens calls "the leprosy of unreality," and awaiting the melodramatic deluge of the Revolution.

The obstructing humors cannot escape from the ritual habits that they have set up to deal with this disconcerting energy that has turned them into mechanical puppets. The heroes and heroines, however, along with some of the more amiable humors, have the power to plunge into the hidden world of dreams and death, and, though narrowly escaping death in the process, gain from it a renewed life and energy. Sometimes this plunge into the hidden world is symbolized by a distant voyage. The incredible Australia that makes a magistrate out of Wilkins Micawber also enables the hunted convict Magwitch to become an ambiguous but ultimately genuine fairy godfather. Walter Gay in *Dombey and Son* returns from the West Indies, remarkably silent, long after he has been given up for dead, and the reader follows Martin Chuzzlewit into a place, ironically called Eden, where he is confidently expected to die and nearly does die, but where he goes through a metamorphosis of character that fits him for the comic conclusion. Other characters, including Dick Swiveller, Pip, and Esther Summerson, go into a delirious illness with the same result. *Our Mutual Friend* has a complex pattern of resurrection imagery connected with dredging the Thames, reviving from drowning, finding treasure buried in dust-heaps, and the like; a similar pattern of digging up the dead in A *Tale of Two Cities* extends from the stately Dr. Manette to the grotesque Jerry Cruncher. We notice too that the sinister society is often introduced in a kind of wavering light between sleep and waking: the appearance of the faces of Fagin and Monks at Oliver Twist's window and the alleged dreams of Abbie Flintwinch in *Little Dorrit* are examples. The most uninhibited treatment of this plunge into the world of death and dreams occurs, as we should expect, in the Christmas Books, where Scrooge and Trotty Veck see in vision a tragic version of their own lives, and one which includes their own deaths, then wake up to renewed festivity. It seems clear that the hidden world, though most of its more direct expressions are destructive and terrible, contains within itself an irresistible power of renewing life.

The hidden world is thus, once again in literature, the world of an invincible Eros, the power strong enough to force a happy ending on the story in defiance of all probability, pushing all the obstructing humors out of the way, or killing them if they will not get out of the way, getting the attractive young people disentangled from their brothers and sisters and headed for the right beds. It dissolves all hardening social institutions and reconstitutes society on its sexual basis of the family, the shadowy old fathers and mothers being replaced by new and livelier successors. When a sympathetic character dies, a strongly religious projection of this power often appears: the "Judgment" expected shortly by Miss Flite in *Bleak House*, for instance, stands in apocalyptic contrast to the Chancery court. Dickens's Eros world is, above all, a designing and manipulating power. The obstructing humor can do only what his humor makes him do, and toward the end of the story he becomes the helpless pawn of a chess game in which black can never ultimately win.

The victorious hidden world is not the world of nature in the Rousseauistic context of that word. The people who talk about this kind of nature in Dickens are such people as Mrs. Merdle in *Little Dorrit*, Mrs. Chick in *Dombey and Son*, and Wackford Squeers—not an encouraging lot. Like most romancers, Dickens gives a prominent place to the fool or "natural"—Smike, Mr. Dick, Barnaby Rudge—whose instincts make up for retarded intelligence. But such people are privileged: elsewhere nature and *social* education, or human experience, are always associated. To say that Dora Copperfield is an un-spoiled child of nature is also to say that she is a spoiled child. Dickens's nature is a human nature which is the same kind of thing as the power that creates art, a designing and shaping power. This is also true of Shakespeare's green world, but Dickens's Eros world is not the conserving force that the green world is, which revitalizes a society without altering its structure. At the end of a Shakespeare comedy there is usually a figure of authority, like Prospero or the various dukes, who represents this social conservation. We have nothing in Dickens to correspond to such figures: the nearest to them are the empty Santa Claus masks of the Cheerybles, Boffin, and the reformed Scrooge. For all its domestic and sentimental Victorian setting, there is a revolutionary and subversive, almost a nihilistic, quality in Dickens's melodrama that is post-Romantic, has inherited the experience of the French Revolution, and looks forward to the world of Freud, Marx, and the existential thriller.

I used the word "absurd" earlier about Dickens's melodramatic plots, suggesting that they were creatively and not incompetently absurd. In our day the word "absurd" usually refers to the absence of purpose or meaning in life and experience, the so-called metaphysical absurd. But for literary criticism the formulating of the theory of the absurd should not be left entirely to disillusioned theologians. In literature it is design, the forming and shaping power, that is absurd. Real life does not start or stop; it never ties up loose ends; it never manifests meaning or purpose except by blind accident; it is never comic or tragic, ironic or romantic, or anything else that has a shape. Whatever gives form and pattern to fiction, whatever technical skill keeps us turning the pages to get to the end, is absurd, and contradicts our sense of reality. The great Victorian realists subordinate their storytelling skill to their representational skill. Theirs is a dignified, leisurely vehicle that gives us time to look at the scenery. They have formed our stock responses to fiction, so that even when traveling at the much higher speed of drama, romance, or epic we still keep trying to focus our eyes on the incidental and transient. Most of us feel that there is something else in Dickens, something elemental, yet unconnected with either realistic clarity or philosophical profoundity. What it is connected with is a kind of story that fully gratifies the hope expressed, according to Lewis Carroll, by the original of Alice, that "there will be nonsense in it." The silliest character in *Nicholas Nickleby* is the hero's mother, a romancer who keeps dreaming of impossible happy endings for her children. But the story itself follows her specifications and not those of the sensible people. The obstructing humors in Dickens are absurd because they have overdesigned their lives. But the kind of design that they parody is produced by another kind of energy, and one which insists, absurdly and yet irresistibly, that what is must never take final precedence over what ought to be.

II. 16

Two Faces of Edward*

RICHARD ELLMANN

Oxford University

VICTORIA STAYED too long, Edward arrived too late. By the time the superannuated Prince of Wales became king, it was evident that a change would take place in literature; it took place, but Edward has somehow never received credit for it, and the phrase 'Edwardian literature' is not often heard. We have to fall back on it, though, because there is no neat phrase in English, like 'the nineties', to describe the first ten years of a century. The word 'Edwardian' has taken its connotations from social rather than literary history. Just what it means is not certain, beyond the high collars and tight trousers which flouted Victorian dowdiness then, and which later became for a time the pedantic signs of juvenile delinquency. Perhaps 'pre-war courtliness' is the closest we can come to the meaning of Edwardian outside literature, sedate Victorianism in better dress. The meaning was present enough to Virginia Woolf for her to declare that 'on or about December 1910,' that is, in the year of Edward's death, 'human character changed.' [1] Edward 'the Peacemaker' had to die before the world could become modern, and she pushed the dead Edwardians aside to make room for the lively Georgians. The distinction was more relevant, however, for describing Virginia Woolf's own accession to purposiveness than George's accession to rule.

While the late Victorians seem to have relished the idea that

* Read at the Institute in 1959. Published in *Institute Essays*, 1960, and in *Golden Codgers: Biographical Speculations* by Richard Ellmann, Oxford University Press: New York and London, 1973. Copyright Richard Ellmann 1973. Text from the latter.

[1] Virginia Woolf, "Mr. Bennett and Mrs. Brown," *Collected Essays*, 4 vols. (London and New York, 1966-7), I, 320.

they were the last, the Edwardians at once declined to consider themselves as stragglers, ghostly remains of those Englishmen who had stretched the Empire so far. The Edwardians had, in fact, a good deal of contempt for the previous reign, and an odd admiration for their own doughtiness. In the midst of the general melancholy over Victoria's death, her son said sturdily, 'The King lives.' To Virginia Woolf the hated Edwardian writers were Bennett, Galsworthy, and Wells, yet even these writers laboured under the apprehension or misapprehension that they were trying something new. Lascelles Abercrombie, in one of the few essays on Edwardian literature, finds the period to be only the decorous extension of tradition, and in his essay is detectable that faintly patronizing note which occurs also in biographies of Edward that prove the king was a worthy man.[2] So for Abercrombie the writers of this time were engagingly discreet; they drew in literature, as Edward in life, upon an ample wardrobe, and perhaps dared to go so far as to leave unbuttoned the lowest button on their literary waist-coats.

That the Edwardians have been discounted is understandable, I think, because of the prevalence of a sociological assumption. If the birth of modern literature is dated back to the century's first decade, what happens to our conviction that it was the Great War which turned the tables? At any cost we have to confine the beginning of the century to the infancy or adolescence of modern writers, so that only when the guns boomed did they become old enough to discern the nature of the world. The admonitory fact, however, is that most of the writers whom we are accustomed to call modern were already in their twenties or older when King Edward died. In 1910 Eliot was twenty-two, Lawrence and Pound were twenty-five, Joyce and Virginia Woolf were twenty-eight, Forster was thirty-one, Ford Madox Ford thirty-seven, Conrad fifty-three, Shaw fifty-four, Henry James sixty-seven. Bennett, Galsworthy, and Wells were in their forties. To dismiss most of the writers I have named as either too young or too old to be Edwardians, as if only men of middle age counted in literary fashion, is one of those historical simplicities like denying that the twenties were the twenties because so many people didn't know the twenties were going on. Neither age nor self-consciousness determines the private character of a period; if anything does, it is the existence of a community between young and old experimental writers. Such a community existed in the Edwardian period. It was a community which extended not only

---

[2] Lascelles Abercrombie, "Literature", in *Edwardian England*, ed. F. J. C. Hernshaw (London, 1933), 185–203.

across the Irish Sea but, spottily at least, across the Channel and the Atlantic; so, if I extend Edward's dominions occasionally to countries he did not rule, it is only to recover the imperial word 'Edwardian' from an enforced limitation.

If a moment must be found for human character to have changed, I should suggest that 1900 is both more convenient and more accurate than Virginia Woolf's 1910. In 1900, Yeats said with good-humoured exaggeration, 'everybody got down off his stilts; henceforth nobody drank absinthe with his black coffee; nobody went mad; nobody committed suicide; nobody joined the Catholic Church; or if they did I have forgotten.'[3] That there was pressure upon them to change was something that the writers of this time were distinctly aware of; it is not only Yeats whose attitudes take a new turn; it is also lesser writers. Even John Masefield was once asked how it had happened that his poetry had moved from the nostalgic rhythms of his early work to the more athletic ones of 'The Everlasting Mercy', and he replied simply, 'Everybody changed his style then.' The Edwardians came like Dryden after Sir Thomas Browne, anxious to develop a more wiry speech. Their sentences grew more vigorous and concentrated. I will not claim for the Edwardians' work total novelty—that can never be found in any period, and many of their most individual traits had origin in the nineties or earlier. But in all that they do they are freshly self-conscious. What can be claimed is that there was a gathering of different talents towards common devices, themes, and attitudes, and King Edward at least did nothing to impede it.

What strikes us at once about Edwardian literature is that it is thoroughly secular, yet so earnest that secularism does not describe it. It is generally assumed that in this period religion was something to ignore and not to practise. Edwardian writers were not in fact religious, but they were not ostentatiously irreligious. In the Victorian period people had fumed and left the churches; in the Edwardian period, becalmed, they published memoirs or novels describing how strongly they had once felt about the subject. This is the point of Gosse's *Father and Son* (1907) as well as of Samuel Butler's *The Way of All Flesh* (written earlier, but published in 1903). It was also part of the subject of Joyce's *A Portrait of the Artist as a Young Man*, much of it written in 1907–8, as it is of Yeats's first autobiographical book, *Reveries over*

---

[3] W. B. Yeats, Introduction to *The Oxford Book of Modern Verse* (Oxford, 1936), xi.

Childhood and Youth, written just before the war. In all these books the intensity of rebellion is past, an incident of an unhappy childhood (and the vogue of having had an unhappy childhood may well have begun with the Edwardians) succeeded by confident maturity.

Because they outlived their passionate revolt, writers as different as Yeats and Joyce are sometimes suspected now of having been reverted Christians or at least demi-Christians. Certainly they no longer make a fuss about being infidels. And they are suspected of belief for another reason, too. Almost to a man, Edwardian writers rejected Christianity, and having done so, they felt free to *use* it, for while they did not need religion they did need religious metaphors. It is no accident that the Catholic modernists, with their emphasis upon the metaphorical rather than the literal truth of Catholic doctrines, became powerful enough in the first years of the century to be worth excommunicating in 1907. There were other signs of a changed attitude towards religion: the comparative mythologists tolerantly accepted Easter as one of many spring vegetation rites; William James's *The Varieties of Religious Experience*, published in 1902, made all varieties equally valid.

In creative writers, this new temper appears not in discussion of religion, which does not interest them, but in vocabulary. Religious terms are suddenly in vogue among unbelievers. Yeats calls up God to be a symbol of the most complete thought. Joyce in *A Portrait* allows the infidel Stephen to cry out 'Heavenly God!' when, seeing a girl wading, he experiences 'an outburst of *profane* joy'. Elsewhere, as in *Ulysses*, he asks what difference it makes whether God's name be Christus or Bloom, and Jesus is allowed into *Finnegans Wake* as one of Finnegan's many avatars. Ezra Pound, newly arrived in London in 1908, immediately writes a canzone to celebrate 'The Yearly Slain', a pagan god, and then a ballad to celebrate the 'Goodly Fere', who turns out to be Christ made into a Scottish chap. All deaths of all gods roused Pound to the same fervour. There was no need to attack with Swinburne the 'pale Galilean', or to say with Nietzsche that 'God is dead'; as a metaphor God was not dead but distinctly alive, so much so that a character in Granville-Barker's play *Waste* (1906–7) asks sardonically, 'What is the prose for God?' T. S. Eliot, if for a moment he may be regarded as an Edwardian rather than as a Rooseveltian, in 'Prufrock' (written in 1910) used John the Baptist and Lazarus as if they were characters like Hamlet, and even in his later life, after be-

coming consciously, even self-consciously Christian, he used the words
'God' and 'Christ' with the greatest circumspection, while unbelievers
used the words much more casually, their individual talents more at
ease in his tradition than he himself. D. H. Lawrence, the same age as
Pound, writes his 'Hymn to Priapus' in 1912, yet remains attracted by
images of Christ and is willing enough, in spite of his preference for
older and darker gods, to revise Christianity and use its metaphors. In
The Rainbow (begun the same year), Tom Brangwen and his wife,
when their physical relationship improves, experience what Lawrence
variously calls 'baptism to another life', 'transfiguration', and 'glorification'. In later life Lawrence would give Christ a new resurrection so he
could learn to behave like the god Pan, and in poems such as 'Last
Words to Miriam' the cross becomes emblematic of the failure to
cohabit properly, an interpretation which I should like to think of as
Edwardian or at least post-Edwardian. Even H. G. Wells played for a
time with the notion of a 'finite God', 'the king of man's adventures in
space and time,' though in the end he granted, too unimaginatively,
that he had been guilty of 'terminological disingenuousness'.[4]

To accept Christianity as one of a group of what Gottfried Benn
calls 'regional moods', or to rewrite it for a new, pagan purpose, seemed
to the Edwardians equally cogent directions. For the first time writers
can take for granted that a large part of their audience will be irreligious, and paradoxically this fact gives them confidence to use religious imagery. They neither wish to shock nor fear to shock. There is
precision, not impiety, in Joyce's use of religious words for secular
processes. About 1900, when he was eighteen, he began to describe his
prose sketches not as poems in prose, the fashionable term, but as
'epiphanies', showings-forth of essences comparable to the showing-
forth of Christ. *Dubliners* he first conceived of in 1904 as a series of ten
epicleseis, that is, invocations to the Holy Spirit to transmute bread and
wine into the body and blood of Christ, a sacramental way of saying
that he wished to fix in their eternal significance the commonplace incidents he found about him. To moments of fullness he applied the term
'eucharistic'. When Stephen Dedalus leaves the Catholic priesthood behind him, it is to become 'a priest of eternal imagination, transmuting
the daily bread of experience into the radiant body of everlasting life.'
One did not have to be a defected Irish Catholic to use terms this way.
Granville-Barker's hero in *Waste* wants to buy the Christian tradition

[4] H. G. Wells, *Experiment in Autobiography* (New York, 1934), 573–8.

and transmute it. Proust, searching for an adjective to express his sense of basic experiences, calls them 'celestial'. Yeats, a defected Protestant, wrote in 1903 that his early work was directed towards the transfiguration on the mountain, and his new work towards incarnation. The artist, he held, must make a Sacred Book, which would not be Christian or anti-Christian, but would revive old pieties and rituals in the universal colours of art instead of in the hue of a single creed.

The re-establishment of Christianity, this time as outer panoply for an inner creed, was not limited to a few writers. In the Edwardian novels of Henry James the words he is fondest of are 'save' and 'sacrifice', and these are secular equivalents for religious concepts to which in their own terms he is indifferent. In the novels of E. M. Forster, mostly written before Edward died, there is exhibited this same propensity. Forster usually reserves his religious imagery for the end of his novels. In the last pages of *Where Angels Fear to Tread*, his first novel (1905), Forster writes of Philip, 'Quietly, without hysterical prayers or banging of drums, he underwent conversion. He was saved.' *The Longest Journey* (1907) concludes with Stephen Wanham undergoing 'salvation'. In *A Room with a View* (1908), there is a 'Sacred Lake', immersion in which, we are told, is 'a call to the blood and to the relaxed will, a passing benediction whose influence did not pass, a holiness, a spell, a momentary chalice for youth.' At the end the heroine derives from Mr. Emerson, who has 'the face of a saint who understood', 'a sense of deities reconciled, a feeling that, in gaining the man she loved, she would gain something for the whole world.'

Even allowing that writers always incline to inflated language for their perorations, Forster obviously intends his words momentously, almost portentously. He is not for Christ or Pan, but with profoundly Edwardian zeal, for the deities reconciled. Some of the same images appear with much the same meaning in his contemporaries. A character in Granville-Barker calls for 'A secular Church'. Shaw's *Major Barbara* (1905) makes similar use of the theme of salvation with its earnest fun about the Salvation Army. Let us be saved, Shaw says, but with less Christian noise and more Roman efficiency. Forster's 'chalice' is like the chalice in Joyce's 'Araby' (written in 1905), which is a symbol of the boy's love for his sweetheart. The 'Sacred Lake' with its subverting of Christian implication is like *The Lake* in George Moore's novel (1905), in which the priest-hero immerses himself in the lake not in order to become Christian, but to become pagan. Forster's deflection of familiar Christian phrasing in having his heroine feel that, in gaining the man she loves she gains something for the whole world, is cognate with Joyce's heroine in 'The Dead' (written in 1907), who says of her pagan lover, 'I think he died for me,' a statement which helps to justify the ending of that story in a mood of secular sacrifice for which the imagery of barren thorns and spears is Christian yet paganized. I do not think it would be useful to discriminate closely the slightly varying attitudes towards Christianity in these examples: the mood is the same, a secular one.

Yet to express secularism in such images is to give it a special inflection. The Edwardians were looking for ways to express their conviction that we can be religious about life itself, and they naturally adopted metaphors offered by the religion they knew best. The capitalized word for the Edwardians is not 'God' but 'Life': 'What I'm really trying to render is nothing more nor less than Life,' says George Ponderevo, when Wells is forty-three; 'Live,' says Strether to Little Bilham, when Henry James is sixty; 'O life,' cries Stephen Dedalus to no one in particular when Joyce is about thirty-four; 'I am going to begin a book about Life,' announces D. H. Lawrence, when he is thirty.[5] It does not much matter whether life is exciting or dull, though Conrad is a little exceptional in choosing extraordinary incidents. Arnold Bennett is more usual in his assurance that two old women are worth writing The Old Wives' Tale (1908) about. The Edwardians vied with each other in finding more and more commonplace life to write about, and in giving the impression of writing about it in more and more common speech. In Ireland there is the most distinct return to simple men for revelation, in the peasant drama, in Lady Gregory's collection of folklore, in Moore's and Joyce's short stories; but there is a good deal of it in England too, in Arthur Morrison for example. It is connected with an increasing physicality in writers like Lawrence and Joyce, as if they must discuss the forbidden as well as the allowed commonplace. In Lawrence and in Yeats there is the exaltation of spontaneous ignorance, the gamekeeper in the one and the fisherman in the other held up as models to those who suppose that wisdom is something that comes with higher education. In 1911 Ford Madox Ford calls upon poets to write about ash-buckets at dawn rather than about the song of birds or moonlight.[6] While Henry James could not bring himself to joy in ash-buckets, he

[5] Quoted by Harry T. Moore in The Intelligent Heart (New York, 1954; London, 1955), 191.
[6] Ford Madox Ford, Collected Poems (London, 1914), 17.

too believed that by uninhibited scrutiny the artist might attract life's secrets.

The Edwardian writer granted that the world was secular, but saw no reason to add that it was irrational or meaningless. A kind of inner belief pervades their writings, that the transcendent is immanent in the earthy, that to go down far enough is to go up. They felt free to introduce startling coincidences quite flagrantly, as in *A Room with a View* and *The Ambassadors*, to hint that life is much more than it appears to be, although none of them would have offered that admission openly. While Biblical miracles aroused their incredulity, they were singularly credulous of miracles of their own. As Conrad said in his preface to *The Shadow-Line*, 'The world of the living contains enough marvels and mysteries as it is; marvels and mysteries acting upon our emotions and intelligence in ways so inexplicable that it would almost justify the conception of life as an enchanted state.' The central miracle for the Edwardians is the sudden alteration of the self; around it much of their literature pivots. In 1907 Yeats began work on *The Player Queen*, a dramatic statement of his conviction that, if we pretend hard enough to be someone else, we can become that other self or mask. That was the year, too, when Joyce planned out the miraculous birth of his hero's mature soul as the conclusion of *A Portrait of the Artist*, and when J. M. Synge, in *The Playboy of the Western World*, represented dramatically the battle for selfhood. At the end of Synge's play, Christy Mahon is the true playboy he has up to now only pretended to be, and his swagger is replaced by inner confidence. In *The Voysey Inheritance* (1905) Granville-Barker brings Edward Voysey to sudden maturity when, like the hero of that neo-Edwardian novel of James Gould Cozzens, *By Love Possessed*, he discovers the world is contaminated and that he may nonetheless act in it. Lawrence's heroes must always shed old skins for new ones. In Conrad's *Lord Jim* (1900), the struggle for selfhood is the hero's quest, a quest achieved only with his death. In Henry James's *The Ambassadors* (1903), the miracles among which Strether moves at first are phantasmagoric, but there is no phantasmagoria about the miracle which finally occurs, the release of Strether from ignorance to total understanding. Though the dove dies in another of James's novels of this time (1902), her wings mysteriously extend beyond death into the minds of the living, to alter their conduct miraculously. The golden bowl (1904) is cracked and finally broken, but by miracle is recreated in the mind.

Miracles of this sort occur in surprising places, even in H. G.

Wells. In *Kipps* the hero is transformed from a small person named Kipps into a bloated person named Cuyps and finally into a considerable person named Kipps. He is himself at last. Less obviously, such a change takes place in George Ponderevo in *Tono-Bungay*. It is part of Wells's favourite myth of human achievement, and trying to express that George Ponderevo says, 'How can I express the values of a thing at once so essential and so immaterial?' To do so he falls back upon the words 'Science' or 'Truth', words as reverberant for Wells as 'chalice' for Forster or 'eucharist' for Joyce. Selfhood—the crown of life, attained by a mysterious grace—forced the Edwardians into their grandest metaphors. It will not seem strange that Bernard Shaw's mind hovers continually about it, as in *Man and Superman* (1901–3) and *Pygmalion* (1912), where miracles as striking and as secular as those in Synge, Joyce, or Yeats, take place. Perhaps we could distinguish two kinds of such miracles: the kind of Shaw and Wells, in which a victory in the spirit is accompanied usually by some material victory, and the kind of James, Lawrence, Conrad, Yeats, and Joyce, in which a victory in the spirit is usually accompanied by some defeat. Shaw complained vigorously to Henry James that James's kind of miracle was not 'scientific'.[7]

If the secular miracle is usually the climax of Edwardian writings, there is also a thematic centre, usually some single unifying event or object, some external symbol which the Edwardians bear down upon very hard until, to use Conrad's unprepossessing phrase, they 'squeeze the guts out of it'.[8] So Forster's *A Room with a View* is organized round the title; Lucy Honeychurch, viewless at first, must learn to see; Forster plays upon the word 'view' at strategic points in the novel, and at the end Lucy attains sight. In Conrad's *Nostromo* (1904) the central motif is silver, established, by Conrad's custom, in the first chapter: silver civilizes and silver obsesses, a two-edged sword, and the different attitudes that silver inspires control the action of the book. The meaning of the hero's name, Nostromo, becomes as ambiguous as silver; a lifetime of virtue is balanced against an ineradicable moral fault, and Nostromo dies an example of Conrad's fallen man, partially at least saved by misery and death. In *The Man of Property* (1906), John Galsworthy, somewhat under Conrad's influence, developed the very name of Forsyte into a symbol, and as if fearful we might miss it, he

7 Letter from Shaw to James, 17 January 1909, in *The Complete Plays of Henry James*, ed. Leon Edel (New York and London, 1949), 643.
8 Quoted by Ford Madox Ford in *The English Novel* (Philadelphia, 1929), 147.

keeps reminding us that the Forsytes were not only a family but a class, a state of mind, a social disease. The use of a symbolic nucleus in these books seems to justify itself by its public quality, a whole society being measured in terms of it. In *The Golden Bowl*, one of those demonstrations of method which Forster found too extreme, Henry James not only invokes the bowl itself several times in the novel, but keeps invoking its atmosphere by repeating the words 'gold' and 'golden'. Verbal iteration is a means by which Edwardian novelists make up for the obliquity of their method, the complexity of their theme, and give away some of their hand. So Conrad in *Lord Jim* speaks of his hero's clothing, on the first page, as 'immaculate', and at the last he is 'a white speck', all the incongruities of the book pointed up by the overemphasis on stainlessness. Joyce plays on a group of words in *A Portrait*, 'apologise', 'admit', 'fall', 'fly', and the like, expanding their meaning gradually through the book. The pressure of this Edwardian conception of novel-writing is felt even in the work of Lawrence. In his first book, written in 1910, Lawrence is still rather primitive in his use of key words. He changed his title from *Nethermere* to *The White Peacock*, and then laboriously emphasized his heroine's whiteness and introduced discussion of the pride of peacocks. By the time he started *The Rainbow* two years later, he had developed this technique so far as to use the words 'light' and 'dark', and the image of the rainbow itself, obsessively, and he does not relax this method in *Women in Love* or his later books. He even does what most Edwardians do not do, writes his essay 'The Crown' to explain what light, dark, and rainbow signify.

A good example, too, is Joyce's transformation of *Stephen Hero* (1904–5) into *A Portrait of the Artist as a Young Man* (chiefly 1907–8). Between writing the two books he read a good deal of Henry James, George Moore, and others, and quite possibly caught up Edwardian habits from them. *Stephen Hero* was to a large extent a Victorian novel, with an interest in incident for its own sake; so Joyce was particularly pleased when he composed the scene in which Stephen asks Emma Clery to spend the night with him. But two or three years later he expunged that scene: it had become irrelevant to his central image. For by then he had decided to make *A Portrait* an account of the gestation of a soul, and in this metaphor of the soul's growth as like an embryo's he found his principle of order and exclusion. It gave him an opportunity to be passionately meticulous. In the new version the book begins with Stephen's father and, just before the ending, it depicts the hero's severance from his mother. From the start the soul is surrounded by liquids, urine, slime, seawater, amniotic tides, 'drops of water' (as Joyce says at the end of the first chapter) 'falling softly in the brimming bowl.' The atmosphere of biological struggle is necessarily dark and melancholy until the light of life is glimpsed. In the first chapter the foetal soul is for a few pages only slightly individualized, the organism responds only to the most primitive sensory impressions, then the heart forms and musters its affections, the being struggles towards some unspecified, uncomprehended culmination, it is flooded in ways it cannot understand or control, it gropes wordlessly towards sexual differentiation. In the third chapter shame floods Stephen's whole body as conscience develops; the lower bestial nature is put by. Then, at the end of the penultimate chapter, the soul discovers the goal towards which it has been mysteriously proceeding—the goal of life. It must swim no more but emerge into air, the new metaphor being flight. The last chapter shows the soul, already fully developed, fattening itself for its journey until at last it is ready to leave. In the final pages of the book, Stephen's diary, the style shifts with savage abruptness to signalize birth. The soul is ready now, it throws off its sense of imprisonment, its melancholy, its no longer tolerable conditions of lower existence, to be born.

By making his book the matrix for the ontogeny of the soul, Joyce achieved a unity as perfect as any of the Edwardians could achieve, and justified literally his description of the artist as like a mother brooding over her creation until it assumes independent life. The aspiration towards unity in the novel seems related to the search for unity elsewhere, in psychology for example, where the major effort is to bring the day-world and the night-world together. Edwardian writes who commented on history demonstrated the same desire to see human life in a synthesis. In 1900 Joyce announced in his paper on 'Drama and Life' that 'human society is the embodiment of changeless laws,' laws which he would picture in operation in Finnegans Wake. H. G. Wells insisted later that 'History is one', and proceeded to outline it.[9] Yeats said, 'All forms are one form,' and made clear in A Vision that the same cyclical laws bind the lifetime of a person, a civilization, or an idea; and this perception of unity enabled him, he said, to hold 'in a single thought reality and justice.'

[9] Wells, Experiment in Autobiography, 619.

When they came to state their aesthetic theories, the Edwardians bore down hard on the importance of unity. To choose one among a multitude of their sources, they were to some extent making English the tradition of the *symbolistes* of whom Arthur Symons had written in 1899. Aggressively and ostentatiously, the Edwardians point to their works as microcosms characterized by the intense apprehension of the organic unity of all things. They felt justified in subordinating all other elements to this node of unity. Events of the plot can be so subordinated, for example, since, as Virginia Woolf declares, life is not a series of gig lamps symmetrically arranged but a 'luminous halo'.[10] Short stories and novels begin to present atmospheres rather than narratives; and even when events are exciting in themselves, as in Conrad and often in James, the artist's chief labour goes to establish their meaning in a painstaking way, and he will often set the most dramatic events offstage or, rather than present them directly, allow someone to recollect them. Time can be twisted or turned, for unity has little to do with chronology. What subject-matter is used becomes of less importance because any part of life, if fully apprehended, may serve. As Ford Madox Ford says in describing the novel of this period, 'Your "subject" might be no more than a child catching frogs in a swamp or the emotions of a nervous woman in a thunderstorm, but all the history of the world has gone to putting child or woman where they are. . . .'[11] Since characters are also subsidiary to the sought-after unity, there is a tendency to control them tightly. Few Edwardian characters can escape from their books. Galsworthy's plays are called *Strife* (1909) or *Justice* (1910), as if to establish the pre-eminence of theme over character. The heroic hero is particularly suspect. He is undermined not only by Lytton Strachey in *Eminent Victorians* (begun in 1912), but by Joyce, who calls his first novel *Stephen Hero* on the analogy of the ballad 'Turpin Hero', as if to guard by awkwardness against Stephen's being thought too glibly heroic; Granville-Barker writes plays in which the heroes do not deserve the name. The Edwardian male, as he appears in the books of this time, is often passive and put upon, like Maugham's Philip in *Of Human Bondage* (published in 1915 but drafted much earlier) or James's Strether, not only because this is the period of the feminist movement, but because it is the period of the hero's subordination. Concurrently, there is a loss of interest in what the hero does for

10 Virginia Woolf, 'Modern Fiction', *Collected Essays*, II, 106.
11 Ford, *The English Novel*, 147.

a living—the emphasis comes so strongly upon their relatively disinterested mental activity that the occupations of Strether, Birkin, or Bloom become shadowy and almost nominal.

The amount of unity which the Edwardians instilled in their work is one of their extraordinary accomplishments. As Edith Wharton aggressively and seriously declared in the *Times Literary Supplement* in 1914, 'the conclusion of [a] tale should be contained in germ in its first page.' Conrad said in his preface to *The Nigger of the 'Narcissus'* that a work of art 'should carry its justification in every line.' There were occasional signs of revolt against this zealous 'desire and pursuit of the whole'. So Wells found Henry James's insistence upon what he aptly called 'continuous relevance' to be objectionable. 'The thing his novel is about is always there,' he said disapprovingly, probably remembering how Joseph Conrad had irritatingly asked several times what Wells's own novels were really *about*.[12] Wells thought himself later to be in favour of irrelevance, but he himeslf said that 'almost every sentence should have its share in the entire design,' and his best books are not thoughtlessly constructed; they are unified, as I have suggested, by the myth of selfhood.

The Edwardian aesthetic is fairly closely related to the imagist movement, or part of it. T. E. Hulme had interested Pound and others in his theory of intensive manifolds, that is, of wholes with absolutely interpenetrating parts instead of aggregates of separate elements. Hulme instructed them to place themselves 'inside the object instead of surveying it from the outside.'[13] This position was that which Yeats also insisted upon when he said that the centre of the poem was not an impersonal essence of beauty, but an actual man thinking and feeling. He threw himself into the drama because he saw in it a rejection of externality, even of scenery, and an invitation to the writer to relinquish his self. Henry James was also convinced that the 'mere muffled majesty of irresponsible "authorship"' must be eliminated, and entered the consciousness of his most sensitive characters so thoroughly as to make possible disputes over where *he* stood.[14]

What is confusing about the first imagist manifestoes is that this theory has got mixed up with another, a notion of objectivity and im-

---

[12] H. G. Wells, *Boon* (London and New York, 1915), 106, 109; *Experiment in Autobiography*, 527–8.

[13] T. E. Hulme, *Speculations*, ed. Herbert Read (London, 1949), 180–1, 213.

[14] Preface to *The Golden Bowl*, in *The Art of the Novel*, ed. R. P. Blackmur (New York, 1950), 328.

personality which, though it receives passing applause from Stephen in
A Portrait, is not Joycean or Edwardian. Most Edwardian writing is
not aloof, and the poems Pound praised for their Imagist qualities were
poems like Yeats's 'The Magi', or Joyce's 'I hear an army', in which the
writer is not at all removed from his image. Pound found a more congenial version of the Edwardian aesthetic in the vorticist movement, for
that was manifestly based upon the absorption of the artist into his
work, rather than his detachment from it. The word 'vortex' was something of an embarrassment. Pound said, with an obvious allusion to its
female symbolism, 'In decency one can only call it a vortex.' [15] But it
had the advantage of implying the death of the poet in his poem: the
ultimate arrogance of the artist is to disappear. This was the point of
view of James and of Yeats as well as of Joyce; Edwardian writers were
not much concerned with the artist as were writers of the nineties; they
were concerned only with the art. They began to put away their flowing
ties. Yeats could never understand the reluctance of some writers to let
him improve their poems for them, since to him the work was all. The
Edwardian writer is an artist not because he proclaims he is, as Wilde
did, but because his works proclaim it. There is much less time for
affectation and eccentricity, the point being to get on with the job. As
Conrad said in his preface to *The Secret Agent*, 'In the matter of all my
books I have always attended to my business. I have attended to it with
complete self-surrender.'

Having yielded up his own identity to write his work, the Edwardian wished the reader to make comparable sacrifices. The *hypocrite
lecteur* whom Baudelaire had arraigned was the reader who thought he
might observe without joining in the work of art. This was to pass
through the house like an irresponsible tenant, and the Edwardian
novelist was too good a landlord for that. The reader must become
responsible, must pay his rent. The sense of the importance of what
their books were doing, the sense that only art, working through religious
metaphor, can give life value, made the writers free to ask a great deal of
their readers, and the literature of the time moved towards greater difficulty, the revival of Donne in 1912 being one of its manifestations, or
towards greater importunacy, as in Lawrence. As Henry James remarked
to a writer who complained that a meeting of authors was dull, 'Hewlett,
we are not here to enjoy ourselves.'

It may seem that, though I have offered to exhibit two faces of

[15] Ezra Pound, *Gaudier-Brzeska* (London, 1916), 106.

Edward, I have in fact shown only one, and that one staring urgently towards the age of anxiety. Yet modern as Edwardian literature was, it was not fully modern. There was a difference in mood, which Yeats hinted at when he said that after 1900 nobody did any of the violent things they had done in the nineties. Can we not detect in this period, so distinguished in many ways, its writers so strict with themselves and with us, a sensible loss of vigour and heat? The Edwardians managed to retain much of the stability of the Victorians, but they did so only by becoming artful where their predecessors had seemed artless. The easy skill of Victorian narrative disappears, and while the Edwardians have good reasons for trying for more awesome effects, their work does not escape the charge of being self-conscious, almost *voulu*. It is the age of prefaces and of revisions. Their secular miracles, which they arranged so graciously, seem too easy now, and the modern equivalents of them, in Malamud or Bellow, for example, are deliberately wrought with far greater restraint. Writers of social protest like Galsworthy seem, as Esmé Wingfield-Stratford points out in *The Victorian Aftermath* (1934), resigned to their own helplessness. H. G. Wells, though so energetic, seems when he is not at his best too devout towards science, towards popular mechanics, and the later history of his writing of novels, which Gordon N. Ray has described, makes us wonder if even earlier he was quite so energetic as he appeared. Bennett presents his slices of life with the assurance of a good chef that life is appetizing, yet he has mastered his ingredients without much flair. *A Portrait of the Artist* is a work of genius, but wanting in gusto; and even Yeats is for much of this time more eloquent than implicated, not so much passionate as in favour of passion. Conrad achieves his effects, yet so laboriously, and with awkward narrators like Marlow who, in spite of his laudable artistic purposes, is a bit of a stick. The repetition of words and images, while helpful to the creation of unity, gives an air of pedantry to this aspiring period; the bird flies, but with leaden wings. I should like to find in George Gissing's book, *The Private Papers of Henry Ryecroft* (1903), a reflection of this diminution of vitality in a period that prided itself on its life. Gissing lived turbulently enough, but in this autobiographical fiction he is at pains to seem full of calm; a writer today might live calmly, but would want his books to be distraught.

The war, for I will not deny that it took place, made everything harder. The Edwardian confidence in artistic sensibility was broken down: the possibility of nothingness seems to replace the conviction of somethingness. Those Edwardian writers who lived through the war found stability less easy to come by. Before the war Yeats could write 'The Magi', with its longing for violence; after the war he wrote 'The Second Coming', in which violence inspires horror. Forster, who had accomplished his secular miracles rather handily in his early books, as by the trick of sending his thinner-blooded characters to lush Italy, descends lower to *A Passage to India*, where there is more brutality, and where the realizations to which he brings his personages are less ample, less reassuring. Pound, content with his troubadours before the war, turns upon himself in *Mauberley* with a strange blend of self-destruction and self-justification. Eliot, after politely mocking Edwardian politeness in 'Prufrock', becomes impolite in *The Waste Land*. Lawrence becomes strident, frantic, exhoratory, almost suffocating his own mind. Virginia Woolf, unable to find herself before the war, discovers at last a tense point round which to organize her books, and this is not so much unity as the threat of the break down of unity. Joyce, content to stay in the conscious mind in his earlier work, descends to a fiercer underworld in the *Circe* episode of *Ulysses*, where Edward VII appears, appropriately now turned to a nightmare figure babbling hysterically of 'Peace, perfect peace'. The miracle of birth was accomplished in *A Portrait of the Artist* without much resistance, but the comparable miracle in *Ulysses*, Bloom's rescue of Stephen in a world where gratuitous kindness seems out of context, is described by Joyce with great circumspection, as if humanistic miracles now embarrassed him. The religion of life keeps most of its Edwardian adherents, but it has begun to stir up its own atheists and agnostics.

II. 17

Poetic Drama and the Well-made Play*

ARTHUR MIZENER

Carleton College

IN LOUIS MACNEICE's very bad verse play entitled *Out of the Picture* there is a parody of a BBC lecture on Aristotle and The Modern Stage in which the lecturer sums up what he calls "the one and only plot of Chekhov" by saying, "To be excluded from the great city, the culture, the caviare, the interminable brilliant conversations—this was something the young men could not face. So they started shooting." Then he adds: "Now Aristotle wouldn't have liked that kind of plot. Aristotle insisted on unity and dignity. Further, Aristotle liked to know where he was. . . . But in these plays of Chekhov and many other plays which have succeeded them, who is to say? . . . [They are] terribly inconsequent; but, ladies and gentlemen, terribly true to life."

I suppose nearly everything wrong with the verse plays written by poets during the last twenty years is evident in the sprightly condescension of that passage. Yet, sadly enough, it has a kind of truth in it, not applicable, perhaps, to Chekhov but to most of the playwrights who, since William Archer's day, have concentrated on that particular conventionalized version of truth-to-life which has been current in their theatre. By now even the simplest intention beyond that leaves Wolcott Gibbs baffled and inclined to ask, in his bluff manly way, whether we do not all agree that Shakespeare or Eliot is, after all—let's be frank now fellows—an old bore.

We all know the air leaked some time ago out of the opinion that

* Read at the Institute in 1949. Published in *Institute Essays*, 1950.

The Second Mrs. Tanqueray is one of the great plays of the English theatre. No one can any longer convince himself that the well-made problem play about the soiled skirt and "a man's life" or public housing projects or what-not fulfills the serious demands of our understandings. Such plays, earnest and well-meaning as they often are, constitute for us only the staple fare of the theatre, the high-grade, book-of-the-month-club product, competent but concerned with ideas and feelings which are too near the surface to move anyone more than temporarily. "You do it," Picasso is supposed to have said, "and then some one else does it pretty." Except for Shaw and perhaps O'Neill, we have been doing it pretty in the theatre for a long time now. Our plays occasionally dress themselves up in technical devices borrowed from the experimental theatre and venture boldly into simplified weekly-news-magazine versions of the ideas of Freud or Marx or whoever happens to be the latest thing going in up-to-the-minute circles. But the technical devices fit them about as well as Macbeth's royal robes did him; and the snappy new ideas turn out to be only trick versions of the old ones.

It is impossible, I think, in the face of Saroyan's good-hearted prostitutes and Tennessee Williams' variations on *Gone with the Wind* not to sympathize with the poets who, in the thirties, came boldly into the theatre to show the old hands what was the matter with them: at least they were right that what the more or less traditional plays had to say was, however pretentious, second-hand; they knew how very mediocre the imaginations of the Elmer Rices and the Maxwell Andersons were. Because they were to this extent right, it is a real misfortune that they had almost no knowledge of how to make a play, as distinguished from a lyric poem, and that most of them were much too cocksure of themselves to think of learning.

This natural incompetence was compounded by the widespread conviction throughout all the arts that in order to do anything big you had to do it differently, experimentally, so that to their natural ignorance of the resources and limitations of the theatre these poets added a fear of doing anything in the way it had been done before, and much of their energy flowed into trying to improve what they would never understand half so well as a Pinero or a Williams, and very little of it into what the journeyman playwrights would never understand half so well as they.

Thus, after all the stew and fuss about the theatre, we are left, for the most part, with unplayable plays by genuine poets and skillfully made plays by men who are, at best, serious journalists. I suspect this difficulty exists—and this is my thesis, for what it is worth—because the drama is a far more demanding form than writers trained in the art of verse or the novel suppose, and potentially a far more eloquent one than the theatrical craftsmen know how to use.

Much of the blundering about this very simple possibility must surely be the result of that vicious term "the poetic drama." Why do we talk so solemnly about "poetic drama" and not about "poetic novel," or "poetic epic," or "poetic *Life* articles"? All the sensible meaning—as the discussion here has shown clearly—contained in that word "poetic" is taken for granted with these other forms, because all we can sensibly mean by it is that a writer has a serious imagination: we ought to mean that by drama anyway. And because the great plays of the Elizabethan theatre were written in verse, the phrase "poetic drama" is positively misleading. It makes us suppose a good deal of the time that if, like Maxwell Anderson, we do up a costumed and vulgarized piece of history real pretty in meter we have poetic drama; or to suppose with Auden and MacNeice that if we have good verse of any kind at all we have poetic drama. These suppositions are about as sensible as our thinking that we will have a poetic novel if we versify *Forever Amber* or that *Paradise Lost* is a great epic only because it is in good verse.

Richard Blackmur remarked recently that what makes *Ulysses* a fine novel is not the Homeric parallels or the fancy footwork of Joyce's verbal experiments but what he called, in a beautiful phrase, "the intransigence of Stephen." In so far as Joyce's technical facility and inventiveness are a means to the ordering and communication of that imagined substance, they are admirable: we would not have the intransigence of Stephen without them. But in so far as Joyce was a man who delighted in playing with language and, losing sight of his book's purpose, introduced into it devices which destroy its basic form, these things are only an interesting and irrelevant game. The general proposition here—that technical facility which is irrelevant to the occasion is frivolous—is commonplace enough: nothing is more familiar when it is asserted of Swinburne, for instance, or the Miltonizing poets of the eighteenth century. But something like this confusion of means and ends is the curse of the contemporary arts, so that with rare exceptions the people with genuine imaginations who have ventured into the theatre in the last hundred years have ignored the art of the theatre. And in the theatre, art—craft—is more necessary than in any of the other kinds of literature.

In what is written to be read the words are everything: they are all we have. We talk about "character" and "setting" and such things in the novel; but these are terms borrowed from the theatre and we are, whether we realize it or not, using them metaphorically when we apply them to other kinds of fictions. In the novel they are secondary things, constructions in the reader's mind which have been built up by the words and sentences and paragraphs he has read. But in the theatre this is not so. In the theatre the audience sees—though under certain con- trolled conditions which are very important—actual, three-dimensional persons moving about in an actual, three-dimensional space. I do not mean to sound here as if I were advocating that theory which holds that drama ideally approaches the condition of the ballet and that the fewer words spoken, the better "theahtah." In the drama people speak, and what they say contributes its share to the total effect, as much as does the visible interplay of concrete persons in concrete places. But even these words are heard words, spoken by particular persons, a part of them in the same way that their facial expressions, their gestures, their movements, are a part of them. I think it is possible to argue that their speech is, like the talking we do in life, the most important single means available to the dramatist for realizing his subject. Still, it is only one of his means; and the dramatist who writes only talk is creating for the stage a blind man's world. Moreover, talk is a means he cannot use without imagining it always very vividly as the speech of the character it is given to, since each character is so overwhelmingly, visibly a person on the stage.

In short, the conditions of the drama, unlike those which exist for some other kinds of fiction, are such that the integrity of the characters must be very strictly preserved. I suspect no convention ever endured very long in any theatre if it ran counter to its society's everyday criteria for determining what conduct is or is not possible for a given person. Take, for example, the soliloquy, which endured in our theatre until the end of the nineteenth century. The soliloquy is generally scorned today for the relatively superficial reason that it requires a character to talk to himself—to say aloud to himself what we suppose he would, in actual life, only think to himself. But if this convention offends against our demand for a lifelike surface, it does not offend against the fundamental requirement of the integrity of character. It is a far sounder device in the context than, say, having firmly established and differentiated type characters, such as the collection that is gathered at Wishwood in the first act of Eliot's *Family Reunion*, suddenly turn somnambulist and recite in chorus a lot of ominous and uncomplimentary notions about themselves which, given their established characters, it is impossible to believe they would ever know at all. No dramatist who understood and respected his medium would think of playing such tricks because he would realize that no one must ever say what the audience will not believe he can know.

Compare Eliot's device with the one used by Philip Barry in *Hotel Universe*. Barry is not in Eliot's class as a writer at all; but he is an intelligent and sensitive man, and a playwright who has by no means had his due, perhaps because he does not, like Williams, trick his plays out in neon lights. When he wanted to do what Eliot wanted to do, he did not make the mistake of writing a lyric and then freezing perfectly sensible characters into dummies so that they might speak it. What he did was to imagine a piece of action.

I do not know how familiar *Hotel Universe* is, so I am going to risk summarizing this piece of business. Three of the characters in the play are men who have known each other since boyhood. We see them first being very "Lost Generation"—as a matter of fact they *are* The Lost Generation, for Barry once said that the starting point of the play was the villa owned by the Gerald Murphys at Antibes where the Hemingways and the Fitzgeralds and the Dos Passoses and such people gathered so often in 1926 and 1927. As soon as Barry has completed his skillful exposition, he has two of these lifelong friends, with an actress named Lily Malone, fall into a bit of play-acting about the third, a man named Norman Rose, who has been an enormously successful businessman. It is started by Rose's getting a little pompous, like this:

NORMAN: No.—I'll tell you, Ann, here's how I see my life.
LILY: Tune in on the Norman Rose Hour.
NORMAN: —There are several angles to it: When a man decides he wants to accumulate a fortune—
TOM: It's going to be a speech.
PAT: —I can't speak to Mr. Morgan just now. Tell him I'll call him back.
TOM: —Nine-thirty A. M. The great Norman Rose enters his office—(*He goes to the table . . . Lily knocks three times upon her book. Tom turns.*) Who's there?
LILY: It's me, Mr. Rose, Little Lily Malone. You know *me*.
TOM: (*Wearily*) Come in, come in! (*Lily enters the great man's office.*)
LILY: —A gentleman to see you, sir.
TOM: I don't like gentlemen. It's ladies I like.—Come closer, Miss Malone. (*Lily stiffens.*)
LILY: —A Mr. Patrick Farley. Morgan and Company. Sleighs and Violins Mended.

TOM: Show him in.

LILY: —Mr. Rose will see you now, Mr. Farley. (*Pat comes in. Lily announces him:*) Mr. Farley, Mr. Rose.—I know you'll like each other. (*Lily retires. Tom indicates a chair. Pat seats himself.*)

TOM: Well, Farley, what is it?

PAT: It's just everything, Doctor. I feel awful.

A moment later Farley is asking Rose about a shipment of ear-marked gold for Sweden. "It's you who are bluffing, Rose," he says. "What *is* ear-marked gold?"

TOM: (*confused*) I—why, it's—I'm not sure, but I *think* it's—

PAT: We have no place here for men who are not sure. . . .

TOM: But who—who are you? (*Pat rises, opens his coat, and points to his badge.*)

PAT: The Chairman of your Board of Directors. (*Tom covers his face. Pat speaks quietly:*) Good afternoon, Mr. Rose.

When this little performance is completed Rose himself laughs and says, "All right! I'll resign!" and one of the women who has been watching says: "It was lovely! Do another—" But Tom's wife says, "No, they mustn't. I'm always afraid they'll slip over the line and turn into the people they're pretending to be." Apart from the bearing this little show has on the underlying natures of the characters involved—and it is considerable—Barry has established for us the idea that such performances are the family joke of the group. Thus, when he wants to show us the inner meaning of these people, to have them say the kind of thing they would not ordinarily say to one another, he is able to have the three men begin to play they are boys together again and slip imperceptibly over the line. In this way, without violating the integrity of their characters, they reveal to us their buried lives.

The poet-playwrights of the thirties not only ignored the basic necessity of maintaining the integrity of their characters. They also ignored the conventions of the drama of their time. Yet the formal conventions are far more important in the drama than in any other kind of fiction. They are important, to be sure, in all kinds. But they are particularly important in those directed to an audience which is not pre-selected, in those, that is, which are "popular" as the theatre is. And they are superlatively important in one which depends on the audience's direct understanding, where the audience cannot go back and mull or read over what was not, at least narrative-wise, clear the first time.

No doubt it is true that such conventions as the chorus in the Greek theatre or the indeterminate stage in the Elizabethan had advantages not provided for our dramatists, and there is, of course, no reason why they should not, in their time and place, have worked just as well as any other conventions; in fact there is every reason to suppose they did. But that doesn't mean they do now; because the one necessary characteristic of a convention is that it should be conventional—that is, like good conventions in any sphere, accepted habitually and unself-consciously. The conventions of theatres not our own make even a learned audience self-conscious, like an anthropologist trying to feel at home on a social occasion in a primitive tribe whose culture he has painstakingly studied.

This is no place to go into the etiology of the conventions of our theatre, even if I knew enough to do so, but it is obvious that there is an important connection between the kind of conventions which become established in a theatre and the culture of the society that theatre serves. The mechanical images which are scattered like autumn leaves through William Archer's *The Old Drama and the New* show clearly enough the connection between the rise of our kind of play, for instance, and the general concern in our society for somewhat mechanical cause-and-effect explanations of experience. I suspect a study of this relationship would show that to be accepted by an audience any set of conventions must circumvent literal reality in the same way the common imagination of its age does so. If this is true, no convention, however ingenious and fruitful, which circumvents literal reality in some other age's way will be viable in our theatre. Theatrical conventions are not, any more than the conventions in terms of which organized society exists, a formal contract. Once established, however, they work like a kind of contract between the imaginations of playwright and audience, and if the playwright evades his contractual obligations, the audience's imaginations are likely to walk out on him.

You cannot, of course, have drama at all without conventions. They allow the playwright to save time in an art where time is immeasurably precious, so that, for instance, a slight pause and a long look between hero and heroine can spare him the time-consuming and—for everyone except the principals—dull process which falling in love so often actually is. And they allow a piece of action to be cleared of all the muddying contingency of real experience and concentrated, so that it can take on meanings larger than those of unordered experience. The real problem is not conventions as such or the degree of artificiality they involve; the real problem is the conditions in which the audience will fulfill its contractual obligation and suspend without self-consciousness its disbelief. A set of conventions may be—in Kenneth Burke's terminology—"stretched"; it may be manipulated in all sorts of new ways. But it must be coherent. We must not be made conscious of the artificiality of a set of conventions by the insertion among them of one devised for different imaginative conditions; and the basic imaginative assumption of the set as a whole must not be violated by the way they are handled.

All this was obvious to a dramatist like Pinero; a man does not write twenty-seven apprentice plays, as Pinero did, without learning his trade. It has not been clear at all to the poet-playwrights of our time who refuse to recognize that a trade exists. Pinero's deficiencies were deficiencies of the understanding. But such understanding as he had he embodied with great skill in a form which is still the form of our theatre. He was, if a minor one, still a genuine poet of the drama, in the only meaningful sense of the word. Within his limits, he even understood the kind of verbal effects required by his theatre. "And besides," says Aubrey Tanqueray to Drummle, "yours is the way of the world."

DRUMMLE: My dear Aubrey, I *live* in the world.
AUBREY: The name we give our little parish of St. James.
DRUMMLE: (*Laying a hand on Aubrey's shoulder*) And are you quite prepared, my friend, to forfeit the esteem of your little parish?

The deficiency of this is not in art but in imaginative grasp.

It was this imaginative grasp that Shaw had, and he provides a fine illustration of "poetic drama" for our theatre. There is nothing conventional about Shaw's imagination; its complications are in fact very great and I am not sure he is not the most difficult writer of our time. But in the dramatic sense of the word he was thoroughly conventional because he knew that you cannot destroy the means your form provides for communication and still expect it to communicate, any more than you can destroy the conventions of language itself and expect it to work for you.

It is fascinating to compare Shaw's uses of the familiar resources of his theatre with those of merely workmanlike playwrights such as Pinero. When, at the end of Act III of *The Notorious Mrs. Ebbsmith*, the curtain comes down on the tableau of Agnes kneeling before the stove with the charred Bible clutched to her bosom and Gertrude and Amos watching her in astonishment, Pinero has summed up in a frozen piece of action all he wants to say about Agnes' character and its rela-

tions to the larger ideas of the play. Thanks to his skill in using the conventional act-ending of our kind of play, he has been able to give the
maximum dramatic focus to his understanding. But what he understands is comparatively little.

Think of that moment at the end of Scene IV in *St. Joan*, where
Shaw uses the same conventional act-ending. We have listened to Warwick and Cauchon discussing the case of Joan from their different points
of view. These points of view are sharply defined as those of the nobility
and the church—Shaw is even capable of a little joke about the patness
of their formulations in now familiar historical terms. Yet so wonderful
is his power of visualizing any idea whatsover in terms of the character
who speaks it, that we feel each speech first as a recognizable product
of the speaker's character and only after that as a general idea. The
scene ends with Warwick's rising, politely but authoritatively. "My
Lord," he says to Cauchon: "we seem to be agreed."

CAUCHON: (*Rising also, but in protest*) I will not imperil my soul. I will
uphold the justice of the Church. I will strive to the utmost for this
woman's salvation.
WARWICK: I am sorry for the poor girl. I hate these severities. I will spare
her if I can.
THE CHAPLAIN: (*Implacably*) I would burn her with my own hands.
CAUCHON: (*Blessing him*) Sancta simplicitas!

And the curtain descends on the tableau. It is a magnificent though
entirely conventional moment—perhaps I ought properly to say, *because* entirely conventional. Without stepping outside the habitual language of its theatre, it even gets most of the advantages of verse. Cauchon and Warwick each speak three declarative sentences which are
parallel in structure and three-stressed. De Stogumber caps their exchange with one more such sentence and Cauchon rounds off the pattern with his comment, which—counting the necessary pause before it
—is also three-stressed.

But what is far more important than the poetry of the language is
the poetry of the action, the amazing variety of implication and irony
within the visually simple pattern of movement. Warwick rises, suavely,
a little wearily, Cauchon's answering movement is polite, too, but almost
violent with controlled indignation; Warwick faces this indignation with
the perfect self-possession of his own sophisticated sincerity. And then
de Stogumber erupts beside them with the uncontrolled and comically
naive violence of his conviction. Each movement, with its accompany-

ing speech, is a comment on all the others, and the Bishop's gesture applies to all three of them. It is beautifully simple and clear, because it is a moment perfectly realized in terms of the theatre with which its audience is completely at ease.

Yet it is a moment which echoes in the imagination because the implications Shaw has embodied in it are so wonderfully varied and penetrating. We can say, of course, that both Warwick and Cauchon are hypocrites, intent on maintaining the power of their orders and pretending otherwise only for appearance's sake; we will then add that de Stogumber exposes their real purpose and that Cauchon's blessing is a sarcastic comment on that exposure. We will be right so far as we go. But we have seen also that Cauchon is a very intelligent man and a deeply sincere Christian, and that he means everything he says about saving Joan. We know too that Warwick is, in his skeptical and cultured way, a very humane man who cannnot endure to watch a heretic burning. Their actions display all the mixed motives of men caught between conviction and practical necessity. For them both, in their different ways, de Stogumber's attitude is the product of stupidity and lack of imagination. But they are too intelligent not to recognize how closely it touches them both. Cauchon's blessing states something of all this for them. But it would be a bold man who would say how much of the irony is a thing the characters themselves are to be thought of as understanding and meaning and how much of it a thing that exists, as it were unbeknownst to them, between play and audience. It would be an even bolder man who would say how the interanimating meanings of this moment add up. It is as impossible to answer the examination question about "what Shaw means" in any serious way as it is to answer that question about any great poet.

Shaw's plays are, in one sense, easy. All their elaborate and necessary artificiality is of a kind which is so familiar that we do not feel it as artificial, and no self-consciousness about means intrudes between us and the action of the play. We are watching the kind of characters we have agreed for decades to think real, moving about familiar sets in the ordinary stage way, and talking an imperceptibly heightened and lovely version of what we have agreed to accept as the real language of men. In another sense, however, Shaw's work has—again like the work of all great poets—the inexhaustible fascination of thought and feeling dramatically suspended in a controlled medium. Meaning thus suspended is always in significant motion and never exists in the fixed relations of exposition and never eventuates in fixed conclusions. Because it is thus in motion it can never be abstracted for translation into other terms; and because it is held within a controlled medium, every great moment in the play echoes the whole play, exactly as do the great moments in a poem. Shaw's great plays are dramatically conventional not only in detail but also as wholes. If a play starts with characters conventionally defined and related to one another in action, it ends by being a completed action. Even Auden, after fiddling around with scenes quite unrelated to his chosen action and long choruses of beautiful and completely undramatic verse to be delivered by Ignoto, eventually brings Alan and Francis back to Pressan Ambo to give the best ending he can to an action which was posited in the first scene but never really begun.

What a completed action looks like in our theatre is, I think, clear from *Heartbreak House*. Here is the familiar drawing room of the English country house inhabited by the cultivated English ladies and gentlemen, who are being visited by a few relatives and friends. The surface action of the play appears to move rather loosely through the familiar series of drawing-room conversations—the surface looseness is about the only important result of Chekhov's much talked-of influence. Only, without violating these conventional elements, Shaw has stretched them until they serve the complex purposes of his imagination, has made them a full and evocative symbol of the world of his time which exposes itself to us bit by bit as I suppose the world of reality would expose itself if we were wise enough and the world well enough made.

He has made the country-house drawing room an old-fashioned ship under at least the nominal command of an eccentric and very old captain, sailing, as we quickly realize, God knows where. The ladies and gentlemen, while beautifully realized as ladies and gentlemen, are something more, something more at which their names hint from the beginning: Captain Shotover, Mazzini Dunn, Ariadne Utterword, Hesione and Hector—not, we notice, Heracles—Hushabye. There is a small drama in the play of ironies between each of these names and the character of the person who possesses it.

Shaw begins with a conventional situation. A pretty and apparently simple girl named Ellie Dunn is about to marry a middle-aged capitalist named Mangan because she believes he has, out of kindness, saved her father's business career. Hesione Hushabye, in the play's first extended scene, struggles to make Ellie see that this pious intention is wicked, because she is not marrying for love. She is in love, as she gradually admits, with a romantic and—to everyone but her—quite implausible stranger who calls himself Marcus Darnley. When none other than this gentleman himself enters, as patly at the clown in the old comedy, and turns out to be Hesione's husband, Ellie's romantic heart breaks. She signals the fact by saying, "Damn!" She is damning neither some one else nor fate but, as she says, herself "for being such a fool" and letting herself "be taken in so." A new, unexpected, and admirable layer of her nature has been exposed by the scene.

In this same way each of the characters is presented and forced to expose a new layer of understanding through a series of scenes which emerge from one another so plausibly and with such a variety and range of revealed meaning that it is as difficult to plot their pattern as it is not to feel their beautiful articulation. As soon as the characters have all been established at a new level of understanding, Shaw repeats the process by recombining them in another series of conversations where the new understanding of each is the instrument for uncovering in another a deeper layer of his nature. The process goes on until everyone has been plumbed to the bottom. "In this house," as Hector puts it, "We know all the poses; our game is to find out the man under the pose." Captain Shotover exposes Mangan's moving-picture conception of himself as a man of force and a husband for Ellie, only to have it emerge that Mangan, having fallen in love with Hesione, does not want to marry Ellie; whereas Ellie, disillusioned about romantic love and thrown back on that practical view of marriage which everyone in Shaw can always espouse so brilliantly, is prepared not only to marry Mangan but to blackmail him into marrying her. Her lack of scruple so exasperates Mangan that he tells her the real motive for his treatment of her father. But he only succeeds in convincing Ellie that she should marry him and recover the money Mangan stole from her father. Ellie goes from this astonishing triumph over Mangan to the exposure of the soft spot in Hesione's romantic view of marriage, so that Hesione is, in her turn, forced to a deeper understanding.

All this is, if you will, merely the stock action of drawing-room comedy, the clever shifting of a set of characters through all the possible permutations of relationship. It is. But because of what the characters are and what they come to understand, the issues involved are the very largest. In this way the play is built up, until the action implicit in its initial situation has completed itself. By its end each important charac-ter—and therefore most of the important attitudes of our time—has clashed with every other. None triumphs—"What did you expect," as Captain Shotover says to Ellie, "a Savior?" On the contrary; because Shaw can see everything there is to be said for as well as against each character, we have been shown the surprising but convincing wisdom of the stupid people like Mazzini Dunn and Lady Utterword and the stupidity of the clever people like Hesione and Hector. Even Captain Shotover, the old, powerful King Lear of the play, has been seduced by the happiness of old age, rest. Then Ellie Dunn says: "There seems to be nothing real in the world except my father and Shakespeare. Marcus's tigers are false; Mr. Mangan's millions are false; there is nothing real or strong about Hesione but her beautiful hair; and Lady Utterword is too pretty to be real. The one thing that was left me was the Captain's seventh degree of concentration; and that turns out to be—" and Captain Shotover says: "Rum."

We have been taken down to the bedrock of these people who so visibly represent—without ceasing to be their particular, individual selves —the possible attitudes in our world, and we have been shown that they are all, even Captain Shotover, helpless and defeated. The best of them has nothing finally to suggest but courage. Shaw closes the play with one of his wonderful tableau curtains. The thunder of the air raid fades into the distance, and the two practical men of business—Mangan and the burglar—are dead, because they had the selfishness and foresight and lack of honor to hide in a cave which, for all their selfish foresight, they did not know contained thirty pounds of dynamite. "Turn in all hands," says Captain Shotover. "The ship is safe"—at least for the moment it is. And he sits down and goes to sleep. But neither Hesione nor Ellie is that old or that capable of irony. "What a glorious experience!" says Hesione, "I hope they'll come again tomorrow night." And Ellie adds: "Oh, I hope so." For a moment they have all lived, as Captain Shotover had lived on his bridge in a typhoon, in the midst of "hardship, danger, horror, and death, that I might feel the life in me more intensely." Their courage will not save them, as Captain Shotover tells them, but it shows that their souls are still alive. It will not save them because there is no one on the bridge of their ship, really. "The Captain is in his bunk drinking bottled ditchwater; and the crew is gambling in the forecastle. She will strike and sink and split," says Captain Shotover. "Do you think the laws of God will be suspended in favor of England because you were born in it?"

It is a wonderful moment. Shaw has imagined a final event which

suggests, visually and aurally, England's striking and sinking and split-
ting; it is also an event which allows each character an opportunity to
sum up himself and his attitude by his response to a moment of violence
and danger. They all do so. Shaw knows just how they will all act, from
Hector with his romantic and despairing courage, through Lady Utterword who cannot imagine the governor's wife in the cellars with the
servants, and Mazzini, the efficient and wholly mistaken subordinate
officer of society, to Ellie who thinks the thunder of exploding bombs
is like Beethoven—which is always an important comparison for Shaw.
They all show some virtue: even Boss Mangan shows that enlightened
self-interest which Shaw, much as he hates its social results, has always
been willing to recognize is effective in most ordinary situations—such
situations, for instance, as Undershaft had to face. The terrible question
is whether, as Captain Shotover put it earlier, any one of them knows
his business. When the curtain finally comes down with Ellie "radiant
at the prospect" of further Beethoven, Randall the Rotter manages to
steady his lips enough to play "Keep the Home Fires Burning" on his
flute—burning with both their courage and their destruction.

This is poetic drama of a very high order, because an imagination
of great range and depth has found its expression completely within the
conventions of its form.

II. 18

EXCURSUS: Poetry in the Theatre and Poetry of the Theatre: Cocteau's *Infernal Machine**

FRANCIS FERGUSSON

Princeton University

THE QUESTION of poetic drama—its possibility in our time—is perhaps *the* question of the contemporary theatre. There is no better way to see into the nature and the limitations of the theatre as we know it, then to ask the perennial question, Why don't we have a living poetic drama?

But this question has occupied some of the best minds of our time and has received a vast variety of answers. It would take a book, at the very least, to handle the matter at all adequately. In a brief paper one can do no more than suggest one approach—expound a sample, more or less arbitrarily chosen from among many—of the attempt to make a modern poetic drama. I have chosen Cocteau's *Infernal Machine* for this purpose. But first of all, I should give a word of explanation of this choice—why Cocteau, who did not even write his play in verse?

When we talk about modern poetic drama in English we think of the long line of poets, beginning with Shelley and Coleridge, and continuing right up to Yeats and Eliot, who have aspired more or less in vain to the stage. But on the continent the picture is quite different.

* Read at the Institute in 1949. Published in *Institute Essays*, 1950.

Ibsen and Wagner, Chekhov and Pirandello, Cocteau and Stravinski and Lorca—one can think of many writers who worked directly for the stage and who produced works, whether in verse or not, which could in some sense be called poetic drama and which are certainly "poetic" in the widest meaning of the term. There is no question that they produced viable theatrical pieces, while the work of poets writing in English for the stage is all too likely to be unstageable. The fact is that on the continent the idea of the theatre is even yet not quite lost. The state-supported theatres, the repertory theatres and art theatres, have kept the ancient art of drama alive and provided the means which poets of the theatre would require. But in English-speaking countries the idea of a theatre has succumbed, except for a few undernourished little theatres, to the stereotypes and the mass-production methods of the entertainment industry. In the shallow medium of our commercialized entertainment the poet is lost, however true his inspiration or authentic his dramatic talent.

It is for this reason, I think, that contemporary poets in English who wish to write for the stage so often look to the continent for their models of dramatic form—and especially they look to Paris in the twenties, Paris between the Wars; and above all to Jean Cocteau who was one of the leaders of that Paris Theatre. I am thinking of Eliot, from *Sweeney Agonistes* to *Murder in the Cathedral*; of the later Yeats —the Yeats of *Plays for Dancers*; of Thornton Wilder, e.e.cummings, the Virgil Thompson–Gertrude Stein operas; of the ballet. It is probable that the theatrical dexterity of these more or less poetic theatre-works is largely due to the influence of the Paris Theatre, and, as I say, especially to Cocteau. In other words it is certain that Cocteau is one of the chief sources of contemporary theatre poetry, or poetry in the theatre, even in English.

COCTEAU'S GROWTH; HIS NOTION OF THEATRE POETRY

When Cocteau started to write in Paris just after World War I, he found artists from all over Europe gathered there; and he found a theatrical life nourished from Russia, Italy, Germany, Sweden, as well as a fairly lively native theatre. Copeau's Théâtre du Vieux Colombier for instance, had been in existence since 1912. Paris in the twenties still looks fabulous to us: Bergson and Valéry, Joyce and Picasso and Stravinski; Pirandello and the Moscow Art Theatre, Milhaud and Gide and

Maritain and Ezra Pound—if we think over some of the names associated with that time and place, we can see very clearly what an impressive effort was being made, in the center of Europe, to focus and revive the culture which had been so shaken by the war. If there was to be a favorable opportunity in our time to build a poetic drama, it should have been there and then, where the most enlightened audience and greatest talent were concentrated.

When Cocteau began to work, his immediate allies were the young French musicians who were to be called *les six*, a few painters, and the Swedish and Russian Ballets. The collection of his early critical writings, *The Call to Order*, throws a great deal of light upon his labors in this period. He was trying to sort out the extremely rich influences which bore upon him; and to select the elements of a contemporary, and *French*, theatre poetry.

In very general terms, I think one may say that he was trying to fuse two different traditions, one ancient, the other modern. What I call the ancient tradition was that of myth, of ritual, and of primitive or folk art. What I call the modern tradition was French—that classical spirit of intelligence, wit, measure and proportion, which the French are supposed to have at their best—especially the French since Racine and Molière. The formula which Cocteau invented to describe the fusion of these two strands was *une poésie de tous les jours*—an everyday poetry. He was looking for a dramatic or theatrical art which should be poetic as myth, ritual, and the inspired clowning of the Fratellinis is poetic—and yet at the same time acceptable to the shrewd and skeptical Parisians in their most alert moments and as part of their daily lives, like red wine, for instance, as an indispensable part of the diet. He wanted to acclimatize mythopoeia in the most up-to-date, rational, and disillusioned of modern commercial cities.

You will I am sure remember that during this period many other artists were trying to nourish themselves upon myth, upon ritual, and upon primitive and popular forms of art. The painters were studying African and South Pacific sculpture; Stravinski was doing *Petrouchka*, *Les Noces*, and *Sacre du printemps*; Eliot was writing *The Waste Land*; Joyce was between *Ulysses* and *Finnegan's Wake*. When Cocteau and his friends began, most of this work was still to come; Cocteau himself was one of the pioneers in the movement. When he looked around for clues to the ancient and perennial theatre art he was seeking, forms which he might imitate or adapt, he found, not the works I have just mentioned, but Wagner and the all-pervasive Wagnerian influence.

Wagner was in a sense a forerunner of this whole movement. He had made use of myth in his operas, elaborated a whole theory of mythic drama, and worked out a singularly potent poetic theatrical form in the very heydey of bourgeois positivism. Cocteau remembered that Baudelaire had greeted Wagner as an ally against the Parisian Philistines of his day. Baudelaire's studies of Wagner remain one of the fundamental documents for any modern theory of poetic drama. Nevertheless Cocteau and his friends found Wagner extremely unsympathetic. The Parisians in Cocteau's day, like the rest of the world, had learned to accept and even to depend on Wagner, as an indulgence whether hypnosis or drug. They had the bad habit of swooning when they heard that kind of music, and this prevented them from listening to the young French composers who were trying to speak to them in their alert, critical, and wakeful moments. Thus for Cocteau and his friends, the Wagnerian taste or habit of mind became the great enemy, in spite of their respect for Wagner's achievement. They saw Wagnerianism as an alien mode of awareness which was impeding the development of native French forms of art. The Wagnerian tradition, Cocteau says in *The Call to Order,* is like "a long funeral procession which prevents me from crossing the street to get home." Probably he felt in Wagner's magic the potent elements which the Nazis were so soon to use for their own purposes—drowning not only the French spirit but the physical life of France also.

However that may be, Cocteau developed his own conception of poetic drama, as it were, in answer to Wagner's. He too wanted to tap the ancient sources of myth and ritual, but without resorting to religiosity, hypnosis, or morose daydreaming. He wanted to bring mythopoeia and some of the ancient myths themselves into the center of the faithless, nimble, modern city—but he sought to establish them there by the clarity and integrity of art.

The Call to Order is a collection of working notes and critical *obiter dicta* from the very beginning of Cocteau's career, between 1918 and 1926. *The Infernal Machine* was published in 1934; and yet that play seems to be exactly the poetic drama which he had planned and foreseen fifteen years earlier. It presents a very ancient myth, the myth of Oedipus, not as a joke, but as a perennial source of insight into human destiny. Yet at the same time the play is addressed to the most advanced, cynical, and even *fashionable* mind of contemporary Paris. It is at one and the same time chic and timeless—rather like the paintings of Picasso's classic period, or his illustrations for Ovid. If one were to try to describe it briefly, one might say it shows the myth behind the modern city: both the mysterious fate of Oedipus and the bright metropolitan intrigues for pleasure and power which go on forever. To have achieved such a fusion of contradictory elements is, of course, an extraordinary feat of virtuosity. And therefore this play illustrates, from one point of view at least, *the* problem of modern poetic drama: that of presentation on the public stage, at a time when poetry has lost almost all public status.

After this prolonged introduction, I wish to look briefly at the play itself, in order to illustrate more concretely what I mean.

The Play: The Myth Behind the Modern City

The story of *The Infernal Machine* is the same as that of Sophocles' tragedy, *Oedipus the King*. Before the curtain goes up, a voice reminds us of the main facts.

Jocasta, Queen of Thebes, was told by the oracle of Apollo that her infant son Oedipus would grow up to murder his father and marry his mother. To avoid this terrible fatality she has the infant exposed on Mt. Kitharon with his feet pierced. But a shepherd finds him on the mountain and saves him, and eventually the young Oedipus makes his way to Corinth, where the childless king and queen adopt him as their son. He is brought up to think he is really their son; but in due time he hears the oracle, and to escape his fate he leaves Corinth. At a place where three roads cross, he meets an old man with an escort; gets into a dispute, and kills him. The old man is, of course, his own father Laius. Oedipus continues his journey, and reaches Thebes, where he finds the Sphinx preying on the city. He solves the riddle of the Sphinx and like other young men who make good, marries the boss's daughter, the widowed Queen Jocasta, his own mother. They rule prosperously for years and raise a family; but at last, when Thebes is suffering under the plague, the fate of Oedipus overtakes him. The oracle reports that the plague is sent by the gods, who are angry because Laius's slayer was never found and punished. Oedipus discovers his own identity and his own guilt—but thereby becomes once more, and in a new way, the savior of the city.

Such are the facts, in Cocteau as in Sophocles. But the question is how Cocteau presents them. What attitudes, what dramatic and theatrical forms does he find to bring the ancient tale alive in our time?

His dramaturgy is utterly unlike Sophocles's; he presents *both* the mythic tale, and, as it were, the feel, or texture, of contemporary life, in which no myth is supposed to have any meaning.

When the curtain goes up we see the stage hung with nocturnal drapes, as Cocteau calls them; in the center of the stage there is a lighted platform, set to represent the city wall of Thebes. The play is in four acts, and each act is set upon that lighted platform. Everything that occurs in the set on the lighted platform is in the easy, agile style of the best sophisticated modern comedy—Giraudoux's *Amphitryon*, or the acting of Guitry. In other words Cocteau tells the story in the foreground in a way that his blasé boulevard audience will accept. Thus he achieves the "everyday" part of his formula for "everyday poetry." But the tinkling modern intrigue is itself placed in a wider and darker setting represented by the nocturnal curtains—and in this vaster surrounding area the cruel machine of the gods, Oedipus's fate, is slowly unrolled, almost without the main actors being aware of it at all. Thus the "poetry" part of the formula is ironically hidden; it is to be found in the background, and in the mysterious relation between the hidden shape of the myth and the visible shape of Oedipus's ambitious career.

The first scene on the lighted platform represents the city wall of Thebes. It is the night when Oedipus is approaching the city. Two young soldiers are on guard. They have seen Laius's ghost, who is trying to warn Jocasta not to receive Oedipus when he comes. Queen Jocasta herself has heard rumors of this ghost, and arrives with the high priest Tiresias to investigate. But the ghost cannot appear to Jocasta; he can appear only to the naive, "the innocent, the pure in heart," such as the young soldiers; and Jocasta departs none the wiser.

The second scene shows the suburbs of Thebes, where the Sphinx lies in wait for her prey. Occurring at the same time as the first act, it discloses Oedipus's interview with the Sphinx. The Sphinx is not only a goddess but a very mortal woman, who falls in love with Oedipus and lets him guess her riddle in the hope that he will fall in love with her. But he is more interested in his career than in love; he takes her mortal remains to town as a proof of his victory, while she departs to the realm of the gods, thoroughly disgusted with mortals. She is willing to let him get away with his heroic pretenses because she sees the terrible fate in store for him.

In both of these scenes the most important characters—Jocasta in the first and Oedipus in the second—are unaware of their fate. It is separated from them as by a very thin curtain; they *almost* see what they are doing, but not quite. Moreover, in both scenes the characters and the dialogue are felt as modern, like the scandals in the morning paper.

In the first scene, for instance, Cocteau gives us the atmosphere of Thebes by means of the slangy gossip of the two soldiers. The soldiers, exactly like any GIs, are fed up with military service and especially with the brass hat who commands them. We hear the music, hot or blue, from the cafés and cheap night clubs of the popular quarter, where the people are trying to forget the rising prices, the falling employment, and the threats of war or revolution. We gather that the authorities do not know how to deal with the Sphinx. To explain their failure there are rumors of bribery, corruption and scandal in high places. In other words, Thebes is wholly familiar and acceptable to our worldly under-standing—it might be any demoralized modern Mediterranean city of our time or any time. In this atmosphere even the Sphinx and the ghost of Laius are scarcely more surprising or significant than our more com-monplace public nightmares. When Jocasta arrives with Tiresias to find out what all this talk of a ghost is about, she, too, is sharply modern: she speaks, Cocteau tells us, with the insolent accent of international royalty. He might have been thinking of Queen Marie of Roumania, or any other Elsa Maxwell character from café society. Jocasta is full of fore-bodings; she is nervous and overwrought; she complains about every-thing—but she does not have the naïveté or the "purity of heart" to grasp her real situation, or to see the ghost which appeared to the soldiers.

In the second act the young Oedipus is also a modern portrait, almost a candid-camera picture in the style of Guitry or Noel Coward. He is an ambitious and worldly young Latin—he might be the winner of a bicycle marathon or a politician who managed to stabilize the franc for a day. It is inevitable that he and Jocasta should get together—two shallow careerists, seekers after pleasure and power. The third scene shows their wedding night. It is set in the royal bedroom, and beside the royal bed is the crib which Jocasta kept as a memento of her lost son. In this scene the tenuous curtain of blindness which keeps them from seeing what they are doing is at its thinnest. But they are tired after the ceremonies of the coronation and the marriage; and they proceed sleepwalking toward the fated consummation.

In these first three acts of his play, Cocteau keeps completely separate the mythic fate of Oedipus and the literal story of his undoing, in so far as Oedipus and Jocasta themselves are concerned. The audience is aware of the fact that the terrible machine of the gods is slowly unwinding in the surrounding darkness; but the audience also sees that the victims are winning their victories and building their careers in total ignorance of it. In this respect the plan of *The Infernal Machine* resembles that of Joyce's *Ulysses.* Joyce also shows the lives of the people of a modern city in the form of an ancient legend which they are quite unaware of. Bloom wanders through his Dublin life according to an abstract scheme like that of the Odyssey; the reader sees this, but Bloom does not. The audience of *The Infernal Machine* sees Oedipus both as a contemporary politician and as the character in the myth. But at this point the resemblance between Cocteau's play and Joyce's novel ends. For Cocteau proposes to bring the two levels sharply together— to confront the city with the myth, and the myth with the city. This he proceeds to do in the fourth and last act.

We have been prepared all along for the sudden shift in point of view—for the peripety and epiphany of the last act. The naive soldiers saw Laius's ghost, though Jocasta did not. In the second scene the Sphinx saw what was happening to Oedipus, though he did not. And on the wedding night, Tiresias almost guessed who Oedipus was, though the bride and groom themselves could not quite make it out. Moreover, at the beginning of the play, and at the beginning of each of the first three acts, a Voice bids us relish the perfection of the machine which the gods have devised to destroy a mortal. The emphasis is on mortal stupidity and upon the cruelty of the gods. But before the last act, the Voice reminds us of a different meaning in these events; the Voice makes the following proclamation: "After false happiness, the king will learn real unhappiness: the true ritual, which will make out of this playing-card king in the hands of the cruel gods, at long last, a man."

The fourth act, unlike the other three, follows fairly closely the order of events in Sophocles's tragedy. Oedipus feels, like an unsuccessful bluffer in poker, that the jig is up; he receives the evidence of the messenger and the old shepherd which unmistakeably reveals him as his mother's husband and his father's killer. Tiresias, who had half-guessed the truth all along, watches this terrible dénouement and explains it to Creon and for the audience. When Oedipus gets the final piece of evidence which convicts him, he runs off to find Jocasta. Tiresias tells Creon, "Do not budge. A storm is coming up from the bottom of time.

The lightning will strike this man; and I ask you, Creon, let it follow its whim; wait without moving; interfere with nothing." As in the Sophoclean tragedy, Jocasta kills herself and Oedipus puts out his eyes, while their bewildered child Antigone tries to understand. Cocteau, like Sophocles, imagines these horrors with great intimacy, sparing nothing. But Cocteau brings the play to an end on a different note. In Sophocles thé final pathos and enlightenment of Oedipus is presented in a series of steps, and by the time we finally see him blind at the end, the chorus has pretty well digested, or at least accepted, the tragic and purgatorial meaning of it all. But Cocteau ends the play with a *coup de théâtre*, a spectacular effect, a piece of theatrical sleight-of-hand, which visibly presents the tragic paradox on which the whole play is based.

The dead Jocasta appears to Oedipus, who is blind and can therefore see—but she appears not as the corrupt queen and dishonored wife of the sordid tale, but as a sort of timeless mother. "Yes, my child," she says to Oedipus, "my little son. . . . Things which seem abominable to human beings—if you only knew how unimportant they are in the realm where I am dwelling." The blind Oedipus, the child Antigone, and the ghostly Jocasta depart on their endless journey. Creon can see Oedipus and Antigone, if not Jocasta, and he asks Tiresias, "To whom do they belong now?" to which Tiresias replies, "To the people, to the poets, to the pure in heart." "But who," asks Creon, "will take care of them?" To which Tiresias replies, "La Gloire"—glory, or renown.

The effect is to remind us, all of a sudden, that Oedipus, Jocasta, Antigone, are not only literal people as we know people, but legends, figures in a timeless myth. We had in a sense known this all along; but during the first three acts we forgot it—we laughed at Oedipus's youthful vanity, grinned with cynical understanding when we saw his shallow ambition, his bounder-like opportunism. Now he and Jocasta are safe from our irony—as poetry and myth are safe—both more human and less human than the intriguing puppets which we found so familiar in the first three acts.

Cocteau, I think, must have learned a great deal from Pirandello before he wrote this play. The final effect, when Oepidus and Jocasta are suddenly taken up into the legend, like saints receiving the stigmata, is very much like the effect Pirandello contrives for his six characters in search of an author. When the six characters first appear on the stage they have some of the quality of masks, of the achieved and quiet work of art; when they fight with each other about their story, they are all too sharply human; and when they leave at the end, their tragic procession is like the procession of Oedipus, Jocasta, and Antigone—a steady image in the mind's eye, and in the light of the stage, of the tragic human condition in general: they have the eternity, if not of heaven, at least of the poetic image.

Moreover the paradox on which the tragedy is based is very much like Pirandello's favorite paradox—the contradiction between myth or poetry on one side, and the meaningless disorder of contemporary lives on the other. We live in two incommensurable worlds, neither of which we can do without—that of myth-making, and that of literal, unrelated, and therefore meaningless facts.

I do not mean to say that this is the only way to understand tragedy. On the contrary, Pirandello and Cocteau write a particular *kind* of tragedy, which is much more closely akin to the Baroque than it is either to Sophoclean or Shakespearean tragedy. Both of these authors may seem to us artificial; certainly they are Latin, rationalistic, deflated; they work with brilliant images, clear and distinct ideas, sharp contrasts, strong chiaroscuro. If we are used to Shakespeare, the plays of Cocteau like those of Pirandello may seem arbitrary and invented to us,

Music and philosophy, curiosity,
The purple bullfinch in the lilac tree,

as Eliot's Thomas of Canterbury says rather scornfully of the refined pleasures of the mind. I do not say that we could ever succeed in making that kind of modernized Baroque tragedy in English—I don't think it fits the genius of our language, or our peculiar habits of mind.

Nevertheless, as I said at the beginning of this paper, many fine playwrights and poets, writing in English, have learned from Cocteau; and I believe that there is much more still to be learned from him, short of direct imitation, about poetic drama in our time. I wish to conclude these remarks with two observations on the dramaturgy of *The Infernal Machine,* which bear upon the problem which concerns us.

The first observation is this: The whole play of *The Infernal Machine,* if properly understood, may be read as a discussion of the most general problem of dramatic poetry in our time: how are we to place upon the public stage, which is formed to reflect only literal snapshots, slogans, and sensationalism, a poetic image of human life? The play, as we have seen, answers this question in its own wonderful way, which cannot be exactly our way in English; but the general question is the same as Wagner answered according to his taste, and Yeats and Eliot according to theirs. *The Infernal Machine* thus takes an important place in the long line of attempts which have been made, for over a hundred years, to build a modern poetic drama.

The other observation has to do with the *nature* of Cocteau's poetry from which, I think, much technical lore is to be learned. The play is not in verse; and though the language is beautifully formed, the poetry is not to be found in the first instance in the language at all. The play is *theatre*-poetry, as Cocteau defines it in his preface to *Les Mariés de la Tour Eiffel*:

The action of my play is in images, while the text is not. I attempt to substitute a poetry *of* the theatre for poetry *in* the theatre. Poetry *in* the theatre is a piece of lace which it is impossible to see at a distance. Poetry *of* the theatre would be coarse lace; a lace of ropes, a ship at sea. *Les Mariés* should have the frightening look of a drop of poetry under the microscope. The *scenes* are integrated like the *words* of a poem.

Though the language in *The Infernal Machine* is of course more important than it is in *Les Mariés* (essentially a dance pantomime), Cocteau's description of the underlying structure applies also very accurately to *The Infernal Machine*. The poetry is to be found in the relationships of all the main elements: the relationship between the lighted platform in the center of the stage with the darker and vaster area around it; between Oedipus's conscious career with the unseen fatality that governs it; between the first scene and the second, which ironically occurs at the same time; and between the first three acts, when we see Oedipus as a contemporary snapshot, and the last act, when we see him as a legend. In other words, the basic structure, or plot—the primary form of the play as a whole—embodies a poetic idea; and once that is established the language need only realize the poetic vision in detail.

If Cocteau, more than any other contemporary playwright, is thus a master of poetic-dramatic form, it is partly because he has learned from the neighboring arts of music, painting and ballet, and partly because he found his way back to a root notion of drama itself, that which Aristotle expressed when he said the dramatic poet should be a maker of plots rather than of verses. If Auden and MacNeice do not succeed in making poetic drama, it is because they do not understand the poetry of the theatre—they take an unpoetic well-made plot from the commercial theatre and add, here and there, a pastiche of verses.

This concludes what I have to say about *The Infernal Machine* as a poetic drama. If there is a moral to the tale, it is this: poetic drama, real poetic drama, comparable to the landmarks of the tradition, when the ancient art has really flourished—cannot be invented by an individual or even a small group. If it is to perform its true function it must spring from the whole culture and be nourished by sources which we may perhaps recognize, but can hardly understand. Will such a drama ever reappear? We do not know. In the meantime, all we can do is pick together the pieces, save and cultivate such lesser successes as have been achieved. *The Infernal Machine* is one of these successes—one of the clues, so to say—to the nature and the possibility of poetic drama in our time.

II. 19

EXCURSUS: Sartre and the Drama of Ensnarement*

VICTOR BROMBERT

Yale University

Tout est piège. *Huis-Clos*

SARTRE, whose central concern is man's freedom, seems almost obsessively drawn to a literature of imprisonment. Man's metaphysical freedom is for him the frightening secret of the gods, that secret which Zeus, in *Les Mouches* (*The Flies*),[1] is so reluctant to share with Orestes. And the function of the writer, much like the compulsion of Orestes in the play, is to proclaim this terrifying and exhilarating truth. In his essay *What is Literature?*, Sartre sets forth this function in explicit terms: "The writer, a free man writing for free men, has only one subject: freedom." Yet in that same essay, he calls for a new dramaturgy of *situations*, which he conceives in fact as a theater of entrapment: "Each situation is a trap, there are walls everywhere."[2]

The very titles of so many of Sartre's works—*Le Mur* (*The Wall*), *Huis-Clos* (*No Exit*), *La Chambre* (*The Room*), *Les Séquestrés d'Altona* (*The Prisoners of Altona*), *Intimité*, *L'Engrenage* (*In the Mesh*), *Les Jeux sont faits* (*The Chips Are Down*)—betray metaphorically an obsession with images of confinement, enclosure, and immurement.

---

* Read at the Institute in 1963. Published in *Institute Papers: Ideas in the Drama*, 1964.

[1] After the first reference in the text to any of Sartre's works, the title of the published English translation is given. Quotations from Sartre's works have been translated from the French original by the author.

[2] *Situations II* (Paris, 1948), pp. 112, 313.

They communicate a sense of the walled-in quality of human consciousness and human existence. Bounded by external contingencies or
by the imperatives of a dilemma, the Sartrean hero often appears inextricably jammed-in.

Literal prisons, or places of detention, occur repeatedly in his works.
The setting of *Huis-Clos* is a cell-like room, symbol of the living hell of
guilt and ceaseless judgment. In this peculiar torture chamber there
are no racks: the conventional torture instruments are absent. But there
are the atrocious tortures of the mind as it is ensnared by itself and by
the relentless glance of the "others"—tortures symbolized by permanent
exposure to light, total absence of sleep, and eternal cohabitation with
inmates who are also one's torturers. *"Fait comme un rat"* (trapped
like a rat), concludes one of the characters. And on one level, the trap is
the very prison of a past life that now—since it has been completely
lived out—rigidly immobilizes the dead. In *Morts sans sépulture* (*The
Victors*) the action takes place in a room where Resistance fighters,
while listening to the cries of their comrades, wait for their turn to be
tortured. Fear and pride, as well as the distance separating those who
have been tortured from those who have been spared, here create prisons
within a prison. And in *Le Mur* we witness the anguished night of a
political prisoner, during the Spanish Civil War, waiting with other
jailed men for dawn and the moment of execution. The cruel tricks of
the imagination, the hallucinations and the visceral reactions provoked
by fear, the sense of alienation and absurdity as the proximity of death
already separates man from his life have perhaps never been treated more
vividly—not even by Leonid Andreev, whose *The Seven Who Were
Hanged* may well have inspired Sartre.

Even when the setting is not a jail, there are in Sartre's works numerous scenes of confinement. Claustration, in one form or another, is
frequently the central motif. Hugo, the young revolutionary intellectual
in *Les Mains sales* (*Dirty Hands*), seeks refuge with Olga and remains
throughout the play, until his final choice, in what could be termed
"protective custody." The prostitute's room in *La Putain respectueuse*
(*The Respectful Prostitute*) is also—for a while at least—an asylum for
the hunted Negro. At times enclosure is self-imposed. Frantz von Ger-
lach, the guilt-ridden former German army officer in *Les Séquestrés
d'Altona*, withdraws into self-inflicted confinement, complicated by an
incestuous relationship with his sister that further entraps him. The
bolted door, the walled-up window are symbols of a refusal of life and

truth, of a hopeless escape from a bad conscience, which ironically provides further deceptions, as the protagonist flirts with his own delirium.
As for "La Chambre," one of Sartre's most successful short stories, it
describes a woman's self-imposed imprisonment with her mentally ill
husband who slowly sinks into total insanity. Here also the author
creates a sense of a prison within a prison. Eve tries in vain to reach her
husband beyond the steadily thickening wall of his madness.

Sometimes, notably in *Les Mains sales,* the dramatic structure of
the play locks the situation within itself, apparently allowing the protagonist no escape whatsoever. Hugo, who has just been released from a
real prison, is hunted down by fellow revolutionaries who have decided
to liquidate him. When the play begins, Hugo is given a last chance.
In a closed room he is to explain to Olga the motives for his ambiguous
murder of Hoederer. The major part of the play is thus a flashback
between a suspenseful beginning and an outcome (life or death) that
will entirely depend on the answer this retrospective examination of
motives will provide. It is difficult to conceive a more immobilizing situation than the one achieved through this dramatic compression of time
and irrevocable action within a "theatrical" time (from 9 P.M. to midnight) that barely exceeds the actual time of the performance.

The theater, to be sure, lends itself to the prison image. The epic
form—whether in the classical epic or in modern fiction—allows and
even calls for movement in time and space. Tragedy, especially in the
French tradition with its "unities," most often focuses on a crisis in
which the protagonists have reached a seeming impasse. Racine's antechambers are not so different from Sartre's cell where characters are
locked together in a death dance. And one could easily show that Greek
tragedy is filled with images of restriction and confinement: the chains
of Prometheus, the fatal webs and nets in *Agamemnon,* the meshes of
fate and the trap of intellect in *Oedipus.* The modern stage, with its
three walls—the fourth wall being the inexorable eye of the public—
may be said to symbolize an issueless situation.

These are no doubt permanent features of the tragic theater. But
in Sartre's plays, the prison motif is closely bound up with psychological
obsessions as well as with philosophical themes. The flashback, for
which Sartre has so marked a predilection, may appear, as in *Les Mains
sales,* as a melodramatic rather than a tragic device: it immobilizes a past
that seemingly cannot be altered. Yet this is a misreading of the play.
The real suspense is not to be summed up by the question: What will
happen to Hugo? but by the far more important one: How will he

choose to give a meaning to his past act? For it is up to him to bestow a meaning upon it. The flashback thus leads not to a sterile investigation but to a choice and consequently to an act *in the present*. The element of surprise—for there is a *coup de théâtre*—is not at all related to Hugo's fate but to his will and to his decision. And the *coup de théâtre* is the hero's breaking out from the imprisonment of what appears like a set, prearranged order.[3] The philosophical implications of such a breaking out are clear. The significance of a human act must not be sought in motivation, which is always muddled, nor in the prison of a given psychology, but in the allegiance to the act itself—for man *is* his acts—and in the meaning man imposes in relation to a present situation. Every heartbeat thrusts into the world a decision through which we reinvent ourselves. When Hugo, at the end of the play, kicks open the door so his murderers can come in, he paradoxically escapes to an authentic freedom.

Sartre's own favorite haunts, as well as the *luoghi ameni* of his poetic universe, are most often both anonymous and walled-in: hotel rooms, dimly lit cafés, night clubs (the French *boîte de nuit* evokes the sealed-in atmosphere), reading rooms in public libraries—all suggest airlessness and reclusion. Camus' work also provides striking illustrations of this *lyrisme cellulaire:* in *L'Etranger* the stranger Meursault in his North African jail, in "Le Renégat" the renegade in the ghastly chambers of the city of salt, in *La Chute* Clamence sitting out his life in the dingy bar surrounded by the concentric canals of Amsterdam like so many circles of hell, an entire city locked in and isolated in *La Peste*. Modern literature from Dostoyevsky's underground man to Beckett's pariahs is filled with lonely and hedged-in figures. It is also filled, since *The House of the Dead*, with penal colonies.

The literary historian with a penchant for political or sociological interpretations might be tempted to generalize about the possible relationship between this cellular lyricism and the collective political and ideological tragedies of our time. Sartre himself has been fully aware that his generation was brutally thrust into the nightmare of history. "We were driven to create a literature of historicity," he explains in an essay on the function of literature.[4] Sartre's generation had indeed learned that this was no longer a time to toy with aesthetic problems or to seek

---

[3] Jacques Guicharnaud very aptly observes this tendency on the part of characters to reject the tyranny of a scenario written in advance. *Modern French Theater* (New Haven, 1961), p. 142.

[4] *Situations II*, p. 245.

private salvation through art—that private salvation was no longer possible, that man was involved in a collective tragedy, and that the very meaning of traditional Humanism was being seriously challenged. The era of concentration camps (*l'ère concentrationnaire*, as it came to be called) reminded the writer that even imprisonment was no longer a private affair. And the concentration camp has haunted the imagination of Sartre ever since the days of the Occupation. This, too, was a lesson in loneliness and solidarity: a period of humiliation and betrayal, a period when deportation, execution of hostages, and torture became a daily reality, when almost daily man was cornered, exposed to extreme situations and extreme choices between heroism and abjection, when moral problems could no longer be comfortably relegated to the classroom but had to be faced, here and now, leaving little room for cozy innocence. It is significant that the most haunting memory associated with the guilty past of Frantz, in *Les Séquestrés d'Altona*, is the construction of a concentration camp on family land sold by his father to Himmler.

This fear of a complicity with evil explains in part why Sartre permanently seeks a complicity with the victims. To be *"dans le coup,"* to be *"dans le bain"* are typical expressions of solidarity, pointing to an involvement and an entrapment with others. They are the social and political equivalent of the metaphysical *"nous sommes embarqués"* of Pascal who, incidentally, also viewed the human condition as a form of collective imprisonment: men in chains, all condemned to die, some of them each day slaughtered in full view of the others. In the eyes of Sartre's generation man must not prefer his private cell to the bitter realities of collective imprisonment. This urge to "be with," this compulsion to enter into a collective prison, has been given its most articulate allegorical form in *Les Mouches* where the inhabitants of Argos are seen as the prisoners of a tyrannized city—prisoners who are, however, willfully blind in the face of their servitude and whose bad faith and secret shame further subjugate them. It will be Orestes' function to carry a lesson of freedom to the inhabitants of Argos. This, however, he will not be able to do unless he himself first becomes a member of the imprisoned community.

The paradoxes, or even contradictions, are apparent enough. How is one to reconcile the self-willed immurement (whose major symptom is incommunicability) with the shame of this private prison and the urge to assume one's role in a collective imprisonment and eventually in a collective liberation? And how are these problems in turn related to the prison metaphor as a structural device whereby the philosopher-playwright stresses the existential responsibility of his protagonists? Or are these problems merely brought together by the coincidence of a persistent prison imagery?

For an answer we may well turn to the one play that, better than any other work of Sartre, dramatizes man's basic dilemma in existential terms—*Huis-Clos*. This play provides a striking illustration of man's double imprisonment: in the self, and through the presence of others. For it is based entirely on a reversed metaphor: it is not hell that is here described as a condemnation to the self under the judging eye of another consciousness, but it is life-in-the-self and in the presence of others that is hell. What the play provides is a figuration of man's simultaneous solipsistic and interdependent condition. "*L'Enfer c'est les autres*," remarks one of the characters. And, significantly, the original title of the play was *Les Autres*. Every character in *Huis-Clos* is trapped in a private world of guilt and shame: the infanticide, the sexual pervert, the coward. They desperately search for a key to innocence and attempt to break out of their confining cell. In the mirrorless room they turn to the "others" as to consoling or flattering mirrors, only to come face to face with their severe glance and cruel judgment. Through what amounts to psychological *voyeurisme* the other becomes at the same time accomplice, witness, and judge, as mutual confessions turn out to be mere pretexts for exercises in bad faith. The eye of the other is woefully needed, but it is also feared. For man's very identity depends on the presence of a mirror. But the mirror allows for no escape. The search for an exit carries its own paradox: one cannot break through a mirror. The protagonists are thrown back within their own limits, as the much wanted other becomes an object of hate. What salvation in this hellish trap? "*Regarder en soi*" (to look into oneself), says Garcin. But this is intolerable, and moreover impossible. For man will necessarily recreate within himself a glance that will substitute the glance of the others, he will interiorize a judgment that will play out the hypothetical judgment of another consciousness. Man is caught. The play symbolically comes to an end with an attempt at an impossible murder. There is no solution but to get on with it. "*Lasciate ogni speranza. . . .*" The fellow inmates are bound to each other forever. Solitary and—whether they like it or not—solidary.

Man is thus, in the Sartrean context, condemned to an inalienable subjectivity from which he cannot extricate himself. Contingent and superfluous, his existence is frequently described through images suggesting viscous, gummous, sticky sensations—"*glu*" and "*englué*" are favorite terms in the Sartrean vocabulary. This adhesion to one's own existence is like the awareness of one's own insipid taste. It is also the fundamental cause of man's anguish. For anguish, abandon, and sweating of blood, explains Sartre in one of his essays, begins when man no longer has any witness but himself. "Then he must drink the bitter cup to the dregs, and experience fully his human condition." [5] And it is more than just anguish. It is like a permanent awareness of guilt: the awareness of the original guilt of being. This "sin of existing" described by Roquentin in *La Nausée* (*Nausea*) is shared by almost all of Sartre's characters who, like Brunet in *Les Chemins de la liberté* (*Roads to Freedom*), feel "vaguely guilty"—guilty "of being alone, guilty of thinking and living. Guilty of not being dead."

This psychological rift within the prison of self has its philosophical counterpart in Sartre's notion of the irreconcilable, and at the same time interdependent, relationship of the *en-soi* and the *pour-soi*. All experience is thus conceived as bipolarized. In his major philosophical work, *L'Etre et le Néant* (*Being and Nothingness*), Sartre, in discussing the stumbling block of solipsism, stresses the double alienation of man, both in relation to the other and in relation to himself.[6] The Sartrean hero is thus subjected to an eye—the eye of the other, but first the eye of his *pour-soi*—before he can attain identity. Stendhal once wistfully complained that the eye cannot see itself. This is a blessing Sartre does not grant his characters. To make their suffering greater, it would seem that they are endowed with precisely such an introverted vision.

The self-torturing potential of the mind and the self-punishing workings of the intellect are permanent themes in Sartre's work. Garcin, in *Huis-Clos*, cries out: "Give me rather a hundred burns and flayings than this agony of mind." Mathieu, in *L'Age de raison* (*Age of Reason*), sees himself rotten to the core: "Thoughts, thoughts on thoughts, thoughts on thoughts of thoughts; he was transparent to infinity." Hugo, the young bourgeois intellectual who has joined the revolutionaries in *Les Mains sales*, knows that he remains trapped and paralyzed by his intellect. He has chosen Raskolnikov as a battle name. The choice is symbolic: the name Raskolnikov in Russian implies a rift. And this is

[5] *Situations II*, p. 250.   [6] *L'Etre et le Néant* (Paris, 1943), p. 277.

true of all of Sartre's intellectuals—and who among his characters is not an intellectual?—all of them compulsive thinkers ensnared by the mirror-disease of thought. Sartre's imagery often suggests a "third degree" type of lucidity: the burning light in *Huis-Clos*, and in *L'Age de raison* the relentless sun in the "lucid sky" dazzling Mathieu and forcing him to blink. The characters of Sartre not only think, they watch themselves think. Their thoughts are reflected and infinitely multiplied in a looking-glass that turns into an instrument of self-torture. And there is no end to it. "Nausea," among other things, is the loathsome weariness that accompanies this pathological cerebration. Consciousness can find no escape from itself. One is reminded here of Baudelaire's self-torturer, "L'Héautontimorouménos."

Huis-Clos illustrates how this rift within the self is further complicated by intolerable relations with the others. Sartre's heroes are prisoners without privacy. And they are caught in an insoluble dilemma: the need for a witness is closely linked with the fear of the judging eye. Thus, in *Les Séquestrés d'Altona* Johanna describes all the members of the family as "jailer-slaves." And Frantz, who at one point says to Johanna: "I will not let myself be judged by my younger brother's wife," later pleads with her to judge him. In the novels there are countless examples of characters fenced about by the other's consciousness at the very moment they seem most withdrawn in themselves. Mathieu, walking through the streets of Paris, suddenly stops aghast: "He was not alone; Marcelle had not let him go. She was thinking of him. She was thinking: dirty bastard. . . . The consciousness of Marcelle remained somewhat out there. . . . It was unbearable to be thus judged, hated." Or this other moment of panic: "Behind him, in a green room, a little consciousness filled with hate was rejecting him." [7] The desire to break through the immurement becomes doubly urgent: the other not only judges us, but refuses us and rejects us.

For almost as basic as the guilt of *being* is the sin of *being another.* The bitter and anguished exclamation of Goetz in *Le Diable et le bon Dieu* (*The Devil and the Good Lord*)—"You are not me, it is unbearable"—is echoed throughout Sartre's writings. It reflects a psychological obsession that is closely bound up with a guilt of class consciousness, namely the shame of being a *fils de bourgeois* that has so persistently haunted the French intelligentsia ever since the middle of the nineteenth century and that the writers of Sartre's generation have felt with

[7] *L'Age de raison* (Paris, 1945), p. 23.

particular acuteness. It is indeed noteworthy how often Sartre refers to the condition of bourgeois as a form of imprisonment. In *Situations II* he explains that the bourgeois writers are trapped: "Born of bourgeois parents, read and paid by the bourgeoisie, they will have to remain bourgeois, for the bourgeoisie, like a prison, has sealed them in." The proletariat is doubly inaccessible to the borgeois revolutionary who yearns to reach out to it and be accepted, for it too is trapped in its own class consciousness. It is, explains Sartre in *What is Literature?*, "encircled by a propaganda which isolates it; it is like a secret society, without doors or windows." [8] Ashamed of his own class, Sartre comes to envy those who, according to him, were born prisoners of a more enviable class. How many of Sartre's protagonists share this sense of alienation! Hugo, in *Les Mains sales*, is a typical déclassé who cannot, however, slough off his *"peau de bourgeois."* Goetz, in *Le Diable et le bon Dieu*, is similarly—though on a more grandiose scale—locked up in his own social conditions: a bastard nobleman who cannot become a plebeian. Nasty, the leader of the mob, explains that Goetz cannot save the poor, only corrupt them. And when Goetz desperately proclaims his solidarity ("I am one of you"), Nasty opposes with a flat "No." What right has Nasty to speak in behalf of the peasants? The answer is equally clear: "I am one of them." And Goetz will never be.

But "they" signifies not merely a social group or a political party. "They" are all those who have undergone what I did not undergo, all those who have suffered what I have not suffered. Between their suffering and myself lies all the distance that separates us. Their very imprisonment confines me and excludes me. This separation created by suffering is perhaps the most important tragic theme in Sartre's work. It is at the very core, for instance, of *Morts sans sépulture*, a play whose brutality shocked and disconcerted the audience. But *Morts sans sépulture* is not what it may appear at first: a melodramatic topical treatment of the torture of Resistance fighters. It is a series of tragic variations on the intolerable human divorce created by the presence of pain. Not only is each character confined to his terror, to his torment, and to his pride, but the glance of the person who has undergone torture becomes unbearable to the one who has been spared. Worst of all: How is one to bear the glance of an individual who has been tortured for our sake? "Must I have my nails torn out to become your friend again?" cries out one of the characters. The Sartrean hero develops an almost morbid

8 *Situations II*, pp. 155, 277.

jealousy of the victim, a paradoxical yearning for pain as a passport to brotherhood. Hugo, in *Les Mains sales*, knows that his new comrades will never forgive him for having been a well-fed child. "They will never accept me," he moans. There is the same feeling of rejection in *Le Diable et le bon Dieu*. Goetz tries in vain to take upon himself the suffering of his dying mistress, as he will try in vain to share the agony of the peasants. An impossibility that marks his bitter isolation ("Why do they always suffer so much more than I will ever suffer?"), but that leads to a further determination to break into the prison of the others. As early as in *La Chambre*, this desire to "break into" assumes an obsessive quality. Only here the compulsion has not yet taken on social and political overtones. Eve feels excluded from her husband's insanity. But she is determined to join him behind his wall. That, of course, is the meaning of her willful confinement to the sick man's room.

At this point one begins to see by what devious but also rigorous logic the Sartrean tragic figure seeks to leave his private cell, only to break into the cell of the other and ultimately into the collective prison of a given group. This attempt at penetrating into an imprisoned collectivity is the subject of *Les Mouches*, a play that was written and performed during the German Occupation, at a time when the concepts of prison and freedom were loaded with a tragic potential. It was impossible not to see a striking parallel between Sartre's city of Argos and the France of Vichy, defeated, guilt-ridden, and degradingly submissive. The play is studded with topical allusions. Orestes returns on a national holiday invented by the rulers to keep collective remorse alive. Aegisthus, like Pétain, is a collaborator. Pétain collaborates with Nazi tyranny and Aegisthus with the tyranny of Zeus. The flies are the very symbol of moral decay. But characteristically, the inhabitants are fond of their flies. The little idiot boy whose eyes are literally covered with flies smiles contentedly. For the flies, like a sterile remorse, can be paradoxically comfortable. In fact, the people of Argos like their running sores so much that they scratch them with their dirty nails to keep them festering. The city of Argos thus appears as the sordid city of *nonfreedom* and *nonresponsibility*. It is also the city of guilt. And Zeus the tyrant, whose nostrils are tickled by the stench of carrion, relishes the odor of guilt— for guilt and shame that blind men to the possibility of their own responsible action are the God's only hope of fighting man's freedom.

Orestes' desire to win the name of guilt stealer represents his attempt to enter into the prison of the collectivity, first to save himself from his own negative freedom, but ultimately, having found his roots, in order to rediscover the meaning of authentic freedom. To achieve this, to belong, he must first commit an irrevocable act: the murder of his mother. What matters is thus not the avenging of past crimes, as in Aeschylus' tragedy, but a binding and at the same time liberating enterprise, which Sartre metaphorically conveys through a whole series of prison images. At the beginning of the play, Orestes' "innocence" is like a wide moat separating him from the people of Argos. He stands, figuratively, *outside*. Looking at the city, he explains to Electra: "It fends me off with all its walls, with all its roofs, with all its locked doors." Orestes dreams of becoming more "weighty." He is attracted to Argos precisely because it is a city of suffering and heaviness. He wants to draw the city around him like a thick blanket and curl himself up in it. Elsewhere, he says to Electra who has just warned him that even if he stayed a hundred years, he would still be a stranger: "I must go down into the depths, among you. For you are all living at the very bottom of a pit." Finally, the breaking-into-the-prison is expressed in a language of violence: "I'll turn into an ax and hew these obstinate walls asunder, I'll rip open the bellies of those bigoted houses. . . . I'll be a wedge driving into the heart of the city, like a wedge rammed into the heart of an oak tree." The simple and perhaps impossible aim is the dream of a human solidarity which would liberate the individual from his false freedom and bind him to the freedom of a solidary group: "To become a man among men." And it is significant that Goetz, in *Le Diable et le bon Dieu*, repeats Orestes' wish word for word: *"Je veux être un homme parmi les hommes."* [9]

Though fundamentally relevant in psychological and social terms, Sartre's prison imagery is closely woven into the philosophical texture of his works. And this not as an illustration but as a metaphoric embodiment of a philosophical dilemma. Thus literature, for Sartre, is never a vehicle for already crystallized thoughts but an experience that probes into its own meaning. Nothing is more revealing than Sartre's statement, made during an interview, that he discovered and developed his concept of freedom in the very process of writing *Les Mouches*. An exploratory exercise, literature for him does not describe a dilemma, it *is* the dilemma. Or rather, to put it in Sartrean terms, it does not describe a "situation," it *is* the "situation." And, of course, every situation is a trap.

Théâtre (Paris, 1947), p. 64; *Le Diable et le bon Dieu* (Paris, 1951), p. 275.

And, to begin with, there is existence itself. For the raw experience of *Dasein*—of "being there"—is that never-ending ensnarement in a perpetual present that Sartre so brilliantly describes in *La Nausée*. By means of a diary method that adheres to the banal, fragmented, and essentially undramatic experience of unfiltered, uninterpreted reality, Sartre shows how Roquentin lives each moment as it weighs on him, in an opaque immediacy, caught in a permanent indetermination. The diary form becomes an exercise in discontinuity, as we the readers, as well as the narrator, become prisoners of a chronic present tense, which also marks a chronic disintegration. Pure existence is thus shown as innocent of meaning. The very imprisonment in the here and the now turns out to be a revelation of absurdity.

But this revelation, this nausea that is almost an ecstasy of horror, is also an apprenticeship in existential awareness. Roquentin discovers that existence is original contingency, that life is not justifiable in its essence, and that man is not only free—terrifyingly free—but, as it were, condemned to freedom. He does not have but *is* his freedom. It is a bitter lesson, a most uncomfortable one—for, if this is so, then there is no escape from this freedom, there being no one in this world to whom man could delegate a responsibility that he, and he alone, must bear. This relation between freedom and responsibility is the cornerstone of Sartre's ethical construction. Like Heidegger, Sartre stresses the "intentional structure" of human awareness.[10] In a key passage of *L'Etre et le Néant* entitled "Freedom and Responsibility," Sartre writes that "man, condemned to be free, carries the weight of the entire world on his shoulders." [11] The very alienation of man, according to Sartre, forces him into a value-creating role. Orestes—so Zeus tells him in *Les Mouches*—is not in his own home: he is an intruder, a foreign body in the world, "like a splinter in flesh, or a poacher in his lordship's forest." What Sartre means is that man has been thrown into this world that he did not create and did not want. But here he is, and only he can provide for himself the values whereby he can live. As Orestes puts it, "human life begins on the far side of despair."

The image of the trap—*"tout est piège"*—is thus potentially dynamic, in so far as man is condemned permanently to seek an exit. But first comes the awareness of being ensnared. *"Nous sommes drôlement*

---

[10] John D. Wild, "The New Empiricism," in *Sartre: A Collection of Critical Essays*, ed. Edith Kern (New York, 1962), p. 139. The chapter originally appeared in *The Challenge of Existentialism*, 1955.

[11] *L'Etre et le Néant*, p. 639.

coincés" (Are we trapped!) says Frantz in *Les Séquestrés d'Altona*. But immediately he adds: "There must be an exit"—and he repeats this twice. Sartre himself, in his essay on the function of literature, asseverates that it is the writer's duty to unveil to man, in each concrete situation, his potential for action; that he must measure man's servitude only to help him transcend it.[12]

This view of "man-in-situation" is reflected in Sartre's literary precepts as well as in his practice, particularly his dramaturgy. In the very passage in which he calls for a new theater of entrapment, Sartre also calls for the end of the theater of "characters." "No more characters: protagonists are entrapped freedoms, like the rest of us. What exits are there? Each personage will be nothing but a choice of an exit and will be worth exactly the exit he chose." And in the passage quoted earlier ("each situation is a trap, there are walls everywhere"), Sartre adds: "I have expressed myself badly: there are no exits to *choose*. An exit has to be invented. And every one of us, by inventing his own exit, invents himself. Man is to be invented every day." [13]

What this means, in literary terms, is that the playwright as well as the novelist must turn away from conventional character study. Malraux, in his preface to *Le Temps du mépris*, had taken the bourgeois novelist to task for eternally exploring the so-called inner world of his protagonists. In his introductory essay for *Les Temps modernes*, Sartre also proclaims the death of the spirit of analysis that isolates human beings in their "differences" and immobilizes them in their pseudo-essences. For Sartre, just as for Malraux, a man is not what he hides but what he does. He is the sum total of his acts. It is the act that defines man. By his acts he creates himself. Thus man is neither subject nor object but an eternal project. This, in fact, is why Sartre scorns the omniscient type of novelist who assumes a God-like privilege of dissecting and explaining his characters. Sartre's heroes may find themselves in a trap, but it is not the trap of their psychology. Their actions are not the expression of what they are, but the means by which they become what they are not yet. A literature of *praxis*, Sartre calls it: one that does not describe or explain but that brings man face to face with his latest dilemma.

Sartre himself is temperamentally drawn to "impossible" situations, as witnessed by the permanent conflict between his philosophical tenets and his political allegiances. Replying to objections raised by George

---

[12] *Situations II*, pp. 311–12.   [13] *Ibid.*, p. 313.

Lukacs in *Existentialisme ou Marxisme,* Sartre explains the precise nature of this dilemma:

We were convinced *simultaneously* that historical materialism supplied the only valid interpretation of history and that existentialism remained the only concrete approach to reality. I do not pretend to deny the contradictions in this attitude. . . . Many intellectuals, many students have experienced and are still experiencing the tension of this double exigency.[14]

Honesty here lies in the refusal to juggle away a difficulty or a contradiction. There is little doubt that Sartre also draws a measure of satisfaction from the tension of double exigencies. But, above all, Sartre welcomes the trap of any dilemma because in it alone can man take the full measure of his inventive and self-liberating potential. Sartre believes that, faced with the two alternatives of any dilemma, man will of a sudden discover a third possibility—a discovery that amounts to an act of creation. Few writers have been more keenly aware of the problematical nature of human existence and of the challenging difficulties man's confined freedom provided.

[14] "Questions de méthode," *Les Temps Modernes,* September, 1957, pp. 338–417. Reprinted in *Critique de la raison dialectique.*

II. 20

The Urban Apocalypse*

HUGH KENNER

University of California, Santa Barbara

THERE IS nothing so appeasing as a category; think how chaotic many eighteenth-century poems would seem if we did not know that we were supposed to call them Pindaric Odes. A name for the kind of poem *The Waste Land* is might have spared criticism much futile approximating. There used to be a kind of conducted tour, in which the student was bidden to observe how checkpoints would align if he closed one eye and sighted in the proper direction. This or that feature —the drowned man, the desert traveller, the unnerving woman—entered one or another thematic system, depending on the part of the terrain you were visiting, and the poem seemed a great feat of civil engineering. When the itinerary of one such tour was laid before Eliot, he remarked that he had not been conscious of being so ingenious, as though to say that the egg will exemplify mathematical shell-analysis of which the hen knows nothing. Yet the drafts, now that we have them, suggest a poem whose author might have described its plan. Though he seems to have found that poem impractical, it was from its wreckage that he salvaged the poem we know, the first exemplar of a category that still has no name. To examine the drafts is to interrogate imperfect traces of a poem that was never achieved. Such an exercise needs no apology. *The Waste Land* is still a determinant of modernist consciousness, post-modernist also if it has come to that, and the profit of yet one more tour of speculation may be that we shall learn a little more about the history of our own minds.

* Read at the Institute in 1972. Published in *Eliot in His Time, Essays on the Occasion of the Fiftieth Anniversary of "The Waste Land,"* ed. A. Walton Litz, Princeton, N.J.: Princeton University Press, 1973. Reprinted by permission of Princeton University Press.

To examine the drafts means for most of us to examine the reproductions in Valerie Eliot's 1971 facsimile edition. I have not been able to see the originals myself. Under even an unskilled eye, though, the reproductions suffice to dispel any notion of a longish poem called *The Waste Land* which its author wrote all at once and later shortened with help from a friend. Some of the handwriting is mature, some youthful—Valerie Eliot [130] [1] dates three of the leaves "about 1914 or even earlier." The typescripts, moreover, have come from at least three typewriters. "Death by Water" and "What the Thunder Said" were both "typed with the violet ribbon used by Pound" [63, 83], hence in Paris after Eliot arrived there with holographs Pound declined to mark up [55].

More interesting, two different machines which I will call "A" and "B" were used for the rest of the copy. The title-page [3] and "The Fire Sermon" [23–47] display the elongated quotation marks and apostrophes of machine "A." But "The Burial of the Dead" [5–9], "A Game of Chess" [11–15], and the cancelled "Death of the Duchess" [105–107] exemplify machine "B," hence a different place and—we shall see—a different stratum of the poem. (As for the two remaining sheets of typescript, the shapes of lower-case "t's" and "f's" would assign "Exequy" [101] to the "A" family and "Song. For the Opherion" [99] to the "B," but these have no further importance for the argument.)

Comparison with typed correspondence would show where and when Eliot used machines "A" and "B." Pending such confirmation—or contradiction—there is reason to deduce that "A" was his London typewriter, "B" the one he used at Lausanne. If so, and I will explain later why I think so, he typed "The Fire Sermon" before leaving London, and took it with him to Switzerland, and its first state as printed in the facsimile edition represents the earliest continuous stretch of the poem.

A few dates next, to help bracket what may have been a catalyzing event. It is on 5 November 1919 [xvii–xviii] that we first hear Eliot hoping to get started on "a poem I have in mind." Six weeks later it is a long poem he has had on his mind "for a long time" [xviii], and nine months after that (20 September 1920) he is still longing for a little time to think about it [xx]. Then by 9 May 1921 something had happened: the poem was "partly on paper" [xxi]. The rest belongs to late

[1] All citations in square brackets refer to the facsimile edition of the original drafts.

1921. In mid-October he went to Margate, where nothing connects with nothing; in mid-November to Lausanne. On 13 December, in Lausanne, he was "working on a poem" [xxii], and in Paris on his way back to London he laid before Pound the poem that he was later to tell John Quinn had been written "mostly when I was at Lausanne for treatment last winter" [xxii].

"Mostly" serves to exclude what he brought with him to Lausanne, notably whatever had been on paper since May. Now by some time in May 1921 Eliot had read Mark Van Doren's *John Dryden*, his review of which appeared in *The Times Literary Supplement* for June 9;[2] and not far into his first chapter we find Mark Van Doren explaining the late seventeenth-century vogue of Ovid, the poet "at once tender and mocking, at once flexible and hard, at once allusive and brisk, [who] taught Dryden his gait, and showed him how to turn all the sides of his mind to the light." Van Doren's explanation of this vogue is worth pondering: "For the first twenty years after the Restoration Dryden's London was to reproduce with a certain amount of accuracy the Rome of Ovid. With civil war just past and a commonwealth overthrown, with court and city beginning to realize their power, with peace prevailing and cynicism in fashionable morals rampant, with a foreign culture seeking the favor of patrons and wits, the new city did for a while bear a strange resemblance to the old Empire." (Third edition, 1946, p. 9.)

A war just past, a rampant cynicism, wits gone wild after continental novelty: we may guess how that could have sounded, in 1921, like contemporary London. Eliot's review does not cite the passage, confining itself as it does to advocacy of Dryden's verse. It does contain two suggestive statements: that "to enjoy Dryden means to pass beyond the limitations of the nineteenth century into a new freedom," and that the book under review is "a book which every practitioner of English verse should study."

Eliot's praise of Dryden in the 1920s, which extended even to calling one book of essays *Homage to John Dryden*, has not been assimilated by his commentators, for the good reason that until the *Waste Land* manuscripts were published in 1971 it was impossible to

---

[2] The review is reprinted in *Selected Essays* as "John Dryden." From the fact [xviii] that on 5 November 1919 he was working on a review which *The Times Literary Supplement* published in its 13 November issue, we learn that its lead time for reviews was a week or less, so Eliot could have written his piece on Van Doren's *Dryden* as late as, say, June 1. I wish I knew how much earlier he was reading in the book, but let us guess several weeks. Its American copyright date is 1920.

know what to make of it. Today, and especially from the first version of "The Fire Sermon," we can see how Dryden entered the conception of the unwritten poem, part of the rich amalgam that gathered in Eliot's mind in the months just before those decisive weeks in Lausanne.

To abridge much tedium of detail, we may summarize under two heads. The long poem was to be an urban poem, a London poem; and it was to be a poem of firm statements and strong lines, traceable to the decorums of urban satire.

Neither proposition need imply that Eliot was contemplating a radical change. He was always a city poet, not a country poet, his affinities rather with Baudelaire than with Wordsworth. And he was always quotable in the single line: "Let us go then, you and I." Still, he was changing. One novelty of the new poem was to be a new specificity: a public focus on his new environment, the City of London. His earlier poems immerse us in a city we cannot name. If we tend to suppose that Prufrock treads the streets of Boston, still his surname and his yellow fogs are from St. Louis, and the Paris of Laforgue has left its impress. But the crowd in the "Unreal City" flows over London Bridge, up the hill and down King William Street with St. Magnus Martyr and the Billingsgate Fish Market to its right, and the Thames Daughters' mortal places are on a map of the greater London area: Highbury, Richmond, Kew, Moorgate. One passage, drafted amid swarms of variants [37], typed into "The Fire Sermon" and finally cancelled, confronted the personified City:

London, the swarming life you kill and breed,
Huddled between the concrete and the sky,
Responsive to the momentary need,
Vibrates unconscious to its formal destiny,

Knowing neither how to think, nor how to feel,
But lives in the awareness of the observing eye.
Phantasmal gnomes, burrowing in brick and stone and steel!
Some minds, aberrant from the normal equipoise
(London, your people is bound upon the wheel!)
Record the movements of these pavement toys
And trace the cryptogram that may be curled
Within the faint perceptions of the noise
Of the movement, and the lights!

Not here, O Glaucon, but in another world. [31, 43]

Though it drew a rude marginal expletive from Pound, this seems to have been meant for a focal passage, suggesting in conjunction with other details that the mythological unity Eliot's notes encourage us to find in the final poem was at one time a geographical unity. (Another passage commencing "O City, City," later used as the basis of lines 259–65, was drafted on the same sheet [37].) London, killing and breeding, Eliot seems to have intuited as a sort of presiding personage, the original Fisher King as well as the original Waste Land, resembling Augustine's Carthage as Dryden's London had resembled Ovid's Rome.

The passage commences with a four-line stanza, set off by a space and rhymed *a b a b*, a stanza that just a little later in "The Fire Sermon" was repeated seventeen more times. This is an uncommon stanza, recognizable to most modern ears because Gray used it in his *Elegy*. Mark Van Doren (pp. 82–84) has something to say about its history, and about Dryden's persisting fascination with its "leisurely authority." Before Dryden, Spenser, Davies, Donne, and Ben Jonson had used it, and D'Avenant in *Gondibert*. Most pertinently, it is the stanza of *Annus Mirabilis*, which just here in "The Fire Sermon" it seems calculated to echo.

Annus Mirabilis (as Van Doren notes) was dedicated "To the Metropolis of Great Britain, the Most Renown'd and Late Flourishing City of London." Dryden commenced his preface with the supposition that he might be "the first who ever presented a work of this nature to the metropolis of any nation," a boldness he justifies by suggesting that no city ever so much deserved such praise. Other cities, he says, have won their fame "by cheaper trials than an expensive, tho' necessary war, a consuming pestilence, and a more consuming fire." The last twelve stanzas of *Annus Mirabilis* are singled out by Van Doren. They "pile themselves up," he says (p. 111), "like the Theban stones that obeyed Amphion's lyre," to prophesy London's illimitable future:

298

. . . The silver Thames, her own domestic flood,
   Shall bear her vessels like a sweeping train;
   And often wind (as of his mistress proud)
   With longing eyes to meet her face again.

299

The wealthy Tagus, and the wealthier Rhine,
   The glory of their towns no more shall boast;
   And Seine, that would with Belgian rivers join,
   Shall find her luster stain'd, and traffic lost.

300
The vent'rous merchant, who design'd more far,
And touches on this hospitable shore,
Charm'd with the splendor of this northern star,
Shall here unlade him, and depart no more. . . .

Such was the prospect before London in 1666. By 1921, having undergone yet one more "expensive, tho' necessary war," and one more "consuming pestilence" which figures in demographic history as the great influenza epidemic, it was playing host to such ambivalently vent'rous merchants as Mr. Eugenides, "unshaven, with a pocket full of currants," and seemed ripe for a Fire Sermon if not for a fire.

Unreal City [wrote Eliot] I have seen and see
Under the brown fog of your winter noon
Mr. Eugenides, the Smyrna merchant . . .   [31]

and he followed this with the apostrophe to London that commences in the stanza of *Annus Mirabilis*, the "heroic stanza," alternately rhymed, which Dryden was to call "more noble, and of greater dignity, both for the sound and number, than any other verse in use amongst us."

It specifies in what respect the City is Unreal: unreal the way sensate accretions are unreal for Plato, to whose *Republic* the line about Glaucon directs us [127–28]. Its whole life has been levelled down to the plane of sensation. To this, to the likes of Mr. Eugenides, to a life of "phantasmal gnomes" and "pavement toys," has the London of Dryden's magniloquent prophecy come: that seems to be the tacit burden of these details, and, after a few lines irregularly rhymed, Eliot wrote seventeen more heroic stanzas, presenting in Dryden's form though not his diction the movements of the typist and the youth with the spotted face who enact an unreal automation of Love itself [31–35, 43–47].

That passage, Tiresias' vision, as we know from the manuscripts, was all in the *Annus Mirabilis* stanza once, and the fine laconic gravity of its present state was achieved by ruthless deletion that cut through quatrains and amalgamated their details. By then the poem's coordinates had so shifted that a tacit allusion to Dryden no longer mattered, and Eliot made no effort to preserve the stanzas' identity. He had dwelt, in the longest portion that got deleted, on the uncivil habits of the young man. A quatrain ran

—Bestows one final patronizing kiss,
And gropes his way, finding the stairs unlit;

And at the corner where the stable is,
Delays only to urinate, and spit.

Pound [47] called the last two lines "over the mark," as they were. As to why Eliot first included them, we may learn less from dwelling on what is called his social snobbery than from weighing his statement that the neglect of Dryden is "not due to the fact that his work is not poetry, but to a prejudice that the material, the feelings out of which he built is not poetic." The urination and the spitting near the stable, like other constellations of low detail—

He munches with the same persistent stare,
He knows his way with women and that's that!
Impertinently tipping back his chair
And dropping cigarette ash on the mat   [45]

—seem meant to affirm, with a confidence perhaps enforced by the reading [xx] of the latter parts of Ulysses in typescript, that material of that order will make poetry, and in the way Dryden made poetry, by making plain statements. "When Dryden became fired," says Van Doren, "he only wrote more plainly. . . . His passion was the passion of assurance. His great love was the love of speaking fully and with finality." Eliot's Tiresias too spoke that way, as well in the strongest parts of the typist passage as in the ones reconsideration discarded.

She turns and looks a moment in the glass,
Hardly aware of her departed lover;
Her brain allows one half-formed thought to pass:
'Well now that's done: and I'm glad it's over.'

This is without doubt the poetry of plain statement, and when Pound helped it toward the form in which we know it he simply made it plainer. Eliot had written, "Across her brain one half-formed thought may pass," and Pound's thick pencil jabbed at the word "may" and scribbled in the margin, "make up yr. mind." The rest of his comment is almost a free-verse stanza:

    you Tiresias
  if you know
  know damn well
      or
    else you
    dont.   [47]

This brings us around to the suggestive fact that collaborative revision was possible at all. It was possible because the main criteria Eliot's verse implied were as easy to formulate as they were difficult to sustain. They were the criteria of the strong line, the ample unflagreed statement, its normative unit the end-stopped pentameter coincident with a closed syntactic member.

> The time is now propitious, as he guesses,
> The meal is ended, she is bored and tired;
> Endeavours to engage her in caresses,
> Which still are unreproved, if undesired.

Such a quatrain proclaims its Restoration ancestry: straightforward syntax, with a high proportion of principal to dependent clauses; Latin precision—"propitious," "endeavours"—lending overtones of wit to its completion of native monosyllables; and the neat closing antithesis, "unreproved, if undesired," establishing a viewpoint which is not that of the innocent eye but that of the Lockean judgment, making distinctions. "Carbuncular," in what is perhaps the most famous line in the passage, is another weightily felicitous Latinism: "He, the young man carbuncular, arrives"; and with still more felicitous wit it follows its noun in the manner of a French adjective, rather a taxonomy than an epithet.

But such verse, so sparse, so centered on its affirmations, cannot justify itself by its wit or its local accuracy, only by a certain authority which is part of what Eliot meant by "impersonality," which may correspond to what is called "sincerity" in the poet, but of which his sincerity is by no means the guarantee. Of verses composed by these canons of statement, Dr. Johnson once remarked that the difficulty was not to make them but to know when you had made good ones. Johnson often helped other poets who were in that difficulty. We learn from Boswell of lines he supplied for Goldsmith, and if we had the manuscript we might find in it lines he deleted, the readiest way to improve imperfect Augustan verse being to take things out. Sense tends to collect itself into metrical units, and build by accumulation; passage-structure is paratactic, and omissions do not show.

So like a pair of bohemian Augustans, Pound and Eliot that winter in Paris worked over passages that recapitulated the literary procedures of a period. Pound mostly removed things; or else he fussed so much at a quatrain's details that Eliot himself removed it rather than recast.

The heroic stanzas which were introduced by an echo of Dryden's apostrophe to London concluded with a parodic allusion to Goldsmith ("When lovely woman stoops to folly"). Goldsmith survived the revision but all identifiable trace of Dryden vanished, the heroic stanzas having become an irregularly rhymed sequence of "strong lines." Also gone was the long opening of "The Fire Sermon," which had imitated Pope. Of this there was nothing left at all, not a line, and there was no way to tell that the whole central section of Eliot's long poem had moved through modes of Augustan imitation.

The Popish passage deserves a moment's attention. At the root of its troubles lay Eliot's deficient grasp of Pope, concerning whom, in the absence of any critic to do what Mark Van Doren had done for Dryden, he was damnably at the mercy of *idées reçues*. Judging (as we learn from his *Times Literary Supplement* leader on Dryden) that Pope's way was to trivialize and to belittle, he adopted what he took to be Pope's idiom for a character who invited belittling, the pretentious lady taking tea in bed.

> Admonished by the sun's declining ray,
> And swift approaches of the thievish day,
> The white-armed Fresca blinks, and yawns, and gapes,
> Aroused by dreams of loves and pleasant rapes.
> Electric summons of the busy bell
> Brings brisk Amanda to destroy the spell;
> With coarsened hand, and hard plebeian tread,
> Who draws the curtain round the lacquered bed,
> Depositing thereby a polished tray
> Of soothing chocolate, or stimulating tea.   [23]

The day is thievish, the rapes are pleasant, the summons (in the best touch in the passage) electric, the bell busy, Amanda brisk, the bed lacquered, the tea stimulating; deprived of their adjectives, none of the perceptions in these ten lines is of interest, their author having supposed Pope to consist of sequential clichés redeemed by adjectival justness. Pound noted on the carbon copy that the couplets (which Eliot was to recall thinking excellent) were "too loose" ("rhyme drags it out to diffuseness"), and on the ribbon copy, after pausing over minute improvements, he slashed out the whole seventy lines. What was built on adjectives was built on sand.

London, perceived through various Augustan modes: that was "The Fire Sermon" originally. It might have been entitled *London: a*

Poem, or even *The Vanity of Human Wishes*. If work on this section was indeed precipitated by the reading of Mark Van Doren's book about Dryden, it may well contain what had gotten on paper by May. Anyhow, it preceded Lausanne, and went there in Eliot's luggage: two typed copies, original and carbon, transcribed on the "A" machine. The rest of the poem seems to have been planned around it, guided by the norms and decorums of an Augustan view of history. When the plan faltered and changed, the historical norms changed too. Still, we can reconstruct them.

Eras and cultures resemble one another, and from their resemblance we can collect a normative sense of what it can mean to live in a civilization. The English Augustans had been encouraged by points of correspondence between their London and the Rome of Augustus. Eliot's parallel is between Augustan London and modern, and it does not hearten. It signifies a relapse into habit. History, Eliot had written in 1919, "gives when our attention is distracted." By this he appears to mean something like what Wyndham Lewis meant in the 1917 "Inferior Religions," an essay Eliot admired: that to fall into the rhythms of an archetype, into "the habit-world or system of a successful personality," is to be guilty of inattention. "A comic type is a failure of a considerable energy," Lewis had written, "an imitation and standardizing of self." Such beings are "illusions hugged and lived in, little dead totems." That elucidates one of Eliot's couplets about the fashionable lady, that

> Women grown intellectual grow dull
> And lose the mother wit of natural trull,   [27]

and such an image as "pavement toys," and such a passage as the one about how things are in Hampstead, which he typed in Lausanne and may have composed just after he got there, the urban satirist's impulse still upon him:

> The inhabitants of Hampstead have silk hats
> On Sunday afternoon go out to tea
> On Saturday have tennis on the lawn, and tea
> On Monday to the city, and then tea.
> They know what they are to feel and what to think,
> They know it with their morning printer's ink
> They have another Sunday when the last is gone
> They know what to think and what to feel
> The inhabitants of Hampstead are bound forever on the wheel.   [105]

And it illuminates his use of historical parallels. In *Annus Mirabilis* Dryden, meaning to enhance the recent war with the Dutch, compares it to the Second Punic War. In *The Waste Land* Eliot introduces an ex-sailor who has fought in some analogue of the First Punic War— "You were with me in the ships at Mylae!"—by way of suggesting that the same dreary wars recur as the wheel revolves. His point seems not to be, what used to be often alleged, that the present is tediously inferior to the past: rather that the present is inferior to its own best potential insofar as it courts resemblance to the past. Tradition, with the whole past of Europe in its bones, ought to be engaged on something new.

The Conrad epigraph Eliot later proposed enforces this theme of paralyzing reenactment: "Did he live his life again in every detail of desire, temptation and surrender during that supreme moment of complete knowledge?" For if history gives when our attention is distracted, so does personal circumstance, and if London had become a kind of jumbled quotation of former cities, he himself too in his unfortunate marriage had become something like a quotation: a character in an over-familiar play, which sometimes seemed to be *The Duchess of Malfi* and sometimes a French farce. "The Death of the Duchess" [105–107] moves between Hampstead farce and Websterian domesticity. Eliot's decision not to include it in his long poem seems to have come early; he gutted it for details—the game of chess, the knock upon the door— to use in the multi-parted work he now thought of calling *He Do the Police in Different Voices*.

This title, a whimsical comment on the poem's polyphony, would have also served to imply that the police news embodied the nineteenth-century's poetic of fact; and would have invoked too at the poem's threshold, for readers who caught the allusion [125] to *Our Mutual Friend*, the Dickens whose art is inseparable from London and whose genre is the urban satirist's as it was Hogarth's and Dryden's.

So across a sheet headed "The Burial of the Dead," we find typed *He Do the Police in Different Voices: Part I*. This comprehensive heading is misaligned with the rest of the page, which suggests a second, probably later, insertion of paper into machine [4]. At the head of Part II, however, the Dickens title sits on the page as though it had been meant to be there from the start. We may guess that Eliot had typed at least the first page of Part I before he thought of the overall title.

His faith in it seems to have wavered. He never crossed it out. On the other hand he did not write or type it on any of the extant copies of Parts III, IV, and V. Only some weeks later did the long poem acquire a title it could live with.

So we have Eliot now in Lausanne, transcribing on the "B" typewriter what he meant for semi-final versions of Parts I and II. Part I commenced with a panorama of his own recent life: an undergraduate spree in Cambridge (Mass.), café talk in Munich, the morning crowd in London. All this was headed "The Burial of the Dead," a less mystifying title when the sequence of personal pasts was more prominent than it later became.

The sequence brings him to the Unreal City, where Mme. Sosostris reads cards, and where a section title, "In the Cage," invites us to see the woman in the ornate chair and the woman in the pub who knows so much about Lil and Albert as lurid extrapolations from an 1890 tale by Henry James.[3] Mme. Sosostris's cards may remind us of the riddling leaves of the Sibyl of Cumae in the sixth book of the *Aeneid*, whose injunction to Aeneas, when he wanted to visit the Underworld, required him not only to locate the golden bough but to perform for a drowned companion the rite of the burial of the dead. As we brood on the first parts of the poem in their first form, points of contact with the *Aeneid* multiply: Carthage and the Punic Wars Dido prophesied, the drowned sailor, the Sibyl and her enigmas, the horn and ivory gates [31: later cancelled], even such a detail as the word "laquearia" (*Aen.* I: 726), which hints that the woman in the chair, rendered in the dead luxurious diction of Huysmans or the Mallarmé of *Hérodiade*,[4] is a kind of Dido,

---

[3] Mrs. Eliot's note connects this title, which Eliot later cancelled, with the Sibyl of *The Waste Land*'s epigraph, hanging "in a cage" (*in ampulla*). But "cage," though the Loeb translator uses it, is a doubtful rendition of "ampulla" (bottle, jar); moreover it remains to be demonstrated that Eliot at that time had any notion of affixing the quotation from Petronius without which an allusion to the decrepit Sibyl would be impenetrable.

[4] Compare:

> Et sur les incarnats, grand ouvert, ce vitrail.
>
> La chambre singulière en un cadre, attirail
> De siècle belliqueux, orfèvrerie éteinte,
> A le neigeux jadis pour ancienne teinte,
> Et sa tapisserie, au lustre nacré, plis
> Inutiles avec les yeux ensevelis
> De sibylles offrant leur ongle vieil aux Mages.

to interfere with the traveller's proper destiny. That would have been one way to imagine Vivien Eliot, whose "Yes & wonderful wonderful" written up the margin of a passage [13] projected from the hell she and Tom inhabited is quite the most unnerving detail in these fifty-four leaves of manuscript.

Multum ille et terris jactatus et alto: Eliot, much impressed by Joyce's use of Homer, may well have had in mind at one time a kind of modern *Aeneid*, the hero crossing seas to pursue his destiny, detained by one woman and prophesied to by another, and encountering visions of the past and the future, all culminated in a city both founded and yet to be founded, unreal and oppressively real, the Rome through whose past Dryden saw London's future.

In "The Fire Sermon" which he neglected to number "Part III" though he must have been counting it when he headed "Death by Water" "Part IV"—London travesties Dryden's vatic prediction. Were Eliot's readers meant to bridge an ellipse by thinking of Dryden as a British Anchises, and the finale to *Annus Mirabilis* as analogus to the famous evocation of Rome's future (*Aen.* VI: 847–53) that Aeneas heard from his dead father's lips in the Underworld? We can hardly expect to know. The "Fire Sermon" typescript apparently preceded such formal decisions as shaped Parts I and II, and needed more work to clarify its status. On the back of its first leaf [25] Eliot drafted a passage in which the last fingers of leaf clutch the river's wet bank. Conceivably one thing that prompted this was Vergil's account of the unburied dead thronging the bank of Acheron,

Quam multa in silvis autumni frigore primo
Lapsa cadunt folia   (*Aen.* VI: 309–310)

In the final version of the poem, "The Fire Sermon" opens with this passage. On the back of its third leaf he drafted lines to be inserted into the Fresca passage, aligning her with Venus Anadyomene and recalling how

Une d'elles, avec un passé de ramages
Sur ma robe blanchie en l'ivoire fermé
Au ciel d'oiseaux parmi l'argent noir parsemé,
Semble, de vols partir costumée et fantôme,
Un arôme qui porte, o rôses! un arôme,
Loin du lit vide qu'un cierge soufflé cachait,
Un arôme d'ors froids rôdant sur le sachet. . . .
                                    —*Hérodiade,* I

> To Aeneas, in an unfamiliar place,
> Appeared his mother, with an altered face,
> He knew the goddess by her smooth celestial pace.   [29]

That would have helped bring Fresca into the myth; but the Fresca passage was cancelled.[5]

In Part IV ("Death by Water") we are still in the Underworld. The speaker is a dead sailor from New England recounting how they ran into an iceberg. By the time he drafted this, we may speculate, Eliot was losing his grip on the poem he had set out to write. The original "Death by Water" [55–61] has trouble with idiom, trouble with rhythm, trouble with tone, and we note mechanical efforts to link it with the rest of the poem by recalling Dante's Ulysses and working in bits of diction from Tennyson's. A typewriter being for some reason inaccessible, Eliot had made a holograph fair copy, which Pound [55] declined to "attack" until he got a typescript. The passage was accordingly typed on Pound's machine, and its imperfections attacked to such effect that the entire narrative portion, eighty-two lines, simply vanished, leaving only ten appended lines about Phlebas the Phoenician, Englished from a French poem ("Dans le Restaurant") that had been published in the *Little Review* three years before.

The decision to scrap the rest was unarguably correct, as much so as the decision to retain "What the Thunder Said" intact, little though that had to do with what seems to have been the poem's working plan. "What the Thunder Said" was virtually a piece of automatic writing. Eliot more than once testified that he wrote it almost at a sitting, apparently so late in his stay at Lausanne that he did not have time to make a fair copy, and the rapid handwriting of the holograph [71–81] bears him out. False starts and second thoughts are few, and later retouching was insignificant. One of the first thoughts is arresting: the fourth line from the end ran, "These fragments I have spelt into my

[5] That these passages were drafted in Lausanne seems a reasonable assumption. After the conference with Pound in Paris, the Fresca passage was marked for deletion, so there would have been no point writing an insert for it. On the other hand, you do not use the back of your typescript for drafts unless you have decided the typescript will have to be done over, so Eliot's decision that Part III needed more work seems to have preceded Pound's major surgery. My guess is that he was trying to incorporate an *Aeneid* parallel he had decided on since he first wrote it. Vivien Eliot was later to insert a version of "Fresca" into a *Criterion* article [127]. The editor [23] calls this an earlier draft, but it reads to me like a later one. Eliot hated to throw things away altogether.

ruins," to imply that the protagonist has visited the Sibyl of Vergil, whose oracles, like those of Mme. Sosostris, were fragmentary and shuffled by the winds. Above "spelt into" Eliot wrote "shored against," but he did not cross out the earlier phrase and opted for "shored" only when he made the typescript.[6]

Some of the materials for these pages had been on Eliot's mind many years; the opening, and the apocalyptic passage with the bats and the whisper-music and the towers upside-down in air, reproduce and improve scraps of verse [109, 113] that Valerie Eliot dates from the handwriting "1914 or even earlier" [130]. For at least seven years, it would seem, an urban apocalypse had haunted Eliot's imagination, its first version tied to such images of walking through a city as we find in "Rhapsody on a Windy Night."

> So through the evening, through the violet air
> One tortured meditation dragged me on
> Concatenated words from which the sense seemed gone—

The as-if-senseless words on this early page [113] include a draft of the familiar passage that begins "A woman drew her long black hair out tight." There was also a Prufrockian bit, not later used, in which a man like Lazarus declines to return to life.

In the remarkable upwelling of language to which the holograph draft of Part v is testimony, this vein of material virtually took possession of the poem. The motifs familiar from commentaries appeared: the nightmare journey, the Chapel, the Quester, the Grail Legend, the Fisher King. Later, the notes would encourage us to perceive their applicability to what revision had left of the earlier sections, and luckily one enigmatic passage in Section i, with "a heap of broken images" and a red rock, would give the opening of the poem the look of having foreseen its closing.

For it is difficult to believe that anyone who saw only the first four parts in their original form would believe that "the plan and a good deal of the incidental symbolism" were suggested by Jessie Weston's book on the Grail Legend, or that The Golden Bough (Frazer's, not Vergil's) had much pertinence. If we were asked to nominate a controlling scheme, we might more plausibly guess that the pages before us

---

[6] One of several reasons for rejecting the suggestion [83] that Pound may have done the typing. In particular, his mannerism of hitting the space-bar twice is nowhere visible. And the spelling of "Hieronymo" has been corrected and the italicization of the Sanskrit regularized—not the sort of detail Pound took care over.

had something to do with the *Aeneid*, notably its sixth book. If we guessed, from Mme. Sosostris, that the Sibyl was present, we should surely connect her with the Sibyl of Vergil, dealing out her fragments of prophecy (*Aen.* III, 444), than with the Sibyl of Petronius, withered and longing to die. The Sibyl of Petronius entered the explicit scheme only via an epigraph that was added later than anything recorded in the manuscripts.

The decision to entitle the poem *The Waste Land* seems also to have come late. Its only occurrence in the manuscripts is on a title-page with the Conrad epigraph, typed neither on the "B" typewriter we have assigned to Lausanne nor on the one with Pound's violet ribbon that was used in Paris, but on the "A" machine, the one on which "The Fire Sermon" was transcribed. And it seems doubtful that the title-page and "The Fire Sermon" were typed at the same sitting. We have seen Pound working over the "Fire Sermon" typescript. On the other hand, his comment on the Conrad citation (D. D. Paige ed., *The Letters of Ezra Pound*, No. 181) implies that he had not seen it before, one indication that this title-page, and incidentally this title, was not part of what he saw in Paris.

This letter was written on 24 January 1921,[7] some time after Eliot's return to London, and clearly pertains to a fresh typescript, received in the mail, one that took nineteen pages to run "from 'April . . .' to 'shantih' without a break." Three short pieces—probably "Song," "Exequy," and "Dirge"—were tacked on at the end, but on Pound's advice Eliot removed them without protest.

There can be no doubt that the poem was retyped. Nineteen pages seems a trustworthy figure—Pound used it again in his 21 February letter to John Quinn—and there is no plausible way to extract it from the existing typed pages. Of these, Parts I, II, and V, plus a page for Phlebas, total only ten sheets, leaving nearly half the total for the recast Fire Sermon, which is absurd.

---

[7] Paige antedates it by a month, which makes the whole chronology impossible. Pound typed "24 Saturnus, An 1," amusing himself with a calendar that terminated the Christian Era at midnight, 29/30 October 1921, when Joyce completed *Ulysses*, and dating subsequent events p.s.U., i.e. *post scriptum Ulixi*. See Letter No. 185, undated letters from Pound to Margaret Anderson at the University of Wisconsin, Milwaukee, and the calendar itself in *The Little Review*, Spring 1922, p. 2 and note, p. 40. October 30 (Pound's birthday) was designated Feast of Zagreus, October 31 Feast of Pan, and the year commenced with Hephaistos (November, old style). December was Zeus and Saturnus was January.

So there was a new typescript, probably double-spaced, the theme of the published correspondence between the two poets, and vanished now. And it is highly probable that the title-page now among the manuscripts was part of it. Since the scrupulous Eliot did not include this typescript among the manuscript materials he sent to Quinn on 23 October 1922 [xxix], we may entertain the probability that it was the emergency copy he had already sent Quinn on July 19 [xxiii] for transmittal to Horace Liveright when the book contract was being negotiated. From the fact that Quinn only gleaned the title of the book from a postscript of Pound's, we infer that the copy he was sent in July lacked a title-page; the most plausible guess is that Eliot was still looking for a new epigraph, and had meanwhile removed the title-page from the typescript. The epigraph would have gone to Liveright later, along with the notes, and the rejected title-page—the one we have—was attached to the other *brouillons* of the poem when they went off to Quinn in October.

It is apparently all that survives of that nineteen-page typescript, and since it was typed on the "A" machine the probability grows very high that the "A" machine was Eliot's London typewriter. And since "The Fire Sermon" was typed on the "A" machine it was typed in London, one ground for inferring that it was one of the earliest parts of the poem. Undisclosed facts that may bring down this card-house of inference are unlikely to make the story of the poem's composition any simpler.

So it would have been about mid-January 1922, in London, that *The Waste Land* received its final form, and likely its title too. The state of the manuscripts Eliot had unpacked after his return from the continent may be readily summarized. "The Burial of the Dead" had lost its Cambridge opening but was otherwise lightly annotated. "A Game of Chess" had had its opening heavily worked over by Pound, to tighten the meter, and Vivien Eliot had supplied a few suggestions for improving the pub dialogue. "The Fire Sermon" was a shambles; it needed much work. "Death by Water" had been cut back to ten lines. "What the Thunder Said" was "OK."

Pondering these materials, Eliot perceived where the poem's center of gravity now lay. Its center was no longer the urban panorama retraced through Augustan styles. That had gone with the dismemberment of Part III. Its center had become the urban apocalypse, the great City dissolved into a desert where voices sang from exhausted wells, and the Journey that had been implicit from the moment he opened the poem in Cambridge and made its course swing via Munich to London had become a journey through the Waste Land. Reworking Part III, and retyping the other parts with revisions of detail, he achieved the visionary unity that has fascinated two generations of readers. He then went to bed with the flu, "excessively depressed." (Pound *Letters*, appendix to No. 181.)

He was anxious. He thought of deleting Phlebas, and was told that the poem needed Phlebas "ABsolootly." "The card pack introduces him, the drowned phoen. sailor." He thought of using "Gerontion" as a prelude, and was told not to. "One don't miss it *at* all as the thing now stands." (Pound *Letters*, No. 182.) What seems to have bothered him was the loss of a schema. "Gerontion" would have made up for that lack by turning the whole thing into "thoughts of a dry brain in a dry season." Later the long note about Tiresias attempted the same strategy: "What Tiresias *sees*, in fact, is the substance of the poem." The lost schema, if we have guessed about it correctly, had originated in a pre-occupation with Dryden as the poem grew outward from "The Fire Sermon." If Vergil had once sponsored the protagonist's journey as Homer sponsors the wanderings of Leopold Bloom, Vergil was per-tinent to a poem prompted by Vergil's major English translator, John Dryden. Ovid, who supplied Tiresias and *Philomel*, and told (*Metam.* xiv) the story of the Sibyl's terrible longevity which may underlie the line about fear in a handful of dust, was a favorite of Dryden's, and (on Mark Van Doren's showing) pertinent to Dryden's London and Eliot's. Wren's churches, notably Magnus Martyr, were built after the fire *Annus Mirabilis* celebrates, which is one reason Eliot works Magnus Martyr into his Fire Sermon. And in disposing ornate diction across the grid of a very tame pentameter, Eliot's original draft of the opening of Part II had rewritten in the manner of French decadence a Shake-spearean passage (". . . like a burnished throne") that Dryden had rewritten before him in a diction schooled by his own time's French decorum. No classroom exercise is more ritualized than the comparison of *Antony and Cleopatra* and *All for Love*.

But the center from which such details radiate had been removed from the poem. What survived was a form with no form, and a genre with no name. Years later, on the principle that a form is anything done twice, Eliot reproduced the structural contours of *The Waste Land* exactly, though more briefly, in *Burnt Norton*, and later still three more times, to make the *Quartets*, the title of which points to a decision that such a form might have analogies with music. That was *post facto*. In 1922, deciding somewhat reluctantly that the poem called *The Waste Land* was finished, he was assenting to a critical judgment, Pound's and his own, concerning which parts were alive in a sheaf of pages he had written. Two years afterward, in "The Function of Criticism," he adverted to "the capital importance of criticism in the work of creation itself," and suggested that "the larger part of the labour of an author in composing his work is critical labour; the labour of sifting, combining, constructing, expunging, correcting, testing." He called it "this frightful toil," and distinguished it from obedience to the Inner Voice. "The critical activity finds it highest, its true fulfillment in a kind of union with creation in the labour of the artist." (*Selected Essays*, "The Function of Criticism," IV.)

For it does no discredit to *The Waste Land* to learn that it was not striving from the first to become the poem it became: that it was not conceived as we have it before it was written, but reconceived from the wreckage of a different conception. Eliot saw its possibilities in London, in January 1922, with the mangled drafts before him: that was a great feat of creative insight.

In Paris he and Pound had worked on the poem page by page, piecemeal, not trying to salvage a structure but to reclaim the authentic lines and passages from the contrived. Contrivance had been guided by various neoclassic formalities, which tended to dispose the verse in single lines whose sense could survive the deletion of their neighbors.

When they had finished, and Eliot had rewritten the central section, the poem ran, in Pound's words, "from 'April . . .' to 'shantih' without a break." This is true if your criterion for absence of breaks is Symbolist, not neoclassical. Working over the text as they did, shaking out ashes from amid the glowing coals, leaving the luminous bits to discover their own unexpected affinities, they nearly recapitulated the history of Symbolism, a poetic that systematized the mutual affinities of details neoclassic canons had guided. Eliot in his *Times Literary Supplement* review had paid Dryden the unexpected compliment, that in being prizeworthy for what he had made of his material he resembled Mallarmé. It was something akin to Mallarmé, finally, that his own effort to assimilate Dryden came to resemble: the ornate *Hérodiade*, or the strange visions ("Une dentelle s'abolit . . .") of unpeopled rooms where detail strains toward detail and we cannot feel sure what the rhetoric portends.

AFTERWORD

I am grateful to Professor Ralph Rader, who heard the English Institute version of this essay, for some confirming suggestions I have worked into the present revision.

And a letter from Prof. Stanley Sultan, received when these pages were in proof, removes any doubt that the "A" typewriter was Eliot's London machine. He used it to address the packet of *Waste Land* MSS to John Quinn. The label bears the typed return address, "From T. S. Eliot, 9, Clarence Gate Gardens, London N. W. 1." and is postmarked "London, October 23 1922." It is reproduced opposite p. 11 of the New York Public Library's 1968 catalogue of its John Quinn Exhibition. Professor Sultan also points to the absence of a part number on the draft of "The Fire Sermon" as confirming evidence that it antedates any decision about the amount of material that should precede it.

With this essay in proof the mail brings *Mosaic* VI-1, where I find that Grover Smith ("The Making of *The Waste Land*," pp. 127–141) has also read the riddle of the typewriters and reached virtually identical conclusions about the sequence of the drafts. Though our notions of what went into the poem differ greatly, I am delighted to have his confirmation of the chronology.

Index